ONE VOICE
My Life, Times and Hopes for Hawai'i

Nicole,
warm Love and
Aloha!
Kenney

14-3-19

Nicole,

wishing you a very

Aloha!

Danny

14-2-17

ONE VOICE
My Life, Times and Hopes for Hawai'i

DAN AKAKA
with Jim Borg

Daniel K. Akaka

WATERMARK
PUBLISHING

After a blessed, inspired and destined life in the Hawaiian spirit of *aloha*, I dedicate this book to Ma—Annie Kaleianuenue Akaka—and Pa—Kahikina Akaka—who delivered me and nurtured my life; to Millie Chong Akaka, who is my warm and loving wife; and to our children, grandchildren and great-grandchildren, who are loving and supportive.

© 2017 Watermark Publishing LLC

All rights reserved. No part of this book may be reproduced in any form or by any electronic or mechanical means, including information retrieval systems, without prior written permission from the publisher, except for brief passages quoted in reviews.

ISBN (softcover) 978-1-935690-92-4
ISBN (e-book) 978-1-935690-93-1
Library of Congress Control Number: 2017948823

Cover photo by Dennis Oda/*Honolulu Star-Advertiser*. Interior photos courtesy of Daniel K. Akaka, the *Honolulu Star-Advertiser*, the Hawai'i Congressional Papers Collection and Kawaiaha'o Church. Excerpts from Jacobs, John, *A Rage for Justice: The Passion and Politics of Phillip Burton*, paperback © 1997, University of California Press, used with permission.

Design and production
Angela Wu-Ki

Watermark Publishing
1000 Bishop St., Ste. 806
Honolulu, HI 96813
Toll-free 1-866-900-BOOK
sales@bookshawaii.net
www.bookshawaii.net

Printed in the United States

Contents

Foreword by Al Gore   8

Prologue: The Light before Morning   11

PART ONE
The Waters of Haʻo   13

PART TWO
In the Footsteps of Kūhiō   89

PART THREE
The One Hundred Club   213

PART FOUR
The New Normal   371

Epilogue: The Light after Twilight   593

Appendices   604

Index   624

Acknowledgments

I would like to thank my family for their support, not only for this memoir but for my entire career.

My "better half," my steadfast loving and lively wife, Millie, who cared for our growing sons while I was in the House of Representatives, filled in many blanks in my memory. So did our daughter, Millannie Kahokuaonani, and sons Daniel Kahikina Jr., Gerard Kapena, Alan Limaikaika and Nicholas Kalaohikina. Special thanks go out to my first grandson, Dr. David Mattson, Millannie's son, for serving voluntarily and with great energy as the curator of my congressional artifacts. He went so far as to commission a replica of my desk in the Senate, which now graces my adjunct offices in downtown Honolulu, along with other much-valued memorabilia. His lovely wife, Elizabeth, helped greatly in this effort. Also thanks to Dr. Jeff Akaka, my nephew, for details of Abe Akaka's adventures in Europe.

Thanks to Governors George Ariyoshi and John Waihee for sharing their perspectives. And a big thank you to John Uchima. I cannot ever repay my debt to John, who took out a second mortgage to jump-start my political career, and later became my House chief of staff. His memories infuse the mosaic here. Thanks also to his wife, Violet, another supporter who endured John's time-consuming dedication to our efforts. A big *mahalo* to my chiefs of staff, committee staff directors, legislative directors, state directors and all of my congressional aides. They worked tirelessly and contributed immensely to my success as a congressman and senator. I will always be grateful to them.

Thank you to the many supporters and volunteers who helped me throughout the years, especially Elizabeth Rathburn, Wayne Yamasaki and Donn Ariyoshi. Of my many stalwart supporters over the years,

Acknowledgments

mahalo nui loa to Walter Dods, Larry Okinaga and Bert Kobayashi. I will always cherish your friendship and support. Mahalo nui loa to Jim Borg for his hours of chatting with me, researching and warmly recording my life on these pages. *Aloha ia kakou apau.*

Former congressman John Burton, chairman of the California Democratic Party, lent colorful context to our time in the House with his brother, Philip.

Entertainer Jimmy Borges, sadly now passed away, helped me recall details of the state capitol services for Governor Jack Burns.

At the University of Hawai'i's Hamilton Library, where my congressional papers are stored in more than 500 boxes, my thanks go to Rachael Bussert for helping us find key documents and photos, to university librarian Irene Herold and to longtime archivist Ellen Chapman. At the Hawai'i State Archives, my appreciation goes to Luella Kurkjian, chief of the Historical Records Branch. Thanks also to Daniel S. Holt of the U.S. Senate Historical Office, the Office of the Historian of the U.S. House of Representatives, the Office of the Architect of the Capitol and 'Auli'i Tenn of the Hawai'i state Office of Elections.

Special thanks to Ken Reyes, a new UH graduate and indefatigable researcher, and to Karen Iwamoto, a keen-eyed copy editor.

Finally, I would like to thank my old friend and 1976 congressional classmate, Al Gore, for writing the thoughtful foreword to this memoir. We would have saved thousands of lives and billions of dollars if he had been our president.

—Daniel K. Akaka

Foreword

When I went to Congress in the 1970s, it was a true privilege to advocate on behalf of the farmers, shopkeepers and families in my home district in Middle Tennessee. At the risk of sounding corny, I could almost hear "The Battle Hymn of the Republic" playing in my head as I arrived on Capitol Hill! The work was meaningful and I loved it, but that time holds a special place in my heart because I also had the pleasure of meeting and working with like-minded colleagues in the freshman class of the 95th United States Congress—colleagues like Daniel Akaka.

From our first meeting in late 1976, I recognized Danny as the embodiment of Hawai'i's treasured spirit of *aloha*. And we soon became close friends. In the House, and later in the Senate, Danny worked quietly, steadfastly and effectively—usually behind the scenes—showing respect for even his most stubborn rivals and, in turn, winning their deep admiration. He didn't grandstand on the floor, a rare quality in Washington even then, but he kept his word and was willing to compromise to make our country a better place. Danny's low-key Hawaiian style—soft-spoken, humble, unfailingly polite—won him admiration and respect, and stands in stark contrast to the bitter, partisan atmosphere that permeates Capitol Hill today. Our friend and fellow classmate, Senator Barbara Mikulski of Maryland, once put it best when she said that Danny "demonstrates that you do not have to be loud to be powerful."

Over the years, I appreciated Danny's hard work, collaborative approach and quiet power. As vice president, I remained grateful for his support on important policies. But perhaps most of all, I enjoyed his friendship and his trademark warm greetings. Not a day went by when Danny didn't show aloha—not only to his colleagues but nearly every person on Capitol Hill! We were all fortunate that he and his wife, Millie, recreated the warm, welcoming environment of their home state in our nation's capital.

A patriot and proud World War II veteran, Danny is also a consummate man of peace, with a quiet reverence for the divine, for humankind and for nature. Throughout his life, he has been a tireless champion of environmental causes and scientific research. He has long been a leader and advocate for renewable energy research and development, to more quickly move us away from dirty fossil fuels. He championed ocean conservation and preservation, national parks and wildlife issues. He was a strong advocate for space exploration, laying the foundation for many of the enterprises we see today. And Danny's time in office was marked by a commitment to protecting our oceans, reefs and forests—some of Hawai'i's most important and exceptionally beautiful resources—and ensuring that they were managed in a sustainable way.

Danny has been a steadfast leader in support of our nation's veterans, working relentlessly to ensure that those who served our country received the recognition, benefits and care they so rightly deserved. As chairman of the Senate Veterans' Affairs Committee, Danny helped secure increased health-care funding for service members returning from Iraq and Afghanistan; he insisted that those charged with caring for our brave servicemen and women when they return home recognized and addressed the psychological wounds of war in addition to the physical ones; and he played a key role in expanding education benefits for service members through a new G.I. Bill. Danny also sought to secure recognition for those communities that protected our nation but had not yet received proper acknowledgment or support. His efforts to do so resulted in long-overdue compensation for the Filipino veterans of World War II who fought bravely on behalf of the United States, and he also prompted the military to review Distinguished Service Cross medals awarded to Asian American veterans of World War II. During that review, twenty-two medals were upgraded to the Medal of Honor, our nation's highest symbol of bravery. These included the Distinguished Service Cross belonging to the late senator Daniel Inouye of Hawai'i, Danny's friend and colleague who, as a captain of the 442nd Regimental Combat Team, lost most of his right arm in combat.

But throughout his tenure, Danny fought most passionately as an advocate for the citizens of Hawai'i and for indigenous peoples across our nation, including American Indians, Alaska Natives and Native Hawaiians. One of his first accomplishments in the Senate was the passage of the

1993 Apology Resolution. I was proud to stand with Danny as President Clinton signed the resolution, acknowledging our nation's role in the overthrow of the Hawaiian monarchy and committing to a long-overdue process of reconciliation. And his work never stopped. Just before he left the Senate, Danny passed legislation protecting women and children across 565 federally recognized reservations, giving tribes jurisdiction over non-Indians who commit crimes on their lands and broadening the authority of tribes and prosecutors to address sexual and domestic violence.

Danny's belief that we could lift each other up drove his efforts to improve the lives of people in every corner of our nation. As an advocate of financial literacy, Danny helped establish the Office of Financial Education and promoted school-based activities to promote sound economic decision-making. He championed what's become known as the Akaka Box—a warning to consumers about how much they'll owe in interest if they make only the minimum credit card payment each month. He fought for fair pay for federal workers in Hawai'i, Alaska and U.S. territories and supported families by promoting telecommuting among federal workers.

For nearly four decades in Congress, Danny displayed the best qualities of our nation. In this vein, he made a lasting esthetic contribution to our nation's capital by rescuing the 15,000-pound, nineteen-foot-tall plaster model of the *Statue of Freedom*—which had sat atop the Capitol Dome since the Civil War—from decades of inglorious storage in the basement of the Smithsonian Institution. The model now resides in the Capitol Visitor Center, where countless visitors pass it every day in fitting tribute to Daniel Akaka's vision for our future.

Quite simply, every time our nation has needed Daniel Akaka, he's been there. He defended our nation in World War II. He protected our natural resources every chance he got. He stood up for underserved and underrepresented communities in all parts of the country time and time again. And he spent decades making each day a bit better for the people he represented and loves.

These pages tell the story of a full life, a kind man dedicated to public service and, for me, a true friend.

Al Gore
45th U.S. Vice President
Nashville, Tennessee
September 2016

Prologue

The Light before Morning

As often happens, I rose early. Cumulus clouds glowed gunmetal gray, the first signs of a new day. A few bright stars and a gibbous moon lingered against the advancing sun. Venus shined like a beacon above the eastern horizon. Silent points of light in the sky by their movement revealed they were not stars but planes on their final approach. The faint hum of the highway had little competition, only a distant rooster.

It's funny. I like the quiet moments before dawn better than dawn itself.

Maybe it's because sunrises are seldom as pretty as sunsets, the light too harsh, too glaring. The whistle of a train coming towards us lends alarm. The sound as it recedes is somehow soothing. The same with light. As the Earth spins eastward, we are all on a collision course with morning, with sunlight, and perhaps the jangle of a bedside clock. Maybe most people are happier at sunset because their day is done. Taps is more restful than reveille. One of the most beautiful songs ever written, "Stardust," is about dusk, not dawn.

But I find comfort in the cold light before sunrise. Despite our familiar routines, no one really knows how a new day will go. Will the baby come? Will our team win? What will the voters decide? What will the new president do? For me, each day holds astounding promise, all captured in the light before morning. We can only pray that the good outweighs the bad. In Shakespeare's *Julius Caesar*, a nervous Brutus muses, before a battle, "Oh, that a man might know the end of this day's business ere it come!" Then, after a reflective pause, he adds, "But it sufficeth that the day will end. And then the end is known."

Tom Brokaw has called mine the greatest generation because

of our service in World War II. And oddly, conflict does bring out the best in many people. As Winston Churchill prepared his fellow Britons for the Blitz, he famously urged them to act in a way that would make future generations look back and say, "This was their finest hour." But we don't have to look to the past for heroes. They are all around us. Every day, everywhere, brave people rise to challenges big and small, ageless and modern, complex and mundane—single mothers, teachers, social workers, first responders, hospice aides, animal shelter volunteers. A restaurant worker who knows the Heimlich maneuver can do more good than most professional athletes. Ordinary people are capable of extraordinary acts. And there is no finer hour than now.

PART ONE

FROM THE WATERS OF HAʻO

CHAPTER

1

The storm struck overnight.

Five of us manned the *Morning Star VI*, a missionary schooner out of Honolulu bound for the Marshalls. The boat was a sturdy two-master, its holds and spare deck space crammed with staples and supplies. Plenty of Sunday offerings had paid for these goods. Our job was to deliver them and shuttle missionaries and natives between the remote Marshall and Caroline Islands.

As we set sail in the fall of 1947, our horizons felt full of promise. We had made it through World War II. Now, in peace, we were going to embrace a broader world, helping and healing.

The *Morning Star VI* was the latest in a string of missionary boats dating back to 1857, part of a movement to spread the Gospel across the Pacific. The first *Morning Star* was commanded by Hiram Bingham Jr., son of one of Hawai'i's first missionaries. He was also the father of Hiram Bingham III, an Indiana Jones-class explorer who stumbled across the ruins of Machu Picchu in Peru. So, for me, a Hawai'i-born former enlisted soldier looking for something to do, the stars seemed aligned. This was my postwar mission.

The Pacific voyages were dangerous, we knew, but our crew welcomed the challenge. The *Morning Stars II* and *III* both crashed on the reef at Kosrae, the easternmost of the Caroline Islands, and ended up in splinters. The *IV* and *V* fared better, but ultimately succumbed to the elements. Number *VI*, built in Boston as the *Norseman*, had classic lines, including gaff-rigged sails and a boom that jutted several feet aft of the transom. It was sixty-three feet long and had a three-cylinder diesel. It sailed for the Pacific via the Panama Canal in July 1947.

Our skipper, Price Lewis, had commanded a destroyer during the war so he knew well the moods of the sea. Also aboard was Loren

Miller, our radio operator and the son of a Navy admiral. And brothers Joe and Al Linish. I was the navigator and engineer.

Our first leg, to Kwajalein, a 2,500-mile trip, brought smooth sailing. Northeast trades filled our sails. We each took turns at the helm, and enjoyed a calm camaraderie as we went about our duties and shared meals in the galley.

"So, Danny, how'd you learn diesels?" asked Loren, as we sat with the Linish boys, savoring hot stew and rice.

"First in high school, then the Army," I said. "Ran tugboats all over the Marianas, Guam, Saipan, Tinian, shuttling supplies, just like now."

"Anything scary?"

"Yes," I said. "I had a very close brush with a shark, diving off Tinian."

They laughed. Like many in the war, I had never been shot at. But in the Marianas, we knew there were Japanese soldiers hiding in the interior, having been told by their superiors the U.S. would slaughter them upon surrender. On Saipan, Captain Sakae Oba and his company didn't surrender until December 1945. On Guam, Private Bunzo Minagawa and his sergeant, Masashi Ito, held out until May 1960. And Shoichi Yokoi, Ito's corporal, wasn't captured until January 1972.

"Tinian. Isn't that the A-bomb planes?"

"Yes," I said. "I was there when the *Enola Gay* took off for Hiroshima."

As engineer, I was in charge of the diesel engine, which we used mostly to get in and out of harbors and reef passages. We had turned it off as soon as we cleared the outer buoy at Honolulu and had relied since on sails. Also in the cramped engine compartment was a gas generator that we used to keep the batteries charged. The batteries in turn ran the refrigerator, radio, cabin lights and running lights at night. The generator was nowhere near as noisy as the engine, but we still tried not to run it when people were sleeping. Within days we were into a comfortable routine.

Miller was frequently on the radio, trying to get information about waves and weather from other vessels. This was long before the days of NOAA weather radio and Coast Guard emergency channel 16, so our information was always sketchy.

❋ ❋ ❋

Our peaceful passage ended between dusk and dawn. First the wind freshened, rich with moisture, as if a squall had us in its crosshairs. As darkness descended, the waves and wind built up. By sunrise we were cowed by howling winds and heaving seas.

"Drop the sails! Secure the hatches!" the captain bellowed.

We weren't quick enough on the first task. Our foresail ripped and went flying off.

After everything else was secured, we all scrambled below except the helmsman, secured by a lifeline, who would try to keep the boat from pitch-poling or turning turtle.

In the galley, plates, cups, pots and pans had fallen out of cabinets and drawers and off wall mounts and were skittering across the table and floor. The coffee pot, its bottom blackened from daily use, was floating in four inches of water aft near the engine. The radio was dead. We did our best to secure what we could, but the boat was heaving so violently that the smallest job seemed insurmountable.

"Akaka, you have the wheel!"

I went to the cockpit to find raw chaos. Towering swells dwarfed the main mast. I had no way to measure the wind speed, but guessed at a gale, more than fifty miles per hour. And as I took in this forbidding seascape, a sickening thought closed in. *Would we get through this?* At no time in my life, not during the Pearl Harbor attack, not in World War II, had I felt such clutching fear.

So I turned my thoughts to home. To Hawai'i. I recalled my brother Abe telling me about the morning I was born. At our modest house in Pauoa, my father delivered me at 3:30 a.m., washed me up, wrapped me in a towel and awakened the family. I was the youngest of eight children. So as dawn crept into the sky, our family was complete.

"This is your new brother," Dad announced. "Ma and I decided to name him Daniel. Because we feel that he is going to be like Daniel in the Bible. One day he'll be in the lion's den. But he will survive."

Pa's prediction proved mildly comforting amid the black walls of water.

We set up a system under which the helmsman, once relieved, would inspect the deck, looking for any signs of trouble. Then he would go below for a cold meal, maybe canned tuna, crackers and a cup of water, with seawater sloshing at his feet.

I was below when I heard the helmsman shout the most dreaded of all alerts.

"Man overboard!"

We rushed up to the cockpit, where Miller pointed helplessly forward.

"He's gone!"

We squinted into the wind and, sure enough, the deck was clear.

We had lost Joe Linish.

We pressed forward anyway, praying for a miracle. Because even if we spotted him in the water, there was no way to get the boat to him. All we could do was toss a life ring in his direction.

Under the whistling wind, the ocean, empty all around, seemed to have claimed a fine sailor and good friend.

Then I saw it. A line trailing off the deck into the sea. As taut as a violin string. Could it be?

I called the others over.

"Hooey, let's haul this in!"

So we pulled, no easy task even for three of us. Foot by foot we pulled, careful not to fall overboard ourselves in the process. The rope must have been twenty or thirty feet long. But finally, there at the end was Joe. Our prayers had been answered. We got him back on deck, him cold and coughing.

He said the wind had snapped loose the spar, which had swung around and swatted him off the deck. As he went over, he was able to grab the line, which saved his life. There was no way we would have found him otherwise.

The storm raged for four more days—we learned it was the worst in twenty-five years. Water started seeping through the hatches. So we were constantly pumping and bailing. Everything was soaking wet, including our bunks. And then the generator went out, so we couldn't run the electrical pump. That meant manning the hand pump on deck, which we pretty much ran constantly. Crate by cask, we lost everything on deck, restraining straps notwithstanding.

The devilish winds eventually subsided, but the ocean stayed unsettled for some time. Finally, exhausted, we turned the helm full starboard and tied it off, so that the boat went around in a circle—we didn't want to bump into anything. And then we tumbled into our soggy sacks and slept. ❇

CHAPTER

2

I woke up with a start, not in the pitching bunk of a boat but secure in our brick townhouse in Alexandria, Virginia. I lifted my wrist and checked the time: 6:20 a.m. As usual, I had awakened about ten minutes before the alarm.

My stirring had shaken my wife, Millie, from her slumber.

"You'd better get up," she commanded. "It's a big day in the Senate."

October 10, 2002. I swung my legs out of bed, feeling an ache in the right knee, and marched to the shower.

My chief of staff, Jim Sakai, picked up Millie and me for the drive in to the District of Columbia. I sat with him in the front as he briefed me on the day's appointments and events.

Millie spouted, "The only reason you want me along is so you can drive in the HOV lane!"

The high occupancy vehicle lane required three people.

"That's right, Millie," Jim said, perhaps for the hundredth time.

Jim, an extremely dedicated and hardworking aide, had been in Honolulu mayor Frank Fasi's cabinet as director of budget and finance. I brought him to Washington in 1980, when Fasi lost the Democratic primary to Eileen Anderson. When Fasi recaptured Honolulu Hale four years later, he asked Jim to come back. Jim said no. Very generous, respectful and soft-spoken, he had been working with me for more than twenty years.

One of the pieces of Senate business this day would be a resolution recognizing the contributions of Hawai'i's late U.S. congresswoman Patsy Mink, whose Title IX legislation established equality for women in collegiate sports. Mink had died September 28.

But the overarching piece of business was a resolution authorizing an invasion of Iraq.

Our route took us past the Pentagon, still showing the scars of the terrorist attacks. September 11, 2001, had been my seventy-seventh birthday, and my Senate staff had arranged for a celebratory cake. We never got to eat it, of course. As soon as the jetliners hit the World Trade Center—followed shortly by the crash of American Airlines Flight 77 into the side of the Pentagon—security personnel whisked all members of Congress and their aides to safe locations. Word was there was a fourth plane out there. And in fact, we later learned, the intended target of United Flight 93 was likely the White House or Capitol Hill. In the end, the heroic passengers rebelled and the hijackers crashed the jet into a field in central Pennsylvania, a bit west of Gettysburg, another turning point. But nobody, even at the highest reaches of government, knew the scope of the attack in those early hours. So I spent the day with a few others, including Senator Robert Byrd of West Virginia, in a windowless room in the belly of the Capitol Police Department, just down from Union Station.

Crossing the 14th Street Bridge over the steel-hued Potomac, the Capitol came into view, and I had a chance to reflect on the changes that had swept the country since 9/11. Air travel had certainly changed forever. And a huge new bureaucracy, under the rubric of homeland security, would soon control once largely independent and efficient agencies such as the Coast Guard and Federal Emergency Management Agency. And would insinuate itself into American lives in ways we then could only suspect. We had invaded Afghanistan, a move that hadn't worked out well for the Soviets in the 1980s. There is a sensible saying about those who don't learn from history. And it would prove to be an expensive lesson. But at least U.S. military action in Afghanistan could be justified by Kabul's look-the-other-way attitude toward the architects of the attack, al-Qaida, believed to be holed up in the high country.

But now the administration of George W. Bush wanted to invade Iraq. That was a different story. Iraq had nothing to do with 9/11. Admittedly, Saddam Hussein had plotted to assassinate the president's father, former president George H.W. Bush, in April 1993. In response, President Bill Clinton had launched a Tomahawk missile attack against the headquarters of the Iraqi Intelligence Service in Baghdad. And yes, Saddam and his sons were decidedly "evil doers," to borrow from Bush. But there were serious questions about whether Iraq posed a threat to U.S. national security.

Today, a cool and humid Thursday, the Senate was preparing to weigh in on the Iraq issue in the form of joint resolution offered by Bush on October 2. The resolution said military force against Iraq was justified by several factors, including his possession of chemical and biological weapons and desire to acquire nuclear arms, and his hostility toward the United States, as evidenced by the Bush assassination attempt and his firing at U.S. aircraft enforcing the "no-fly" zone after the first Gulf War. The resolution also mentioned Iraq's "brutal repression of its civilian population." That phrase caught me up short. If brutal repression were reason enough for invading a country, then there were plenty of other candidates, including North Korea, Myanmar, Somalia—even Saudi Arabia. But no one was talking about parachutes over Pyongyang.

Our car pulled up to the Hart Senate Office Building and Millie and I made our way to my office, no. 720. Along the way we greeted other senators and staffers we had come to know since 1990, when I was appointed by Governor John Waihee to fill the seat left vacant by the death of beloved Senator Spark Matsunaga.

"Danny, Millie, how are you?"

It was Ted Kennedy.

"You going to be speaking today on the Iraq resolution?" Kennedy asked.

"Absolutely."

"See you on the floor," he said.

Kennedy was one of my closest friends in Congress, our desks only a few feet apart. By 1990, he had built up quite a few years of seniority, so under the rules deserved a desk closer to the speaker's podium, the center of action. So I was puzzled to see him out in the "boonies" where freshman members like me resided.

"Ted, what are you doing way out here?" I asked.

"This was my brother's desk and I'm keeping it," he said, referring to John. Bobby had also been a senator, but representing New York, not Massachusetts.

※ ※ ※

Once in the office, Millie took off her shoes. She wasn't on my payroll, but served nearly every day in an unofficial capacity, greeting visiting constituents—yes, in bare feet—and taking on other routine tasks, and lending otherwise stuffy spaces an island flavor. She even eschewed her shoes when Bill Clinton stopped by for a chat. Millie religiously kept the office stocked with Hawaiian snacks, including chocolate-covered macadamia nuts, spicy rice crackers—mochi crunch, and li hing mui Chinese candy.

That afternoon, the Republican-led House of Representatives passed the Iraq invasion resolution, 297–133, with three abstentions. Eighty-two Democrats voted yes. Only six Republicans voted no.

In the Senate, the acting pro tem was Jean Carnahan of Missouri, appointed to fill her husband's seat after he died in a plane crash in October 2000.

"The senator from Hawai'i is recognized," she said.

I stood and voiced support for the resolution only if key conditions were met.

"Before the United States wages war against Iraq, President Bush and the Congress owe it to the young Americans who face death or injury in that conflict to ensure that every effort has been made to obtain our ends without endangering them," I said. "Every ounce of preparation must be taken to ensure a swift and efficient outcome should war become necessary. As another president, Herbert Hoover, once said, 'Older men declare war. But it is youth that must fight and die.' The burden is on our leaders to justify why young men and women need to risk their future now."

I had seen figures from the Congressional Budget Office that a war with Iraq could cost $13 billion per month.

"Remember, in the first Persian Gulf War, it was our allies who paid for the war," I said. "The cost of the war this time will be borne largely by the American treasury, unless we are supported by an international coalition. With a battered economy, it will be difficult to fund two wars at once for an indefinite period of time. Already our funds are stretched."

I also argued that a unilateral war with Iraq would eliminate much if not all of the good will and empathy that the United States enjoyed after the September 11 attacks.

"Traditionally, America has never sought war by striking first, nor has America eagerly sought foreign entanglements," I said, referring to George Washington's admonition as he left office in 1796. "This would be a preemptive war and one in which we could have few allies. Not since the Spanish-American War would the United States be fighting a war so far from our borders with so few friends."

Finally, I questioned our strategy and objectives, remembering General Colin Powell's famous Pottery Barn rule, "If you break it, you own it."

"A rush to battle without a strategy to win the peace is folly," I said.

Ultimately, the Senate defeated the amendments that would have made the resolution acceptable to me. After midnight on Friday, October 11, the historic vote began on House Joint Resolution 114.

"Mr. Akaka."

"Nay."

By alphabetical fluke—my name beginning with A—I became the first senator to vote against the Iraq War.

One view. One voice. It's the bedrock of democracy.

I was quickly joined by Senators Jeff Bingaman of New Mexico, Barbara Boxer of California and Byrd of West Virginia. Joining us was Lincoln Chafee—the sole Republican—and Jack Reed of Rhode Island, Kent Conrad of North Dakota, John Corzine of New Jersey, Mark Dayton and Paul Wellstone of Minnesota, Dick Durbin of Illinois, Russ Feingold of Wisconsin, Bob Graham of Florida, my Hawai'i colleague Dan Inouye, James Jeffords—an independent—and Patrick Leahy from Vermont, Ted Kennedy, Carl Levin and Debbie Stabenow of Michigan, Barbara Mikulski and Paul Sarbanes of Maryland, Patty Murray of Washington and Ron Wyden of Oregon.

Our twenty-three votes fell to seventy-seven on the other side. And so was endorsed one of the most monumental blunders in American history. ❖

CHAPTER

3

The corridors of Congress, where I spent thirty-six years, are a far cry from the life of a boy in Pauoa, a once-verdant valley behind Punchbowl, an extinct volcanic cinder cone that now serves as a national cemetery.

In those days, the 1920s and 1930s, Pauoa was known for its taro patches, watery farms that produced a staple in Hawaiian called *kalo*. Today, it's a crowded residential neighborhood, but back then there were no paved roads nor sidewalks. Children walked barefoot across fields and neighbors' yards, laughing in anticipation of their next adventure.

My parents, three brothers and four sisters shared a two-bedroom house. The wood-fueled kitchen was outdoors, and to keep food cool we had an ice box, literally a cabinet with a large block of ice in it. That meant frequent trips to the icehouse on Booth Road in the valley. We were poor in possessions but rich in spirit.

Under the guidance of my father, Kahikina Akaka, who was part Hawaiian, part Chinese, and my mother, Annie Kahoa, pure Hawaiian, our family worshipped daily. Pa would wake us up before he went to his job at the Honolulu Iron Works and we would have "*'ohana*," a devotion period with all of us sitting in the parlor. When my father looked at us, each in turn, in no particular order, we had to recite a verse from the Bible. So we had to be up on our verses. In a pinch, we could get away with John 11:35, "Jesus wept." After the verses, we would recite the Twenty-Third Psalm in Hawaiian.

The Lord is my shepherd; I shall not want.
'O Iēhova koʻu Kahu hipa; ʻAʻole oʻu mea e nele ai.

He maketh me to lie down in green pastures; he leadeth me beside the still waters.
Nāna nō wau i hoʻomoe iho ma nā ʻāina uliuli: Ua alakaʻi ʻo ia iaʻu ma kapa wai lana mālie.

He restoreth my soul; he leadeth me in the paths of righteousness for his name's sake.
Ke hoʻāla mai nei ʻo ia i koʻu ʻuhane: Ke alakaʻi nei nō ʻo ia iaʻu ma nā ala maikaʻi no kona inoa.

Yea, though I walk through the valley of the shadow of death, I will fear no evil, for thou art with me; thy rod and thy staff they comfort me.
ʻOiaʻiʻo, inā e hele au ma ke awāwa malu o ka make, ʻAʻole au e weliweli i ka pōʻino: no ka mea, ʻo ʻoe pū kekahi me aʻu; ʻO kou mana, a me kou koʻokoʻo, ʻo koʻu mau mea ia e ʻoluʻolu ai.

Thou prepares a table before me in the presence of mine enemies: thou anointest my head with oil; my cup runneth over.
Ke hoʻomākaukau mai nei ʻoe i ka papa ʻaina naʻu ma ke alo o koʻu mau ʻenemi: Ua kāhinu mai ʻoe i kuʻu poʻo me ka ʻaila; Ua piha a hū koʻu kīʻaha.

I always found it curious that the Hawaiians had to borrow the English word for enemies, having no equivalent of their own.

Surely goodness and mercy shall follow me all the days of my life; and I will dwell in the house of the Lord forever.
ʻOiaʻiʻo, e hahai mau ana iaʻu ka pono a me ke aloha i nā lā a pau o koʻu ola ʻana; A ma loko o ka hale o Iēhova ʻo wau e noho mau loa aku ai.

After that Pa would start singing a hymn of his choice and the family would join in. Over the years we started to sing in harmony, creating a lovely chorus.

One of our favorites was "Iesū Nō Ke Kahuhipa" ("Jesus is Our Shepherd"), which we sang in four-part harmony. After the hymn, Pa would kneel on the floor, facing his chair, and we would do the same, and pray silently. And we would end with the Lord's Prayer in Hawaiian. We did that every morning and afternoon. It kept us close as a family.

Although we sang and prayed in Hawaiian—and Pa and Ma spoke Hawaiian to each other, they encouraged us to speak English as our first language. And so we kids never became fluent in our native tongue, which I regret. But my parents insisted that we know English well to properly compete in the world.

On Sundays, we would walk from Pauoa Valley down Lusitana and Punchbowl Streets to Kawaiahaʻo Church, the first Christian church in the islands. Before the missionaries arrived in 1820, this was all empty land with a spring reserved for royalty. The chiefess Haʻo often used the freshwater pool, so the area became known as "the waters of Haʻo," or Kawaiahaʻo. Thatched huts served as the first places of worship. The current building, commissioned by Queen Kaʻahumanu and designed by the Reverend Hiram Bingham, was built between 1836 and 1842 from 14,000 slabs of coral rock. Part of the United Church of Christ, this was our second home.

We would arrive at 9 a.m. for Sunday school and then the service, which ran from 10:30 to 12. Then we would go home for lunch. At 2 p.m., we would attend service at a small branch church up on Pauoa Road next to the graveyard. After that we would go home and, at about 5, would get ready to go back to Kawaiahaʻo to attend what we called Christian endeavor meetings, held at 6 p.m. for different age groups. Following that was the regular evening service. And then we went home. That was our Sunday. When I was an adult, some of the old-timers at Kawaiahaʻo would tease me, "You know, you came to church when you were in your mother's womb and you're still coming to church." I guess it was no surprise that in the late 1950s I would become choir director and minister of music at Kawaiahaʻo, and my brother Abe its pastor.

❋ ❋ ❋

Pa would bring his pay home and he and my mom would say a prayer of thanks. Then they would put the coins into a shoebox that had separate sections. The first was for the church, ten percent, tithing. Then food. Then clothes. But new clothes were never a priority. As the eighth child, I got all the hand-me-downs from my brothers. I remember one time at Pauoa Elementary School my mother gave me pants that had a hole, in Hawaiian a *puka*.

"I don't want it," I told her, embarrassed to wear the pants.

"You use it because this puka pants is clean," she said softly. There were never any raised voices in our family, except in song.

And so I put on the puka pants and went to school.

I owned one pair of shoes, but they were for special occasions. No kid in those days wore shoes to school.

We bought our *poi* down on Kuakini Street, I think for fifteen cents a bag. So we got a lot of poi, and to stretch the poi, we would pick *'ulu*, breadfruit, from the trees and bake it and pound it and squash it and mix it with the poi, so we had more for the family to eat. We would also catch *o'opu*, gobies, in the stream and cook them in *ti* leaves. There were times when we didn't have food, but we accepted this. There were times when I didn't have lunch money, so I would go to school and skip lunch. It really made my siblings and me realize that we must be grateful for what we have.

My mother, being full-blooded Hawaiian, was very sociable. We had a *lānai*, and when people passed by she would say, "Hooey! Hele mai e 'ai!" Meaning, "Come eat!" And I would pull her skirt and whisper, "Ma, we don't have anything to eat!" And she would tell me, "That's all right. They can drink water." So they would come on the porch and sit down and talk and she would give them water.

Our valley was very diverse—Hawaiians, Japanese, Chinese, Koreans, Portuguese—and our family had many friends. I remember a Japanese boy, Kaoru, who would come to our house to play. And I guess his family was having problems. So it got to the point where my mother talked to the family and she said, "Kaoru, you're staying with us." So he came and lived with us and was part of our family. Later, he opened a Chevron station at Waialae Avenue and St. Louis Drive. And the family would go there to fill gas to give him business. And he would say, "No pay." And the family would say, "Eh, we not going pay, we not going come!" He had a mechanic shop there and did very well.

In the 1920s and '30s, Pauoa Valley also had lots of Hawaiian medicinal plants growing wild. So whenever we needed medicine we'd go look for the plant. Like *pōpolo*, with small dark lavender fruit that we liked to eat. We would pick the leaves and in some cases we'd pound it and in other cases boil it and drink it as tea. Good for colds, good for the body. And of course the *kukui* nut tree. Every time you picked a kukui nut, the juice would emerge and we scooped the juice out and that was the medication. Hawaiians believed that the tongue was the bellwether of health. So they'd say, "Let me see your tongue." We would stick out our tongue and they would look at the color and say, "Oh, you need kukui. Go get kukui." So they would grab it and scrape it on and it didn't taste good but it was supposed to be good for you, like castor oil.

As a child, from my siblings' perspective, at least, I was notoriously inquisitive, *nīele*, always asking, "What's this, what's that?" My sister Annie once told me that when I was three years old, I picked some buds from a tree and placed them on the edge of our outdoor stove.

"And what are you doing that for?" she asked.

"Because I want the flowers to bloom early," I said.

"Why do you put it on the stove for it to bloom early?"

"Because it's hot," I said, obviously equating the warmth of the oven to the warmth of spring, when in Hawai'i plumeria, African tulips and golden roseodendron erupt in magnificent color.

She could only shake her head, amazed that anyone would make that connection.

When I was old enough, my friends and I would take the streetcar into Waikīkī, which then had only two hotels, the Moana and the Royal Hawaiian. From Pauoa, the streetcar went down Lusitana, down Punchbowl, and then turned right on King Street, went through town all the way to Liliha, and then up to Pu'unui. So when we got to King Street, we'd get off and transfer to the Waikīkī line, which would go down McCully. It was cheap, five, ten cents, and opened up a new world to us.

We'd spend the whole day there, swimming and surfing, and come back late in the afternoon. Sometimes we would spend the night there, sleeping on the beach, and I remember one time awakening to the gentle tap of a policeman's billy club on my feet. He told us not to sleep there anymore.

At the far end of Waikīkī, what is now Kapiʻolani Park was occupied by polo grounds and stables. Sometimes we would marvel at the matches and incredible displays of horsemanship. Other times we would pick *limu*, or take a swim in the World War I memorial natatorium, then a very popular spot where the legendary Duke Kahanamoku had competed. In August 1937, when I was nearly thirteen, he sponsored a three-day swim meet there. Many times we would go down to the bleachers and watch people swim, or swim there ourselves. It was nice because it had men's and women's changing rooms with showers—and still does to this day, although the saltwater pool itself has long been left to ruin.

In the middle of Waikīkī, at Kalākaua and Paokalani Avenues, was the Lalani Hawaiian Village, a cultural *hula* center operated by the Mossman family. There were a few stores on the *mauka* side of Kalākaua and some places to eat—local places. For fifteen cents we could get a meal. If we had fifteen cents.

My formal financial education began in the fourth grade at Pauoa Elementary School. My teacher, Mrs. Dung, made sure every student had a piggy bank on his or her desk. Any time we had loose change we were required to bring it in and drop it in the piggy.

"All right, class," she announced one day. "I want you to write down how much money you have in your piggy bank. And I want you to write and tell me what you want to buy with your money."

I decided I wanted a yo-yo, which must have cost about $1.25. That doesn't seem like a lot now, but this was back in the thick of the Depression, when a gallon of gas cost ten cents, a loaf of bread eight cents.

Then Mrs. Dung asked, "How many of you don't have enough money in your piggy bank?"

All of us raised our hands.

"What are you going to do to get that money?" she pressed.

And so she had us write what we proposed to do to get the money. Working with numbers helped our arithmetic. Writing it out helped our composition.

I began shining Pa's shoes, five cents.

Afternoons, my brothers and I would hawk the *Star-Bulletin*, then the dominant daily.

"Pape!" we yelled, shortening paper to one syllable.

We tried to get as close to central downtown as possible, because that's where the action was. But my brothers told me in no uncertain terms to avoid the intersection of King and Bishop Streets, "owned" by a curmudgeon named Maui. He would rotate those corners trying to sell papers and didn't want any kids selling there.

Whatever we made, we saved.

And by the end of the fourth grade, I had my yo-yo. I learned to keep it down, and jerk it and throw it up, so I really enjoyed it. But the lessons from Mrs. Dung were the greater reward. She had a huge influence on my life. She would always tell us, "Keep track of your money!" I found her advice useful years later as a member of the U.S. Senate Banking Committee. ✤

CHAPTER

4

The tradition in my family was for the kids to go to Pauoa Elementary School, Kawananakoa Middle and McKinley High. My brother Abe, the first, and oldest sister, Annie, went on to the University of Hawai'i. Abe was always in good shape and would often leap up and grab on to a tree branch and do pull-ups. Later, he went off to divinity school in Chicago. Annie was smart and beautiful and played the piano. She got a bachelor's degree and a master's degree—unusual for women at the time, and went on to become a teacher, first in Kona and later for many years at Waipahu High School. My oldest brother, John, went to community school by Dole Cannery and became a mailman and then worked at the Richards Street post office with Anne Burns, the mother of our future governor, Jack Burns. Her friends called her Flo. Brother John was also a musician and became vice president of the musicians union. My brother Joe went to work as a rigger at Pearl Harbor. My sisters Susan and Phoebe went to work for state social services. Another of my sisters, a baby who was never named, died in the hospital soon after birth. From then on, Pa delivered all the kids at home.

At Kawananakoa, they explained to us new kids that each class would need someone to represent them on the student council. For some reason, that interested me, and I was able to get the class to support me. I liked trying to find ways to help the school. In the eighth grade, I was elected again. In the latter part of eighth grade, they elect a student council president, who assumes that role in the ninth grade. So I got some of my buddies together and said, "Eh, you know, I want to try to become president." And I ran for president and won. While I was president, the school built the auditorium that's still there by Pauoa Road. I took part in the dedication ceremony.

The school is named for Prince David Kawānanakoa, the nephew of Queen Kapiʻolani. He was in line to be king around the time the monarchy was overthrown in 1893. His brother was Prince Jonah Kūhiō Kalanianaʻole, the territory of Hawaiʻi's delegate to Congress. One of his children was Princess Abigail Kapiʻolani Kawānanakoa, who had long taken an interest in our school.

So when I was in the ninth grade, the princess took me under her wing, I'm guessing, in part because I was the first Hawaiian to preside over the student council. Back then, I really didn't realize that she was connected to the monarchy. I just thought she was a nice lady. On occasion, she would invite me to her house on Pensacola Street, where the Hawaiian Mission Academy is now. Their home was huge and had a big lānai that wrapped around two sides of the house.

"Please, sit," she would say.

So we sat on the lānai and talked, mostly about her family, which included her daughter Abigail Kekaulike Kawānanakoa, whom I didn't meet until much later.

And she noticed I never wore shoes. This was quickly remedied.

At schools in Hawaiʻi, May Day is a big celebration, with music and pageantry. And when I was selected May Day king at Kawananakoa, the princess bought me white shoes, white pants, a white shirt with long sleeves and a red waist sash.

"You wear that," she said.

It certainly was a new style for me, but I took them and wore them proudly, standing next to the May Day queen, Hannah Ho, from Don Ho's family.

Near the end of the year, I got an unsolicited visit from a Mr. Banning, the admissions director at Kamehameha Schools, a campus for Hawaiian children established by Princess Bernice Pauahi Bishop.

"We would like you to come to Kamehameha," he said.

"Well, thank you very much, Mr. Banning," I said. "But I want to go to McKinley." I explained that that was our family tradition.

"You know, we really want you," he said.

Three times he came to see me and three times I turned him down.

I wanted deeply to go to McKinley because all my brothers and sisters went there and when they'd come home, they'd talk about the teachers. So I felt like I knew all the teachers. I especially liked Doris Keppeler. She was Hawaiian and, of course, her husband, Herbert, became a trustee of Bishop Estate, the trust set up by Princess Pauahi to support Kamehameha Schools. My siblings raved about Mrs. Keppeler, so I thought, *I want her for a teacher.*

I also didn't know how much Kamehameha would cost, and didn't want my father to have to pay for it since my brothers and sisters all had a free public education.

So then Mr. Banning went to talk to my father.

And not long after that, my dad sat me down.

"You know, Danny, I think you should go Kamehameha," he said.

"Eh, look, Pa, thanks. But I shouldn't go to Kamehameha because I don't want you to pay for me going there."

"No. They told me if you go to Kamehameha, I don't have to pay a cent. I think you'd better go."

So I accepted and went to Kamehameha in the tenth grade. ✽

CHAPTER

5

In those days, the late 1930s, Kamehameha School for Boys was down at the site now occupied by the Bishop Museum, not up on the hill. The current campus on Kapālama Heights had opened in 1931, and was undergoing expansion when I arrived. They had four levels of high school—tenth grade, low eleventh, high eleventh and senior—part of a two-track system, academic and trade skills. Because of the two tracks, we had to go to school on Saturdays. In the tenth and low eleventh grades, on the trade side, we had to attend shops: carpentry, electrical, engineering, agriculture. And then in the high eleventh year we had to select one shop and stick with it.

The classes were split in half, and for six weeks half of the students were in academic classes and half were in shops and related apprenticeships. As part of the engineering shop, I was assigned to the Hawaiian Electric power plant down at the waterfront. During those work weeks, we ate breakfast on campus, where we boarded, and then they had bag lunches all lined up for us. I would grab my bag lunch, walk down to King Street, catch a streetcar, get off at Bishop Street and walk down to the plant. It was a pleasant routine.

There I worked with a terrific welder named Mau, a gregarious but no-nonsense Chinese gentleman. I learned so much from him because he would pass on tips as we worked.

"Look," he told me, "in the power plant the welding has to be tight because there cannot be any leaks. The steam pipes have to withstand pressure. You gotta be a good welder over here. You learn to be a good welder."

So I fired up my torch, pulled down my faceguard and watched the sparks fly.

I would say in the two years I was there I became equal to what they called in those days a certified welder, capable of very sophisticated work. And I learned it from Mau. We even had to go into the boiler sometime. They'd shut it down for several days beforehand to let it cool off. And, of course, it had to be tight welding. I really liked it. Because I was a young kid, the older guys took care of me. When we ate lunch, we sat together, and I'd listen in on whatever they talked about. Hawaiian Electric paid me thirty-five cents an hour. So I worked there two years under Mau and Mr. Olson, the superintendent, a kind local *haole*.

The other six weeks we would spend in school.

The world was discovering Hawai'i back then. On Boat Days, the glorious, white-hulled Matson ships would pull into Aloha Tower, greeted by hula girls in grass skirts and the Royal Hawaiian Band. Streamers would fly off the ships as the passengers lined the rails. As a tugboat edged the ship up to the pier, passengers would toss coins into the water and Hawaiian boys would dive for them, following the reflective glint of sunlight off the metal. On occasion, I would walk down from the power plant, a short distance away, to view this vibrant spectacle. Typically, we think life is always going to be the way it is. But Boat Days long ago disappeared, and those of us lucky enough to witness them must be content with the memory.

By the late 1930s, visitors began to arrive also by air, led by some early pioneers. In January 1935, Amelia Earhart became the first person to fly from Honolulu to Oakland, California. In March 1937, she attempted to fly solo around the world, taking off from Oakland and landing at the Navy's Luke Field on Ford Island, in the middle of Pearl Harbor. But when she tried to resume her trip three days later, a mysterious accident—perhaps a blown tire or collapsed landing gear—sidelined her Lockheed Electra. The round-the-world flight was scrubbed.

Two years later, though, she tried again, this time heading east from Oakland. It was big news in Hawai'i—and the subject of many excited conversations in the halls of Kamehameha—when Earhart reached New Guinea near the end of June 1937 and set out across the Pacific. Honolulu was to be her next-to-last stop on the way to Oakland, but on July 2, she and her navigator, Fred Noonan, vanished on their way to a refueling stop at Howland Island, part of the Phoenix Islands, 1,900 miles southwest of Honolulu. Despite an extensive and lengthy search by the Navy and Coast Guard, the pair was never seen nor heard from again. And the mystery endures to this day.

Those valiant adventures, and more by the military, set the stage for the Pan American World Airways Clippers. The famous "Flying Boats" were the first to provide passenger air service to the Pacific, the first one arriving in Hawai'i on a practice run in April 1935. The route was San Francisco to Honolulu to Midway to Wake Island to Guam, then to Manila and Macao/Hong Kong, a six-day trip with sixty hours of flying time. Then back again. I watched the Pan Am Clippers land and take off from the vantage point of a small farm my mother's family owned in Pearl City. The arriving planes would fly in from the east and circle Pearl Harbor, landing to the northeast on typical trade wind days, touch down on the aquamarine waters with a healthy splash, then taxi over to the airline's new base on the Pearl City Peninsula, where the passengers, all first class, would disembark. The planes augured an exotic new era, one filled with glamor and romance.

To get to the farm, the lower parts of which we leased to Chinese families growing rice, I would hop aboard the OR&L rail line at A'ala Park. The railroad in those days carried sugarcane, freight and passengers in what we called the White Train because it was painted white. The rails went right through our property, formally the John Edward Kahoa estate, which was bounded by Lehua Avenue on the east and Waiawa Stream on the west. The tracks then continued around Pearl Harbor to the Wai'anae Coast, around Ka'ena Point, up to Kahuku and ending in Laie. It was a marvelous and scenic trip through mile after mile of unspoiled terrain. I hold a lot of nostalgia for the OR&L, which was gradually dismantled over the years.

Toward the end of the 1930s, of course, there were war clouds over Europe. We saw the headlines almost daily in the *Star-Bulletin* or morning *Advertiser*. In March 1938, Germany invaded neighboring Austria. In March 1939, they took over parts of Czechoslovakia, and Germany's other neighbors understandably were anxious about what would happen next.

In the summer of 1939, my brother Abe, then twenty-two, was selected to represent Hawai'i at the first World Conference of Christian Youth in Amsterdam, the Netherlands. It was during that conference—attended by more than 1,000 young people from dozens of nations—that he decided to become a minister. But no one in the family suspected, as he set off for San Francisco on a Matson ship, the risks that the trip presented. A train ride across country brought Abe to New York, where he boarded a second ship for Southampton, England, and Le Havre, France. From there he made his way to Amsterdam and the embrace of his fellow Christian delegates and sponsors. Abe relished the fellowship during the conference, held July 24 to August 2. But by August Europe was turning increasingly ugly. Germany invaded Slovakia, and the other nations were bracing for the worst. When Abe went to catch his ship back to the United States, they told him, "We're not sailing." He was stuck, and potentially about to be swept up in war with nothing to his name but a passport, a guitar, some cash and a worthless ship ticket home.

At the harbor, he happened to run into a poised and well-dressed black man, who, perhaps sensing Abe's distress, asked him what was wrong. Abe hesitated, unsure of the wisdom of sharing his woes with a stranger, but then went ahead and explained.

"Give me your passport and $50 and meet me back here at one o'clock," the man said.

Abe thought, *What do I have to lose?* He gave the man the money and passport.

Back at the pier at 1 p.m., there was no sign of the mysterious black man. He waited until 2 p.m., then decided to go to the American embassy for help.

He described the black man to a consular official, who said, "That's the Black Eagle. He's an international smuggler."

Oh, mercy, Abe thought.

"I guess that's that," he muttered to himself on his way out. "Goodbye money, goodbye passport. At least I have my guitar. Maybe I can play on the sidewalks for francs."

On a whim, however, he went back down to the harbor. And there was the Black Eagle.

"Where have you been?" the man demanded. "Here's your ticket. Here's your passport."

Abe was astounded and delighted at the same time.

Then the Black Eagle pulled out a package.

"Can you do me a favor?" he asked. "Can you deliver this package in New York?"

Oh, brother, Abe thought. *He wants me to smuggle something for him in return.*

In as innocent a tone as he could muster, Abe asked, "What's in the package?"

The Black Eagle assessed him with a steely-eyed gaze.

"Never mind," he said, and put the parcel away.

And that's how my brother left Europe as the Nazis prepared to invade Poland. ✤

CHAPTER

6

In the fall of 1940, during my high eleventh year, we moved up to the Kapālama campus, where I had a room in dormitory D.

And in the fall of 1941, I entered my senior year with thirty-five other boys, all boarders and all in the Junior Reserve Officer Training Corps. We dressed in either khakis, fatigues or a dress uniform. Our school day was compact and disciplined. It began with a bugle call at 6 a.m. By 6:10 a.m. we were assembled for roll call, orders of the day and calisthenics. We fell out for breakfast at 6:30 a.m. in the dining room. At precisely 7:10 a.m. the cadet officers inspected our dorm rooms. At 7:25 a.m. we reported for assembly with the principal and sang Hawaiian songs.

Classes began at 8 a.m. and ended at 2 p.m. At 2:30 p.m. we reported for custodial duties. At 3 p.m., we had ninety minutes of athletics, either varsity or junior varsity sports or intramurals. At 5:30 p.m. we fell into company ranks to lower the flag. Dinner was at 6. At 7 p.m. we had club meetings. At 7:30 p.m. we had study hall. And 9 p.m. was lights out. That was our day.

One of my good friends was Kekuni Blaisdell, whom my kids would later call Uncle Dicky. He was a healthy, handsome young Hawaiian—caring, responsive, curious, intelligent and prompt on assignments. He was consistently an honor student who earned gold and silver pins for his academic achievements. I can't ever recall him being in trouble. He was a serious, competitive athlete on the first string as left guard on the varsity football team. He played in all the games sponsored by the Interscholastic League of Hawai'i, then and now the private school league. But he had a softer side, too: he loved to sing as a second tenor. We were partners in a project in Mr. E.R. Burmeister's Metallic and Engineering Shop that won special acclaim. Our nickname for it was "Kuni and Kina." He would later go on to become a distinguished doctor and a founder of the UH School of Medicine.

Something awoke me from a sound sleep before dawn on Sunday. I went to the window. The air was fresh. The usual sounds. A dog barking in the distance. There was no clue that the world was about to change. I went back to bed.

In the morning, we were in our dorm rooms getting ready for breakfast, after which we would typically all go to church, boys and girls together. But that was not to be a typical Sunday. At about 7:50 in the morning, we heard explosions.

"What is going on!" Kekuni exclaimed.

The school was high on a ridge, perfectly perched to look down at Pearl Harbor. And we could see smoke. One ship, which we later learned was the *Arizona*, had been bombed and was listing to one side. It was sending up billows of smoke—and did so for days. At about 8 a.m., a squadron of planes came over us and we saw that it was the Japanese. Each plane had a red ball—a sun symbol—on the wings. We didn't know it until later, but that was the squadron heading over to attack the naval air base at Kāneʻohe. Not knowing what else to do, we went to breakfast and then to church. But the whole time we were wondering, what's going to happen? And of course, things were happening very quickly.

Before the day was out, our territorial governor, Joseph Poindexter, had relinquished his authority to martial law under the Army commander, Major General Walter Short. Our ROTC commander, Colonel Ainsley Mahikoa, received orders to place an armed rifle unit in the Koʻolau Mountains above our school. So my company at Kamehameha was mobilized, issued World War I rifles and ammunition and sent up to scout for paratroopers. The nearly universal fear was that an invasion would soon follow the air raid. Our secondary mission was to guard the island's water system, a series of pipes and flumes, from sabotage. So we pulled together some gear and twenty-nine of us seniors, Kekuni included, trudged up into Kuahiwi ʻAlapaki above Keōpūolani in the Koʻolau range, making camp before nightfall.

We weren't allowed a cooking fire—the military authorities had ordered a total island blackout—so we fairly froze in the dampness. As we lay in our sacks contemplating sleep, with sentries posted, every rustle of a leaf or creak of a tree limb in our minds became the enemy inching closer.

"What was that?!" someone whispered in the darkness after a particularly loud grunt rose from the forest.

The beam of a flashlight revealed our invader: a 200-pound *pua'a*, a pair of piglets in tow. She vanished as quickly as she appeared, leaving behind as evidence only the pounding on our eardrums.

Colonel Mahikoa kept us supplied with water and rations. The food was bland and cold but plentiful. And that remained our mission until just before Christmas, when we were ordered to stand down, having never fired a shot.

A plaque at Kamehameha Schools still bears our names: Richard Aea, Louis Agard (we knew him as Buzzy), Daniel Akaka, Henry Awana, Richard Blaisdell, Carl Bode, William Campbell, William Crabbe, Joseph Daniels, John De Guair, Arthur Doo, Robert Douglas, Robert Gomard, Herbert Heu.

The list goes on:

Henry Kahanu, Donald Kauka, Thomas Kealoha, Keanahou Ludloff, Albert MacDonald, Theodore Morrison, Lionel Muller, Jack O'Brien, Calvin Ontai, John Sabey, Mack Taylor, Leonard Warner, Benjamin Williams, Abraham Won, Llewellyn Wong.

Quite a variety of names for boys all or part Hawaiian.

What followed in Hawai'i and places on the Mainland was one of the cruelest chapters in American history, when people of Japanese ancestry were rounded up as possible spies or saboteurs and placed in internment camps. Hundreds of Japanese, including whole families, were sent from Hawai'i to camps like Manzanar in the California desert. In all, more than 100,000 Japanese Americans were incarcerated. In 1943, Hawai'i got its own camp, Honouliuli, on the far side of Pearl Harbor. Honouliuli held 320 internees at a time and nearly 4,000 total by the time it closed in 1946. But Japanese Americans in Hawai'i fared better than their Mainland counterparts, thanks in large part to the efforts of one man, Jack Burns. As tensions with Japan grew in the year before Pearl Harbor, Burns, then with the Honolulu Police Department, was assigned as head of the department's Espionage Bureau. In that capacity, he investigated whether the local Japanese community, then nearly forty percent of the population, posed any threats. In so doing, he got to know the community well and was able to vouch for their loyalty in the aftermath of the attack. He remained close to the local Japanese populace after the war, and it would in fact become one of the pillars of his political success.

It wasn't until 1988 that the United States offered an apology for the internment camps. That's when President Ronald Reagan signed the Civil Liberties Act, which also paid out $20,000 to each surviving victim. In 2015, President Barack Obama named Honouliuli a national monument for its historical significance, but to date there is nothing there, only empty scrub land.

The first months of World War II brought unrelentingly grim news from the western Pacific. Coincidentally with the Pearl Harbor raid, Japanese forces had attacked Guam and Wake Island, Thailand, Singapore, Hong Kong, Malaya and the Philippines. In January 1942, Japan invaded Burma, the Dutch East Indies, New Guinea, the Solomon Islands and captured Manila.

Although not many people know it, Oʻahu was the target of a second Japanese air attack in March 1942. The plan was to hit the U.S. carrier fleet and disrupt repairs to the damaged battleships in Pearl Harbor. On March 4, two huge Kawanishi H8K1 "Emily" flying boats took off from Wotje in the Marshall Islands without fighter escort. The distance to Honolulu was too great—2,500 miles—for their fuel tanks, so the planes landed near French Frigate Shoals in the Northwestern Hawaiian Islands, where they were refueled by two submarines modified to hold aviation gas. Then they took off again and approached Honolulu under cover of darkness in the early hours of March 5.

The massive airboats were picked up by radars operated by the Women's Air Raid Defense Corps, and P-40 Warhawk fighter planes scrambled to intercept them. Searchlights soon sliced across the overcast sky. Even with radar vectors, the fighters failed to find the intruders in the rainy, moonless darkness. But the poor conditions also worked against the flying boats. Each plane had to drop its four 550-pound bombs blindly. Two hit off the harbor entrance with no damage. More landed in Makiki Heights, about 1,000 feet from Roosevelt High School, shattering windows and digging craters up to ten feet deep. At that point, the flying boats beat a hasty retreat, both incredibly making it back home intact. As inconsequential as it was, the bombing run was yet another incident that rattled our lives in those desperate and confused early months of the war.

A brief ray of hope interrupted the dismal headlines when Air Force Lieutenant Colonel Jimmy Doolittle, in April 1942, led a squadron of B-25 bombers in a surprise raid on Tokyo. The bombers took off from aircraft carriers—an unprecedented feat—and landed—or crashed—in China. They inflicted substantial damage, and the effect on American morale was huge. "War Strikes Japan! Planes Raid 4 Industrial Areas," screamed the headline in the *Star-Bulletin*. "TOKYO, YOKOHAMA, KOBE BLASTED IN ALLIED RAID," echoed the *Advertiser*.

In the Philippines, U.S. and Filipino forces resisted until May 1942, when more than 80,000 soldiers surrendered. General Douglas MacArthur, the allied commander, escaped from Corregidor in a PT boat, eventually reaching Australia, where he promised, "I shall return." The Philippines campaigns were of great interest to me later as chairman of the Senate Veterans' Affairs Committee.

A month later, June 4–6, 1942, the tide of the war turned with the Battle of Midway, where U.S. carrier-based forces defeated their Japanese counterparts who had much superior strength. Had we lost Midway, we all felt certain, an invasion of the Hawaiian Islands was next. ✤

CHAPTER

7

As the war raged during my final semester at Kamehameha, I continued working for Hawaiian Electric at the downtown power plant.

When my class graduated in June 1942, several of my classmates were drafted into the Army, but I was not because I worked for a utility. Even though I enjoyed working with Mau, there came a point where I felt like a new challenge. So I talked to Mr. Olson, the superintendent. As it happened, the Army Corps of Engineers was looking for welders. So I thought that was a good time to make a move. And with Olson's blessing, I left Hawaiian Electric and joined the Corps of Engineers as a civilian.

My first project was the construction of Pier 39 in Honolulu Harbor. We had to drive all the piles before putting in the pier, and they were steel piles, so a lot of welding was involved. And we also had shops for anything that needed welding.

And because I was working for the Corps of Engineers, the draft board left me alone. For the time being. The superintendent of the Pier 39 project had me doing all kinds of things, including working on diesel engines. I studied diesels and they put me in the diesel shop and I guess I did well because they put me on a tugboat, the *Eads*. We operated out of Honolulu and also Pearl Harbor, and eventually I was put in charge of the engine room.

The corps kept me occupied from 1942 until 1944.

During that time, in the interest of maintaining a social life, I cofounded the Hawaiian Junior Civic Club, which met periodically at the Richards Street YWCA. Other times we had picnics, at Kailua

Beach Park, Kalama Beach Park, that sort of venue. As a director of the civic club, I was among those who interviewed potential new members. One day in the fall of 1944 a pretty Chinese Hawaiian girl, a senior at Roosevelt High School, sat down across from me. I can't really remember what we talked about. But I do recall her outgoing nature, so different from my own quiet reserve. Her name was Millie and her family lived in Makiki. To hear her tell it years later, I "never had a chance." Part of it was I had gone to Kamehameha School *for Boys* and didn't know a lot of girls—or a lot about girls.

"He's warm and has that face you can trust," she told our curious grandchildren decades later about how we got together. "An untouched Christian boy from Kawaiahaʻo. Clean-cut and good-looking. I thought he was the ideal person to be the father of my kids." Millie was never one to mince words or skirt around a point.

After we began seeing each other, we never really saw anything in anyone else, although Millie insists other girls were always pursuing me. Personally, I don't recall any.

So life was looking pretty good.

And then they drafted me. I did my six weeks of basic at Schofield Barracks, later made famous by James Jones' novel *From Here to Eternity* and the movie starring Burt Lancaster, Deborah Kerr, Frank Sinatra and Montgomery Clift. And then, likely because of my welding and diesel experience, they assigned me back to the Corps of Engineers in the western Pacific. I bid a fond goodbye to Millie and my family and boarded a troop ship at Pier 7. That's right where the HECO power plant is, so I felt that, in a sense, Mau and Olson were also there to see me off.

We went to Guam and then Saipan. By then it was 1945. On Saipan I was assigned to another tug. While there, I recall, there was a particularly stubborn diesel engine that just wouldn't start. So they came to me and said, "Eh, we want you to look at this engine. We need to get it running." And so I went in with the best of my ability and did everything that I knew, but it wouldn't start. At the time, there were these ships that would come in to deliver goods, and the chief engineer of one of these ships was a guy named Von Hulu Donlin. He had papers to operate on any engine, steam or diesel.

"Hey, come, I have an engine I've been working on," I told him.

When he arrived at my shop, I told him all the things I had tried.

"And it still won't start?" he asked.

"No."

So, not following any formal procedures, he began fiddling with the thing.

This, that. And I was right there, helping him with each unorthodox step.

Then, with a flip of a switch, the hibernating bear roared awake.

Wow! Everyone in the shop was amazed. They couldn't believe the thing had started and came over for a closer look.

"Eh, don't touch this thing!" I warned them, only half joking. "It's working now. Let it work!"

I was saddened to learn of the death on April 12 of Franklin Roosevelt, the only president I had ever really known. I was too young to have a real awareness of his predecessor, Herbert Hoover, apart from selling newspapers. And I knew very little about Roosevelt's successor, Harry Truman, but had to trust that he would do the right thing for us troops. In Europe, the war was winding down. Allied forces had won the Battle of the Bulge, the German's desperate—and almost successful—counterattack, and Hitler's hordes were on the run. His own staff tried to assassinate him, and on April 30 Hitler took his own life. The war ended in that theater on May 8, Victory in Europe Day.

But in the Pacific we were preparing for a long haul. The invasion of Japan, which everyone anticipated before hostilities could cease, promised to be a long and bloody undertaking. The Japanese had already started using suicide pilots—*kamikazes*—against allied ships. We had no doubt they would defend every inch of their homeland with the same selfless ferocity.

Our tugboat missions, hauling barges laden with building materials and supplies, took us back and forth between Guam, Saipan and a small island in the Northern Marianas called Tinian. We had captured the island from the Japanese after an amphibious landing and subsequent battle from July 24 to August 1, 1944. But a garrison on

Aguijan Island just offshore was still in the hands of the Japanese, commanded by a die-hard lieutenant. And an untold number of Japanese soldiers and civilians were in hiding on the main island, convinced by the military leadership that the Americans would slaughter them. (In fact, the last holdout on the island, Murata Susumu, did not surrender until 1953.) Time and again, we would come across families in hiding and promise them safety. Some families, including small children, all hand in hand, jumped to their deaths off a cliff rather than face expected American brutality.

In 1945, Tinian was a bustling place, with 50,000 troops. Thousands of Seabees had built six 8,000-foot runways to support B-29 bombers, which conducted runs against the Philippines and Japan, including the March 1945 firebombing of Tokyo. One of the pilots was a Hawaiian boy, last name Stewart, a graduate of Kamehameha, but we had no time to socialize.

The bombers would leave at 5 a.m. and fly to Japan and come right back without stopping. Some of them didn't make it back. Some came back with holes in their wings. We never got any after-action reports, but had the sense that we were really hurting Japan.

And then came scuttlebutt of a special kind of bomb. Some people called it a "uranium" bomb, others an "atom" bomb. We had no sense of its devastating nature, but favored anything that would shorten the war. Truman was supposedly deciding whether to use it.

One of the B-29s was the *Enola Gay*. Its payload was kept underground, and when they loaded it, they brought the bomb up from below into the bomb bay. I learned later the bomb was called Little Boy and its destination was Hiroshima. I didn't see the *Enola Gay* take off, but word got around once it had.

I was back on Saipan when we heard the war was over. As far as I know, I am the only person to have glimpsed both the beginning of World War II for America and the bomber that helped end it. ❖

CHAPTER

8

In December 1945, I returned to Pearl Harbor on a so-called LSM, landing ship/medium, much like the ones used in the D-Day invasion. We called it a slapstick because as you sailed you slapped the swells. All the way. It was a rough ride. Curiously, I could smell the land before I actually saw it. As we rounded Hospital Point, the golf course at Hickam Field was a fond sight after more than a year away.

Looking back, I think I might have been suffering from a bit of post-traumatic stress disorder, what we called battle fatigue back then. My dis-ease—and I use the hyphen deliberately—manifested itself in a sort of restlessness.

On Maui, I scaled the 10,000-foot summit of Haleakalā, the House of the Sun, and soaked in the Pools of Oheʻo, popularly called the Seven Sacred Pools, near Hāna, hitchhiking most of the way. Often I stayed with strangers, Hawaiian families that took me in as one of their own. I rambled through the rainforests of Kīpahulu, which would become part of Haleakalā National Park in 1961. In his final years, aviation pioneer Charles Lindbergh adopted that area as his home and was buried there in 1974. I marveled at the lush landscape of ʻIao Valley and saw my first *nēnē*, a descendant of Canada geese likely blown here in a storm. The village of Lāhainā, once the kingdom's capital and a bustling port of call for whalers, was again a sleepy scene in the years before large-scaled tourism transformed the coast. When Mark Twain described Hawaiʻi as "the loveliest fleet of islands anchored in any ocean," he may well have been sitting along the shore in Lāhainā, where Lānaʻi and Molokaʻi frame sunsets across Kalohi Channel. On a clear day on Oʻahu, you can see Molokaʻi on the horizon, less often Haleakalā and Lānaʻi. But on the West Maui coast, I had my first solid sense of occupying an archipelago. North of Lāhainā, where the high-rise hotels of Kāʻanapali and luxury resorts of Kapalua now line the shore, the land back then was all rainforest, farms and modest residential. I explored as far as Kahakuloa, a village punctuated by a 630-foot-high promontory. The narrow, winding, unlit road in and out was then and remains today one of the most harrowing in Hawaiʻi, topping even Hāna Highway.

On Hawaiʻi island, the Big Island, I tramped through dank lava tubes home to albino crickets, creatures that had lost their color—and their eyesight—through evolutionary adaptation to a lightless habitat. I sat with legs dangling over the edge of Halemaʻumaʻu Crater and stared into the maw of a slumbering volcano. I haunted tiny cafés in Hilo, a rainy, rustic setting worthy of a Somerset Maugham novel. A few weeks after my visit, on April 1, 1946, most of the Hilo waterfront was wiped out by a tsunami from an 8.6 magnitude earthquake in the Aleutian Islands. The seismic sea waves killed 165 people—159 in Hawaiʻi and six in Alaska, and caused more than $26 million in damage. That's about $240 million in today's dollars.

Had the waves hit a day earlier, Millie and I could easily have become victims back on Oʻahu. On March 31, a Sunday, the Hawaiian Junior Civic Club held a picnic at Kailua Beach. Going to Kailua in those days was a hair-raising adventure. There was no Pali Highway and no Pali tunnels in those days. We drove slowly up Nuʻuanu Pali Drive, two lanes surrounded by lush rainforest, then as now. At the top was a small parking area with a wall and you could look out over the windward side, much as people do at the Pali Lookout now. And of course, the winds could be vicious. Then you'd start down. It was very narrow, one lane up, one lane down, and they drew a line down the middle, but I always felt that, even though you hugged the one side, two wheels were on the other side of the line. So when you passed a car going the other way, it had to be in certain spots and often it was a matter of millimeters.

"Be careful, Danny."

Obviously, we drove slowly. So getting to Kailua took quite an investment of time, an all-day outing.

It was a bright, sunny day, the bay its typical hue of green and blue. There was no hint of the destruction that would hit the next morning. A series of nine waves rolled into Kailua Bay and Lanikai, the newspapers said. One family that lived below the Lanikai pillboxes recalled seeing a piano floating in the bay. Elsewhere, a large rowboat wound up in someone's living room. Monday was trash pickup day, so all the neighborhood rubbish was swept across yards and deposited on the beach and inland. Calls to the radio stations about the disaster were dismissed as April Fool's jokes.

July 1947 found me in Oslo, Norway, at the second World Conference of Christian Youth. I was already an adult, but the conference, attended by some 300 of the faithful, included many twenty-somethings such as myself. This was the same conference that my brother Abe had attended in Amsterdam in July and August 1939 as the Nazis began invading their neighbors.

It was after the World Conference of Christian Youth that the *Morning Star* opportunity arose. The church elders were familiar with my wartime work on diesels and so asked me to serve as engineer. When I met the captain, Price Lewis, he asked me also to navigate. I quickly agreed. ✤

CHAPTER

9

When we awoke from our post-storm slumber aboard the *Morning Star*, I took some bearings with the sextant and set a course under sail for Kwajalein. In the meantime, we cleaned up and repaired what we could. I spent much of my time massaging the moribund engine, hoping it would ultimately cough to life like a near-drowning victim responding to CPR. At least we had the mainsail and the jib.

The only trouble was, on the day we were to arrive at Kwajalein… it wasn't there.

I had miscalculated the course.

Captain Lewis studied me with a raised brow.

"Akaka, where are we?" he demanded.

The only explanation was that we had slept longer than we imagined—an entire day longer. So I redid the figures and at dawn the next day took a cloud-free sextant bearing. I plotted a new course and a day later we reached Kwajalein. Like war-weary buccaneers, we sailed into the lagoon and tied up at the battered pier.

The place was a mess, with windows shattered, houses missing roofs, debris and shards of glass in the streets. Some of the Marshallese and the U.S. Navy captain in charge of the atoll told us that it was the worst storm in a generation.

So that was the beginning of our mission in the Marshalls and the Carolines. We shuttled missionaries out to these little islands, dropped them off, picked others up. Our first stop in the Carolines, in February 1948, was the easternmost isle of Kosrae, then called Kosaie, much like Hawai'i with green volcanic peaks. There we were met by the Reverend Eleanor Wilson, a native of Cambridge, Massachusetts, who had been ordained in February 1946 at Kawaiaha'o Church. She would become captain of the *Morning Star VI* in 1950.

In her 1956 book about Wilson, *The Lady was a Skipper*, Maribelle Cormack recounted the greeting.

> There were handclasps between welcomers and welcomees. Captain Price Lewis and his youthful crew were bearded like pirates. They had had a rough passage out from Honolulu and a bad storm before reaching Kwajalein. The sails were worn and patched. It was well that rigging was woven wire. Rope must have parted under the strain. They were bone weary and thankful to be here. The young captain watched with satisfaction as the anchors were dropped over the side.
>
> "What do you want more than anything else?" Eleanor asked the captain and crewmen as they were paddled to the mission station by the shore.
>
> "A drink of water, a bath and a shave, and something to eat besides canned beans!" the captain answered laughing.
>
> "You can have all of these!" she told them. What luck that there was something special for them! Only yesterday her cook had fried a great batch of doughnuts, and they were safely stored in tin boxes to protect them against the ever-present cockroaches.
>
> Being Sunday there could be no noisy celebration; shouts of welcome did not count! But there was rejoicing everywhere on the four inhabited islands of the Kusaie [Kosrae] group and the word was going out, almost by frigate bird, it seemed, over thousands of miles of sea. Soon on every island in the Carolines they would be saying, "The *Star* is back! The *Star* is back!"

It had been forty-two years since the *Morning Star V* had plied these seas.

❈ ❈ ❈

It was on Kosrae, of course, that the famous pirate Bully Hayes was shipwrecked and stranded. His ship, the *Leonora*, was hit by a storm in Lelu Harbor in March 1874. He spent the next several months abusing the natives, and word of his misdeeds finally reached the British navy. The HMS *Rosario* arrived that September and the crew arrested Hayes, but he escaped in a boat made from the timber of the wreckage. Bully, aptly named, was notoriously cruel to his crew, and was ultimately murdered by his cook in 1877. Some say he left treasure behind in the jungles of Kosrae, but no one ever found it. Unfortunately, as busy as the *Morning Star* crew was, we never had a chance to look for it ourselves.

To me, the fascinating thing about the eastern Carolines is that each island, relatively close by, has a distinct language. The language of Kosrae is very different from that of Pohnpei, which in turn is very different from that of Chuuk. This is quite unlike the Polynesian tongues, which have clear similarities, even though the Polynesian Triangle extends from Hawai'i to New Zealand (Aotearoa) to Easter Island (Rapa Nui). House is *hale* in Hawaiian, *fale* in Samoan. Sea wind is *makani* in Hawaiian and *matangi* in Tahitian. There are countless examples: taro, kalo; taboo, *kapu*. It's amazing to me how many cultures (including ancient Egypt) call their sun god Ra or La. But the only language uniting the eastern Carolines in those days was Japanese. Almost everyone spoke it, thanks to Japan's longtime prewar occupation.

The natives dressed simply, the men wearing shorts and a short-sleeved shirt, the women plain dresses, mostly cotton and not particularly colorful. No one wore shoes, not even the chief and his wife, whom we met as a courtesy on our first day. A typical meal included breadfruit, maybe some yams, bananas or taro. And of course there was plenty of fish.

Education was universal, as the missionaries had set up schools. The most common mode of transportation was the canoe, which commonly plied an extensive network of rivers, much like a canal system. In fact, the waterways in those days were an impediment to foot and bicycle traffic. So one boy from Hawai'i, Manny Sproat, made it his business to build bridges over the streams. Manny had been an engineer in the military and I guess he decided to retire there. The natives helped him get the timber and set up these uncovered spans so they didn't have to wade through the water. He made a huge difference. I guess he lived on several of the islands and went to wherever he had work to do. But when we got there, he was on Kosrae and so I got to meet him and talk story.

I loved my months on the *Morning Star*, but by the time I left I was ready for home. They had an airport on Chuuk, so I was able to fly out. Captain Price left soon after, I heard, and they turned the schooner over to Eleanor Wilson. I was surprised to learn that the *Morning Star VI* sank in 1951 while under tow between Pohnpei and the Marshalls. A storm hit, the tow line broke and the captain at the time, Creston Ketchum, couldn't keep the vessel afloat with the pumps. So he and his mate dove into the stormy seas and swam for the tow boat, the *Torry*. And the once-proud schooner went under. There never was a *Morning Star VII*. But a decade later, from 1959 to 1962, ABC aired a show called *Adventures in Paradise*, created by James Michener (whom I would later meet) and starring Gardner McKay as the captain of the South Pacific schooner *Tiki III*. It was a series that resonated robustly with this old salt. ❧

CHAPTER

10

On May 22, 1948, a sunny Saturday, not long after I returned to Honolulu, Millie and I were married at Kawaiahaʻo Church by the Reverend Edward Kahale. It was a small ceremony. My best man was Richard Aea, whom I knew from Kamehameha, and Millie's maid of honor was Harriet "Wunnie" Lau Akana. We had no honeymoon. And, sadly, I couldn't afford to give her a diamond ring, but promised that I would someday! Millie graciously accepted that vow.

We moved in with Millie's grandmother, or Popo, who had a good-sized house to herself at Nuʻuanu Avenue and Iliahi Lane, just above School Street. And that fall I enrolled at the University of Hawaiʻi at Mānoa on the G.I. Bill, which had helped so many World War II veterans get a college education.

On October 22, our daughter was born. Millie and I agreed that I would name our girls and she would name the boys. So I decided to name her after Millie and also my mother, Annie. I put the two names together as Millannie, which has sort of a Hawaiian lilt. And for her middle name, I drew on my days as a schooner mate: Kahokuaonani, the beautiful morning star.

To make ends meet, I worked weekends at the Pacific Club, the first private club of its kind west of the Mississippi. The older part of the club, on Queen Emma Street, is the former estate of Archibald Cleghorn, a Scottish businessman who married Princess Miriam Likelike, the sister of David Kalākaua. Under King Kalākaua, Cleghorn's daughter, Victoria, became an heir to the throne as Princess Kaʻiulani. Queen Liliʻuokalani later named her crown princess, and the beautiful and gracious Kaʻiulani would have ruled Hawaiʻi had the monarchy not been overthrown in 1893—ironically by some prominent club members, including Sanford B. Dole, the first provisional governor.

Sadly, Kaʻiulani died in 1899 at age twenty-three. But her understated family home, with an early 1960s expansion by the noted architect Vladimir Ossipoff, stands in mute testament to some of Hawaiʻi's most pivotal history.

Back in the late 1940s, and for many decades afterward, the Pacific Club was for white men only, mostly Big Five businessmen, some of whom lived in cottages on the property. The only people of color there were the workers. The first Asians weren't admitted until 1968, and the first woman didn't come aboard until 1984. Anyway, they paid me a modest wage to staff the reception desk and keep track of the payment chits the members signed. This was harder than it sounds as some of the members had really bad handwriting. I suspected in some cases this was intentional. But as my first weeks passed I learned to recognize their scrawls and directed the monthly bills appropriately.

Millie went to work for her mother, who had a children's shop in the Palama Theater complex, across from Kaumakapili Church.

During the summer, I worked as a foreman at the Libby Cannery off Houghtailing Street. I also worked in the tire shop for the Army in Āliamanu Crater. So with all that, and my G.I. Bill pay of $133.50 a month, and living rent-free with Popo, we got by. Popo and her husband, Gunggung, had worked for the family that owned a house where the Baptist academy is now. He was a chef and she was a maid until Gunggung passed away. She didn't speak English very well, all those years. She would spend time going to Chinatown. It was so easy from School Street to walk down to Chinatown and visit the whole day with her friends and come back home. So that was the kind of life she had. But she was a big help to our children as they grew up.

At UH, I first went into the arts and sciences because I really didn't know what I was going to pursue. But by the end of my second year I was gravitating toward teaching. So in my junior year I switched to education, with a minor in music, and got a B.A. and a fifth-year professional certificate as well. My internship was at Kaimuki Intermediate School and my first job was at Kahuku High, where I spent two years.

On May 3, 1953, our first of four sons was born. Millie named him Daniel Jr.

Politics was the furthest thing from my mind, but no one could ignore the seismic shift that was taking shape in 1953 and 1954. Largely because of people like me—returning vets educated by the

G.I. Bill—the ranks of the Democratic Party in Hawai'i were swelling. And in the election of 1954, the Democrats took over the territorial legislature for the first time. The new lawmakers included World War II veterans Dan Inouye and Spark Matsunaga, George Ariyoshi, and from Hawai'i Island, my future nemesis, Nelson Doi.

Gone were the days of Republican Party dominance at the hands of white tycoons, many of them descendants of the first missionaries. One of the architects of the victory was Jack Burns, a former Honolulu police captain and chairman of the Democratic County Committee. Jack had his sights set on Congress, a goal that eluded him in 1952 and 1954. But he would ultimately make an indelible mark on the Islands' political landscape—and on my own career path. ❖

CHAPTER

11

When I was growing up, my family was very musical. We sang daily. So music was a natural thing for me. When I was at Kawananakoa Intermediate, in the seventh grade, I became interested in band. The instructor was a woman at that time, Helen Cunningham, and she took to me and I guess I was an easy kid to teach. So I worked with her and I really liked the band. I learned to play trumpet.

When I went to Kamehameha, of course, I took band there, too, under Mr. Otto Helbig. And when I went to college, I thought I wanted to really study music academically, so I took that as a minor. I was in the UH band, playing at all the football games and at concerts as well, loving every note and moment of color and drama. I also was in the chorus as a tenor, but I took pride in saying I was a "blender" type because I could sing different parts.

Also at UH, I became part of a deputation team that puts students together to travel to schools throughout the state, telling high school students what the university had to offer and what we did there. They would set up an assembly and we'd sort of take over the event and we had to sing and entertain the kids. We had some good people in that group. One was George "Scotty" Koga, who later became a Honolulu city councilman. And Jimmy Shigeta, who went on to act in such movies as *Flower Drum Song*, *Midway* and *Die Hard*. And we had George Shimabukuro, who was famous even at that time as a local boy who sang Japanese songs. Other members included Satoru Izutsu, who would go on to become a medical school professor; Ted Yanagihara, who would become a teacher at Farrington High; and Eppy Yadao, father of TV reporter Elisa Yadao. That was a good activity for me because I met people on the Neighbor Islands and also got a good sense of what various schools were like, which helped me in my teaching career. Those were good years.

Music continued to be a large part of my life after I received my diploma at Andrews Amphitheater. As part of my teaching internship, I handled the band at Kaimuki Intermediate School. And I taught social studies and ran the band and chorus at Kahuku High School after that, in 1953–54. My work in music really got me friendly with a lot of families. Hiroshi Togo, the owner of the Kahuku Theater, the only one in town, had two daughters in my class, Ellen and May.

My goal was to switch jobs every two years so that I could experience as many schools as possible toward the goal of becoming school superintendent, which was my highest ambition for many years. After Kahuku, I went to Pearl Harbor Intermediate for two years, then Aina Haina Elementary. So I had all three levels at that point—elementary, intermediate and high school.

Millie, meanwhile, landed a well-paying civilian job with the Army at Fort Shafter. Our son Gerard was born a few days before Christmas 1954. And our son Alan came into the world in June 1956. Millannie, then eight, was at Kamehameha Schools Preparatory Department, which is what they called the elementary grades.

In 1957, I went back to my alma mater, Kamehameha, where I stayed for three years. The late 1950s were a particularly interesting time in politics and in education. There were very strong rumblings for statehood. But there was opposition in Congress, particularly among southern Democrats led by Senator Lyndon Johnson, our future president. When Jack Burns succeeded in his quest to become the territory's congressional delegate, going to Washington in January 1957, some there accused him of being a communist.

That October, an event of a different nature stunned the world: the launch of Sputnik. Suddenly there was fear that the Soviet Union had achieved technological superiority over the United States, an edge that might extend to nuclear weapons, which both countries were pursuing aggressively in those years, along with the means to deliver them. In the ensuing national self-analysis, it was decided that our schools were to blame. *That's* why the Soviets were ahead. One of the changes that came about was more hands-on science labs, which remains standard today. It could be argued that no single factor had such a profound influence on our schools, particularly in science education, as that beeping satellite.

At Kamehameha, I started with a sixth grade class. That year, Millannie also was in sixth grade, although not in my class, of course. It was fun to see her every day on campus. After a year, I shifted to the intermediate school, and again had the band and the chorus.

Our family continued to be active at Kawaiahaʻo Church, where my brother Abe became pastor in 1957. A year later, I became director of the Kawaiahaʻo Church choir, or more formally the minister of music. This group dated back to 1836. My predecessors included Princess Victoria Kamāmalu and Lydia Kamakaʻeha, who became Queen Liliʻuokalani. The queen was also the first organist. The singers included Princess Bernice Pauahi Bishop, whose will established the Bishop Estate to support Kamehameha Schools. When I took over, we had about fifty-five singers of all ages. Promotional materials of those days touted my "mastery of the trumpet, horn, trombone, tuba, clarinet and saxophone." But, honestly, the organizational aspects of the job kept me so busy I rarely had time to play. Our staples included "O Ka ʻIlima," "Pūpū A ʻO ʻEwa," and "ʻĀinahau," usually to ʻukulele accompaniment. The song "Mauna Kaʻala" described the beautiful Mount Kaʻala, and "ʻŪlili Ē" was about the antics of the kōlea, or Pacific golden plover.

Interest in the Islands grew even more when Congress passed the Hawaiʻi Admission Act in March 1959, establishing Hawaiʻi as the fiftieth state. The legislation, quickly signed into law by President Eisenhower, would not take effect until August, pending the results of referendum in the isles, but most everyone accepted statehood as a sure thing, if not universally a good thing.

Fireworks lit the skies and sirens sounded when news of the vote came down.

At the urging of Mayor Neal Blaisdell, a crowd of about 1,000 people gathered at Kawaiahaʻo Church for quiet reflection. And at services the next morning, Friday the 13th of March, my brother Abe delivered what would become known as his statehood sermon, which Burns entered into the Congressional Record.

"'One nation under God, indivisible, with liberty and justice for all'—these words have a fuller meaning for us this morning in Hawaiʻi,"

Abe said. "And we have gathered here at Kawaiahaʻo Church to give thanks to God, and to pray for his guidance and protection in the years ahead.

"I would like today to speak the message of self-affirmation: that we take courage to be what we truly are, the Aloha State." Later, he defined aloha: "Aloha consists of this new attitude of heart, above negativism, above legalism. It is the unconditional desire to promote the true good of other people in a friendly spirit, out of a sense of kinship. Aloha seeks to do good, with no conditions attached. We do not do good only to those who do good to us. One of the sweetest things about the love of God, about aloha, is that it welcomes the stranger and seeks his good. A person who has the spirit of aloha loves even when the love is not returned. And such is the love of God."

But statehood would be no panacea, he warned.

"There are some of us to whom statehood brings great hopes, and there are some to whom statehood brings silent fears. One might say that the hopes and fears of Hawaiʻi are met in statehood today. There are fears that Hawaiʻi as a state will be motivated by economic greed; that statehood will turn Hawaiʻi into a great big spiritual junkyard filled with smashed dreams, worn-out illusions; that will make the Hawaiian people lonely, confused, insecure, empty, anxious, restless, disillusioned—a wistful people."

He recited an ancient *mele* that describes an underground fire pit that produces both dark smoke and light.

"We need to see statehood as the lifting of the clouds of smoke, as an opportunity to affirm positively the basic Gospel of the fatherhood of God and the brotherhood of man. We need to see that Hawaiʻi has potential moral and spiritual contributions to make to our nation and to our world. The fears Hawaiʻi may have are to be met by men and women who are living witnesses of what we really are in Hawaiʻi, of the spirit of aloha, men and women who can help unlock the doors to the future by the guidance and grace of God."

Abe's sermon hit the perfect note for that momentous event.

※ ※ ※

One of the most popular TV shows at the time was *The Dinah Shore Chevy Show*, which each week hosted entertainers of various stripes. In the spring of 1959, word reached us at Kamehameha that the show would be sending scouts to Hawai'i for an upcoming program celebrating Hawai'i as the fiftieth state. Kamehameha would be one of the places they would look for talent. The choir, which I directed, was thrilled and nervous at the same time.

For the scouts, I had two of my better soloists, Joe Recca and Zillah Young, perform "The Hawaiian Wedding Song." Zillah was an incredible contralto who later went on to become a professional opera singer. Joe, a soprano, came from a famous musical family in the islands, the Brights, and became a professional entertainer as well. The scouts were blown away by their duet, and by the full choir as well, and so we were invited to perform on the live broadcast on NBC on April 12, 1959.

At the old Honolulu Airport, the family members of the choir lined the railing to wish us goodbye and good luck. And some of the students, who had never been away from their families before, actually shed tears at the parting. But very soon they were caught up in the excitement of the trip. This would be no vacation, of course. We had a platoon of chaperones and teachers along with us; the kids were expected to keep up with their studies and attend class for four hours a day.

After a comfortable flight on Pan Am to Los Angeles, we boarded a bus to the Biltmore Hotel, our headquarters during the journey. When it opened in 1923, the Biltmore was the largest hotel west of Chicago. While there, we saw several prominent stars of the day, and one of them, Jack Benny, a beloved and enduring comedian on radio and television, came up to talk to us, chomping a cigar.

"You kids are from Hawai'i, right?"

"That's right, Mr. Benny!" they chimed.

Before he left, Benny put out his cigar in one of the lobby planters. One of the kids, Joe Guerrero, took it home as a souvenir. In his luggage. His mother later complained that it stunk up all of his clothes.

We rehearsed every day leading up to the show and the producers made it clear that seconds counted; we could not go over our allotted time. Toward the end of the week, I was actually asked to shave ten seconds off our performance, no easy task. But the week was not all work, either. As a group, we had a chance to visit Disneyland, which had opened less than four years earlier in a county then best known for its oranges. We also trod on the Hollywood Walk of Fame and visited Grauman's Chinese Theatre. We typically had breakfast and lunch in the NBC Studios cafeteria and dinner at the hotel or a nearby restaurant.

On the second or third day of rehearsal, we met Dinah herself. She was shorter than I expected, I guess because she was such a powerful personality on TV, and incredibly sweet. She said she was happy that Hawai'i would become a state, adding, "I hope you enjoy yourself while you're here!"

Dinah's guests that episode included Gary Crosby, son of Bing and a crooner himself; Red Norvo, aka "Mr. Swing," a big band and jazz artist; and actor Tony Randall, who was then working on *Pillow Talk* with Rock Hudson and Doris Day. We didn't really get a chance to meet them, but did say hi to another entertainer from Hawai'i, Charles K.L. Davis.

Along with Joe and Zillah, my group of twenty-four students included Fenner Marie Akaka, Abe's daughter; and Bina Mossman. Joe was particularly nervous as he had been suffering from a sore throat. One of the chaperones, Blossom Neary, brought him hot tea and lemon.

"Here, drink this," she told him.

The wife of the principal, Mrs. Kent, always very protective of the students, came up and said, "And what is that you are giving Joseph?"

"This is for his throat so he can sing tomorrow," Blossom said.

"I don't know," said Mrs. Kent. "Joseph, is that all right with you?"

They were like two mother hens.

As the show began, we were tucked away in our holding room, waiting for our turn on stage. So we didn't really see the performances, but they were described in detail by columnist Eddie Sherman, who saw the show on two TVs, in color and black and white. One *tūtū* from Don the Beachcomber taught Tony Randall the hula. Dinah sang "Lovely Hula Hands" with a chorus of five girls led by Leilani Bermudez. Dinah then sang "Song of Old Hawai'i" and then it was our turn. Joe's solo was "Pua Carnation," an early twentieth-century classic by Charles E. King, a part-Hawaiian composer and lyricist who had studied music with Queen Lili'uokalani. Together, the choir then sang "Niu Haohao" ("Young Coconut"), written by Bina Mossman, the grandmother of our choir member. If the kids were nervous, they didn't show it. Their performance was excellent and wonderfully representative of Hawai'i.

Afterwards, as he sat under a palm tree, Tony sang "Little Grass Shack" as Leilani fanned him with a frond. A bit campy, but that's Hollywood! Martin Denny then played "Quiet Village" and "Burma Train." Davis and Dinah sang "The Wedding Song," and then the entire cast gathered for "Aloha 'Oe."

And in this fashion the eve of statehood brought an adventure of a lifetime for this group of young performers, and I was proud to be a part of it. ❖

CHAPTER

12

While I was at Kamehameha I got my master's degree in education and the public schools offered me a job as vice principal at 'Ewa Beach Elementary School. So I left Kamehameha in 1960 after teaching there three years. Things were going pretty well and I could have stayed another year, but I was past my personal, arbitrary schedule of two years per job.

And at 'Ewa Beach I again exceeded my schedule, staying another three years as vice principal. Part of the reason—and this was very unusual—each year I had a different principal. Helen Tanga was my first principal. Edna Stevens was my second and Edward Sakai was my third. Each had a different style, so I benefited from that exposure and I believe I truly grew as an educator. 'Ewa and 'Ewa Beach were growing rapidly back then, and in the fall of 1963 we had to take over some classrooms at Barbers Point Elementary at the naval air station. I was put in charge of that group. The principal at Barbers Point was a close friend, Joe Kuroda.

Meanwhile, our family expanded once again in August 1961, when our fifth child and fourth son, Nick, was born.

These were the so-called "Camelot" years, of course. Since his election in 1960, President John F. Kennedy, riding on a kind of cult of personality, drew comparisons with the magical, mystical King Arthur, the subject of a popular Broadway musical at the time. Kennedy's youth, vitality—touch football on the White House lawn!—and easy charm, and his glamorous wife and small, well-behaved children didn't undercut the comparison. In truth, those years were anything but rosy. It was arguably the most dangerous period of the Cold War. When U-2 reconnaissance flights confirmed the presence of Soviet missiles in Cuba, the U.S. in October 1962 launched a naval blockade. A very tense time. Fortunately, the Soviets backed down.

Both the United States and Soviet Union were busily testing nuclear weapons—in the atmosphere and oceans, no less, which seems ludicrous now. People in Honolulu got a ringside seat on atmospheric testing in July 1962, when the U.S. detonated a 1.4-megaton hydrogen bomb in space above Johnston Atoll, 825 miles to our south-southwest. The blast, codenamed Starfish Prime, turned night to day, and the electromagnetic pulse fried sections of the island's power grid, a phenomenon later documented in detail by Alan Lloyd of Hawaiian Electric. About 300 streetlights blinked out, and countless burglar alarms blared. We didn't know it then, but it was a dramatic finale to the age of above-ground nuclear explosions. A treaty signed between the U.S. and Soviets in August 1963 banned nuclear testing in the atmosphere, in outer space and underwater. But a lot of damage to the environment and people of the Marshall Islands, a place I knew well, had already been done.

Most everyone who was alive back then remembers where they were when they heard the news that Kennedy had been assassinated. I was in a conference with some of my teaching staff at Barbers Point on November 22, 1963, when someone interrupted the meeting and told us the grim news that Kennedy had been shot and killed in Dallas. Someone found a transistor radio and we listened intently as the first reports came in, our sense of disbelief coloring the accounts. As with the 9/11 attacks many decades later, we felt that the world had just changed monumentally. Our new president, sworn in almost immediately, was Lyndon B. Johnson, whom we recalled as one of the vocal opponents of Hawai'i statehood. Camelot had ended in an eye blink.

In the summer of 1964, I took the Kawaiaha'o choir on a Mainland tour, including Pasadena, California; New York and Washington, D.C. At the New York World's Fair, I was struck by the iconic beauty of the Unisphere, a thirty-five-ton, 140-foot-tall stainless steel sculpture of the Earth. It was a celebration of the space age, with three rings around it: one for Russian Yuri Gagarin, the first man in space; one for John Glenn, the first American to orbit the earth; and Telstar, the first U.S. communications satellite. Dramatically illuminated at night, it really captured the hopefulness of those times. In the decades since, it has resided in Flushing Meadows, in the Queens borough of New York, and has appeared in several movies.

In our hour-long performances, the first half was devoted to anthems and religious songs, and then we switched to Hawaiian. In Washington, we stopped by Capitol Hill and were met by Senator Dan Inouye. When I reached out to shake his hand, he grabbed it with his left hand. Of course, he had lost part of his right arm in combat in World War II. The Inouye-style handshake was probably one that he had to repeat with countless people over the course of his long career. We all assembled on the Capitol steps—I guess I had about thirty-five men and women with me—and sang "Aloha 'Oe." That drew a small crowd and we got a smattering of applause at the end.

Around that time, 'Ewa Beach Elementary was badly overcrowded, with two shifts of students, morning and afternoon. It was really difficult. The Department of Education recognized that a new school was badly needed in the area and I was offered the job of principal. I quickly accepted because the superintendent also wanted me to have a role in designing the school itself. I proposed the name Pohakea, which means to give forth light. The Board of Education accepted the name, so it became the first school in Hawai'i to be named after a concept rather than a place.

While the school was being built on Fort Weaver Road, about 1,200 feet from the ocean in what used to be a sugarcane field, we used empty classrooms at Campbell High School. Oh, I had grand plans for Pohakea! First, I wanted to focus on Hawaiian culture. One way to reach a child and get him or her excited about education is to work through the cultural traits of the community. So I wanted gardens with both indigenous plants and plants that arrived by canoe. So the kids could learn which plants are native and which are Polynesian and watch them grow and also have a place to lounge.

I pictured a two-story building with six classrooms on each floor. And I wanted the kindergartners and first graders and possibly also the second graders up on the second floor, with a bathroom with small toilets and easy-to-reach sinks. I wanted the younger kids up on the second floor because there would be no noisy foot traffic by the older kids, who would all be down on the first floor. The youngsters would have more privacy that way and would less likely to be awakened during their naps. I also wanted the second-floor classroom desks and other furnishings to cater to small children.

'Ewa Beach is typically dry. So I wanted outdoor classrooms as well in areas with plenty of shade and attractive landscaping. And I wanted a sprinkler system so the custodian could just flip a switch and the sprinklers would come on. My father-in-law was a horticulturist and agronomist, so I asked his advice about the kind of plants and trees we should have and he drew it all out for me.

I envisioned a school newspaper, *Kalamalama*, that would keep students and parents informed about events on campus. I felt that families were very important to education and wanted a school where parents were free to visit classrooms and possibly volunteer.

Well, the first thing the board of education shot down was the sprinkler system. Too expensive. I didn't want to argue with them. The second thing they shot down was putting the younger students on the second floor. The concern was they might get hurt going up and down the stairs. This I did argue. I said the smaller kids would be more careful traversing the stairs than the older kids! And when the smaller kids go out to recess, they always have a teacher with them to supervise. But the board was not persuaded. Before long, it became clear that very few, if any, of my ideas were going to be implemented, other than the name. This board, like others before and after, simply could not warm to new ways of doing things. A pity.

Around that time, I was offered a job as principal of Kaneohe Elementary School, then the largest elementary school in the state. So I left Pohakea and went to Kaneohe and served there three years. In June 1966, I was named Father of the Year by the state Department of Education. This came as a complete shock to me. There was a small item in the paper, with my grinning face. "We're a kissing family," I was quoted as saying. The paper went on: "Akaka, who is principal of Kaneohe Elementary School, was speaking of the affectionate relationship he has with his five children. They are, in chronological order: Millannie, 16; Dan, Jr., 13; Gerard, 12; Alan, 10; and Nicky, 4." It took that notice in the newspaper to make me realize suddenly how fast my kids were growing up!

At Kaneohe Elementary, I became more involved with other principals around the state. I liked to work with people and so they elected me president of the elementary school principals' association. In that role, I attended conferences sponsored by the National Education Association. Within three years I was elected to the national board of elementary school principals. And that meant more trips to the Mainland.

In my second year, they put me up to run for vice president of the national elementary school principals. So I started to build up a campaign for that. But then I got word that the Hawai'i Department of Education wanted me to join the state superintendent's office. Since from early on my goal was to become superintendent, I thought that might be a good experience. So I made that move in 1968, serving as a program specialist. Superintendent Ralph Kiyosaki set me to work on the Model Cities Program, part of President Johnson's War on Poverty, so I got more experience and new connections at the national level. ✽

CHAPTER

13

January 22, 1968, marked a sad day for Hawai'i with the passing of Duke Kahanamoku. It was as if the "old days" of Hawai'i died with him. More than 1,000 mourners filled St. Andrew's Cathedral for memorial services five days later. Arthur Godfrey delivered the eulogy for Paoa, as Duke was known, saying, "He gave these islands a new dimension, winning the respect of the world for himself and his people." The sixty-five-member Kamehameha Schools glee club sang, "Hawai'i Aloha." Afterwards, a motorcade with a large police escort glided somberly toward Waikīkī, where perhaps another thousand waited on the beach. Among them, at the Royal Hawaiian Hotel, was brother Abe, barefoot and wearing shorts and a cross made of two small wooden surfboards.

"It is written God is aloha," he said after sprinkling sand on Duke's urn. "And Paoa was a man of aloha. His life was gentle, and the elements so mixed in him that nature might stand up and say to all the world, 'This was a man.'" The assembled beach boys sang "Aloha 'Oe." Then a flotilla of canoes, including Duke's paddling team from the Outrigger Canoe Club, made its way offshore to consign his ashes to the sea.

The year 1968 epitomized a tumultuous time in our national history. The war in Vietnam was escalating, and January brought the Tet Offensive, the strongest campaign yet by the Viet Cong and North Vietnamese against the South and U.S. forces. The war was increasingly the source of unrest at home, and Minnesota senator Eugene McCarthy, who was vocally against the war, announced in late November 1967 that he would challenge Johnson, a fellow Democrat.

Although McCarthy initially was given little chance of defeating the incumbent, a campaign by thousands of college students boosted his numbers in New Hampshire, where in the primary he received a creditable forty-two percent of the vote, compared to Johnson's forty-nine percent. With Johnson so clearly vulnerable, New York senator Robert Kennedy jumped into the race days later. On March 31, Johnson shocked the nation by announcing that he would not be running for reelection. That prompted a flurry of last-minute candidates, including Vice President Hubert Humphrey and South Dakota senator George McGovern. Johnson's name was still on the ballot in Wisconsin, where he lost to McCarthy fifty-six to thirty-five percent, on April 2.

* * *

In 1968, the civil rights movement was in full flower, led by the Reverend Martin Luther King Jr. But like a one-two punch, within days of Johnson's announcement King was shot and killed in Memphis, and once again the world seemed to be spinning off its axis.

Kennedy went on to win the Indiana and Nebraska primaries, but McCarthy won in Oregon, setting up the California primary in early June as the must-win match. There, Kennedy prevailed, outpolling McCarthy by forty-six to forty-two percent. But in the early morning hours after the primary, Kennedy was shot and killed after his victory speech at a hotel in Los Angeles. Another Kennedy gone. I was not alone in wondering what further price this family might pay for its tradition of public service.

Humphrey won the nomination, then lost in the general election to former vice president Richard Nixon, one of the most enigmatic characters ever to strut the political stage. My first impression of Nixon came during the televised debates in 1960, when he came off as petulant and pasty. After losing to Kennedy, he went on to challenge California governor Pat Brown (father of later two-time governor Jerry Brown) in 1962. When he lost that race, he vowed never to run again. "You won't have Dick Nixon to kick around anymore!" he told reporters. But now reporters had Dick Nixon to kick around again!

And ultimately they would. ❋

CHAPTER

14

It was while I was in the superintendent's office that I got to know Jack Burns, our governor since 1966. Burns was a very engaging fellow, who, of course, knew my brother Abe, and we hit it off immediately. Right from the start, he never called me anything but Danny.

"You should come to work for me, Danny!" he took to saying. He had white hair by then, and stood tall and rail thin, with a firm handshake and a grin that could light up any room.

"Thanks, Governor," I said. "But I think I'm still making a difference at the DOE."

And of course my ambition remained to become superintendent of schools.

"You like helping people, Danny," he said. "And you can help a lot more people working for me than you can at the DOE."

Finally, in 1971, I relented, and went to work for Burns as director of the Hawai'i Office of Economic Opportunity. This was much like a state version of the Model Cities Program, with the goal of improving education and the livelihoods in the state's most disadvantaged communities, many of them in remote locales with very little, if any, infrastructure. Even into the 1970s, more than a decade after statehood, there were still places in Hawai'i with dirt or coral roads, no electricity, no sewer system, no telephone. My job was to try to turn that around as a kind of troubleshooter. Sometimes a community had a problem that didn't fall precisely into the *kuleana* of a particular state agency, such as the Department of Health or Department of Transportation. So I would become the catalyst that would bring those agencies together for a solution. The job took me frequently to the Neighbor Islands and to rural O'ahu communities like Wai'anae and Waimānalo, where I made lifelong contacts that proved invaluable later in my run for Congress.

We started care programs for senior citizens, Head Start programs for children and Maui's first public bus system, part of an effort run by a young, ambitious Democrat named Joe Souki, later two-time Speaker of the Hawai'i House of Representatives. On the Big Island, my counterpart was George Yokoyama, a mover and shaker whose diminutive stature belied his considerable influence. He seemed never without a cigarette.

Years later, when I got to know him better, I would urge him to quit smoking.

"Danny, if I quit, I'll die," he insisted well into his nineties.

In 1972, Burns sent me to represent him at the ground breaking for the Queen Ka'ahumanu Highway on the Big Island. Laurance Rockefeller's Mauna Kea Beach Resort had opened in South Kohala in 1965, and the resort could be reached easily from Kawaihae and Waimea. But there was no speedy access to South Kohala from Kailua-Kona to the south. This highway was intended to change that and, in fact, to open up what Burns envisioned as a Gold Coast in West Hawai'i. That proved to be prescient. When the highway opened in 1975, the Mauna Kea hotel was followed by the Mauna Lani Beach Resort and several other five-star destinations. All that was Burns' doing, and I was honored to be part of it. My son Danny made a career as the Hawaiian cultural adviser to the Mauna Lani resort.

But the highway had humble beginnings, I recall: the speakers' platform was a hastily decorated flatbed truck. I can't remember everyone we crammed onto the back of that truck, but I'm sure it included Mayor Shunichi Kimura and George, doubtless smoking through the entire dedication.

※ ※ ※

On May 22, 1973, our twenty-fifth wedding anniversary, Millie and I renewed our vows at Kawaiaha'o Church. Because she's Catholic, we had a parallel ceremony over at Sacred Heart Church on Wilder Avenue. And finally, after a quarter century, I was able to keep my promise and present her with a simple diamond ring to go with her wedding band.

※ ※ ※

Burns and I had a very easy relationship. My office was just down the corridor. My neighbors included Don Horio, Burns' communications specialist, and Myron S. "Pinky" Thompson, the director of administration and Burns' liaison to the Legislature. Of course, Thompson would go on to cofound the Polynesian Voyaging Society, an important pillar in the impeding Hawaiian cultural renaissance.

Sometimes Burns would call me in at 7 p.m. and ask me to come over to his office and we'd chat about things, often just the two of us. Sometimes it was work related—improving the bridge over the Hanalei River on Kaua'i, for instance. And sometimes it related to his personal interests, which embraced Hawaiian history and culture. He was extremely interested in the achievements of Kamehameha the Great, including a legendary, miles-long irrigation tunnel the king dug to bring water to his *loʻi,* or taro patches, in North Kohala. We both admired Kamehameha for his innovations in battle. Well into the nineteenth century, armies traditionally marched headlong against each other across open fields. Kamehameha, by contrast, perfected the flank attack. And at sea, warships at the time would typically pull abreast of each other and fire broadside at close range. Kamehameha mounted his cannons on the bow and fired at his adversaries lengthwise at a distance; that way, the round's range to target—how high you point the cannon—did not have to be as precise, increasing the chances that the first shot would hit.

Burns had a strict daily routine. He would get up every weekday at 4 a.m. and meditate and pray. Then he would walk from Washington Place over to Our Lady of Peace Cathedral on Bishop Street, where, as a devout Catholic, he would attend the early morning Mass. Then he would walk back to Washington Place and tour the grounds, talking to the gardener and custodians about what he wanted done that day. Then, precisely at 7:27 a.m. (we never learned why it had to be that hour), he would enter an alcove off the kitchen for breakfast. Anyone he had invited for breakfast was expected to be there.

A typical breakfast was papaya, scrambled eggs, sticky rice and Kona coffee. The first time I had breakfast with Burns, I was astounded to watch him pour ketchup on his papaya. Over the years I got used to it.

Then he would pick up the morning paper and scan it.

A few minutes into the paper, he would start talking. "Danny, what do you think about this? What do you think of that?"

And after breakfast we would walk across Beretania Street to the capitol and go to work.

It was in that setting, breakfast before work, that Burns first suggested that I run for office.

Again, I was astounded.

"Governor, I'm flattered, but..."

"Think about it," he said. "You have time. Hawaiians need one of their own in office. They need a leader. You're it."

Although he never said it, Burns, I suspected, was looking for solidarity on the next "ticket," although Hawai'i's governors and lieutenant governors run independently in the primary. His first lieutenant governor, Tom Gill, had challenged him in 1970, but Burns managed to win the primary, fifty-three to forty-five percent. He then went on to beat Sam King, son of a territorial governor. King ran as a Republican with my old boss, Ralph Kiyosaki. His second and current lieutenant governor, George Ariyoshi, was widely expected to run for governor in 1974. Ariyoshi could use a loyal number two, Burns might have been thinking, but he never said so specifically. Still, he broached the subject of elective office more than once, and even had Donald Ching, the Senate majority leader, talk to me about running.

"You know," I said, "I love my work and I'd like to stay and continue what I'm doing." And I meant it. And I thank Burns for that.

Burns never told me he had colon cancer. So it was a surprise when he announced, in October 1973, that he would be stepping down for health reasons. Ariyoshi took his place as acting governor. ✤

CHAPTER

15

Ariyoshi had been a reluctant politician from the outset. He told me the only reason he ran for the state Legislature in 1954 was that he felt that the Big Five companies had too tight a lock on the state. "The community I want was for fairness, where every person was judged and advanced on the basis of ability, not on the basis of what contacts they had," he recalled years later.

George had wanted to become a lawyer ever since the eighth grade. And he truly enjoyed the practice of law. As a legislator, then and now a part-time job, he could continue his practice. But then Jack Burns asked him to run as his lieutenant governor in 1970. That was a different story, and Ariyoshi balked. "Being a lawyer, practicing law, was something I really looked forward to, and I was enjoying it in 1970," he recalled.

He told Burns, "What you're asking me to do is give up my law practice. That's a very hard sell for me."

Burns said, "Listen to me very carefully. No person other than a white person has ever been governor of Hawai'i."

Burns told him that a lot of local people felt that the top political jobs in Hawai'i were beyond them, but that would change if Ariyoshi prevailed.

"Shoot, Governor, you've really put me on the spot," said Ariyoshi, then forty-four. "You're asking me to give up my law practice at a time when I can make a few dollars."

"Well," Burns told him, "some people have to make that kind of sacrifice."

And the discussion essentially was over.

Burns and Ariyoshi took office in December 1970 and Ariyoshi earned a reputation as a behind-the-scenes workhorse. He was not by nature a political animal. I suspected he had probably been more comfortable crunching numbers as chairman of the Senate Ways and Means Committee than working a crowd at a stew and rice fundraiser. But he was genuine, no phony, and that worked to his advantage. I can't remember at what stage he came up with the campaign slogan "Quiet But Effective," but that suited him. He was not the kind of officeholder who would have his staff dash off a press release at every minor achievement. He was nonconfrontational, very much in the local Hawai'i way, and would rather work collaboratively offstage than engage in loud public debate. I liked him right away.

When Burns took ill, Ariyoshi could have brought in his own people, but chose to retain many of us aides. So I kept my office and responsibilities, but missed my breakfasts at Washington Place and evening brainstorming sessions with Burns.

With 1974 an election year, Ariyoshi almost immediately found himself in a fight for his job. He had help from Burns' machine, notably Bob Oshiro, a famously influential political operative. And he needed the help, frankly.

In 1974, he was facing a primary challenge from Tom Gill, who had lost to Burns in 1970 and who doubtless saw Ariyoshi as an easier target. It's unclear how those two would have fared head-to-head, because there was another formidable Democrat in the race, feisty Honolulu mayor Frank Fasi, a former marine who made his fortune after World War II selling Quonset huts and other military surplus gear. Fasi liked to tell a joke about a marine who was supposedly at the side of John Paul Jones during the Battle of Flamborough Head. Jones, captain of the *Bonhomme Richard*, famously informed the British, "I have not yet begun to fight!" At which point the marine stomped off, muttering, "There's always some poor SOB who doesn't get the word." That was vintage Fasi. He was always ready to fight.

Also in the race was state Senate president David McClung, so the Democratic field was crowded.

These rivals were far more dangerous than the leading Republican candidate, Randy Crossley, a former state senator who had been out of office for ten years. Burns' 1970 GOP opponent, Sam King, by now was comfortably settled in as a U.S. district judge, a position he would hold with distinction for decades.

In the race for lieutenant governor was Democrat Nelson Doi, fifty-two, a former circuit judge on the Big Island. Like Ariyoshi, U.S. senator Dan Inouye and then U.S. representative Spark Matsunaga, Doi had become a state lawmaker in the game-changing election of 1954. He went on to become state Senate president, where he often clashed with Burns. It was no secret that Ariyoshi didn't like him—or his strong-arm style. At one point during their Senate days, for instance, Doi asked Ariyoshi to support a certain piece of land legislation.

"I got a lot of pressure," Ariyoshi recalled. "All the unions came to me, and I told Nelson, 'Nelson, I can take the pressure. I'm not going to be bowled over.' So he sent me a note telling me if I didn't go along I was going to lose my (Ways and Means) chairmanship. What he was telling me was, he was going to force me to vote in a way that I didn't want to."

The threat proved idle, but the prospect of having Doi as his number two gave Ariyoshi heartburn. Already, on February 14, they had exchanged sharp words during a candidate forum at 'Iolani School. Doi accused Ariyoshi of abiding a conflict of interest as a board member of the Honolulu Gas Co. when he was chairman of the Senate Public Utilities Committee. Ariyoshi admitted both roles, but insisted that he always abstained from voting on matters concerning the company. "I also abstained from taking part in committee hearings that affected the company," he told the 'Iolani seniors. "I turned the committee over to the vice chairman."

So there was no love lost there.

When he announced his candidacy in December 1973, Doi had allied himself with Gill, declaring, "We want to heal the divisions in our community. We want to bring excitement and purpose to the people; and we want the people to feel that, together, we can make government serve the people—not the people serve the government." But by May they had had an apparent falling out that was never fully explained. We had our suspicions.

In March Doi attracted a record 8,000 people to a fundraiser at the National Guard Armory in Hilo—the largest political gathering in Hawai'i island history. Mayor Kimura declared it "amazing," adding, "I think he's running for the wrong office." Gill attended the rally but did not speak. Earlier, state senator Duke Kawasaki, a highly respected F-4 Phantom jet fighter pilot in the Vietnam War, also suggested that Gill and Doi should swap positions on the unofficial "ticket," an idea that Doi brushed off. Still, that might have been the source of the friction.

As the governor's race heated up, Ariyoshi called me in.

"Danny," he said.

"Yes, sir."

"I want you to run for lieutenant governor."

I was flattered but floored. This was July; the primary was less than three months away, on October 5. So I had little time, no money and no organization. But I thought back at the encouragement I had gotten from Burns, then fighting for his life, and that gave me courage.

I told him I would give it serious consideration.

"Terrific," he said, and we stood and shook hands.

On July 15, I called George and told him I planned to resign as director of the Hawai'i Office of Economic Opportunity, to avoid any appearance of a conflict of interest. Word got out immediately—a new realization for me, a lifelong out-of-the-spotlight worker—and soon I got a call from the *Honolulu Advertiser*.

I conceded to the reporter I was weighing a run at lieutenant governor. "I'm not yet fully committed," I said, "but I expect to make a final decision within a week."

The same reporter reached Ariyoshi, who said he was "happy to see him considering the race this year."

On July 26, I took out nomination papers, essentially declaring my candidacy, and on August 1 made a formal announcement alongside my family and brother Abe at the 'Iolani Palace Bandstand. Although only one Ariyoshi aide, Scott Stone, attended, it was clear to most observers that my candidacy was preferred by that camp. Political reporter Gerry Keir wrote, "One idea behind the push for Akaka is to try to avoid the prospect of a racially unbalanced, all-Japanese ticket of Ariyoshi and Doi. This seems to be one of the main assets that newcomer Akaka brings to the contest, in addition to the fact that he has been on the Burns-Ariyoshi team as head of the Office of Economic Opportunity."

Millie and the kids took my decision with maybe equal measures of excitement and worry; becoming a public figure in the media age has clear advantages and risks. I also quickly pulled together some old friends and colleagues from the Department of Education, notably John Uchima, my former boss in the Compensatory Education Unit, the office that handled federal funds for poverty. The core group included Joshua , who would later become a state labor director; Gerald Greer, Jeanne Shida, Paul and Les Kobayashi, Masao Osaki and Rose Yamada. We garnered the support of Frank Hata, whose family owned Y. Hata & Co., a large food service wholesaler. Only years later did I learn from Uchima that these friends of mine took out personal loans to finance the campaign. With those loans, each about $2,000, and a donation from Hata, we came up with about $30,000.

Our headquarters was in the Gaspar Building, 1270 Queen Emma Street, across from Saint Andrew's Priory. The building, which looks like it was made from ill-fitting bricks, had DOE offices as well, so we all felt quite at home. Today it's called the Queen Emma Building.

We hired a San Francisco media company, Rowan, Deicker, Sanders & Bleich, who for $14,000 created five thirty-second commercials with a retired TV news announcer doing the voice-overs.

We also contacted Mary Isa, Burns' secretary, to solicit support from the ailing governor. Burns told Ariyoshi to do what he could for me, but George had his hands full with his own campaign. We did go to George's stew and rice fundraisers and made contacts that way. David Trask, executive director of the powerful Hawai'i Government Employees Association—the state's white-collar government workers union, and Russell Okata, also with HGEA, agreed to help.

We set up Neighbor Island offices.

On Kaua'i, we had Turk Tokita, who won two Purple Hearts fighting with the 442nd Regimental Combat Team in World War II. Turk went on to become a political protégé of Burns, and led Burns' gubernatorial campaigns on Kaua'i. He did the same later for Ariyoshi, John Waihee and Ben Cayetano. His 2014 obituary in the *Star-Advertiser* called him "the patriarch of Democratic politics on Kaua'i." So he was a vital man to have on board. We also had Ed Morita and Champ Ono, title-winning coach of the Kaua'i High School Red Raiders. On Maui, we had Shigeo Ogawa, who sold construction materials for Alexander & Baldwin, and Rose Ohashi; and in Hilo we had George Yokoyama, head of the Hawai'i County Economic Opportunity Council. Years later, state representative Clift Tsuji, in an interview with *Star-Advertiser* reporter Richard Borreca, called Yokoyama "the Pied Piper of economic opportunity in the war against poverty." These folks were tremendously influential on their individual islands.

And we waved signs along roadways—me, Millie and the kids, then in their teens and twenties. Sign-waving, especially during rush hours, has always been a political institution in the isles and a decent way to get name recognition with little expenditure of funds; only the cost of making the signs.

Amidst all this, on August 8, President Richard Nixon announced his resignation in the culmination of the Watergate scandal. All six of the gubernatorial hopefuls took the news somberly. "No one can take any partisan joy in the tortured decline of the president's fortunes," Ariyoshi said. McClung said, "In these troubled times, I think we might say a prayer of gratitude for the wisdom of the men and women who laid the foundations of our democratic society." Gill was a bit more pointed. "I am not a Nixon supporter, and never have been," he said, "but I can sympathize with those of our people who voted for him and now feel betrayed by his immoral and unconstitutional behavior."

Back in June, word had gotten around that a third candidate was poised to enter the race. It was Herman Lemke, fifty-seven, an accountant and former chairman of the Honolulu City Council. Lemke lost to Fasi in the 1968 mayoral election, but was as widely known as Doi. He was part Hawaiian—in fact, his brother Paul was a classmate of mine at Kamehameha—so there was concern in our ranks that he would draw away some Hawaiian votes. Some of my supporters, unbeknownst to me, approached him to try to dissuade him from running. But he jumped in anyway, announcing his candidacy at Magic Island—an area he as a councilman had helped preserve—on August 20, the same day that Ariyoshi formally declared.

Lemke was a staunch supporter of a third freeway connecting Honolulu with Windward Oʻahu. This was known at the time as TH-3. Today, of course, it's the H-3 freeway through Hālawa Valley. But back then it was slated to go through Moanalua Valley and was very controversial. Fasi and Gill were both fervently against it, a conflict that Lemke acknowledged. He argued that if it were not built, H-1 and H-2 would eventually be overloaded.

"I don't think it really affects the environment because we have many valleys nearby just as beautiful as Moanalua," he told the *Advertiser*, adding, "If transportation bogs down, it's going to affect the young people trying to make a living."

During the race, which was conducted very civilly, Lemke also called for campaign finance reform, making, for instance, $100 fundraising dinners illegal. And he wanted candidates to report any contribution over twenty-five dollars. This would have scuttled me and Doi, a fundraising master. In late March, Doi had drawn in 1,000 people to a $100-per-plate Chinese dinner at the Hilton Hawaiian Village's Coral Ballroom. Gill was there and together they put on a show of unity. So was Senate president McClung. So was a prominent Republican, D.G. "Andy" Anderson. After expenses, according to the newspapers, Doi cleared $80,000 that night.

Doi made better public education part of his platform. He wanted more music and sports in the schools. He also favored a low-cost interisland ferry system. He also advocated for providing what he called "professional parents," much like foster parents, for children who have become delinquents because of inadequate parental supervision. That notion seemed to carry some weight because of his years as a judge.

For my part, I campaigned in favor of better state programs to help immigrants get jobs, housing and legal assistance. That plank was a natural outgrowth of my experience in the Office of Economic Opportunity. I also supported diversified agriculture, knowing that we could not rely permanently on sugar and pineapple, given cheap foreign competition.

But I also emphasized my collaborative style.

"I believe one strength I have is working with people," I told *Advertiser* reporter Doug Woo, who noted: "This general theme of harmony is strikingly familiar to the style of Ariyoshi, who has inherited from Gov. John A. Burns and maintains a 'consensus government' image in running the State."

On September 9, a couple of days before my birthday, we held our own $100-a-plate fundraising dinner at the Coral Ballroom. About

500 people attended, including Ariyoshi and a surprise guest—Burns, who seemed in excellent spirits. We also attracted the same group of entertainers who had been openly supportive of Ariyoshi. These included Don Ho, Danny Kaleikini, Zulu, Bill Kaiwa, Leinaʻala Kalama Heine, the Kihei Brown Trio and Hui O Hana. Bill Kaiwa and I joined Burns in singing two of Burns' favorite Hawaiian songs, "Waipiʻo" and "Nānākuli." Brother Abe delivered the invocation, and three of my boys provided background music during the dinner: Danny Jr., then twenty-one, on rhythm guitar; Gerard, nineteen, on bass; and Alan on steel guitar. My son Nick was not on stage because he played the drums, not exactly consistent with the mood we wanted during the meal. It was a wonderful family event that we knew we would cherish long after and regardless of the election results.

The polls were showing that we were gaining ground quickly in the final weeks.

Our last grand event was a *lūʻau* rally September 28, a Saturday, at McKinley High School. Several thousand people turned out for the event, at which we asked for two-dollar donations. Ariyoshi attended, and I took the occasion to speak in support of his candidacy.

"George is the kind of man with whom I would feel most comfortable and with whom I know there would be a sense of mutual trust and aloha in carrying out the responsibilities of the executive branch of government." I concluded, "I am convinced that we are of the same heart, the same sentiment and of the same mold in terms of our hopes, our desires and our aspirations for the people of Hawaiʻi."

George did not speak, but when approached by the *Star-Bulletin*, said, "I know him well. He is an able administrator and would be an attractive running mate for any candidate."

Doi was victorious, but not by much. He received 92,841 votes, or nearly forty-nine percent, to my 77,475 votes, almost forty-one percent. Lemke likely proved the spoiler, pulling in 19,547 votes, slightly more than ten percent. Without him in the race, I might well have won. In fact, we were told that if the primary had been held two or three weeks later, we would have pulled it out. As it happened, Doi outspent me almost two-to-one: $114,364 overall, as he reported to the state Campaign Spending Commission. My spending: $61,756. Of the $69,282 my campaign had collected, only $9,456 was in contributions of $100 or more. Burns had kicked in $500.

Not long after, I ran into Nelson.

"If I had known how fast you were catching up, I would have campaigned harder!" he said, clapping me on the shoulder.

In the governor's race, George received a plurality of thirty-six percent, holding off both Fasi at thirty-one percent and Gill at thirty percent. On Oʻahu, it was nearly a three-way tie, at more than 48,000 votes each. Ariyoshi did particularly well on the Big Island, where he outpolled Fasi, Gill and McClung combined.

With the election over, I went back to work as a program specialist for the Department of Education. So, on the bright side, I had a paycheck again. And I had established name recognition, mostly from TV commercials, as well as a statewide organization. Both would prove useful two years later. ✤

CHAPTER

16

When Jack Burns died in April 1975, everyone in the state recognized the huge void left behind. It wasn't just his contributions to the territory, state and Democratic Party. Many of us felt a deep sense of personal loss. No matter what your politics were, you recognized that a true friend and champion of Hawai'i had left the stage.

Burns lay in state for twenty-two hours in an open casket in the rotunda of the state capitol. The casket arrived at 10 a.m. on Tuesday, April 8, and was placed in the center of the "Aquarius" mosaic in the glow of two blue spotlights. It was draped with the Hawai'i flag. Greeting the coffin in a brief ceremony was Burns' wife, Bea, their three children and other family members, as well as Ariyoshi and his wife, Jean, Supreme Court chief justice Bill Richardson, and Mary Isa, Burns' longtime secretary. Bea Burns placed the first floral wreath, followed by the Ariyoshis, Senate president John Ushijima, state House Speaker James Wakatsuki, Richardson, Hawai'i U.S. senator Hiram Fong, U.S. House Speaker Carl Albert, Admiral Noel Gayler—commander in chief of U.S. Pacific forces, as well as other government and consular officials. After a twenty-minute tribute, led by Monsignor Charles Kekumano, a close friend of Burns, the family left.

Throughout the day and into the night, a steady stream of mourners filed past to pay their respects to one of Hawai'i's finest leaders. His younger son, Jim, later a distinguished jurist, walked among them for much of the evening, thanking each in turn.

❋ ❋ ❋

Ariyoshi had put me in charge of arranging live music as the crowds filed by. I had set up two stages on the second floor, because I wanted continuous music coming from "on high." One group would be performing, and toward the end of their allotted time another group would set up on the opposite stage and begin as soon as the others ended. I had the University of Hawai'i choir and a lot of church choirs, including the one from Kawaiaha'o, as well as high school glee clubs and civic groups.

More than once, the groups performed Burns' favorite Hawaiian song, "Kahana Bay."

Jimmy Borges, the jazz singer, arrived in the late afternoon. Jimmy and Betty Loo Taylor in those days were playing at Keone's on Lewers Street in Waikīkī. Jimmy chose to sing a cappella from the fifth floor because he wanted to achieve a "ghostly" effect. "I wanted to do something different so I would have kind of an echo," he said later.

He started off the "The Star-Spangled Banner," then, as his last notes faded into silence, followed up with Billie Holiday's "I'll Be Seeing You."

> *I'll be seeing you*
> *In all the old familiar places*
> *That this heart of mine embraces*
> *All day through.*
> *In that small café,*
> *The park across the way*
> *The children's carousel,*
> *The chestnut trees, the wishing well.*
> *I'll be seeing you*
> *In every lovely summer's day*
> *In everything that's light and gay*
> *I'll always think of you that way.*
> *I'll find you in the morning sun*
> *And when the night is new*
> *I'll be looking at the moon*
> *But I'll be seeing you.*

The music went on from late morning into the evening, and then after midnight other Waikīkī performers arrived as they got off their club shifts.

One of them was Don Ho.

He and I called Governor Burns "Papa," and earlier I had told him, "Hey, I want to give you as much time as you need to pay tribute to Papa."

"Thanks," he said, clearly pleased.

"How much time do you want?"

"Oh, at least an hour," he said.

So he sang his favorites, among them the Kui Lee classic, "I'll Remember You," and between songs shared his memories of the governor, often addressing Burns personally as Papa. It was very touching.

At 4 a.m. I stopped the music for two hours because that was the time that Burns had devoted daily to meditation and prayer.

We started up again at 6 a.m. with the Royal Hawaiian Band and at 11 they took his body up for burial at the National Memorial Cemetery of the Pacific. But at precisely the time the music stopped at the capitol, I had the UH choir begin singing up at Punchbowl. The Kamehameha Schools choir sang the national anthem and then "Hawai'i Pono'ī" as five motorcycle policemen led the funeral procession into the crater. Eight of Burns' closest friends and allies carried the coffin to a section of Punchbowl known as the Garden of the Missing, where Kekumano conducted a funeral Mass.

I had to stay down at the capitol to help break down the stages, but Ariyoshi's emotional tribute was recounted in both dailies.

"A giant has walked among us," he said, "and we have been privileged to walk with him. He taught us that the highest form of love is not the fatherhood that is paternalistic, but rather that which fosters individual freedom and independence. In all his work, he sought no personal recognition. He wanted all of Hawai'i's people to take part in the process by which his successes were achieved, and he gave to them the full measure of credit for shaping their destiny."

Then the coffin was driven slowly over to a nearby burial site, coincidentally near some of the Nisei veterans that Burns had known. The site was actually selected as a matter of convenience for Bea Burns, who had used a wheelchair since contracting polio as a young woman. Kekumano gave a final blessing. Then the Hawai'i Army National Guard delivered a thunderous, nineteen-round cannon salute that I heard all the way down at the capitol. Then four F-102 Delta Dagger fighter jets from the Hawai'i Air Guard roared overhead, one breaking off in a "missing man" formation. And then two buglers played the ever-mournful taps, one echoing the other.

And that was the end of an era. ❖

PART TWO

In the Footsteps of Kūhiō

CHAPTER

17

The mid-1970s were a fascinating period, perhaps the most gripping since the tumultuous year of 1968, and not just in Hawai'i.

The Watergate scandal had toppled the presidency of Richard Nixon, who waved farewell from the White House lawn in August 1974. He was succeeded by the so-called "caretaker" president, Gerald Ford. Ford pardoned Nixon for unspecified crimes. That was to spare the country from more angst after the Watergate hearings on Capitol Hill had played out on live television from May 1973 to June 1974. Preserved forever in history are the phrases "unindicted co-conspirator," "expletive deleted," and "What did you know and when did you know it?" The hearings made celebrities out of the Watergate committee's chairmen: down-home, no-nonsense Senator Sam Ervin of Texas; Senator Howard Baker of Tennessee—the ranking Republican; and the number two Democrat after Ervin, our very own Dan Inouye, who represented Hawai'i on this international stage with grace and good sense.

The divisive Vietnam War ended in April 1975 and home came our largely unheralded troops, many of them suffering from post-traumatic stress syndrome, a condition that wasn't widely recognized then by the medical community. Some had been exposed to the defoliant Agent Orange, later determined to be a carcinogen. In Hollywood, the immensely unpopular war would spawn such anti-military films as *Coming Home* (1978), *The Deer Hunter* (1978) and Francis Ford Coppola's *Apocalypse Now* (1979). This litany both reflected and reinforced the mood of the country. In fact, after Vietnam, it wasn't until 1986, with *Top Gun*, that Hollywood portrayed the U.S. military in a positive light. It was a long time coming for under-appreciated veterans.

In Hawai'i, a renaissance of Hawaiian culture had begun on several fronts. In music, one of the key players—and long one of my favorites—was Gabby Pahinui. Gabby, born in 1921, spent much of his youth selling newspapers and shining shoes for spare change. His first recording, "Hi'ilawe," in 1946, about a waterfall in Waipi'o Valley on Hawai'i island, remains a classic today, the first Hawaiian song recorded with slack key guitar. That led to other gigs, including appearances on Webley Edwards' *Hawaii Calls* radio show. But it wasn't until the 1970s that Gabby gained his greatest influence. From 1972 to 1976, the Gabby Band produced four cutting-edge albums. The songs included the haunting "Moonlight Lady," "Lāhainā Luna," and another favorite of mine, "'Akaka Falls," about another scenic cascade (not my 1974 primary bid).

There were many other musicians of note around this time, including Nedward and Ledward Kaapana, Dennis Pavao, Keola and Kapono Beamer, Cecilio and Kapono, Kalapana—which drew 25,000 people to the Waikiki Shell for a three-concert performance in June 1976—and Jerry Santos and Robert Beaumont of Olomana, whose album *Like a Seabird in the Wind* featured that namesake song as well as "Ku'u Home O Kahalu'u," enchanting, sentimental melodies still often heard on island radio.

> *I remember days when we were younger*
> *Used to catch o'opu in the mountain stream*
> *'Round the Ko'olau hills we'd ride on horseback*
> *So long ago it seems it was a dream.*

Those lyrics take me back to my own youth, when I caught gobies at the back of Pauoa Valley. And while we never owned a horse, I had plenty of experience with the city equivalent, the Honolulu streetcars.

In the mid-1970s, my old friend and state capitol colleague Pinky Thompson and his son, Nainoa, became actively involved with the Polynesian Voyaging Society, another pillar of the Hawaiian renaissance, which was was formed in 1973 by UH anthropologist Ben Finney, Honolulu waterman Tommy Holmes and Big Island artist and cultural historian Herb Kawainui Kane. The Polynesian Voyaging Society built a traditional double-hulled canoe called *Hōkūle'a*, complete with Polynesian crab-claw sails, and recruited a master navigator named Mau Piailug from Satawal in the Caroline Islands to teach a new generation of sailors the techniques of non-instrument ocean voyaging. The goal was to reproduce the round-trip voyages from Tahiti and the Marquesas that took place when Hawai'i welcomed its first humans. Hōkūle'a is the Hawaiian name for the star Arcturus, which in ancient voyaging was as important as Polaris, the North Star, or Hōkūle'a. As Earth rotates, Hōkūle'a reaches its zenith precisely over Hawai'i. When that happens at night at certain times of the year, the star is the perfect guidepost. The navigators simply wait for the star to reach its highest point in the sky—and steer in that direction. When Hōkūle'a is at the top of the sky, you and Hawai'i are in the same place!

In 1976, the Polynesian Voyaging Society put these techniques to the test, sailing the canoe with a small crew to Tahiti, navigating only by the stars, ocean currents and seabird sightings. The Tahitians greeted these modern voyagers with wild acclaim and erected a monument marking the occasion at Papeete Harbor. It was a fantastic achievement that stirred pride in every Polynesian, myself included.

Perhaps the most emotionally charged issue of the day was the Navy's use of the island of Kaho'olawe as an artillery and bombing range.

The smallest of the eight main Hawaiian Islands, Kaho'olawe had once been home to a small Hawaiian settlement, as evidenced by petroglyphs and a quarry at Pu'u Moiwi, where the Hawaiians mined stone for use in adzes, and in turn used to carve out logs for canoes. One promontory, Ke Awe a Kahiki, by its name evidently was used as a navigational guide for voyages to Tahiti. But the island has no fresh water and in fact lies in the trade wind shadow of Haleakalā, which means there is also little rain. In the mid-1800s, under King Kamehameha III, the island was used as a men's penal colony—a cruel fate for anyone! Some prisoners reportedly risked the seven-mile swim to Maui to escape. Later it supported a series of ranching ventures. But overgrazing soon left little vegetation, and the winds ultimately blew off much of the topsoil, leaving the isle badly eroded. When martial law was declared after the Pearl Harbor attack, the military took control of Kahoʻolawe and had used it as a "Target Isle" ever since. From Maui or Lānaʻi, one could see occasional tufts of smoke from bombs or naval gunfire, a distressing sight to many Hawaiians.

On January 4, 1976, nine men and women occupied the island for part of a day before they were removed by the Coast Guard. They were Emmett and Kimo Aluli, Walter Ritte, George Helm, Gail Prejean, Stephen Morse, Karla Villalba, Ellen Miles and Ian Lind.

"All my life I had heard and read that Kahoʻolawe was just a rock in the ocean, that it had no value, so let the Navy bomb it," Morse recalled years later in *First Landing*, a memoir. "But, for the first time, seeing it close and upfront, it made a lasting impression. This was no rock. This was an island, 44 square miles of it, an island that was part of the Hawaiian archipelago; a place kapu to us for far too many years."

At a press conference at Kawaiahaʻo Church, Ritte said he sent a telegram to President Ford demanding that the bombing be halted immediately.

"We will go back," he vowed. "It's much easier now because there is a deeper feeling."

A second, smaller landing occurred on January 16. These were peaceful protests. Meanwhile, members of the newly formed Protect Kahoʻolawe ʻOhana filed suit in federal court to stop the bombing. It was the start of a long legal process.

The winds of change were blowing on the political front as well. President Ford had a host of Democratic challengers, including the former governor of Georgia, Jimmy Carter, who variously described himself as a peanut farmer and nuclear engineer. Both were true; in the Navy he had served on nuclear submarines.

In Hawaiʻi, the bombshell was the announced retirement of U.S. senator Hiram Fong, a Republican who had represented Hawaiʻi in Congress since statehood. Fong had survived for so long in a predominantly Democratic state because he seemed truly nonpartisan, working comfortably with both sides of the aisle. Fong could safely be described as a liberal Republican—a vanishing breed—much like Nelson Rockefeller, the former New York governor whom Ford tapped as vice president, or California congressman Pete McCloskey, who ran against Nixon for the GOP nomination on an anti-war platform in 1972. Fong also had a reputation as a man of the people, having co-founded Finance Factors, which provided mortgages to Hawaiʻi's ethnic minorities, and a man of the soil, running a plantation on Windward Oʻahu that eventually was turned into a tourist attraction.

With Fong's announcement, U.S. representative Spark Matsunaga quickly threw his hat into the ring. So did Congresswoman Patsy Mink, who represented Hawaiʻi's Second District—rural Oʻahu and the Neighbor Islands. So did former Republican governor Bill Quinn. With both of Hawaiʻi's U.S. House seats open, more candidates surfaced, including broadcasting executive Cecil "Cec" Heftel and John Craven of the University of Hawaiʻi, both declaring for Sparky's First District seat.

Craven had a particularly intriguing background. He first began working for the Navy as an applied physicist on nuclear submarine design. After the loss of the sub USS *Thresher* in 1963, he helped the Navy develop rescue mini subs, called Deep Submergence Recovery Vehicles. He also had a hand in the recovery of an atomic bomb lost at sea off Palomares, Spain, in 1966, the result of a B-52 bomber colliding with its refueling tanker. Involved in that search was the submersible *Alvin*, from Woods Hole Oceanographic Institution on Cape Cod, the same vehicle that helped find the wreck of the *Titanic* twenty years later. His team also found the wreck of the nuclear sub USS *Scorpion* in 1968. Craven was involved in a lot of secret Cold War projects that he couldn't talk about. Word is he helped U.S. subs tap into Soviet communications cables on the seafloor. Off Hawaiʻi, the Howard Hughes Corp. research ship *Glomar Explorer* was involved in a mission in 1974, ostensibly to test the feasibility of mining manganese nodules from the ocean bottom. It turned out the ship was actually salvaging a sunken Soviet submarine, the K-129, and its nuclear missile. That had Craven's fingerprints all over it. In 1975, he became dean of UH marine programs and a year later was appointed head of the UH Law of the Sea Institute. He eventually led the effort to create the Natural Energy Laboratory of Hawaiʻi, which has found multiple uses for the deep, cold water off Keāhole Point near the Kona Airport.

Not long after Fong's announcement and the resulting political flurry, Ariyoshi called me into his office. By then I was his special assistant for human resources and director of the Progressive Neighborhoods Program.

"Danny, you should run for Patsy Mink's seat," he told me. "This is your chance." ✤

CHAPTER

18

On June 17, a Thursday, I announced my candidacy at the state capitol courtyard.

I said I had decided to run in the Second District because it offers not only the major remaining opportunities for economic growth but our last chance of preserving our open spaces, a strong Hawai'i agriculture and the ties of our people to the land.

I still had my statewide organization in place from 1974, consisting largely of my "DOE mafia," as we jokingly called it. And the run for lieutenant governor had given me some name recognition as well. Also, unlike 1974, we had some time to get the ball rolling. There was one immediate potential obstacle, however. I lived in the First Congressional District. Was I qualified to run to represent the Second District? John Uchima and I promptly asked for an informal opinion from state attorney general Ron Amemiya. His answer: yes.

A second hurdle arose with the announced candidacy of my old friend Joe Kuroda, a well-respected state senator and retired Army officer. When I saw him next, I said, "Ho, Joe, if I knew you were going to run for Congress, I wouldn't have thrown my hat in the ring!" I can't remember his exact response, but he made it clear that politics would not get in the way of our amicable relationship. Joe also had DOE connections as a former Big Island teacher and Barbers Point principal. John was worried Kuroda would erode some of our support among current and former educators. So he contacted three former superintendents of education; Ralph Kiyosaki, who ran the department from 1967 to 1970, Shiro Amiyoka (1971–74) and Teichiro "Tim" Hirata (1974–75) and had them sign a letter of support that we sent out in a mass mailing. I have no way of knowing for sure, but I think that helped a lot.

"It makes a statement," John agreed.

We had essentially the same team in place, with Gerald Greer as treasurer and the addition of Amoi Miller and Arlene Sumimoto in the core group. We suspected from 1974 that Hawai'i County was key. In the gubernatorial primary that year, Fasi and Gill together had outpolled Ariyoshi on O'ahu, Maui and Kaua'i, but not so on the Big Island. In Hilo we were counting again on George Yokoyama, who had worked closely with me on anti-poverty programs. George had had a colorful upbringing and career, some of which he recounted in his 2015 book, *Memoir of a War on Poverty in Paradise*.

During the waning months of World War II, when George was at Hilo High School, the principal caught him and others smoking behind the cafeteria. But the principal singled George out for a lecture.

"America is at war with Japan," he told him. "You are at war with Japan. You are Japanese and you have to behave yourself."

The second time George received this rebuke, he punched the principal! The principal did nothing at the time, but two weeks later George received a letter from President Harry Truman. "Welcome to the Army!" it said. Turned out that the principal was on the draft board.

That was his junior year, so George never graduated from high school. Instead, he donned a private's uniform, which ultimately proved a good move. "The Army, with its strict adherence to a daily routine, its insistence on conformity and discipline, and its chain of command organizational structure, helped me tremendously as I became a young adult," he recalls.

By the time he got out of basic training, the war in Europe was over, so George went to Germany as part of the occupation forces and spent four years there. After a stint in Korea during the war, he wound up in Japan in 1952, staying there even after he left the Army. He worked as a civilian fire chief on an army base outside Tokyo and, after passing an entrance exam—since he had no high school diploma, went to Sophia University on the G.I. Bill. Later he went into military surplus sales and was doing quite well until he lost $200,000 to a crooked customer in the Philippines. That wiped him out, so at the urging of his sister he moved back to Hilo in 1968 with his wife, Mieko, and son, Paul, then three.

At first they struggled. Mieko didn't even speak English. But eventually with the help of family and friends the pair was able to make ends meet. Then came along a job that George considered "the opportunity of a lifetime." The Hawai'i County Economic Opportunity Council, a nonprofit, federally funded community action agency, was looking for an economic development specialist. In his interview, he argued that the only way people on welfare could become self-sufficient was to change their attitudes toward work, family and the community through training and placement. And he said it was important to work with the children of people in poverty so that they don't repeat the cycle. George was hired almost immediately and started work on April 1, 1971.

That led to a long and storied career in community involvement, helped in large measure by his talent for writing successful grant applications. I met him through my work with Burns and Ariyoshi, and in 1974 Ariyoshi's campaign coordinator, Bob Oshiro, gave George huge credit for their victory in the governor's race. Not long after, I ran into George and he apologized for not being able to help me more, but that he had had his "hands full" with the Ariyoshi campaign.

"Don't worry about it," I told him.

But 1976 was different. There was no question that we needed George on full court press, especially since Kuroda had Big Island ties as a former teacher at Kalanianaole Elementary and Intermediate Schools in Papa'ikou. In mid-June 1976, I quit my state job once again to avoid the appearance of a conflict in the congressional race, and one of the first things George had me do was talk to a group of about 200 at the Papa'ikou Senior Center. After my brief remarks—basically introducing myself as a candidate, George took the microphone and addressed the crowd in Japanese. I understood very little of what he said, but trusted him to say just the right thing.

In his memoir, he recalls: "I began my speech by pointing out the positive—that most of the members present had immigrated to Hawaii as sugar plantation workers and eventually became naturalized citizens of the U.S. Their sons, daughters and grandchildren, some of whom were now young adults, were gainfully employed and had attained economic self-sufficiency.

"Hawaii had been good to them. The Native Hawaiians have graciously accepted all immigrants to their lands without resistance or a fight. Where else could this have happened?

"Some people in the crowd were nodding in agreement.

"There was one group of people, I told them, that was still living in poverty and occupying the lowest rung of the social and economic ladder—the Native Hawaiians. We had an obligation, I implored, to lift at least one of them up to become a congressman of the United States as an example for other Hawaiians to follow.

"More nodding.

"I said that for the sake of returning a lifelong obligation (*onegaeshi no tame ni*) to the Hawaiians, we should put Dan Akaka in the U.S. Congress."

"Will you help us?" George asked.

"*Hai!*" the crowd answered loudly and enthusiastically.

The response left me feeling immensely grateful, but also humbled at support from so many strangers. But they weren't finished. About three weeks later, they invited me and George back to the center and offered up a campaign donation: 199 dollar bills.

※ ※ ※

On our road to victory that year, we hit more than a few potholes. Early polling showed Oʻahu a tossup, with me leading slightly on Kauaʻi and in Maui County. But Kuroda's numbers were very strong on the Big Island. Influential party leaders urged me to get rid of George Yokoyama and replace him with Burns-Ariyoshi old-timers to try to turn things around. I phoned George personally and told him I had faith in him. He later admitted to being vastly relieved.

But the party at least wanted him watched closely and so dispatched former schools superintendent Tim Hirata to Hilo to urge George to shake up the campaign organization. In an apparent test of George's fundraising prowess, Tim asked him to prepare a stew and rice dinner for 1,000 people to be served *the next day*! Reservations were made at Moʻoheau Park pavilion in Hilo. George quickly borrowed the money for ingredients from the local credit union and recruited fifteen volunteers to chop and cook. At 4:30 p.m. the next day, the steaming hot dinners were delivered to the park. Unfortunately, only seven people—not 1,000—showed up, along with the fifteen volunteers. So George quickly distributed the food to local low-income families, compliments of Dan Akaka. George had an uncanny way of turning potential disaster to our advantage. Tim didn't bother him again.

There was another example. George had arranged a fundraiser for me at the old Kona Airport. In a rare lapse in judgment, he entrusted the ticket sales to a man he had just met who went by the name Masa, who had assured him he had vast experience in such matters. So George trustingly gave him all 500 tickets. And never saw him again. By the day of the event, all was in order. Our Kona coordinator, Lily Kong, and other volunteers had erected a stage. They bought twenty-five cases of beer, now chilling in coolers. And another stew and rice dish awaited our 500 hungry ticketholders. But where were they?

When I arrived, the only one there besides the campaign volunteers was Roland Higashi, a candidate for Hawai'i County Council.

"George, where is everyone?" I asked.

A painful realization darkened his face: Masa, if that was his name, had disappeared with the tickets, selling not a one! He said he later learned that Masa was a Kuroda supporter, but I know that Joe never would have endorsed a dirty trick—even if he knew about it, which he likely didn't.

Anyway, George remembered that there was a huge canoe regatta that day up the road at Kawaihae Harbor, so he drove me there and persuaded the commodore, Charlie Rose, a Hawaiian police officer, to introduce me to the paddlers. So Captain Charlie took me around and I got to shake a lot of new hands. That's how George salvaged the trip.

On O'ahu, meanwhile, Kuroda was running a high-energy, high-profile campaign. Looking back, it's clear that his most creative tactic was to enlist supporters to pick up litter along roadsides. Then they would leave the trash-filled bags along the road to be picked up later—with his name printed prominently on the bags. That cast him as a dedicated environmentalist, someone who cared for the *'āina*. That resonated particularly strongly in rural O'ahu, where "Keep the Country Country" remains an enduring slogan. Joe also outspent us on advertising.

Election night, October 2, was tense by any measure. Millie and I and the kids stayed home until the results started coming in on TV. Early returns showed I was about 1,400 votes behind on O'ahu and running neck-and-neck on Maui and Kaua'i. The votes from Hawai'i County were still out, but we felt sure we had to win there. George later recalled, "The vote tally on the other islands told us that if Akaka did not win the Big Island of Hawai'i, he was doomed to lose. Our headquarters was very quiet and on edge, with a feeling of predestined failure."

At about 9 p.m., we headed down to the campaign headquarters at a Savings and Loan on School Street in Kalihi and to a greeting by about 300 supporters. We had set up tents in the parking lot to accommodate the crowd. There was plenty of food and nearly continuous music. We knew that the night could go either way.

In the end I lost O'ahu by more than 1,500 votes, but did well on Maui, winning by 1,900, and Kaua'i, winning by more than 1,300. My victory on Hawai'i island was razor-thin: 294, but we pulled it out. Overall, I won by 2,015 votes out of more than 100,000 cast. One of the ironies of politics is that we could have lost Hawai'i island—by a comparably narrow margin, anyway—and still won the election, something we never dreamt possible during the course of the campaign.

To his great credit, Joe Kuroda stopped by my headquarters to congratulate me. We shook hands, embraced and together sang "Hawai'i Aloha."

Elsewhere on the ballot, Sparky handily beat Patsy Mink in the U.S. Senate primary; Heftel had picked off Craven despite Ariyoshi's backing for the brilliant marine scientist; and Fasi held off my previous opponent, Lieutenant Governor Nelson Doi, in the mayoral race. Given that the state was, and remains, heavily Democratic, those primary results were all but certain to be repeated in the November general election.

So the celebration began. Hawai'i very likely was going to get its first Hawaiian representative in Congress since Prince Jonah Kūhiō Kalaniana'ole was elected a territorial delegate in 1902. ✤

CHAPTER

19

It was a tough decision, but Millie and I came to the conclusion that it would be best if she stayed in Honolulu rather than come with me to Washington. Our daughter, Millannie, was a grown woman of thirty, working for Hawaiian Telephone Co. Danny Jr., twenty-three, and Gerard, twenty-two, were finishing up at the University of Hawaiʻi. Alan, twenty, was still in college as well, and Nick, fifteen, was a sophomore at Roosevelt High and had no interest in transferring to the Mainland. Staying in Honolulu would also allow Millie to care for her aging grandma, Popo, who was living alone in Nuʻuanu. So it was decided. I told Millie I would visit on weekends as often as I could.

I set out with my top aide, John Uchima, a veteran of both campaigns, for Washington in December 1976. Initially, we had decided to stay in a hotel until we found a suitable apartment to share. At first, I didn't even have an office, but fortunately I was adopted, in a manner of speaking, by Congressman Jim Lloyd, who represented a district in Orange County, California. I don't remember precisely how we met, but he said he loved Hawaiʻi and had visited often. Jim became my instant "big brother" in the House. He let me and John use his office and his phones, and he gave us a valuable tutorial on how things worked on Capitol Hill.

Also of huge help was the gregarious House majority leader, Tip O'Neill, a character really larger than life.

When he found out Millie had remained in Hawaiʻi, he shared his own experience.

"My wife never moved to Washington," he told me, hand on my shoulder. "She's always lived in Massachusetts." He went back home most weekends, as I intended to do, although his commute was considerably shorter than mine. In any case, his comments made me feel better about the separation.

In those early weeks, we made contact with quite a few Hawaiʻi people living in Washington and the suburbs of Maryland and Virginia. One of them, Myrtle Nelson, was born in Keaukaha and brought up there. She married a Minnesota lawyer and when Burns was a delegate to Congress she helped set up the Hawaiʻi State Society, a booster group. She and her husband had a five-bedroom home in Virginia.

"Hey, why don't you come stay with us instead of a hotel?" she said. "Because we have lots of room."

So we went to her house and looked it over and decided to move in, John and myself. The commute proved very convenient. We stayed with Myrtle for several months until we found another place, in Alexandria, Virginia.

That December, even before the congressional session began, one of the first pieces of business before us was to select new House Democratic Party leaders. Speaker Carl Albert had resigned, leaving a void that was clearly going to be filled by Tip.

According to custom, the majority whip would then move up to be majority leader. But the whip, John McFall of California, had fallen out of favor. Tall, thin, congenial and perennially polite, he was seen as simply too nice a guy for the job, which required occasional arm-twisting. He had also become caught up in Koreagate. McFall had accepted $2,000 from a Korean businessman named Tong-sun Park, who was spreading money around town, trying to buy influence. McFall didn't take it as a campaign donation but rather applied it to his office fund, used to entertain visiting constituents. The *Washington Post* reported the donation a few days after the November election. It was all legal but still hurt.

Another, more aggressive contender was Dick Bolling of Missouri. Bolling had been a protégé of Speaker Sam Rayburn and was unabashedly ambitious. He was handsome and intelligent, but many members considered him arrogant, aloof and a bit of a know-it-all. When a member of Congress meets another in the corridor, and one member is with constituents, it's considered common courtesy to stop and greet your colleague's constituents. Bolling couldn't be bothered with that.

Also in the running was Jim Wright of Texas, perhaps the best orator in the House and a talented floor manager. Wright, a wily politician whose bushy brows made him look appropriately foxlike, had won untold favors by campaigning for other congressmen in their districts, which often required driving several hours each way. Those favors were not forgotten. Before the 1976 general election, he also courted dozens of candidates that he thought had a good chance of winning; I was not among them. And he got his Texas donors to write checks, typically $500, for those candidates, which Wright then presented to the candidates himself.

He also had a geographical advantage. With Tip as Speaker, Wright would further the "Boston-Austin" partnerships that had characterized the House leadership since 1931. (Albert was from Oklahoma, but an oil-rich state next door to Texas was considered close enough.) Wright had a checkered record, however. He had, for instance, voted against the Civil Rights Act of 1964, a misstep that still haunted him a dozen years later.

I favored Phil Burton of California, chairman of the Democratic Caucus and a colleague I would become very close to over the next few years. He was well acquainted with Pacific issues, including Micronesia, a region close to my heart, American Samoa, and atmospheric nuclear testing by France in the Tuamoto Archipelago, which had begun in 1974. Phil was well over six feet tall and had an expansive personality to match. Some members, including Tip, found him to be unpolished, loud and a bit of a loose cannon. He also had been an ally of outcast Wayne Hays of West Virginia. Burton defended Hays when some members tried to remove him as chairman of the powerful House Administration Committee a year or so earlier. Then, in May 1976, the *Washington Post* reported that Hays kept his mistress on the committee payroll. Elizabeth Ray told the *Post* that she did very little work for her $14,000 secretary's salary. "I can't type," she admitted famously. "I can't file. I can't even answer the phone." Although Hays resigned from Congress September 1, the scandal continued to infuse the political atmosphere well into the fall. Nevertheless, most people thought the election was Phil's to lose.

Phil's brother, John, a congressman who represented a neighboring Bay Area district, also had Hawai'i ties. His wife, Michele, was the daughter of Jack Hall, the firebrand leader of the Hawai'i longshoremen's union who challenged Hawai'i's Big Five companies in the 1950s and 1960s.

Working for Wright energetically was Dan Rostenkowski, a Chicago pol who had seen his own leadership ambitions derailed. From Rostenkowski's perspective, he belonged in Tip's shoes. When Albert became Speaker, Rostenkowski was working hard to ensure that Hale Boggs of Louisiana would become majority leader. Usually, the Speaker allowed the majority leader to choose the whip, and Boggs had promised the job to Rostenkowski. Boggs won, but Albert balked at his whip choice, perhaps due to bad blood with Rostenkowski over the tumultuous 1968 convention in the Windy City. Boggs then suggested Tip, who got the job.

Tip's path to leadership opened up by dark chance, and with mystery and intrigue worthy of a Robert Ludlum novel—literally. In October 1972, Boggs was in Alaska, campaigning for Nick Begich, who was in a tight race with his GOP challenger, Don Young. They boarded a flight from Anchorage to Juneau—and were never seen again. The search was called off after thirty-nine days. Conspiracy theories abounded, most of them focused on Boggs' service on the Warren Commission investigating the assassination of John F. Kennedy. Boggs had disagreed with the "single bullet" theory adopted by the majority. The popular notion was that Boggs was killed to prevent him from discovering the truth about the assassination. This was actually a plot point in Ludlum's 1979 novel, *The Matarese Circle*. Boggs and Begich were both reelected posthumously, and in January 1973 Congress officially recognized Boggs' presumed death. That cleared the way for Tip to move up as majority leader. Now he was set to be the next Speaker. All that still stuck in Rostenkowski's craw.

He knew he would never get anywhere with Burton and Bolling, both adversaries. So he urged Wright to run and, after Wright declared his candidacy in July, backed him full measure. Wright's strategy centered on the caucus voting process, multiple rounds of secret balloting. After each ballot, the candidate with the fewest votes is eliminated. Then that losing candidate's backers are free to vote for someone else. So the plan was this: knock off McFall on the first round, then let Burton and Bolling split the liberals while he, Wright, more moderate, picked up the rest. Then face Burton or Bolling—probably Burton—in the final round.

Wright had the twenty-one-member Texas delegation behind him, except for Bob Eckhardt and Jack Brooks, who had early on committed to Burton. He also had allies on the House Public Works Committee, where he was in line to become chairman. He had solid support in the South. Although I didn't know this at the time (and neither apparently did Wright), he also had the indirect support of Tip O'Neill through Tip's aide Leo Diehl, whose use of crutches from polio belied his robust influence. A phone call from Diehl was as good as one from Tip. But what was truly brilliant about Wright's strategy, in my view, is that he asked members who were committed to Burton, Bolling or McFall to vote for him *after the first round*. That way they could honor their promise to vote for their candidate—if only once, or maybe twice.

And by December Wright and Burton already knew many of the forty-eight new Democrats coming in. In August, at the Democratic National Convention in New York, Wright brought twenty-four congressional challengers in one by one for informal chats in a small hospitality room at the Essex House, off Central Park. One of them was Allen Ertel of Pennsylvania, whose district had been hit by recent floods. Later, Wright made twenty-three campaign appearances for him in one day. That generates an immense amount of loyalty. In his own memoir, *Balance of Power*, Wright recalled that sixteen of the twenty-four candidates he met with committed to support him in his bid for majority leader. Burton also had a hospitality suite where challengers could drop by, but by all accounts it was a less aggressive effort. I was neck deep in my own congressional campaign back home so did not go to New York.

On Sunday, December 5, the day before the vote, Wright invited the freshmen Democrats to a luncheon in Washington—I don't recall the spot. Surprisingly, he also invited his three competitors and graciously introduced them. Each had a chance to say a few words. It was the only event where we could see all four at once. Burton and Wright were by far the most domineering personalities, each with his own distinct style. Burton seemed brimming with confidence; Wright had a humble yet crafty smile, like he had a secret that no one else knew.

On Monday, the caucus met on the floor of the House. In his book on Burton, *A Rage for Justice*, John Jacobs recalls that Burton and Rostenkowski exchanged vote estimates, although not names. Burton figured he had 117 on the first ballot. Rostenkowski had calculated 111 for Burton and seventy-eight for Wright, with another twenty maybes.

"How we gonna do?" Rostenkowski asked.

"I'm going to win this," Burton told him. "I'm going to haul your ashes."

"If it ain't us, I hope it's you," Rosty replied, and they shook hands.

Then Burton ran into Wright at the back rail.

"Well, Phil, you got the horses in and the barn door locked?"

"Yeah, Jim, I think so."

The first formal piece of business was Burton's resignation as caucus chairman. He did so, and handed the gavel to Rostenkowski. Tom Foley of Washington State was elected chairman over Shirley Chisolm of New York.

Then we elected Tip as Speaker of the House.

Then came what *Washington Post* political columnist David Broder called "the second most important election of 1976." The first, of course, was Carter's win over Ford.

Peter Rodino of New Jersey nominated Bolling. The seconds included Tim Wirth of Colorado, who said, "When I was a new member last year, Dick Bolling was for me teacher and leader a colleague," adding, "He knows the rules and knows how to help others understand them. He has been the point man on the tough issues."

Bernie Sisk of California nominated McFall. John Murtha of Pennsylvania called McFall "the most helpful person I have met in this House."

Yvonne Burke of California nominated Burton. Abner Mikva of Illinois seconded and said, "We have an agenda to make government work better. That is why I think Phil Burton is the right candidate... He is a doer. Phil looks for ways of getting the problem solved. Phil is a coalitionist. He puts people together. Sometimes odd couples, but that is the way the process works."

Charlie Wilson of Texas (played by Tom Hanks in the 2007 movie *Charlie Wilson's War*) nominated Wright. "He has voted for the Civil Rights Act of 1957, 1959, and 1960," Wilson said, not mentioning the watershed Civil Rights Act of 1964. "He has consistently supported home rule for the District of Columbia. He has supported every anti-sex-discrimination act in his tenure. He spoke from this very well for the Voting Rights Act of 1965, which was about as popular in Fort Worth as terminal cancer, and it was that voting rights act that gave Jimmy Carter his victory in Florida, South Carolina, Alabama, Mississippi, and certainly my state of Texas."

Then the balloting began. In the first round, Burton had 106 votes—including mine, Bolling had eighty-one, and Wright, seventy-seven. McFall was out with thirty-one.

At that point, Dawson Mathis of Georgia came up to Burton.

"Should we throw some votes to Wright?" A final matchup against Wright was seen as preferable to a head-to-head with Bolling.

"Are you crazy?" Burton said. "No. We play straight football."

But Mathis and Charlie Rose of North Carolina admitted years later that they, and possibly others, threw their votes to Wright on the second ballot anyway. It made a difference.

The tally was Burton, 107; Wright, ninety-five; and Bolling, ninety-three. Bolling was out—barely, and Burton had picked up only one vote. Most of McFall's backers had gone for Wright or Bolling, it seemed. And, of course, Mathis and Rose et al had picked off Bolling, seen as the major threat.

The tension in the chamber could have been sliced with a knife.

The third round of voting began. At this point, Wright and Burton brazenly sent their allies out to peer over the shoulder of certain members to see what name they were writing down. One of Burton's people went up to Norman Mineta of California, a future transportation secretary.

Mineta showed him his card with the name Burton on it.

"Go tell Uncle Phil," he said.

Rostenkowski saw that Tom Ashley of Ohio had written Burton's name.

"What did you do that for?" Rosty pressed.

"Wright doesn't have a chance, but if you want me to vote for him, I will," Ashley replied to his occasional golfing partner. He changed his vote.

There were three ballot boxes. In one, Burton was up by five. In the second, Wright was up by five. The third box had one ballot left uncounted.

"I reached out my hand like it was dead weight and turned up the last card," Charlie Wilson recounted. "It was Jim Wright."

Wright had won by a single vote, 148–147.

Over the next several months, even years, Burton obsessed over which of his supposed supporters sold him out. Many Democrats refused to say how they voted out of fear of retaliation. At one point Burton cornered me, towering over me, and pumped his finger at my chest.

"Danny, did you vote for me?"

His pale blue eyes were lasers, scanning every muscle movement of my face.

"Yes, Phil, I did," I said.

He nodded and stalked away.

I think he might have confronted each of his assumed allies in that fashion.

As for Rostenkowski, all his machinations never got him very far. Turned out Tip had promised the job of whip to John Brademas of Indiana. Rosty was named chief deputy whip. He ended up, by virtue of seniority, chairman of the House Ways and Means Committee, but went to prison on felony fraud charges as part of what became known as the House Post Office Scandal. As the Chinese say, may you live in interesting times. ✤

CHAPTER

20

On January 3, 1977, with Carter as president-elect, I joined sixty-three others as the freshman class of the 95th Congress. My classmates included Hawai'i colleague Cec Heftel as well as Dick Gephardt of Missouri, a future Democratic majority leader; Leon Panetta of California—a future defense secretary, CIA director and White House chief of staff; Dan Quayle of Indiana, a future vice president; and Dan Glickman of Kansas, a future secretary of agriculture. Dan was our class treasurer. Then, of course, there was Al Gore. He was outgoing, very friendly and with a young family. From the way he carried himself I sensed ambition, so I wasn't surprised when he ran for president in 1988 and then became Bill Clinton's vice president four years later. In Congress, he worked hard for Tennessee.

Speaker O'Neill swore us in all together, then had pictures taken with us individually in reenactments. A kind gesture to us newcomers.

My office was in the Cannon House Office Building, room 514, across the hall from Congressman Silvio Conte, a gregarious and big-voiced Republican whose district covered the western end of Massachusetts, including the Berkshires. We quickly became friends despite our party affiliations. He was also a close friend of Tip's; they hailed from the same state. I often went over to his office to chat. It might have been from Silvio that I learned about the weekly House Prayer Breakfast, a tradition since 1942. It was held every Thursday in one of the rooms in the Capitol. Members only, no staff allowed; we wanted to keep it as intimate as possible. The dining room served breakfast, which you could order in advance. So we'd eat together, share a prayer and then one of the members would say a few words, typically relating a memorable experience or something about his or her family. Then we'd sing. In time I became the guy who decided on the songs or hymns. I tried to keep the selections simple, like Steve Green's "He Holds the Keys." One hard and fast rule was when you come in the door, you leave your baggage behind. We were not there to discuss legislation. I found it to be a very uplifting experience and didn't miss more than a few prayer breakfasts during my entire time in Congress. It also deepened the relationships among us, allowing us to work more cordially. This way, I also got to know well quite a few congressmen from the South that I otherwise might not have.

Meanwhile, my staff was coming together, with Bob Ogawa as legislative aide and Karen Koyonagi as my press secretary.

In the House, the Steering Committee decides committee assignments and I introduced myself to some of the more influential and senior members, including Tom Foley of Washington and Charlie Rangel of New York. But I knew my freshman status meant I probably not get a committee like appropriations or armed services. I could only hope that my assignments would bear some relevance to Hawai'i. Foley and Rangel were very approachable and friendly and took interest that I was from the Aloha State.

My two committee assignments were agriculture, and Merchant Marine and fisheries. The first made sense given Hawai'i's stake in the sugar industry, and I made it an early goal to try to keep the islands' plantations viable through price supports or whatever other means necessary. Pineapple back then was also still a major crop, but also was facing stiff foreign competition, even with a three percent trade duty. The second assignment made sense because Hawai'i imports nearly all of its goods, mostly by cargo ship, and has a robust longline tuna fishing fleet. But I was also quite interested in promoting aquaculture in Hawai'i.

※ ※ ※

The early issues back then also included welfare reform and possible federal reparations to Hawaiians for the overthrow of the monarchy in 1893.

Back at home, still making headlines was Kahoʻolawe, the island the Navy used for target practice. On January 30, 1977, George Helm, Walter Ritte, Charles Warrington, Francis Kauhane and Richard

Sawyer launched their second civil-protest invasion. Helm, Warrington and Kauhane were arrested February 2, but Ritte and Sawyer managed to elude the military authorities for weeks, traveling mostly on goat paths so as to avoid stepping on unexploded ordnance. In mid-February, Helm, Kauhane and three others—Pae Galdeira, Martial Kaanoi and the Reverend Charles Hopkins—took their case to Washington, a trip Helm called "a gesture to show we mean business." They met with White House officials but were not allowed in to see Carter.

Kauhane told the Gannett News Service, "The legislators here, with the exception of Akaka, are trying to play down the seriousness of this. They have been insensitive to our problems. Of course, they're not Hawaiians."

But I knew that Inouye, Matsunaga and Heftel were sensitive to the issue. While Helm and the others were in Washington, the four of us flew to Maui to meet with the PKO and also to hear the military's side. The military, of course, argued from a practical standpoint that the island was needed for training; that, without it, our sailors, soldiers, airmen and marines would be unprepared for battle. While the Vietnam War was over, the Cold War was still raging. The Soviets also had their eyes on Afghanistan.

Later in the day, I flew to Moloka‘i to talk to a group of about thirty-five PKO members. They included Loretta Ritte and Zenadia Sawyer, whose husbands were still hiding out on the island, and Mae Helm, George's mother.

"George doesn't even know what it is, but something is driving him," she told me.

Zenadia Sawyer was particularly emotional.

"No one hears us," she said. "Please try to make others hear us. We hurt inside and it's very deep."

Loretta Ritte said her husband was on the island because he considers it a sentient entity.

"Every time a bomb is dropped, he feels for her because she is alive," she said. "Go back to Congress and tell them man cannot live without land. The ‘āina is the giver of life."

I told the group that while I could not condone illegal acts such as trespassing, I was proud of their spirituality and their prayers. I told them I was happy to see more Hawaiians caring for the land, part of a renaissance of culture in the islands.

"Be proud of our roots," I urged. "Understand who we are. Find our identity."

Less than a month later, tragedy struck when George Helm and Kimo Mitchell disappeared in the channel between Kahoʻolawe and Maui. A stone marker at Hakioawa Bay on Kahoʻolawe attests to their contributions to the cause. ❖

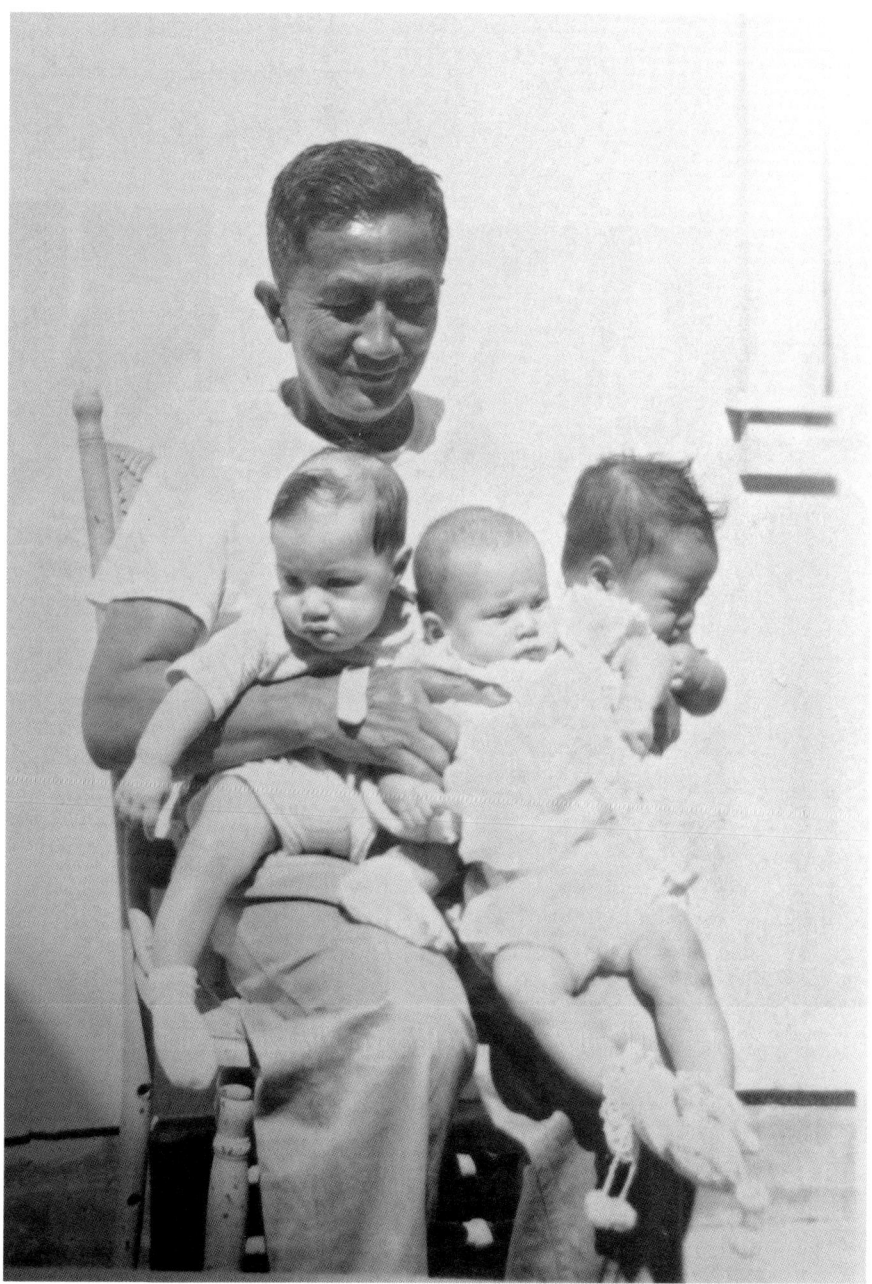

At the Lusitana Street house in 1949, Kahikina Akaka holds grandchildren Patrick Taylor, Pualani Akaka and Millannie Akaka.

Above: In 1933 Dan stands second from right, top row, in his third grade class photo at Pauoa Elementary School. Opposite: Dan at age five in 1930.

116   One Voice

Opposite top (left to right): Brother Joe's wife, Violet, holds son Godfrey; brother Abraham's wife, Mary Lou, holds daughter Pualani; Dan's wife, Millie (Mary Mildred), holds Millannie; and sister Susan Taylor holds son Patrick on Lusitana Street in 1939. Opposite bottom: The University of Hawai'i Deputation Team. Above: Kahikina Akaka (here at age ninety-one) often sat for hours in the family's Hook Chu Cemetery in Pauoa.

Top: More members of the UH Deputation Team:
(front, left to right) Jimmy Ohashi, Eppy Yadao and Satoru Izutsu,
(back, left to right) Ted Yanagihara, John Giltner, Scotty Koga and Dan.
Above: Kamehameha Schools ROTC with Dan at front row center.

Dan and fellow missionary Loren Miller aboard the *Morning Star VI* in 1947.

Dan poses for a graduation photo at Kamehameha Schools in 1942.

CHAPTER

21

Among the many accomplishments of the 95th Congress, one that gives me particular pride is the passage of a law recognizing as veterans the women aviators who served during World War II. These so-called WASPs, for Women Airforce Service Pilots, were pressed into service in 1942 when male pilots were needed for combat overseas. Eventually, they flew every type of army aircraft, including P-51 Mustangs—the top-of-the-line fighter, and B-17 and B-24 bombers. Typically they ferried the planes from the factory to the docks in Newark, New Jersey, where they were shipped to Europe. Initially, twenty-eight women pilots signed up for this duty. By the end of the war, their ranks topped 1,000. Their experiences are documented in a compelling exhibit at the Pacific Aviation Museum Pearl Harbor, a taste of history that I highly recommend.

Although far from the war front, these women pilots accepted the risks that accompany any type of aviation. And thirty-eight of them made the ultimate sacrifice. One of the most acclaimed WASPs was Cornelia Fort, who as a civilian pilot at Pearl Harbor inadvertently became the first to encounter the Japanese aircraft on the morning of December 7. She was giving a flying lesson to a young student and they found themselves flying directly at the attacking squadrons. She grabbed the controls and managed to land at John Rodgers Airport near the entrance to Pearl, where her plane was strafed by a Zero. Fort survived that harrowing incident but not the war. In March 1943, while part of a group ferrying aircraft from a factory in California, she died in a crash in Texas when another plane, flown by a male colleague, sliced off her wing with his landing gear.

In June 1944, General Henry "Hap" Arnold, commander of the Army Air Forces, asked Congress to designate WASPs as members of the military. But many other male pilots objected, and Congress declined. The WASP program ended in December 1944 without this much-deserved recognition. But decades later we were able to remedy that egregious oversight with House Resolution 8701, sponsored by Democrat Olin Teague of Texas, which President Carter signed into law as the G.I. Bill Improvements Act of 1977. The act also expanded benefits for Vietnam veterans.

※ ※ ※

In addition my committee assignments on agriculture and the Merchant Marine, Tip named me to the House Select Committee on Population and the Select Committee on Narcotics Abuse and Control.

The rapid growth of the world's population had become a prominent issue since Paul Ehrlich, a Stanford University biologist, had published *The Population Bomb* in 1968. Ehrlich predicted that humans faced mass starvation if the world's numbers were allowed to increase unchecked. And in fact the rate of increase took a sharp uptick after World War II. It took the world 123 years—from 1804 to 1927—to go from a population of 1 billion to 2 billion. It took only thirty-two years—from 1927 to 1959—to reach 3 billion, another fifteen years to hit 4 billion, in 1974, and the population was on track to hit 5 billion by 1986, a span of only twelve years. Of course, Ehrlich's chief prediction—mass starvation—had not come to pass, thanks in large measure to the Green Revolution, a research and development effort that increased food production worldwide, mostly in developing nations, beginning in the 1960s. For his role in that initiative, biologist Norman Borlaug won the Nobel Peace Prize in 1970. Without the Green Revolution, by some estimates, 1 billion people would have starved, so Ehrlich's warning was a serious one.

The population committee was led by Jim Scheuer of New York and included Dick Gephardt, Pete McCloskey and twelve others, including David Stockman, a Minnesota Republican who would go on to become a controversial director of the Office of Management and Budget under Ronald Reagan. We had a staff of nine.

The narcotics committee had an equally serious focus. The main concern was the importation of dangerous drugs like heroin, principally through Mexico but also through the Golden Triangle of Asia.

The percentage of heroin arriving from Southeast Asia had risen from two percent in 1972 to twenty-five to thirty-five percent in 1977. In Hawai'i, marijuana was a thriving industry and in the late 1970s would prompt Operation Green Harvest, a joint effort by federal, state and county vice officers, using Hawai'i Army National Guard helicopters to root out hidden growing operations, initially on the Big Island, but eventually statewide. Hawai'i's marijuana had a reputation for being particularly potent, so there was a thriving market for these illegal harvests. Of course, this was long before "crack" cocaine and "ice"—crystal methamphetamine—arrived on the scene. These scourges make marijuana seem, in retrospect, as menacing as shave ice. But at that time I was a strong advocate of cannabis crop eradication.

The committee had eighteen members, led by Lester Wolff of New York. They included Peter Rodino of New Jersey; Kika de la Garza of Texas, a state through which much of the imported drugs passed; Charlie Rangel of New York; Pete Stark of California and Tom Railsback of Texas. We had a staff of three. It became clear that first year that drugs were largely not a homegrown problem but one of foreign imports—that is, smuggling. The pressing question was whether the United States could do more to halt the shipments before they reached our borders. On May 17, 1977, Wolff took a bold move and entered the names of eight major drug lords in Thailand in the Congressional Record. Within months, most had fled the country or gone into hiding.

Just after the holidays we set out on a three-week, round-the-world, fact-gathering mission, leaving January 2. There were five of us from the narcotics committee, including Wolff and Rangel, and six others from all around the country, Republicans and Democrats. With us was Adolph Dubs, deputy assistant secretary of state for Near Eastern and South Asian Affairs; James Free, special assistant to President Carter; and an Army lieutenant colonel, our escort officer, who made most of the arrangements. Many of the members brought their wives along, myself included. Millie was excited about the trip.

Our first stop was Japan, where we looked at drug abuse among American military personnel. The problem there was relatively small and largely confined to marijuana and alcohol use. In 1977, of the 3,562 personnel who were given urine tests for drugs, only eighty-three tested positive. Among the Japanese, methamphetamine abuse was rampant. A gram of meth bought for $10 in Korea could be sold in Japan for

$1,000. A lot of those profits was fueling the *yakuza*, organized crime. Japanese authorities had only lately come to tackle this problem. U.S. Drug Enforcement Administration agents in Japan had recently shifted their attention from meth to heroin from Southeast Asia with Japan as a transshipment point. Japan was also a major producer of the chemical acetic anhydride, which has many industrial uses but is needed to make heroin from opium. We made clear to the Japanese that it was essential to prevent the diversion of the chemical to the heroin factories in Malaysia, Thailand and Burma.

The Philippines, our next stop, were another potential avenue for drugs headed for the United States. However, the imposition of martial law by President Ferdinand Marcos in 1972 had limited the use, production and trafficking of dangerous drugs—and had limited travel and the flow of goods in general. As with our forces in Japan, personnel at Clark Air Base north of Manila had gravitated mostly to alcohol and marijuana, grown in the mountainous region of Luzon and available for $10–20 per ounce. But our commanders there did not view these problems as so large as to affect combat readiness. Same for Subic Bay Naval Base. However, the Naval Investigative Service had run a successful anti-smuggling effort called Operation Stableboy. In 1977, the NIS, working with Philippines authorities, arrested 173 servicemen and 316 Filipinos and seized 172 grams of heroin, 14,000 grams of marijuana and 443 cannabis plants.

After a stop on Papua New Guinea, which had no major domestic drug abuse problem, we arrived in Australia, where drug abuse had been steadily rising, notably among young adults. An estimated half million Australians use marijuana at least once a week. There were also 30,000 to 40,000 heroin addicts. Australian officials said they had no record of any heroin coming into the country for transshipment, but the potential was there: Australia has 12,000 miles of coastline, and plenty of abandoned airstrips left over from World War II.

In Singapore, five members of the delegation attended a regional narcotics conference, at which Rangel lauded the Carter administration for attempting to deal with the drug plague on an international level. We also got a briefing by DEA agents, who told us that a key to stopping drugs from the Golden Triangle (Burma, Thailand and Laos) was regulation of acetic anhydride and knocking out the refineries, which could only be done by the respective governments. In Burma (now

Myanmar), however, more than a third of the heroin was produced on land in the hands of insurgents.

The story was pretty much the same everywhere we went. The drug trade was hugely profitable. A pound of heroin in Malaysia, for instance, cost $1,500. By the time it reached Europe it was worth $17,000. By the time it reached the United States, it was worth $40,000 to a dealer and much more on the streets.

Thailand had undergone a coup in October, and the new prime minister, Kriangsak Chamanan, had stepped up anti-drug efforts. In fact, the crackdown had led to a buildup of heroin in the Thai border with Burma and Laos. We met with Kriangsak and he promised to keep up the good fight. He also asked us for more U.S. helicopters, something that was not in the budget.

India, we learned, is the world's largest producer of legal opium, used in the production of morphine and codeine. U.S. companies bought more than a fifth of the Indian supply. The government had strict controls on production. It was one of the bright spots on an otherwise sobering sojourn.

One of our last stops was the most fascinating. Iran in January 1978 was still in the hands of the shah, Reza Pahlavi, whose father had run the country before him, starting in 1925. But the shah was increasingly unpopular for human rights abuses, using his secret police, the Savak, to control the country. The leader of the opposition, Ayatollah Ruhollah Khomeini, was in exile in France. Demonstrations had started in October, when Khomeini's son, Mustapha, was found dead under mysterious circumstances. The Savak declared the cause of death a heart attack, but many people suspected the agency itself. On January 7, an article in the national daily accused the ayatollah of being a British spy. In protest, 4,000 seminary students in the city of Qom demonstrated. The police responded with weapons drawn and the protesters dared them to fire, which they did. The number of fatalities varies widely, but the opposition claimed seventy were killed.

We were elsewhere on the trip at the time, but that was the mood of the country when we arrived for a four-hour stopover on January 17. Over lunch, prime minister Jamshid Amougezar—who would resign in August after only a year on the job—complained about the ineffectiveness of the U.N. Fund for Drug Abuse Control. He also was unhappy that opium production was out of control in neighboring Afghanistan and Pakistan. There was already a serious problem of opium passing through Iran into Turkey. Of his country's 400,000 addicts, most got their heroin from Afghan sources, he said. But Iran soon would have bigger problems than drugs. The revolution that was brewing also would have a profound effect on the United States, including presidential politics. ✤

CHAPTER

22

In February 1978, much to my satisfaction, the House voted 234–130 to approve the National Aquaculture Policy Act, a measure that I cosponsored. The bill was aimed at drastically expanding fish farms by consolidating federal programs that led to a fragmentation of resources, redundancies and unproductive turf wars. The bill went on to passage in the Senate, and I was hopeful President Carter would sign it promptly. However, that October, after Congress had recessed, Carter used his first "pocket veto" and refused to sign the measure, effectively killing it. He said he supported aquaculture, but was reluctant to begin any major new government subsidies such as loan guarantees.

On October 19, I wrote to Carter to express my disappointment.

"Dear Mr. President, I note with profoundest regret your veto of H.R. 9370, the National Aquaculture Act of 1978. Mr. President, the United States is at a pivotal point in the development of aquaculture. At present, we import more than fifty percent of all the fish and shellfish we consume. While aquaculture provides for less than three percent of our needs, 'fish farms' supply countries such as Japan and Czechoslovakia with more than ten percent of theirs. The U.S. has an annual fish and fish product deficit of approximately one billion dollars." In Hawai'i alone, I said, "various operations are presently researching or are engaged in the culturing of algae, mullet, milkfish, catfish, baitfish, shrimp, prawns, oysters and numerous other types of aquatic plants and animals. The state of Hawai'i has done all it can to assist in these efforts, but its efforts are limited. Everyone has been looking to the federal government for some indication of support. I am certain the same holds true throughout America."

I called our current position with respect for aquaculture "shameful" and said that the measure would have encouraged business investment and created jobs.

"Mr. President, I would sincerely hope that the action you have taken on this bill is not a reflection of a belief that, with respect to aquaculture, the status quo will adequately serve our aspirations."

I offered to meet with him to discuss the matter, adding, "I trust that this situation can be resolved and look forward to working closely with you toward the expedient formulation of a comprehensive national aquaculture policy." But Carter never took me up on my offer.

Soon I was back home with the general election just weeks away. I had sent John Uchima back to Honolulu in late September to mind the local office and help with the campaign, which was in the able hands of Norman Taira, chairman, and Michael Tanaka, treasurer. I had two general election opponents, Republican Charlie Isaak and Libertarian Amelia Fritts. Even I was surprised at my margin of victory: eighty-six percent. Especially considering I had a budget of about $20,000. I had gone into debt to finance the $170,000 campaign in 1976 and didn't want to repeat that exercise. Most of that debt was now paid off, thanks in part to a fundraiser at the Neal S. Blaisdell Center where 600 people paid $50 for an inexpensive meal.

I had kept my promise to Millie and the kids to visit the isles frequently, although often in concert with other engagements. With the time away, however, it seemed to me that Honolulu was changing fast. On June 4, addressing the biennial general assembly of the Hawai'i Government Employees Association in Honolulu, I warned that Hawai'i was facing serious population pressure. "Hawai'i is in danger of becoming overpopulated. The state is already straining at the seams of its social and economic fabric. The first symptoms of this overcrowding are beginning to show. Crime is on the rise. Drug and alcohol addiction is prevalent. Air, noise and water pollution—every phase of environmental pollution—are becoming evident. Privacy is being eroded, and with it the gentle spirit of Hawaiians that distinguishes them from the rest." Back then, the population of Hawai'i was just over 890,000; in 2016, it topped 1.4 million—enough to make me miss the 1970s!

While I still stung from the defeat of the aquaculture bill, I could look back on an instructive, if not highly productive, first term.

On a historical note, on June 12 the proceedings of the House were broadcast on live radio for the first time. "Our action today, opening floor debates to regular, continuous coverage by the broadcast media, will give the American people the chance to hear for themselves exactly what is said here in this chamber," said my fellow freshman Al Gore, one of the champions of the change.

I was proud to have cosponsored, after hearings in Honolulu, the Agricultural Land Retention Act, which would prevent prime farm land from going to nonagricultural uses, an issue that also remains at the forefront of public debate today. The bill, sponsored by Jim Jeffords of Vermont, was approved by the House Agriculture Committee on July 28, but never went up for a vote before the full chamber.

On the drug front, the Select Committee on Narcotics Abuse and Control, at my urging, had hearings in Honolulu June 30–July 5 on drug trafficking in and through Hawai'i and Guam. At the hearings, at which I held the gavel, we heard testimony from Governor Ariyoshi, agents of the DEA and U.S. Customs inspectors. The bottom line: the growing demand for drugs, especially on the Mainland, had increased the drug problems in the islands. Part of the problem was personnel. Drug enforcement officials were spread too thin to adequately cover Honolulu airport, Hawai'i's seven commercial harbors, twenty-one public harbors, three military harbors and five recreational boat harbors. "If we want to keep narcotics from reaching the Mainland, we must be willing to provide Hawai'i with adequate personnel to cope with this increasing problem," I said in a statement after the hearing. I also vowed to push for marijuana eradication and better programs in drug prevention, particularly in the schools.

Meanwhile, Inouye, Matsunaga, Heftel and I kept fighting for sugar. In late July, we complained to Agriculture secretary Bob Bergland that Hawai'i's sugar producers were being discriminated against under the department's price support program. We were especially upset by the "location differentials" for Hawai'i and Puerto Rico included in the regulations for the 1978 price support loan program, issued June 7. We argued that the price support level should be applied equally for all areas of the country, with no exceptions for offshore areas. Hawai'i at the time was getting just over fourteen cents per pound. In the House, I cosponsored the Sugar Stabilization Act of 1978, and the Agriculture Committee began final markup in late July. The bill had a price objective of seventeen cents a pound. "Sugar prices continue to maintain an unprofitable level with no signs of immediate recovery," I said in a statement. "It is imperative that the Congress step in and assure a fair price to sugar growers." Unfortunately, the House and Senate passed the measure in different versions on October 12 and the differences were never resolved.

Heftel and I also failed to achieve two other important goals, establishing a commission for Native Hawaiian claims and banning competitive bidding in military moving contracts. But I hoped in the future that my loyalty to the House Democratic leadership would pay off. The Congressional Quarterly reported that in my first term I voted with the Democratic majority eighty-nine percent of the time. By comparison, I voted with President Carter sixty-eight percent of the time. So I showed more loyalty to Tip than the top.

One important victory: The House had come up with $5 million for construction of a deep draft harbor at Barbers Point. Inouye managed to raise that to $6.5 million in the Senate Appropriations Subcommittee on Public Works. I was frankly in awe of how well Inouye took care of Hawai'i through his membership on appropriations. I myself had early aspirations to join the House Appropriations Committee, but was told by Tip, Tom Foley and Charlie Rangel that those seats were highly coveted and reserved for more senior members.

I didn't know Leo Ryan, but had heard nothing but good things about the industrious, conscientious congressman who represented Pete McCloskey's old district in the East Bay. Phil Burton and his brother John, also a California congressman, knew him well. With Jim Jeffords, Ryan had gone to Newfoundland to investigate the slaughter of baby seals. He was also a vocal critic of the CIA. So I was as shocked as everyone else in Congress to learn of his death November 18 in Guyana. Ryan had gone down to check on the welfare of the members of the Peoples Temple, a commune led by one Jim Jones. This was in his capacity as a member of the International Relations Subcommittee on International Operations, tasked with keeping an eye on U.S. citizens living abroad. Ryan had become interested in Jonestown when the son of one of his friends, Sam Houston, turned up dead near railroad tracks a day after he decided to leave the cult. Ryan had obtained affidavits from former Temple members that described a bizarre culture of guns and violence. He had asked other members of the Bay Area delegation to join him on the trip, but they declined, as did his friend Dan Quayle. John Burton recalls the invitation, made at the last minute. He also knew Jim Jones, he said, "before he went bonkers." His group included seventeen Bay Area relatives of Temple members and the news media. The atmosphere down there was tense from the start. Several members expressed a desire to defect. Ryan was arranging for that on two planes when one devout Temple member, posing as a defector, opened fire on the passengers. Other Temple members, serving as escorts, followed suit, killing Ryan, three journalists and one Temple defector and wounding nine others. By the time the Guyanese army reached the site the next day, more than 900 people were dead in a mass murder-suicide involving poisoned Kool-Aid. Ryan is the only member of Congress to be killed in the line of duty. In a eulogy, Jim Wright called him "a friend of the disadvantaged, the disenchanted and the dispossessed—those who most need a friend in high places," adding, "He took on their habiliments, tasted their anguish with them, and in their service he went literally to the ends of the earth."

In January 1979, my first order of business was to introduce the Native Hawaiian Education Act, which had passed the Senate in the final days of the last session, thanks to Dan Inouye. But it had not yet been introduced in the House. The bill provided $22 million in Native Hawaiian education programs through 1983. That would provide financial aid for schools with high Hawaiian enrollment, adult education programs, graduate fellowships and special training for teachers who work with Native Hawaiians. Inouye had tried for years to include Hawaiians in the education programs for American Indians, but had to take another tack when the Indians balked at sharing the money with Hawaiians.

Days later, Jim Scheuer of New York, the chairman of the Select Committee on Population, and I held a press conference to announce the findings of a committee report. We argued that Hawai'i should get special federal aid to cope with a booming population, while New

York should get aid to deal with a population decline. (California had passed New York as the most populous state with the 1970 census.) I noted that Hawaiʻi already had a population density of sixty people per square mile—twice the national average.

Scheuer said, "My own city of New York has made serious mistakes in trying to cope with population declines. We lost just under one million people and 750,000 jobs. Then, instead of adjusting to a smaller city and fewer jobs, 100,000 new public housing units are being built in the South Bronx. This is not management. This is not planning. This is sheer unadulterated waste."

The report said that population size alone should not be the only criterion for federal aid to localities. That ignores the effects on the demand for services of changing population characteristics associated with growth or decline. It was clear that the days were gone when Americans were born, grew up, raised a family and died in the same city or town. We were a country on the move.

In August, I joined eight other members of Congress on a trip to Vietnam, which was experiencing a huge exodus of refugees. Acting foreign minister Nguyen Co Thach told the delegation, led by Congressman Ben Rosenthal of New York, that he was willing to discuss letting the refugees go via American aircraft, but would continue cracking down on illegal departures by sea. He said fleeing refugees had already made off with half the nation's fishing fleet. Some of those who were captured were put to death, he said.

He also said Vietnam had dropped its demand for reconstruction aid as a condition of normalizing ties with the U.S., a goal that he was "very, very anxious" to attain. That goal had become complicated by the refugee crisis and Vietnam's invasion of Cambodia in December to install a pro-Hanoi regime.

Other dramatic events abroad led to the passage of the first piece of legislation for which I was the primary sponsor. In the face of mounting civil unrest, the shah and his family had left Iran for exile in January. Within weeks Ayatollah Khomeini returned to rule the country and by mid-February the shah's regime had collapsed. But months of turmoil ensued as Khomeini battled other factions on ideological grounds. In October, the shah entered the United States for cancer treatments, which angered the ayatollah, who considered America the "great Satan." He demanded that the shah be returned to Iran for trial for his brutal leadership. To add fat to the fire, on November 1, Khomeini's interim prime minister, Mehdi Bazargan, was photographed shaking hands with U.S. national security adviser Zbigniew Brzezinski at a meeting in Algeria. Radical media in Tehran warned of the "return of American influence."

On November 4, Islamic students occupied the U.S. embassy in Tehran, taking fifty-two American diplomats and staff workers hostage. But six diplomats got out of the embassy and hid in the home of a Canadian diplomat, John Sheardown. The Canadian ambassador to Iran, Kenneth Taylor, arranged for the government to issue passports to the Americans. CIA agents posing as a movie crew managed to sneak the six out of Tehran on a flight to Zurich, Switzerland, on January 28, 1980, after seventy-nine days of fear and apprehension. This so-called "Canadian caper" was the basis for the 2012 movie *Argo*, starring Ben Affleck and Bryan Cranston.

On January 30, 1980, I introduced House Resolution 6374, which authorized the president to present on behalf of the Congress a specially struck gold medal to Ambassador Taylor. The measure flew through the House Banking, Finance and Urban Affairs Committees and on March 6 it became Public Law 96-201. President Reagan presented the medal to Taylor on June 6, 1981. ❖

CHAPTER

23

In June 1980, with the death of Japanese prime minister Masayoshi Ohira, I got an invitation from the White House to join President Carter on Air Force One on the trip to Tokyo to attend the state funeral. At first I was puzzled by the invitation, but finally concluded—this was never confirmed—that someone in the West Wing thought I was Japanese! Ironically, Congressman Norm Mineta, a Japanese American who represented a district in Silicon Valley, was not aboard the flight.

Carter had a bit of history with Ohira, having met him in Tokyo a year earlier at an economic summit also attended by the leaders of Canada, France, West Germany, Italy and the United Kingdom. On that occasion, Carter also met Emperor Hirohito, as he would again this trip, along with President Ziaur Rahman of Bangladesh—who would be assassinated less than a year later; Australian prime minister Malcolm Fraser; the new prime minister of Thailand, Prem Tinsulanonda; and Chinese premier Hua Guofeng, who succeeded Mao Zedong.

We took off from Andrews Air Force Base in Maryland and flew nonstop. I was impressed with the size of the plane. It seemed even bigger, outside and in, than the way it is portrayed in films. The president had his own compartment and in the back were staff and communications people. As it happened, I shared a lounge with the new secretary of state, Edmund Muskie, a former senator from Maine who ran for president in 1972. He was sitting with Brzezinski, Carter's national security adviser, by all appearances an extremely energetic individual. The staff would bring them folders marked "For Your Eyes Only." Muskie and Zbig, as he was known, would look over the folders with some discussion and then the staff would come and pick them up and bring more. It was that kind of trip. I hardly spoke to them. I was so junior in the Congress I didn't know what I'd talk about. In the room were a couple of other people, also quiet. One of them I think was associated with the House Foreign Affairs Committee.

At one point, Carter came back to talk to Muskie and Brzezinski and then came over and said hello. I stood and shook his hand.

"It's a pleasure to meet you, Mr. President," I said. "Thanks for having me along."

"Hawai'i's so beautiful," he said, soft-spoken, pronouncing it "Ha-wai." He had lived on O'ahu in 1949 and 1950 as a naval officer assigned to the submarine USS *Pomfret*, his first shipboard duty. His second son, James Earl III, known as Chip, was born in Honolulu. So he had fond memories from those pre-statehood days when the islands were uncrowded, unhurried and unsullied.

Somehow the subject came around to recreation, and I mentioned that before I came to Congress I would go out fishing on the weekends with Millie's stepfather, Nick Tong. That caught his attention.

"What kind of fishing do you do?" he asked.

I told him we had a nineteen-foot boat with an outboard that we launched from Ke'ehi Lagoon boat ramp, looked for a good spot to anchor, sometimes off Barbers Point, sometimes off Diamond Head, then set heavy tackle using shrimp for bait. If we were lucky, we would catch a *kāhala*, or amberjack, or a nabeta, a prized deep sea parrotfish that would bite you if you didn't hold it by the head. I found that out the hard way. We'd go out early in the morning and then quit around noon. Those were good memories for me. I didn't tell Carter this, but sometimes we were joined by Kats Miho, a 442nd veteran who became a legislator and circuit judge. We got to know his family really well, especially his son. He was a staunch Republican and a friend of Hiram Fong's, but we never talked politics, only fishing.

"Do you fish?" I asked him.

"Oh, yeah," he said. "I love fishing."

"In Georgia there must be plenty of rivers and lakes," I said.

"Oh, yes." He had learned to fish as a child, but only took up his current passion, fly fishing, in the early 1970s. As governor, he made frequent trips to the nearby Chattahoochee River, a frigid retreat for brook trout. As president, he and Rosalynn had fished the upper Potomac River for smallmouth bass, and had found a small stream full of trout near Camp David. And they had fished for trout in streams as far away as West Virginia. He tied his own flies. He said he had a pair of high coveralls and would walk out into the water as far as he could before casting.

His favorite kind of fishing: "Dry fly, rising trout, long leaders, fine tippet, deep water."

On his way back from Japan, he and Muskie were going to fish for grayling in Alaska.

Then he said, "Just a moment."

He walked off and in a minute came back with a brown polyester jacket. Inside it was covered with hooks and lures.

"All these hooks!" I said.

Each was designed for a particular type of fish, he said. I spent a good minute admiring the collection.

Muskie and Zbig didn't seem to be paying any attention to us.

"So what's your best hook?" I asked.

And I think he really liked that question. After a moment's reflection, he said, "Okay," and reached inside the vest and pulled out a hook.

It looked like a regular hook, but had little, dark brown hairs attached.

"What are those hairs?"

"Oh, they're special hairs," he assured me. "There is only one place you can find these hairs." That place, he said, was under the hoof of a deer.

"What's special about those hairs?"

"Well, you can't really see it, but these hairs are hollow."

So when he casts, he said, the hook floats. (Thus, the term dry fly.) When he jerks the pole, the fly skips along the surface.

"Boy, it really attracts the fish," he said.

"How often do you go fishing?"

"As often as I can. Wherever I go, if there is a place where I can fish, I do. And that's why I always carry this."

"How much fish do you catch, usually?"

"I catch a lot," he said with his trademark toothy grin.

"Well, then, Mr. President, you must take home a lot of fish!"

His grin faded.

"I never take the fish."

"Never?"

He said when he catches a fish, he looks it over and always

throws it back. That was a different philosophy from mine and I found it mildly disappointing—as if we had fallen short of a bond. He caught many fish and tossed them back, alive if bloodied. Hawaiians caught a few fish. And ate them.

But I guess he was in it for the relaxation and sportsmanship. Heaven knows he needed it, with the Iranian hostage crisis now in its ninth month. Only two months earlier, Carter had mounted a rescue mission that ended catastrophically, with a fiery helicopter crash and eight dead in the Iranian desert. And on the home front, he was facing a challenge from Senator Ted Kennedy for the presidential nomination. I was amazed at his resilience. ✤

CHAPTER

24

On July 12, at the lieutenant governor's office in Honolulu and surrounded by my family and supporters, I announced my candidacy for a third term. In a short statement, I expressed concern about runaway federal spending, an issue I had been addressing for months. Early in the year, in fact, at the Democratic Party's biennial convention at the Sheraton Waikiki, I had warned 700 fellow Democrats about the ravages of inflation. "Our years of random spending, both on a personal level and in government, are gone," I said. "Today calls on us to pay the debts which we have accumulated over the last twenty years. If we are to live responsibly, we must hold ourselves accountable to our present, so our children and their children may live in a time of prosperity and world peace and not in a time of constant crisis, shortage and doubt."

Now I voiced opposition to a proposed tax cut, which would only "fan the fires of inflation" and drive up the deficit. But I argued against a new tax on gasoline, which I felt would place undue hardship on Hawai'i residents. I also argued against a proposed import quota on Japanese cars, which would drive up the cost of American cars and not solve Detroit's chief problem—too little workplace productivity.

I had only one challenger in the race, Libertarian D. Gordon "Don" Smith, the morning newscaster at KGU Radio. So I was hoping I could get by spending as little as possible, since I still owed some money—about $5,500—from the 1978 race. On July 18, I held a stew and rice fundraiser, which helped replenish the coffers.

On the national front, Jimmy Carter beat back challenges from fellow Democrats Ted Kennedy and William Proxmire, a senator from Wisconsin. When he conceded at the convention at Madison Square Garden in August, Kennedy said, "For me, a few hours ago, this campaign came to an end. For all those whose cares have been our concern, the work goes on, the cause endures, the hope still lives and the dream shall never die." Carter again had Walter Mondale of Minnesota as his running mate.

At the Republican convention in Detroit, former California governor and movie actor Ronald Reagan got the nod, and Reagan picked his former rival George H.W. Bush, a former Texas congressman and CIA director, as his running mate.

It was shaping up to be an interesting fall campaign. Overshadowing everything, of course, was the Iranian hostage crisis.

A crowd of about 4,000 gathered on September 7 at Aloha Tower for a meet-the-candidates rally sponsored by the Office of Hawaiian Affairs. Steve Kuna, coordinator of volunteers for OHA, introduced me as "the only Hawaiian congressman," and I stepped up to the microphone. "Hawaiians have a message for our country," I told the crowd, many of them fanning their faces with candidates' brochures. "For the first time in their history, the Hawaiian people have been granted the rare opportunity to direct their own destiny." But I said democracy only works when people actually show up at the polls.

"I'm dismayed when I study the voter turnout from the 1978 election," I said. Statewide, it was seventy-five percent in the primary and seventy-four percent in the general. For the general, that was the lowest since statehood. "If our voices are to be heard, then it is very important that we go to the polls on Election Day. We have OHA. Let us use this office to the fullest extent possible. Through OHA, we can preserve our cultural heritage, we can enrich our children's educational possibilities and improve our economic circumstances. Since 1778, the people of Hawai'i have lived under a variety of government structures. One was the chiefdom, another was the kingdom, another was a territory and now we are under statehood." This was a journey, I said, from "a feudal, close-to-nature, no-wheel system" to an industrialized democracy in less than 200 years. Because "we know we cannot return to an earlier era," I said, OHA represents the best way to improve life for Hawaiians today.

As with the first, my second term was characterized by loyalty, voting with the party leadership eighty-six percent of the time. I had backed President Carter's initiatives seventy-six percent of the time, according to Congressional Quarterly.

On energy issues, I supported Carter's decision to stop price controls on domestic oil, and voted for a six-month moratorium on the construction of nuclear power plants. That made sense in light of the partial meltdown in March 1979 at the Three Mile Island plant in Pennsylvania. With my vote, Congress also passed a bill to streamline licensing procedures for ocean thermal energy conversion. OTEC is a process that generates electricity by exploiting the temperature differences between warm sea surface water and deep, cold water, as found relatively near shore off Keāhole Point on the Big Island. There, the Natural Energy Laboratory of Hawai'i had become a leading test facility for the technology.

I also backed Carter's proposed tax on windfall profits in the oil industry, but supported an amendment that reduced the tax by ten percent and set it to expire after a decade. I voted to fund the Panama Canal treaties of 1978, and served on a special committee working on welfare reform. I also backed a new U.S. Department of Education, and $1.5 billion in loan guarantees for Chrysler Corp., which was teetering on the edge of bankruptcy. Further, I strongly supported the National Tourism Policy Act, which would have created a cabinet-level board to carry out U.S. tourism policy. That was of keen interest to Hawai'i, where tourism was down in 1980. In fact, the year would bring the first drop in annual visitors figures since 1949. Unfortunately, the bill would be pocket-vetoed by Carter on Christmas Day.

In the primary election, turnout was even more dismal than two years earlier, at just under sixty-nine percent, perhaps because there was a University of Hawai'i football home game that Saturday. In any case—surprise!—Eileen Anderson, Ariyoshi's budget and finance director, beat Frank Fasi in the mayor's race with seventy percent of the vote.

In the general, we did better than in 1978, with a turnout of seventy-nine percent, still nowhere near the historic highs in the early years of statehood. My opponent, Don Smith, won ten percent of the vote, a decent showing for a Libertarian.

Carter eked out a victory in Hawai'i, one of only six states he won, including his native Georgia, Mondale's Minnesota, Maryland, West Virginia and Rhode Island. Even Kennedy's Massachusetts, which is on par with Hawai'i as a liberal state, went for Reagan. So it proved a rather significant end run for "the Gipper." If you exclude Gerald Ford, who was never elected president, Carter was the first incumbent to lose since Herbert Hoover fell to Franklin Roosevelt in 1932.

In December, Jim Sakai, Fasi's outgoing budget chief, agreed to be my administrative assistant, replacing John Uchima.

And on January 20, 1981, Inauguration Day, as Reagan took the oath of office, the Iran hostage crisis came to an end with the release of fifty-two embassy workers after 444 days. The Reagan Revolution had begun. ✤

CHAPTER

25

With Reagan's victory, the Republicans took control of the Senate, 53–46, with Howard Baker of Tennessee assuming the majority leadership. It was their first congressional majority since 1954. Ted Stevens of Alaska became majority whip, which was good for Hawai'i because Stevens was very close to Inouye; they cooperated on a lot of legislation affecting the forty-ninth and fiftieth states. In the House, the Democrats' majority held, 244–191, with Tip and Jim Wright still at the helm.

The exciting prospect for me even before my third term was that a seat had opened up on the Appropriations Committee. Longtime committee member John M. Slack, who had taken over Robert Byrd's West Virginia House seat in 1959, had died of a heart attack the previous March.

I immediately made my interest known to Tip, Tom Foley and Charlie Rangel, powerful members of the Steering and Policy Committee. Foley was a fellow member of the Agriculture Committee and a close friend of mine. So I felt like they were in my corner, although they both, with patient smiles, warned me that it was a long shot. Others on the twenty-nine-member panel included Phil Burton, Geraldine Ferraro of New York, Dick Gephardt, Norman Mineta, Dan Rostenkowski, Jamie Whitten of Mississippi—the chairman of the Appropriations Committee, Charlie Wilson and Tim Wirth of Colorado. Tim kindly nominated me for the vacancy, but Rangel informed me that there were seventy-seven applicants with more seniority.

"You're number seventy-eight," he said starkly.

Tom and Charlie kept me apprised of the process, which took months. Week after week, the Steering Committee would knock off names. Someone from the committee told me it was the longest they took in selecting somebody for Appropriations. Finally, it came down to two people, myself and a member from West Virginia. I think there was strong sentiment to keep the seat in the Mountain State.

So I thought, *Oh, boy*. My last stand was to talk to the Speaker. So I waited for a good time and then approached Tip on the floor.

"Mr. Speaker," I said. "I'm here really to tell you thanks. I know I would not have survived on the list without your help. I think you know that I support you whenever I can."

"Danny, you are one of my greatest supporters," he said.

"Thank you so much, Speaker. I'm glad you feel that way because I've really tried. I really want to thank you for what you have done for me."

The next day, Rangel came looking for me.

"Danny! Danny!" he said. "You're it!"

"It?" I said. "What?"

"You are going to be on the Appropriations Committee!"

My assignment still had to be cleared on the House floor, but with Tip's support that would be almost automatic.

"You are going to be the first and the last guy from Hawai'i to be on the House Appropriations Committee," he said. That's how tough the competition was.

My appointment took effect January 7, 1981. As a result, I had to give up my seats on the Agriculture and Merchant Marine Committees, but I felt that I was now in a position to do in the House what Inouye had so long done in the Senate—keep the federal dollars flowing to the isles.

I was stunned, along with the rest of the world, when a would-be assassin shot President Reagan and his press secretary, James Brady, outside the Washington Hilton Hotel on March 30, 1981. One of my staffers had heard the news and we quickly turned on the television. The images of Reagan waving as he left the hotel were followed by shots and bedlam. A Secret Service agent and District of Columbia police officer also were wounded. Reagan was taken swiftly to George Washington Memorial Hospital, where, fortunately, he recovered. The gunman, John Hinckley, it turned out, acted out of a crazed desire to impress a Hollywood actress. To my mind, this was another example of senseless handgun violence. Hinckley had used a small, .22-caliber pistol, easily available in the United States.

Just three months earlier, on December 8, 1980, another sad fellow, Mark David Chapman, had gunned down former Beatle John Lennon in New York. Chapman, a former Honolulu resident, had bought his .38 Special at a gun shop on Young Street. The purchase was perfectly legal. Struck by these two events, I was proud on April 9 to cosponsor the Handgun Control Act of 1981, introduced by Peter Rodino of New Jersey. The bill called on the attorney general to identify those models of handgun that were suitable for "sporting purposes," that is, hunting and target shooting. All other handguns would be illegal, except for relics and other collector's items. The measure also had strict language on permits and transporting handguns. There were fifty-four other cosponsors, including Heftel, Phil Burton, Pete McCloskey, Charlie Rangel, Shirley Chisolm, Geraldine Ferraro and Jim Scheuer. On April 20, it was referred to the House Judiciary Subcommittee on Crime, where it never again saw the light of day.

No measure better illustrates the often byzantine workings of Congress than that year's farm bill, formally the Agriculture and Food Act of 1981. This bill, introduced on April 7 by Republican senator Jesse Helms of North Carolina, established price supports for farmers, assured consumers of food at reasonable prices and continued the food stamp program for low-income families for the next four years. It was of keen interest to the Hawai'i delegation because our sugar plantations were on the ropes. We badly wanted sugar included in the price supports. The original bill covered dairy products, wheat, feed grains (corn, barley, oats, sorghum and rye), upland cotton, rice, peanuts, soybeans, even wool and mohair. But no sugar. It was referred to the Senate Agriculture, Nutrition and Forestry Committee, which approved it on May 13 with sugar included. The price support for sugar was set at no less than 19.6 cents per pound, with a market price of ninety-six cents per pound.

Typically, only one in four bills is reported out of committee, so this was a major hurdle cleared.

The full Senate passed the bill on September 18, but dropped the market price for sugarcane to eighteen cents per pound, rising to 19.5 cents in the fourth year. The measure then went to the House.

The House passed the bill on October 22 but without any mention of sugar!

The bill then went to a House-Senate conference committee to hammer out the differences. During that process, we were able to include sugar again, with price supports of 16.75 cents per pound, and market prices of seventeen cents, rising to eighteen cents by 1985. But then the compromise measure had to go back to the full House and Senate again for approval.

Heftel and I were not at all sure of passage in the House and set about lobbying our colleagues. It was clear there were a lot of "nays" out there, especially among Democrats. The whole process was extremely nerve-wracking.

On December 10, the Senate approved the measure, 63–31.

Six days later, the House approved it by a bare 205 to 203. A two-vote margin. Those voting yes included eighty Democrats and 125 Republicans. The naysayers included 143 Democrats. We got some surprise support from Phil Burton, Mineta and Leon Panetta of California. For some reason, John Burton did not vote. Carter signed the measure three days before Christmas. Almost immediately, the price of sugar rose to 17.6 cents per pound.

"It was a miracle," I told some constituents back home in Hilo. "This is a first step, not a total step to keep the sugar industry in business." This was more than a problem just for the plantations, I added. "If sugar goes, it means the death of communities. This is life and death for us." ❖

CHAPTER

26

In addition to committee assignments, members of Congress typically worked with one or more caucuses. For instance, Cec Heftel and I early on joined the House Tourism Caucus, for obvious reasons. In 1981, I had occasion, with Republican congressman Newt Gingrich of Georgia, to found the House Space Caucus.

Space had long been an interest of mine, ever since the Apollo astronauts used Hawai'i island as a training ground for the moon landings. The Apollo crews also splashed down in the Pacific at the end of their missions. Helicopters plucked them from the sea and transferred them to an aircraft carrier. The first terra firma they touched after the moon was Hickam Air Force Base in Hawai'i.

But U.S. spaceflight programs had largely gone on hiatus since the last moon landing in December 1972. When the space shuttle *Columbia* lifted off from Kennedy Space Center in Florida in April 1981, it was the first U.S. manned spaceflight since the Apollo-Soyuz docking in 1975. The shuttle, of course, was geared to low Earth orbit. It seemed to me that NASA was abandoning planetary exploration.

The caucus was born out of an informal association called the Congressional Staff Space Group. In early 1981, a bunch of pro-space staffers, some close to Gingrich and Republican Paul Trible of Virginia, had sent out a notice to find like-minded individuals. A few Democrats joined, including my aide Diana Hoyt, who was married to a NASA astronomer. Jim Muncy, a self-employed lobbyist for what he called the Action Committee on Technology and later an aide to Gingrich, also was active in that effort. The group held semi-regular meetings in 1981 with various space experts from NASA, industry or academia.

Gingrich's interest was a bit more futuristic than mine. He loved science fiction, especially Robert Heinlein—*Stranger in a Strange Land, Starship Troopers, The Moon is a Harsh Mistress*—and Isaac Asimov's

Foundation trilogy. As a teenager, he read *Missiles and Rockets* magazine and had been profoundly influenced by Sputnik. Even as *Columbia* completed its second mission in November, he agreed that the administration was letting space exploration slip. In one interview, he declared, "The space program is always in trouble because it has never been championed by a politician. I want to be that politician." Muncy once observed, "Gingrich sees space as a place, not a program. To him, space is a natural extension of the Earth's frontiers; and opening space to human enterprise and settlement is a uniquely American response."

Defense Daily had already reported that Gingrich and Trible wanted to develop "space interceptors" to shoot down enemy missiles—foreshadowing Reagan's 1983 Strategic Defense Initiative, as well as a space-based solar power system and a permanently manned space station. Earlier, Gingrich had sponsored the National Space and Aeronautics Policy Act of 1981. The bill "set forth provisions for the government of space territories," among other things. A historian by vocation, he had based the measure on the Northwest Ordinance of 1787, which set out rules for governing the territory northwest of the Ohio River. The legislation never made it out of committee, but the proposals seemed so outlandish for that time that his hometown newspaper took to calling him Newt Skywalker.

As the notion of a caucus congealed, Gingrich understood that he needed a Democrat as cofounder—someone with the majority party. Initially, he discussed it with Tim Wirth of Colorado. But then Wirth lost interest. With Diana's stellar work at the Congressional Staff Space Group, I was an obvious second choice, and as a member of the Appropriations Committee I would lend the organization some credibility. Although we were seen as a bit of an "odd couple," Newt and I got along well.

As Muncy recalled years later, "They would catch up on the House floor occasionally and maybe Newt would call Dan or vice versa, but mostly they tag-teamed since they have very different personalities. Dan was always a gracious host to me in his office and was great at introducing VIP scientists like Carl Sagan and others to speak at caucus events. Newt is much more 'type A' and into the nuts and bolts of policy. So Newt would testify to the Space Subcommittee about an insanely high NASA budget while Dan would hold court at a reception with NASA types. They had complementary strengths that made them a good team."

On November 20, 1981, Gingrich and I sent out the first of our "Dear Colleague" letters to other House members. The letter was cosigned by Democrats Wirth, Tom Bevill of Alabama and Norman Mineta of California and Republicans Wayne Grisham of California, Ken Cramer of Colorado and Joe Skeen of New Mexico. We called for support of "the common goal of revitalizing America's space program." Without a new agenda, the U.S. could well lose its supremacy in space, we warned. "Space has become a commonplace contributor to an integral part of our everyday life, but this is just the beginning," we said. "Space offers staggering opportunities for solving major global problems and the development of vital new industries." Not long afterward, Gingrich wrote to Reagan, urging him to support a $9 billion budget for NASA in fiscal 1983—an increase of $2.4 billion. Not only would that support the shuttle fleet, he said, but it "will allow us to begin a permanent space station and an industrial park around the Earth that will create jobs on Earth by creating jobs in space… Why, in a time of tight budgets, do I propose an expanded space effort? It's because I believe true conservatism has to offer hope and prosperity for the future."

Reagan effectively ignored his request, but Gingrich had succeeded in one of the caucus's informal goals—"making noise on the Hill" in support of space.

I had already fought my own battle for NASA funding. The summit of Maunakea is one of the premiere spots in the world for ground-based astronomy because it is dry and there is very little light pollution and an elevation of nearly 14,000 feet places it above much of the light-bending atmosphere. In 1979, NASA opened its Infrared Telescope Facility there. But the conditions at the summit often were harsh, with thin air and freezing temperatures in the winter. So the agency wanted to build a dormitory and kitchen at the 9,300-foot level where astronomers could acclimate and recuperate without having to drive to the nearest town, Hilo. But then the money for the mid-level facility ran out. I had to fight hard to get the funds for construction in the fiscal 1982 budget.

On February 23, 1982, I was given a minute to speak on the House floor.

"Mr. Speaker, once, we were clearly leaders in the field of space and space-related technology," I said. "Once, we had a bold plan for the future with long-range policy goals. Today, we are in danger of losing our leading edge to countries which recognize the importance of long-term space policy goals. I strongly believe that whether or not America rises to the space challenge of the future and commits itself to a vigorous space effort depends on whether or not Congress takes a strong lead in promoting the U.S. space enterprise."

With the caucus up and running, Hoyt was named executive director, a job she held while also serving as my press secretary and legislative assistant. She was in charge of the day-to-day caucus activities, including recruiting members, drafting the "Dear Colleague" letters and arranging events. She sent out a letter at least once a week, with enough copies for every member of the House and Senate. McDonnell Douglas Corp., which manufactured spacecraft and boosters, proved helpful in encouraging membership, Hoyt found. By March 1982, we had forty-two members. ❖

CHAPTER

27

One of our first orders of business in 1982 was to authorize a Congressional Gold Medal for Admiral Hyman Rickover, the so-called father of the nuclear Navy. After sixty-three years of service, Rickover had been forced to retire on January 31 at age eighty-two by Navy secretary John Lehman. Rickover's influence could be felt profoundly at Pearl Harbor, home to some two dozen nuclear-powered attack submarines. The latest two Los Angeles-class subs in the production line at Newport News Shipbuilding in Virginia were the USS *Olympia* and USS *Honolulu*, both headed to Pearl. On March 8, I was proud to become one of 250 cosponsors of the measure, introduced by Democrat Sam Stratton of New York.

As the year progressed, I became increasingly concerned with another issue close to home: the long-term solvency of Social Security. In December, Congress had passed a measure to get the retirement fund through 1982 by allowing it to borrow from Medicare and disability accounts. But now President Reagan was proposing cuts to the benefits to current retirees. I found that unacceptable.

In April, in a talk to the Hawaiʻi chapter of the National Association of Retired Federal Employees, I insisted that the current Social Security outlays remain sacrosanct. The troubled system needed immediate action, I said, but a "quick fix" would not be enough. Expenditures could be reduced in several ways: raising the retirement age or offering incentives for later retirement, including government employees in the program, or changing the way cost-of-living raises are calculated.

"What we must do is come up with a method which will not only ensure long-term financial stability, but which will also do the least amount of damage to our nation's retirees. From the studies which I have read, the proposal which appears to have the lightest impact on retirees and the greatest financial return lies in the area of changing the way the formula for benefits is computed," I said. Reagan, I added, has "made it clear to older Americans that the financial planning they did while working is no longer relevant to the fiscal realities of the 1980s. What the president is really saying is that he will sacrifice the interests of older Americans on the altar of political expediency."

Another issue of grave concern that year was the discovery of the chemical heptachlor in Hawai'i's milk. The pesticide had been routinely applied to pineapples. Then the leftover pineapple tops, called "green chop," were fed to dairy cattle. The result: poison milk. At the height of the crisis, more than $200,000 in milk was being dumped every day. I felt that more research was badly needed into alternative means of pest control. While the U.S. government did fund some of that research, there was inexorable pressure to cut back on government spending in areas that don't pay off in the near-term—areas like basic research. In Washington, it had been a major struggle this year to obtain support for basic research in the area of pest control. It was clear that federal spending in that field must continue at meaningful levels, but it was obvious that using dangerous chemicals to control bugs was no longer the ultimate answer.

In August 1982, I was part of the U.S. delegation to the Second United Nations Conference on the Peaceful Uses of Outer Space, or UNISPACE '82, in Vienna, Austria. The group included four other congressmen, as well as representatives from NASA, NOAA and the State Department. Ninety-four nations, developed and undeveloped, also sent delegates to the twelve-day meeting. The goals were to assess the current and future state of space science and technology; consider the applications for space technology for economic and social development, and evaluate international cooperation, especially that which would benefit developing countries.

Along with the conference was an exhibition at the Trade Fair Palace. The U.S. exhibit, "Working Together to Benefit Spaceship Earth," emphasized that American leadership in space arose from both government and private sector contributions. In fact, not just government and academia but all the major space and defense companies—Ford Aerospace, General Dynamics, Lockheed, etc.—had a hand in the displays. The exhibit featured projects to develop electricity from sunlight the space shuttle program and several remote sensing projects. There was a moon rock that people could touch, a full-scale model of the Viking Mars lander, and large models of the shuttle and Landsat D spacecraft. Visitors could also walk through a room where photos of planets were projected. Each day, more than 10,000 Austrians and visitors from around the world viewed these exhibits.

On August 10, a Tuesday, the United States sponsored a gala dinner at the Volkstheater, built in 1889. Author James Michener, who had just published his fourteenth book, *Space*, was the keynote speaker, discussing "The Impact of Space on Mankind." Michener, whose novels included *Hawai'i*, introduced me to the delegates. I was surprised at the level of interest that other countries, many of them small, had in the high frontier.

A series of deaths in September 1982 forever changed how drug companies package over-the-counter medications. A twelve-year-old girl from Elk Grove Village, a suburb of Chicago, came down with a cold and her mother gave her one capsule of extra strength Tylenol. Within hours she was dead. It turned out the Tylenol had been contaminated with potassium cyanide, a potent poison. Over the next few days, six more residents of the greater Chicago area also died from poisoned Tylenol. By early October, investigators had made the connection, and the manufacturer, a subsidiary of Johnson & Johnson, quickly recalled more than 31 million bottles of Tylenol. The company also warned the public through the media. In very short order, tamper-proof packaging became the new standard. They never caught the killer.

* * *

Before long, the political season was upon us once again. Up for election every two years, members of the House of Representatives are almost always campaigning. My twice-monthly trips back to Hawai'i, leaving Friday and returning by Monday, allowed me to keep in touch with my family and my constituents, to speak at meetings and to try to rustle up some votes, even though I had no Democratic challenger. Of more interest that year was the governor's race. Jean King, elected lieutenant governor in 1978, was challenging Ariyoshi in the Democratic primary. Running to fill her post as LG was John Waihee, a Big Island native who was among the first graduates of the UH law school in 1976. Two years later, he took part in the state Constitutional Convention that helped establish the Office of Hawaiian Affairs. Now, as a first-term state representative, he was on the eve of a meteoric political rise. Also challenging Ariyoshi were Frank Fasi, running as an independent Democrat, and state senator and local businessman D.G. "Andy" Anderson, a Republican.

After beating King in the primary, fifty-four to forty-five percent, Ariyoshi went on to win his third term with forty-five percent of the vote. Fasi and Anderson almost evenly split the rest. Anderson's running mate, Pat Saiki, was out her state Senate seat, but her political career was far from over. In time she would become one of my most formidable opponents. And Ariyoshi's running mate, Waihee, became the first lieutenant governor of Hawaiian ancestry.

On the heels of the November election, literal winds of change approached in the form of Hurricane Iwa. The Pacific hurricane season runs from June 1 to November 30, so this was a very unusual, late-season storm. The year 1982 was the first in which tropical cyclones forming in the Central Pacific were given Hawaiian names; Iwa had followed tropical storms Akoni, Ema and Hana, and was named for the great frigate bird or "thief," often seen stealing fish from other birds. Iwa developed near the equator on November 19 and zigzagged north, becoming a hurricane on November 23, a Tuesday. Before day's end, it passed within twenty-five miles of Kaua'i, packing 90 mph winds and gusts up to 120 mph. The breadth of the storm covered both Kaua'i and O'ahu, and damage was immediate and extensive. On Kaua'i, nearly 6,000 people fled to storm shelters; on O'ahu the number was roughly 1,000. I was in Washington at the time, but followed the events as closely as I could through the news outlets. Phone calls to O'ahu were difficult if not impossible. My whole staff was worried sick about their family members back home. Fortunately, in the end, all were safe.

I caught the first plane out and arrived the next day, Wednesday, the day before Thanksgiving. At Hickam Air Force Base, I boarded a Hawai'i Army National Guard UH-1H Huey helicopter to tour the damage. With me was Thomas Hamner, the federal emergency relief coordinator, and representatives of Hawai'i State Civil Defense, including Major General Art Ishimoto, the state adjutant general. At the Lihue Airport, closed to normal air traffic, we picked up Sonny Gerardo, the Kaua'i County civil defense chief. Other duties kept Kaua'i mayor Tony Kunimura busy elsewhere.

The southwest side had taken the brunt. Downed trees and telephone poles left some roads impassable. The old, two-story wooden wing of the Sheraton Poipu was demolished, as were oceanfront suites of the Amfac hotels, the Waiohai and the Poipu Beach Hotel next door.

On the chopper, we had to communicate with microphones and headsets because of the noisy thump of the rotors.

"Garden Island Apartments," someone said, pointing.

Splintered wood was all that was left of the cottages, toppled by the winds and then pushed by the sea surge into a narrow mauka gorge. Along the coast, once-beautiful houses had vanished, with only the concrete foundations left behind. Beautiful Brennecke's Beach, gone. Just rocks remaining. Beach House, a restaurant, gone. But the most striking damage to me was in Waimea Canyon. The trees were all down, all pointing in the same mauka direction, like toothpicks. I couldn't imagine the power that had caused that. One funny thing. At the Puakea Golf Course in Nawiliwili, debris covered the links, but that didn't prevent one golfer from swinging his clubs.

Although property damage on Kaua'i was severe, most injuries blessedly were minor. There was one incidental death. The Navy destroyer USS *Goldsborough*, which had only hours before returned to Pearl Harbor after a six-month deployment, was among fifteen vessels leaving the harbor to weather the storm at sea. Just outside the harbor entrance, a sailor lost his balance in rough seas, fell against a stanchion and was fatally injured. One of the ship's officers, a young lieutenant, was thrown overboard and swam two miles to shore with a broken hand and leg. Days later, the damage was assessed at $250 million, making Iwa the most destructive storm to hit Hawai'i to date. This Iwa was less a thief, more a vandal.

Kaua'i had no power for days. Interestingly, the submarine USS *Indianapolis* sailed for Nawiliwili to offer its nuclear reactor as a possible source of electricity for the island. While that plan never materialized, the gesture was another demonstration that the Navy was in many ways a good neighbor. And it was a praiseworthy and unprecedented disaster relief effort by Rickover's nuclear fleet. ❖

CHAPTER

28

On December 13, 1982, I introduced the Space Commerce Act to provide encouragement and the necessary regulation for the commercial development of space. The bill, the first of its kind, directed the secretary of commerce to issue licenses for launching private-sector space objects. It also set out the conditions for issuing such a license, including the ability to meet liability insurance requirements. And it established criminal penalties for anyone who conducted a private space launch without a license. I had fifty bipartisan cosponsors, twenty-five of them members of the Space Caucus. They included Democrat George Brown and Republican Wayne Grisham of California and Democrat Ronnie Flippo of Florida; all three had been with me in Vienna. Others were Newt Gingrich, Al Gore, John Burton, Norman Mineta, Shirley Chisolm, Mo Udall, Jack Kemp, Joe Skeen, Jim Scheuer, Steny Hoyer and Cec Heftel. A week later, the measure was referred to the House Science and Technology Subcommittee on Space Science Applications, where after one hearing it was roundly ignored.

The stark truth was, in those early years, the House Space Caucus got a less-than-enthusiastic reception from both NASA and the House Science and Technology Committee. The space science subcommittee had jurisdiction over NASA, turf the members guarded jealously. As Jim Muncy put it, "They felt we were stepping on their toes." To NASA, the caucus was just another legislative hoop to jump through. And agency officials were also worried that the caucus was made up of "flaky space enthusiasts," according to Diana Hoyt. In a letter the previous March to Jack Murphy, NASA's congressional liaison, Hoyt said, "Apropos of the caucus, bits and pieces of puzzling intelligence have been coming my way. Apparently, the folk at NASA HDQ (headquarters) view the caucus as possibly 'troublesome' and mildly L-5ish. Do we need to talk?"

L-5 referred to the L-5 Society, established in 1969 by a Princeton University professor who advocated for space colonization. One of the society's biggest backers was Udall. And the society's political action committee, the L-5 Spacepac, contributed to eleven pro-space candidates in the 1982 election. The biggest chunk of cash, $1,000, went to Gingrich. For those reasons, there might have been suspicion at NASA that the caucus was just an arm of the L-5 Society.

I reintroduced the Space Commerce Act on January 27, 1983, with sixty-five cosponsors, fifty-two of them members of the Space Caucus. This version made it slightly farther, to a markup session, but still bogged down in committee. Part of the problem was that the White House Office of Management and Budget wanted the program under the Transportation Department, specifically the Federal Aviation Administration, not the Department of Commerce.

On September 21, I introduced the measure a third time as the Commercial Space Launch Act with forty-nine cosponsors. On May 23, 1984, the House Science, Space and Technology Committee passed the bill and the full House passed it by voice vote in June. On October 9, the Senate gave its approval.

At some point in this process, I got a call from Reagan.

"How are you, Mr. President?"

"Well, Danny," he said, very personably, "I'm calling because I just want you to know that I'm going to veto the bill."

"Gee," I said, "can you tell me why?"

"Well, the bill has it where the Department of Commerce is the lead agency. And I want Transportation to be the lead agency." Elizabeth Dole of North Carolina—Senator Bob Dole's wife, was transportation secretary at the time.

"Is there anything else in the bill that you don't like?"

"No, just that one thing," Reagan said.

"Mr. President, let me explain to you why I put that in that way. To me, Transportation is a regulatory agency for water, air, land transportation. This has to do with bringing in new ideas from the private sector as well as their resources to help, and so I felt Commerce was the place."

"Well, I just wanted to call you and tell you this. I'm going to veto it the way it is."

I thanked him and we said cordial goodbyes.

And I thought to myself, *Well, if that's the only thing, I'll change it.* So I did, making the Transportation Department the lead agency. It had to go back to committee with that change, but the process was smooth.

Reagan signed the measure on October 30. The Commercial Space Launch Act of 1984 became the first of my introduced bills to become law. I would say that that really turned the space program around. Muncy went as far as to call it *the* seminal commercial space legislation in this country. Hoyt remained convinced years later that without a space caucus, the legislation would have gone nowhere. The only one who was unhappy about the whole thing was NASA, which didn't like being cut out of the process. But NASA slowly came to appreciate the caucus, as did the members of the House Science and Technology Committee. NASA, for its part, realized that the committee system was such that they dealt directly with relatively few congressmen. The caucus gave them a much larger congressional audience. And the committee, in Hoyt's view, "realized that the caucus built a strong constituency in support of a lot of their legislation." By 1984, twenty-five members of the forty-three-member House Science and Technology Committee were also on the Space Caucus, then with a roster of 158.

In his State of the Union address on January 25, 1984, Reagan had called for the development of a space station.

"America has always been greatest when we dared to be great," he said. "We can reach for greatness again. We can follow our dreams to distant stars, living and working in space for peaceful, economic and scientific gain. Tonight, I am directing NASA to develop a permanently manned space station and do it within a decade." His speech called to mind President Kennedy's 1961 challenge to put a man on the moon by the end of the decade. Of course, Gingrich and Paul Trible had been calling for a space station since March 1981. And in August 1981, Wayne Grisham introduced a resolution promoting the establishment of a space station in low Earth orbit. His cosponsors included Gingrich and Charlie Wilson of Texas. So the idea wasn't new. But having Reagan on board would surely give it momentum.

The House Space Caucus quickly took up the cause. In his 1984 book, *Window of Opportunity*, Gingrich called Reagan's proposal "an important step in the right direction," but that it did not go far enough. He wanted more planetary exploration.

After serving as cochairmen for three and a half years, Gingrich and I stepped down on March 28, 1985. We were replaced by Democrat Mike Lowry from Washington State and Republican Herb Bateman from Virginia. I made the announcement to Tip O'Neill.

"Mr. Speaker," I said, "as cochairman of the Congressional Space Caucus since its inception, I have witnessed a renewed interest and commitment to the challenge of space. This growing public and congressional interest was given a dramatic boost by the president's mandate last year to develop a permanently manned space station within a decade and to begin research in earnest into the strategic defense initiative. We are again taking the first step towards a new era in space."

In October 1985, the Space Caucus and the Space Subcommittee sponsored a three-day conference on the future of space science that brought together eminent scientists from a myriad of disciplines. It was well attended by House members, senators, NASA officials and industry experts. But that conference, which Gingrich and I had largely planned, pretty much was the caucus's last hurrah.

Still, with the energetic Diana Hoyt at the helm, the caucus remained active until 1986, when she joined the staff of the House Science and Technology Committee under Republican Manuel Lujan of New Mexico. After that, it was largely rudderless. ✤

CHAPTER

29

On January 3, 1983, Kīlauea Volcano began its historic modern eruption on the east rift zone, natural pyrotechnics that, at last check, showed no signs of stopping. Lava fountains quickly built a cinder and spatter cone more than 800 feet high, Puʻu ʻŌʻō. While the lava was moving away from Hilo, I knew that could change at any moment with as fickle a goddess as Pele. (In fact, when Kīlauea and Mauna Loa erupted in tandem in March 1984, lava from the latter did advance toward Hilo.) With that in mind, on April 27 I introduced the Hawaiʻi Rivers and Harbors Act. The bill called for the Army Corps of Engineers to build an emergency lava flow control project near Hilo. It also called for a flood control project on the ʻAlenaio Stream on Hawaiʻi island, a dredging project at Hilo Harbor and a hydroelectric power project on the Wailua River on Kauaʻi. It was referred to the House Transportation Committee, where it languished in the Subcommittee on Water Resources and the Environment. However, the Hilo Harbor and ʻAlenaio Stream projects, as well as a flood control project for Kalihi Stream, passed three years later as part of the Water Resources Development Act.

It was a great shock to learn, in April 1983, of the death of my friend and ally Phil Burton. Only fifty-six years old, Burton died of an aneurysm while at home in San Francisco. Tip led a delegation of 117 members out to the memorial service, myself included. Richard Conlon, executive director of the Democratic Study Group in the House, told those assembled: "Half of you are here to pay your respects, the other half to make sure he's really dead."

Phil's ashes were interred at the Presidio, where he could watch over his beloved Golden Gate National Recreation Area, which he helped create in 1972. In June his wife, Sala, won a special election to finish out his term. I had great respect for Sala, but in Phil Burton the Pacific had lost a particularly effective advocate.

※ ※ ※

Sadly, before the year was out, we would lose another member, much more violently. I knew Larry McDonald, a conservative Democrat representing a suburb of Atlanta, from the House Prayer Breakfasts, although we were not close. While I did not agree with a lot of his politics—he was opposed to school integration, welfare programs and gun control—I had great respect for his medical degree and service as a Navy flight surgeon. Although he hailed from Georgia, McDonnell was never a supporter of Jimmy Carter. He was also a staunch anti-communist and opposed to the establishment of the Martin Luther King holiday because he—and Senator Jesse Helms of North Carolina—thought King was a communist sympathizer. But he did arrange for statutes of two prominent African Americans, Booker T. Washington and George Washington Carver, to be placed at the Capitol.

In August, McDonald was invited to South Korea to attend ceremonies marking the thirtieth anniversary of the U.S.-Korea mutual defense treaty. Also on the guest list were Helms, Senator Steve Symms of Idaho and Congressman Carroll Hubbard of Kentucky. Because of bad weather, McDonald's flight from Washington to New York was diverted to Baltimore, and by the time he got to JFK he had missed his flight to Seoul. He could have taken Pan Am to Korea, but opted to wait for a cheaper flight on Korean Air Lines. Helms had wanted to join McDonald on that same flight, but it didn't work out. On August 31, McDonald boarded Korean Air Lines Flight 007, a Boeing 747 jumbo jet. The plane made a refueling stop in Anchorage, where Helms arrived on another Korean Air flight. Helms invited McDonald to join him on Korean Air Lines Flight 015, but McDonald declined.

En route to Seoul, the plane strayed into Soviet airspace and was shot down by a fighter plane near Sakhalin Island, just north of Hokkaido, Japan. McDonald and 268 other passengers and crew members died. The American public and international community rightly erupted in outrage. Tip condemned the act as "unbelievably barbaric." And U.S.-Soviet relations, which had dimmed with the Soviet invasion of Afghanistan in 1980, plummeted further at the height of the Cold War.

In Honolulu, which has a large Korean community, the reaction was swift and vehement. On September 4, a Sunday, about 600 members of the Korean community marched at the state capitol, carrying anti-Soviet signs and shouting slogans. Homemade hammer and sickle flags were slashed and torched along the Beretania Street sidewalk. "Long live Korea!" the demonstrators shouted in their native tongue.

Over the next few months, Navy ships and the Honolulu-based Coast Guard cutter *Munro* searched for the plane's black box. Hopes rose on September 15, when the first electronic pings from the box were picked up on Navy sonar equipment northwest of Moneron Island, a rock the size of Koko Head just west of Sakhalin. They continued on and off for about nine days. The United States asked Moscow for permission to search inside the twelve-mile territorial circle around Moneron, but the request was met with stony silence. In all, some 235 square miles of ocean bottom were scoured for debris. This despite a full-court press by Soviet warships and trawlers, which tried to intimidate the search vessels and disrupt their sonar sweep patterns. Finally, on November 5, the search for the black box and other debris was called off, a disappointing end to a $22 million effort.

Like Sala Burton, McDonald's wife, Kathy, ran to fill his seat, but lost to George "Buddy" Darden, a Georgia legislator and former Cobb County district attorney.

✻ ✻ ✻

On November 2, 1983, Reagan signed legislation establishing the Martin Luther King holiday, one of the highlights of the 98th Congress. The previous July, I had been one of 108 cosponsors of the bill, introduced by Katie Hall of Indiana. In August, it passed the House 338–90. In October the Senate passed it 78–22. The holiday was set for the third Monday in January.

✻ ✻ ✻

On Thursday, January 19, 1984, as part of the Select Committee on Narcotics Abuse and Control, Charlie Rangel and I joined five other congressmen on a visit to the Vatican. We were hoping that Pope John Paul II could be drawn into the anti-drugs discussion. Worldwide pressure from the pulpit, we felt, could go a long way toward reducing demand, as big a problem as supply. We were encouraged by the fact that the United States, on January 10, had reestablished formal diplomatic ties with the Holy See. President Reagan had yet to name an ambassador, but that would happen in due time.

Rangel, a former altar boy, was particularly excited about the audience, as was Millie, among several wives that joined the delegation. She had brought her new dress from Carol & Mary just for the occasion. It was black, with long sleeves, simple but stylish. Millie wore it to evening events in Washington with either her pearls, her jade necklace or shells.

"Oh, boy, an altar boy meeting the Pope!" Rangel enthused as we fought noisy, chaotic Rome traffic on our way to Vatican City. He and I had become close friends over the years.

A handsome church official, possibly a monsignor, met us at the gate and escorted us to the Apostolic Palace, not far from St. Peter's Basilica and the Sistine Chapel. In the ornate hallways we passed Swiss Guards in elaborate blue and yellow uniforms and red feathered helmets. The Papal Apartments occupy two sides of the third and top floor of the palace. His Holiness was waiting for us in his study, with two windows overlooking St. Peter's Square. From this room, the pope greets and blesses the crowds in the square every Sunday. The pontiff seemed in good spirits and good health—even though he would die of a massive heart attack a little more than six months later. We were introduced in turn. The others included Democrat Frank Guarini of New Jersey, Democrat George Crockett and Republican Harold Sawyer—both of Michigan, Republican Harold Rogers of Kentucky and Democrat Louis Stokes of Ohio.

"Welcome," he said in near-perfect English, one of several languages he spoke, including his native Italian.

In the end, his answer to us was that addiction was a family problem, not one for the church.

"As public officials you are charged with promoting and safeguarding the common good of your fellow citizens, and thus it is your task to protect the good of the whole of your society, while at the same time preserving the rights and liberties of the individuals who make up that society," he told us. "Hence it is by no means extraneous to your work as public servants to foster social conditions in which individuals may grow and develop in a way commensurate with their human dignity, unencumbered by threats to their authentic realization as persons. Among those factors which menace the individual and impede the growth of a healthy social climate is the problem which brings you together in this assembly: namely, the scourge of narcotics trafficking and drug abuse. Obviously this problem is not unique to the United States. The flow of narcotics has reached immense proportions, so that no nation is immune from its debilitating effects.

"The church's interest and pastoral concern, both for the individuals whose lives are marked by devastating personal tragedies and for the societies which must come to grips with an increasingly dangerous phenomenon, is focused on the crucial role that the family must play in the solution to the problem. Faced with a world and a society that runs the risk of becoming more and more depersonalized and therefore dehumanizing, with the negative results of many forms of escapism—a principal one being the abuses associated with drugs—the family possesses formidable energies capable of taking the individual out of his anonymity, keeping him conscious of his personal dignity, enriching him with deep humanity and actively placing him, in his uniqueness and unrepeatability, within the fabric of society.

"The family stands at the very foundation of society, and through its role of service to life is vitally linked to society's advancement. It provides the primary forum for the fostering of authentic and mature communion between persons, and is the place of origin and the most effective means for humanizing and personalizing society. With the conviction therefore that the good of the family is an indispensable value for the civic community, the church encourages the public authorities to do everything possible to ensure that families have all the help that they need in order to fulfill their responsibilities.

"I would invite you this morning to favor unhesitatingly all initiatives which aim at strengthening the family in American society. As you try to make your fellow citizens more and more conscious of the dangers of drug abuse; as you promote legislation, on the national and international level, which seeks to draw up a comprehensive plan of deterrence against trafficking in narcotics, may you ever strive to meet the needs of the family, for it is a key element in establishing stable, loving relationships and in offering to every person the support needed for a fulfilling life.

"May Almighty God bless you in your efforts."

Before we left, he blessed us, making the sign of the cross in the air.

On the way out, Millie asked the monsignor if it was just she who was blessed, or her clothing as well.

"You are blessed and everything on you," he replied.

She never wore the Carol & Mary dress again. It hangs in her closet to this day. ✤

CHAPTER

30

The arrival of the year 1984 struck many people as strange, given that it was the title of George Orwell's novel, published in 1949, about a distant future dominated by an authoritarian Big Brother under whom individualism and independent thinking were crimes. This was long before the National Security Agency and the FBI could conduct warrantless searches of domestic email and cell phone records. Those technologies didn't exist, of course; even personal computers were crude and rare. Traffic cameras and closed-circuit security cams, today easy pickings for law enforcement agencies, were the exception rather than the rule. Even U.S. Keyhole spy satellites, state of the art for their time, still took photos on Kodak film, dropping the canisters over the Pacific to be retrieved by a remarkable outfit with a stodgy name, the 6594th Test Group. On descent through the atmosphere, the canister, about the size of a trash can, would pop a parachute. Then the Test Group crews, operating out of Hickam Air Force Base, would catch the package, chute and all, in a big net trailing behind their modified C-130 Hercules aircraft. Their motto: "Catch a Falling Star," after a 1957 Perry Como hit. These missions were invaluable, but this Air Force unit got little recognition. In fact, its work was largely secret until the Corona program, which operated the Keyhole fleet, was declassified in 1995. In one important case, photos retrieved by the Test Group provided the United States with vital information on a huge explosion at the Soviet base at Severomorsk, home to the Northern Fleet on the Arctic Ocean, in May 1984. The blast, which killed perhaps 300 people, was so strong that it was first thought to be an accidental nuclear detonation. It turned out to be a fire at a warehouse storing naval surface-to-air missiles. We captured the disaster from 200 miles up. So I guess Big Brother was watching after all.

In the nonfictional 1984, individualism and independent thinking remained robust, if the candidates arrayed against President Reagan gave any indication. On the Democratic side we had Walter Mondale, the former Minnesota senator who was Carter's vice president. We also had Gary Hart, a senator from Colorado with movie-star good looks. We also had the Reverend Jesse Jackson, a black activist who had been close to Martin Luther King, and Senator John Glenn of Ohio, one of the original Mercury astronauts who in 1962 became the first American to orbit the Earth. I knew him well from the Space Caucus, where he had been a featured speaker. Then there was former South Dakota senator George McGovern, who had challenged Nixon in 1972. I wasn't sure why he thought he could do better against the immensely more popular Reagan. Finally we had Senators Alan Cranston of California and Ernest Hollings of South Carolina and former Governor Reuben Askew of Florida. On the Republican side, there was perennial candidate Harold Stassen, the former governor of Minnesota who had run for president in 1944, 1948, 1952, 1964, 1968 and 1980. But the early primaries have a way of thinning out the herd. By mid-March, Cranston, Hollings, Askew, McGovern and Glenn had dropped out.

Hart had stunned Mondale by handily winning the New Hampshire primary, and the candidates traded victories well into the spring. Hart was seen as the individual with "new ideas" (independent thinking) while Mondale rallied the establishment. But a silly line from a Wendy's hamburger commercial proved to be Hart's undoing. At one debate, Mondale looked at him squarely and said, "When I hear your new ideas, I'm reminded of that ad, 'Where's the beef?'" That really resonated. After that, Mondale pulled ahead in the delegate count. At the convention, Mondale took the bold step of naming the first female vice presidential running mate, Congresswoman Gerry Ferraro of New York.

Nationally for the Democrats, the November election felt like Severomorsk. Reagan won every state except for Mondale's Minnesota, which he nearly won. Mondale also won in the District of Columbia. That was it. Even Democrat-dominated Hawai'i went for Reagan, fifty-five to forty-four percent. In state races, Cec Heftel and I were reelected with more than eighty-two percent of the vote over Republican and Libertarian candidates. Inouye and Matsunaga were not up for election that year. In a final twist, Fasi got his old job back, running as a Republican! Apparently, Andy Anderson had persuaded Frank to switch parties. That way, he didn't have to face Eileen Anderson in the primary, held on a Saturday, when his supporters might be tailgating at Aloha Stadium. So Frank surfed in on part of the Reagan tsunami, winning fifty-two to forty-six percent.

* * *

In late January 1985, Hawai'i-born astronaut Ellison Onizuka invited me down to Cape Canaveral to watch the launch of the space shuttle *Discovery*. Ellison, whom I had known for years, was to be among a crew of five aboard the fifteenth shuttle flight, STS-51C. It was a classified mission, the first for the Department of Defense, so they couldn't give me a precise launch date, but I went down anyway with Senator Quentin Burdick, a Democrat from North Dakota.

At Kennedy Space Center, just outside Daytona Beach, we were greeted warmly and escorted into a building where they asked us to change clothes as part of, I think, a quarantine system. Inside we found Ellison and the other astronauts.

Retired Navy Rear Admiral Ken Mattingly, the mission commander, was a lean former fighter pilot with a big grin. He had been scheduled to fly on the problem-plagued Apollo 13 mission in 1970, but was grounded when he was exposed to German measles. He later flew on Apollo 16. Loren Shriver, a retired Air Force colonel, test pilot and red-blooded Iowan, was the shuttle pilot. He would later fly on the mission that launched the Hubble Space Telescope. Also aboard were mission specialist James Buchli, a Marine colonel from North Dakota who had invited Burdick, and payload specialist Gary Payton, also an Air Force colonel. All smart, friendly gentlemen.

Ellison showed me all the rooms where they trained for their mission. And he took me to his room and showed me his chopsticks and a little Hawaiian flag.

"I'm taking this up with me," he said.

Back out in the main room, Mattingly suddenly appeared in the doorway and fired a starter's pistol, apparently to get everyone's attention. It worked.

"Dinner is served," he said.

And so we went in and there was a huge table set up and, of course, Mattingly was in the middle and in front of him was a cake with the crew members' names. And the crew members sat on each side of him. I sat at one of the ends and Burdick at the other and we had dinner. They were lighthearted, friendly, talkative and so I stayed there as late as I could and then I went back to my hotel.

The next day, Thursday, January 24, we were told that the launch was taking place that afternoon. At 2:50 p.m., on a crisp winter day under blue skies, we assembled for the spectacle, the Atlantic Ocean shining in the distance. As usual, the shuttle was upright, attached to its two solid rocket boosters and giant orange external fuel tank.

The countdown began at "T minus 17."

At T minus 10, the announcer said, "You're go for a main engine start."

Flames shot from the main engine as it burned through liquid hydrogen and liquid oxygen propellants.

With a loud rushing sound, white smoke spread out horizontally from the pad. At zero, the metal supports fell away and the spacecraft lifted off, slowly at first, then gaining speed as it traced a smoky arc across the sky. The shuttle then rolled on its back and headed ever higher over the ocean. Success! It was the 100th human spaceflight to reach orbit. And Ellison was the first Asian American to go into space.

Elllison's job was to take care of the primary payload. To this day, it's still hush-hush. The Air Force would only say the shuttle successfully launched its payload with an inertial upper stage on the eleventh orbit. The internet says the payload was probably a Magnum/ORION ELINT satellite, placed into orbit 22,236 miles up, a distance that keeps it above the same spot over the equator—so-called geosynchronous orbit. After forty-eight times around the planet, the *Discovery* returned to Kennedy Space Center, landing like an airplane, on January 27. The crew had spent seventy-four hours in space.

Ellison was born just after World War II in Kealakekua, the Big Island hamlet perhaps best associated with the death of Captain Cook. He led a typical rural boyhood, joining the Boy Scouts and eventually making Eagle. He was active in the 4-H Club and Future Farmers of

America, although farming was not in his future. He graduated from Konawaena High School in 1964. He studied aerospace engineering at the University of Colorado, where he got a bachelor's degree and a master of science. He then joined the Air Force, working as a test pilot on a wide variety of aircraft.

I was aware, in the late 1970s, that a Hawai'i boy had applied for the astronaut corps. And when he was selected in January 1978, I decided I would visit his mother, who still lived in North Kona.

I knew there was an M. Onizuka Store in Holualoa, on the mauka road, Route 180. When I found the place, I saw it was one of those old mom-and-pop shops with a lānai and one double door. Inside, a bare bulb was hanging by a wire from the ceiling. The light was on, but there was no one in sight. On the shelves were 100-pound sacks of rice, bags of salted codfish, Saloon Pilot Crackers, plastic tubs of shoyu, glass jars of candy, cases of soda.

"Hooey! Hooey!" I called. "Anybody there?"

No answer. So I took a look around and, sure enough, nobody was in.

The backdoor was open, so I walked to the door and saw the landscape dropped off to some houses, with wooden stairs leading down. I stepped onto a little porch at the rear of the store and called again.

"Hooo! Anyone home?"

A woman with neat, short hair and glasses stood up in the garden.

"Oh, I'll be right up!" she said. "Just a moment. I'll be up."

So she came up. It was Ellison's mom, Mitsue. She had been running the store since her husband, Masamitsu, died in 1968.

And so I told her who I was and said, "I'm here because of your son Ellison."

"Oh, yeah, yeah," she said.

"You know, we're so proud of Ellison," I said.

"Oh, you know, he was a good boy," she said, recounting how he walked to school without shoes—an experience I could relate to.

"I'm here to tell you that he was selected to be in the space program as an astronaut," I said.

"Oh!" she said. She hadn't heard the news.

After that, we became really good friends, and I got to know

Ellison's brother, Clyde, as well. When the family visited Washington they would come by my office, as did a lot of constituents.

When Ellison returned from his first mission, we kept in touch. And fairly soon afterward, he was selected for a second mission, which was to include tracking Halley's Comet, set to approach the Earth in early 1986, as it did every seventy-five years. His training took him to Fort Meade, Maryland, not too far from Washington, so we would see each other from time to time.

And he invited me down to Cape Canaveral again for the launch of the space shuttle *Challenger*, on January 28, 1986. The mission was to carry the first teacher into space, Christa McAuliffe, and five others. But I couldn't make it.

"Well, when I get back from that trip, I'm going to have a lūʻau," he said. "I want you to come to the lūʻau."

"Fine," I said, looking forward to a taste of home.

One of my staff members, maybe Patrick McGarey, rushed in with the news.

In stunned disbelief, we watched the footage over and over again on television, the shuttle lifting off, then, a few seconds later, exploding, its boosters flying off in all directions, and the shuttle itself plummeting to the sea. Seven lives cut tragically short. Ellison was only thirty-nine.

That winter, every time I would look up and see Halley's Comet, like a star with a tail, I would think of Ellison.

He was buried June 3 after a Buddhist ceremony at the National Memorial Cemetery of the Pacific, Punchbowl, not too far from the resting place of Ernie Pyle, the famous World War II correspondent. About 700 mourners attended, including his widow, Lorna, daughters Janelle and Darien and mother, Mitsue. Also there were Loren Shriver, the pilot of the *Discovery* in January 1985, and Lieutenant Governor Waihee.

Norman Sakata, Ellison's scoutmaster, gave the eulogy.

"Ellison made nearly ninety appearances throughout the state after his first shuttle flight," he said. "He touched the hearts of everyone who met him by his expressions of humility. He was an inspiration not only to the young, but to all of us."

An honor guard fired a twenty-one-gun salute, a bugler played taps and four F-4 Phantom fighter jets from the Hawai'i Air National Guard flew overhead in a "missing man" formation.

I had frequent follow-up talks with Lorna, who decided to stay in Texas. We would chat about the family and how she was doing. I offered to help in any way I could, and she thanked me.

Eventually, we named Hale Pohaku, the mid-level facility on Maunakea, the Onizuka Center for International Astronomy. On November 3, 1986, Congress approved a bill promoting Ellison posthumously to bird colonel, but the measure came with no pay raise for Lorna. ✤

CHAPTER

31

Soon after Reagan was sworn in for his second term, on January 21, 1985, his administration proposed to slash sugar price supports. They wanted to cut the federal loan rate of eighteen cents per pound in half over the next five years, and impose a $10,000 limit on the benefits granted to any one grower.

Cec Heftel and I saw a fight coming.

"Profits for Hawai'i's cane producers are now break-even at best due to the depressed price for sugar in the world market," I said in a statement on January 29. "The administration's plan would be a mortal blow."

On April 3, Heftel and I made our case before a key agriculture subcommittee.

"The president's sugar proposal is a prescription for disaster," I testified. "Since the administration's sugar program is so inadequate, it is up to the House Agriculture Committee to fashion a program that is responsive to the needs of sugarcane and sugar beet producers."

Heftel said, "Sugar production and marketing is regulated by more governments and to a greater degree than any other commodity... In only a few countries do consumer prices reflect the world market. Removal of the sugar program would not result in free trade. On the contrary, there is ample indication that sugar will never be freely traded."

In the end, the farm bill, formally the Food Security Act of 1985, continued price supports for sugarcane and sugar beets. Reagan signed the measure on December 23, but he wasn't happy about it.

"Earlier this year, my administration proposed a market-oriented farm bill designed to correct past farm policies that have often worked at cross purposes," he said in a statement. "We have encouraged farmers to produce more commodities by artificially propping up prices while, at the same time, forcing farmers to set aside more and more land to reduce production so prices would not drop. As a result of years of such counterproductive farm policies, the American farmer has become less competitive in the international marketplace, the cost of our farm programs has risen to unsustainable levels, and farm income has stagnated. Clearly, our past policies have failed."

The bill corrected some of those problems, he said, but added that it had "several highly objectionable features that must be changed."

These included, he said, a "mandatory reduction in the size of the sugar quota that threatens to severely disrupt the economies of the Caribbean Basin countries and the Philippines," adding, "This provision is inconsistent with the foreign policy objectives of our country and may also be violative of our obligations under international trade agreements. I find it difficult to ask other countries to bear the cost of our sugar program while encouraging them to maintain a stable course toward development with democracy."

So Heftel and I won the battle, but Reagan made it clear the war was not over.

Another major piece of legislation that year was the Graham-Rudman-Hollings Balanced Budget Act. The chief sponsors were Senators Phil Graham of Texas, Warren Rudman of New Hampshire and Ernest Hollings of South Carolina. Graham-Rudman, as the bill was called, aimed to reduce the federal budget deficit, which at the time was the highest in U.S. history as measured in dollars, as opposed to percentage of gross national product. The bill created a series of deficit targets meant to balance the budget by 1991. If these targets were not met, a series of across-the-board spending cuts would automatically kick in. After a lot of hashing back and forth with the Senate, the House on December 11 voted on a conference report that raised the statutory limit on the deficit to $2.079 trillion, but with an annual decline over the next five years. Heftel and I voted for it, among 118 Democrats to do so. Another 130 Democrats voted against it, but the bill passed 271–154. The measure passed 61–31 in the Senate, with Sparky voting no and Inouye abstaining. Reagan signed it the next day. Graham-Rudman never really worked as advertised, and in fact was declared unconstitutional a year later by the U.S. Supreme Court.

* * *

I was proud also to have cosponsored a bill establishing the Korean War Veterans Memorial in Washington, and another to rename the Point Reyes National Seashore Monument in California the Phillip Burton Wilderness. Both measures became law.

* * *

As a political year, 1986 has had few rivals. Ariyoshi was facing the end of his third full term as governor and was barred from running again. On July 16, Heftel resigned from Congress to run for governor. Also in the Democratic mix was Lieutenant Governor Waihee and former congresswoman Patsy Mink. On the Republican side, Senator Andy Anderson led the pack.

In late August 1986, I met with the editorial board of the *Honolulu Star-Bulletin*. I think Bud Smyser and Chuck Frankel were there, and maybe John Simonds. The first question had to do with criticism raised by my Republican opponent, Maria Hustace, a Moloka'i cattle rancher.

"First a comment from your opponent, who said you were elected because of your brother's name; and that you are a nice man but that you've been in Congress for ten years and it's time for you to retire. She says we need someone with a little more vigor, imagination and creativity, someone who's going to stand up and be counted. What is your answer to that attack by your opponent?"

"'A nice man,'" I said. "At least she got one thing right."

Over the next several weeks, Heftel outspent Waihee by four-to-one and picked up the endorsement of the *Honolulu Advertiser*. In a poll published by the newspaper on September 14, Heftel led Waihee by forty-nine to twenty-nine percent, with a margin of error of four percent. By any measure, that was a commanding lead. But less than a week later, on September 20, Waihee won the primary election with forty-five percent of the vote. Heftel drew thirty-six percent and Mink sixteen percent. More people voted against Waihee than for him, but Mink and Heftel effectively split the opposition.

"Tonight is a miracle!" Waihee, forty-one, shouted to his supporters at his campaign headquarters that Saturday night.

With Heftel's resignation, a special election was needed to fill his seat for the remaining weeks of the term. That race drew six candidates, including Democratic state senators Neil Abercrombie and Steve Cobb; Republican state senator Pat Saiki; Mufi Hannemann, a former aide to Ariyoshi and President Carter; my old Kamehameha classmate "Buzzy" Agard; and nonpartisan candidate Blase Harris. Abercrombie edged out Saiki by fewer than 1,000 votes of more than 140,000 cast. Hannemann came in a close third.

But in the Democratic primary election *that same day*, Mufi beat Neil by 1,162 votes. Saiki, the Republican, was unopposed, so a vote for her was wasted. Since Hawai'i has an open primary, thousands of Republicans likely pulled a Democratic ballot to try to stir things up. That's really the only explanation for the mixed results. With the special election so close, Abercrombie didn't find out he won until he got a phone call at 7:30 Sunday morning.

In the general election, Mufi lost to Republican state senator Pat Saiki, who drew fifty-nine percent of the vote. So Neil served in Congress from September 20, 1986, to early January 1987, when Saiki took the seat.

In my own race, I received seventy-six percent of the vote, compared to thirty-five percent for Hustace and two percent for Libertarian Ken Schoolland. So the GOP dominance in the First Congressional District did not carry over into the Second District, but Saiki's lopsided victory gave Republicans a lot of hope for the future.

Also in the November general, Waihee squeaked by Anderson, fifty-two to forty-eight percent, to become the state's first governor of Hawaiian ancestry when he took office December 20. His lieutenant governor was another legislative veteran, Ben Cayetano.

Elsewhere on the military side, the MX missile and B-2 bomber programs were up for funding. I was in favor of a new stealth bomber to supplement our aging fleet of B-52s, which had been around since I was a bachelor. On the MX, I initially supported the ten-warhead behemoth. Our current, top-of-the-line missile, the three-warhead Minuteman III, had been in service since the early 1970s. I felt that our ICBM fleet also could stand some modernization. But in the crazy calculus of the Cold War, I came to realize that the hugely expensive MX would never be used. Of course, we prayed fervently that we would never have to use our strategic weapons. We built them as a deterrent, to assure adversaries that, if they attacked us, the result would be "mutual assured destruction," or MAD, in the fitting parlance of the day. The United States had long pledged never to start a nuclear war. This so-called "no first use" policy meant that we have to wait until nukes hit us before we respond. Of course, the Soviets would target the MX silos first. We would then have bombers and missile subs to retaliate. But why pay billions of dollars for a weapon that will surely be the first casualty in a conflict? In fact, the MX would be such a lucrative target, some in Congress maintained that it might actually invite an attack! So the chief value of the MX seemed to be as a first-strike weapon, our policy notwithstanding. That is what made the Soviets nervous. And nervousness in the Cold War served no one well.

In his budget request for fiscal 1985, Reagan had asked for forty new MX missiles. The House Armed Services Committee cut that to thirty. But the MX opponents in the House, led by Democrats Charles Bennett of Florida and Nicholas Mavroules of Massachusetts, wanted to cut all MX funding. Les Aspin of Wisconsin crafted a compromise that would allow the production of fifteen missiles. On May 16, 1984, that was approved by a vote of 229–199, with Heftel and me voting no. Tip then put together a team to fight against the MX, led by Dick Gephardt and including Mavroules, Tony Coelho of California and Marty Russo of Illinois. The Gephardt group wanted to delay MX production until April 1985 to give the Soviets time to come back to the strategic arms bargaining table. If they did, no production would take place. When the next key vote came up, on May 31, I happened to be on the phone in the House cloakroom. Russo found me there and literally lifted me out of the phone booth and escorted me into the House chamber for the impending roll call. The MX foes, including myself, won that vote, 199–197. But in the end, Reagan got his "Peacekeepers."

Among the debates ongoing then was the fate of Fort DeRussy. Congress had approved legislation allowing the secretary of the Army to sell forty-five acres of the Waikīkī military recreation area after

August 1, 1987, after giving sixty days' notice to Congress. Hawai'i's delegation was very much opposed to that.

Internationally, Reagan wanted to provide aid to Nicaraguan "Contras," or rebels, in an ongoing civil war with the Sandinista government. But Congress had put the clamps on that through legislation known as the Boland Amendment, after Democrat Ed Boland of Massachusetts. We didn't know it at the time, but the Reagan administration was in the process of side-stepping that prohibition through a secret program run out of the National Security Council.

On September 25, Abercrombie and I split our votes on the tax reform bill, with me voting against it. A congressional study had found that about half of the 20 million taxpayers who would end up paying more in 1987 and 1988 would make a paltry $30,000 per year or less. The bill also eliminated charitable deductions unless you filed an itemized return. I thought that would hurt charitable donations. But the House passed it 292–136, the Senate passed it 74–23 and Reagan signed it into law on October 22.

But we voted together for the Comprehensive Anti-Apartheid Act of 1986, aimed at ending white-dominated racial discrimination in South Africa. Reagan vetoed this legislation on September 26, but Congress overrode his veto with a 313–83 tally in the House and 78–21 in the Senate. ❖

CHAPTER

32

For Hawai'i, perhaps the biggest controversy of the day was the proposed H-3 freeway. Originally called TH-3, it was intended to provide a third route across the Ko'olaus, in addition to the Pali and Likelike Highways. The idea dated back to at least 1963, when a transportation study called for a thirteen-mile "national defense" highway linking Pearl Harbor with Kaneohe Marine Corps Air Station. The state began public hearings on possible routes in January 1965 and concluded that Moanalua Valley best fit the bill. But that route met with almost immediate opposition.

In 1970, the Damon family created the Moanalua Gardens Foundation with the express purpose of blocking the highway. They warned that the route would displace an ancient petroglyph stone, Pōhaku ka Luahine, listed on the National Register of Historic Places. So the state decided to go ahead and build a two-mile section at the other end, near the Marine base, at a cost of $5.4 million. In July 1972, the foundation filed suit in federal court seeking to block construction in Moanalua Valley. Joining it as plaintiffs were the Stop H-3 Association, the Haiku Community Association, the Moanalua Valley Community Association and Life of the Land. In 1972 U.S. district judge Sam King ordered all work to stop pending an environmental impact study. He lifted the ban two years later. By then, the state was looking at Hālawa Valley instead of Moanalua.

In a huge legal milestone, the Ninth U.S. Circuit Court of Appeals in March 1976 overturned King's decision, ruling that the historic significance of the valley was enough for the state to have to prove there was no "feasible and prudent alternative." The judges refused to reconsider and the Supreme Court declined to hear an appeal. On Pearl Harbor Day 1976, the *Honolulu Advertiser* editorialized bluntly: "Let's end H-3." In early 1977, in the final days of the Ford administration,

Transportation secretary William Coleman told the state transportation director, Alvey Wright, to find another route.

So Hālawa Valley it was. The opponents shifted gears. Now they questioned what effects the freeway would have on the city's Hoʻomaluhia Botanical Garden on the Kāneʻohe side. They said the freeway would bring urban sprawl to the windward side, and drive the rare Achatinella tree snail to extinction. They also suggested that radio waves from the Coast Guard's Omega Station transmitter in Haʻikū could disrupt drivers' pacemakers. In the waning weeks of the Carter administration, Transportation secretary Neil Goldschmidt, the former mayor of Portland, approved the environmental impact statement for the Hālawa route. The opponents had lost an important ally in Fasi when Ariyoshi's budget director, Eileen Anderson, won the mayoral race in 1980. Anderson favored H-3, as did the governor. Fasi won the job back four years later, but by then momentum for the project—and its projected cost—had grown. Judge King lifted his injunctions against construction in April 1982. In November, the U.S. Transportation Department okayed the freeway's location and design, and notified ʻIolani School that it intended to condemn ninety-six acres of its Kāneʻohe property that lay in the freeway's path. The school in turn moved to evict fifteen banana farmers in Luluku.

Again, the appellate court weighed in, ruling in 1984 that construction had to stop until the federal government explained why the route had to go so close to Hoʻomaluhia. Boyce Brown, the lawyer for the Stop H-3 Association, called the decision "the nail in the coffin for H-3." When the high court let that decision stand, Inouye and Matsunaga quickly introduced legislation to exempt the freeway from all environmental laws. Heftel and I introduced a similar bill in the House.

The measures were the subject of a heated hearing in November 1985 before the Senate Committee on Environment and Public Works, led by Republican Robert Stafford of Vermont. During his testimony, Inouye pointed to a four-foot-high stack of environmental reports and public hearing transcripts.

"We have already met all the requirements of the environmental impact laws, the Endangered Species Act and the National Environmental Protection Act," he said.

Stafford asked for the motivation behind his bill.

"I sincerely believe the opposition is obstructionist," he said.

"The opposition will use whatever law it can to stall construction."

Federal Highway administrator Ray Barnhart agreed, saying that opponents have used the courts to "abuse a well-intended law"—namely, section 4(f) of the Federal Aid Highway Act, which says a freeway, with its noise and exhaust, cannot impinge on a park.

Matsunaga testified that the only alternative left would be "a more expensive, more dangerous and less convenient route that would displace numerous homes and community buildings."

I testified that the H-3 would actually help Hoʻomaluhia by acting as a buffer zone. Because the freeway and park were cheek by jowl, there could be no development next to the park.

Honolulu lawyer Cynthia Thielen, representing the Stop H-3 Association, read a telegram from Fasi that was also signed by council members Patsy Mink, Marilyn Bornhorst and Welcome Fawcett. "We are in complete agreement that this issue should be resolved at the local level," they said. Council member Leigh-Wai Doo remained opposed to H-3 but didn't sign the letter. Fasi, who had once supported the project, now opposed it in favor of other transportation projects, notably light rail in the urban corridor.

But state Transportation director Wayne Yamasaki led a four-member delegation to the hearing to support H-3 construction.

That's how divided the field was.

Meanwhile, a new issue had emerged in November 1985: archaeological sites. When Bishop Museum experts surveyed the Luluku banana patch, they found ancient terraces that had evidently been used to grow kalo. And elsewhere along the proposed route they found a burial ground that dated back to the year 1250. State officials promised to redesign the freeway to avoid the area, but that didn't satisfy everyone, notably the Office of Hawaiian Affairs.

A larger threat to the project loomed in 1986. About four miles of the freeway was done, but the money for the remaining 10.7 miles—about $716 million—had to be transferred by the end of the fiscal year, September 30, or the state would lose it. Matsunaga and Inouye were concerned enough that they told the state to start making a list of alternative transportation projects. Transportation secretary Elizabeth Dole sounded a similar alarm.

Both the city and the state started angling for an extension of the deadline. Fasi didn't want the money to disappear before the city had a chance to apply it to other projects. His managing director, Andy Anderson, and other city executives spent the last week of January 1986 in Washington lobbying for the extension.

So now we had two issues in play: the exemption and the extension.

In May 1986, the other shoe dropped at the city council. Five members—a majority—wrote to Stafford urging him to approve the exemption. They were Donna Mercado Kim, Randy Iwase, Arnold Morgado, David Kahanu and Tony Narvaes. Morgado voiced concern that the Senate had misinterpreted the earlier letter by Mink and the others as unanimous council opposition to H-3.

Their appeal fell on deaf ears. In a May 28 letter to the National Wildlife Federation, Stafford said exempting H-3 would be "particularly objectionable" because it would skirt a court decision that had been reviewed and tacitly approved by the Supreme Court. In a joint letter to Congress in June, the National Wildlife Federation and ten other environmental groups urged denial of the exemption. They included the Natural Resources Defense Council, the National Audubon Society and the Sierra Club.

Within days, though, the exemption gained the backing of the Transportation Subcommittee of the House Committee on Public Works. This was terrific news. "Judging by today's action, it is quite clear that the subcommittee recognizes the extraordinary nature of the H-3 controversy, and supports the state of Hawai'i's efforts to complete construction of the highway," I said in a statement to the press on June 19. The full committee approved the exemption on June 25.

Predictably, Stafford's Senate committee rejected the exemption when it passed a $13.4 billion highway bill in July. True to form, Fasi, wearing a clerical collar, conducted a mock funeral for the freeway. Over a coffin and headstone that said "H-3 R.I.P.," he told reporters in his office, "We are here today to commit the remains of H-3."

Cheryl Soon, the state deputy transportation director, had this to say: "I don't know how many funerals they've given this project," adding, "I'm not at all discouraged. We are in the House still. We have an excellent chance on the Senate floor."

She was partly right. On August 15, the full House passed the H-3 environmental exemption by a vote of 345–34. "The passage of this bill is a message to the Senate that the House is in favor of H-3,"

I remarked. "Prior to this, we weren't sure whether the H-3 had a chance, even with the support of the governor and Legislature and a majority of the city council."

However, the measure failed in the Senate.

We were back to square one.

All that month, the city's transportation director, John Hirten, spoke to community groups about the need for alternatives to H-3. He pointed out that commuters from Windward Oʻahu would get off the H-3 more than seven miles from downtown. He said the money could be better used for widening roads, building underpasses and overpasses and a rapid transit system. However, the Hawaiʻi Poll, sponsored by the *Honolulu Advertiser*, found that sixty-eight percent of respondents wanted the freeway.

In September, the state and Stop H-3 Association filed papers in federal court that allowed the state to connect the completed section of the freeway, extending from the Marine Base entrance, to Kamehameha Highway, the so-called Halekou Interchange. Once those were linked, Kailua commuters would have an alternative to the long lights at Castle Junction.

As the fate of the H-3 looked ever more uncertain, the Oʻahu Metropolitan Planning Organization on September 12 unanimously approved a resolution in support of transferring the H-3 money to other transportation projects. While the decision on H-3 still rested with Ariyoshi, the panel wanted to be ready in case the governor abandoned the freeway rather than lose the money on September 30. The agency's approval was mandatory in order for the change request to go to the U.S. Department of Transportation.

As the deadline approached, Ariyoshi called me from Japan, where I think it was two in the morning.

"Dan," he said, "I'm not going to cave in." He wanted H-3. "If it doesn't come through, I'm going to lose it—lose the money for Hawaiʻi. Dan, I really need Congress's approval and I've got to feel that you're going to deliver for me."

"I'm going to deliver," I promised.

So I focused on the Appropriations Committee, where I had some influence. I was close to the chairman, Jamie Whitten, a friendly Democrat from Mississippi who was elected in 1941. Like me, he was a former educator.

I told him Ariyoshi badly wanted the freeway, but we needed the environmental exemption.

"You know, Danny, we have our last meeting for the fiscal year coming up. If we don't do anything at that meeting, that's it."

So I told him I wanted to put the exemption in the $562-billion omnibus spending bill necessary to keep the government operating for the next fiscal year.

"Why don't you talk to Bill Lehman and Neal Smith?"

Lehman, a Florida Democrat, was chairman of the transportation subcommittee. Smith, an Iowa Democrat, was chairman of the Subcommittee on the Interior and the Environment.

Lehman, a former used car salesman, was very approachable.

"Danny, how can I help?"

I told him my plan and that Whitten had suggested I discuss it with him.

"What do you think of the idea?" I asked. "Will you support it?"

"Yeah, I'll support it."

So I went back to the chairman.

"He'll support it," I said.

Whitten suggested we slip the amendment in quietly during markup of the continuing resolution.

"Look, Danny, we have fifteen items on the agenda in that last meeting. I'm not going to announce anything else but this is what I suggest we do. As soon as we finish with the fifteenth item, call for my attention and ask me about this amendment. I'll take it up. Now that Lehman is supporting it, have him make a statement supporting what you're doing."

Smith, also supportive, helped me write the amendment. The wording was important because it had to pass legal muster and would have to be acceptable to the Senate. We had no time for a conference committee to hash out the issue.

Markup day came, September 16. And I can tell you this thing was heavy on my mind. After we finished the fifteenth item, sure enough, everybody thought that was it. They stood up and started to talk and the room got noisy.

"Mr. Chairman," I said.

"The congressman from Hawai'i."

"Mr. Chairman, I have an amendment that I'd like to propose."

Nobody was listening except Whitten and Lehman.

"And I have the support of the chairman of the transportation subcommittee."

"The chair recognizes the congressman from Florida."

"We've discussed this and I support it," Lehman said.

"Are there any objections?" Whitten asked.

Nobody heard him except me and Lehman.

"I move that we pass the amendment," I said.

"Without objections, the amendment is passed," Whitten said and rapped his gavel.

The room fell silent.

A couple of committee members, opponents of H-3, came up to me.

"Danny, what was that?"

I told them.

So they went up to the chairman.

"There were no objections," Whitten said dryly. "So it passed."

Inouye attached the amendment to the U.S. Surface Transportation Act, which the Senate took up on September 23. Stafford tried to remove it, but his resolution was voted down 78–16. That same day the amendment cleared the Senate.

Next came the House vote on the spending bill. There was a lot of sentiment against it for various provisions and Reagan had threatened to veto it, although in the end he didn't. It passed by the narrowest margin, 201–200, and our "temporary" congressman, Abercrombie, voted for it despite his stated opposition to H-3. He said he backed the overall bill, that the government needed money to keep running.

So we had the exemption. And then we got the extension.

Ariyoshi had his freeway. ✤

CHAPTER

33

They still must make Teflon pans. I hope so, anyway. Teflon pans were great because, back when I was cooking for myself, or Uchima was cooking, you could stir-fry chicken and vegetables, maybe tofu, or fry an egg, sear ahi, with a little shoyu, olive oil or—if we wanted to live dangerously—butter, and the chicken, egg or fish wouldn't stick to the pan! Easy to clean. We loved Teflon.

In the fall of 1986, everybody loved Reagan. But his party took a beating in the elections. In the Senate, the Democrats won eight seats held by Republicans, including seven freshmen who rode Reagan's coattails in 1980. Fiddle-playing Robert Byrd of West Virginia became Senate majority leader once again.

With the impending retirement of Tip O'Neill, Jim Wright was set to become House Speaker and Tom Foley of Washington the majority leader. I was sad to see Tip go because we had worked well together.

Shortly after the election, on November 13, Reagan went on national TV. He had some explaining to do.

A newspaper in Lebanon had reported that the United States had shipped missiles to Iran via Israel. Iran was under a U.S. arms embargo, so that was a problem. In addition, the shipments were reportedly part of a deal to win the release of seven American hostages held in Lebanon by Hezbollah, a terrorist group with ties to Iran. So the U.S. in effect was negotiating with terrorists, something Reagan said he would never do.

"Good evening," the president said, looking earnestly at the camera.

It was a Thursday. Congress was in recess and I was at home in Honolulu with Millie. We exchanged a glance. How would Reagan sort this out?

"I know you've been reading, seeing and hearing a lot of stories the past several days attributed to Danish sailors, unnamed observers at Italian ports and Spanish harbors and especially unnamed government officials of my administration. Well, now you're going to hear the facts from a White House source, and you know my name.

"I wanted this time to talk with you about an extremely sensitive and profoundly important matter of foreign policy. For eighteen months now we have had underway a secret diplomatic initiative to Iran. That initiative was undertaken for the simplest and best of reasons: to renew a relationship with the nation of Iran, to bring an honorable end to the bloody six-year war between Iran and Iraq, to eliminate state-sponsored terrorism and subversion and to affect the safe return of all hostages. Without Iran's cooperation, we cannot bring an end to the Persian Gulf War; without Iran's concurrence, there can be no enduring peace in the Middle East. For ten days now, the American and world press have been full of reports and rumors about this initiative and these objectives. Now, my fellow Americans, there's an old saying that nothing spreads so quickly as a rumor. So, I thought it was time to speak with you directly, to tell you firsthand about our dealings with Iran. As Will Rogers once said, 'Rumor travels faster, but it don't stay put as long as truth.' So, let's get to the facts.

"The charge has been made that the United States has shipped weapons to Iran as ransom payment for the release of American hostages in Lebanon, that the United States undercut its allies and secretly violated American policy against trafficking with terrorists. Those charges are utterly false."

"He's lying," Millie said.

"Millie."

"He's lying!"

Well, she was right.

This became known as the Iran-Contra scandal, and it overshadowed the final years of Reagan's second term.

At its heart lay twin desires by Reagan. The first was to bring home the hostages in Lebanon. The second was to overthrow the Sandinista government in Nicaragua. He didn't want another Cuba in the hemisphere. He called the Nicaraguan rebels, or Contras, "the moral equivalent of our Founding Fathers."

However, Congress had forbidden the U.S. government from aiding the Contras.

Iran and Iraq had been at war since 1980, and Iran had made a secret request for weapons from the United States. National security adviser Robert "Bud" McFarlane took the request to Reagan, who consulted with his top aides. Defense secretary Caspar Weinberger and Secretary of State George Schulz were against the idea. McFarlane and CIA director William Casey were for it. Reagan gave the go-ahead with the stipulation that moderates in Iran try to get Hezbollah to release the Americans.

On November 21, the House and Senate Intelligence Committees began hearings into the matter. At the same time, Attorney General Ed Meese told Vice Admiral John Poindexter, McFarlane's successor as national security adviser, to gather all the relevant documents. Instead, Poindexter proceeded to cover his tracks. One of his aides, Marine Lieutenant Colonel Oliver North, got busy shredding documents.

Meese found out that only $12 million of the $30 million the Iranians paid out could be accounted for. North later confirmed that he had been diverting funds from the arms sales to the Contras, with the full knowledge of Poindexter. He said he assumed that Reagan knew as well.

On November 25, Reagan announced Poindexter's resignation and the firing of North. He denied that he knew about the diversion of money to the Contras, claiming that he had not been "fully informed" about events. A week later, he appointed a panel to look into the scandal: former Republican senator John Tower of Texas; former secretary of state Ed Muskie; and Air Force Lieutenant General Brent Scowcroft, national security adviser under President Ford. They eventually concluded that Reagan was so out of touch with the workings of the White House that the Contra payments could easily have been made without his knowledge. North's conviction was overturned on a technicality, and Reagan pardoned six culprits, including McFarlane. Poindexter's conviction was reversed on appeal.

Dan Inouye became chairman of the Senate Select Committee on Secret Military Assistance to Iran and the Nicaraguan Opposition. He concluded famously that there existed under Reagan "a shadowy government with its own air force, its own navy, its own fundraising mechanism and the ability to pursue its own ideas of the national interest, free from all checks and balances, and free from the law itself."

None of this ever stuck to Reagan. That's why Colorado congresswoman Pat Schroeder called him the "Teflon president." ✻

CHAPTER

34

On Capitol Hill, sometimes legislation moves with lightning speed. Other times it's as slow as a slug. The 100th Congress saw classic examples of each.

Early in the year, we took up the Water Quality Act of 1987. The bill, introduced on January 6 by Democrat James Howard of New Jersey, provided more money to municipalities for sewage treatment plants and aimed to limit, for the first time, "nonpoint source" pollution like fertilizer and pesticide runoff. Howard had 167 cosponsors and the measure passed the House, 406–8, within two days. The Senate passed it on January 21 by a vote of 93–6 and it went to the president that same day.

Reagan didn't like it. In his veto statement January 30, he said it would be too expensive, unnecessary and a bad example of big government.

"The real issue is the federal deficit—and the pork-barrel and spending boondoggles that increase it," he said. "The Clean Water Act construction grant program, which this legislation funds, is a classic example of how well-intentioned, short-term programs balloon into open-ended, long-term commitments costing billions of dollars more than anticipated or needed. Since 1972, the federal government has helped fund the construction of local sewage treatment facilities. This is a matter that historically and properly was the responsibility of state and local governments. The federal government's first spending in this area was intended to be a short-term effort to assist in financing the backlog of facilities needed at the time to meet the original Clean Water Act requirements."

When the program started, he said, the estimated cost was $18 billion. At last count, it had cost $47 billion.

"Despite all this money, only sixty-seven percent of all municipalities have actually completed the construction needed to comply with the Clean Water Act pollution limits," he said. "On the other hand, non-municipal treatment systems, which have received no federal funding, have completed ninety-four percent of the construction needed for compliance with federal pollution standards."

He also thought the bill gave the EPA too much power.

"If farmers have more runoff from their land than the Environmental Protection Agency decides is right, that agency will be able to intrude into decisions such as how and where the farmers must plow their fields, what fertilizers they must use and what kind of cover crops they must plant."

But support in Congress was strong. The House overrode Reagan's veto four days later, 401–26, with Pat Saiki and me in the majority—even though she was a Republican. The Senate followed suit the day after that, 86–14, with Sparky and Inouye both voting to override.

Reagan was happier about a bill I cosponsored that increased federal assistance to schools, especially those in poor areas, on Indian reservations and for Hawaiians. The Hawkins-Stafford Elementary and Secondary School Improvement Amendments also aimed to extend programs for the disadvantaged and other students with special needs, stimulate education innovation and reform, enhance local control and flexibility, improve accountability and focus benefits on those with the greatest need. Introduced on January 6, 1987, it also established greater flexibility in bilingual education. Later that year, Sparky served on the conference committee. It took more than a year to get it to the president's desk.

"We've encouraged a return to basics and common sense in primary and secondary education," Reagan said when he signed the bill on April 28, 1988. "And we have shifted authority away from distant federal bureaucracies and returned it to parents, principals and school boards."

Title IV of this legislation became known as the Native Hawaiian Education Act of 1988. This groundbreaking law had its roots in 1981, when the Senate ordered a comprehensive study on

Native Hawaiian education. The report was funded by the Bishop Estate in large measure thanks to trustee Pinky Thompson and was submitted to Congress in 1983. It found that low achievement levels among Hawaiians were related directly to cultural factors. The Select Committee on Indian Affairs, of which Inouye was a member, subsequently held hearings on the issue. The result was a bill that focused on improving education for Hawaiians in preschool, elementary school, special education, higher education and through gifted/talented programs. The $60 million measure also funded the Kamehameha Schools Family-Based Education Centers and a curriculum research project, a Hawaiian language immersion program called ʻAha Pūnana Leo, a special education program within the public schools called Pihana Nā Mamo and a gifted/talented program through the University of Hawaiʻi called Na Pua Noʻeau. All were founded on the understanding that Hawaiians are a "distinct and unique indigenous people."

The water quality bill wasn't the only time Saiki voted against Reagan. That spring she sided with the Democrats in overriding Reagan's veto of an $87.9 billion highways bill. Of that money, $135 million was earmarked for Hawaiʻi. After his veto, Reagan went to Capitol Hill personally twice to urge lawmakers not to override. When she was lobbied by the White House, Saiki said she was sympathetic to Reagan's attempts to rein in the deficit. "I explained that I had to take care of the needs of my district," she recalled.

I also cosponsored bills that banned employers from forcing workers or prospective workers to take a lie-detector test; extended protections for the elderly against abuse, neglect and exploitation; restricted a certain type of toxic, anti-barnacle hull paint; increased federal assistance to states during major natural or manmade disasters or other emergencies; tightened protections to consumers in the area of home equity loans; made it illegal for landlords to refuse to rent to people with disabilities; required commercial fisheries to dramatically reduce the deaths or injuries to marine mammals; assured that hearing-impaired and speech-impaired people have reasonable access to federal agencies and information; and established the Department of Veterans Affairs, formerly the Veterans Administration. All of these became law.

Not so successful was my bill to improve the health status of Native Hawaiians. House Resolution 1136, introduced February 19 and cosponsored by Saiki, directed the secretary of health and human services to provide funds for Native Hawaiian organizations to establish and administer programs that promote health and disease prevention. I envisioned a battalion of outreach workers who would fan out across Native Hawaiian communities like Waiʻanae, Waimānalo and Papakōlea to talk persuasively about the benefits of a high-fiber, low-fat diet, exercise and regular checkups. This was especially important, I felt, among Hawaiian children. Hawaiians and other Pacific Islanders were at particularly risk of diabetes, for instance. In fact, they are more than three times more likely to contract type 2 (adult-onset) diabetes than non-Hispanic whites. But on March 2 it was referred to the House Energy and Commerce Subcommittee on Health and the Environment, where it died. Fortunately, Inouye had sponsored a companion bill in the Senate. Inouye's version specified Papa Ola Lokahi, the Native Hawaiian Health Board, as the recipient of federal grants. It passed out of committee fairly quickly, on March 19, but then it took nearly a year and a half to get full Senate approval, on October 1, 1988. The House passed it eleven days later and Reagan signed it on Halloween. This became known as the Native Hawaiian Health Care Improvement Act of 1988.

On July 16, 1987, Inouye interrupted the Iran-Contra hearings so that 200 senators and congressman could take the train up to Philadelphia, where they convened a special session of Congress at Independence Hall. The occasion was the 200th anniversary of the Constitution. Inouye represented the Hawaiʻi delegation. It was the first meeting outside Washington since 1800, when Congress left Philadelphia. We had selected the date because it marked the "great compromise" in which the Founding Fathers approved a two-chamber legislative branch. "That compromise saved the convention from collapse," Speaker Jim Wright said at the ceremony. "It made the Constitution, with all of its other delicately balanced compromises, possible."

※ ※ ※

Back home, the key issues included the proposed irradiation of papayas to kill fruit flies. Hawai'i's fruit flies were the reason that papayas, mangoes, lychee and other local crops could not be sold on the Mainland. The other states did not want to risk importing Hawai'i's crop pests. There were three main culprits: the melon fruit fly, the oriental fruit fly and the Mediterranean fruit fly—the "tri-fly" problem. The Malaysian fruit fly, the latest to arrive in 1983, had not yet become a big concern. These bugs would lay eggs in fruit. When the maggots hatched, they would feast, leaving a mushy mess. Pesticides were expensive and not always effective. A brief, hot water bath would kill fruit fly eggs in papaya, but the fruit was never quite as good afterward. And hot water didn't always work, either. Same with harvesting them underripe, before they were infested; they just weren't as tasty. That's why I was in favor of irradiation, a method approved by the Food and Drug Administration in April 1986. This was a low dose of gamma rays to kill any eggs. Trouble was, people have a natural fear of radiation. That's why doctors, in the 1970s or '80s, changed the term "nuclear magnetic resonance," something like an X-ray, to "magnetic resonance imaging" (MRI). Even though radiating fruit was not the same as irradiating a person, some people still worried about eating fruit treated with gamma rays.

Of course, consumers were fine with microwaved spaghetti, popcorn and water for coffee or tea. So there was a move afoot at one point to say the papaya had been treated with "picowaves." Like MRI, it's all in the name, right? But the term picowaves never caught on.

All these waves are just an invisible extension of the rainbow. If you spin a basketball as you drop it, it will bounce farther on the court. The greater the spin, the longer the bounce. Violet light packs more energy than blue, green, yellow, orange and red, so it bounces farther when it hits water vapor in the atmosphere. The colors spread out based on their energy. Ultraviolet light, which causes sunburn, is invisible at wavelengths measuring in billionths of a meter, or nanometers. So you could say your skin turned red because of nanowave exposure. Picowaves lie in the trillionth of a meter range. Microwaves, as in the radiation in your countertop oven, are misnamed for the purposes of marketing. "Micro" means one millionth, but the oven waves have much longer wavelengths than that, from a meter to a millimeter. The oven waves are called "micro" just because they're small.

On March 18 in Washington, D.C., at a hearing before the Appropriations Subcommittee on Agriculture, I wanted more on the science from Frank Young, commissioner of the FDA. The agency planned to build six experimental irradiators at a cost of $10 million and Hawai'i was one of the participating states. The others were Washington and Florida for fruit, Iowa for pork, Oklahoma for curing cattle hides and Alaska for produce. Young said there were "a lot of myths" about irradiation, including that it was the same as radioactivity. He said he had no second thoughts about approving a dose of up to 100 kilo-rads on fruits and vegetables, calling that a "particularly low level."

"We made the right choice," he said.

A few weeks later, the FDA issued a fact sheet on irradiation, which I provided to the media back home. The fact sheet said irradiation causes no molecular changes in food, leaves vitamins intact and forms no toxic chemicals.

"I do not think anyone can honestly say that irradiated food is unhealthy," I said. "It is clear that the FDA has done a very thorough job of investigating the safety of irradiation. Many people who have raised questions about irradiation will be reassured by the FDA response."

I added, "Treating locally grown papaya with irradiation is a viable alternative to current food preservation processes."

While sugar and pineapple would remain Hawai'i's top crops for years, I thought the isles could benefit greatly from diversified agriculture. Sure, Kona coffee and macadamia nuts had a worldwide market, but that only scratched the surface. I wanted to see Hawai'i guava, cherimoya, atemoya, mountain apples and melons sold overseas. That couldn't happen until we won the fruit fly wars. But a long road lay ahead. The first irradiated foods from Hawai'i didn't reach Mainland markets until 1995.

✳ ✳ ✳

A second issue back home was the proposed sale of part of Fort DeRussy, an Army recreation area in Waikīkī. The state wanted to build a convention center on forty-five acres mauka of Kalia Road. The Hawai'i delegation favored the sale, as did the Pentagon. However, in April, the House Armed Services Committee voted against the sale. I was annoyed that they had taken the vote before the issue had been thoroughly studied. However, in May, looking at the larger picture, I voted in favor of omnibus military spending bill, which included the no-sale provision. Other parts of the measure were good for Hawai'i, I felt. Saiki voted against it, but it passed the House. This issue also would be hotly debated for years. In the end the land sale never went through. The Hawai'i Convention Center opened in 1998 on the corner of Kalākaua Avenue and Kapi'olani Boulevard.

As fall rolled around, rumors arose that I was about to resign from Congress to become president of Kamehameha Schools, succeeding Jack Darvill, set to retire December 31, or maybe join the board of the Bishop Estate, which ran the schools. These scenarios fit my former work as an educator. But no one ever approached me about those possibilities, and on October 5 I announced my intention to run for reelection.

With Reagan a lame duck, a huge pool of candidates was gathering for a stab at the White House. They included, on the Democratic side, my congressional classmate Al Gore, who had moved to the Senate in 1985; my classmate Dick Gephardt of Missouri; Gary Hart; Jesse Jackson; Senator Joe Biden of Delaware; former governor Bruce Babbitt of Arizona and Governor Michael Dukakis of Massachusetts. On the Republican side, we had Vice President Bush; Senator Bob Dole of Kansas, President Ford's running mate in 1976; Congressman Jack Kemp of New York; former secretary of state Alexander Haig; former secretary of defense Donald Rumsfeld; and televangelist Pat Robertson.

Sparky had no Democratic rivals in his bid for reelection, but Moloka'i cattle rancher Maria Hustace and Libertarian Ken Schoolland had set their sights on him in the general. Saiki had no Republican rival, but a number of Democrats were looking to run for her First District seat, including state senator Russell Blair and Mary Bitterman, former executive director of PBS Hawai'i and director of the state Department of Commerce and Consumer Affairs. I also had no formal opponent, although there was speculation in the newspapers that state senator Rick Reed, who represented East Maui, was contemplating a campaign.

※ ※ ※

December was rainy, with five times the average monthly precipitation. By New Year's Eve, the ground was saturated. The day started out rainy, then got worse. Around 3 p.m., the skies opened up with lightning and thunder. Many people canceled parties as a result; driving was dangerous. At 5 p.m., the National Weather Service was still insisting that the threat of imminent flooding was low, even though two to four inches of rain was falling per hour.

Up in Nuʻuanu Dowsett, we were fine, our family gathered around. But on Windward Oʻahu, the rainfall was at levels expected only once every century—a 100-year storm. The weather service issued its first flash flood warning at 8 p.m., and the Oʻahu Civil Defense Agency promptly opened its emergency operations center, but had trouble reaching people to staff it. The water in Kawainui Marsh rose steadily into the evening, then, right around midnight, overtopped the levee and flooded much of the Coconut Grove section of Kailua. Flash floods also hit low-lying farmland in Waimānalo. With streets cut off by water and debris, a lot of revelers couldn't get home, so the Red Cross opened several shelters, where about 1,100 people spent New Year's Eve and part of New Year's Day.

In the morning, houses in Coconut Grove had water lines four feet up the walls. Boulders littered Kahena Street in Hawaiʻi Kai. In all, more than 1,250 houses suffered some kind of damage, 300 of them major damage. Unfortunately, only one in ten of the homeowners had flood insurance. Miraculously, there were no injuries. Overall damage: $34 million, the worst disaster since Iwa.

And so arrived 1988. ✤

CHAPTER

35

In his last State of the Union address, on January 25, Reagan praised the "freedom fighters" in Nicaragua and Afghanistan. No mention of Iran-Contra.

"We support the Mujahidin," he said at a joint session of Congress with Bush and Wright directly behind him. "There can be no settlement unless all Soviet troops are removed and the Afghan people are allowed genuine self-determination. I have made my views on this matter known to Mr. Gorbachev. But not just Nicaragua or Afghanistan—yes, everywhere we see a swelling freedom tide across the world: freedom fighters rising up in Cambodia and Angola, fighting and dying for the same democratic liberties we hold sacred."

Mikhail Gorbachev, the president of the Soviet Union, had brought important changes to his country since he assumed power in 1985, calling for *glasnost*—openness—and *perestroika*—reform. Events of his making would change the world dramatically in a few short years.

Reagan also emphasized his efforts to reduce the budget deficit.

"For the first time in fourteen years, the federal government spent less in real terms last year than the year before," he said. "We took $73 billion off last year's deficit compared to the year before. The deficit itself has moved from 6.3 percent of the gross national product to only 3.4 percent. And perhaps the most important sign of progress has been the change in our view of deficits. You know, a few of us can remember when, not too many years ago, those who created the deficits said they would make us prosperous and not to worry about the debt, because we owe it to ourselves. Well, at last there is agreement that we can't spend ourselves rich."

That said, I was annoyed to learn, in May, that the administration had refused to release $2.4 million in aid to the farms in Waimānalo damaged during the New Year's Eve flood. Here was Reagan trying to save money again. But to me it was double talk. In his budget message he said he would seek supplemental funding from Congress whenever there arose "true emergencies." Now the Soil Conservation Service, part of the USDA, was telling me that the emergency watershed repair account was bone dry.

I pledged to get the money through the Appropriations Committee if possible. "It appears this administration has its priorities mixed up," I said in a statement. "It sees the eradication of plant pests or contagious animal diseases as 'true emergencies' worthy of supplemental aid. Human needs in the form of damage assistance, however, are conveniently ignored."

If you believe in miracles—as I do—then that's the likely explanation for the safe landing of Aloha Airlines Flight 243. On April 28, the passenger aircraft, a Boeing 737, left Hilo for Honolulu. Shortly after takeoff, at an altitude of 24,000 feet, a huge section of the upper fuselage tore off, leaving the cabin exposed. A veteran flight attendant, Clarabelle Lansing, fifty-eight, was swept to her death. But the passengers, all belted in the seats, survived the explosive decompression. The cockpit crew, Captain Robert Schornstheimer and First Officer Mimi Tompkins, immediately brought the plane down to altitude where the passengers and flight attendants could breathe air that wasn't freezing. And despite the aerodynamic challenges posed by the plane missing part of its roof, they landed without further incident at Kahului, where the inflatable exit slides deployed. Sixty-five people were hurt, eight of them seriously, from flying debris. The National Transportation Safety Board blamed the accident on metal fatigue due to repeated exposure to salt and humidity—a wakeup call for the industry. As with many things, depending how you look at it, Aloha 243 was either the luckiest or unluckiest flight in Hawai'i history. But history has a way of repeating itself. Less than a year later, a similar incident happened to a United Airlines flight out of Honolulu. On February 24, 1989, a cargo door flew off a United Boeing 747 that had just left for Auckland, New Zealand. The door peeled off a large, vertical piece of the starboard fuselage. The explosive decompression at 22,000 feet swept out several rows of seats, killing nine passengers. The cockpit crew at first thought a bomb had gone off because this was just two months after Libyan terrorists blew up a Pan American plane over Lockerbie, Scotland. United 811 Captain Dave Cronin, days away from retirement, managed to fly the crippled aircraft back to Honolulu.

In the presidential race, Inouye had thrown his support behind Biden and served as national chairman of the Biden campaign. But after a topsy-turvy primary season, the race had narrowed down to Bush and Dukakis. One issue that gained prominence was the Massachusetts prison furlough program, which had allowed the release of a convicted killer named Willie Horton. After a year on the loose, Horton was back in custody in April 1987 after committing violent assaults and a robbery in Maryland. The first candidate to criticize the furlough program was Gore, in a debate before the New York primary on April 19. But once Dukakis sewed up the nomination, Bush adopted the issue as his own. Horton came up in nearly every speech he delivered. The *Baltimore Sun* quoted Lee Atwater, Bush's campaign manager, as saying, "By the time we're finished, they're going to wonder whether Willie Horton is Dukakis' running mate." Horton was also mentioned prominently in Bush's television commercials that fall.

Bush also gave Dukakis heat for vetoing a bill, eleven years earlier, that would have required public schools to start each day with the Pledge of Allegiance.

In the House, John Rowland, a Republican from Connecticut, caught that ball and ran with it. On Friday, September 9, he introduced a resolution requiring that each legislative day open with the pledge. Speaker Pro Tem Kenneth Gray, a Democrat from Illinois, shot this down as an improper change to the rules of the House.

"Mr. Speaker," said Rowland.

"The gentleman from Connecticut."

"Mr. Speaker, I respectfully appeal the ruling of the chair."

Gray took a voice vote.

"Shall the opinion of the chair stand? Those in favor of that question vote aye."

There were a few ayes, including mine.

"Those opposed, vote no."

"No!" the chamber resounded.

Steny Hoyer rose to object to the vote in that we lacked a quorum, and Gray accepted his objection. But the issue had riled so many members that Jim Wright took the podium a couple of hours later to calm them down.

"I think most members recognize that the ruling of the chair was correct," Wright said of Gray. "None of us objects to the Pledge of Allegiance. All of us embrace the Pledge of Allegiance. But I think it is very important that all of us recognize that the Pledge of Allegiance to the Flag is something intended to unite us, not intended to divide us."

This brought a standing ovation, with loud applause and whistling.

"I think all of us and each of us, in our heart of hearts, would subscribe to the belief that patriotism knows no political party."

More applause.

"All of us believe in America. All of us want to defend this country."

Still more applause.

"And nothing would be more reprehensible than for any of us to suggest that another member, or another citizen, simply by adhering to the principles of the other political party, was less patriotic that ourselves. Judge Learned Hand said it well. He said, 'That society is already in the process of dissolution where neighbors begin to view one another with suspicion or that nonconformity with an accepted creed becomes a mark of disaffection.' Let that not be the epitaph of this civilization."

Wright then announced that on Tuesday, September 13, after the opening prayer and the approval of the minutes, he would ask Sonny Montgomery, a conservative Democrat from Mississippi, to lead the House in the Pledge of Allegiance.

Another standing ovation.

On Wednesday, he went on, he would ask Republican Jerry Lewis of California to do the same.

More applause.

"So let us all reaffirm, let us seriously reaffirm that the rules of the House are important. And the rules of the House are not subject to temporary emotions and sudden whims." He pointed back at Gray. "And whoever he be that sits in the chair has the responsibility to uphold the rules of the House. And the rest of us have a responsibility to sustain him when rightly he rules. And that all of us embrace the flag and the Constitution of the United States, one nation, under God, indivisible. And may we recite it as a vehicle of our unity. And never may it be used as an instrument of disunity."

With that, he walked off to more applause.

This was vintage Wright. Not many people could have pulled it off—a soft but pointed public scolding that made everyone feel better. The House added the Pledge to its rules in 1995.

Hawai'i held its primary election a few days later. In the Democratic race for the First House District, Mary Bitterman held off council member Leigh-Wai Doo, forty-eight to thirty-three percent. On the Republican side Pat Saiki was unopposed. In the Second District, I also was unopposed, but sixteen percent of the votes were blank, nearly 18,000—a reflection, I guess, of a lack of excitement in a one-way contest. Maria Hustace won the Republican race to face Sparky.

As the fall political season heated up, military service arose as another issue in the presidential campaign. In World War II, Bush was the Navy's youngest dive bomber pilot. He won the Distinguished Flying Cross for completing a bombing run after his plane had been hit by Japanese anti-aircraft fire. Dukakis had served unremarkably as an Army draftee in the late 1950s, in peacetime South Korea. Bush tried to paint him as soft on defense. When Dukakis had some footage shot showing him driving around in a tank, the Bush strategists had what they wanted. The result was a scathing TV ad.

With a helmeted Dukakis circling in the tank in the background, the announcer says, "Michael Dukakis has opposed virtually every defense system we developed. He opposed new aircraft carriers. He opposed anti-satellite weapons. He opposed four missile systems, including the Pershing Two Missile deployment. Dukakis opposed the Stealth Bomber and a ground emergency warning system against nuclear attack. He even criticized our rescue mission to Grenada and our strike on Libya. Now he wants to be our commander in chief." Dukakis is shown smiling and pointing at the camera. "America can't afford that risk."

The Dukakis campaign never recovered from that ad.

In the November balloting, Bush and his running mate, Senator Dan Quayle, won fifty-three percent of the vote. Dukakis and Senator Lloyd Bentsen of Texas, the vice presidential nominee, won forty-five percent. The electoral vote was even more lopsided, 426–111. Dukakis won only nine states, including Massachusetts and Hawai'i.

In Hawai'i, Sparky beat Hustace, seventy-seven to twenty-one percent. Saiki defeated Bitterman, fifty-five to forty-three percent. And I won my sixth term, beating Libertarian Lloyd Mallan eighty-nine to eleven percent. Fasi won reelection as a Republican, beating former city councilwoman Marilyn Bornhorst. There were a couple of surprises on the Neighbor Isles: environmental activist JoAnn Yukimura beat Mayor Tony Kunimura on Kaua'i, and Bernard Akana beat Mayor Dante Carpenter on Hawai'i island. ✤

CHAPTER

36

Heavy winds hit Oʻahu on the night of March 2, 1989, toppling trees and tearing off roofs. At the height of the storm, which also generated fifteen-foot seas, the oil tanker *Exxon Houston* broke free from its mooring off Barbers Point and ran up on the reef about 2,000 feet offshore. In the process, the tanker spilled some 117,000 gallons of oil into the ocean.

It could have been much worse. Initially, the 800-foot ship had been loaded with 490,000 barrels of crude—or 20.5 million gallons. But 400,000 barrels had been off-loaded. The oil spilled from a rupture in the ship's fuel tank; this was bunker fuel, used to power the ship. Some washed ashore at the beach where they hold Germaine's Luau. Some ended up on the reef. Six commercial tugs, two Navy salvage ships and the Coast Guard cutter *Sassafras* eventually managed to pull the tanker free.

On March 16, Saiki and I signed on to the Oil Pollution Act of 1990, sponsored by Walter Jones, a Democrat from North Carolina. It established an Oil Spill Compensation Fund and made the owner of the ship, rig or refinery that caused the spill responsible for the cleanup and for the cost of associated economic and environmental damage. There was much more to it, of course. In all, the bill attracted seventy-nine cosponsors and moved quickly through the committees, House and Senate.

But before the month was out, on March 24, another tanker, the *Exxon Valdez*, ran aground at Prince William Sound, east of Anchorage, Alaska, spilling as much as 32 million gallons of oil. This was an environmental catastrophe of jaw-dropping proportions that could just as easily happened in Hawaiʻi. You could say we dodged a bullet with the relatively small *Exxon Houston* spill.

Bush signed the Oil Pollution Act into law on August 18.

Of course, sugar was in trouble again. During his campaign, Bush had promised to keep import quotas on foreign sugar until "the international sugar market becomes a level playing field." But many in his administration favored free trade. I was surprised and angry when I learned that U.S. Trade Representative Carla Hills, in a May 24 letter to the ambassador from El Salvador—another sugar-producing country—said that the administration wanted to dismantle the sugar quota program.

"Hawai'i sugar growers can compete head to head against any growers in the world," I said June 7 on the House floor. "But if we allow foreign subsidized sugar to flood our market, the U.S. sugar industry will wither and die. Then we will be at the mercy of cut-throat world market prices." The Farm Bill was set to expire in 1990, and I wanted to be sure to keep the sugar quotas alive.

On June 27, over breakfast with constituents in Washington, I speculated that, if named a Bishop Estate trustee, I might try to hang on to my congressional seat, just as Henry Peters, appointed in May 1984, continued to serve in the state House. "It would be possible, through modern technology, to participate in Bishop Estate deliberations," I remarked. "With teleconferencing, I could sit at my desk in Washington and take part in all discussions and votes." I was also concerned, if I were to resign from Congress, that the Democrats would split the vote in a special election. That could lead to a second Republican in the House. Already, a large number of candidates were waiting for a possible shot at the Second District seat, including Patsy Mink, Mary Bitterman, state senators Michael Crozier and Ron Menor, Mufi Hannemann and city managing director Jeremy Harris—Fasi's number two. When my remarks made the front page of the *Advertiser* the next day, both Sparky and Waihee commented that they didn't think it was a good idea for me to keep both positions, at least in the long term. But the fact remained that nobody had approached me about the job, and I hadn't made up my mind to take it even if it were offered. So this fuss proved all for nothing. On December 15, almost a year after Richard Lyman's death, the justices selected Oswald Stender, who went on to do a creditable job during a very hard time for the estate.

The end of the 1980s marked the rise of crystal methamphetamine, or "ice," and the fall of the savings and loans, or "thrifts."

The S&L disaster could be pinned squarely on the Reagan administration. In Reagan's effort to penny-pinch the budget, he cost us billions.

Until 1989, savings and loans came under the regulation of the Federal Home Loan Bank Board and were insured by the Federal Savings and Loan Insurance Corporation. That set them apart from banks. Typically, they would offer low-interest mortgages. Because these loans were low interest, the savings accounts had to be low interest, too. In 1980, the Federal Reserve cut back on the money supply to fight inflation, which had risen into the double digits. With money in short supply, demand rose and so did interest rates. A lot of people took their savings out of S&Ls because they could get better rates elsewhere. That started the snowball. As more and more S&Ls found themselves in trouble, the Reagan administration decided the answer was deregulation. At the same time, the Reagan folks cut back on the number of regulators in a move to help fight the deficit, a familiar theme. Under less oversight, more and more S&Ls tried to turn things around with riskier but potentially higher-paying investments, like questionable real estate and junk bonds. By 1989, more than 1,000 of them had failed. The Federal Savings and Loan Insurance Corporation had nowhere near enough money to cover the $20 billion in losses.

So Bush, now president, and Congress decided something had to change. We came up with a taxpayer-financed bailout called the Financial Institutions Reform, Recovery and Enforcement Act. It provided $50 billion to close failed S&Ls and stop more losses. And it set up a new agency called the Resolution Trust Corporation to resell S&L assets, and use the money to pay back depositors. The new law also changed S&L regulations to help prevent more bad investments. But this ended up costing taxpayers $132 billion.

Along the way, several of my colleagues got caught up in the mess.

Senators Alan Cranston of California, John Glenn of Ohio, Dennis DeConcini and John McCain of Arizona, and Donald Riegle of Michigan had all accepted donations from Charles Keating, chairman of the Lincoln Savings and Loan Association, based in Irvine, California. McCain had even taken some vacations at Keating's expense. The so-called Keating Five were accused of intervening with the Federal Home Loan Bank Board, which was investigating Lincoln Savings for shady deals. A Senate ethics panel eventually cleared Glenn and McCain, accusing them only of "poor judgment." Lincoln's parent company, American Continental Corporation, went bankrupt in 1989 with losses of $285 million, wiping out the life savings of 21,000 elderly Americans.

Speaker Jim Wright was formally accused of influence peddling related to Vernon Savings and Loan in his home state of Texas. The owner was Don Dixon, who would be convicted in December 1990 of twenty-three counts of fraud. U.S. Attorney General Dick Thornburgh called him "the highest of the high fliers among the savings and loan crooks." To protect the thrift from investigation, Wright tried to get William Black, deputy director of the Federal Savings and Loan Insurance Corporation, fired. After a critical report by the House Committee on Standards of Official Conduct, Wright resigned from office on May 31, 1989. Tom Foley became Speaker and Dick Gephardt, who entered Congress with me in 1977, majority leader.

In Hawai'i, there were two notable success stories: Territorial Savings, which became Territorial Savings Bank, and American Savings and Loan, which became American Savings Bank, bought by Hawaiian Electric.

While Hawai'i was infamous for its marijuana crops, a new and far more dangerous drug gained popularity around the time that Green Harvest had cut into the weed fields. Crystal meth, when smoked, provided a euphoric high and heightened awareness at a terrible cost to the body. Amphetamines or "uppers" had been around since the 1880s and in prescription doses have been used to treat attention deficit hyperactivity disorder, obesity and narcolepsy—falling asleep during the day. In Japan after the war, under pressure to produce, a lot of workers took meth.

But in the United States until the 1980s it was something mostly produced and distributed by California biker gangs. In Hawai'i, ice gained popularity through imports from the Philippines, where it was called *batu*. By the late 1980s it qualified as an epidemic. In Hawai'i, it was sold in $50 cellophane packets that contain about a tenth of a gram, good for one or two hits. But smoking ice provides a high for eight hours or more, compared with less than thirty minutes for crack cocaine. It was just as addictive as crack, and also produced bouts of severe depression and paranoia as well as convulsions. Chronic use also ruins the mouth and teeth.

In January 1990, the House Select Committee on Narcotics Abuse and Control held hearings on the subject in Honolulu. Despite the alarming evidence, the Bush administration failed to take the problem seriously, dismissing it as mainly a Hawai'i problem that wouldn't catch on on the Mainland.

In Washington in February, Dr. Herbert Kleber, deputy director of the Office of National Drug Control Policy, told the committee that heroin and marijuana would continue to be the most popular drugs in the 1990s—not ice or crack cocaine. I found this position extremely short-sighted.

"The Mainland may be caught with its pants down due to the administration's hunch," I said in a statement. "The administration should not overlook the dangerous consequences of ice abuse. We're in a unique position to head off ice's destructive threat before it begins."

On the legislative scoreboard, the 101st Congress had the usual mix of victories and "nice tries."

One victory was the Cranston-Gonzalez National Affordable Housing Act. This put forward a number of provisions to make it easier for American families to afford a decent home in a suitable environment. I was one of forty-two cosponsors of the measure, which became law in late 1990, after I had left the House.

Congress also approved and Bush signed a compact of free association with the Pacific island nation of Palau.

Also successful was the Augustus F. Hawkins Human Services Reauthorization Act of 1990, which expanded the Head Start program. I was one of 104 cosponsors, so it had broad support.

A few bills that I strongly favored came up short. Maybe they were ahead of their time.

One was the Hydrogen Research and Development Act, introduced by George Brown of California. It called for a five-year R&D program into the use of hydrogen as a fuel. The beautiful thing about hydrogen is that it is so abundant; every water molecule has two atoms of hydrogen. And Kīlauea Volcano, erupting for eighteen years now, remained a prolific generator of hydrogen in the form of sulfides. But the bill died in the House Science, Space and Technology Committee.

Another unfortunate failure was the National Global Warming Policy Act, which sought to reduce the amount of heat-trapping greenhouse gases in the atmosphere. The bill, introduced by Democrat Vic Fazio of California, called for a twenty percent drop in CO_2 emissions by the year 2000. It also called for the United States to host an international conference on climate change and to encourage multilateral agreements. The measure also sought to encourage the development of green technologies, and help protect tropical rainforests worldwide. In April 1989 it was referred to the House Subcommittee on Energy and Power, where it was dead on arrival.

A related environmental measure, the Stratospheric Ozone Protection Act of 1989, aimed to ban chlorofluorocarbons and other chemicals responsible for creating the ozone hole over Antarctica. The bill, sponsored by Jim Bates of California, had nominally wide support, with 159 cosponsors including myself. It died in the House Energy and Commerce Committee. The CFC ban eventually would come, but not for years. ✤

CHAPTER

37

Health problems began to afflict Sparky in 1988, notably his back and a serious case of the flu that caused him to lose twenty pounds and miss the Democratic National Convention. Despite that, he made eighty-seven percent of the Senate roll call votes, according to the Congressional Quarterly. So he was upset with rumors that he was more seriously ill than he let on. "It was nothing to be alarmed about," he complained to the *Star-Bulletin*. "The fact is, I've gained all the weight I lost back—and maybe a few extra ones."

But then, in January 1989, he fell down a flight of stairs, breaking a leg and two ribs. Then he came down with a bad case of shingles, a painful recurrence of the chicken pox virus. By July he was hospitalized at Walter Reed Army Medical Center, in Bethesda, Maryland. Still, I didn't sense that his legislative agenda had been hampered by his illnesses.

He had cosponsored, along with Inouye, the landmark Americans with Disabilities Act, introduced by Senator Tom Harkin of Iowa on May 9, and was able to take part in three roll call votes on amendments September 7. He also voiced support for a bill that provided reparations for Japanese Americans sent to internment camps during World War II, a measure that he championed.

But by the late fall, he was slowing down again. In November, he was hospitalized for a fever and swollen leg, and missed some key votes. In its year-end issue, the Congressional Quarterly reported that the worst Senate voting records belonged to Sparky and Al Gore, whose son was hit by a car as they left a Baltimore Orioles game. Sparky missed eighty-five of 312 roll call votes; Gore, twenty-three.

Then in January 1990, just when you thought things couldn't get any worse, Sparky fell again at his home in Maryland and broke his arm. Back in the hospital.

Within weeks, he confirmed that he had prostate cancer, but was determined to beat it. "I cannot conclude at this juncture that my condition is debilitating to the extent that I should step down," he said in a statement January 19. "I deeply regret the fact that 1989 marred my twenty-seven-year record in Congress for roll call voting attendance, and if it appears that my attendance in the second session of the 101st Congress does not show marked improvement over the record of the first session, I will reassess my present intention of fulfilling my term of office."

If the seat were to become vacant, speculation ran high that Saiki and I would face each other. A poll in late March showed the race would be close.

By then, the cancer had spread to his bones, and Sparky had decided to try an alternative treatment in Toronto, where he died April 15, Easter Sunday morning. He was seventy-three. The Aloha State had lost a good and loyal friend.

"Sparky warmed our state and our country with his humanitarianism," said Waihee, who had learned the news via a phone call from Sparky's widow, Helene. "He will be remembered most for his vision of peace and his faith in the human spirit. In his memory, we will carry on his quest. In his spirit, we will strive for the highest of principles and the brightest of worlds."

The next day, a sunny Monday, more than 300 people, including twenty-five senators, crowded into St. Joseph's on Capitol Hill, a Gothic brownstone on the corner of Second and C Streets, NE. Dating to the 1860s and with a 200-foot spire, St. Joseph's is diagonally across from the Hart Senate Office Building, where Sparky had his office. Helene thanked those attending, including his Senate staff members. The Reverend Richard Halvorson, the Senate chaplain, called Sparky "an uncommon man," adding, "I loved him and I miss him very much." And so we said goodbye to a great patriot.

The task to name a replacement fell to Waihee. Some people wondered if he might appoint himself. Open Senate seats in Hawai'i don't come along very often. Another possibility was Lieutenant Governor Ben Cayetano. Whomever Waihee named would have an advantage in a special election to fill out the rest of Sparky's term, which ran through 1994. The winner would likely face Saiki.

For me, this was not an easy decision because, in my thirteen-plus years in the House I had gained seniority. If I stayed in the House, I would be up for two appropriations subcommittee chairmanships. That was a lot of power for Hawai'i. After giving it considerable thought, and discussing it with Millie and the family, I announced on April 24 that I would be running in the special election regardless of Waihee's choice.

"The unfortunate death of my dear friend Spark Matsunaga presents a new challenge and a greater opportunity for me to serve all the people of Hawai'i," I told the press. "My Hawaiian parents taught me and my family the importance of hard work and achievement. I now have the opportunity to demonstrate that their son can be elected and excel in the U.S. Senate."

Cayetano immediately endorsed me. "I'm leaning toward running for reelection, but I haven't made up my mind yet," he told Bill Kresnak of the *Advertiser*. "The governor and I have worked well together." He added, "I think it's best to put forth our best candidate. He deserves the appointment because of his experience and the contacts that he has in Washington."

Days later, Waihee made it official. At his office at the capitol, with Cayetano and Inouye standing by, he named me as Sparky's temporary replacement. He had some kind words to say. "I think the congressman has demonstrated that he is a person of extremely high integrity in his personal and professional dealings," Waihee said. "He's an individual of proven experience in the U.S. Congress."

I immediately accepted and vowed to continue the senator's work.

"I find that many of the things that we were doing have been overlapping," I told reporters. "So I'll continue his agenda on alternate energy, and I want to continue his agenda on veterans' affairs also."

Inouye expressed confidence that I would be a "great asset to the state."

Cayetano, the state's chief elections officer, announced that a special election to fill my seat would be held on August 22, primary election day.

When asked if I had someone in mind to succeed me, I said no.

"I have so many friends seeking that seat," I said. "I wish them all well."

That same day, Waihee issued a disaster declaration for Kalapana, where a lava flow from Kīlauea Volcano was rolling through the town, so far destroying nearly one hundred homes. Emergency workers prepared to move the famous Painted Church to save it from a fiery demise. Before Pele was through, the entire development of Kalapana Gardens would be covered, as would be Kalapana's celebrated black sand beach. ✤

PART THREE

※

THE ONE HUNDRED CLUB

CHAPTER

38

On May 16, 1990, Senate President Pro Tempore Robert Byrd swore me in as Hawai'i's junior senator. Millie was there, of course, wearing a white carnation *lei* and breadfruit-pattern dress. So was Dan Inouye and George Mitchell, the majority leader. With our kids all grown, Millie now was able to join me in Washington full-time. No longer would I have to commute to Hawai'i on weekends twice a month. Honestly, I enjoyed those trips home, but at sixty-five I could do without the jet lag.

With a tough campaign ahead of me for the first time in fourteen years, however, I knew I would be spending a lot of time in Hawai'i through the special election. President Bush had made a personal appeal to Pat Saiki to run for the Senate. She had yet to jump into the race, but everyone expected her to do so.

On May 5, before winging off to Washington, I appealed for help at the O'ahu Democratic convention.

"Retaining Sparky's seat will be no minor task," I assured the delegates at the Sheraton Waikiki Hotel. "Of course, I really need not tell you that. We face the power of the presidency and financial resources we could never hope to match. Yet, they face the power of the people and grassroots resources beyond any they could equal. The times are both rife with glorious promise and fraught with potential peril. One thing and one thing alone will spell the difference for us: unity. Believe me, there is going to be more than enough for all of us to contend with. Let us not have to contend with ourselves."

On my last day in the House, May 15, I led the members in the Pledge of Allegiance and said a quick goodbye.

"I have come today to bid aloha to my friends and colleagues," I said. "My service here has been one of the most rewarding experiences of my life, and I thank my constituents for enabling me to serve in this honored body."

Then I handed my resignation letter to Speaker Tom Foley. "It has been a distinct honor to serve with you and our fellow House colleagues for the past thirteen years," it said. "While I am eager to take on new challenges in the Senate, I will always cherish my years in the House."

Two friends, Steny Hoyer of Maryland and Dick Durbin of Illinois, came up to offer heartfelt congratulations and hugs. Of course, with me leaving, they were up for coveted chairmanships on appropriations subcommittees. That was no secret and we laughed about it.

The first order of business was moving. The staff, led by receptionist Pat Kim, later Pat Hill, packed up all of our files and photos, no small task.

At one point Pat told me I had a call from Ted Kennedy.

"Put him through," I said.

Ted just wanted to chat and welcome me to the Senate.

"Anything I can do, Senator, let me know," he offered.

"Call me Danny," I said.

"All right, Danny. Call me Ted."

Kennedy embodied aloha, and before the year was out would prove to be a valuable political ally.

I also stopped by Matsunaga's office and told the staff that I would take on as many of them as I could. I left with several résumés.

On May 22, I announced my staff lineup. From the House, I brought Jim Sakai as administrative assistant, Patrick McGarey as legislative director, Peter McClaran as press secretary and, of course, Pat Hill as office manager. As legislative assistants I brought aboard Dale Sakai, Debra Wada, Paul Cardus and Kaloa Robinson. Mary Beth Aoyagi was my visitors liaison. Gregg Takayama, formerly with Inouye, joined the staff as communications director. And from Sparky's staff I picked up Darci Tokioka; legislative assistants John Tagami, Amy Fujimoto, Nancy Langley, Cora Yamamoto, Kristy Kusumoto and Glenn Leong; along with support staffers Terri Byers, Kelli Kauinui and Scott Richter; and assistants Gladys Karr, Joan Ohashi—daughter of my Maui stalwart

Rose Ohashi, and Pearl Takahashi. Running my Honolulu office as state administrator was Bob Ogawa, with help from Juliette Sagum, Michael Kitamura and Carlene Flores.

❊ ❊ ❊

In the Senate, my assignments were the Committee on Energy and Natural Resources—a perfect fit for Hawai'i, the Committee on Governmental Affairs—also good because of all the federal employees in Hawai'i, and the Committee on Veterans' Affairs, another avid interest. I felt like I'd been dealt a poker hand with three aces.

Almost immediately, however, I found a battle brewing.

On February 7, Kennedy had introduced the Civil Rights Act of 1990. This amended the historic Civil Rights Act of 1964 in important ways. The measure put up more barriers to discrimination in the workplace on the basis of race, color, religion, gender or national origin. The bill was prompted by recent Supreme Court rulings that made it harder for minorities and women to win job discrimination suits. It also banned racial harassment in the workplace. The initial cosponsors included such respected members as Howard Metzenbaum of Ohio, Republican Mark Hatfield of Oregon, Paul Simon of Illinois, Gore, Biden, Barbara Mikulski of Maryland, Chris Dodd of Connecticut, John Kerry of Massachusetts and Inouye. At Kennedy's urging, I joined the forty-nine other cosponsors on May 17, my second day in the Senate.

On June 8, the bill went to the Senate Committee on Labor and Human Resources, then on July 18 passed the Senate by a 65–34 vote, just short of a two-thirds majority. On August 3, the bill passed the House with amendments and went to conference committee. By mid-October the committee had hammered out the differences, and the bill landed on Bush's desk on October 20. Bush didn't like it. He claimed the measure "employs a maze of highly legalistic language to introduce the destructive force of quotas into our national employment system." We disagreed about the quotas, but were willing to take a look at an alternative bill that Bush sent over. He wanted, among other things, to cap the damages in successful discrimination lawsuits at $150,000. In the end, we stuck with our version.

Bush vetoed it.

"I deeply regret having to take this action with respect to a bill bearing such a title, especially since it contains provisions that I strongly endorse," he said in his veto message. Bush became only the second president since the 1950s to veto a civil rights bill. The first was Reagan.

Ron Brown, chairman of the Democratic Party, remarked, "At the crossroads of his presidency, George Bush has made clear where he and the Republican Party really stand."

Kennedy called the veto "tragic and disgraceful."

On October 24, less than two weeks before the November elections, the Senate held an override vote. It was a cliff-hanger, with sixty-seven votes needed to override. The clerk logged a "yea" next to my name and that of the Senate's fifty-five other Democrats. We also picked up the support of ten Republicans, eight of them cosponsors: Lincoln Chafee of Rhode Island, Bill Cohen of Maine, John Danforth of Missouri, Dave Durenberger of Minnesota, Arlen Specter of Pennsylvania, Jim Jeffords of Vermont and Bob Packwood and Hatfield of Oregon. Two other Republicans, Pete Domenici of New Mexico and John Heinz of Pennsylvania, also voted to override. But Inouye's frequent ally, Ted Stevens of Alaska, voted "nay." So we came up one vote short, 66–34. For me, it proved an early and pointed lesson in the politics of the One Hundred Club. ✤

CHAPTER

39

On Thursday, May 31, 1990, at a rally in her hometown of Hilo, Saiki announced her candidacy for the Senate. A crowd of about 100 supporters, including former U.S. senator Hiram Fong, joined her at Moʻoheau Park Pavilion.

"Hawaiʻi needs a senator who can make the people on Pennsylvania Avenue and Constitution Avenue understand the people on Kamehameha Avenue," she said, referring to Hilo's main street. "My opponent is a cordial gentleman. But this is a Senate race, and the stakes are far greater than personality. I offer an independent vote for Hawaiʻi and something more, a respected voice that can be heard in the Oval Office."

That was true. Saiki already had the strong backing of Bush, and had met with him May 2 at his request at the White House. She was also urged to run in a letter signed by forty-three senators.

The race looked close. On the same day of her announcement, a poll sponsored by the *Star-Bulletin* and KGMB-9 News found that we had nearly even appeal among voters. Of those surveyed, seventy-one percent had rated her performance in Congress as good or excellent; my number was fifty-seven percent. Nine percent viewed her unfavorably, compared to seven percent for me. Where we really differed was finances. Just a week earlier, we had made pubic our congressional disclosure reports. Saiki reported assets of between $740,000 and $1.5 million. Mine ranged between $220,000 and $575,000. In addition to our House salaries of $89,000, Saiki and I reported state pensions of $9,000 per year from our days as educators. I was certain her campaign would benefit greatly from Republican interests on the Mainland. The Republicans thought that this was one of best chances they had of claiming a seat held by a Democrat.

Wendy DeMocker, communications director for the National Republican Senatorial Committee, told the *Advertiser* in June: "With the entrance of Mrs. Saiki into the race, this race immediately becomes one of the top national Senate races for 1990. It will be a very competitive race."

Her counterpart on the Democratic side concurred. "The Hawai'i race is one of the top Senate races in the country," said Anita Dunn. "Certainly, we feel that Senator Akaka winning in November is a top priority for the committee and for the Senate majority."

The Democrats had a 55–45 majority, but the Republicans wanted to win a few seats this year with an eye toward retaking control in 1992.

On June 11, the U.S. Supreme Court overturned as unconstitutional the Flag Protection Act of 1989, which banned U.S. flag burning, a form of protest. Now the only way to ban flag burning would be to amend the Constitution, which required a two-thirds vote in Congress and ratification by thirty-eight states. This became an early, minor issue in the campaign.

"I find it repugnant that some may defile the American flag," I said in a statement. "However, I cannot support a constitutional amendment to restrict the freedom of speech. We should not tamper with the Constitution for political gain. As much as I abhor the desecration of our nation's flag, I believe that this symbol of our nation is strong enough to withstand the misguided actions of those few who would abuse it."

Saiki said she was in favor of a constitutional amendment, so that was one area where we differed.

Once again, sugar was in trouble and on that issue Saiki and I agreed. In May, Richard Crowder, undersecretary of Agriculture for International Affairs and Commodity Programs, said the Bush administration opposed the sugar price support program and would be pushing for a ten percent reduction. The House Agriculture Committee, however, kept the price supports at eighteen cents per pound as part of an omnibus farm bill, which Bush threatened to veto.

In a letter to Bush in June, I wrote: "I urge you to disavow published comments by members of your administration that the farm bill would be the subject of a presidential veto if the support program for sugar is continued at the current level."

Saiki promised to use her influence with the White House to keep the supports in place. And in fact she extracted a promise from Agriculture secretary Clayton Yeutter on June 20 that the current price supports would remain intact. I was happy to hear that, but a bit surprised. That's because the Senate Agriculture Committee had just rejected two amendments supported by the administration that would have cut sugar supports. So maybe Saiki's new clout as a promising Senate candidate was making a difference.

Sparky left so many important legacies. In the early 1980s, he had played a huge role in establishing the U.S. Institute of Peace, akin to the military academies, near the State Department in Washington. This was a goal he shared with Senators Mark Hatfield of Oregon and Jennings Randolph of West Virginia, along with Congressman Dan Glickman of Kansas. Sparky led a commission, named by President Carter, to study the possibility, which led to enabling legislation signed by Reagan in 1984.

After Sparky died, while I was still in the House, I sponsored a bill to rename the U.S. Institute of Peace after him. I also introduced a bill to establish a scholarship in his name. The Spark M. Matsunaga Peace Studies and Conflict Resolution Scholarship Act would set up a federal foundation to award undergraduate scholarships and graduate fellowships and make annual grants to outstanding educators in the field. This very fitting tribute was referred on May 7 to the House Subcommittee on Postsecondary Education, which took no action. A pity.

On June 27, I introduced the Peace Institute bill in the Senate. This attracted thirty-nine cosponsors, including Inouye, Kennedy, Gore, Biden and Byrd and a number of prominent Republicans. Despite the bipartisan support, this also went nowhere. But in Honolulu, the University of Hawai'i Board of Regents voted to name the UH Institute for Peace after Sparky. And the VA medical center in Honolulu also adopted his name. I was very pleased with those tributes to a fine American.

Matsunaga's major post-mortem success story had to do with alternative energy.

He had supported hydrogen research as far back as 1981, when he saw the country in the grip of rising oil prices. Not everyone was as forward-thinking in those days. In March 1989, he sponsored the Hydrogen Research, Development and Demonstration Act, with a goal of speeding up efforts to produce hydrogen as a fuel. That would in turn reduce the nation's dependence on fossil fuels, which puts the United States at the mercy of overseas oil producers. Burning oil and gasoline also generates heat-trapping atmospheric carbon dioxide that threatens to bring about catastrophic climate changes. Hydrogen fuels would be particularly helpful in Hawai'i, where electricity is produced largely by burning oil from Southeast Asia and the Mideast. The major problem with hydrogen remained that it was highly combustible, as the world learned dramatically from the explosion of the airship *Hindenburg* over Lakehurst, New Jersey, in May 1937. But it is abundant and clean. Sparky's bill directed the secretary of energy to come up with a five-year R&D plan and budgeted $20 million for the first three years.

His cosponsors were Inouye, Tim Wirth of Colorado, Claiborne Pell of Rhode Island, Joe Lieberman of Connecticut and Republican Rudy Boschwitz of Minnesota. The bill cleared with the Committee on Energy and Natural Resources on July 23, 1990, and the full Senate in October. That was followed by swift approval in the House, with Saiki remarking, "This legislation to develop hydrogen as an energy resource is definitely a positive step toward a secure energy future." The measure landed on Bush's desk on November 9, three days after the election, and he signed it into law on November 15.

I'm sure Sparky was there in spirit for the signing in the Oval Office. ❖

CHAPTER

40

In early July 1990, I opened up my new campaign headquarters on Kapiʻolani Boulevard, just ʻEwa of the Flamingo Chuckwagon. This happened to be downstairs from the state Democratic Party headquarters, which opened at the same time.

Inouye told those assembled not to be fooled by my gentle demeanor.

"Don't you think he's too gentle, too soft-spoken," he warned. "That is Daniel Akaka's strength."

Also on hand were Millie and some of our grandchildren; brother Abe, who blessed the place; Waihee, Cayetano, city councilman Neil Abercrombie; Mufi Hannemann, who was vying for my old House seat; Senators Norman Mizuguchi and Matt Matsunaga, son of Spark, who were running for Saiki's First District seat; as well as local businessmen and union leaders. Days earlier, I had picked up the endorsement of the powerful International Longshore and Warehouse Union.

On July 5, a Thursday, the day after the Independence Day holiday, Saiki and I made it official, filing papers at the lieutenant governor's office for the U.S. Senate election. Pat kept pounding the drum that she had the ear of the president, that Hawaiʻi would have entrée at the White House should she win. My view was, so what? "The president hasn't been a friend since 1980," I told reporters at the state capitol, referring to the last full year of the Carter administration. Sugar provided the perfect example. I had recently written to the U.S. Department of Agriculture, saying that it was obvious that the administration lacked a coherent policy on price supports and loan rates.

"I don't see any benefit of just having a pipeline for White House bad news," I added. "I'm sure she can call the president and talk to him, but whether that would change policy is the question."

There was one note of promise, however. A month earlier, Saiki had announced that she had raised the issue of Kahoʻolawe when she met with Bush in the White House. This is how she described the meeting in a 2008 interview with Leslie Wilcox of PBS Hawaiʻi. Bush was very eager for her to run.

"It's going to be a tough race, so I am thinking it over. I'm looking at possibly running," she told Bush.

"Well, is there anything I can do?" Bush asked,

"Yes, Mr. President, there is something you can do."

"What is it?"

"Well, the first thing you have to do is stop the bombing of Kahoʻolawe."

"Kahoʻo-what?" Bush said.

He called in his chief of staff, John Sununu, the former governor of New Hampshire.

"Now, Pat, will you spell this out?"

She told them that Kahoʻolawe had been used for target practice since World War II and the Hawaiians—and the Hawaiʻi state government—wanted the island returned.

"Mr. President, it's very simple," Saiki said. "I did my research, and the bombing was permitted by executive order of the president. Therefore the president can rescind the executive order, and the bombing can stop."

She told him that when the bombs and shells hit Kahoʻolawe, the windows rattle in Lāhainā.

"And one day a bomb is going to go astray, Mr. President, and I don't think you want to be responsible for that. I think it's time for us to return the island, a sacred island, to the Hawaiian people."

"Well, I don't see why we can't do this," Bush told her. "We'll have to tell the Navy to go find someplace else to bomb."

As a result of that conversation, she said, Bush asked the National Security Council to look into the possibility of returning the island to the state.

Under the 1953 executive order, signed by President Eisenhower, Kahoʻolawe had to be returned in a "habitable" condition. But Inouye and Waihee were working on a plan that would avoid a lengthy and costly cleanup. Waihee wanted the island reforested and used as a religious, archaeological and recreational attraction. Inouye remarked in June, "The fact that there's a possibility of returning that island without having to clean it all up makes a vast difference. Instead of being out of reach and costing billions of dollars, it becomes a reasonable goal. The possibilities are much greater now."

We couldn't know it then, but the possibilities would play out very swiftly, thanks in large measure to the Senate race.

Not only was the president firmly in Saiki's camp, but I was fighting big money as well.

Soon after she filed papers, Saiki won the endorsement of the U.S. Chamber of Commerce, based in Washington, D.C.

"Patricia Saiki's record demonstrates her strong commitment to fiscal responsibility," said the chamber's president, Richard Lesher, in making the announcement in Honolulu. "She has a strong voting record on issues that are important to the business community in Hawai'i and throughout the country."

When asked for reaction by the newspapers, I downplayed the endorsement, "Hawai'i's special needs are often not understood by outside organizations like the U.S. Chamber of Commerce," I said.

But it quickly became clear that Saiki was going to raise more campaign funds than I could. Our filings with the Federal Election Commission, for the six-month period ending June 30, bore that out. Pat raised $422,000—about $120,000 more than I did. She also had spent $142,000 to my $96,000. Her individual supporters included former Republican governor Bill Quinn; William Borthwick, vice chairman of HonFed Bank; John Couch, chairman of C&H Sugar; and Thurston Twigg-Smith, president of the *Honolulu Advertiser*. She also got $15,000 from the National Republican Senatorial Committee and $5,000 from Campaign America, Senator Bob Dole's political action committee.

My contributors included my old friend Pinky Thompson and fellow Bishop Estate trustees Henry Peters—state House Speaker, Oswald Stender, Matsuo Takabuki and former chief justice William Richardson. I also got $5,000 each from the Fund for a Democratic Majority and the Senate Majority Fund, and also hefty donations from the political action committees of the National Committee to Preserve Social Security and Medicare, the American Federation of Teachers and the United Auto Workers.

I was counting on raising more at a fundraiser at Aloha Tower in August.

In late July, the National Republican Senatorial Committee introduced their favored candidate to the national press corps in Washington. "I am running because the people of Hawai'i should be represented in both the Republican and Democratic caucuses," she told them. "Their concerns should be heard by the White House, members of the cabinet and all of the agencies and commissions that make decisions affecting Hawai'i." Clearly, she was going to play the White House card all the way to November.

But first we had to get past the primary on September 22. On the Democratic side, I had one opponent, Big Island resident Paul Snider. On the GOP side, Saiki was facing former state representative Richard "Ike" Sutton, Moloka'i rancher Maria Hustace and author and consultant Bob Zimmerman.

Meanwhile, a flurry of competition had erupted over our House seats. Abercrombie had entered the First District House race, running against Mizuguchi and Matsunaga. On the Republican side, it was Mike Liu, Frank Hutchinson and John Sabey. For my old Second District seat, Patsy Mink was running against Mufi and state senators Ron Menor and Mike Crozier. On the Republican side, perhaps the best-known candidate was Councilman Andy Poepoe.

From the air over the whitecaps of the central Pacific, Johnston Atoll looks like an aircraft carrier scuttled in a green lagoon. Two miles long and a half mile wide—about the size of the Honolulu airport reef runway, the concrete and coral island stands about six feet above sea level. Its dominant feature, an airfield, takes up nearly the entire length. In 1962, the isolated speck provided the launching pad for the Starfish Prime nuclear test that lit up the night sky in Honolulu, 825 miles to the northeast.

Now Johnston was home to outdated chemical munitions, mostly sarin and VX nerve gas rounds for artillery and mortars, but also many mustard shells. This was all very nasty stuff, housed in hardened bunkers on either side of the runway. Rising above the island was a large incinerator, a complex industrial facility that looked like nothing so much as the villain's lair in an action-adventure movie. This was the Johnston Atoll Chemical Agent Disposal System, or JACADS ("JAY-cads"). The Army's plan was to disassemble the munitions, separate the chemical agents and then incinerate the whole arsenal. But there was more. Not only would the weapons on the atoll be destroyed, but the Army planned to ship to Johnston chemical munitions currently stored in Europe. Those, too, would be destroyed at JACADS. So, for me and for Saiki as well, two safety concerns arose. First, could the agents be destroyed safely? Second, could the chemical arms from Europe be transported safely to Johnston? What if there were an *Exxon Valdez*-type accident with one of the ships?

For those reasons, we both opposed the shipments from Europe. I added language to the defense appropriations bill that would make those shipments the last.

※ ※ ※

On July 13, 1990, I was proud to cast my vote to approve the Americans with Disabilities Act, one of the landmark pieces of legislation before the 101st Congress. In the Senate we voted 91–6 to approve the conference committee report. Among other things, the measure prohibited discrimination against the disabled in job application procedures, hiring or firing, compensation, promotion and training. It also required that public amenities—like buildings and sidewalks—be able to accommodate wheelchairs. Thus the now-ubiquitous term "ADA-compliant." Bush signed the bill into law on July 26.

※ ※ ※

On August 2, Iraqi leader Saddam Hussein invaded neighboring Kuwait with some 100,000 troops. No one knew how far he would go. Could Saudi Arabia be next? Egypt began mobilizing its armed forces against the possibility, and the Bush administration weighed a military response. Bush sent his secretary of defense, Dick Cheney, to the Mideast to scope out the situation. Chemical warfare was a risk, some leaders felt, because Saddam was thought to have used chemical agents in the 1980–88 war with Iran and also against domestic Kurds.

Such was the preoccupation of the nation as the state primary election approached. A public opinion poll, published by the *Advertiser* on August 6 and cosponsored by KHON-2, showed Saiki way ahead, forty-three to thirty-five percent, with twenty-one percent undecided and one percent backing Libertarian Ken Schoolland. In urban Honolulu, Saiki's lead was even larger, forty-eight to twenty-nine percent. I had a small advantage on the Neighbor Isles and rural Oʻahu—the Second Congressional District, forty-one to thirty-eight percent. But Saiki was also leading among Caucasians (51–30), Japanese (40–34), men (44–33), women (42–37) and non-union households (47–32). I led only among Hawaiians and part Hawaiians (46–37) and union families (43–33). Although many in the Japanese American community remained undecided—twenty-six percent—Saiki was seen to have an advantage there because of shared ethnicity—maiden name Fukuda. Honestly, the numbers were quite disappointing and it took every ounce of spirit I could muster not to let it get me down.

Obviously encouraged by the numbers, the Republicans promptly sent Bob Dole of Kansas, the Senate minority leader, to stump for Saiki in Hawaiʻi. In the 1988 presidential election, Saiki had supported Dole initially, before switching to Bush when Dole dropped out. At a news conference at the state capitol, Dole said that Republicans had a solid chance of winning in seven Senate races across the country.

"This is number one," he said.

Smiling at his side were Liu, who hoped to replace Saiki; state senator Fred Hemmings, who was running for governor; and Senator Mary George. The Senate Republicans "really want someone with a fire in their belly, and she's one of them," Dole said, referring to Saiki.

To the press, a quick retort came from Dennis O'Connor, the state Democratic Party chairman. "Bob Dole is no friend to Hawaiʻi," he said. "When local people find out his position on issues that directly affect Hawaiʻi, it's going to hurt her campaign." For instance, O'Connor said, Dole had voted for a measure that would have cut federal price supports for sugar. Inouye and I voted against the amendment, which thankfully failed. Dole was also anti-abortion and opposed the Equal Rights Amendment.

At his news conference, Dole, a World War II hero, was also asked about the conflict in the Middle East. He said he thought economic sanctions against Iraq would be the best approach.

"If we can squeeze Saddam Hussein and shut off everything going in and coming out, he'll be on his knees without (us) firing a shot."

That was, alas, not to be.

Saiki looked a little less invincible when, on August 16, the 300-member Hawai'i Women's Political Caucus left her name off the list of endorsements. They didn't back me, either, deciding to stay silent on the Senate race. They did back Waihee for governor and Mink for my old seat in the House.

* * *

As the race heated up, both Pat and I brought in political consultants from the Mainland. I hired Kam Kuwata, from Oakland, California, until recently a spokesman and adviser to Senator Alan Cranston. Although Kam was only thirty-six, my campaign chairman, Steve Arashiro, was impressed with his political savvy and expertise with both the "air" and "ground" games, that is, television and neighborhood canvassing. Saiki hired Anne Stanley as her campaign manager. Stanley, forty-seven, her neighbor in Alexandria, Virginia, was former vice president of the GOP consulting firm Russo Watts & Associates. She was Midwest regional director for the Reagan-Bush campaign in 1984 and then moved on to the Republican National Committee as director of political planning, education and research. In the 1988 presidential campaign, she worked in Iowa, home of the nation's first caucuses, for Congressman Jack Kemp of New York.

My TV ads began to air in late August. Both thirty-second spots showed me with a smile, talking with local people, with the narrator summing up my record.

Saiki's first TV ad showed an empty Senate desk.

"For over 200 years, the United States Senate has shaped the American dream and changed the world," the narrator says. "War and peace, life and death, freedom and equality are at stake. That's why we have to send our best to the United States Senate—to stand up for Hawai'i, the nation and the future. Saiki. Send Hawai'i's best."

I was happy we both chose not to go negative.

* * *

At the Ala Moana Hotel that month, I addressed bedrock Democratic constituencies—teachers and labor.

"Hawai'i needs to be represented by someone who shares our values and our priorities," I said to a gathering of the Hawai'i State Teachers Association. "Not someone who says one thing and votes another way."

I mentioned I had a 100 percent rating with the National Education Association and the Children's Defense Fund, while Saiki had scores of sixty-seven and fifty percent from those groups, respectively.

"I am a cosponsor of the Child Care Act to expand Head Start to all disadvantaged preschoolers and to provide child care programs, while my opponent voted to cut them," I said.

In late August, I addressed some 300 labor leaders. State AFL-CIO director Gary Rodrigues introduced me to the crowd. I recognized a lot of faces. Before I finished, I received two standing ovations.

"For ten years, working men and women have been under attack by the Republican Party," I said. "Their taxes have been raised. Their unions have been broken. The price of housing and health care and a college education skyrocketed while wages just barely kept up. In the meantime, the Republicans threw themselves a party. They cut taxes for the rich. They watched quietly while a bunch of New York bond traders and investment bankers went on a buyout binge that cost billions of dollars and thousands of jobs. And now they want us to pay."

I told them I favored legislation that would protect pensions and keep companies from replacing striking workers with scabs.

"When I get back to Washington," I told them, "I'm going to be working for legislation that protects Hawai'i's union members. The Republicans will be working for a capital gains tax cut for the rich."

I said the stakes were high.

"The Republicans have poured a lot of money and other resources into my opponent's campaign," I said. "This race—here, in our state—is the Republicans' number one targeted race in the country. If they gain this seat, they will be one step closer to taking control in the Senate."

❊ ❊ ❊

On my birthday, September 11, Bush addressed a joint session of Congress. Among the attendees was Army General Colin Powell, chairman of the Joint Chiefs of Staff.

"We gather tonight, witness to events in the Persian Gulf as significant as they are tragic," Bush said. "In the early morning hours of August 2, following negotiations and promises by Iraq's dictator, Saddam Hussein, not to use force, a powerful Iraqi army invaded its trusting and much weaker neighbor, Kuwait. Within three days, 120,000 Iraqi troops with 850 tanks had poured into Kuwait and moved south to threaten Saudi Arabia. It was then that I decided to check that aggression.

"At this moment, our brave servicemen and women stand watch in that distant desert and on distant seas side by side with the forces of more than twenty other nations. They are some of the finest men and women of the United States of America. And they're doing one terrific job...

"Our objectives in the Persian Gulf are clear, our goals defined and familiar: Iraq must withdraw from Kuwait completely, immediately and without condition. Kuwait's legitimate government must be restored. The security and the stability of the Persian Gulf must be assured. And American citizens abroad must be protected."

This was Operation Desert Shield, the run-up to Operation Desert Storm, later to be known as Gulf War I.

Back in Washington, on Thursday, September 20, I introduced a measure to establish a commission to study and recommend terms and conditions for returning Kahoʻolawe to the state of Hawaiʻi and prohibit any further use as a target range. The measure earmarked $1.5 million for that effort. The legislation also directed the secretary of commerce to study the feasibility of establishing a national marine sanctuary in the adjacent waters. The bill, Senate 3088, cosponsored by Inouye, was referred to the Senate Armed Services Committee. But the whole issue would soon be "overtaken by events," as they say.

Two days later, Pat and I both handily won our primary races.

I received more than 180,000 votes, or eighty-one percent. Pat got eighty-two percent, but her vote total was just under 40,000, showing the huge disproportionality that Democrats enjoyed in the state, then as now. Elsewhere on the ballot, Waihee and Lieutenant Governor Ben Cayetano easily prevailed, and would face Hemmings and Billie Beamer in November. Abercrombie beat Mizuguchi and Matsunaga in the First District race, and would face Liu in the general. Together, Mizuguchi and Matsunaga drew more than 52,000 votes, compared to Abercrombie's 43,480. So you had to wonder what would have happened if only one, not both, had run. In the Second District race, Mink edged out Mufi, thirty-eight to thirty-six percent. But again, Menor and Crozier split another twenty-one percent. So more people voted against Mink than for her, yet she won. "Divide and conquer" is an undying principle. Maybe less prominent contenders should get together and jan-ken-po to decide who takes on an Abercrombie or Mink, former incumbents with wide name recognition. Mink also won the special election to finish the last three months of my House term, beating Mufi by a hair, 34.6 to 33.5 percent. ❖

CHAPTER

41

First Lady Barbara Bush charmed a crowd of about 1,500 at a $50-per-head dinner for Saiki on October 2 at the Hilton Hawaiian Village.

"Pat will give Hawai'i its first bipartisan Senate delegation since Hiram Fong retired, and it's so important for Hawai'i to have that balance," she said. "Senator Saiki is going to have real direct access to the people and the groups in Washington whose decisions influence the state of Hawai'i because she has shown she can work with everyone on both sides of the aisle."

And then she upped the ante, promising that the president himself would soon be out to stump for Pat.

Senator Saiki? Many people—both in Hawai'i and on the Mainland—thought it was a clear possibility. Our contest, which the *Advertiser* described as "too close to call," continued to attract national attention. The *Washington Post* called the matchup the closest among seventeen in which Democratic senators were up against GOP challengers. I was the only incumbent who was not ahead, the *Post* said. Not very encouraging, but my team remained focused and energetic.

With Mink back in Congress for the first time since 1976, Hawai'i now had two females in the House. That was unique. Women remained a tiny minority in Congress, with only twenty-nine among 435 members. In the Senate, we had only two, Nancy Kassebaum of Kansas and Mikulski of Maryland. Even corporate boardrooms had better gender balance.

"We're glad to have Patsy back in town," Sharon Rodine, president of the National Women's Political Caucus, told the *Star-Bulletin* by telephone. "It was like a flashback to some really great times to see her there again. We are looking forward to her leadership. We need a breath of fresh air on Capitol Hill."

The caucus had endorsed Mink in the general election, which she needed to win to stay in Congress past January 3. The caucus had not endorsed Saiki, but Rodine had high praise for her.

"Pat Saiki is a very engaging candidate," she said. "She is tough and strong and articulate and caring. We have been very impressed with her."

The Hawai'i chapter apparently was less impressed.

Judy Sobin, president of the Hawai'i Women's Political Caucus, confirmed days later that her group had declined to endorse Saiki. Under national rules, the group could not endorse men in federal races, so I didn't get the nod, either. But the decision infuriated the national caucus, which filed a formal grievance as a step toward having it overruled. Around the same time, state representative Carol Fukunaga announced the formation of a Women for Akaka Committee. She said my congressional record "shows that he shares our commitment to issues of importance to women, children and families." So the women's vote appeared divided in the race, although Saiki had the support of the National Organization for Women (NOW) and other Mainland groups, most of them interested in abortion rights.

With Bush in her corner, Saiki found herself in a somewhat awkward position when she joined the House majority in shooting down the president's budget package. Pat called the vote on October 5 "one of the most difficult I have made in Congress," adding, "Our deficit is real and begs for real solutions. I do not, however, share the conclusion of some that the bill before that will accomplish that end."

Pat was right. The plan called for more taxes on gasoline, cigarettes, liquor, airline tickets and cars and yachts worth more than $30,000; it also called for $60 billion in cuts to Medicare. I argued that Bush had forced the budget summit members to accept a deal that was too harsh on the elderly, too easy on the wealthy and passed too much of the price tag on to working Americans. It was doomed to fail. Mink also voted against it.

The savings and loan bailout was an area where Pat and I parted.

In fact, my campaign put together a TV spot on the issue. It opened with a backdrop of the Capitol, with Saiki's photo on the left, mine on the right.

"November 8, 1989," the narrator said. "Congress votes on who will pay to clean up oil spills. Democrat Dan Akaka votes to force oil companies to pay. Republican Pat Saiki sides with the oil companies to force taxpayers to pay.

"August 4, 1989. Congress votes on bailing out Mainland S&Ls. Democrat Dan Akaka votes against the bailout. Republican Pat Saiki votes for it, costing every taxpayer in Hawai'i $2,500.

"Akaka or Saiki? Real differences that really matter."

I quite liked the piece, but Saiki objected, writing me a stinging letter that she shared with the press.

"Less than three weeks ago on the floor of the House of Representatives, you gave me your personal assurances that you had instructed your Mainland media consultants to run a positive campaign," she scolded, referring to Squier-Eskew-Knapp Communications, our Washington-based strategists. "This commercial, Dan, is definitely not positive."

I let Kam Kuwata respond.

"The commercial compares the record of Senator Akaka and Congresswoman Saiki on two issues, oil spill liability and the S&L bailout," he said. "The comparison is necessary, fair and not at all negative." And the $2,500 figure was right on the mark.

※ ※ ※

Then the second shoe dropped.

"Danny, I want to help you."

"Well, thanks, Ted. That's so nice of you. I could sure use the help!"

Kennedy, hearing that Bush was going to come out and campaign for Saiki, offered to ride to my rescue. Initially, through state party chairman O'Connor, we booked the evening of October 30, the Tuesday before the election, for a rally at McKinley High School. But his presence—and personality—would be felt at much broader and more intimate venues.

Bush's agenda also was taking shape. Ostensibly, the reason for his visit was a meeting with leaders of Pacific Island nations at the East-West Center. The White House confirmed that invitations had been sent to the leaders of the Cook Islands, Fiji, Kiribati, the Marshall

Islands, the Federated States of Micronesia, Nauru, Niue, Papua New Guinea, the Solomons, Tonga, Tuvalu, Vanuatu and what was then called Western Samoa. The White House would not confirm the reason of this Pacific "mini summit," set for October 27, but the speculation was that the topics would include the chemical weapons at Johnston Atoll. Already, two ships carrying U.S. chemical artillery shells from Germany were en route to Johnston, due to arrive between October 31 and November 10, according to the Army.

Note I said *Germany*, not West Germany. East and West had just united, yet another milestone at the close of the Cold War. An amazing time in history.

On Saturday, October 20, much to my delight, my Kahoʻolawe plan cleared a House-Senate conference committee. The plan placed a two-year moratorium on the bombing while a five-member, federal-state commission studied the cost of clearing the island of ordnance, possible future uses and jurisdictional issues. Waihee promptly named Maui mayor Hannibal Tavares and Dr. Emmett Aluli of the Protect Kahoʻolawe ʻOhana as his appointees to the panel. The Office of Hawaiian Affairs named trustee Frenchy DeSoto. The other two were up to the feds.

Then came the bombshell from the White House. On Monday, October 22, before Inouye and I could boast about the progress of our Kahoʻolawe legislation, Bush ordered an immediate halt to the bombing. He allowed Saiki to make the announcement locally, a shrewd political move.

In a letter to Defense secretary Dick Cheney, Bush said:

"You are directed to discontinue use of Kahoʻolawe as a weapons range effective immediately. This directive extends to use of the island for small arms, artillery, naval gunfire, support and aerial ordnance training. In addition, you are directed to establish a joint Department of Defense-state of Hawaiʻi commission to examine the future status of Kahoʻolawe and related issues."

This apparently took the Navy by surprise. A spokesman at Pearl Harbor said a fax from Saiki and a copy of Bush's letter were enough to shut down the range—even as four Marine F/A-18 Hornet fighter jets from Kāneʻohe were on a bombing run, quickly aborted. Some construction battalions sailors, Seabees, remained on the island for routine maintenance.

But some confusion remained. Was this a permanent or temporary ban? If permanent, then why did Bush not also lift President Eisenhower's executive order? Walter Ritte, one of the main opponents to the bombing and shelling, reacted skeptically.

Bush, he said, "is not doing it because he loved the Hawaiian culture," adding, "If it turns out that the bombing will stop forever, then God bless politics. But right now, keep the beer cold—not time to celebrate yet."

I, too, had some concerns about the wording of Bush's letter.

"My primary concern with the presidential order is that any findings issued by an administration-appointed commission may be biased against the return of Kahoʻolawe," I said in a media statement. "My legislation, on the other hand, would create a commission to recommend the terms and conditions for the island's return, not just the future status of the island. In response to his directive, I have asked the president to go one important step further and return Kahoʻolawe to the people of Hawaiʻi."

As Election Day approached, Saiki and I were spending money like there was no tomorrow—about $14,000 a day each, by one estimate, mostly on airtime. Our campaign spending reports through October 17 showed that she had raised more than $1.4 million and spent $1.3 million. I had raised and spent just over $1.2 million. But in the forty-five-day period ending October 17, she had me beat, raising $739,000 to my $432,000. In the same period, she had spent $753,000 to my $673,000.

The National Women's Political Caucus had overruled the Hawaiʻi chapter and was prepared to announce its endorsement of Saiki on Wednesday, October 24. But some members of the Hawaiʻi organization took matters into their own hands. A splinter group, along with top officials of the Hawaiʻi State Teachers Association, held a news conference that same day to pledge support for me. The HSTA endorsement was particularly poignant because Saiki was a former educator as well.

"I believe the women of Hawaiʻi feel that it's pretty strange that others outside of the state are really deciding for us," said Amy

Agbayani, chairwoman of the caucus' Democratic Task Force. "We decided we did not want to endorse a woman in this race, and that's the way we want to continue, and we stand by that position." She called Republican policies "anti-family and anti-women" on issues such as cuts in Medicaid services, the minimum wage and the civil rights bill, which Bush had vetoed two days earlier. The Hawai'i caucus gave me a 100 percent rating for my voting record; Saiki scored a seventy-five.

Bush arrived just after 6 p.m. Friday, October 26—eleven days before the election—with Air Force One pulling up to Hangar 5 at Hickam Air Force Base. Greeting him with lei and handshakes were Fasi, Hemmings, Liu, Poepoe, Mary George, city councilman David Kahanu and former senator Hiram Fong, along with military brass. Fasi and Hemmings rode with Bush in a black limo, part of a twenty-five-car motorcade, to the Hilton Hawaiian Village, where the president headlined a fund-raiser that drew 1,500 donors to the Coral Ballroom. Ironically, Saiki couldn't make it, having gone back to Washington for a vote on a deficit-reduction package, which passed against her opposition. (Inouye, Mink and I voted for the measure, aimed at reducing the national deficit by about $500 billion over five years.) But she delivered a videotaped message on a ten-foot screen. "For the first time in history, you will gather together the leaders of the Pacific Island nations who deserve to be heard," she said. "Together, you will begin to shape the policies of the future as they affect all of us who live in this most beautiful region of the country."

Bush in turn hailed Saiki as "a great teacher" and a "great leader" who worked well with others. "If we had more people like Pat on our side of the aisle, and we had more like her elected to the Senate, I can guarantee you we wouldn't be back year after year in a deficit mode," Bush said.

Coincidentally, on the day of Bush's arrival, the Army released a report saying leaks had been found in 120 weapons at Johnston Atoll since the arsenal arrived from Okinawa in 1971. Specifically, the leaks were found in thirty-eight 750-pound bombs and five 500-pound bombs; twenty-nine 155mm artillery rounds containing VX nerve agent; twenty-one 105mm rounds containing mustard, a blistering agent; twenty-one GB nerve gas rockets; four VX nerve gas rockets; and two one-ton containers of mustard. This news heightened anticipation that Bush would offer the Pacific leaders some assurances on safety measures at the atoll. And that he did.

But first, early Saturday morning, Bush left the Hilton Hawaiian Village and took a jog along the shore with his Secret Service entourage. Then, in a move that apparently surprised his agents, he took a quick dip in the ocean—without even removing his shoes or T-shirt. A photo of a beaming Bush, neck deep in water, hair wet and askew, made the UPI wire.

With an Army Black Hawk helicopter hovering overhead, Bush arrived at the East-West Center around 9:15 a.m. The two-and-a-half-hour meeting took place on the ground floor of the Imin Conference Center, with a tranquil view of a brook bubbling through an oriental garden. About 100 soldiers patrolled the adjacent hillside as part of the elaborate and tightly orchestrated security measures. A luncheon followed the meeting.

In a public statement afterwards, Bush pledged that the chemical weapons incinerator would not become a fixture on the Pacific horizon. He said the incinerator would be used to destroy only those weapons already there, those en route from Germany, and any World War II era munitions that turn up in the Pacific.

"We emphasized our common interest in ridding the world of these terrible weapons and asked for their understanding and support in this significant step toward peace and disarmament," Bush told reporters. "We confirmed that these munitions will be destroyed safely, on a prioritized schedule, and that once the destruction is completed, we have no plans to use Johnston Atoll for any other chemical munitions purpose or as a hazardous waste disposal site. We also assured the leaders that safeguards we're employing ensure there will be no associated environmental damage."

He also said he had invited the South Pacific Forum to send a team of technical experts to visit the atoll and monitor the operation independently.

Speaking for the Pacific leaders, Geoffrey Henry, prime minister of the Cook Islands, whose main island is Rarotonga, thanked Bush for "replenishing the pool of good will" between the United States and the nations of Oceania. He admitted the leaders didn't get all they wanted from Bush.

"We wish you could tell us that you would break down JACADS

tomorrow," he said. "We know, of course, that cannot be done. That is not sensible."

Henry also said Pacific Islanders are anxious for a better exchange of information on possible greenhouse global warming, with many low-lying islands vulnerable to rising seas.

"We certainly hope that the opportunity would be taken to bridge this huge gulf of misunderstanding or misinformation that apparently exists," he said.

The Bush administration, claiming the verdict was still out on the climatic effects of carbon dioxide emissions, has balked at the strict measures favored in Europe. But Bush told the Pacific Isle heads of state he would spend $1 billion annually to study the issue.

That evening, clad in an untucked aloha shirt, Bush took a Diamond Head sunset cruise aboard the *Holokai*, a glass bottom catamaran. The hour-cruise included Fasi; East-West Center president Victor Li; and Kenny Brown, chairman of the East-West Center Board of Directors. Most of the other thirty guests were from Washington, D.C.

After the budget vote, Saiki and I hurried back to Hawai'i for the final days of campaigning. Pat got back in time to have a twenty-minute chat Sunday with Bush in his suite at the Hilton. Saiki then joined those bidding Bush aloha at Hickam.

On Monday, back in Washington, Bush formally signed an executive order ending the bombing on Kaho'olawe. That gave us a little more clarity on the issue. I felt strongly that my efforts had forced the president's hand, but what counted was that the island was now officially protected. ✽

CHAPTER

42

Ted Kennedy arrived in Honolulu that evening. It was good to see my old friend in the islands. He seemed relaxed and in good spirits, his complexion slightly pink under a mane of silver hair, his green eyes sharp.

After he rested up at his hotel suite, our first stop Tuesday morning was the office of Honolulu prosecutor Keith Kaneshiro, who, with other county prosecutors, gave Kennedy and me a briefing on the crystal meth epidemic.

"I think every member of the United States Senate ought to hear what is happening in Hawai'i," Kennedy said. "Because what is happening in the area of 'ice' abuse in these groups of islands is clearly going to happen on the Mainland."

Then we motored over to Kapi'olani Medical Center for Women and Children, where we got a briefing on treatments for drug-exposed babies and a tour of the Neonatal Intensive Care Unit. I got to cradle one of the infants, wrapped in a soft white blanket, for a moment as the camera flashes went off. Oh, my heart went out to those poor kids, gravely ill through no fault of their own. What a way to start out life! A former patient and success story, six-year-old Reneisha Courtney, presented Ted and me with maile and pikake lei on behalf of the staff.

"This is the kind of area where we ought to be investing, rather than in some of the gold-plated weapons systems, which draw down so much of our resources," Kennedy, chairman of the Senate Health and Human Services Committee, told the TV crews.

I said I wanted Kapi'olani to be at the forefront of a new study on how to treat drug-addicted newborns.

Our next stop was far more upbeat, lunch with youngsters at the Early School, part of the Church of the Crossroads, just 'Ewa of University Avenue, below the freeway. I had picked the school because

I thought it represented the kind of education that every child in Hawai'i deserved. A pleasant setting, excellent teacher-student ratios, hands-on learning. In a classroom after, with the kids cross-legged on the floor, Ted led them in a rousing round of "The Eensie Weensie Spider," or, as he bellows it, "itsy-bitsy."

> *The itsy-bitsy spider climbs up the water spout.*
> *Down comes the rain to wash the spider out!*
> *Out comes the sun and dries up all the rain.*
> *And the itsy-bitsy spider goes up the spout again.*

A lesson in persistence! He sang it himself the first time to familiarize the kids with the words and gestures. He made a diamond with his thumbs and index fingers, rotating and rising to denote the climbing spider. He made a circle with his hands for the sun. Hands sweeping broom-like low was the rain drying up. Then he sang it again with the whole class joining in.

"Come on, Danny!" he regaled me, so I had to sing and do the gestures, too, but with far less confidence.

He also told the kids a couple of stories, one involving bunny rabbits and a fox in the forest. All this with a grave face, as if he were running a committee hearing. For kids, it is a tremendous compliment to receive an adult's full and serious attention.

Outside, as I stood with him, he told reporters I was "making an important contribution to the country," adding, "I just think it's very, very important that he be returned. I know that he's fighting a difficult and challenging race, but he's doing it by bringing the issues to the people. And I think the people are increasingly knowledgeable about the difference that he's making."

That evening, he gave a rousing speech before 1,500 noisy supporters at rally at McKinley High School. Waihee was there to kick off the event with all the vigor of a Tigers gridiron coach. Supporters in pink T-shirts waved red, white and blue pom-poms.

"I say it's time for the people of Hawai'i, it's time for America to veto the Bush administration!" Kennedy said to loud applause.

He called me a champion for child care and the war on drugs, and—a slight exaggeration—"one of the most outstanding candidates for the United States Senate that the Democratic Party has produced."

He also heaped scorn on Bush.

"I understand there was a sighting of President Bush out here the other day," he said to laughter. "We started to wonder where he was in the final stages of the budget debate. People back in Washington were beginning to ask, 'Where's George?' With the trouble he is in and all the mess he put the country in, he wanted to get as far away from Washington as possible!"

"Where's George! Where's George!" the rowdy crowd responded.

Kennedy said I was the only senator up for election who had the "guts" to vote for the deficit-reduction package. After the hour-long rally, we told the media that we hoped that Bush would consult with Congress—now in recess—before going to war with Iraq.

"I think Senator Akaka and I feel strongly this should be a shared responsibility," he said. "If we're going in on the landing, we ought to be in on the takeoff."

The next day, at the UH Biomedical Institute, Kennedy picked up an award from the Asia-Pacific Academic Consortium for Public Health for his work to improve health in the Pacific. Then he gave a talk at Kennedy Theatre, named for his brother John, at the University of Hawai'i at Mānoa. He once again decried "gold-plated weapons," to include the B-2 bomber and new Chobham ceramic armor for the Abrams tank.

"The debacle of the budget summit has demonstrated in the starkest terms the differences between Republicans and Democrats," he said. "Republicans wanted another decade of what we've endured for the last ten years—lower taxes on the rich, higher taxes on working Americans and the middle class." From a discussion of the budget mess, his addressed evolved into soaring oratory on the greatness of our nation. The crowd loved it, as did I.

After that speech, backstage, he told me, "Danny, I gotta go."

I walked him to his car.

"Ted, thanks so much for this. Please let me know how much this cost you. I'll pay you for your trip."

He gave me a big hug.

"Danny, this is on me."

And he took off.

❋ ❋ ❋

Later that day, I addressed an energy conference at the Ala Moana Hotel, emphasizing my support for hydrogen fuel and wind and ocean energy technology. Republicans, I pointed out, had backed cuts in renewable energy research.

"The sad reality is that my opponent, Pat Saiki, joined in these efforts," I said. "She has been part of the problem, not part of the solution. Her philosophy is summed up by the phrase, 'Less is more.' And her strategy is best described as 'cut, cut, cut.' In the drive for clean, renewable energy, Pat just ran out of gas."

By Wednesday, Saiki was distancing herself from Bush, emphasizing to a crowd on the Big Island that she was "independent" from the administration, citing her support for sugar. Her vote on the budget showed that as well, but not, I thought, for the good of the country.

Meanwhile, the voter surveys had us neck and neck. The Hawai'i Poll, commissioned by the *Advertiser* and Channel 2, had her ahead forty-five to forty-two percent, within the margin of error. The poll was taken during Bush's visit, but before Kennedy's, so did not reflect any bump from Ted.

The weekend before the election was a whirlwind. I paid two visits to the Voter Education Fair at the Bishop Museum and also hit the swap meet at Aloha Stadium and Ohikilolo Ranch. I also flew to Maui for the Democratic Unity Rally in Wailuku. Saiki, meanwhile, was campaigning with Elizabeth Dole, our dynamic and photogenic U.S transportation secretary and the wife of the senator. They were the main attraction at a luncheon at the Ala Moana Hotel that included Billie Beamer, Fred Hemmings's wife, Suzy, and Frank and Joyce Fasi.

By all accounts, Dole stole the show.

She said her husband had reservations about her next job, president of the American Red Cross, which she would assume in January.

"Does this mean I'm going to have to keep eating frozen dinners?" he asked.

"You bet, Bob, that's exactly what it means."

She also quipped that he wouldn't be of much help to her in her new role.

"He said these budget negotiations have been so rough that he doubted he had any blood left to give."

※ ※ ※

As the polls were about to close on Election Day, Tuesday, November 6, I hopped in the car to go down to my campaign headquarters. The phone rang.

"Hello?"

"Danny!"

I recognized Ted Kennedy's voice instantly.

"Hi, Ted."

"Danny, congratulations. You won!"

"Hey, Ted, our polls haven't closed yet."

"But you won!"

"How do you know?"

"The exit polls! They show you won!"

Sure enough, despite the voter surveys, I won by a comfortable margin, fifty-three to forty-four percent.

Only one Republican did well that night—Linda Lingle, the new mayor of Maui and our future governor. Also victorious were Abercrombie in the First District and Mink in the Second District. Waihee easily won a ticket back to Washington Place.

Bush ultimately appointed Saiki director of the Small Business Administration, where she did an outstanding job. ❧

CHAPTER

43

The year 1990 closed out with all eyes on the Middle East. On Thanksgiving Day, Bush visited the U.S. troops staging in Saudi Arabia. By then we had more than 400,000 assembled under General Norman Schwarzkopf. Bush had cobbled together a coalition of thirty-four nations to defend the Saudis from Saddam and possibly invade Iraq, but was also working diplomatic channels, including the United Nations. On November 29, the U.S. Security Council passed a resolution that gave Iraq until January 15 to get out of Kuwait. After that, it authorized "all means necessary" to remove the despot's minions. The measure passed 12–2, with only Cuba and Yemen voting no and China abstaining.

But on Capitol Hill, the sentiment remained "not so fast."

From conversations with and letters from my constituents, I became convinced that an overwhelming number of Hawai'i residents wanted to hold out for a peaceful solution.

"The Bush administration hasn't come to Congress and presented a justifiable case to use force against Iraq," I said in a press statement. "Congress has not fully debated the issue." Under the Constitution, the authority to declare war rests solely with Congress. In early January, Abercrombie, newly assigned to the House Armed Services Committee, got a briefing from Defense secretary Cheney and General Powell, chairman of the Joint Chiefs of Staff. "I was very disappointed with their attitude, which reflects that of the president, that they do not need a declaration from Congress to go to war," he lamented.

Even Inouye, widely viewed as the most hawkish member of the delegation, agreed that Bush could not launch a first strike without an OK from Congress. He, too, felt that the folks back home in Hawai'i wanted the crisis to be resolved, if possible, without bloodshed.

In the end, after two days of debate that ended on a Saturday, January 12, Congress gave its approval for Bush to act once the Security Council deadline passed.

On the Senate floor, Inouye had argued most eloquently against the measure.

"Mr. President, those who know me know that I am not one to shrink from a fight or retreat from the field of battle," he said. "The defense of freedom, I believe, is a duty which falls to every individual who cherishes our way of life. My generation paid a terrible price to safeguard our nation—a price which tragically has been paid many times since. It is for this reason that I feel compelled to counsel caution as we move ever closer to the January 15 deadline set by the United Nations for the withdrawal of Iraqi forces from Kuwait."

The vote was 52–47 in the Senate and 250–183 in the House, which had debated for twenty hours straight, the longest debate on a single issue in the history of that body. Inouye, Abercrombie, Mink and I all voted with the minority. Rather, we favored an alternate resolution that called for more time to allow economic sanctions and diplomacy to work. That fell 53–46 in the Senate and 250–183 in the House.

On January 17, 1991—two days after the U.N. deadline, Bush launched Operation Desert Storm, beginning with a full-scale air assault campaign. The missions were flown mostly from Saudi Arabia and six coalition aircraft carriers offshore. The priority targets were Iraqi aircraft and anti-aircraft guns and radars, command and communications facilities, and Scud-missile launchers and tanks. The coalition flew more than 100,000 missions, dropping 177 million pounds of ordnance. On February 24, the ground war began and within five days the American forces declared Kuwait liberated. But before they left, the Iraqis set the oil fields on fire. This apocalyptic panorama abided for weeks. Some U.S. troops crossed the border into Iraq, but Bush pulled them back. He had concerns that the carefully crafted coalition would not support an invasion of Iraq. Besides, if Saddam fell, many observers worried that the country—an uneasy conglomeration of Shiite and Sunni Muslims and Kurds in the north—would devolve into anarchy. Although the casualties among the Iraqi forces was high—an estimated 20,000 to 22,000 dead, the toll on the U.S. side was relatively low: 148 deaths, including thirty-five from "friendly fire," a misnomer if ever there was one. Almost as many Americans, 145, died in accidents during the blitz.

※ ※ ※

Back in Washington, I set out my legislative priorities. One was the renewal of the two-year Mortgage Revenue Bond Program, which offers low-interest notes to home buyers across the country. In Hawai'i we called it Hula Mae. More than 5,600 Hawai'i families took advantage of the program in 1990, and I wanted to make it permanent. I also wanted to secure funding, at least $120 million, for a veterans hospital in Honolulu, to be named after Sparky. This would be up by Tripler Army Medical Center. Another priority was the speedy cleanup of the Superfund hazardous waste sites recently discovered at Schofield Barracks. And I wanted reauthorization of the Higher Education Act to facilitate college loans and other support.

As a matter of philosophy as much as policy, I also wanted the federal government to apologize to Native Hawaiians for the overthrow of the monarchy in 1893. I had introduced a joint resolution to that effect on August 3, 1990, but it never made it out of the Committee on Governmental Affairs. So I reintroduced it on February 6, with Inouye as my sole cosponsor, for consideration by the new 102nd Congress. The measure, drafted with the help of my staffer Esther Kia'aina, also would require the federal government to declare a "trust relationship" with Native Hawaiians. When the republic of Hawai'i was annexed by the United States in 1896, becoming a territory, the U.S. assumed ownership of more than 2 million acres of crown and government lands that had belonged to the republic and the kingdom. "The health and well-being of the Hawaiian people is intrinsically tied to their deep feelings and attachment to the land," I noted in the text of the measure. I wanted Congress to acknowledge the "fundamental injustice" of the U.S. participation in the overthrow and the land grab.

On the Senate floor, I pointed to our readiness to defend the sovereignty of other countries, notably Kuwait.

"It is time that Congress and the administration reflect upon America's own history and her actions, which have affected the self-determination and freedoms of her native people," I said.

From an environmental standpoint, high among my concerns was the possible introduction to Hawai'i of the brown tree snake from Guam. Accordingly, on May 23, I introduced a pair of bills requiring the Defense Department and the Department of Agriculture to institute an aggressive screening program for the pest, which had devastated the native bird population on Guam. We just couldn't afford to have this creature established in the isles. It would ruin the environment and in turn decimate our largest industry, tourism. Yet in the last decade, four brown tree snakes had reached Hawai'i in the cargo holds or wheel wells of aircraft. Fortunately, they were either frozen en route or were captured before escaping Hickam. Unfortunately, neither of my bills moved out of committee.

* * *

When Sparky was in the Senate, starting in 1977, one of the traditions he forged was daily lunch reservations at the largest table in the Senate dining room. This sat ten people, and Sparky regularly would fill all nine seats, besides his own, with visiting constituents. Whenever a visitor arrived or called to say they wanted to come down to the office, Sparky would invite him or her to lunch, and rarely did he get a refusal. This was a wonderful opportunity for him to get to know his voter base, and vice versa. And typically Inouye would stop by the table to say hello to everyone as well as they tackled their senate bean soup, double thick new york strip or mahi mahi bella vista. By contrast, the other tables sat four or six. Over the years, other senators asked if they could reserve the table. But no. Sparky had it reserved already, Monday through Friday, seemingly ad infinitum. I frankly don't know how he got away with it, but he did.

When I arrived in the Senate, I wanted to continue Sparky's tradition and went to the dining room maître d' to make the arrangements.

"You know, I would like to continue Senator Matsunaga's tradition of reserving the big table daily for lunch," I said.

"Sorry, Senator," I was told. "We're not going to do that anymore."

From now on, he said, the big table would be open for all senators to reserve—including me, he added equitably.

* * *

On another front, I was delighted that the Senate had a weekly prayer breakfast, as did the House. The senators held theirs on Wednesday, whereas the House Prayer Breakfast was every Thursday.

Dan in uniform with brother Abraham and his daughter, Fenner Marie, in 1944.

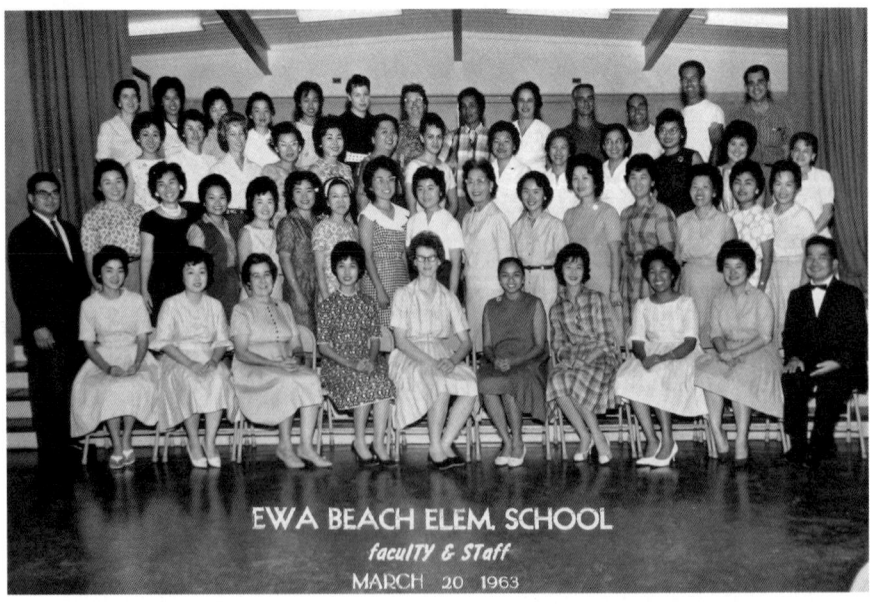

Top: Millannie, Millie and Dan in 1950.
Above: The faculty and staff of 'Ewa Beach Elementary School
(Dan at far left) in 1963.
Opposite: Dan and Millie, Kawaiahaʻo Church.

THE ONE HUNDRED CLUB 253

Opposite bottom: In 1959, Kamehameha Schools' choir
(rehearsing on campus, opposite top) boards a flight for a live broadcast
appearance on *The Dinah Shore Chevy Show* in Los Angeles.
Above: Dan meets with Dinah Shore before the show.

Opposite top: Corinthia Puaʻa Harbottle, Louise Pohina Tolles, Abraham Akaka and Dan work on a Waikiki Shell benefit for the Kawaiahaʻo Church choir in 1963. Opposite bottom: Dan and Millie pose with Governor George Ariyoshi and wife Jean at an early Akaka rally. Above: Dan poses for a McInerny newspaper ad for Kahala Sportswear's ʻOkole Maluna ("Bottoms Up") Hawaiian cocktail shirt.

Abe and Dan celebrate an Akaka victory on election night in November 1976.

But unlike the House, the senators didn't sing. I had found our hymns so uplifting during the House Prayer Breakfasts that I promptly pushed to have the Senate embrace them as well.

"No, we don't sing," one member said flatly.

"Yes, but *can* we sing?" I pressed.

In the end, I won. As in the House, I selected the song each week. Each prayer breakfast had a speaker, so I would ask the speaker if he had a favorite song or hymn. If he didn't, I would make the pick, usually something simple that everyone likely knew. Some of our standbys were "America the Beautiful," "Amazing Grace," "The Old Rugged Cross," "What a Friend We Have in Jesus" and "How Great Thou Art."

And as with the House, the rule remained that you left your baggage at the door. No politicking allowed. The prayer breakfasts were a great way to get to know your counterparts across the aisle in a nonconfrontational, uplifting setting. ✤

CHAPTER

44

From Millie's perspective, I'm sure, one of the highlights of 1991 was the stop in Washington by Queen Elizabeth II on her thirteen-day visit to the United States. On May 16, the queen addressed a joint session of Congress, becoming the first British monarch to do so.

Elizabeth and her husband, Prince Philip, received a standing ovation as the entered the House chamber, where about 800 people awaited. She wore a pale orange dress and matching hat, a three-strand white pearl necklace and white gloves. She took the lectern and waited for the applause to die down. Behind her stood Vice President Dan Quayle and House Speaker Tom Foley.

Foley remained standing as everyone else sat.

"Members of the Congress," he said, "it is my great privilege, and I deem it a high honor and personal pleasure, to present to you Her Majesty Elizabeth the Second."

The audience rose once again in applause. When everyone was seated and quiet, she began, "I do hope you can see me today from where you are."

That brought laughter and a third standing ovation. It was a reference to her five-foot-four-inch frame being obscured by a forest of microphones during an address at the White House two days earlier. The press had dubbed her "the talking hat" in that appearance.

"Some people believe that power grows from the barrel of a gun," the queen said. "So it can, but history shows that it never grows well nor for very long. Force, in the end, is sterile. We have gone a better way: our societies rest on mutual agreement, on contract and on consensus."

She went on, "I want to take this opportunity to express the gratitude of the British people to the people of the United States of America for the steadfast loyalty to our common enterprise throughout this turbulent century. The future is, as ever, obscure. The only certainty is that it will present the world with new and daunting problems. But if we continue to stick to our fundamental ideals, I have every confidence that we can resolve them.

"Recent events have proved that it is possible to do just that. Both our countries saw the invasion of Kuwait in just the same terms—an outrage to be reversed, both for the people of Kuwait and for the sake of the principle that naked aggression should not prevail. Our views were identical and so were our responses. That response was not without risk, but we both have learned from history that we must not allow aggression to succeed."

That drew applause.

"I salute the outstanding leadership of your president and the courage and prowess of the armed forces of the United States. I know that the servicemen and women of Britain, and of all the members of the coalition, were proud to act in a just cause alongside their American comrades. Unfortunately, experience shows that great enterprises seldom end with a tidy and satisfactory flourish. Together we are doing our best to reestablish peace and civil order in the region and to help those members or ethnic and religious minorities who continue to suffer through no fault of their own. If we succeed, out military success will have achieved its true objective.

"For all that uncertainty, it would be a mistake to make the picture look too gloomy. The swift and dramatic changes in Eastern Europe in the last decade have opened up great opportunities for the people of those countries. They are finding their own paths to freedom. But the paths would have been blocked in the Atlantic alliance not stood together, had your country and mine not stood together. We must never forget that lesson."

Applause.

"Britain is at the heart of a growing movement towards cohesion within Europe and within the European Community in particular. This is going to mean radical economic, social and political evolution. NATO, too, is adapting to the new realities in Eastern Europe and the Soviet Union and to changing attitudes in the West. It is Britain's prime concern to ensure that the new Europe is open and liberal and that it works in growing harmony with the United States and the other members of the Atlantic community."

She quoted Ralph Waldo Emerson on England's resolve in times of trouble: "'I feel, in regard to this aged England, with a kind of instinct, that she sees a little better on a cloudy day, and that, in storm of battle and calamity, she has a secret vigor and a pulse like a cannon.'"

She ended with "May God bless America."

We had been advised by British Embassy officials that, at the reception afterwards, we should not extend our hand to the queen. But when Elizabeth saw Millie's ʻilima lei, she reached out her hand and greeted Millie with a smile.

"You're from Hawaiʻi, aren't you?" the queen said.

"Yes, I am!" Millie said.

That made our day.

On the international stage, these indeed were heady times for historians, with the impending dissolution of the Soviet Union. Most people alive in 1991 couldn't remember a time when the United States hadn't viewed the USSR as a dangerous adversary kept at bay by the threat of "mutual assured destruction," that is, nuclear holocaust. But now the Cold War was coming to an end. One by one, the Eastern bloc "republics" were voting for independence. This didn't sit well, apparently, with some of the Communist Party hard-liners, who in August attempted a coup. This failed, chiefly by the opposition of Russian president Boris Yeltsin, who promptly outlawed the party.

The implosion of the Soviet Union had implications for U.S. military and domestic policy as well. Since the 1950s, the United States had kept up an effective but expensive nuclear "triad" of missiles, long-range bombers and ballistic missile submarines—the last designed to stealthily survive a first strike. But now, with the credible threat diminishing, perhaps some of the Pentagon's money could be spent on domestic programs—schools, health care or cleaning up the environment. A bill introduced by Senator Tom Harkin of Iowa—and undeclared candidate for president—called for transferring $3.1 billion from the defense budget to fund health, education and low-income programs. I voted for it; Inouye voted against it—a rare split.

"Intelligence experts tell us that we should be prepared for another coup or many other coups in the Soviet Union," Inouye said on the Senate floor in arguing against the measure. "And if this loose confederation of sovereign nations becomes a reality, then we will have ten more nuclear nations added to the rostrum."

The measure was defeated 69–28.

※ ※ ※

Nature also was having an effect on our military posture.

In the spring and summer of 1991, Mount Pinatubo in the Philippines rumbled to life after untold eons of dormancy. Earthquakes and spectacular plumes of ash and grit were followed on June 15 by a cataclysmic eruption, the second largest in the twentieth century, bested only by one on the Alaskan Peninsula in 1912. Nearly 850 people were killed, mostly when wet ash accumulated on roofs, causing them to collapse. The hazard was exacerbated by the arrival of Typhoon Yunya. Some 200,000 acres of rice paddies were destroyed. The ash also killed some 800,000 farm animals. More than 8,000 houses were destroyed and another 73,000 damaged. The U.S. Air Force airlifted thousands of military service personnel and their families from Subic Bay Naval Base and Clark Air Base, which was ultimately shuttered. Pinatubo put more ash into the atmosphere than any volcano since Krakatoa in 1883, scientists estimated. As a result, the amount of sunlight reaching the surface of the earth dropped by ten percent, and average temperatures in the far latitudes dropped by a full degree Fahrenheit. Sunsets in Hawai'i were intensely spectacular for years afterward, but that was the only upside. It was a powerful reminder of the destructive force of nature, which Hawai'i all too often sees firsthand.

Hawai'i also had a front-row seat on a stunning solar eclipse July 11. What made the event all the more significant scientifically was that the shadow of totality passed directly over Maunakea, home to some of the world's best observatories. Haleakalā on Maui also has some fine observatories. In fact, any mention of an eclipse calls to mind the LURE Observatory atop Haleakalā.

For years, LURE, which stands for Lunar Ranging Experiment, fired lasers at the moon, where they bounced off mirrors left there by the Apollo astronauts. By measuring the time it takes for the laser light to return, scientists were able to measure the distance to the moon with incredible accuracy. That allowed them not only to track the movements of the earth's tectonic plates, but also to calculate the date of every eclipse going back thousands of years. Turns out there was a total eclipse over much of the Mideast on Friday, April 3, 33 AD.

"And when the sixth hour came, there was darkness over the whole land." Mark 15:33. ✤

CHAPTER

45

In the summer of 1991, I was happy to win acknowledgement from the League of Conservation Voters, a highly respected environmental group, which had rated the members of the twenty-member Senate Committee on Energy and Natural Resources. They gave me a grade of seventy-five out of 100, third highest on the committee. The grade, the group said, was in large measure due to my opposition to proposed oil drilling in the Arctic National Wildlife Refuge. The grade would have been higher had I backed greater fuel efficiency for cars. But I had concerns that the fuel standards as proposed would make cars so light that they would be unsafe for the occupants in a crash. On other environmental issues, I remained deeply concerned about the loss of native plant and animal species in Hawai'i, and was determined to prevent the establishment of the brown tree snake in the isles. My anti-snake bill, fortunately, was wending its way through the Senate.

By the fall of 1991—with the Iowa caucuses and New Hampshire primary less than six months away—the presidential race was already heating up. Conservative columnist Pat Buchanan had the most gravitas of Bush's GOP challengers, which included Ku Klux Klansman David Duke of Louisiana, perennial candidate Harold Stassen of Minnesota and comedian Pat Paulsen. Had I been a Republican, my vote would have been with Paulsen. Of course, Bush had left himself vulnerable by famously declaring, in 1988, "Read my lips. No new taxes," and then raising taxes. On the Democratic side, there were Senators Bob Kerrey of Nebraska, Harkin of Iowa and Paul Tsongas of Massachusetts; Governors Bill Clinton of Arkansas and Douglas Wilder of Virginia and

former governor Jerry Brown of California; and—shades of 1968—
Gene McCarthy. Not in the race was Gore, who had made a stab at
the White House in 1988, carrying seven states in the primaries. Gore
was sitting this one out because in April 1989 his son Albert, then six,
was hit by a car and nearly killed. "I would like to be president," he
announced in August. "But I also am a father and feel deeply about my
responsibility to my children." He also felt a deep responsibility to the
planet. His book *Earth in the Balance*, published in June 1992, became
the first by a senator to make the *New York Times* Best Sellers list since
John F. Kennedy's *Profiles in Courage*.

With the impending retirement of associate justice Thurgood
Marshall, a brilliant jurist and the first black justice on the Supreme
Court, Bush appointed another African American, Clarence Thomas,
to fill the vacancy. From his contentious, 107-day confirmation hearings, I became convinced that he was not the right man for the job. And
in early October both Inouye and I announced we would be voting
against the nomination. Although I found him engaging and informed,
I was disturbed by his refusal to answer questions about individual
rights. "His retreat from past speeches causes me great concern," I said
in a statement. "And I remain unconvinced that he would protect older
workers from age discrimination." This was all the more unsettling
because Thomas was a former chairman of the Equal Employment
Opportunity Commission. There was also a lengthy paper trail showing his disregard for basic constitutional rights. Inouye and I chose not
to mention the testimony of attorney Anita Hill, Thomas's underling
at the EEOC, who accused him of sexual harassment. I believed Miss
Hill. No one would subject themselves to that degree of public scrutiny—and yes, sadly, scorn—without knowing in their soul it was the
right thing to do. But Inouye and I had more *pono*, righteous, reasons to
oppose Thomas' confirmation.

This was not my first problem with a Bush appointee. A year
earlier, I had voted against David Souter, Bush's choice to replace Justice

William Brennan, on the court since Eisenhower nominated him in 1956. Three senators voiced their opposition in floor speeches—Brock Adams of Washington, Alan Cranston of California and Kennedy, the sole dissenting vote on Biden's Judiciary Committee. "If nominees do not meet the test of demonstrating a convincing good faith, in-depth, abiding commitment to the core constitutional values of the kind so obviously at stake at this turning point in our history, they can, and should, be rejected by the Senate," Kennedy said. But in the end Souter was confirmed 90–9. The other no votes came from Democrats Bill Bradley and Frank Lautenberg of New Jersey, John Kerry of Massachusetts, Quentin Burdick of North Dakota and Mikulski of Maryland.

The vote for Thomas was much closer—52–48. Only two Republicans voted no—Bob Packwood of Oregon and Jim Jeffords of Vermont. But eleven Democrats voted yes. It came down to an ugly racial litmus test. The *New York Times* put it best. "Seven Southern Democrats, many of them dependent on black voters for their political survival because of the flight of whites to the Republican Party, held firm in support of the nominee, along with four from other parts of the country, and that made the difference. Judge Thomas had repeatedly invoked racial themes in his own defense, and, in a move that seemed to gain sympathy among blacks, he accused the all-white Senate of conducting a 'high-tech lynching.'" The non-Southern Democrats who voted for Thomas were David Boren of Oklahoma, Alan Dixon of Illinois, Dennis DeConcini of Arizona and Jim Exon of Nebraska.

Shortly before we went home for the holidays, the Senate passed a resolution recognizing the contributions of the federal civilian employees during and after the attack on Pearl Harbor. The measure, which I introduced, had fifty-five cosponsors. Sixty-eight of the 2,403 people killed in the attack were civilians, as were thirty-five of the 1,178 wounded.

"When the first bombs fell on Ford Island in Pearl Harbor, our armed forces were not the only ones to respond bravely to this aggressive action," I said in a press statement. "Our federal civilian employees, as well, boldly answered the call to duty and exhibited the highest order of patriotism and performance under fire."

On the eve of December 7, 1991—the fiftieth anniversary of the attack, I attended a reception on the lawn of the Royal Hawaiian Hotel. The event was hosted by Admiral Charles Larson, commander in chief of U.S. Pacific forces, whose headquarters was up at Camp Smith, and his wife, Sally. Also attending were the only two other members of Congress who had witnessed the attack: Inouye and Congressman Bernard Dwyer, a New Jersey Democrat. Inouye recalled he was at home in McCully, getting ready for church, when he heard news of the attack on the radio. He and his father went outside and saw dive bombers with the rising sun symbol. Dwyer, then nineteen, was a radioman aboard the destroyer USS *Dale*, anchored near Ford Island. "It was a surprise, very much of a surprise," Dwyer recalled. "And it was also, in retrospect, a surprise how quickly everyone turned to and went to general quarters and how quickly we got using the guns."

In all, twenty-six members of Congress—seventeen of them veterans—were in Hawai'i for the fiftieth anniversary remembrance of the attack. Aboard the USS *Arizona* Memorial on December 7, a sunny Saturday, were President and Mrs. Bush; Defense secretary Cheney and his wife, Lynne; Joint Chiefs chairman Powell; Admiral Larson; and other dignitaries. At the precise time of the attack, 7:55 a.m., the USS *Chosin*, a new, Pearl Harbor-based Aegis missile cruiser, with its crew lining the deck, sounded its horn. We then observed a moment of silence, followed by the roar of four F-15 Eagles from the Hawai'i Air National Guard, slicing the sky overhead in a "missing man" formation.

At Larson's command, a bugler sounded "attention," and the audience stood.

Then, as the flag was hoisted at the memorial, singer Danny Kaleikini sang the national anthem to the accompaniment of the Pacific Fleet Band.

At Larson's invitation, Bush and his wife, wearing a pink suit with gold buttons, stood and walked to the memorial well, a hole in the floor where you can see the hulk of the *Arizona* and its rainbows of extruding oil. They tossed flowers and wreaths of maile into the water, then returned to their seats silently, except for the clack of Barbara's heels.

"We are fortunate to have as the senior leader of our Department of Defense a man with the wisdom to look backward for lessons, and the foresight to look forward with solutions," the admiral said. "In his time as secretary of defense, he has seen the world transformed as dramatically as after the Pearl Harbor attack. But this time the change was brought on by our success—success in deterring global conflict, success in ending the Cold War, success in rolling back Iraqi aggression and showing the world that America stands by its word. With these realities of the present in mind, he has created a vision of our armed forces for the future, a force to secure our interests and advance our ideals in a world of both uncertainty and opportunity. Ladies and gentlemen, it is my honor and privilege to introduce our secretary of defense, the Honorable Dick Cheney."

Frankly, I thought Larson was laying it on a bit thick. Cheney was not responsible for the victory in Kuwait as much as were Powell and Schwarzkopf. Likely Larson's introduction was written at the Pentagon, under Cheney aides' careful approval. In any case, his remarks were a poignant reminder of the scope of the changes we had seen the last few years.

After brief remarks, Cheney in turn introduced retired Navy Captain Donald Ross, a crewman on the battleship USS *Nevada* during the 1941 attack. The *Nevada* was the only battleship to get underway that day. Ross won the Medal of Honor, the first in World War II, for his work getting the engine running in blinding smoke and steam. The ship ran aground on purpose at Hospital Point rather than risk being sunk and blocking the harbor channel.

After Ross, Bush stepped up to the lectern.

"At first, to the American sailors at Pearl, the hum of engines sounded routine, and why not? To them, the idea of war seemed palpable but remote. And then, in one horrible instant, they froze in disbelief. The abstract threat was suddenly real. But these men did not panic. They raced to their stations, and some strapped pistols over pajamas, and fought and died. And what lived was the shock wave that soon swept across America, forever immortalizing December 7, 1941.

"Ask anyone who endured that awful Sunday. Each felt like the writer who observed: 'Life is never again as it was before anyone you love has died; never so innocent, never so gentle, never so pliant to your will.'

"Today we honor those who gave their lives at this place, half a century ago. Their names were Bertie and Gomez and Dougherty and Granger. And they came from Idaho and Mississippi, the sweeping farmland of Ohio. And they were of all races and colors, native-born and foreign-born. And most of all, of course, they were Americans. Think of how it was for these heroes of the harbor, men who were also husbands, fathers, brothers, sons. Imagine the chaos of guns and smoke, flaming water and ghastly carnage. Two thousand four hundred and three Americans gave their lives. But in this haunting place, they live forever in our memory, reminding us gently, selflessly, like chimes in the distant night... Look at the water here, clear and quiet, bidding us to sum up and remember. One day, in what now seems another lifetime, it wrapped its arms around the finest sons any nation could ever have, and it carried them to a better world. May God bless them. And may God bless America, the most wondrous land on Earth." ❧

CHAPTER

46

In late 1981, when I was still in the House, I received a visit one day from an internationally acclaimed *kupuna*, Morrnah Nalamaku Simeona. Morrnah was an expert in *hoʻoponopono*, the Hawaiian tradition of forgiveness and reconciliation. But she had updated it for modern times, developing a self-help and self-identity system by promoting a hoʻoponopono-style balance between the three parts of the mind: the id, ego and superego. In her words, "Hoʻoponopono is a profound gift that allows one to develop a working relationship with the Divinity within and learn to ask that in each moment, our errors through word or deed be cleansed. The process is essentially about freedom, complete freedom from the past."

In the 1960s, she had started out giving *lomilomi* massages in her spas at the Kahala and Royal Hawaiian Hotels, and her clients included Lyndon Johnson, Jackie Kennedy and Arnold Palmer. Later she expanded into the field of *lāʻau lapaʻau*, or Hawaiian healing. Through her Pacifica Seminars, she had lectured across the country, including at the United Nations, and in many foreign lands about her inner peace technique. In 1983, she was named a Living Treasure by the state Legislature and won similar recognition from the Honpa Hongwanji Mission, a Buddhist temple in Honolulu.

Morrnah usually stopped by my office whenever she was in Washington.

On a visit in 1984, freedom was on her mind, but not in the sense of personal liberty. Since 1863, during the thick of the Civil War, a nineteen-foot bronze statue, the *Statue of Freedom*, sometimes called the *Lady of Freedom*, has stood atop the dome of the U.S. Capitol. It's a classic female figure with long hair under a battle helmet with nine stars and a crest of an eagle's head and feathers. She wears a classical dress with a brooch that says "U.S." Her right hand rests on the hilt of a sheathed sword. Her left hand grasps a laurel wreath and the shield of the United States with thirteen stripes. Interestingly, the person who approved the design was Secretary of War Jefferson Davis, who left Lincoln's cabinet to become president of the Confederacy. The statue, which stands on a pedestal more than eighteen feet high, tops out at 288 feet above the Capitol's East Front Plaza.

Morrnah found herself drawn to the statue. She would stare up at it and get, in her words, "messages," a feeling that something was incomplete. She said she came to me because she felt I was the only one who could help her.

Honestly, at first I didn't know what to think. But I looked into it for her and learned that the white plaster model that was used to make the statue was lying in storage somewhere in the basement of the Smithsonian Institution. The 15,000-pound model had been moved and mothballed several times since its creation, finally ending up at the Smithsonian in 1890. From 1900 to 1967, it was on display in the Smithsonian's Arts and Industries Building. Then it was cut up and put back into storage.

"We need to get that model back to the Capitol, where it should be on display for visitors," Morrnah asserted. That would be good because the statute itself was way too high for people to appreciate, she said.

The Smithsonian said it would try to find the model. Years went by. No word. Finally, they said, "Oh, yeah," they had found the plaster model in five pieces. I spoke with the architect of the Capitol at that time, George M. , and mentioned that I would like to see it refurbished, restored and mounted someplace on the Hill.

"How can we do that?" I asked.

"Well, it's under the jurisdiction of the Smithsonian," he said. "If we want to put it in the Capitol, we have to move the ownership or jurisdiction to the Capitol."

We put this idea to the Smithsonian, and were surprised that they were resistant.

Another problem arose. There was no mechanism at the time for the Capitol to receive a gift or donation of that kind. So I introduced an amendment to the fiscal 1988 Legislative Branch Appropriations bill that said that the Architect of the Capitol, under the jurisdiction of the Joint Committee on the Library, is authorized to accept donations to restore and display the *Statue of Freedom* model. Since this was breaking new ground, I had asked for an opinion on the language from the House legal counsel. By the time I got it, on the morning of June 18, 1987, the deadline for submitting amendments was in about ten minutes. This is no exaggeration. So I ended up literally running down the corridors of the Rayburn Building to the committee hearing in room 2360. But I made it in time. The House passed the measure June 29. Reagan signed the measure as Public Law 100-458.

Ultimately the model was transferred to the Capitol, and White and I discussed where we could put it. We had no idea how much it would cost to put the pieces back together and refurbish it. One initial estimate was $300,000.

Morrnah herself raised $25,000 through her foundation, the Foundation of I, Inc. At first, in March 1991, Tom Foley, the House Speaker, and Robert Byrd, the president pro tem of the Senate, turned down the donation because it came nowhere near the estimates presented by the Capitol Preservation Commission. But then this tale took one of its uncanny turns. In a letter to Morrnah on April 18, Byrd and Foley changed their tune. "Since we last wrote to you, we have received a new cost estimate for this project from the Architect of the Capitol. It now appears that the repair and placement of the plaster model can be accomplished for $25,000 with the use of in-house resources available to the Architect. We therefore will apply your $25,000 donation to this project as originally intended by your foundation. Again, we are very grateful for the generous assistance of the Foundation of I in making possible the restoration of this important original plaster model of the *Statue of Freedom.*"

Ken Riley, the chief painter for the Architect of the Capitol, was quite active in the restoration, which took place on the loading dock of the Russell Senate Office Building. Under his supervision, a work crew exfoliated nearly every square inch of the statue's leaded paint surface. "The biggest challenge was (avoiding) damaging the brittle—and historic—plaster substrate," Riley recalled. The paint crew also put on a primer undercoat to preserve the original plaster and to provide a barrier coat of protection. Small voids and imperfections were filled with a spackle-type compound and sanded smooth. Riley also filled in and sanded the model's shield.

"Because I'd worked on the restoration of the pedestal on top of the Capitol, I'd seen the bronze statue's shield up close with its beautiful concise straight lines," he's quoted on the website of the Architect of the Capitol. "I knew that the plaster model must have at one time looked like that so I ended up spending a lot of time working to correct the alignment of the thirteen stripes on the shield."

From the loading dock, the model, still in two large pieces, was crated and transported to the Russell Building's basement rotunda, where it spent about seven years. But for me that was a temporary solution. I wanted it at the Capitol.

Morrnah envisioned a place near a staircase, where visitors could view the statue at different levels, top to bottom.

Around that time arose the notion of creating a Capitol visitor center, where people could come and relax. On March 18, 1998, I wrote to Tom Daschle, the Senate Democratic leader, expressing my "deep interest" in relocating the statute from the Russell Building rotunda to the proposed visitor center. "I believe that the cast model would be an ideal focal point for the visitor center by serving as an educational resource and representation of renewed hope for our country," I said. Daschle agreed. Construction of the visitor center began in the fall of 2001.

So I worked with the architect on the design of the center to create a place where visitors could view the model from the ground floor but also a second-story mezzanine. So he pulled out a pencil and quickly drew a sketch, and his design is what you see today at the visitor center, which opened in 2008. It is now the centerpiece of Emancipation Hall. Beautiful. It brings back the image of freedom to the people of the United States.

I wish Morrnah could have seen it, but unfortunately she died in February 1992. In a tribute, on March 25, I put these words in the Congressional Record:

"We all shall miss her quiet but strong presence and leadership, her friendship and most of all her understanding and compassion. We take solace that she has departed from this world and is going home to life eternal… Morrnah gave freely of her spirituality to others throughout her life… We are better today for having known her, and the world a better place for her having passed through." ✤

CHAPTER

47

In the presidential race, Doug Wilder of Virginia, the first black governor of any state, surprised everyone by throwing in the towel in early January 1992, even before the Iowa caucuses. Beginning in February, the presidential primaries and caucuses were tit-for-tat, with candidates typically winning their home turf and neighboring states. This proved true for Tom Harkin, who won Iowa with seventy-seven percent of the vote. The rest of the field had conceded Iowa. New Englander Paul Tsongas won the next contest, the all-important New Hampshire primary, with thirty-three percent in a crowded field, but the surprise was the strong, second-place showing by Clinton. Jerry Brown edged out Tsongas in neighboring Maine. Bob Kerrey took South Dakota, and Brown beat Clinton and Tsongas by single digits in Colorado. So by the end of February, all the major candidates had a piece of the pie.

On Super Tuesday, March 3, Clinton took Georgia, fifty-seven percent, with Tsongas far back at twenty-four. Things looked bad for Tsongas and Kerrey. Brown edged out Tsongas and Clinton in Colorado, and Harkin slid past Tsongas in Idaho and Minnesota. But Tsongas managed to stay in the game with victories in the Washington and Utah caucuses. After finishing fourth in Colorado, Kerrey dropped out.

Tsonga also took Arizona on March 7 and Brown picked up Nevada the next day. After Nevada, Harkin quit.

Then Clinton went on a roll. He won South Carolina, Wyoming, Florida, Louisiana and Hawai'i—fifty-one percent, with Brown and Tsongas each at fourteen. Tsonga picked up his home state at sixty-six percent. But then the Clinton machine kicked into high gear with wins in Mississippi, Missouri, Oklahoma, Texas, Illinois, Michigan and North Dakota, showing he was competitive outside the South. After North Dakota on March 19, Tsongas quit. That left Brown and Clinton.

From March into April, Brown showed promising momentum, winning Connecticut, Vermont and Alaska. But then Clinton blew it open, dominating the remaining major contests. The only race he didn't win was Delaware, where on May 5 voters backed Tsongas even though he was out.

With the nomination wrapped up, Clinton on July 9 tapped Gore as his running mate. That went against the conventional wisdom of creating a regional see-saw, where a Southerner picks a Northerner—Johnson-Humphrey, Carter-Mondale—or vice versa—Kennedy-Johnson, Dukakis-Bentsen. Gore was from Tennessee, right across the Mississippi from Arkansas. Clinton and Gore were from the same generation, too. But Gore brought other balance to the ticket. After graduating from Harvard, he enlisted in the Army and served in Vietnam. Clinton had no military service. Gore also had foreign policy credentials as a member of the Senate Armed Services Committee and a former member of the House Intelligence Committee. And he was a famous technology buff, one of the so-called "Atari Democrats," after the pioneering video games of the day. He was the first member of Congress to appear, in 1979, on C-Span. I was proud of my friend and 1976 classmate.

As a longtime educator, I find history quirky. Maybe that's why I got along with Newt Gingrich, a college history professor before he ran for office. In the election of 1792, we had an incumbent president named George who was challenged by a Governor Clinton. That was George Washington, of course, and Governor George Clinton of New York. Now, 200 years later, we had an incumbent named George challenged by a Governor Clinton.

On the legislative front we had, once again, a mixed bag of successes and setbacks.

Inouye called me into his office one day, a fairly frequent occurrence.

"Danny, we need to do more to help working families," he said. "They are really on the ropes, especially with a new baby or when a child gets sick."

So we signed on as cosponsors of the Family Medical Leave Act of 1991, introduced by Chris Dodd of Connecticut. The bill aimed to protect jobs for workers in businesses with at least fifty employees who take up to twelve weeks of unpaid leave to care for a newborn, adopted or ill child. It also covered time off for personal medical emergencies, including caring for family members. To be eligible, the worker must have been on the job for at least twelve months and had worked 1,250 hours during that year. There were a lot of ifs, ands and buts, but that was basically it. The House and Senate passed slightly different versions in late 1991, and the bill went to a conference committee in late July 1992. The conferees included some heavy hitters—Kennedy, Dodd, Harkin, Howard Metzenbaum of Ohio and Orrin Hatch of Utah. It also included both of the women in the Senate at that time, Mikulski and Nancy Kassebaum of Kansas. The point being, you could trust these lawmakers to reach a respectable compromise, which they did in August. On September 10 the House approved it 241–161. Abercrombie and Mink voted with the majority. But on September 22, Bush vetoed it, saying he supported the concept but that leave was a matter for labor-management negotiations. He objected to the bill's "rigid, federally imposed requirements." On September 24, the Senate overrode the veto, 68–31. The House needed 290 to override, but the votes just weren't there: 258–169. So it goes.

A bill with a happier outcome was the Energy Policy Act of 1992, which encouraged states to make residential and commercial buildings more energy efficient, and set deadlines for doing so. This was introduced in the House by Phil Sharp, a Democrat from Indiana. After committee markups that spring, the bill passed the House, 381–37, in late May. It sailed through Lloyd Bentsen's Finance Committee in June and the Senate passed it, 93–3, with an amendment, on July 30. The naysayers were Paul Wellstone and Dave Durenberger, both of Minnesota, and Bob Smith of New Hampshire, another place where heat leaks out windowpanes in the winter, making energy efficiency difficult. Back to conference committee. Finally, on October 5, the House approved the conference report, 363–60. The Senate followed suit three days later by voice vote, my voice among the ayes. And Bush signed the measure October 24.

Then a Hawai'i bill made it past the president's pen. I was pleased, on May 7, to sponsor a measure on a topic that was then and remains today very dear to my heart: Hawai'i's native forests. The Hawai'i Tropical Forest Recovery Act cleared Congress with atom-smasher speed—the House action all came on a single day, October 2. Bush signed it on October 29 as Inouye and I looked on. "This act demonstrates our intent as a nation to conserve and protect irreplaceable tropical forests and to provide world leadership in stemming the decline of these forests," Bush said in his signing announcement. "Almost two-thirds of Hawai'i's original forest cover has been lost over the last three centuries. This loss has severely affected the state's diverse ecosystems, which are among the most fragile and complex in the world. To better understand these changes and to develop means to conserve these forests for human ecological needs, this act authorizes the establishment of the Hawai'i Experimental Tropical Forest. This experimental forest will serve as a center for long-term research and a focal point for developing and transferring knowledge and expertise for the management of tropical forests." The law also called for the expansion of the Institute of Pacific Islands Forestry in Hawai'i to serve as a center for disseminating scientific, technical, managerial and administrative assistance to organizations at home and abroad.

Throwing a possible monkey wrench into the presidential race was the independent candidacy of Texas billionaire Ross Perot. In the early 1960s, Perot was a top salesman at IBM. He quit to start his own business, Electronic Data Systems, EDS, which signed lucrative government contracts. When he took the company public in 1968, his fortune was made.

Just before the Iranian revolution, the government of the shah jailed two EDS employees in a contract dispute. Perot hired a team of former Special Forces commandos to rescue them, which they did dramatically via a mountain crossing into Turkey. Ken Follett detailed that exploit in a 1983 nonfiction thriller, *On Wings of Eagles*, after which Perot became a household name.

As his running mate, Perot had picked James Bond Stockdale, a retired Navy vice admiral who had been a prisoner of war in Vietnam for more than seven years. That experience he shared, of course, with John McCain and Jeremiah Denton, who represented Alabama in the Senate from 1981 to 1987. Denton's book, *When Hell Was in Session*, was turned into a 1979 TV movie starring Hal Holbrook, who actually looks a bit like Denton. I knew two other former Vietnam POWs, retired Navy Captain Jerry Coffee and retired Marine Colonel Orson Swindle, both of whom would run for Congress in Hawai'i. In 1992, Swindle served as Perot's campaign spokesman.

On September 11—my sixty-eight birthday—Hurricane Iniki, a Category 4 storm with 145-mph winds, slammed into Kaua'i, a direct hit, causing massive destruction. Six people were killed, thousands of houses were destroyed, and power outages were widespread. In all the damage reached $1.8 billion. It would be months before most of the island would recover. And some places did not recover. The Coco Palms Resort, where Duke Kahanamoku had been a guest and where Elvis Presley filmed scenes for *Blue Hawaii*, remained shuttered for decades.

Bush, Clinton and Perot held three debates, on October 11 in St. Louis, on October 15 at the University of Richmond, and October 19 in East Lansing, Michigan. Clinton appeared more relaxed and smoother than either Bush or Perot. But, you know, this was the guy who, on June 3, wearing sunglasses, had played "Heartbreak Hotel" on his saxophone on the *Arsenio Hall Show*. It was at the second debate, in a town hall format where the audience asked questions, that Clinton distinguished himself.

A black woman in the audience asked, "How has the national debt personally affected each of your lives? And if it hasn't, how can you honestly find a cure for the economic problems of the common people if you have no experience in what's ailing them?"

Perot said, "It caused me to disrupt my private life and my business to get involved in this activity. That's how much I care about it. And believe me, if you knew my family and if you knew the private life I have, you would agree in a minute that that's a whole lot more fun than getting involved in politics."

Not exactly the answer she was hoping for, I suspect.

"Thank you, Mr. Perot," said the moderator, Carole Simpson of ABC. "Mr. President."

"Well, I think the national debt affects everybody. Obviously it has a lot to do with interest rates."

"She's saying you, personally," said Simpson.

The woman in the audience repeated, "On a personal basis, how has it affected you—has it affected you personally?"

Bush said, "Well, I'm sure it has. I love my grandchildren and I want to think that—"

"How?" the woman pressed.

"Are you suggesting that if somebody has means that the national debt doesn't affect them?"

That is exactly what she was suggesting.

"I'm not sure I get it," Bush said. "Help me with the question and I'll try to answer it."

"Well," the woman in the audience said, "I've had friends that have been laid off from jobs. I know people who cannot afford to pay the mortgage on their homes; their car payment. I have personal problems with the national debt. But how has it affected you? And if you have no experience in it, how can you help us if you don't know what we're feeling?"

"Everybody cares if people aren't doing well," Bush said. "But I don't think—I don't think it's fair to say, 'You haven't had cancer, therefore you don't know what it's like.'"

"Governor Clinton."

Clinton stood and addressed the woman directly.

"Tell me how it's affected you again. You know people who've lost their jobs and lost their homes."

"Well, yeah, uh-huh."

"Well, I've been governor of a small state for twelve years. I'll tell you how it's affected me. Every year, Congress and the president sign laws that makes us—make us do more things and gives us less money to do it with. I see people in my state, middle-class people, their taxes have gone up in Washington and their services have gone down while the wealthy have gotten tax cuts. I have seen what's happened in this last four years when in my state, when people lose their jobs, there's a good chance I'll know them by their names. When a factory closes I know the people who ran it. When the businesses go bankrupt, I know them. And I've been out here for thirteen months in meetings just like this ever since October with people like you all over America, people that have lost their jobs, lost their livelihood, lost their health insurance.

"What I want you to understand is the national debt is not the only cause of that. It is because America has not invested in its people. It is because we have not grown. It is because we've had twelve years of trickle-down economics. We've gone from first to twelfth in the world in wages. We've had four years where we've produced no private-sector jobs. Most people are working harder for less money than they were making ten years ago. It is because we are in the grip of a failed economic theory. And this decision you're about to make better be about what kind of economic theory you want. Not just people saying I want to go fix it but what are we going to do. What I think we have to do is invest in American jobs, American education, control American health-care costs and bring the American people together again."

While Clinton was talking, the camera occasionally panned over to Bush, who looked increasingly vexed. At one point during the forum, he looked at his watch, as if to say, how much longer do I have to endure this? The near universal impression was that Bush was out of touch with ordinary Americans.

On Election Day, Clinton won nearly 45 million votes. Bush drew 39 million and Perot nearly 20 million. But of course the national popular vote doesn't really matter. In the Electoral College, Clinton won 370 votes—100 more than he needed. Bush's tally was 168. Perot: zero, because he won no states.

It was going to be a new day in Washington. ❖

CHAPTER

48

In early January 1993, Senator J. Bennett Johnson of Louisiana and I traveled to China as unofficial envoys of President-elect Clinton. Relations between China and the United States had soured since the military crackdown on the student-led, pro-democracy movement at Tiananmen Square in June 1989. More recently, the U.S. had announced its intention to sell F-16 Falcon fighter jets to Taiwan, a $6-billion deal that China vehemently opposed. I can't recall how the arrangements were made, but the Chinese People's Institute for Foreign Affairs picked up the tab for our trip, which included Millie and a staffer. In turn, I was asked to speak to the institute about the new administration and the workings of Congress. In Beijing, Johnson and I had a fruitful meeting with Li Peng, the premier, who told us he would like to see improved ties between our two nations. "There is no reason for China and the United States not to develop a friendly relationship of cooperation," Li said through an interpreter. But in an apparent reference to the F-16s, and perhaps also Tiananmen, he added that our relations should improve on a foundation of "mutual respect and non-interference with each other's internal affairs." When I mentioned our concerns over human rights in China, he said, "China is willing to have a dialogue with America on the differing perceptions of this issue." During the election, Clinton had criticized Bush for failing to revoke China's "most-favored nation" trade status in the wake of the violent crackdown. But if Li was worried about losing that status under Clinton, he didn't show it.

"I didn't get any negative vibes," I told the *Advertiser*.

When a diplomatic meeting breaks down into vehement arguments, the State Department calls it "a frank exchange of views." When the meeting is cordial but produces no breakthroughs, the State Department calls it "useful." I guess our meeting with Li was near the "useful" side of the spectrum.

※ ※ ※

Thousands of people took part in a five-day ceremony embracing to the 100th anniversary of the overthrow of the Hawaiian monarchy, on January 17, 1993. There were reenactments, vigils, marches and singing. On January 14, a Wednesday, more than 1,000 people attended the opening ceremony at the Queen Lili'uokalani statue, between the state capitol and 'Iolani Palace. During the ceremony, Governor Waihee announced that he was banishing the American flag from state buildings during the events as a reminder of U.S. involvement in the ouster.

This stirred up intense emotions, especially from veterans groups. By mid-afternoon the next day, the governor's office had recorded 210 phone calls against the removal and 173 supporting the decision. Inouye immediately appealed to Waihee to reconsider. And by Thursday Mink and I also urged the governor to change his mind, saying it sent the wrong message.

"Understandably, to some, the flag of the United States of America stands for wrongs that have been perpetrated against Native Hawaiians for a century," I said in a press statement. "Equally beyond dispute, it is also a revered symbol honored by innumerable past, present and potential comrades in the fight for justice for Native Hawaiians. It would be regrettable if our fervor causes the perception, however mistaken, that there is yet another artificial barrier being raised between us and those I firmly believe are at the brink of acknowledging and rallying to the righteousness of the Hawaiian cause."

Mink said, "I am stunned by the intensity and number of people who have expressed shock and dismay. Given the overwhelming objection voices from all quarters, I respectfully ask the governor to rescind his order. The objection comes from the feeling that the removal of the American flag diminishes its importance as the symbol of our love and respect for our country. I know this was not what was intended by the governor."

Abercrombie, on the other hand, supported Waihee, saying, "The governor's action is an acknowledgment of history, of the inescapable past that shapes the present and the future." And the U.S. attorney for Hawai'i, Dan Bent, said Waihee broke no federal laws by ordering the U.S. flag removed. In the end, Waihee stood by his decision.

* * *

On January 21—the day after Clinton's inauguration, I introduced for the fourth time a resolution calling on the U.S. government to apologize for its role in the overthrow. Maybe the fourth time would be the charm. The resolution said Congress "apologizes to Native Hawaiians on behalf of the people of the United States for the overthrow of the kingdom of Hawai'i on January 17, 1893, with the participation of agents and citizens of the United States, and the deprivation of the rights of Native Hawaiians to self-determination."

The first time I introduced the so-called Apology Resolution, in August 1990, it went nowhere, languishing in the Senate Committee on Government Affairs. The second time, in February 1991, same result. The third time, in August 1992, I had two cosponsors, Inouye and Democrat Paul Simon of Illinois. The resolution also acknowledged the impending 100th anniversary of the overthrow. The bill made it out of the Judiciary Committee and then Inouye got it through the Committee on Indian Affairs. On October 7, it passed the Senate by voice vote. In the House, it was referred to the Interior and Insular Affairs Committee. On October 9, it died on the House floor due in large measure to objections by William Dannemeyer, a lame-duck Californian, and a few other Republicans. I found that regrettable and very frustrating.

Now, there were important differences with version three. For one, it dropped any mention of a "fiduciary duty" on the part of the United States to the Hawaiian people. For another, it emphasized "reconciliation." Specifically, it expressed the commitment of Congress to "acknowledge the ramifications of the overthrow of the kingdom of Hawai'i, in order to provide a proper foundation for reconciliation between the United States and the Native Hawaiian people." And it urged the president to acknowledge such as well.

The fourth iteration retained that language about reconciliation. The apology itself came after a long preamble giving some historical highlights on the kingdom and the overthrow. Inouye, again a cosponsor, ushered it through the Indian Affairs Committee. But I was getting stiff resistance from four Republican senators: Slade Gorton of Washington State, John Danforth of Mississippi, Hank Brown of Colorado and Connie Mack of Florida. All were worried where the resolution might lead. "I'm afraid the logical consequence of this resolution is independence for the state of Hawai'i," Gorton said. Mack pointedly asked, "Where do you draw the line and stop making apologies?" And what, he wanted to know, comes next—compensation?

On the Senate floor, I defended the measure.

"The deprivation of Hawaiian sovereignty, which began a century ago, has had devastating effects on the health, culture and society of Native Hawaiians with consequences that are evident throughout the Islands today. The acts of villainy that occurred a century ago have never been remedied, and no official apology has ever been made by the United States for its complicity." Looking around, I could see a lot of skeptical faces.

Fortunately we had the support of the GOP minority leader, Bob Dole of Kansas.

On October 27, 1993, the Senate approved it 65–34 in a roll call vote. As an alphabetical fluke, I cast the first "aye." Of the fifty-seven Democrats, only two voted no—Jim Sasser of Tennessee and Richard Shelby of Alabama, a conservative "boll weevil" Democrat who had beaten Jeremiah Denton, the former Vietnam POW, in the election of 1986. (In fact, Shelby would switch to the Republican Party in 1994.) These two were far outnumbered by the Republicans who voted in favor: Dole, Conrad Burns of Montana, Lincoln Chafee of Rhode Island, Thad Cochran of Mississippi, Pete Domenici of New Mexico, Mark Hatfield of Oregon, Nancy Kassebaum of Kansas, Frank Murkowski and Ted Stevens of Alaska, Larry Pressler of South Dakota, Arlen Specter of Pennsylvania and John Warner of Virginia. Democrat Sam Nunn of Georgia did not vote.

On November 15, the measure passed the House by voice vote and went to the White House.

On November 23—two days before Thanksgiving—Clinton signed the measure in the Oval Office, with Gore, Inouye, Mink, Abercrombie and me looking on.

"This is a spectacular moment for Hawaiian history," Mink remarked.

I added, "This is a great time for Hawai'i. "One hundred years ago a powerful country helped overthrow a legal government. We've finally come to the point where this has been acknowledged by the United States. I'm elated at what happened today." ❖

CHAPTER

49

Two events in 1993 for me set the tone for those tumultuous times: the World Trade Center bombing and the FBI siege at Waco, Texas. Both, of course, foreshadowed more dire things to come.

Just past noon on February 26, a Friday, a 1,200-pound truck bomb went off in the basement of the North Tower of the Trade Center. The plan was to send the North Tower topping into the South Tower, bringing both down. That didn't happen, but six people nonetheless were killed and a thousand injured. Hundreds of people were stuck in elevators when the power went out, including a group of seventeen kindergartners who didn't get out for five hours. Can you imagine being their teacher? Combing through the rubble, investigators found the vehicle identification number of the Ryder truck that had carried the bomb. They traced it to a rental agency in Jersey City, New Jersey. It had been rented by Mohammed Salameh, who reported the truck stolen. When he went back to pick up his rental deposit, on March 4, the FBI arrested him. Ultimately, six terrorist plotters, including Salameh, were tried and convicted. A seventh suspect, Abdul Rahman Yasin, remained at large.

Two days later and 1,600 miles away, agents with the federal Bureau of Alcohol, Tobacco and Firearms tried to raid a ranch run by a sect called the Branch Davidians, led by David Koresh, northeast of Waco. Koresh was suspected of abusing children in the compound and had allegedly taken multiple underage brides. The group was also suspected of stockpiling illegal weapons. A year earlier, a deliveryman accidentally dropped a package and saw that it was filled with grenades. As the agents closed in, a shoot-out ensued, claiming the lives of four agents and six cultists. At that point, the FBI sealed off the ranch, like knights surrounding a medieval castle, and waited. Weeks went by, then a month. When the FBI moved in to end the siege on April 19 with tear gas, a fire broke out somehow. Koresh and about two dozen others shot themselves to death or were shot before the fire engulfed the compound. In the end, eighty Branch Davidians died in the fire or rubble of buildings that collapsed. Only eleven survived, of whom eight were convicted on various charges.

Americans are used to violence in time of war—even now we had troops on the ground in Somalia—but here we had examples of violent extremism, of militant radicalism, on our own soil in time of peace.

Against this troubling backdrop arose one positive sign of the times: Clinton announced that he would lift the ban on gays in the military. I joined the rest of the congressional delegation in applauding this decision. "The present policy is discriminatory and advances no end but to deprive our country of talented and dedicated individuals," I said. But I noted the difference between sexual orientation and conduct. "There is no place in the military for anyone of either gender guilty of sexual harassment, assault or rape." With opposition from General Powell, his Joint Chiefs chairman, and Sam Nunn of Georgia, chairman of the Senate Army Services Committee, the Clinton policy would be watered down into the less-than-ideal "Don't Ask, Don't Tell" approach, but at least it was a step in the right direction.

In another major shift in policy, Clinton was easing tensions with Vietnam, the subject of an eighteen-year trade embargo. Normalizing relations with Vietnam was a political risk for Clinton, who as a college student avoided service in Vietnam. Veterans and POW-MIA groups opposed any liberalization of ties, insisting that Vietnam was still withholding information about Americans missing in action. Orson Swindle, for one, called any such move "a total catastrophe," adding, "It's de facto recognition and it means we'll have lost our leverage to get information about our MIAs."

Clinton was also determined to clean up the savings and loan mess. I had serious doubts about Resolution Trust Corporation, the entity set up to bail out the failed S&Ls across the country. A bill before the Senate authorized up to $34.3 billion for that purpose. I simply wasn't confident that those billions would be spent effectively. Inouye and I split our votes on this issue, which didn't happen often. He joined the majority in approving the measure, 61–35. Inouye and

I were united in opposition to Clinton's deficit-reduction package, which we thought shifted too much of the burden away from businesses and the rich.

On many other issues, I was pleased with the direction of the administration. This was the first time since 1980 that Democrats held both the Congress and the White House, and we were looking to make important progress on energy self-sufficiency, particularly non-fossil-fuel energy and the environment.

While I had very little seniority, I was pleased to be elected chairman of an important subcommittee of the Senate Energy and Natural Resources Committee: mineral resources development and production. And I had persuaded my colleagues to assign any bills relating to Native Hawaiians and Pacific territories to that subcommittee, a double victory.

Meanwhile, a great deal of speculation was circulating around my political agenda—that is, would I run in 1994? Some observers suspected I had made a deal with Waihee when he appointed me to fill Sparky's seat: that I would step down in 1994 so he, Waihee, could run. His second term as governor was to end in 1994 and he could not by law run again. Or maybe, some thought, I had my eye on a Bishop Estate trusteeship. So I decided to put all the guesswork to rest. In May, at the dedication of a new open-cycle ocean thermal energy plant at Keāhole Point, I announced my intention to run for reelection.

I also said I would like to see a new research and education center at that spot "to achieve sustainability of our natural resources in an environmentally acceptable fashion." To me, the prospects of OTEC remained quite exciting. In open-cycle OTEC, the sea water itself is used for heat exchange, rather than an intermediate fluid. Not only did the plant generate electricity, but it brought up cold water that could be used for cooling, and it produced fresh water that could be used for crops and aquaculture. John Craven, the marine scientist who ran for Congress in 1976, jumped right on these possibilities, forming a company called Common Heritage Corporation. Within a year, he would be growing strawberries, eggplants and other specialty crops using cold, clean, nutrient-rich OTEC water.

In early June I attended the dedication of the Keālia Pond National Wildlife Refuge, fronting Māʻalaea Bay, on Maui. The refuge serves as a vital natural habitat for two rare Hawaiian birds, the *aeʻo* or Hawaiian stilt and *ke'oke'o*, the Hawaiian coot. Over the years, the ponds gave nesting, feeding and resting space for nearly 600 coots and more than 1,000 stilts. Today, a 2,200-foot boardwalk and kiosk with self-guided interpretive exhibits let visitors learn about the many native and visiting birds at the wetlands. Also at the dedication was Mayor Linda Lingle, who had replaced Hannibal Tavares in 1991. Although a Republican, Lingle was an up-and-coming political figure in the islands, very thoughtful, dynamic and decisive. ✣

CHAPTER

50

In early July, Clinton went to Tokyo for his first Group of Seven, or G-7, economic summit. There he met with counterparts Prime Minister Kiichi Miyazawa, Francois Mitterand of France, Helmut Kohl of Germany, John Major of Great Britain, Kim Campbell of Canada and Carlo Ciampi of Italy. After Tokyo, he flew to South Korea, and visited the heavily fortified demilitarized zone, only the second president, after Reagan, to do so.

Then the family converged on Hawaiʻi!

They had invited the public to an open-air party at the Hilton Hawaiian Village Hotel. Set for Sunday, July 11, this initially was to have been an indoor event with some 2,000 guests. But at the last minute—Thursday—the White House threw it open to everyone and moved it to Duke Kahanamoku Beach, near the Rainbow Tower. Officially called the Aloha Celebration, it became known simply as the Speech on the Beach. It was a huge production. An advance team of organizers came out from Washington. Workers set up bleachers and a stage. The state Democratic Party, then led by Dennis O'Connor, sent out about 3,500 invitations, which said, "You are invited to an Aloha Celebration honoring the president of the United States in the company of Governor John Waihee and Senator Daniel Inouye, Senator Daniel Akaka, Representative Neil Abercrombie, Representative Patsy Mink. Aloha or Casual Attire. Validated Parking."

At 1 p.m. Sunday, the beach near the stage was cleared for a security sweep and remained closed until 4 p.m., at which time the crowds were let back in. The first thousand—those closest to the stage—had to pass through metal detectors. Millie and I arrived about 4:30 p.m., when the entertainment kicked off: the Makaha Sons of Niʻihau, with the legendary Israel Kamakawiwoʻole; Teresa Bright; Palani Vaughan and Gabe Baltazar's jazz quartet. Our seats were in the sun, but we wouldn't have missed this event for anything.

This capped a full day for the Clintons, who had arrived that morning aboard Air Force One. Chelsea, who had arrived Friday with friends, was waiting for them at Hickam Air Force Base. Clinton visited sailors at Pearl Harbor and paid his respects at the USS *Arizona* Memorial, met for about ninety minutes with Admiral Larson, and then checked in to the Kahala Hilton, where he had a swim with Chelsea. A cute photo of her getting a piggyback ride moved on the Associated Press wire. Leaving the Kahala Hilton, Clinton paused to pose with newlyweds. He arrived at the Hilton Hawaiian Village about 6 p.m.— an hour late—wearing a blue and pink aloha shirt. Hillary joined him on stage in a bright floral dress. The White House put the crowd at 21,000. Hillary gave a short talk, mentioning Hawai'i's health-care system—a model, she said, for the rest of the nation, and the enduring damage on Kaua'i from Hurricane Iniki. Then Bill started speaking about 6:30 p.m., about forty-five minutes before sunset.

He was introduced by Mayor Frank Fasi to much applause.

"Thank you. Thank you very much. Thank you so much. Thank you, Mayor Fasi, Congressman Abercrombie, Congresswoman Mink, Senator Akaka, my longtime and good friend Governor Waihee." Clinton and Waihee had gotten to know each other at meetings of the National Governors Association.

"When I look out here at this wonderful scene tonight, it is almost impossible for me to remember that in the snows of New Hampshire in 1992, when many people thought I had no chance to be elected president, John Waihee left this scene and came to that snow to campaign for me, and I'll never forget it. Thank you very much."

He was a perfect public speaker, really—cadence, tone, message, all right. Riveting, even when you couldn't see his eyes.

"I want to thank all of you for coming out and all the people behind me. I can't turn around and face them or the sound will go off. I am so glad to be home. How's this?"

He showed the people behind him his profile and they laughed and applauded.

"Like that?"

More applause.

"It is wonderful to be home after my first trip overseas as your president. I went to Asia to a meeting of the world's seven great industrial nations. I also went to meet in Japan and Korea and here today in Hawai'i with the people who are in charge of the national security interests of the United States in Asia and the Pacific region. This morning I ended that trip with a visit to the *Arizona* Memorial and a briefing by the commander in chief of our forces in the Pacific and his senior officers.

"As Hillary said, yesterday we were in Korea along the demilitarized zone. And I walked out further than any American president ever had onto the Bridge of No Return, about ten yards from the line separating South and North Korea. And with my binoculars I looked into the other side, and I saw some young North Korean soldiers looking back at me. And I thought to myself, I wish you could walk over this bridge, and I hope it won't be long until you can, until we put down the threat of nuclear war and open up the hand of friendship."

He touched on the topic of international trade.

"I want to tell you what this trip meant for America and what it means for Hawai'i. First of all, we agreed among ourselves, these seven nations, that we would support the reduction in tariffs in the trade of manufacturing goods all across the world on a level that we have not seen in many years. That could mean literally millions of jobs in the global economy, hundreds of thousands of jobs in the American economy where manufacturing is coming back. We are now the high-quality, low-cost producer of many products and services again. Our automobiles are regaining market share here in America and are more attractive than they have been in decades.

"The second thing we did was to agree to invest some money, including some of your money, to keep democracy and a free market going in Russia. Why? Because it's in our interests for them to reduce their nuclear arsenals instead of build them up, because it's in our interests for all those people over there to become customers for United States products and travelers to Hawai'i someday.

"And finally, in what could prove to be an historic breakthrough, we agreed on a framework to change the terms of trade between the United States and Japan. The Japanese made a good-faith commitment to bring down the enormous trade surplus between the United States and Japan and to help work with us to sell more products and more services and to equalize the imbalance in the global economy. They have been saying to us for ten years, 'You've got to bring your budget deficit down.' I went to Japan and I said, 'OK, we did that. Now bring your trade surplus down.' And they said yes. They said yes."

He noted that no state was closer to Japan than Hawai'i.

"Finally, since presidents don't often come to Hawai'i, let me make a couple of remarks about this wonderful state. Let me say first, thanks for the support you gave to me and to the vice president in the last election. Thank you for setting a model for health care and in many other areas. And let me say that I have been benefited enormously by the work that your congressional representatives have done in informing me about issues of concern to Hawai'i.

"Number one, my wife, as she said, is going to Kaua'i to view the hurricane damage in a couple of days. Just a few days ago, I signed a bill to provide $40 million in extra assistance to the victims of the hurricane in Hawai'i. And I have instructed the secretary of the Department of Housing and Urban Development to devote an enormous amount of his time to work to repair the damage here. And he will be doing that as well as taking some of the money that they have to rebuild some of the houses on that troubled island. So we hope we can be good partners with you in rebuilding Hawai'i.

"The next thing I would like to say is that, as Governor Waihee said, this is the 100th anniversary of the overthrow of the Hawaiian monarchy. Your governor has talked to me for months and months, going way back last year, about issues of concern to Native Hawaiians. And I pledge to you that I will work with him, with Senator Inouye, with Senator Akaka, with Congressman Abercrombie and Congresswoman Mink to address these concerns in a positive way. We will not forget them.

"Finally, let me say that, as Hillary said, we have learned a lot from Hawai'i's health-care system, but you should know that your governor has asked us to give him permission to do some more things to fully cover all Hawaiians and to manage this system better.

"And so I want to close with this thought: We will never bring the government's budget deficit down to zero, we will never restore full health to the American economy until we find a way to provide basic health security to all American families and bring the cost of health care in line with inflation. It is the single biggest long-term drag on our budget deficit and our economic performance. And I pledge to you, building on the example of Hawai'i, preserving the right of people to choose their doctor and to keep the medical system that works so well, we will find a solution to this problem, and we will begin soon. We must do it to bring the American people together and restore the economic health of America."

At this point, members of Ka Lāhui Hawai'i, a sovereignty group, interrupted his speech by shouting, "Justice for Hawai'i! Justice for Hawai'i! Justice for Hawai'i!"

Clinton replied calmly. "I hope we can provide it. Thank you for being here in such numbers. We want to get out and visit with you. This is probably the longest political speech any of you ever listened to on a vacation in your lives.

"So to close, I'll give you a laugh. I told my mother about this trip, and I said, 'You know, Mother, when we come back we pick up nineteen hours, and I'll have two whole Sundays.' And she said over the phone, 'Son, you need it.'"

That brought peals of laughter from the crowd.

"Thank you all, and God bless you. I'm glad to see you."

That was Clinton's last formal appearance of his visit, but he did manage to get in several rounds of golf before leaving Wednesday. On Monday, I joined him at Hickam's Mamala Bay Golf Course, a fine course next to the ocean across from the Honolulu airport reef runway. The president's foursome included Cayetano, Admiral Larson and General Skip Rutherford, commander of Pacific Air Forces. My group included Waihee, and, if I recall correctly, Admiral Bob Kelly, commander of the Pacific Fleet, and the three-star general from Fort Shafter. Clinton at his best is a very good golfer, but not always consistent. Cayetano remarked on his "pretty strong language whenever he muffed a shot." In the afternoon, Clinton played another eighteen holes with Waihee and Ariyoshi at the Waialae Country Club.

He also got in some snorkeling at Hanauma Bay before heading back to the Mainland and a tour of flood-ravaged Des Moines, Iowa, and to Washington, where Congress was in full-throated debate on his $500-billion deficit-reduction plan. Hillary and Chelsea stayed on for some time on the Neighbor Islands.

In all, Clinton would visit Hawai'i seven times while in office, more than any other president until Obama. ❖

CHAPTER

51

In my view, the nation owes no greater debt than to the men and women who served in uniform. Yet all too often our veterans leave service without an adequate support system in place. That is why I was proud to be one of eleven cosponsors of the Veterans' Compensation Rates Amendments of 1993, a bill introduced by Senator Jay Rockefeller of West Virginia. This measure increased, as of December 1, the rates of veterans' disability compensation, additional compensation for dependents, the clothing allowance for certain disabled adult veterans, compensation for surviving spouses and children and supplemental compensation for disabled adult children. The Senate passed the bill by voice vote in July and it breezed through the House. Clinton signed it into law, appropriately, on Veterans Day.

Another measure that Clinton signed around that time was the California Desert Protection Act, introduced by Dianne Feinstein. This established Death Valley National Park and Joshua Tree National Park, both of them jewels in the Southern California interior. This had wide support, with forty-nine cosponsors, myself included.

Another worthy bill, in my estimation, would have created a Department of Environmental Protection, essentially elevating the EPA to cabinet-level department, much as we had done with the Department of Veterans Affairs in 1988–89. Sponsored by John Glenn of Ohio, this measure had twenty-five cosponsors, including myself and two Republicans, Bill Cohen of Maine and Jim Jeffords of Vermont. One of the goals was to increase cooperation with other countries in environmental programs, working with the Department of State to participate in international agreements and organizations, conduct research on and develop responses to international environmental problems and provide assistance to foreign countries and international bodies to improve the environment. This passed the Senate overwhelmingly, 79–15, with only one Democrat voting no—Bob Kerrey of Nebraska. But it never found any traction in the House.

Perhaps the most sweeping measure approved by the 103rd Congress was the $30-billion Violent Crime Control and Law Enforcement Act. Amid a crack cocaine epidemic and rising violent crime, this legislation provided federal grants to states, local governments, Indian tribes and other public and private entities to put more police on the streets and to expand and improve cooperation between law enforcement agencies and local communities. It also budgeted billions for regional high-security prisons, as well as boot camps for young offenders and other programs to free up more prison space for hard-core violent criminals. It also made mandatory a life sentence for three-time violent felons, and greatly expanded the eligibility for the death penalty to include sixty offenses. This was introduced in the House in October 1993 by Jack Brooks of Texas, chairman of the House Judiciary Committee. Brooks quickly got the bill to the House floor, where it passed by voice vote in early November. In the Senate, where it had the robust support of judiciary chairman Joe Biden, the bill also moved fast, passing 95–4, but with some changes.

The Senate version, for instance, called for $8.9 billion over five years to put 100,000 new police officers on the streets. The House version calls for $3.45 billion for 50,000 officers. The Senate version banned the manufacture, sale and possession of nineteen types of semi-automatic assault weapons and clips holding more than ten rounds. Hunting rifles were exempt. The House version had no language on assault weapons. These and other differences were hammered out in conference committee over the summer of 1994.

Finally, on August 21, in a rare Sunday session the House vote on the conference report, Congressman Ronald Machtley, a Rhode Island Republican, declared grandly: "Mr. Speaker, six days shall we labor and do all of our work, but on the seventh day let us do the work of the people in this country. Let us on this day gladly work together to pass a crime bill." It passed 235–195, with Mink and Abercrombie with the majority. Four days later, the Senate approved it, 61–38, with the ban on military assault weapons in civilian hands intact.

Clinton signed it on September 13 in a ceremony attended by big-city mayors, police chiefs, lawmakers and relatives of crime victims.

"Today the bickering stops," Clinton said. "The era of excuses is over; the law-abiding citizens of our country have made their voices heard. Never again should Washington put politics and party above law and order."

But decades later Clinton reversed himself on the law, saying it led to an "era of mass incarceration."

"I signed a bill that made the problem worse," he said in July 2015, as his wife was beginning her second presidential campaign. "I admit it."

There is no better example of how thinking on an issue can change over time.

In March 1994, I called a hearing of the Government Affairs Committee on what I felt was a dire threat to Hawai'i: invasive species. On average, eighteen new pests arrived each year in Hawai'i, some more potentially destructive than others but all of them unwelcome.

"With so many statutes and so many agencies, federal alien species policy resembles swiss cheese," I said at the hearing. "And alien pests continue to stream through the holes in policy and enforcement."

B. Glen Lee, administrator of the Animal and Plant Health Inspection Service, one of the agencies charged with controlling alien invaders, admitted to the problem. He said he agreed with a new report from the congressional Office of Technology Assessment that concludes that "a dynamic national agenda is needed to effectively address non-indigenous species in the United States."

As the midterm elections approached, there was a growing sense that the Republicans were poised to do well. Few sensed how well.

In Hawai'i, I was up for election, with no opposition from within my party. I had a half dozen challengers on the GOP side, notably Maria Hustace, and one Libertarian, Richard Rowland. There had been intense speculation that Orson Swindle would run as a Republican; he was the favorite of state GOP chairman Jared Jossem. But in May Swindle, a five-year Hawai'i resident, said he would not throw his hat in the ring after all.

"I've done a lot of talking to an awful lot of people in Hawai'i, people of all backgrounds, people of both parties," he told the *Star-Bulletin*. "Without exception, they said I ought to run. But unfortunately, not a single one thinks I can win." Ultimately, he would opt to take on Abercrombie.

In the state races, Cayetano was running for governor, as was Waihee's director of health, Dr. Jack Lewin, another Democrat. On the Republican side, Saiki had decided to take a shot. And Fasi had created his own party, the Best Party, as his springboard for yet another run, hoping to fare better in the general than with in-party opposition in the primary. It was very amusing, then, that he quickly attracted challengers within the Best Party, including John Craven, the marine scientist and 1976 congressional candidate, and gay pride activist Bill Woods. As his running mate, Fasi named famed entertainer Danny Kaleikini.

Two Democrats were interested in the lieutenant governor's job, Senator Mazie Hirono and Representative Jackie Young, as were four Republicans, including Fred Hemmings, Stan Koki and Ike Sutton.

✽ ✽ ✽

One of the things that Hawai'i does right is health insurance. Anyone who works twenty or more hours per week gets medical coverage through their employer, so pretty much everyone is covered. This had been in place since 1974. Clinton was looking to set up something similar at the federal level. So on August 10, 1994, Waihee gave a briefing at the White House with Erskine Bowles, who had followed Saiki as head of the Small Business Administration. Waihee was introduced by Clinton's press secretary, Dee Dee Myers.

"Thank you, Dee Dee. It's been a pleasure this morning to be able to spend some time with the meeting here in Washington and with the president talking about the Hawai'i health-care system. You know, in Hawai'i we're doing what the president hopes to achieve nationally. We have a system designed to provide 100 percent universal health-care coverage, and we are covering approximately ninety-six to ninety-eight percent of our people. He described the Hawai'i system as a "twenty-year demonstration project" showing the efficacy of a mandate for employers.

"This demonstration project has proven that it is possible to have quality health care at lower costs while minimizing cost shifting and keeping a healthy business climate," he said. "First, universal coverage and a focus on primary and preventive care means Hawai'i residents get earlier medical treatment. And, as a result, we can demonstrate some very outstanding health statistics. We have the same instances of cancer, heart disease and diabetes as the rest of the nation, for instance, but among the lowest morbidity rates in the nation for these same conditions. We have higher rates for tuberculosis and smoking, but the morbidity rate that is one-half the national average.

"And, second, lower costs. Universal coverage and primary care means less hospital and emergency utilization. Indeed, those rank about one-third of the national average."

Since the coverage is universal, the cost of coverage puts no business at a disadvantage, he added. But apparently the system was being portrayed nationally as bad for small businesses.

"Now, I am here, though, to say that we are extremely aggravated by the misinformation and the like that is being spread about the Hawai'i system, the mischaracterization of the Hawai'i employer mandate, and we would like very much to clear that up."

Bowles picked it up from there.

"As I have traveled throughout the country from state to state, I have looked for states that would serve as a good model to go forward. And, clearly, since 1974, Hawai'i has had real health-care reform; they have been in the forefront of this effort. And, don't forget, ninety-four percent of the businesses in Hawai'i are small. And of that, eighty-two percent of those small businesses—eighty-two percent—are satisfied with the way the employer mandate works in Hawai'i."

Bowles took issue with a recent report from a small business group.

"Here it says that, 'It is significant that Hawai'i led the nation in job loss in 1993. In 1992 the number of business failures in that state increased by 290 percent.' Now, one of the facts they leave out was that in 1992 they had something called a hurricane, Hurricane Iniki. That devastated the small business populace in Hawai'i in 1992 and carried forward into 1993. But still with Hurricane Iniki, the business failure rate in Hawai'i was below the national average, and the trend in it has been less than half the national average each and every year."

Despite such overtures, the Clinton administration never managed to put a universal coverage plan into place.

* * *

On Thursday, September 15, two days before the primary election in Hawai'i, Clinton went on national, prime-time television to call for U.S. military intervention in the Caribbean island of Haiti. In 1990, the Haitians elected as president Jean-Bertrand Aristide, a Catholic priest who received almost seventy percent of the vote. But eight months later he was overthrown in a coup by a general named Raoul Cedras. The country was now in control of a military junta.

"Resistors were beaten and murdered," Clinton said. "The dictators launched a horrible intimidation campaign of rape, torture and mutilation. People starved; children died; thousands of Haitians fled their country, heading to the United States across dangerous seas. At that time, President Bush declared the situation posed, and I quote, 'an unusual and extraordinary threat to the national security, foreign policy and economy of the United States.' Cedras and his armed thugs have conducted a reign of terror, executing children, raping women, killing priests. As the dictators have grown more desperate, the atrocities have grown ever more brutal."

Clinton said he had ordered Defense secretary William Perry to ready the troops. He had also ordered two aircraft carriers, the USS *Eisenhower* and USS *America*, into the Caribbean.

"I issued these orders after giving full consideration to what is at stake," the president said. "The message of the United States to the Haitian dictators is clear: 'Your time is up. Leave now, or we will force you from power.'"

I was willing to give Clinton the benefit of the doubt, assuming he had reviewed all the options available before making his decision. Inouye had met privately with Perry on the matter and was keeping mum. Mink and Abercrombie were among 140 House members who wrote to Clinton, saying he should get congressional authorization before waging war.

But Clinton wasn't waiting. On Monday, as U.S. forces prepared to invade as part of Operation Uphold Democracy—and with elements of the 82nd Airborne Division already in the air—Jimmy Carter pulled off a diplomatic coup. Along with Colin Powell, former chairman of the Joint Chiefs, and fellow Georgian Sam Nunn, Carter had made a direct appeal to Cedras to step down. The negotiations lasted about two weeks and ended only after they showed Cedras video of paratroopers boarding planes at Fort Bragg. With Cedras' capitulation, the intervention became a peacekeeping and nation-building mission that led to the return of Aristide as president.

Whereas he had gone down in rather lopsided loss in 1980, Carter was turning out to be one of the best ex-presidents our nation has ever had. ✤

CHAPTER

52

The Hawai'i primary produced no surprises. Fasi won the right to represent the Best Party in the governor's race, and with Kaleikini would face Cayetano-Hirono and Saiki-Hemmings in the general. Orson Swindle won the Republican race for the First Congressional District and would face Abercrombie in November. Into the fall, Swindle was raising money on par with Abercrombie, which must have worried Neil. Mink also had GOP opposition but her seat seemed safe. In the Senate race, Hustace defeated five opponents to win the Republican nomination with 28.5 percent of the vote. That put her second only to blank votes at thirty percent. On the Democrat side, I drew nearly eighty percent of the vote, but the blank votes still numbered a staggering 43,393. I never knew how to interpret blank votes—as a vote against me or merely a muted cry for more choices.

A few days before the general election, I was saddened, along with the rest of America, to hear that Ronald Reagan, at age eighty-three, had a diagnosis of eventual dementia.

"My fellow Americans," he wrote in a letter to the public on November 5, "I have recently been told that I am one of the millions of Americans who will be afflicted with Alzheimer's disease... At the moment, I feel just fine. I intend to live the remainder of the years God gives me on this earth doing the things I have always done. I will continue to share life's journey with my beloved Nancy and my family. I plan to enjoy the great outdoors and stay in touch with my friends and supporters. Unfortunately, as Alzheimer's disease progresses, the family often bears a heavy burden. I only wish there was some way I could spare Nancy from this painful experience. When the time comes, I am confident that with your help she will face it with faith and courage.

"In closing, let me thank you, the American people, for giving me the great honor of allowing me to serve as your president. When the Lord calls me home, whenever that may be, I will leave the greatest love for this country of ours and eternal optimism for its future. I now begin the journey that will lead me into the sunset of my life. I know that for America there will always be a bright dawn ahead. Thank you, my friends."

Reagan and I hadn't always seen eye to eye, but I always had great admiration for him and my heart went out to him and to Nancy, whom, as he said, would bear the burden.

Since Hawai'i was six hours behind the East Coast and three behind the West Coast, it became clear by early afternoon on Election Day—even before our polls closed—that it would be a Republican rout. Before the night was through, the GOP gained eight Senate seats and fifty-four House seats, winning a majority in both chambers for the first time since 1954. That was a pivotal year in Hawai'i history, too.

In Arizona, Democrat DeConcini retired as a result of the Keating Five scandal, and Republican Jon Kyl picked up the seat. In Maine, with the retirement of majority leader George Mitchell, Republican Olympia Snowe dominated the landscape. Republicans also won the seat of retiring Democrat Howard Metzenbaum of Ohio, and defeated incumbent Jim Sasser in Tennessee. Also in Tennessee, actor Fred Thompson (*Law & Order, The Hunt for Red October*) easily beat his Democratic opponent to fill a vacant seat. The litany went on. Even powerhouse Kennedy had a fight against businessman Mitt Romney in Massachusetts. And it was likely only thanks to a three-way race that Chuck Robb of Virginia (the son-in-law of Lyndon Johnson) held off conservative gadfly Oliver North (of Iran-Contra notoriety). The new majority leader would be Bob Dole.

In the House, thirty-four incumbent Democrats lost, including Speaker Tom Foley, a thirty-year incumbent; Jack Brooks of Texas, a forty-two-year incumbent and the judiciary chairman; and Dan Rostenkowski, a thirty-six-year incumbent and Ways and Means chairman. The new Speaker would be none other than Newt Gingrich, my old cofounder on the House Space Caucus.

In Hawai'i, Cayetano won 135,000 votes, or thirty-six percent, to claim the governorship. Fasi came in second at thirty percent and Saiki third at twenty-nine percent. Abercrombie held off Swindle, 51–41 percent. Mink won sixty-five percent of the vote. And I polled at sixty-eight percent to win my first full term. So Hawai'i bucked the national trend.

But I knew the new majorities would make it more difficult to push my legislative agenda, including promotion of aquaculture and making sure oil-dependent Hawai'i had access to the national strategic petroleum reserve. I also wanted the return of—or compensation for—30,000 acres of Hawaiian homelands that the federal government had acquired during the territorial years. That included 1,356 acres at Lualualei used for munitions storage and radio antennas.

On November 16, returning from Indonesia and the Philippines, the Clintons arrived back in Hawai'i for a three-day vacation at the Marine base in Kāne'ohe. I was at Hickam when the plane pulled up, and Clinton addressed the crowd, which included kids waving little flags and music by the Fleet Marine Force Band. Also on hand were Waihee and his wife, Lynne; Cayetano in his capacity as governor-elect; Hirono, the lieutenant governor-elect; Harris; Commerce secretary Ron Brown and the military brass. We took seats behind Clinton on the podium. A couple of hundred men and women in uniform also awaited the commander in chief's words.

"To all of you here and all of your counterparts around the world, I say the world knows that the skills of our fighting men and women have never been higher," Clinton said. "Your capacity to carry out our missions has never been greater. Your commitment to liberty has never been stronger. The world is more peaceful and secure because of you. And the most important thing I came here to say tonight is thank you.

"You know, the world is changing profoundly. There are still threats out there, and they are significant, threats of proliferation of weapons of mass destruction, threats of terrorism, the growing international drug trade and the rise of international organized crime in the wake of communism's fall.

"But if you really look around the world, you'd have to say that security, peace and freedom are on the march, that all these children here today holding their American flags will in all probability grow up in a world where they will have less fear than their parents and their grandparents faced because of you.

"If you look at what's happened from the Persian Gulf and the Middle East to North Africa and Northern Ireland and South Africa to Haiti, if you look at the fact that with North Korea we just concluded an agreement to make certain that that nation becomes a nonnuclear nation, not selling nuclear materials to others, if you look at the agreement we reached with China to stop the proliferation of missiles, and if you look at the fact that in Russia for the first time since nuclear weapons came on the face of the earth, there are no Russian missiles pointed at American children, you'd have to say we're on the move."

Of course, the pact with North Korea didn't take. They were to test nuclear weapons within a decade.

"The world of America at home is changing, too, in ways that are both good and troubling," Clinton went on. "We've had problems in our system that are profound: sixty percent of American wage earners are earning the same or less today that they were earning fifteen years ago when you adjust for inflation. We know that this has been especially hard on working men with limited educations. We know that our country still has rates of crime, violence, and family and community breakdown that are too high and unacceptable. We know that a lot of people have a deep sense that our government—except for you, in which they have confidence—only works for organized special interests and is too often unable to protect the interests or the values of the ordinary Americans. The deep concern and frustration of our people about these conditions led to the changes they voted for in both 1992 and in 1994."

But the recent elections were a call for cooperation, not gridlock, he said.

"If you look at what makes a strong country, it's a lot of what makes a strong military: strong families, good schools, safe streets, good-paying jobs, the kind of things that allows people to live up to the fullest of their God-given potential. We've made a beginning on that, and we've got to keep going. We've got more jobs, a smaller deficit, a smaller national government doing more for the American people than we had two years ago, thanks to Senator Akaka and Senator Inouye, Congressman Abercrombie and Congresswoman Mink, and a lot of other people who helped."

✻ ✻ ✻

Before the 104th Congress convened, I had to say goodbye to an old friend. Bob Ogawa, a Maui boy, had been with me for eighteen years. He and his wife, Sharon, were heading back to Hawai'i to help raise their eleven-year-old granddaughter. For two years when I was in the House, he was my legislative director. Then he went back to Hawai'i to run my district office. When I was elected to the Senate in 1990, he came back with me as director of communications, a catch-all position that included speech writing. But he was a valued adviser as well, someone I trusted implicitly with the media, with constituents and my colleagues on the Hill. He was very much at home with the political climates in Hawai'i and in Washington. Esther Kia'aina, my legislative director, once described Bob as "walking institutional memory." She explained: "He was sort of like a bridge—a bridge between the ages, between the senator's days now and his days in the House, between the different elements of the office." He was the glue.

I would very dearly miss his good counsel and our camaraderie. ✻

CHAPTER

53

With GOP lawmakers in charge, these were lean times for a liberal agenda. Under their "Contract with America," signed on the steps of the Capitol September 27, the Republicans outlined legislation they wanted passed by the House within the first 100 days of the new session. These included tax cuts, tax relief for the middle class, line-item veto power for the president, measures to reduce crime and constitutional amendments mandating term limits and a balanced budget. All of it passed except term limits.

One of the last official acts of President Bush had been to sign the North American Free Trade Agreement. On the strength of that pact, which went into effect in January 1994, investors gained more confidence in the Mexican economy. But violence in the state of Chiapas and the assassination of a high-profile presidential candidate undermined that confidence, and investors once again grew cautious. To keep the foreign money flowing, the Mexican government propped up the peso, linking it to the dollar. Under increasing pressure, nuts, bolts and screws in other parts of the Mexican economy started popping, and in December 1994 the government was forced to devalue the peso. By then it was too late; the country faced ruin. Inflation soared.

So, in January 1995, Clinton met with Treasury secretary Robert Rubin, Undersecretary Larry Summers and fed chairman Alan Greenspan to discuss options.

Summers at one point tossed out a bailout figure of $25 billion.
"Larry, you mean $25 million," one of Clinton's aides said.
"No, I mean $25 billion."
That brought stunned silence.
One of Clinton's other aides offered: "Mr. President, if you send

that money to Mexico and it doesn't come back before 1996, you won't be coming back after 1996." This was Summers's recollection, anyway.

In the end, Clinton and his advisers came up with a $20 billion plan, which proved to be one of the most contentious issues before Congress that year. One of the biggest critics: an independent congressman from Vermont, Bernie Sanders.

At one point on the House floor he railed, "At a time when members of Congress are proposing cutbacks in school lunch programs, in breakfast programs, in programs that (help) the most vulnerable people in our society—because the claim is we don't have enough money to provide these programs, it seems to me to be absolutely irresponsible to put one penny at risk in attempting to bail out the unstable Mexican economy." I wholeheartedly agreed.

As if the World Trade Center bombing two years earlier weren't bad enough, America suffered its first massive case of home-grown terrorism with the bombing of the federal building in Oklahoma City on April 19. In all, 168 people died and 680 others were injured when a huge bomb went off in a Ryder truck in front of the Alfred P. Murrah Building. Damage extended sixteen blocks in every direction. Detective work narrowed the suspects to two militants, Timothy McVeigh and Terry Nichols, who had acted in retaliation for the Waco siege, and an earlier incident at Ruby Ridge, Idaho. In fact, the Oklahoma blast came on the second anniversary of the deadly Waco fire. Both men were convicted in 1997. Nichols got a life term. McVeigh died by lethal injection in June 2001.

In the wake of the bombing, Clinton ordered the Department of Justice to assess the vulnerability of all federal buildings, including the already-fortress-like Prince Jonah Kūhiō Kalanianaole Federal Building in Honolulu. The result: security at those buildings was never again the same.

The Clintons arrived back in Honolulu on August 31, 1995, for ceremonies marking the fiftieth anniversary of V-J Day. The president made some brief remarks at Hickam Air Force Base after stepping off Air Force One. I was there to greet him, along with Inouye; Cayetano; Abercrombie; Mayor Harris; Admiral Richard Macke, commander of U.S. Pacific forces; and General John Lorber, commander of Pacific Air Forces. Clinton hailed the "bravery" and "professionalism" of our troops who were with the U.N. contingent fighting Bosnian Serbs in Sarajevo. And he praised the service members who helped the nation prevail in World War II.

"Here on this island of peace that knows all too well the horror of war, let us vow to carry forward their legacy. The World War II generation taught us that when the American people find strength in their diversity and unity in a common purpose, when we stop arguing about our differences and start embracing what we have in common, nothing, nothing, can stop us. And so I say to you, if we apply the lessons that the World War II generation handed down to us to the challenges of the twenty-first century, nothing will stop us. Thank you, and God bless you, and God bless America."

On September 2, a warm, rainy Saturday with light trades, in Pearl Harbor on the flight deck the aircraft carrier USS *Carl Vinson*, Clinton laid a wreath to mark the anniversary of the Japanese surrender.

"Fifty years ago today, on the other side of this Pacific Ocean, the war ended," he said. "It was a war that erupted in smoke and horror aboard the battleship *Arizona* and concluded with peace and honor aboard the battleship *Missouri*. Today we gather to offer a commemoration and to renew a commitment. We commemorate the men and women of the Navy, the Marine Corps, and their sister services who gave everything they had to the cause of freedom. And we commit ourselves to their legacy by meeting the great demands of this age with the same determination and fortitude."

Afterwards, he unveiled a set of commemorative postage stamps, the fifth and final set honoring the men and women who fought in World War II. Helping him were two veterans, Herbert Carter of the Tuskegee Airmen, and Rita Howard of the Navy Nurse Corps.

It was good to be among my fellow World War II vets. But it was hard to believe half a century had passed since the war. I recalled coming home from the Marianas on a bumpy landing craft, passing Hospital Point, which I could see here from the flight deck. As the current conflict in Bosnia and Kosovo showed, as had the Kuwait conflict and Vietnam, war was different now, smaller in scale, if just as intense and ugly. Today's threats were increasingly "nonlinear," meaning terrorism and guerrilla strikes, the opposite of the Civil War cavalry charge or the trench warfare of World War I. The key phrase these days—since Somalia, really—was "exit strategy." Critics of the war in Bosnia claimed Clinton had no clearly defined goal that, once achieved, could allow for withdrawal. Of course, Clinton didn't start Bosnia-Kosovo. That was Bush. But people forget, or don't care. Having no exit strategy would be a charge leveled at the next two presidents as well. ✣

CHAPTER

54

As House Speaker, Gingrich was all about saving money. I guess that was an offshoot of the Republicans' Contract with America, which called for fiscal responsibility and an independent audit of Congress for fraud, waste and abuse of taxpayers' dollars. One of the things he did to save money was lay off the Members' Dining Room staff and replace them with an outside contractor. This nearly broke my heart. Some of those dining room staffers had been there for decades. They had known Sam Rayburn and John McCormack—or their fathers had. For some families, these were legacy jobs, handed down from one generation to the next. They worked with tremendous pride. I knew them all by name.

The contractor came in—all business, no sense of tradition—and eventually up went the contract price until we weren't seeing any savings at all. I didn't need an auditor to tell me that was truly a waste.

It was one of Gingrich's fellow Republicans from Georgia, Bob Barr, who came up with the Defense of Marriage Act. This was in response to a case in Hawai'i, *Baehr v. Miike*, a lawsuit by same-sex couples who wanted to get married. In 1993, the Hawai'i Supreme Court ruled that the state had to show a compelling interest to prohibit same-sex marriages. That raised fears nationwide that Hawai'i would ultimately allow such marriages, which would have to be recognized by other states. Introduced on May 7, 1996, Barr's measure defined marriage as "a legal union between one man and one woman" and the word spouse as "a person of the opposite sex who is a husband or a wife." The bill also said that no state, territory, U.S. possession or Indian tribe had to recognize a same-sex marriage performed elsewhere.

The bill attracted 117 cosponsors, including thirteen Democrats. Ten of the Democrats were from the South or border states: Sonny Montgomery, Mike Parker and Gene Taylor of Mississippi, James Hayes of Louisiana, Charlie Stenholm and Pete Geren of Texas, Pat Danner, Harold Volkmer and Ike Skelton of Missouri, and Nick Rahall of West Virginia. Alcee Hastings, whose district included Miami Beach, had been a cosponsor but withdrew within a week.

The House Judiciary Committee passed it on July 9, after hearings before the Subcommittee on the Constitution. Barney Frank of Massachusetts, who is openly gay, tried twice to amend the bill, once to shoot down the definition of marriage. That failed after seventy-five minutes of intense debate. Then he tried to amend it to say a state's definition of marriage supersedes the federal definition if they differ. That failed, 103–311. The House passed the bill on July 12 by a vote of 342–67, with Abercrombie and Mink—and Hastings—voting no.

The bill moved to the Senate, where it passed on September 10 by a vote of 85–14. Joining me among the "no" votes were Inouye, Russ Feingold of Wisconsin, Barbara Boxer and Dianne Feinstein of California, Kennedy, Bob Kerrey, John Kerry, Carol Moseley-Braun and Paul Simon of Illinois, Daniel Patrick Moynihan of New York, Claiborne Pell of Rhode Island, Chuck Robb of Virginia and Ron Wyden of Oregon. Not a Republican among us.

Then the measure moved to the White House.

Now, Clinton was the first president to openly campaign for support among the gay community. He had gay friends and advisers. He appointed James Hormel, the openly gay heir to the Spam empire, as an envoy to the U.N. Human Rights Commission (and later ambassador to Luxembourg). He supported AIDS research. He also had tried to get the military to allow gays to serve openly before settling on "Don't Ask, Don't Tell." He didn't want to sign the bill, but felt trapped by the Republicans just weeks before the election. To veto it, he knew, would bring a firestorm down on his head and Congress would override it anyway. So, just before 1 a.m. on Saturday, September 21, with no cameras recording the event, he signed the bill, releasing this statement in the morning: "Throughout my life I have strenuously opposed discrimination of any kind, including discrimination against gay and lesbian Americans. I am signing into law H.R. 3396, a bill relating to same-gender marriage, but it is important to note what this legislation does and does not do. I have long opposed governmental recognition of same-gender marriages and this legislation is consistent with that position. The act confirms the right of each state to determine its own policy with respect to same-gender marriage and clarifies for purposes of federal law the operative meaning of the terms 'marriage' and 'spouse.'"

Many in the gay community felt betrayed. And seventeen years later, in 2013, as the U.S. Supreme Court was about to take up the issue of gay marriage, Clinton would express regret for his action. But the mood of the country was very different in 1996.

Clinton did add one warning: "I also want to make clear to all that the enactment of this legislation should not, despite the fierce and at times divisive rhetoric surrounding it, be understood to provide an excuse for discrimination, violence or intimidation against any person on the basis of sexual orientation. Discrimination, violence and intimidation for that reason, as well as others, violate the principle of equal protection under the law and have no place in American society."

The Defense of Marriage Act, or DOMA, wasn't the whole picture back then. On September 5, Kennedy had introduced the Employment Non-Discrimination Act, aimed at extending discrimination protections to gays and lesbians in the workplace. It exempted the military and religious organizations, except for their for-profit activities. The bill attracted three cosponsors; Joe Lieberman of Connecticut, Republican Jim Jeffords of Vermont and Democrat Richard Bryan of Nevada. Five days later, it failed by one vote, 49–50. Inouye and I voted in favor, of course. So did seven Republicans: Lincoln Chafee of Rhode Island, Bill Cohen and Olympia Snowe of Maine, Al D'Amato of New York, Mark Hatfield of Oregon, Alan Simpson of Wyoming and Arlen Specter of Pennsylvania. Five Democrats voted no: Byrd of West Virginia, Jim Exon of Nebraska, Wendell Ford of Kentucky and Sam Nunn of Georgia. David Pryor of Arkansas abstained.

No vote better illustrates how divided the country was on the issue of gay rights in those days.

Better news for the country came in the form of the Small Business Job Protection Act of 1996, which simplified the 401(k) retirement plan so small businesses could take better advantage of it. It also increased the minimum wage from $4.25 per hour to $4.75, then to $5.15 on September 1, 1997. It also set up important tax credits.

Introduced in May 1996 by Republican Bill Archer of Texas, the measure quickly cleared the House Ways and Means Committee and was approved by the House by a vote of 414–10, with Abercrombie and Mink in the majority. With my vote and Inouye's, it passed the Senate 74–24 with amendments, then went to conference committee for a month. Kennedy, Kassebaum and Jeffords crafted a sensible compromise that the House and Senate overwhelmingly approved. Clinton signed it in August 1996.

My only successful legislation was a bill that called for more research into seafloor minerals. The ocean makes up seventy percent of the Earth's surface, yet we know so little about the resources there, other than fish. As we overfished the oceans—prompting my interest in aquaculture—we were underutilizing seabed minerals such as manganese, phosphates, cobalt, metal sulfides, even sand and gravel. That was the motivation behind my Marine Mineral Resources Research Act of 1996. Republican Trent Lott signed on as cosponsor; that helped in the GOP-led Senate. Mississippi, of course, has a coastline on the Gulf of Mexico.

The bill directed the secretary of the Interior to set up a research program, award R&D grants and contracts to private industry, state governments and academia; and designate three hubs for this research, one near the Eastern Seaboard continental shelf, a second in Arctic waters and a third in the near-shore environment of islands. The measure was referred to the Committee on Energy and Natural Resources, now led by Frank Murkowski of Alaska, who approved it in June 1996. The House gave its approval in September 1996 and the president signed it in October. But this turned out to be largely a paper victory. Decades later, due to insufficient funding, marine minerals research—much less actual ocean mining—remains nowhere near where it should be. But an important organization, the International Marine Minerals Society, founded in 1987, maintains administrative officers at the University of Hawai'i at Mānoa and sponsors an Underwater Mining Conference somewhere around the world once a year.

* * *

That summer the United States hosted the Olympics in Atlanta. This was the 100th anniversary of the first modern Olympic Games, held in Athens in 1896. Amazingly, Atlanta beat out Athens for the centennial. The games began with boxing legend Muhammad Ali lighting the torch. Sadly, terrorism struck once again, by way of a bomb at the Centennial Olympic Park, which killed two and wounded 111 others. To many Americans, such tragedies were becoming all too commonplace.

* * *

Over that same summer, a Native Hawaiian plebiscite took place on the issue of sovereignty. Ballots were sent out to 80,000 eligible Hawaiians and 30,000 were returned by the August 15 deadline. The simple question: "Shall the Hawaiian people elect delegates to propose a Native Hawaiian government?" By a three-to-one margin, the respondents said yes. The results, released in mid-September, meant that groups that favor sovereignty could proceed with plans for a constitutional convention, possibly in 1998, to decide what a Native Hawaiian government would look like. Tara McKenzie, executive director of the Hawaiian Sovereignty Election Council, which the state had created to organize the balloting, called it "the dawn of a new age." But not everyone was happy. The Hawaiian rights group Ka Lāhui Hawai'i said the low turnout showed that Hawaiians had largely boycotted the vote. And attorney John Goemans objected for other reasons and had gone to federal court to try to stop the process.

The question of sovereignty would remain contentious well into the next century. ❖

CHAPTER

55

With Clinton viewed as vulnerable, the Republicans thought they had a pretty good shot at the White House with Bob Dole, the Senate majority leader. Like Inouye, Dole had fought in World War II and had been wounded in the right arm. But while Inouye was missing his hand, Dole's was intact but disabled. To keep people from trying to shake his hand, he kept a pen in it. Dole's wife, Elizabeth or "Liddy," a very capable and charming Southern Belle from North Carolina, ran the American Red Cross. A Harvard law graduate, she had been transportation secretary under Reagan and labor secretary under Bush. She was a real asset to the campaign. Eventually, with the retirement of Jesse Helms, she would win election to the Senate herself.

As his running mate, Dole had tapped Jack Kemp, a former nine-term congressman from western New York. He had been secretary of housing and urban development under Bush. He was a big supporter of so-called supply-side economics, a philosophy he shared with Reagan, and in 1981 was the sponsor of the Economic Recovery Tax Act of 1981, commonly known as the Kemp-Roth tax cut. Before entering politics, Kemp was a quarterback for the San Diego Chargers and the Buffalo Bills, a team he led to consecutive American Football League championships. After football, he settled down in the Buffalo area.

Ross Perot was in the mix again as standard-bearer of the Reform Party.

But while Dole had to slug it through the primaries, Clinton faced no serious opposition from within the Democratic Party. He was able to focus on the general election early, and it paid off. Clinton took thirty-one states and the District of Columbia, for a total of 379 electoral votes, 109 more than he needed. Dole carried nineteen states for 159 electoral votes. Perot won no state.

In the Senate, Nebraska Republican Chuck Hagel (a future defense secretary) picked up the seat left open by the retirement of Jim Exon. In Alabama, Republican Jeff Sessions won the seat left open by the retirement of Democrat Howell Heflin. And Republican Tim Hutchinson picked up the seat vacant by the resignation of David Pryor of Arkansas. The lone Democratic victory came in South Dakota, where Tim Johnson narrowly beat Larry Pressler, the only incumbent to be ousted. So the Republicans still controlled the Senate, 55–45.

In the House, the Democrats did better, picking up eight seats, but the Republicans still enjoyed a majority, 228–206. Dick Gephardt of Missouri, my 1976 classmate, continued to serve as minority leader.

In Washington State, Gary Locke, son of an immigrant Chinese grocer, became the first Asian American to be elected governor of a Mainland state.

Back home, Election Day, November 5, brought heavy weather, figuratively and literally. As voters went to the polls, a series of showers soaked much of Oʻahu, prompting evacuations in ʻEwa and closing the H-1 freeway in two places due to ponding. In ʻEwa Beach, twelve inches of rain fell between 9:30 a.m. and 2 p.m.—a rate expected once a century, the National Weather Service said. A flash-flood warning issued midday encompassed communities from Waikīkī to Mākaha. By early evening, civil defense had started evacuating residents of Puʻuloa and Renton Roads and sending them to ʻEwa Beach Community Park. To give people more time to vote, Cayetano extended the polling hours from 6 to 7 p.m.

The big surprise of the night was the reelection of Jeremy Harris as mayor. Much of the Democratic establishment, including Cayetano, had thrown its support behind Harris' rival, city council veteran Arnold Morgado. Harris won by fifty-six to forty-two percent. Fasi, who had finished third in the primary, also had urged his supporters to back Morgado. Cayetano had also backed David Arakawa in the race for Honolulu prosecutor. But former deputy prosecutor Peter Carlisle won handily, 51–46. Abercrombie fought off a tough challenge from Orson Swindle, 86,732 to 80,053 votes, with 6,576 ballots blank. In fact, Abercrombie's victory wasn't clear until the last vote-tally printout. Mink won reelection over attorney Tom Pico.

At the Legislature, however, a number of incumbents lost: Donna Ikeda, chairwoman of the powerful Senate Ways and Means Committee, fell to Republican Sam Slom. Democratic House member Marshall Ige picked off Senate Republican leader Mike Liu. In the state House, majority floor leader Annelle Amaral lost to Republican Mark Moses, a retired marine. Two other incumbent senators had gone down in the primary: Consumer Protection Committee chairman Milton Holt to Suzanne Chun Oakland and judiciary chairman Rey Graulty to Norman Sakamoto.

In a sad twist, Maui voters reelected four-term Hāna councilman Tom Morrow, who died in a plane crash on Moloka'i the previous Friday. Also killed were pilot Robert McCarthy, council candidate Alfred Deloso, Maui Democratic corresponding secretary Mitchell Katz, and his wife, Suzanne.

As O'ahu mopped up after the floods, the damage picture became clearer. Farmers in 'Ewa took a huge hit. Flood waters carried honeydew melons and cantaloupe from Aloun Farms miles away to Honouliuli. A mudslide had hit the back of Makaha Valley Towers, bending cars, as Cayetano put it, "like pretzels." The state Health Department warned people to stay away from flooded areas, particularly in Hale'iwa and Waialua, because of cesspool overflows that raised the risk of contracting hepatitis A or E. coli infections. To make things worse, the rainy weather continued, making it the wettest November for O'ahu since record keeping began in 1874. The eventual damage tally reached $13 million. Cayetano announced he would ask Clinton to declare parts of O'ahu disaster zones.

The Clintons had planned to vacation in Hawai'i right after the elections, but put off their trip when four cabinet members resigned: Secretary of State Warren Christopher, Defense secretary William Perry, Commerce secretary Mickey Kantor and Energy secretary Hazel O'Leary.

The Clintons arrived finally on Friday, November 15, at Hickam with Cayetano and Waihee there to greet them. This was their fourth visit, a short one—three days—after which they were off to

Australia, the Philippines and Thailand and planned meetings with the leaders of China, Japan and South Korea. Despite the sketchy weather, Clinton managed to play eighteen holes at Luana Hills Golf Course in Maunawili. With him were Cayetano, Waihee, Larry Johnson, chairman of the Bank of Hawai'i, and contractor Bert Kobayashi. Unfortunately, I couldn't make it, because I always enjoyed golf with Clinton. The president also was spotted ordering takeout at the McDonald's in Waimānalo, ordering a large fries and Diet Coke. The governor later hosted a lū'au for the First Couple at Waialae Country Club, with Kobayashi's firm picking up the tab. The entertainment: Tahitian hula by Tihati Productions.

Amid this atmosphere, Clinton declared a state of emergency for O'ahu, releasing $5 million in disaster relief funds. With further irony, within three weeks Cayetano would declare a drought emergency for Maui, Moloka'i and Hawai'i Island because of a lack of rain. ❈

CHAPTER

56

It was bad year for cane. Waialua Sugar Company closed down in October 1996 after more than 120 years of continuous production. Part of Castle & Cooke, it was the last sugar plantation on Oʻahu. On Kauaʻi, McBryde Sugar Company, founded in 1899, closed in September. C. Brewer & Co also harvested its last crop on the Big Island. Over the last five years, the number of acres planted in sugar had been cut in half, from 162,000 to 84,000. Four plantations remained, Amfac Sugar and Gay & Robinson on Kauaʻi, and Pioneer Mill and Hawaiian Commercial and Sugar Co. on Maui. If there was a bright side, it was that more companies were diversifying. In 1992, for the first time, sales of diversified crops in Hawaiʻi topped the value of sugar and pineapple. These crops included coffee, macadamia nuts, guava, bananas, kalo, bell peppers, basil, Chinese cabbage, corn, seed corn, cucumbers, ginger, green beans, green onions, sweet potatoes, watercress and zucchini. Timber also was showing some potential.

Plus, more Hawaiʻi families were getting into farming, the opposite of the trend nationally.

"On the Mainland, there has been more and more corporate farming, where once there were family farms," J.W.A. "Doc" Buyers, chairman and chief executive of C. Brewer, told the *Los Angeles Times*. "In Hawaiʻi, it's just the opposite. Corporate farming has dominated, and now all of a sudden, with land coming available, you have all these little family farms growing niche crops."

One key function of the Senate is "advice and consent," that is, to vote on presidential appointees. These include cabinet members, undersecretaries, deputy secretaries and general counsels, Supreme

Court justices, heads of regulatory agencies like the EPA and FAA, the directors of NASA and the National Science Foundation, U.S. attorneys, U.S. marshals, ambassadors, generals and Navy flag officers. Confirmation hearings can prove contentious, especially when the president's party does not control the Senate.

So it was unusual that two of Clinton's appointments breezed through the confirmation process. These were Madeleine Albright as secretary of state and William Cohen as secretary of defense. Both were approved 99–0 on January 22, 1997, with Jay Rockefeller of West Virginia not present. Albright, former U.S. ambassador to the United Nations, became the first female secretary of state. Cohen, a Republican senator from Maine for eighteen years, but who spent no time in the military, was barely challenged during his hearing before the Senate Armed Services Committee, although McCain took the opportunity to criticize Clinton on Bosnia. The one-year deadline for getting U.S. troops out had been extended for eighteen months, a development McCain didn't like.

"I am convinced," Cohen said, "that President Clinton is determined to transcend party lines and labels in formulating his national security policies and that he recognizes the importance of hearing the voices of those who might differ with him or other advisers, so he can be assured that the actions he takes are well reasoned and grounded, and not simply the product of predisposition."

In contrast, Clinton's nomination of his national security adviser, Tony Lake, as director of central intelligence fared poorly. The Senate Intelligence Committee held three days of contentious hearings, March 11–13. Critics focused on two foreign policy areas: Lake's failure to alert Congress to the administration's approval of Iranian arms shipments to Bosnia in 1994 and his role when U.S. troops were killed in the Battle of Mogadishu, Somalia, in 1993. They also questioned his delay in selling some energy stocks as demanded by the White House lawyers. It soon became clear the nomination was in jeopardy. Less than a week after the hearings, after meeting with Clinton, Lake took his name out of consideration and joined the faculty of Georgetown University.

❋ ❋ ❋

The welfare of our combat veterans remained one of my uppermost concerns. These "small" wars—Bosnia, Somalia, Kuwait—took a toll on our troops no less than the big ones—World War II, Korea, Vietnam. On May 5, I introduced a measure to help our veterans on several fronts. The Veterans' Benefits Act of 1997 improved outreach to veterans suffering from serious mental illness, including homeless veterans, with proper care, rehabilitation and transitional housing. It also required the Veterans Affairs Department, in cooperation with local governments and nongovernmental organizations, to keep better tabs on homeless veterans and their needs. The bill made it easier for veterans to file complaints about employment discrimination and assured prompt investigation and resolution of those complaints. It also extended, until the end of 2001, a pilot program under which the department could make housing loans to Native American veterans. I also wanted female veterans to have better access to mammograms when appropriate. The bill also authorized improvements to various medical centers around the country, particularly in Memphis and Sacramento. It also called for improved care and new approaches for Persian Gulf veterans suffering from undiagnosed and ill-defined disabilities. A lot of them had been exposed to smoke from the blazing oil fields that I felt could account for a lot of illnesses, respiratory and otherwise.

My cosponsors included five Democrats—Inouye, Tom Daschle and Tim Johnson of South Dakota, Ernest Hollings of South Carolina and Paul Wellstone of Minnesota; and three Republicans—Jim Jeffords of Vermont, Larry Craig of Idaho and Alphonse D'Amato of New York. It was referred to the Veterans' Affairs Committee, then led by Arlen Specter of Pennsylvania, who held a hearing on July 25. The bill was amended to make the Native American housing loan program permanent, a very happy development. The Senate passed it November 5 and four days later the House approved it by voice vote after forty minutes of discussion. It landed on the president's desk on November 13—two days after Veterans Day, and Clinton signed it November 21.

※ ※ ※

There had been a lot of speculation in the press in the mid-1990s that I would leave the Senate to take a lucrative seat on the board of trustees of the Bishop Estate, Hawai'i's largest private land owner, the trust set up by Princess Bernice Pauahi Bishop to fund Kamehameha Schools. I imagine I was a logical candidate because I was both a Kamehameha graduate and former teacher. And my kids had gone there. I knew the school intimately. But in retrospect, I was very happy I didn't make the jump. The board was in for a very rocky ride.

On the board in 1997 were Dickie Wong, former Senate president; Henry Peters, former state House Speaker; Lokelani Lindsey, a former state educator on Maui—and one of my students when I taught at Kahuku High School; attorney Gerard Jervis; and businessman Oswald Stender. A lot of Kamehameha alumni were unhappy with the board, most notably musician-composer Nona Beamer and Roy Benham, a former Office of Hawaiian Affairs trustee.

On August 9, the *Star-Bulletin* published a scathing critique of the board by federal judge Sam King; former U.S. attorney and state appellate judge Walter Heen; University of Hawai'i law professor Randy Roth; former Kamehameha School for Girls principal Gladys Brandt, who was also former chairwoman of the University of Hawai'i Board of Regents; and Monsignor Charles Kekumano, chairman of the Queen Lili'uokalani Trust. Titled *Broken Trust*, the critique said the community "has lost faith in the Bishop Estate trustees, in how they are chosen, how much they are paid, how they govern."

They said each trustee had averaged $900,000 in annual compensation over the last three years. "Given the estate's ability to pay big-league compensation, one would expect to find an array of phenomenally talented trustees," they said. "Yet somehow, with the exception of Oswald Stender, the Bishop Estate trustees simply don't measure up to the job." They went on to list a number of bad investments the trustees had made, losing many millions of dollars for the estate, including a Texas methane gas deal that lost some $65 million.

There were also "attitude problems" among the board members, they said. "It's been widely reported that trustee Lokelani Lindsey used Bishop Estate people to survey her North Shore property, process her permits and supervise the rebuilding of her house. To our knowledge, she hasn't repaid the estate," the report said. Lindsey was also said to have insisted that every student at Kamehameha be able to recognize her and greet her as "Trustee Lindsey."

Finally, they listed six steps needed to regain the trust of the public, including an investigation into trustee conduct by the state attorney general.

Three days later, on August 12, Cayetano asked Attorney General Margery Bronster to do just that. Less than a month later, on September 10, Cayetano released her preliminary report, saying the allegations against the trustees were "credible" and her inquiry would continue. This delighted the alumni and the *Broken Trust* authors. Eventually, all five board members would resign.

In early September 1997, we got word that Abe had suffered an apparent heart attack and was in critical condition at the Queen's Medical Center. I was in Washington at the time. Abe had turned eighty in February. Our brother Joe, a retired Pearl Harbor Naval Shipyard worker, had died in June 1992 at age seventy. Our sister Annie died in December of that year at eighty-two. She had been a longtime teacher at Waipahu High School and was also the musical director at Kealaokamalamalama Church in Kona, where her husband, the Reverend Francis Akana, was the pastor. Our brother John and sister Susan were doing fine.

I had last seen Abe on a trip home in August; he and Millie and I had breakfast at Wisteria and he seemed fine. Abe had retired as pastor at Kawaiaha'o in 1984, but had remained active in blessings, christenings, weddings and other events, dispensing water from a koa calabash that had belonged to Kamehameha I. He had collapsed September 9, a Tuesday, while conducting a funeral at Hawaiian Memorial Park in Kāne'ohe. He was rushed to Castle Medical Center, then transferred to Queen's for an emergency cardiac catheterization. We remained hopeful that Abe would pull through, and at first things looked good. The family issued a statement that he was "recovering well." But it turned out it wasn't a heart attack but a bulge and subsequent tear in the aorta, the main heart artery. He died late the next evening—a day before my seventy-third birthday.

At Kawaiaha'o, the Reverend William Kaina, who had taken over for Abe, announced: "*Kē'hea 'ia 'o kahu aloha 'o Kahu Abraham Akaka i ka homelani.* Our beloved shepherd, Pastor Abraham Akaka, has been called to his heavenly home."

Millie and I made plans to return to Honolulu for the services, scheduled for September 19, the next Friday, at Kawaiahaʻo, with the burial Saturday. But before we could hop a plane, I got a surprise in the mail. A card from Abe. He had mailed it a couple of days before he died. As always, it was a Kawaiahaʻo Church postcard placed inside a business envelope. His minuscule scrawl marched across the card like files of fire ants.

"Dear Brother Dan, here is wishing you once again a most joyous birthday. May the Lord continue to bless you with good health, wisdom and peace of mind as you go about your important work for our Aloha State and nation. God bless you and all the ʻohana. Bro Kwai." Kwai was his family nickname. Our dad thought Abe looked a bit Chinese at birth, so he gave him a middle name from our Chinese progenitors, Kwai Sing. The rest of the siblings have Hawaiian middle names.

The family held a small private service at 2:30 p.m. Friday, when the koa casket arrived at Kawaiahaʻo. We then opened the church for visitation at 4 p.m. About 3,000 people turned out for the wake, the line stretching out to Punchbowl Street. Flower arrangements surrounded the casket: torch ginger, anthuriums and protea. Abe's widow, Mary Louise, received condolences and hugs from almost everyone. A light breeze caressed the mourners.

"Daddy radiated the hard light of truth and justice and he glowed with the soft light of hope, peace and love," said my niece, Pualani Akaka.

When my turn came, I read a brief letter of condolence from the Clintons, then began my own remarks.

"Aloha ke Akua! Mama Kahu—Mary Lou, Fenner, Pua, Sally, Sandy, Jeff—the family of Abraham Akaka, spiritual, community, governmental, business leaders of Hawaiʻi, our sister states and the world and friends, all who were personally touched by the ministry of this man of God, Reverend Dr. Abraham Kahikina Akaka.

"Aloha! I rise on behalf of my family, the descendants of Simeon, Pulu and Kahikina Akaka to give honor and pay tribute to Brother Abe. He was truly a distinguished human being who believed deeply in God, our Lord Jesus Christ and 'pono' as the destiny for mankind—those with needs on every level of human existence. He was the kahu, the shepherd to all people."

Then I sang Abe's favorite Hawaiian hymn, "A'ole No I Pau Loa," first as a solo and then accompanied by the Kawaiaha'o choir. The song describes a never-ending City of God, with streets paved with gold.

The ceremony combined Christian Scripture with Hawaiian hymns, and made use of four elements that Kahu used in his sermons: the 'ukulele, with the strings representing people who must find harmony with the Creator; the kukui nut, the oil of which is used in candles to light the way; the canoe, symbolic of life's journey; and a star for guidance.

The service also included Abe's favorite childhood hymns, including "Jesus Loves Me." Scripture readings included the Twenty-Third Psalm.

On Saturday, we laid Abe to rest in Hook Chu Cemetery in Pauoa Valley, where our parents are buried as well as Joe and Annie. ✤

CHAPTER

57

After thirty-seven years of planning, protests, court battles, environmental studies, archaeological digs, route changes and design changes, the H-3 freeway opened on December 12, 1997. The $1.3-billion freeway truly was a wonder to behold, passing up through picturesque and otherwise pristine Hālawa Valley, through the mile-long Harano Tunnel, and then into Haʻikū Valley, offering a breathtaking Windward Oʻahu panorama.

About 500 invited guests attended the 11 a.m. Friday dedication near one of the tunnel entrances. They included Ariyoshi, of course, Waihee and E. Alvey Wright, a retired rear admiral who was state transportation director under Ariyoshi and Burns. He was a staunch H-3 supporter. In many ways, this was Alvey's day. The overcast skies contributed their own "Hawaiian blessing"—a smattering of rain. But that didn't dash the mood of jubilation. It seemed like an eternity since I had helped secure the startup funding for H-3 in the House. In his remarks, Cayetano said the freeway's history spanned from "statehood to the new millennium" and provided a "drive into the future." Truly, the tunnel structures yawned like some alien base in a science fiction film, but that is not what Ben meant. The sixteen-mile freeway offered "a quicker and shorter route to economic development and new job opportunities on both sides of the island," he said. He also referred to the long construction delays.

"We have learned to make sure that environmental assessments are objective," he said. "We have learned that we must take care to preserve our ancient Hawaiian sites. And have learned to be aware of escalating costs." In fact, the freeway was the most expensive in U.S. history, $81 million a mile.

The H-3 officially opened at 3 p.m., in time for the afternoon commute. Over the weekend, the car trips totaled 100,000, the state estimated. (Some cars certainly, perhaps many, made more than one trip.) On the Haʻikū side, many drivers pulled over for the scenery. The police had to keep the gawkers rolling. On Monday morning, some commuters reporting travel times cut in half! Between 5 and 9 a.m., the peak hours, 6,381 vehicles used the roadway, which meant twenty-one percent less traffic on Pali and Likelike Highways. Transportation officials had estimated 12,000 to 18,000 vehicles would use H-3 during a twenty-four-hour period. But the morning numbers—covering only four hours—showed that figure would be much greater. The highway was a hit.

"Well, George?" I said to Ariyoshi when we had a moment alone at the dedication.

He took in the view and nodded.

"Yeah." ✽

CHAPTER

58

On February 5, 1998, I had the honor to serve as master of ceremonies of the National Prayer Breakfast at the Hilton International Ballroom in Washington.

At the head table were President Clinton and the First Lady, with Millie to Hillary's right. Also Army General Hugh Shelton, the chairman of the Joint Chiefs of Staff.

I was ready to introduce everyone, but two seats remained empty: Al and Tipper Gore.

"O Lord, our strength and our redeemer, we come together today to pray for strength and guidance in a difficult and challenging world," Shelton said in his opening prayer.

Amen, I said to myself.

I thanked Shelton and told the crowd, "Please enjoy your breakfast."

Tradition, starting with President Eisenhower in 1953, called for a "sturdy" breakfast of eggs, sausage and grits.

I took the podium again a bit later.

"Good morning, ladies and gentlemen. It is a wonderful privilege for me to welcome all of you this morning to the National Prayer Breakfast. I particularly want to greet our international guests who represent over 160 nations. And to everyone attending the prayer breakfast for the first time, I say again, welcome.

"This morning we gather almost 4,000 strong from all fifty states, commonwealths and the U.S. territories and nations around the world to reaffirm our faith, seek spiritual support for our president and leaders in our country, and share fellowship and friendship with one another.

"We are honored to have the president and First Lady and the vice president and Mrs. Gore as our guests."

The Gores, in fact, still had not arrived. There were two empty chairs at the head table to my left. But I had to press on with the introductions.

"Permit me to introduce the people sitting at the head table," I said. "And I'll do it quickly from my left to my right. Randy and Gae Hongo." The Hongos were inspirational singers who flew out from Hawai'i at my invitation. They would be performing later.

"General Hugh Shelton and Mrs. Carolyn Shelton. Dr. Dorothy Height." Height was with the National Council of Negro Women.

"Mrs. Marilyn Gevirtz, Ambassador Don Gevirtz." Gevirtz was the former U.S. envoy to Fiji, Tonga and Tuvalu.

Suddenly chuckles erupted from the crowd. Just as I was introducing the Gevirtzes, out from stage right came the Gores, walking briskly. Tipper sat down and smiled sweetly at Gevirtz to her left and Al filled the empty chair to her right.

"And in a timely fashion, Vice President and Mrs. Gore."

More laughter, including from Congressman Bobby Scott, sitting next to the vice president. I finished the introductions, including the Reverend Billy Graham and Senator Connie Mack of Florida and his wife, Priscilla. Mack would be the keynote speaker.

"Looking upon this august and joyful assembly," I continued, "I see the universality of the prayer breakfast, the coming together of people of different nations, faiths and cultures, and the power of love and consideration for one another. I am reminded of the passage from Psalm 33, verse 12:

> *Blessed is the nation whose God is the Lord, the people he chose for his inheritance. From heaven, the Lord looks down and sees all mankind. From his dwelling place, he watches all who live on Earth. He forms the hearts of all and considers all their works.*

"God's love for all of us is everlasting, for all men and women from all nations. This perfect love fills our hearts, prepares us for the challenges we face each day and opens our minds to God's wisdom. As we seek to love God and one another, let the spirit of this prayer breakfast enrich us, strengthen us and lead us on life's journey, where we are never alone."

In between readings from the Old and New Testament, I called on Randy and Gae. They were joined by their son Andrew, a Yale University student, singing a musical reflection of their own arrangement, *"Ua Mau ke Ea o ka 'Āina i ka Pono"*—"The life of the land is perpetuated in righteousness," our state motto, first articulated by Kamehameha III.

Gore was up after the Scripture readings.

I said, "The vice president and I entered Congress together as members of the class of 1976," I said. "As a congressman and senator, he faithfully participated in both the House and Senate breakfast groups. Today we are honored to have him offer the prayer for our national leaders. So it is with pleasure that I welcome the pride of class of '76."

That brought a smattering of laughter.

"And an esteemed friend, the vice president of the United States, Albert Gore Jr."

Vigorous applause.

"Thank you very much," Gore said. "I'm glad to be introduced by the pride of the class of '76."

More laughter.

"Thank you very much, and to Mrs. Akaka, to the president and First Lady."

He also greeted the others at the head table.

"It is, of course, humbling to join with so many people of all faiths to rededicate ourselves to God's purposes and to reaffirm the ultimate purpose of our lives, to glorify the Creator and to love the Lord our God with all our hearts, with all our souls and with all our minds, and to love our neighbors as ourselves.

"I believe God has a plan for the United States of America and has since our founding. Our mission has always been to advance the cause of liberty and to prove that religious, political and economic freedom are the natural birthright of all men and women and that freedom unlocks a higher fraction of the human potential than any other way of organizing human society. And I believe that God has given the people of our nation not only a chance, but a mission to prove to men and women in all nations that people of different racial and ethnic backgrounds, of all faiths and creeds, can not only work and live together but can enrich and ennoble both themselves and our common purpose and to prove, in the words of Jesus, 'that they all may be one, as thou, Father, art in me, and I in thee.'

"Yet too often we lose sight of our common purpose and seek to make our public discourse one of meanness and not of meaning, one of bitterness and invective, not of faith and love."

Connie Mack, a mainstay of the Senate Prayer Breakfast group, described being born again on an otherwise unremarkable day in October 1995. That experience, of giving up a sense of control and turning his life over to God, left him with "a sense of joy" that he had not felt since before his brother Michael had died of cancer seventeen years earlier.

Clinton was up next.

"For five years now, Hillary and I have looked forward to this day. For me it's a day in which I can be with other people of faith and pray and ask for your prayers, both as president and as just another child of God. I have done it for five years, and I do so again today."

Finally, Billy Graham rose to deliver the benediction.

"Help us remember that you teach us that we're all sinners and everyone who is in this place needs repentance and forgiveness, including me," he said. He did not look at Clinton as he said this.

I took the podium and waited for the applause to subside.

"Thank you very much, Dr. Graham. This concludes the forty-sixth National Prayer Breakfast. I ask all of you to please rise and remain standing until the president and Mrs. Clinton and vice president and Mrs. Gore depart from the ballroom."

The departure protocol came at the insistence of the Secret Service. The Clintons and Gores got more applause as they left.

"I thank all of you for your participation and your cooperation," I concluded. "Trust in God and carry His love with you and share it with others today and every day."

Later, I entered the entire transcript of the breakfast prayers and addresses into the Congressional Record. The event stands as one of the highlights of my years on the Hill. ❖

CHAPTER

59

On the foreign policy front, Clinton remained determined to improve relations with China through a process he called "constructive engagement." While there were wide concerns over China's human rights record, the year 1997 had brought some hopeful developments. In June, Gore visited Beijing and he and the premier Li Peng signed $685 million worth of contracts for Boeing. In October, President Jiang Zemin visited Washington for a successful summit with Clinton. In November, the Chinese released a widely known dissident, Wei Jingsheng, and allowed him to fly to New York. And the U.S. softened its human rights drumbeat. Each year since 1991, at the annual meeting of the U.N. Commission on Human Rights, the United States had sponsored a resolution condemning China's human rights practices. But this year, in March, we didn't do it. We let it go. In April, another dissident, Wang Dan, was released and flown to the United States.

Then Clinton announced he would make an eight-day visit to China in June and July. This brought a hailstorm of criticism that he defended June 11 in a talk at the National Geographic Society.

"The role China chooses to play in preventing the spread of weapons of mass destruction or encouraging it, in combating or ignoring international crime and drug trafficking, in protecting or degrading the environment, in tearing down or building up trade barriers, in respecting or abusing human rights, in resolving difficult situations in Asia, from the Indian subcontinent to the Korean Peninsula, or aggravating them—the role China chooses to play will powerfully shape the next century," he said. "A stable, open, prosperous China that assumes its responsibilities for building a more peaceful world is clearly and profoundly in our interests. On that point, all Americans agree. But as we all know, there is serious disagreement over how best to encourage the emergence of that kind of China and how to handle our differences, especially over human rights, in the meantime. Some Americans believe we should try to isolate and contain China because of its undemocratic system and human rights violations and in order to retard its capacity to become America's next great enemy... (But) choosing isolation over engagement would not make the world safer. It would make it more dangerous."

I was among three senators that Clinton invited along. The others were Jay Rockefeller of West Virginia and Max Baucus of Montana. We also had three House members: Lee Hamilton of Indiana, John Dingell of Michigan and Ed Markey of Massachusetts. With us were Secretary of State Albright, Treasury secretary Robert Rubin, Commerce secretary William Daley and Agriculture secretary Dan Glickman—one of my 1976 classmates. We also had Janet Yellen, chairwoman of Clinton's Council of Economic Advisers, and Mark Gearan, former White House director of communications and now director of the Peace Corps. Except for Hillary Clinton, no spouses accompanied us. Chelsea, then eighteen, also tagged along.

We arrived in Xian, Central China, on June 25. Situated in the fertile valleys of the Wei and Yellow Rivers—the so-called "cradle of Chinese civilization"—Xian was the capital of the Chinese Empire at various times for 1,100 years.

The most famous attraction is the terracotta warriors. Peasants digging a well discovered these pottery pieces in 1974. They are regarded as one of the most spectacular archaeological finds of the twentieth century. The soldiers represented Emperor Qin Shi Huang's imperial guards. More than 3,000 soldiers, nearly 100 horses and eleven chariots have been unearthed so far.

Because we were part of a presidential party, the Chinese authorities allowed us to go down into the archaeological pit, where we could see the soldiers up close. I was astounded: each face was different and exquisitely detailed. One of them looked like he had a cleft palate. They were different heights, too, some of them towering over me. I wondered if they were modeled after actual individuals. In any case, this was no cookie-cutter project but an incredibly creative and painstaking effort. Rank after rank, file after file—just to look down the rows was incredible.

I was equally impressed, days later, to see the Great Wall at

Mutianyu. I had seen it before, on a visit twenty years earlier, but the sight never ceases to amaze. The sheer length of it, stretching over hill and dale as far as they eye can see, and sturdiness attest to a true wonder of the world.

Our trip included three days in Beijing, where the Clintons were greeted to the blare of trumpets at the Great Hall of the People by President Jiang. Clinton and Jiang reviewed the troops and then shared toasts, entertainment and a banquet. While President Clinton held high-level meetings but also met with simple villagers, Hillary had her own agenda, much of it health-related. She attended, for instance, a signing ceremony for a new partnership between the Chinese Ministry of Health and the U.S. Centers for Disease Control and Prevention. She also had a dialogue with Chinese women on challenges in a changing society. We spent two days in Shanghai, a day in Guilin, which included a boat ride up the majestic Li River, surrounded by cliffs, and a day in Hong Kong, which had joined Mainland China the previous July.

For me, one of the most memorable experience was Clinton's speech to students at Beijing University. This was on June 29, a chilly and overcast summer day, outside the campus library. I had mentioned to Clinton that Beijing University, nicknamed Beida, was the Harvard of China. Clinton immediately used that as comedic relief.

"Thank you very much," he said after his introduction. "Well, first, let me thank all of you for coming out to see us on such a nice, warm day."

That brought laughter.

"I thank President Chen, Chairman Ren, Vice President Chi, Senator Akaka and the members of Congress who are here, and all the members of the university community who have made my wife and our daughter and our whole delegation feel so very welcome today. Thank you very much. Now, when Senator Akaka said that some people thought of 'Beida' as the Harvard of China—"

Laughs from the crowd.

"—all of us Americans who did not go to Harvard were thinking, perhaps Harvard was the 'Beida' of the United States."

In another address the same day, at the university's Bangong Lou Auditorium, Clinton called for more attention to democracy and human rights in China, but did so without sounding preachy.

"One of our Founding Fathers, Benjamin Franklin, once said,

'Our critics are our friends, for they show us our faults.' Now, if that is true, there are many days in the United States when the president has more friends than anyone else in America."

Widespread laughter.

"But it is so," Clinton said.

After his remarks, he took questions and, of course, nearly every hand went up. The fifth question was a bit sharper than the rest.

"Mr. President, with regard to the question of democracy, human rights and freedom, actually this is an issue of great interest to both the Chinese and the American peoples. But to be honest, our two countries have some differences over those issues. In your address just now, you made a very proud review and retrospection of the history of America's democracy and human rights. And you have also made some suggestions for China. Of course, for the sincere suggestions, we welcome... So now I'd like to ask you a question. Do you think that in the United States today, there are some problems in the area of democracy, freedom and human rights, and what your government has done in improving the situation?"

Clinton said, "I do, and first of all, let me say I never raise this question overseas in any country, not just China, without acknowledging first that our country has had terrible problems in this area—keep in mind, slavery was legal in America for many years—and that we are still not perfect. I always say that because I don't think it's right for any person to claim that he or she lives in a perfect country. We're all struggling toward ideals to live a better life. So I agree with the general point you made.

"Now, I will give you two examples. We still have some instances of discrimination in America, in housing or employment or other areas, based on race. And we have set up a system to deal with it, but we have not totally eliminated it. And in the last year, I have been engaging the American people in a conversation on the subject, and we have tried to identify the things that government should do, the things that the American people should do, either through the local government or through other organizations, and the attitudes that should change the minds and hearts of the American people."

His second example had to do with a family in New York City that felt trapped by neighborhood violence. Fear kept them from letting their ten-year-old son walk to school.

"I think that's important, because, you see, in America, we tend to view freedom as the freedom from government abuse or from government control. That is our heritage. Our founders came here to escape the monarchy in England. But sometimes freedom requires affirmative steps by government to give everyone an equal opportunity to have an education and make a decent living and to preserve a lawful environment. So I work very hard to try to bring the crime rate down in America, and it's now lower that it has been at any time in twenty-five years, which means that more of our children are free. But the crime rate is still too high, there is still too much violence."

To me, that was such a great response: America has problems, but tries honestly to correct them. But I would say his main message to the students was that the future belonged to them.

"You know," he said, "political leaders of my generation talk a lot about the future and the twenty-first century, but it is you, the students who are here, who will live in it and who must build it. A child born today will not even remember the twentieth century. Indeed, a child born today may think of people like me as relics of an ancient dynasty."

And the laughter was universal. ✤

CHAPTER

60

In June, I introduced the Hawai'i Volcanoes National Park Adjustment Act of 1998, which amended federal law to allow land next to the national park to be purchased with either appropriated or donated money. I thought it would be an effective and valuable way to expand the park, home to many endemic and indigenous species. Inouye was my cosponsor. In September it cleared the Committee on Energy and Natural Resources with the help of Frank Murkowski of Alaska. The bill passed without amendments in both the Senate and House, and Clinton signed it into law on November 12. This paved the way for a historic expansion of the park in 2004, when 115,788 acres were added from adjacent Kahuku Ranch. That increased the size of the park by more than half. At the time, it was the largest land acquisition in state history. The Nature Conservancy financed the $22 million deal with the Damon Estate.

On August 7, 1998, the United States got its first taste of international terrorism since the 1993 World Trade Center bombing. Nearly 300 people, including twelve Americans, died and 5,000 were wounded when truck bombs went off simultaneously at the American embassies in Nairobi, Kenya, and Dar es Salaam, Tanzania. The attacks were traced to members of the Egyptian Islamic Jihad and to al-Qaida, led by Osama bin Laden and Ayman al-Zawahiri, who, unfortunately, would become household names all too soon. The FBI quickly put bin Laden on its ten most-wanted list.

In response, on August 20, Clinton ordered a battery of cruise missile strikes on targets in Afghanistan and the Sudan, part of what was dubbed Operation Infinite Reach.

"Our target was terror," Clinton explained on national prime-time television, speaking from the Oval Office. "Our mission was clear: to strike at the network of radical groups affiliated with and funded by Osama bin Laden, perhaps the preeminent organizer and financier of international terrorism in the world today. The groups associated with him come from diverse places but share a hatred for democracy, a fanatical glorification of violence, and a horrible distortion of their religion to justify the murder of innocents. They have made the United States their adversary precisely because of what we stand for and what we stand against.

"A few months ago, and again this week, bin Ladin publicly vowed to wage a terrorist war against America, saying, and I quote, 'We do not differentiate between those dressed in military uniforms and civilians. They're all targets.' Their mission is murder and their history is bloody. In recent years, they killed American, Belgian and Pakistani peacekeepers in Somalia. They plotted to assassinate the president of Egypt and the pope. They planned to bomb six United States 747s over the Pacific. They bombed the Egyptian embassy in Pakistan. They gunned down German tourists in Egypt."

It was unclear how effective the missile strikes proved. We know they didn't take out bin Ladin or al-Zawahiri.

In Hawai'i, it was yet another political year, with Inouye and Cayetano up for reelection. In the primary September 19, Cayetano easily fought off five relatively unknown Democrats. But Ben's vote tally, at nearly 96,000, was actually below that of his Republican rival, Linda Lingle, who outpolled Fasi roughly 109,000 to 48,000. That didn't bode well for the general election. Abercrombie handily won the Democratic nod for his U.S. House seat and would face Republican Gene Ward, a state House member, in the general. Mink had no credible competition in either party.

The general election on November 3 proved kind to incumbents, with Cayetano holding off Lingle with a slender plurality, 49.5 to 48.2 percent. On Maui, Democrat James "Kimo" Apana won the mayor's race over Republican Alan Arakawa. On Kaua'i, Republican mayor Maryanne Kusaka won a second term.

Nationally, in the Senate, the Republicans maintained a 55–44 seat majority. Among the new faces: Evan Bayh of Indiana; Chuck Schumer of New York, who defeated veteran Al D'Amato; and John Edwards of North Carolina. In the House, the Democrats made a modest gain of five seats. The Republicans still held control of the House, but the election was an embarrassment for Gingrich, who had been assured huge gains thanks to the problems besetting Bill Clinton. Accordingly, he announced his resignation from Congress.

Clinton's woes had begun with the Whitewater investigation, relating to real estate investments he and Hillary had made in Arkansas around the time of the savings and loan meltdown. In May 1995, by a vote of 96–3, the Senate convened a special committee to look into the allegations, with D'Amato as chairman. The no votes came from Jeff Bingaman of New Mexico, John Glenn of Ohio and Paul Simon of Illinois. Inouye and I voted with the majority. Nothing in the Whitewater probe ever stuck to the Clintons, but the independent counsel, Kenneth Starr, expanded the investigation into other, unrelated matters, including Clinton's alleged affair with a White House intern. Clinton denied the affair publicly and repeatedly. But Starr concluded that Clinton had lied about the affair during a sworn deposition in a civil case. If so, that made it a crime.

After testifying before a grand jury for four hours, Clinton on August 17 went on national television to admit the relationship and that he "misled" the nation and his wife about it for seven months.

He got prompt support from Gore, who happened to be vacationing on Kauaʻi with his family. Wearing khakis and a short-sleeved blue shirt, Gore gave an impromptu press conference at his hotel in Līhuʻe.

"Aloha," he said as he walked out to the podium, complete with vice presidential seal. With Tipper at his side and potted palms behind him, Gore read from a prepared statement.

"Late last night, after his televised address to the nation, I spoke to President Clinton and expressed to him that I felt he showed courage in acknowledging his mistakes before the American people and accepting full responsibility for his actions," he said. "I am proud of him because he is a great president, and I am honored to have him as a friend. And Tipper and I continue to keep him and his family in our thoughts and prayers."

But now it was time to move on, he said.

"I believe it is time to put this matter behind us once and for all and move forward with the business of the country."

But that was not to be.

On September 9, Starr sent his report and eighteen boxes of documents to the House, making a case for impeachment on eleven grounds, including perjury, obstruction of justice, witness tampering and abuse of power.

On December 19, during the lame-duck session after the election, and after fourteen hours of debate, the House approved two articles of impeachment. By a vote of 228–206, Clinton was impeached on the grounds of perjury to a grand jury. By a 221–212 vote, the members added obstruction of justice. Two other articles failed. Abercrombie and Mink voted no on all four. This was only the second time in history a president had been impeached, the first being Andrew Johnson in 1868.

Again Gore came to Clinton's defense, appearing with Bill and Hillary at the White House. Blaming "excessive partisanship" in the House, Gore said, "What happened as a result does a great disservice to a man I believe will be regarded in the history books as one of our greatest presidents."

In the Senate, Clinton's trial began on January 8, 1999. With chief justice William Rehnquist presiding, thirteen Republicans from the House Judiciary Committee, led by Henry Hyde of Illinois, made the case against the president. With the courtroom atmosphere, this was unlike any other Senate proceeding I had ever experienced.

On February 4, we decided to accept videotaped testimony rather than bringing the witnesses into the chamber. Two days later, we watched more than two dozen excerpts from the intern, Monica Lewinsky. I felt very sorry for her. I am sure she never imagined her mistakes would play out on such a massive stage. During closing arguments on February 8, Hyde said: "A failure to convict will make the statement that lying under oath, while unpleasant and to be avoided, is not all that serious... And now let us all take our place in history on the side of honor, and—oh, yes—let right be done."

A two-thirds majority—sixty-seven votes—was necessary to convict, but it never came close to that. On the perjury charge, the vote was forty-five in favor and fifty-five against conviction. All forty-five

Democrats voted "not guilty" on both charges. We were joined on both votes by Republicans John Chafee of Rhode Island, Susan Collins and Olympia Snowe of Maine, Jim Jeffords of Vermont and Arlen Specter of Pennsylvania. On the perjury charge, we also picked up the votes of Ted Stevens of Alaska, Fred Thompson of Tennessee, Slade Gorton of Washington, Richard Shelby of Alabama and John Warner of Virginia. The obstruction of justice vote was 50–50.

And so concluded a sad chapter in American history. ✣

CHAPTER

61

In the 106th Congress, Congressman Dennis Hastert of Illinois succeeded Gingrich as Speaker of the House. Dick Armey of Texas stayed on as majority leader, while Gephardt led the Democrats. In the Senate, Trent Lott of Mississippi continued as majority leader, with Tom Daschle of South Dakota and Harry Reid of Nevada serving as minority leader and whip, respectively.

I had an aggressive legislative agenda, but with the Republicans in control it was tough to get bills out of committee. My first effort, the Plant Protection Act, targeted invasive species. The measure authorized the secretary of agriculture to restrict the importation and movement—including by mail—of plants, plant products, biological control organisms, plant pests and noxious weeds in order to prevent their introduction into the United States and movement between states. The second, the Disaster Victims Protection Act of 1999, aimed to curb fraud or gouging by opportunistic retailers or contractors. Following a disaster declaration by the president, under the bill, federal, state and local law enforcement officials would be required to determine the extent to which victims of the disaster were being further victimized by fraudulent or otherwise unscrupulous suppliers of consumer goods and services. Neither of those measures went anywhere, although I had Inouye as a cosponsor on the second.

Another measure encouraged research and development involving an important resource called methane hydrate, ice that has molecules of methane, a natural gas, trapped inside. Typically these deposits, which can be several hundred yards thick, occur beneath the ocean floor and under the Arctic permafrost. When brought to the earth's surface, one cubic yard of gas hydrate releases 164 cubic yards of natural gas. My version passed the Senate, and a companion bill in the House, introduced in May by Democrat Mike Doyle of Pennsylvania, went on to become law.

* * *

Three bills directly related to Hawai'i also made it to the president's desk.

The first designated the Ala Kahakai Trail (Trail by the Sea) as a national historic trail. Also known as Ala Loa, or long trail, this circles the island of Hawai'i and was a major route connecting some 600 communities on the island from 1400 to 1700. Armies used the 175-mile-long trail to reach battlefields, and it played an important role in the rise of Kamehameha I. Inouye cosponsored the measure, which cleared Murkowski's Energy and Natural Resources Committee in June. The full Senate passed it in early July, but then it languished in the House for more than a year.

The second was the Hawaii Volcanoes National Park Adjustment Act of 2000, which allowed for the expansion of the park via the donation or exchange of land, not just by purchase. That bill experienced the same fate as the Ala Kahakai Trail bill. But they both finally cleared the House in the fall of 2000 and Clinton signed them into law on November 13.

The third, which I introduced October 6, was the Hawaii Water Resources Act of 2000. The bill directed the secretary of the interior to study irrigation and other water delivery systems used in farming and look for opportunities for recycling, reclaiming and reusing the water. The study costs would be shared with the state. It also extended drought relief programs through fiscal year 2005 and included Hawai'i in those programs. The bill didn't move until March 2000, but then it made relatively swift progress. Clinton signed it as a lame duck two days before Christmas.

I was a cosponsor on another successful water bill, the Estuaries and Clean Waters Act of 2000, introduced in April 1999 by John Chafee of Rhode Island. That called for the Army to serve as a lead agency in restoring river deltas, an important habitat for birds and other wildlife.

* * *

With the Oklahoma City bombings four years earlier, the United States had already been the target of domestic terrorism, but the year 1999 accentuated a new form of terror: mass school shootings. Until 1966, nearly all school shootings in America had one or two victims, maybe three, rarely more. Then came the sniper shootings at the University of Texas at Austin, with seventeen dead and thirty-one wounded. For decades nothing rivaled that. On April 20, 1999, two disaffected students, Dylan Klebold and Eric Harris, shot up the campus of Columbine High School in Littleton, Colorado, killing twelve students, one teacher and then themselves. In all, twenty-one people were wounded. As a result, the gun-control debate flared anew, but the incident also sparked discussions about youth subcultures, bullying and violent video games. In May 2002, the Secret Service issued a report that looked at thirty-seven U.S. school shootings, including Columbine, and came up with some counter-intuitive conclusions. First, metal detectors provide a false sense of security because most mass attackers don't try to hide their weapons. Second, most attacks are planned, not spontaneous, and the attackers usually exhibit suspicious behavior beforehand. In other words, some people should have seen this coming. I guess that was the lesson going forward. Whatever the case, here arose yet another worrisome tear in the fabric of American society.

By year's end, Hawai'i would get its own taste of mass bloodshed, with seven people dead from gunshots by a coworker at the Xerox Corp. office on Nimitz Highway. The Founding Fathers surely could not have suspected what havoc would result when they drafted the Second Amendment. The freedom to bear arms, including assault rifles and semi-automatic pistols, comes at a dreadful cost.

Of course, Hawai'i's natural beauty masks many hazards as well. On an otherwise pleasant and sunny Sunday, Mother's Day, May 9, 1999, eight hikers were killed by boulders at Sacred Falls on O'ahu's upper Windward Coast. Another fifty sustained non-life-threatening injuries. The state promptly and permanently closed the attraction, one of the most popular on the island, and in December 2003 settled legal claims by the surviving family members for more than $8 million. The plaintiffs claimed they were not sufficiently warned of the hazard. But at some point people have to rely on their own good sense when heading to Hawai'i's mountains, valleys and scenic shorelines. One particularly dangerous spot is Hanakapiai Stream on Kaua'i's Nā Pali Coast. In heavy rains the stream suddenly builds to where it is unsafe to cross. People who tried have died. Another is Hālona Blowhole, Oʻahu's version of Old Faithful. In one painfully memorable case, an eighteen-year-old tourist from California—a recent high school graduate, leaned over the blowhole and a jet of water hit him in the chest. It shot him up into the air, turned him upside down and he plummeted headfirst down the hole. Such deaths are senseless. But they continue—and in fact would increase in the age of easy internet access and selfie sticks.

✻ ✻ ✻

It was with shock and sadness that we learned of the disappearance of John F. Kennedy Jr., his wife and sister-in-law on a flight to Martha's Vineyard in July 1999. Kennedy was flying a small plane, a Piper Saratoga, to the island to attend the wedding of his cousin, Rory. Kennedy became disoriented while flying the plane over water at night, the National Transportation Safety Board concluded. Navy divers found the wreckage and their bodies five days later on the ocean floor, 120 feet down.

On July 19, before the wreckage was found, I joined ninety-eight other senators in cosponsoring a resolution introduced by Trent Lott. I can think of no other resolution that had ninety-nine cosponsors—that is, the backing of the entire Senate.

"Whereas it is with profound sorrow and regret that the Senate has learned that John Fitzgerald Kennedy Jr., his wife Carolyn Bessette-Kennedy and her sister Lauren Bessette have been missing since the early morning hours of Saturday, July 17, 1999; Whereas John Fitzgerald Kennedy Jr., is the son of the late John Fitzgerald Kennedy, the thirty-fifth president of the United States of America and senator from Massachusetts, and nephew of the late Robert Francis Kennedy of New York, and of Senator Edward Moore Kennedy of Massachusetts and a beloved member of the Kennedy family, which has given countless years of service to this country; and Whereas the heart of the nation goes out to the Kennedy and Bessette families as search efforts continue in the waters off Martha's Vineyard: Now, therefore, be it resolved that the Senate, when it adjourns on Monday, July 19, 1999, does so as a further mark of respect for the grieving families, and directs the secretary to transmit a copy of this resolution to the Kennedy and Bessette families."

Tragedy had struck yet another generation of this family of devoted public servants. ✤

CHAPTER

62

Since Jimmy Carter, who started campaigning in Iowa almost two years before the 1976 election, presidential campaigns have started early. That remained true in the 2000 race. Among the Democrats, Al Gore was the odds-on favorite, but he got an early challenge from former senator Bill Bradley of New Jersey.

On March 9, 1999, on CNN, Wolf Blitzer asked Gore, "Why should Democrats, looking at the Democratic nomination process, support you instead of Bill Bradley?"

Gore said, "I'll be offering my vision when my campaign begins. And it will be comprehensive and sweeping. And I hope that it will be compelling enough to draw people toward it. I feel that it will be. But it will emerge from my dialogue with the American people. I've traveled to every part of this country during the last six years. During my service in the United States Congress, I took the initiative in creating the internet. I took the initiative in moving forward a whole range of initiatives that have proven to be important to our country's economic growth and environmental protection, improvements in our educational system."

For the record, Gore never claimed to have "invented" the internet, merely to have gotten the ball rolling.

On the Republican side, there was former vice president Dan Quayle; Senators John McCain of Arizona, Orrin Hatch of Utah and Bob Smith of New Hampshire; former labor secretary Elizabeth Dole; businessman Steve Forbes; Governor George W. Bush of Texas, son of the former president; former governor Lamar Alexander of Tennessee; Congressman John Kasich of Ohio; author Pat Buchanan and a smattering of others. Half of them dropped out before the year 2000 even rolled around: Kasich in July 1999; Alexander in August; Quayle in September; Buchanan, Dole and Smith in October. All of them endorsed Bush.

When we breezed into Y2K—without the feared computer catastrophe—the campaigning began in earnest.

Gore dominated the early contests and had the nomination clinched by mid-March.

Bush won the Iowa caucuses in January with forty-one percent of the vote, with Forbes second at thirty percent and McCain far back at five percent. But McCain rebounded to beat Bush in the New Hampshire primary, 49–30, with Forbes a distant third. After another third-place showing in Delaware, Forbes quit. Then a string of big-state victories on Super Tuesday, March 7, gave Bush the momentum he needed and McCain dropped out.

This was an election year for me as well. Four Republicans wanted my seat, chief among them John Carroll, a former state senator, lawyer, pilot for Hawaiian Airlines and a Korean War veteran. I also had a Democratic challenger, Art Reyes.

On May 9, I held a fund-raising reception at the Hay-Adams Hotel, overlooking Lafayette Square, across Pennsylvania Avenue from the White House. A lot of people from Hawai'i showed up to offer support. Business people, union leaders. I could tell they were impressed with the venue. The walls are rich, dark wood. Several crystal chandeliers hang from the high ceilings, but overall the lighting was low, augmented by a pair of gas-fueled fireplaces. The circular tables can accommodate about 175 people.

Tom Daschle, our Senate minority leader, was there, as was former congressman Norman Mineta, Clinton's pick to be the next secretary of commerce. Smart, hard working, humble. As a boy during World War II, Mineta had been sent with his family to an internment camp in Wyoming. Now he was at the top echelons of government. Among former internees, I have never seen a better record of U.S. government service.

President Clinton arrived after all the guests had gone through the security procedures set up by the Secret Service. When he entered the room the energy in the room spiked noticeably. One person even cried when she saw him because she was so honored to be in the same room as him and to meet him. Daschle introduced him, praising his record as president, and Clinton stepped up to warm applause.

After an obligatory but fullhearted "aloha," Clinton said, "I want to tell you that I'm here for two reasons tonight, besides the fact that I've never had a bad day in Hawai'i."

That brought laughs.

"And I knew that if I came here tonight, Danny would do as much as he could to simulate Hawai'i. You know, I would have music, I'd have a lei, people would say 'aloha,' everybody would be relaxed. And by the time I left, no matter what I was worried about, I'd be in a good mood. And sure enough, that's happened. The second reason I'm here is on behalf of one of the finest people in the United States Senate and one of the most popular people in the entire Congress. Dan Akaka is not only a good senator, he is a good man. And I have yet to meet the first human being who didn't love him who knew him. And I want to thank him for being my friend. The third reason I'm here is because he asked me, and I owe him."

More laughs.

I hope he didn't think he owed me for looking the other way during some of his golf shots.

He talked about his record on the economy, 21 million new jobs, four percent unemployment, a $355 billion reduction in the national debt in the last three years, lower crime rates despite Republican opposition to the Brady Amendment and a ban on "cop-killer" bullets. But he honed in on giving disadvantaged kids a better chance in schools, thanking me as an ally.

"Race, ethnicity, income and location are not destiny if we can give all of our children a world-class education. And the role we played in that would not have been possible if it hadn't been for the supporters I had in our party and Congress, including Senator Akaka. So I'm proud to be here tonight for him." ✤

CHAPTER

63

Robert Kuroda was an Army staff sergeant assigned to the 442nd Regimental Combat Team, made up of second-generation or Nisei Japanese Americans. Born in 'Aiea, he trained to become an electrician, but joined the Army in March 1943. Japanese American soldiers were, of course, sent to Europe, where they could not be confused with the enemy.

On October 20, 1944, during the Battle of Bruyeres in northeastern France, Kuroda and his squad advanced through thick forest brimming with German snipers and machine-gun nests. Occasional artillery shells exploded in the trees, raining down shrapnel and shards of wood. More than one soldier got a piece of tree in his neck. This was less than five months after D-Day, yet already allied troops were pushing toward the German border. Bruyeres was only forty-two miles from the Rhine. Suddenly, heavy machine-gun fire hit the soldiers from a thickly wooded slope. The nest was too far back in the trees to see, so Kuroda led his men into the hail of bullets and made the crest of the ridge.

There he spotted the machine gun, rattling away at his comrades. Kuroda crawled within ten yards of the nest and lobbed grenades, killing three gunners. With his rifle, he killed or wounded at least three more. And then he ran out of rounds. But at least the gun was silenced. When he looked around, he noticed a U.S. officer had been hit on the next hill. He went to help him, but when he got there, the officer was clearly dead. So Kuroda grabbed the officer's submachine gun and pressed toward the second nest. He destroyed that one as well. Not content, he turned to fire on more Germans...and a sniper felled him. He died there in the forests of the Vosges Mountains. I have always hoped that, as he lay dying, he was looking up through the trees, under the fold of copper beech leaves. He was twenty-one.

For his actions that day, Kuroda was awarded the Distinguished Service Cross, the service's second-highest honor. He eventually had a hero's burial at the National Memorial Cemetery at Punchbowl, back in Honolulu.

The 442nd very soon went on to rescue the trapped "Lost Battalion," formally the 1st Battalion, 141st Regiment, originally part of the Texas National Guard's 36th Infantry Division. The battalion became surrounded by German troops in the Vosges. From October 26 to 30, the 442nd broke through German defenses and rescued 211 men. But in doing so the 442nd suffered more than 800 casualties. One company went in with 185 men and only eight walked out unharmed. The 442nd became one of the most decorated units in U.S. history. This was a matter of monumental pride for Japanese Americans in a war that saw thousands of their kin shipped away to internment camps, their loyalty suspect.

But decades later, it struck me as odd that the 442nd, and its companion unit, the 100th Infantry Battalion, had relatively few Medals of Honor, our nation's highest award for valor. I wondered if it had to do with the prejudice of the day. For instance, no black soldier won the Medal of Honor during World War II.

So, in 1995, I inserted language in the National Defense Authorization Act that asked the secretaries of the Army and Navy to review the records relating to the award of the Distinguished Service Cross and Navy Cross, respectively, to Asian Americans or Pacific Islanders who served in World War II. I wanted them to determine if any should be upgraded to the Medal of Honor. The language also waived the time requirements and other restrictions on awarding the Medal of Honor.

Formally Senate Bill 1124, introduced in August 1995 by Senator Strom Thurmond of South Carolina, the bill initially went to the Senate Armed Services Committee and sailed through. The Senate passed it on September 6. The House passed it on January 5, 1996, and it went to conference committee. It cleared the conference committee with my language still intact. The measure went to the White House on January 30, and Clinton signed it on February 10.

The research took more than two years. On October 12, 1998, the Army Center of Military History forwarded the names of 104 Asian American recipients of the Distinguished Service Cross—including Inouye—to a board of senior officers for review. The board sent twenty-two names to the president for final consideration.

On June 21, 2000, in a late afternoon ceremony in muggy heat on the South Lawn of the White House, Clinton presented the Medal of Honor to Inouye and twenty-one other World War II veterans or their families. I was there, of course, as were many members of the Senate and House. Major General David Hicks, chaplain of the Army, said a brief prayer.

"Let us pray. Almighty God, as we begin this award ceremony for these great heroes of our freedom, we offer you our thanksgiving and pray. Knowing that the price of freedom is extremely high, and has always required that people step forward and do the seemingly impossible, we come to you with a deep sense of gratitude for the gift of life, which we enjoy as a result of the heroic deeds of these special soldiers and others like them."

That set the tone.

Clinton stepped up to the podium and greeted Hicks, as well as Defense secretary William Cohen and his wife, Veterans Affairs secretary Togo West and Health and Human Services secretary Donna Shalala.

"I thank all of you for being here on this profoundly important day," Clinton said. "In early 1945, a young Japanese American of the 442nd Regimental Combat Team lay dead on a hill in Southern France—the casualty of fierce fighting with the Germans. A chaplain went up to pray over him, to bless him, to bring him back down. As the chaplain later said, 'I found a letter in his pocket. The soldier had just learned that some vandals in California had burned down his father's home and barn in the name of patriotism. And yet, this young man had volunteered for every patrol he could go on.'

"In a few moments I will ask the military aides to read individual citations, detailing the extraordinary bravery of twenty-two Asian American soldiers—some still with us, some to be represented by family members. We recognize them today with our nation's highest military honor, the Medal of Honor. They risked their lives, above and beyond the call of duty. And in so doing, they did more than defend America; in the face of painful prejudice, they helped to define America at its best."

He introduced Senator Bob Kerrey of Nebraska—a Medal

of Honor winner himself for service in Vietnam—and General Eric Shinseki, the Japanese American chief of staff of the Army.

Shinseki got a standing ovation.

I had known Ric Shinseki, a Kauaʻi native, for years. In fact, his daughter, Lori, was an aide of mine when I was in the House. Shinseki asked me to pin on his eagles when he made full colonel. I was happy to do so. Now he was wearing four stars.

"In 1942," Clinton continued, "a committee of the Army recommended against forming a combat unit of Japanese Americans, citing—and I quote—'the universal distrust in which they are held.' Yet, Americans of Japanese ancestry, joined by others of good faith, pressed the issue and a few months later President Roosevelt authorized a combat team of Japanese American volunteers.

"In approving the unit FDR said, 'Americanism is a matter of the mind and heart. America is not, and never was, a matter of race or ancestry.' That statement from President Roosevelt, so different from the executive order of just a year before, showed a nation pulled between its highest ideals and its darkest fears. We were not only fighting for freedom and equality abroad, we were also in a struggle here at home over whether America would be defined narrowly, on the basis of race, or broadly, on the basis of shared values and ideals.

"When young Japanese American men volunteered enthusiastically, some Americans were puzzled. But those who volunteered knew why. Their own country had dared to question their patriotism and they would not rest until they had proved their loyalty.

"As sons set off to war, so many mothers and fathers told them, 'Live if you can; die if you must; but fight always with honor, and never, ever bring shame on your family or your country.' Rarely has a nation been so well served by a people it has so ill-treated."

He mentioned Inouye in particular.

"As their heroic efforts forced back the Nazis in Europe, news of their patriotism began to beat back prejudice in America. But prejudice is a stubborn foe. Captain Daniel Inouye, back from the war, in full uniform, decorated with the Distinguished Service Cross, the Bronze Star, Purple Heart with Cluster and twelve other medals and citations, tried to get a haircut and was told, 'We don't cut Jap hair.' As Captain Inouye said later, 'I was tempted to break up the place,' but he had already done all the fighting he needed to do.

"People across the country had learned of his heroism and that of his colleagues, and loyal Americans were eager to teach others the difference between patriotism and prejudice. A group of Army veterans who knew firsthand the heroism of Japanese American soldiers, attacked prejudice in a letter to the *Des Moines Register*. It said, 'When you have seen these boys blown to bits, going through shellfire that others refused to go through, that is the time to voice your opinion, not before.'"

Then he addressed Inouye directly.

"Senator Inouye, you wrote that your father told you as you left at age eighteen to join the Army and fight a war that the Inouyes owe an unrepayable debt to America. If I may say so, sir, more than half a century later, America owes an unrepayable debt to you and your colleagues."

The crowd applauded.

Clinton mentioned that the report of the Presidential Commission on Wartime Relocation and Internment of Civilians, issued some twenty years ago, called internment an injustice based on "race prejudice, war hysteria and a failure of political leadership," and suggested remedies.

"Some years later, many leaders backed legislation sponsored by Senator Daniel Akaka, to review the combat records of Asian Americans in World War II to determine if any deserving service members had been passed over for the Medal of Honor," Clinton said. "The review found, indeed, that some extraordinarily brave soldiers never did receive the honors they clearly had earned. So today, America awards twenty-two of them the Medal of Honor. They risked their lives, on their own initiative, sometimes even against orders, to take out machine guns, give aid to wounded soldiers, draw fire, pinpoint the enemy, protect their own. People who can agree on nothing else fall silent before that kind of courage."

We then heard the citations and Clinton presented the medals for Rudolph Davila, Barney Hajiro, Mikio Hasemoto, Joe Hayashi, Shizuya Hayashi, Inouye, Yeiki Kobashigawa, Kuroda, Kaoru Moto, Kiyoshi Muranaga, Masato Nakae, Shinyei Nakamine, William Nakamura, Joe Nishimoto, Allan Ohata, James Okubo, Yukio Okutsu, Frank Ono, Kazuo Otani, George Sakato, Ted Tanouye and Francis Wai.

Of the twenty-two, only seven were still alive, five of them from Hawai'i: Inouye, Okutsu, Kobashigawa, Hajiro and Shizuya Hayashi.

Davila, a Texan who fought with the 3rd Division in World War II, and Sakato, a 442 member from California, also were there. The rest were awarded posthumously. Robert Kuroda's medal was accepted by his brother, Joe—my congressional opponent in 1976.

After the ceremony, I told the *Star-Bulletin*: "I am so elated. I am overjoyed that it has come to this point, where we finally recognize these veterans and give them the proper recognition. That's all I hoped for."

In the follow-up, more than one person said to me, "Oh, so you did it for Inouye."

But I didn't. When I started the process those many years ago, I didn't know that Inouye would qualify for a Medal of Honor.

In late November 2012, as I was preparing to leave Washington, I received a letter from Joe Kuroda. He congratulated me on my years of service and said I deserved a "quiet retired life with Millie."

He recalled our early days as principals—him at Barbers Point Elementary and me at adjoining Pohakea.

"What is important today is we remained friends and we served Hawai'i and our people in our own designated elected official capacity," he said, referring to his seventeen years in the Legislature. "And, Danny, a special 'mahalo' for your great successful effort in the review of the WWII record of U.S. military veterans of Asian ancestry DSC recipients, which resulted in the 'upgrade' to twenty-two Medals of Honor (MOH): twenty AJA, one Filipino American and one Chinese American in the year 2000. I marvel at the thought that I was a UH freshman in the veterans dormitory in 1947 when I met and chatted with UH upper classman WWII hero Dan Inouye, who went on to become our senior U.S. senator, your mentor and MOH recipient. Good luck, God bless you and God bless America!" ✸

CHAPTER

64

Long before President Barack Obama lifted the travel ban on Cuba, three of us in the Senate attempted to ease trade barriers with the communist nation on our own.

Senators Max Baucus, a Montana Democrat; and Pat Roberts, a Republican from Kansas and a member of the Agriculture Committee; and I contacted the Cuban government and were told we were welcome to visit. But oddly we were unable to set up a firm appointment with Fidel Castro. We decided to take a chance and go down anyway, and arrived on Saturday, July 15, 2000, on a chartered flight. American carriers weren't allowed into Cuban airspace.

We three weren't the only ones on Capitol Hill who thought the trade ban with Cuba ought to be scrapped. In August 1999, the Senate voted 70–28 in favor of an amendment by Senator John Ashcroft to remove agricultural trade sanctions against Cuba, Libya, Sudan and North Korea. This was, of course, before North Korea began testing nuclear weapons. Ashcroft, a Missouri Republican who later would become attorney general under George W. Bush, and others argued that unilateral food and medicine sanctions don't work and only hurt American farmers. For soybean farmers alone, we heard, opening up those markets would generate up to $147 million in new income a year. The Ashcroft amendment was attached to the 2000 farm spending bill, surprisingly, with the blessing of Jesse Helms, chairman of the Senate Foreign Relations Committee and a longtime opponent of closer ties with Cuba. Helms, a North Carolina Republican, remarked, "The impetus for this reform comes from our farm community, which is hurting today, and which is asking us in Congress to look at ways in which we can expand markets for American farm products." Ultimately, the measure was dropped in conference committee.

We were greeted at Jose Marti International Airport, nine miles southwest of Havana, by protocol officers from the Foreign Ministry. They spoke excellent English. We repeated our desire to speak directly with Castro, and they indicated with serious nods that it might be possible.

Once in Havana, we passed El Capitolio, the seat of government in Cuba until the revolution in 1959. It bears a striking resemblance to the United States Capitol, with a central dome and dozens of steps leading up to the main entryway. It was now the home of the Cuban Academy of Sciences and houses the National Library of Science and Technology. Funny, but Americans don't really associate Cuba with technology—unless it's rum distillation! I was increasingly sure this visit would fell other stereotypes as well. The city itself, from my brief impression, had an old-world feel, more reminiscent of Europe than the Americas. I had imagined a slow-paced, even sleepy city, but Havana appeared vibrant. Many of the low-rise buildings had louvered shutters and wrought-iron railings.

I can't remember at what ministry we ended up, but we met with both the foreign minister and the minister of economics and planning. The economics minister told us bluntly that there was no move afoot to privatize the economy because capitalism does not work. Only "pure socialism" does, he said. Before we were done, it was abundantly clear that the Castro government had no interest in economic reform, even in the fashion of China or Vietnam. We were at this for hours and finally a telephone call came in.

"*El Jefe* will see you at four o'clock."

We arrived promptly at the *palacio*, not really a palace in European sense but a grand home nonetheless. And there, waiting to meet us at the entrance, was Castro, casually dressed but wearing a light sport jacket. With him was an interpreter, an attractive woman on the young side of middle-aged. I believe he introduced her as Juana or Juanita. And I'm not exaggerating when I say Castro greeted us like old friends. Now, we were warned that Castro liked to talk. But I could never have imagined how much. He didn't stop. We listened to him for at least an hour—before we went inside! Essentially, he was bragging about Cuba, how well the country was doing. Then he paused.

"Oh. *Por favor, entran,*" he said.

Please come inside.

He escorted us into an open-air living room, with comfortably upholstered chairs and sofas and tables holding flowers in colorful ceramic pots. There were side tables in a dark wood, perhaps mahogany. The paintings were mostly landscapes—Cuban, I assumed—in a modern style. The decor was subtle, not ornate and put us instantly at ease.

"*Sientese*, sientese."

Sit down, sit down.

And he kept talking. Cuba and its people. How well they are doing! Almost without taking a breath. Baucus and I exchanged a worried glance. Because it became increasingly clear that if we wanted to say anything, we were going to have to interrupt Castro. Somehow, without being rude, we were able to get across to him that we were there to try to see how we could work with Cuba.

But he took it the wrong way.

"*Oye, no necesitamos ninguna ayuda,*" he said.

Hey, we don't need any help.

"How's the drug problem?" I asked.

"We have it controlled," he said, without seeming to take offense. "We don't need any help."

"How about other health issues? Maybe the U.S. can help improve your country's health care?"

He changed the subject to Havana's night clubs. In fact, he spent a considerable amount of time singing the praises of one particular club, the Tropicana.

"You should go to that night club," he told us. "You'll enjoy it. Hey, I will arrange for you folks to go there tonight!"

Then it was time for dinner.

The large table was, again, glass, with more floral decorations. The placemats looked like linen, off-white, matching the napkins and the silverware looked like, well, real silver. It was fabulous. I want to say we started out with a small bowl of black bean soup laced with onions and garlic. The main dish might have been steak in a tomato sauce served with peas, olives and red peppers over a bed of rice. Fried plantain, a cousin of the banana, I learned, is a popular side dish.

Cuba doesn't need any help! We're doing fine! The people are happy!

This went on for hours.

At one point, he remarked that he didn't think that Cuba could survive as a member of the International Monetary Fund, which he called "the world's most subversive organization."

Then Castro looked at his watch.

"Oye! *Lo siento mucho!*"

Oh, boy! I'm so sorry!

"It's too late for the night club," he said.

By my watch it was 2 a.m. We'd been listening to him for ten hours straight.

"When you come back to Cuba, you should visit the night club," he said.

We said our goodbyes and left Havana the next day. I came away convinced that the Cuban government did not want the American embargo lifted because the lack of economic ties allows the government to blame the United States for its own economic failures. Were the embargo lifted, they would lose that excuse.

Back in Washington, days later, Baucus, Roberts and I received mail from Castro. It was promotional material for the Tropicana. ❖

CHAPTER

65

Ernest F. "Fritz" Hollings was a gracious Southern gentleman, a conservative Democrat from Charleston. He had a firm handshake, straight teeth revealed by a ready grin, and, by the time I knew him, hair the color of freshly fallen snow. I intend the metaphor: he was also cool-headed. He was a decorated veteran of World War II in Europe. His arguments on legislation were unfailingly civil. He never bullied, only cajoled. I liked him.

We were unlikely allies.

As governor of South Carolina in the early 1960s, he opposed integration and flew the Confederate flag over the state house, where it remained until the year 2000. He sent death-row prisoners to the electric chair. In 1967, as a senator, he voted against the appointment of Thurgood Marshall as the first black Supreme Court justice. Later, in perhaps a mistake of equal measure, he voted for Clarence Thomas. He and Howell Heflin of Alabama were the only two Democrats to vote against the Family and Medical Leave Act of 1993. Hollings and Strom Thurmond were peas in a pod for many years.

But on one important issue we did agree: protection of the ocean. Hawai'i's shores look far different from those of South Carolina, but anyone who has been to Hilton Head or the Francis Marion National Park knows they are both beautiful. When I was young, everyone thought the ocean was too vast to be affected by human activity. For some time now, we have known that is untrue. The plastic debris that washes up on Hawai'i beaches attests to a global pollution problem. And some species of fish are on the brink of extinction.

On March 29, 2000, Hollings introduced the Oceans Act of 2000. I immediately signed on, along with twenty other cosponsors, among them Inouye, Kerry, Murkowski and Stevens of Alaska, Feinstein and Boxer of California, Schumer and Moynihan of New York and

Mary Landrieu and John Breaux of Louisiana. I won't go on. Let me just say that all of the cosponsors came from a state with a shoreline. The bill established a federal Commission on Ocean Policy that would look at natural hazards like hurricanes, the responsible stewardship of fisheries, the protection of the marine environment, the role of the oceans in climate change and the enhancement of ocean transportation and commerce. The measure itself didn't solve the problems, but it was an important step in the right direction, with a call for presidential action when the studies were done.

In all my years in Congress, I can't recall any measure moving faster. McCain passed it out of his Committee on Commerce, Science and Transportation on May 23, the full Senate approved it unanimously on June 26, the House passed it by voice vote on July 25, and Clinton signed it into law on August 7. On Capitol Hill, that equates to the speed of light. I think it was a reflection of how seriously we all took of the fate of the seas.

During this process, coincidentally, on May 26, Clinton took steps to protect the coral reefs of the Northwestern Hawaiian Islands.

"The world's coral reefs—our tropical rainforests of the water—are in serious decline," he said in a memorandum to the secretaries of commerce and the interior. "These important and sensitive areas of biodiversity warrant special protection. While the United States has only three percent of the world's coral reefs, nearly seventy percent of U.S. coral reefs are in the Northwest Hawaiian Islands. Many of the Northwest Hawaiian Islands' coral, fish, and invertebrate species are unique, and the area is home to endangered Hawaiian monk seals and threatened turtles."

In August 2000, during the congressional recess, I underwent hip replacement surgery at the Queen's Medical Center. Thanks to a bum right knee that I ignored too long, the right hip joint had deteriorated to the point where it was very painful and made walking difficult. With my new "bionic" hip in place, I underwent five days of rehab at the Rehabilitation Hospital of the Pacific. I regretted missing the Democratic National Convention in Los Angeles—and missing out on some golf rounds, but I was confident of a swift recovery. Eventually, I had both knees replaced as well, a likely legacy of my football days at Kamehameha Schools.

In September, Hawai'i's sugar industry took another hit when Amfac/JMB Hawai'i, the second-largest private landowner on Kaua'i, said it would end all agricultural operations on the island later in the year, close its two sugar mills in Līhu'e and Kekaha, lay off all 400 workers and sell more than 17,000 acres of land mauka of Līhu'e.

"We regret having to take this action, but with losses mounting and no end in sight, we really had no choice," Amfac president Gary Grottke said in a statement. Amfac's plantations had been a fixture on Kaua'i, operating since the nineteenth century, so this was a sad announcement indeed. For some time, however, it had been evident that the company needed cash. In January, Amfac had sold 1,400 acres of farm land mauka of Kapa'a for $4.5 million to singer-actress Bette Midler, a Honolulu native. It didn't help that sugar prices had dropped by five cents a pound, or about twenty percent, over the last year. Amfac's impending departure left only Robinson Family Partners, the island's largest private landowner, as the last sugar plantation on Kaua'i with 51,000 acres. A&B had closed its McBryde Sugar Co. on Kaua'i in 1996.

In fact, the only good news in the agricultural arena came in December, when Steve Case, another Hawai'i native and the founder of American Online, bought Grove Farm on Kaua'i for $26 million and promised not to lay off any workers. Seven months later, he bought another 18,000 acres, once part of Lihue Plantation, for a total of 38,000 acres. Diversified crops and housing were the new focus.

On July 20, I introduced the first of several measures that would eventually evolve into the so-called Akaka Bill. The balky working title was, "A bill to express the policy of the United States regarding the United States' relationship with Native Hawaiians, and other purposes." Inouye was my sole cosponsor. The measure called for the establishment of Office for Native Hawaiian Affairs within the office of the secretary of the interior. It required the attorney general to designate someone in the Justice Department to work with the office on legal and political issues. It also established a Native Hawaiian Interagency Task Force to coordinate federal policies that affect Native Hawaiians. And it established a process for development of a membership roll for organizing a Native Hawaiian Interim Governing Council and for election of a Native Hawaiian government. It recognized the right of the Native Hawaiian people to adopt organic governing documents. And it required the elected officers of the government to submit such documents to the secretary for certification. Once certified, the Hawaiian government would get federal recognition. The bill was referred to the Committee on Indian Affairs, led by Senator Ben Nighthorse Campbell of Colorado, a member of the Northern Cheyenne Tribe. In September he recommended its passage, but it was never taken up by the full Senate. In April 2001, I introduced it again in the 107th Congress with much the same result.

There were few surprises in the Hawai'i primary election on September 23. Russ Francis, a Hawai'i boy who went on to shine as a pass receiver for the New England Patriots and San Francisco 49ers, won the Republican race to challenge Mink. I had three opponents: Carroll and one each from the Libertarian and Natural Law Parties. In the mayor's race, Jeremy Harris beat Hannemann and Fasi. On the Big Island, longtime civil defense director Harry Kim led the Republicans candidates for mayor and would face Democrat Fred Holschuh and Keiko Bonk of the Green Party in November.

The big surprise—shock, really—came on November 7, the beginning of a lengthy, drawn-out ballot count and legal challenges in the presidential race in Florida. It played out in agonizing detail for weeks on network television. Nationwide, Gore and his running mate, Senator Joe Lieberman, narrowly won the popular vote, just under 51 million to 50.5 million for Bush and Dick Cheney. But, of course, the national vote means nothing.

In the Electoral College, it all came down to Florida, where poll minders were forced to decide if partially punched holes—"hanging chad"—counted as a vote. Without Florida, Gore led in electoral votes 255–246, so Florida's twenty-five votes would make the difference.

In the end, Bush led by a whisker-thin 537 votes. (More than 97,000 Floridians voted for Green Party candidate Ralph Nader.) Gore asked for a hand recount in Broward, Miami-Dade, Palm Beach and Volusia counties. Florida's secretary of state, Katherine Harris, said she would not accept any revised totals beyond a deadline of November 14. The Florida Supreme Court extended that deadline until November 26, when Bush was certified as the winner, but the recounts continued under a series of legal challenges. Finally, in December, the U.S. Supreme Court stepped in and, by a 5–4 vote, effectively shut down the recount. The majority included Chief Justice Rehnquist and Justices Sandra Day O'Connor, Anthony Kennedy, Antonin Scalia and Clarence Thomas. I was disappointed in Kennedy and O'Connor. The four in the minority were Stephen Breyer, Ruth Bader Ginsburg, David Souter and John Paul Stevens. Breyer and Ginsburg were Clinton appointees; the others were appointed by Republicans Ford, Reagan or Bush.

So now, for better or worse, we had another Bush.

In Hawai'i, Mink beat Francis, 57–33. Abercrombie also won reelection to the House. Harry Kim won the Big Island mayor's race. And I won my second full term in the Senate, where there was now a 50–50 split between Democrats and Republicans. The Senate lineup also was a bit of a cliff-hanger, with the race in Washington State undecided until December 1. Maria Cantwell, a Democrat, won by a slim 2,229 votes, largely on the strength of her Native American support. That placed her among thirteen female senators, the most in history. The others included Hillary Clinton and Jean Carnahan, who replaced her husband, Mel, killed in a place crash.

As incoming vice president, Dick Cheney, also president of the Senate, would have a tie-breaker role. But the choice of a Senate majority leader proved a bit tricky, as there was no majority. Republican leader Trent Lott and his Democratic counterpart, Tom Daschle, ended up in a kind of power-sharing agreement, but there would be more political surprises to stir the pot in the months ahead. ✣

CHAPTER

66

In his inaugural address, Bush said, "As I begin, I thank President Clinton for his service to our nation, and I thank Vice President Gore for a contest conducted with spirit and ended with grace." He called for better schools, lower taxes, reforms in Social Security and Medicare, but also for civility among Americans.

"America at its best is also courageous..." he said. "We will build our defenses beyond challenge, lest weakness invite challenge. We will confront weapons of mass destruction, so that a new century is spared new horrors. The enemies of liberty and our country should make no mistake: America remains engaged in the world, by history and by choice, shaping a balance of power that favors freedom."

He would soon face very formidable enemies.

Bush's first foreign policy challenge came on February 9, when the Pearl Harbor-based nuclear submarine USS *Greeneville*, on a cruise for sixteen VIPs south of Oʻahu, demonstrated an emergency "blow" of its ballast tanks, a maneuver to lift it quickly to the surface. The bow of the sub burst skyward and collided with a Japanese high school training ship, the *Ehime Maru*, cutting it in two. It sank within minutes. Nine people aboard died, including four students. The tragedy was compounded by the fact that the *Greeneville* had had a sonar contact for the *Ehime Maru*, designated as Sierra 13. So the fire control technician knew a ship was up there, if not exactly where. Unfortunately, when the captain, Commander Scott Waddle, did his periscope sweep before diving, he had no visual contacts, perhaps because the *Ehime* then was hidden in mist. The fire control technician, Patrick Seacrest, knew that Sierra 13 was within 4,000 yards, but figured that Waddle would have seen it if it were close. At that point, about 2 p.m., the sub was also behind schedule and the crew was in a hurry to get back to Pearl, according to testimony at the court of inquiry.

I have been aboard a nuclear submarine, the Pearl Harbor-based USS *La Jolla*, also a Los Angeles-class "hunter-killer" boat, so I am familiar with the VIP experience. The crew does an excellent job of showing off the sub's maneuverability, including a series of sharp turns and dives known as "angles and dangles." Typically, one or more of the guests is allowed to handle the controls during some of the maneuvers. We also got to look through the periscope as the sub is just below the surface. Mine was a startlingly clear view of Tamura's Super Market on Farrington Highway in Waiʻanae. I could see the customers going in and out of the store like I was across the street. I am sure they never suspected they were under surveillance. During our cruise, the crew exuded competence. However, years earlier, in February 1998, off South Korea, this very sub, under another crew, collided with and sank a twenty-seven-ton fishing trawler. The sub managed to rescue all five sailors from the trawler. But it only takes one incident like that to ruin a Navy captain's career. Waddle's was over, everyone knew. Or rather, everyone except Waddle. In his book, *The Right Thing*, he admitted surprise when he was abruptly fired by his friend and mentor, Rear Admiral Al Konetzni, commander of the Pacific Fleet Submarine Force. For some, the sea is a cruel mistress.

The Coast Guard and Navy pulled twenty-six *Ehime Maru* survivors from the sea. But the sinking of Sierra 13 created significant friction between the United States and Japan, which already had a long history of criminal complaints against U.S. service personnel stationed in their nation. Prime minister Yoshiro Mori got word of the deadly accident during a golf game. He continued playing for another ninety minutes, for which he was roundly criticized by lawmakers and the press. Within months he would resign.

Bush called Mori to apologize, then repeated the apology on national television.

"I want to reiterate what I said to the prime minister of Japan: I'm deeply sorry that the accident took place. Our nation is sorry." Public apologies also came from the new secretary of state, Colin Powell, and defense secretary, Donald Rumsfeld, and our ambassador to Japan, former House Speaker Tom Foley. Bush sent the vice chief of naval operations, Admiral William Fallon, to Japan to personally apologize. "I sincerely and humbly request—on behalf of the United States government, the United States Navy and the American people—that the government and people of Japan accept our apology for the tragic loss of the *Ehime Maru*," he said. "I know my words cannot express the profound sorrow and regret that the American people feel over this tragic event." And Admiral Tom Fargo, commander of the Pearl Harbor-based Pacific Fleet, apologized in person to the families of the victims who arrived in Hawai'i in the accident's aftermath. This was an especially difficult encounter because, at that point, several of the bodies had yet to be recovered.

Through his lawyer, Commander Waddle sent a statement to Japanese TV network NHK. "It is with a heavy heart that I express my most sincere regret," Waddle said. "I know that the accident has caused unimaginable grief to the families of the *Ehime Maru*'s missing students, instructors and crew members…and to all of the Japanese people." He would later venture to Japan to express more regret in person.

But some of the victims' family members remained unsatisfied with the U.S. response. And the governor of Okinawa, home to a large U.S. Marine contingent as well the Air Force's 18th Wing at Kadena Air Base, formally asked that the Japanese government negotiate a reduction in the number of American troops there. Waddle, a 1981 Annapolis graduate, left the Navy with an honorable discharge, wrote the book and went on a speaking tour, on which he discussed the redemptive power of contrition.

Salvage crews later raised the wreck of the *Ehime Maru* and recovered eight bodies. The body of student Takeshi Mizuguchi, seventeen, was never found. The United States paid $8 million to the Ehime Prefecture to replace this ship, and another $20 million or so to the victims' families. Within a year of the accident, an *Ehime Maru* memorial was completed at Kaka'ako Waterfront Park in Honolulu, and for years many of the victims' family members have visited on the anniversary.

※ ※ ※

On June 14, 2001, with Inouye as a cosponsor, I introduced a measure to expand the Pu'uhonua o Hōnaunau National Historic Park, the City of Refuge on Hawaiʻi island, with the addition of two parcels totaling nearly 400 acres. This passed the Senate unanimously in October, but it was Mink's companion bill in the House that went on eventually to become law. In Hawaiian culture, the refuge is a deeply spiritual place, so I was gratified to be able to expand it. In ancient Hawaiʻi, Puʻuhonua was a sanctuary for those who had broken the kapu, the laws imposed by chiefs, or for defeated warriors. While the many carved wooden images, or *kiʻi*, may seen threatening, it is traditionally a place of peace and forgiveness.

In the years to come, peace would prove to be a rare commodity.

On September 10, 2001, in Australia, Clinton told a group of businessmen that he had had a chance in 1998 to kill Osama bin Laden, but decided against the strike because the civilian death toll would be high.

"I nearly got him," Clinton said. "And I could have killed him, but I would have to destroy a little town called Kandahar in Afghanistan and kill 300 innocent women and children, and then I would have been no better than him. And so I didn't do it."

In fact, Clinton had several opportunities to kill bin Laden, and tried to do so on one occasion. The 9/11 Commission report offers details on nine instances. Here are three of them:

In August 1998, after the embassy bombings in Africa, the CIA learned that al-Qaida leaders, possibly including bin Laden, would be meeting at a camp near Khowst, Afghanistan. There would be no civilians nearby. The Pentagon briefed Clinton on the plans on August 12 and again two days later. On Clinton's orders, four Navy surface ships and the Pearl Harbor-based submarine USS *Columbia*, all in the Arabian Sea, launched seventy-three Tomahawk cruise missiles at the camp. Most of them hit their targets, but neither bin Laden nor any other terrorist leader was among the twenty to thirty casualties. The CIA later concluded they had missed bin Laden by a matter of hours.

In December, the CIA got word that bin Laden would be spending the night at a residence called Haji Habash, part of the governor's mansion in Kandahar. But the head of the military's Central Command, General Anthony Zinni, predicted more than 200 civilian deaths would result. He was also worried an attack would damage a nearby mosque. The strike was called off. This is the one that Clinton mentioned.

In May 1999, spies in Afghanistan had very detailed information on bin Laden's location around Kandahar over the course of several days. One senior military officer told the 9/11 Commission the attack would have been "a home run." But CIA director George Tenet balked, leaving the military dumbfounded. The caution might have arisen from the ongoing NATO war against Serbia. Flawed CIA targeting coordinates had just led U.S. aircraft, on May 7, to bomb the Chinese embassy in Belgrade, 440 yards from the intended target. Three dead, with the Chinese denouncing it as a "barbarian act." That might make anyone gun shy. So bin Laden had his nine lives.

When American Airlines Flight 77 slammed into the Pentagon, Isaac "Ike" Hoʻopiʻi was driving his dog, Vito, to the vet. Of Hawaiian, Chinese and Portuguese ancestry, Hoʻopiʻi was born and raised in Waiʻanae and had graduated from Waiʻanae High School. Now he lived in McLean, Virginia, and worked with as an officer with the Pentagon police. His specialty: bomb-sniffing dogs. I had known Ike for more than a dozen years, since I was in the House. We shared a love of music. On many occasions, my family and I had spent time with Ike and his wife, Gigi, and their children, Emily, Bess, and Jeff. He often performed with his twin brother, Ivan.

Suddenly, the shocking news came from his radio dispatcher: an airliner had crashed into the side of the building.

"A plane hit the Pentagon! Emergency! A plane hit the Pentagon!" she cried.

Ike spun around and was one of the first officers on scene. Few nightmares could rival what greeted him: a gaping, smoking chasm, the aircraft wreckage, rubble. Cries of pain. Without hesitation, he rushed into the building. With no protective gear, he made his way past collapsed interior walls, sparking wires, shards of glass, flaming debris, burnt bodies, paint peeling off the walls from the heat. He could barely see through the smoke, so he started calling out to survivors.

"If you can hear me, head to my voice!" he shouted.

Later, he recalled, "My job was just to react, and when you react, it is more like tunnel vision. You try to focus and your adrenaline just kicks in. You really don't realize what you're doing, except just to save lives."

He led or carried several survivors out to safety, depositing them on a section of lawn about 100 yards from danger. Some of the people he helped died, but Isaac early on was credited for saving at least eight lives. Later the tally rose to eighteen. Among them was a Pentagon computer contractor, Wayne Sinclair, who told the *Washington Post* he crawled toward the voice of a "guardian angel" with a Hawaiian accent. "Most people were in a state of panic and shock," Sinclair recounted. "I said, 'Let's head toward that voice. There is somebody outside. There's got to be.' So we kept heading toward it and, sure enough, we got outside." Sinclair and Hoʻopiʻi later met on NBC's *Today* show and became fast friends.

Altogether, 189 people died in the attack on the Pentagon. But the toll certainly would have been higher absent the actions of this brave Hawaiian. He and Vito worked thirty-six hours straight after the crash, searching through the rubble.

When I spoke to him later about his split-second decision to respond with little concern for his safety, he downplayed his heroism. I was told by others that Isaac felt badly that he could not have saved more people. But I am sure that the people he did help—and their families—are very thankful for his willingness to risk his life.

On October 16, Inouye paid tribute to Ike in the Congressional Record.

"Out of the rubble of destruction, countless Americans rose and demonstrated great courage and selflessness," he said. "One such American was Mr. Isaac Hoʻopiʻi… Minutes after a hijacked plane crashed into the Pentagon, Mr. Hoʻopiʻi raced into the burning building and carried out eight people. His calm resolve in the face of danger equaled his physical prowess. Unable to see the terrified victims, but knowing that they were amid the debris, smoke and darkness, Mr. Hoʻopiʻi repeatedly called out: 'Head toward my voice'… I have had the opportunity to hear Mr. Hoʻopiʻi's voice. He is a musician with the Aloha Boys, a Hawaiian musical group that has performed on Capitol Hill. His singing is melodious and resonant, but I believe Mr. Hoʻopiʻi's voice had never before sounded more beautiful than it did on that September morning."

In March 2002, I attended the ceremony at which Isaac received the Secretary of Defense Medal of Valor, the department's highest honor for civilians. Thirty-eight others also were recognized. At the ceremony, Paul Haselbush, director of Pentagon facilities, basically the landlord or mayor, mentioned a letter he received from a woman who had been stranded with a flat tire for three hours in the cold. This was before cellphones. When Ike happened by to help her, she recognized him as the "voice" featured on CNN and the *Today* show, so she wrote to the Defense Department to formally express her thanks.

After the ceremony, I told Ike how very proud I was of him. He smiled and said he was just trying to be a good Hawaiian and to share the spirit of aloha. Isaac is a wonderful Hawaiian, a wonderful American, and his actions and attitude reflect the essence of the people of my home state. ✽

PART FOUR

THE NEW NORMAL

CHAPTER

67

On September 20, nine days after the attacks, Bush addressed a joint session of Congress.

"Tonight we are a country awakened to danger and called to defend freedom," he said. "Our grief has turned to anger, and anger to resolution. Whether we bring our enemies to justice, or bring justice to our enemies, justice will be done."

That drew applause.

Bush said all the evidence so far pointed to al-Qaida as the culprits.

"They are the same murderers indicted for bombing American embassies in Tanzania and Kenya, and responsible for bombing the USS *Cole*," he said. "al-Qaida is to terror what the mafia is to crime. But its goal is not making money; its goal is remaking the world—and imposing its radical beliefs on people everywhere."

He called the new rulers of Afghanistan, the Taliban, brutal, repressive and extremist.

"The United States respects the people of Afghanistan—after all, we are currently its largest source of humanitarian aid—but we condemn the Taliban regime," he said to more applause. "It is not only repressing its own people, it is threatening people everywhere by sponsoring and sheltering and supplying terrorists. By aiding and abetting murder, the Taliban regime is committing murder.

"And tonight, the United States of America makes the following demands on the Taliban: Deliver to United States authorities all the leaders of al-Qaida who hide in your land. Release all foreign nationals, including American citizens, you have unjustly imprisoned. Protect foreign journalists, diplomats and aid workers in your country. Close immediately and permanently every terrorist training camp in

Afghanistan, and hand over every terrorist, and every person in their support structure, to appropriate authorities. Give the United States full access to terrorist training camps, so we can make sure they are no longer operating.

"These demands are not open to negotiation or discussion. The Taliban must act, and act immediately. They will hand over the terrorists, or they will share in their fate."

He also announced a new cabinet-level position, director of homeland security, and named former Pennsylvania governor Tom Ridge to the position. As a member of the Senate Committee on Government Affairs, that caught my attention. I sensed another bureaucracy brewing.

"And tonight, a few miles from the damaged Pentagon, I have a message for our military: Be ready. I've called the Armed Forces to alert, and there is a reason. The hour is coming when America will act, and you will make us proud."

More applause.

"This is not, however, just America's fight. And what is at stake is not just America's freedom. This is the world's fight. This is civilization's fight. This is the fight of all who believe in progress and pluralism, tolerance and freedom. We ask every nation to join us."

The Taliban denied Bush's demands, of course. So on October 7 he launched Operation Enduring Freedom. It seemed like only yesterday that we were boycotting the 1980 Summer Olympics in Moscow. The reason: the Soviets had invaded Afghanistan! Now, here we were, in the fall of 2001, invading Afghanistan ourselves.

As if the new millennium didn't deliver enough drama, we soon had an anthrax scare on our hands. Letters containing the deadly biological toxin had been sent anonymously to media outlets, including one addressed to news anchor Tom Brokaw. Twenty-two people contracted anthrax, most dangerous when the spores are inhaled, and five died. Understandably, many people thought this was the second wave of the 9/11 terrorism attacks.

In mid-October, letters containing anthrax spores in white powdered form were delivered to Senator Tom Daschle of South

Dakota. The accompanying note, handwritten in capital letters, said, "9-11-01. YOU CANNOT STOP US. WE HAVE THIS ANTHRAX. YOU DIE NOW. ARE YOU AFRAID? DEATH TO AMERICA. DEATH TO ISRAEL. ALLAH IS GREAT." Several of Daschle's staffers and interns were exposed, as was one of my staffers, Dave Chun. They were among 200 lawmakers and staff members who ended up taking an anti-anthrax medication called ciprofloxacin, or Cipro for short.

Daschle and I both had offices in the Hart Building, which was evacuated as the Capitol Police in hazmat suits and Environmental Protection Agency investigators assessed the situation. In the immediate aftermath, my staff and Inouye's decamped to the Indian Affairs Committee hearing room in the nearby Dirksen Building. Inouye was chairman of the committee at that time. His staff took up one half of the room, my staff the other. As my people left our Hart suite, Pat Hill, my appointments secretary, collected our two mascots, Manu and Laki, cockatiels that we kept in a tall cage at the rear of the suite. She ended up taking them home and keeping them permanently.

All of the Senate mail was collected, quarantined and examined for anthrax. In mid-November, as a part of that batch, a letter addressed to Senator Pat Leahy of Vermont was found to have the same kind of finely milled, "weapons-grade" anthrax powder that had been sent to Daschle. And the handwriting looked the same.

The FBI launched what it called one of the "largest and most complex" investigations in history, but never got to the bottom of it. A couple of suspects eventually were exonerated. Finally, the focus turned to an Army scientist named Bruce Ivins, who worked at a lab in Fort Detrick, Maryland, which apparently gave him access. Ivins never confessed and committed suicide in 2008 as the government was preparing to charge him on circumstantial evidence.

Anyway, these were tense months at the Capitol. In his 2003 memoir, *Like No Other Time*, Daschle described the 107th Congress as "the two years that changed America forever." I told my staff to stay alert for anything unusual. Eventually, spores were found in twelve of the fifty Senate suites in the Hart Building as the EPA conducted a careful and time-consuming decontamination process. Fortunately, my offices were spared. The Longworth Building reopened on November 5, the Ford Building a day later. The nine-story Hart Building eventually was fumigated—much like how they tent for termites in Hawaiʻi—

with chlorine dioxide gas. After extensive follow-up testing, the building reopened on January 22, 2002.

"Why Tom and Pat?" I asked Inouye at one point during the drawn-out crisis.

"No one can figure that out," he said.

Daschle was now majority leader. That's because in June, Jim Jeffords of Vermont, a lifelong Republican, defected. He didn't like Bush's tax cuts for the wealthy and the refusal of Republicans to fully fund the Individuals with Disabilities Education Act. Plus, the Bush White House and the Republican leadership had launched a campaign of petty retribution against him for his perceived disloyalty. One example: the annual National Teacher of the Year Award. This is always a big celebration in the White House Rose Garden, with the president honoring the winner before a crowd of friends, family members, invited members of Congress and the media. This year, for the first time, the winner was from Vermont, a social studies and history teacher from Middlebury, Michele Foreman. Jeffords, a senator from her home state and a staunch proponent of education, didn't make the guest list. This was the kind of thing that was going on with the Bush White House.

"Increasingly, I find myself in disagreement with my party," Jeffords said. "Given the changing nature of the national party, it has become a struggle for our leaders to deal with me and for me to deal with them."

He became an independent. That gave the Democrats a 50–49–1 majority, which made Republican leader Trent Lott almost apoplectic. But the Republicans largely brought it on themselves.

So Daschle was in a high-profile position, although not as high as the Senate president pro tempore, a position now held by Byrd of West Virginia. The Senate president pro tem is third in line to the presidency, after the vice president and Speaker of the House. As such, Byrd had Secret Service protection.

But Leahy? With Jeffords' switch, Pat had assumed the chairmanship of the Senate Judiciary Committee, which handled law-enforcement legislation. By why not others as well? Why were he and Daschle the only ones targeted? It didn't make sense. That said, I was not envious of the attention.

As you might imagine, this led to profound changes in our Capitol Hill security procedures. Hazmat suits became standard issue for the Capitol Police, because several of those first on the scene at the Daschle incident became exposed. Every envelope and parcel now had to be screened and irradiated by private contractors in New Jersey and Ohio. Then each piece was checked by newly trained Senate mail handlers before it was delivered to us.

"Is it ever going to be normal again?" one of my female aides asked me.

"I think this might be the new normal," I said. ✽

CHAPTER

68

On December 4, 2001, Senator Sam Brownback of Texas and I served as cochairman of a National Day of Reconciliation for members of Congress. The aim was to come together in a difficult time and seek the blessings of Providence for forgiveness, unity and charity for the people of the United States. We gathered at 5 p.m. on that Tuesday in the Capitol Rotunda and were joined by cabinet members, justices of the Supreme Court and the chaplains of the House and Senate.

In my welcoming remarks, I said, "Historically, our nation's leaders have gathered for prayer to strengthen and renew America and her leaders during times of turmoil and in thanksgiving for the blessings His Providence has bestowed on us. President Lincoln, on the eve of the Civil War, said it best in his first inaugural address when he reminded his countrymen, and I quote, 'intelligence, patriotism, Christianity and a firm reliance on Him, who has never forsaken this favored land, are still competent to adjust, in the best way, all our present difficulty.'

"As freedom faces this mighty challenge at the beginning of the new century, our nation's leaders need the blessings and spiritual renewal made possible by prayer and reflection through God's grace. I am reminded of Psalm 145, 'The Lord is righteous in all His ways, gracious in all His words. The Lord is near to all who call upon him in truth.'"

In 2002, surfer Andy Irons of Hanalei, Kaua'i, made us all proud, winning the World Championship, the Triple Crown and the Pipeline Masters. All three of the top contests in the sport.

* * *

With shock, I learned of the death of Patsy Mink on September 28. Patsy had been admitted to Straub Clinic and Hospital weeks earlier for chicken pox. Back when I was young, everyone got chicken pox. And mumps and measles. Nowadays there is a vaccine. But chicken pox, merely itchy when you are a child, can be quite serious when contracted as an adult. The virus, herpes zoster, also can revive in adults as painful shingles. We were all praying for Patsy, but then she developed viral pneumonia. We have antibiotics for bacterial pneumonia, but nothing much for viral. She was seventy-four.

Mink had an extraordinary career. Born on Maui and a graduate of Maui High School, she was the first Asian American woman elected to Congress, where she first served from 1965 to 1977. When she lost to Sparky in the Senate race to replace Hiram Fong, she became assistant secretary of state under Carter. Her kuleana was the ocean and environmental and scientific affairs—perfect for Patsy and for Hawai'i. When Reagan came in, she returned to Honolulu and ran for the city council, ultimately becoming chairwoman. She then ran successfully for my Second District House seat when Waihee appointed me to the Senate.

Patsy and I had a great relationship, unfailingly cordial and collegial. She could be a tough talker—her speeches could make the rafters shake—but she was never combative. She was a perfect fit for a delegation that doggedly pursued Hawai'i's interests.

The tributes poured in from every quarter.

"Patsy was a vibrant, passionate and effective voice for the principles that she believed in," said Republican John Boehner, chairman of the House Education Committee and a future House Speaker. "She was a true leader on our committee, and I am deeply saddened by the news of her passing. As chairman of the committee over the last two years, we worked together on the historic No Child Left Behind Act, as well as bipartisan legislation to improve access to higher education for our nation's youth. Patsy fought tirelessly for the causes she supported, and I think we are all grateful for her long record of public service. Her passing is a significant loss for our committee, the people of Hawai'i and the people of the United States. I offer my sincerest condolences to her family and her constituents. She will be greatly missed."

"We are going to miss Patsy Mink because she was a lady with great righteous indignation against injustice," said Congressman Major Owens of New York. Nearly every member of Congress had something to say about Mink.

On September 30, I said my piece in the Senate. I'll include a small part here.

"I feel a tremendous sense of loss," I said. "Her passing leaves a void in the House of Representatives, the Hawai'i congressional delegation and the political life of our nation. It is difficult to put her spirit into words, but those that come immediately to mind as fitting characterizations of the woman we honor today include courageous, forthright, tenacious, gutsy, outspoken, bold, meticulous and determined. She was my friend, a dedicated public servant for Hawai'i, a strong pillar in our state's delegation, and an advocate for those in America who feel scared, small, alone, mistreated, neglected or forgotten."

Back home in early October, Mink's body lay in state at the Hawai'i Capitol for twenty-two hours as mourners filed by. Twenty-five current and former members of Congress flew in for the services.

Gephardt, the House minority leader, called Mink a pioneer who successfully battled discrimination against women and minorities.

"And as a result, literally millions of young women have been able to get scholarships and to participate in sports and get to college and have an opportunity because of her work in the Congress," he said. "That will be a lasting monument to her name forever."

Representing President Bush was his transportation secretary, former California congressman Norm Mineta, one of several speakers who mentioned Title IX.

"Her contributions to that act is nothing less than an Emancipation Proclamation to the women of America," he said. Among Asian Americans elected to the House, Mineta followed Inouye, Matsunaga and Mink.

Governor Cayetano called her "an extraordinary leader, a leader before her time."

After the speakers, I led those assembled in singing, "Hawai'i Aloha." Then the family went up to Punchbowl, where she was buried under a towering shade tree. A bugler played taps and a rifle squad fired a twenty-one-shot salute.

✳ ✳ ✳

Mink's death wasn't the only one that hit us hard on the Hill that fall.

My colleague and friend Paul Wellstone died in a small plane crash with his lovely wife and daughter. Wellstone, a Minnesota Democrat and leading progressive, had entered the Senate just a few months after me, in January 1991, after he upset Republican Rudy Boschwitz. His office was right next to mine in the Hart Building, and Millie and I became very close to him and his wife, Sheila.

In his early years, he had protested the Vietnam War, was arrested twice and the FBI actually started a file on him. Looking back at the career of this patriot, that's amusing. In the mid-1980s, he took part in a labor protest at the Hormel meat packing plant in Austin, Minnesota, home of Spam. As a candidate, he drove around Minnesota on a green bus, much like Abercrombie drove a checkered cab around Honolulu.

As a senator, he was a big supporter of campaign finance reform, but his initiatives eventually were tossed out by the Supreme Court in the infamous 2010 Citizens United decision that gave "super PACs" so much power. Just a few weeks before his death, he had joined us in voting against the Iraq War—the only senator up for reelection to do so.

On October 25, a little over a week before the election, Paul passed up a Democratic fundraiser in Minneapolis headlined by Kennedy and Mondale. Instead, he took off for the north woods to attend the funeral of an old friend, Martin Rukavina, a retired steelworker. Later that night, Paul was scheduled to debate his Republican opponent, Norm Coleman, the former mayor of Saint Paul, in Duluth. The Beechcraft King Air twin turboprop, a nine-seater with plush interior, took off for Eveleth, Minnesota, with eight aboard: Paul; Sheila; their daughter, Marcia Markusun, thirty-three; the pilot and copilot; and staffers Tom Lapic, Mary McEvoy and Will McLaughlin. His two sons, David and Mark, were not aboard, fortunately.

Two miles from the airport, in socked-in conditions that required the pilots to fly on instruments, the plane crashed into the forest. The FBI eventually dismissed sabotage; that had to be ruled out because Wellstone had received steady death threats since entering office. Progressives considered him "the conscience of the Senate," which, of course, drew equally many detractors. The National Transportation Safety Board concluded that the pilots, clean and sober, let the airspeed drop too low. As the plane descended toward the air field in zero visibility, it clipped a treetop. Paul was fifty-eight.

Half the Senate, myself included, attended the services in Minneapolis. Bush had offered to send Cheney, but Wellstone's sons said no. Cheney had encouraged Coleman to run. So Bush instead sent Tommy Thompson, secretary of health and human services. At the White House, before signing the Voter Rights Act, Bush led a moment of silence. "I would like to pause and remember a devoted public servant who was taken from us last Friday, along with his wife and his daughter and several other Americans," Bush said, according to press reports. "Paul Wellstone was a deeply principled and a good-hearted man. He'll be missed by all who knew him and by all who had the privilege of serving with him."

The service, on a chilly and overcast day at the University of Minnesota's Williams Arena, drew 20,000 people—including Clinton, Gore, Mondale, Senator Tom Harkin of neighboring Iowa, Jesse Jackson, Governor Jesse Ventura and Republican senator Trent Lott. The event was covered by 110 newspapers, twenty-two television stations and seventy radio outlets. The local mourners wore green Wellstone buttons on their black suits. The *New York Times* called the ceremonies "part folk festival, part family reunion, part political convention, opening with a video montage, set to 'Forever Young,' by fellow Minnesotan Bob Dylan." The montage mixed snapshots with footage from a recent Wellstone campaign ad. In the ad, Paul said, "Politics is not about winning for the sake of winning. Politics is about the improvement of people's lives."

He and Mink would be sorely missed.

On the national level, there was more *pilikia*.

With great acclaim, Minnesota Democrats picked Mondale to replace Wellstone in the race. He lost.

Jean Carnahan of Missouri, appointed to the Senate seat of her husband, Mel, after he died in a plane crash in 2000, lost narrowly to Republican Jim Talent.

In Georgia, Senator Max Cleland, a Vietnam war hero and multiple amputee, lost to Republican Saxby Chambliss in an ugly campaign.

The Republicans again had control of the Senate, 51–49, with Ted Stevens the Senate president pro tem and Dennis Hastert the House Speaker.

Mink's constituents reelected her posthumously, 100,671 votes to 71,661 over very-much-alive Republican Bob McDermott. Elsewhere on the ballot, Lingle beat Lieutenant Governor Hirono to become the first GOP governor of Hawai'i since Bill Quinn in 1962—a half century earlier.

A special election to fill Mink's seat, held November 30, drew a whopping thirty-eight candidates, including John Mink, Patsy's widower and a respected water scientist. But a majority of the votes—fifty-one percent—went to a legislator from Mānoa, Ed Case, who had run for governor that year. In the primary on September 21, Mazie edged him out by about 2,600 votes out of more than 180,000 cast. Coming in a distant third was Andy Anderson, once a political powerhouse in the isles. The governor's campaign had greatly raised Case's name recognition and profile. That helped him incalculably in the special election for Congress. So, with politics often ironic, Hirono won in September, but as of November she was out and Case was in. ✤

CHAPTER

69

On January 14, 2003, the Senate Committee on Government Operations held a confirmation hearing on the nomination of former Pennsylvania governor Tom Ridge as secretary of the nascent Department of Homeland Security. I knew Ridge well from his dozen years in the House, starting in 1983. He was an intelligent and competent gentleman. But I had severe reservations about the huge new bureaucracy he was slated to lead. It was to incorporate the Coast Guard, the Federal Emergency Management Agency, the Secret Service and the Customs Service—agencies that had operated so far very well with relative independence. It would also gobble up the Animal Plant Health Inspection Service, which played an instrumental role in keeping alien species out of Hawai'i. Not since Truman shook up the military in the late 1940s had the federal government undergone such a massive restructuring. Moreover, some of the department's 170,000 employees would have no customary civil service protections. That bothered me—and many other Democrats.

On November 20, the Senate approved the creation of this monster by a vote of 90–9. Of course, I was among the nine. You can probably guess a few of the other eight. "Round up the usual suspects," as Claude Rains says at the end of *Casablanca*. They were Inouye, Kennedy, Byrd, Levin, Jeffords, Paul Sarbanes of Maryland, Russ Feingold of Wisconsin and Fritz Hollings, who continued to surprise me with his political metamorphosis. Frank Murkowski of Alaska was not there for the vote. Bush signed the measure into law on November 25.

At the hearing, I told Ridge exactly how I felt.

"Governor Ridge, I offer my sincere congratulations on your nomination to be secretary of the Department of Homeland Security... You have an enormous and historic task before you in leading this new department. Although I voted against the Homeland Security Act for several reasons, I want you to know that I stand prepared to help you as much as I can to ensure the creation of the new department enhances our security."

I had raised my concerns with him in a private, one-on-one meeting earlier, but wanted them on the record here.

"First, the cost of creating this new department cannot be at the expense of our fundamental freedoms. The department's mission to help prevent, protect against and respond to acts of terrorism is clear. To accomplish these goals, the department plans to collect, coordinate and store vast amounts of personal data. Legitimate fears have been raised that the price of security may be our constitutional freedoms. Those freedoms are essential to the preservation of our democracy. I urge you to take every precaution to uphold the rights of citizens.

"Second, we cannot afford to lose the critical non-homeland security missions of the agencies being merged into the new department. I am particularly concerned that resources going to first responders, including the Federal Emergency Management Agency and the Coast Guard, may be sacrificed. This is not a zero-sum game."

I had already heard from officials in Hawai'i who were uncertain of whom to contact in this new department in event of a natural disaster or terrorist attack.

"Third, as we further protect America by reorganizing the government, we must not overlook the fundamental rights of our federal employees, who will staff this new agency. The department should not be used as a vehicle to advance untried management initiatives nor erode the rights afforded to federal workers. They deserve the right to collective bargaining, a fair grievance system, equitable pay and protection from retaliation for disclosing waste, fraud and abuse."

I knew I was fighting an uphill battle.

As a founder of the House Space Caucus and a longtime advocate of the commercial space flight, I had watched closely the progress by NASA since the *Challenger* explosion. After the disaster, the shuttle fleet was grounded for two years. The Russians stayed active, though, launching the *Mir* space station. The satellite-launching business had long been

Dan at the keyboard.

Top: The Akaka family—(left to right), Dan, Mikey Akaka (Alan's son), Anthony Mattson (Millannie's son), Renard Mattson (Millannie's brother-in-law), Alika Mattson (Millannie's son), Millie and Melodi Akaka (Alan's daughter)—greets the crowd on election night, 1976.
Above: Hawai'i's congressional delegation (left to right: Dan Inouye, Cec Heftel, Spark Matsunaga and Dan Akaka).

President Jimmy Carter greets Dan at the White House, 1978.

Top: Governor George Ariyoshi and Lieutenant Governor Nelson Doi lend their support to the Akaka for Congress campaign in 1976.

Top: With President Ronald Reagan, 1981.
Above: Dan surrounded by his congressional office staff.

Above and opposite top: Kahu Abraham Akaka was
one of Dan's staunchest political supporters.
Opposite bottom: Dan with Anwar Sadat and Tip O'Neill.

Dan and Walter Mondale in 1980.

dominated by Intelsat, a government-backed global consortium. That started to change in June 1988, when PanAmSat launched its first satellite aboard a European Ariane rocket. The shuttle program revived in May 1989, when *Atlantis* blasted off and launched the *Magellan* spacecraft to explore the surface of Venus. That fall, *Atlantis* launched the *Galileo* probe to Jupiter. The Hubble Space Telescope, launched in April 1990 by the shuttle *Discovery*, marked a game-changer for astronomy, providing images even clearer than those from Maunakea.

In April 1992, NASA achieved another milestone with the Cosmic Background Explorer. This stemmed from research done in the 1960s by two scientists at Bell Labs in New Jersey. Arno Penzias and Robert Wilson set up antennas—crude by today's standards—to scan the sky in the microwave wavelengths. With every scan, they found a faint hum in the background. At first they couldn't explain it, and wondered if it might be something coming from the nearest big city, New York. They consulted another physicist, Robert Dicke, who recalled theories that there might be cosmic residue from the big bang, the explosion that created the universe. The three published companion papers on their findings in the *Astrophysical Journal*. This stunning affirmation of the big bang theory won Penzias and Wilson a share of the 1978 Nobel Prize in Physics. The Cosmic Background Explorer, with much more sensitive and wider-field instruments, was able to precisely chart the early universe. It was a virtual time machine, as are all deep-space telescopes.

Over the next dozen years, space science and technology made huge strides thanks to the shuttle fleet and private enterprise. Among the milestones: DIRECTV, satellite radio, the Iridium mobile phone network and GPS, the landing of the *Mars Pathfinder* on the surface of the Red Planet and construction of the International Space Station. In April 2001, American investment tycoon Dennis Tito became the world's first space tourist, spending a reported $20 million to ride a Russian Soyuz spacecraft up the space station. In July 2001, Intelsat went private, a sign of the times.

On January 16, 2003, the shuttle *Columbia* lifted off from Cape Canaveral with a crew of seven. During the launch, unbeknownst to the crew, a piece of foam insulation broke off from the external fuel tank and hit the left wing, damaging the heat-resistant tiles. Foam had fallen off previous shuttles, resulting in minor damage, so this did not cause panic. Some NASA engineers suspected this case was worse, but if it was, there was no way for the shuttle crew to make the necessary repairs. So, best to just ride it out, NASA concluded. It was a bad ride.

Over the next fifteen days, the crew conducted the usual array of experiments, including one concocted by Australian students to test the ability of the garden orb spider to spin a web in zero gravity.

When the shuttle reentered the atmosphere over the Pacific on February 1, hot gases built up inside the wing. The spacecraft started to shake, rattle and roll, literally, and broke up at an altitude of thirty-seven miles, leaving a debris field stretching from Nacogdoches, Texas, to western Louisiana and parts of Arkansas.

On Capitol Hill, this second catastrophe in the shuttle program generated tremendous anguish, a sentiment shared by the nation and Bush when he went on TV.

"My fellow Americans, this day has brought terrible news and great sadness to our country. At 9 a.m. this morning, Mission Control in Houston lost contact with our space shuttle *Columbia*. A short time later, debris was seen falling from the skies above Texas. The *Columbia* is lost; there are no survivors."

He named the five men and two women who lost their lives. Six were Americans; one was a colonel in the Israeli Air Force.

"These men and women assumed great risk in the service to all humanity.

"In an age when spaceflight has come to seem almost routine, it is easy to overlook the dangers of travel by rocket, and the difficulties of navigating the fierce outer atmosphere of the Earth. These astronauts knew the dangers, and they faced them willingly, knowing they had a high and noble purpose in life. Because of their courage and daring and idealism, we will miss them all the more.

"All Americans today are thinking, as well, of the families of these men and women who have been given this sudden shock and grief. You're not alone. Our entire nation grieves with you. And those you loved will always have the respect and gratitude of this country. The cause in which they died will continue. Mankind is led into the darkness beyond our world by the inspiration of discovery and the longing to understand. Our journey into space will go on."

Important work would go on—the Mars rovers high among them—but the shuttles would be grounded for two years.

※ ※ ※

Bush's chief rationale for wanting to invade Iraq was the contention that Saddam Hussein had weapons of mass destruction. He pressed his case for war with Iraq in his State of the Union address, as usual before a joint session of Congress.

"As we gather tonight, our nation is at war; our economy is in recession; and the civilized world faces unprecedented dangers. Yet, the state of our union has never been stronger," he said, Cheney and Hastert seated above and behind him. "We last met in an hour of shock and suffering. In four short months, our nation has comforted the victims, begun to rebuild New York and the Pentagon, rallied a great coalition, captured, arrested and rid the world of thousands of terrorists, destroyed Afghanistan's terrorist training camps, saved a people from starvation and freed a country from brutal oppression.

"The American flag flies again over our embassy in Kabul. Terrorists who once occupied Afghanistan now occupy cells at Guantanamo Bay. And terrorist leaders who urged followers to sacrifice their lives are running for their own."

But the fight is far from over, he said.

"Our discoveries in Afghanistan confirmed our worst fears and showed us the true scope of the task ahead. We have seen the depth of our enemies' hatred in videos where they laugh about the loss of innocent life. And the depth of their hatred is equaled by the madness of the destruction they design. We have found diagrams of American nuclear power plants and public water facilities, detailed instructions for making chemical weapons, surveillance maps of American cities and thorough descriptions of landmarks in America and throughout the world."

Equally troublesome, he said, are "regimes that sponsor terror." He named three: North Korea, Iran and Iraq, members of what he termed an "axis of evil."

Iraq, he said, "continues to flaunt its hostility toward America and to support terror. The Iraqi regime has plotted to develop anthrax and nerve gas and nuclear weapons for over a decade. This is a regime that has already used poison gas to murder thousands of its own citizens, leaving the bodies of mothers huddled over their dead children. This is a regime that agreed to international inspections, then kicked out the inspectors. This is a regime that has something to hide from the civilized world."

* * *

Bush's case for war against Iraq rested mainly on the contention that its leader, Saddam Hussein, possessed weapons of mass destruction, or WMD, an acronym we all came to know. To make the case, he trotted out his secretary of state, the highly respected Colin Powell, who on February 5 addressed the United Nations General Assembly. He insisted that the Iraqis had hidden WMD from international inspectors in defiance of a U.N. resolution.

"In the middle of January, experts at one facility that was related to weapons of mass destruction, those experts had been ordered to stay home from work to avoid the inspectors," he said. "Workers from other Iraqi military facilities not engaged in elicit weapons projects were to replace the workers who'd been sent home. A dozen experts have been placed under house arrest, not in their own houses, but as a group at one of Saddam Hussein's guest houses. It goes on and on and on."

He showed very impressive satellite photos indicating what he said were chemical weapons bunkers, decontamination vehicles and ballistic missile sites.

"The issue before us is not how much time we are willing to give the inspectors to be frustrated by Iraqi obstruction," he said. "But how much longer are we willing to put up with Iraq's noncompliance before we, as a council, we, as the United Nations, say: 'Enough. Enough.' The gravity of this moment is matched by the gravity of the threat that Iraq's weapons of mass destruction pose to the world."

Of course, there were no WMD in Iraq, a fact that Powell conceded years later.

But Powell was not alone. CIA director George Tenet had declared that the proof that Iraq had doomsday devices was a "slam dunk."

Although a war with Iraq appeared inevitable, Congress still had questions.

* * *

On February 25, my old friend Eric "Ric" Shinseki put in his two-cents' worth. Born and raised on Kaua'i at the height of the plantation days, Ric took inspiration from uncles who served in the 442nd Regimental Combat Team, along with Inouye, in World War II. He went to West Point, graduating in 1965, just as the Vietnam War was heating up. He served two tours there, including one with Hawai'i's 25th Infantry Division. While in Vietnam in 1970, he stepped on a land mine, which blew off the toes of his right foot. It could have been far worse. He was able to return to active duty within a year. And then nothing could stop his career. When he was promoted to full colonel, I went down to the Pentagon and pinned on his eagles. Now he was the first Asian American to reach the rank of four-star general. Clinton had named him chief of staff of the Army in 1999, and Bush had kept him on in the Army's top job.

Now he was addressing the Senate Armed Services Committee. I stopped in to listen. His remarks became the top story of the day and indeed echo through history.

The chairman, Carl Levin of Michigan, asked him, "General Shinseki, could you give us some idea as to the magnitude of the Army's force requirement for an occupation of Iraq following a successful completion of the war?"

"In specific numbers, I would have to rely on combatant commanders' exact requirements," Shinseki replied, "but I think..."

"How about a range?" Levin pressed.

Shinseki had some solid experience in this, having led the postwar NATO peacekeeping forces in Bosnia. There the formula was one soldier per fifty Bosnians.

"I would say that what's been mobilized to this point, something on the order of several hundred thousand soldiers are probably a figure that would be required. We're talking about post-hostilities, control over a piece of geography that's fairly significant, with the kinds of ethnic tensions that could lead to other problems, and so it takes a significant ground force presence to maintain a safe and secure environment, to ensure that people are fed, that water is distributed, all the normal responsibilities that go along with administering a situation like this."

"What effect would that type of an operation, to that extent, have on two things—one is our optempo (operational tempo), which you've talked about, already stressed, and also on the ability of the Army to fulfill the other missions that we have?"

"Well," Shinseki said, "if it were an extended requirement for presence of U.S.-only army forces, it would have significant long-term effects, and therefore I think the kind of assistance from friends and allies would be helpful."

Shinseki's estimate produced an immediate and vehement hailstorm of criticism from Rumsfeld and his top lieutenant, Paul Wolfowitz.

"The idea that it would take several hundred thousand U.S. forces, I think, is far off the mark," Rumsfeld declared.

Wolfowitz echoed that two days later to the House Budget Committee: "Some of the higher-end predictions that we have been hearing recently, such as the notion that it will take several hundred thousand U.S. troops to provide stability in post-Saddam Iraq, are wildly off the mark. It is hard to conceive that it would take more forces to provide stability in a post-Saddam Iraq than it would take to conduct the war itself."

Shinseki stood by his estimate, and ultimately would be proven right.

In mid-March, on the Senate floor, I argued that the country was not ready for the consequences of a war with Iraq. The administration had failed to persuade key allies, was not prepared for a lengthy occupation and had no exit strategy. American soldiers, I said, should not be sacrificed in the "vain pursuit of ill-defined objectives."

On March 20, the United States and Great Britain attacked Iraq with a "shock and awe" bombing campaign. The ground war began not long afterward. By April 2, coalition forces reached the outskirts of Baghdad, which fell a week later. With the capture of Tikrit, Saddam's hometown, on April 15, the coalition declared victory. On May Day, just off San Diego, Bush went on TV from the flight deck of the aircraft carrier USS *Abraham Lincoln*. Under a large sign saying "Mission Accomplished," Bush, wearing a red tie, white shirt and blue jacket, announced that major combat operations had ended. "We have difficult work to do in Iraq," he conceded. "We are bringing order to parts of that country that remain dangerous."

But by month's end, the United States would make one of its biggest blunders in Iraq: disbanding the army. This was done with

Rumsfeld's permission by the leader of the Coalition Provisional Authority, Ambassador Paul Bremer, without consulting Powell, General Peter Pace, chairman of the Joint Chiefs, or national security adviser Condoleezza Rice. That move put some 300,000 trained soldiers out of work, with no way to feed their families. Many doubtless went on to fuel the anti-U.S. insurgency that persisted for several years.

But this was not the fault of our brave troops. By a vote of 99–0, the Senate passed a resolution, introduced by Bill Frist of Tennessee, commending Bush and our Armed Forces for their actions in the Persian Gulf, and expressing condolences for those who lost their lives. Congress also approved a Congressional Gold Medal for British prime minister Tony Blair, our rock-solid ally in Operation Iraqi Freedom.

On June 12, Shinseki quietly retired from the Army after thirty-eight years. Neither Bush nor Rumsfeld attended the ceremony.

"You must love those you lead before you can be an effective leader," he told his Pentagon audience on a hot spring morning. "You can certainly command without that sense of commitment, but you cannot lead without it. And without leadership, command is a hollow experience, a vacuum often filled with mistrust and arrogance."

In the Senate, I introduced a resolution, passed by unanimous consent, commending Shinseki for his outstanding service.

"General Shinseki provided the vision to set the Army on a path of transformation that will provide the nation with an army that is more lethal, agile, deployable and flexible; capable of fighting and winning this nation's wars in all future threat environments," the resolution said. The general, it added, "is a remarkable man of integrity, courage and honor...an American hero who has been selfless in his service to his country through war, peace and personal trial, and epitomizes the spirit of aloha."

I would miss the occasional visits from my friend. ✤

CHAPTER

70

Amid the tragedy of the shuttle crash, the war in Iraq and the massive reorganization of the federal government, I introduced, once again, the so-called Akaka Bill, the Native Hawaiian Recognition Act of 2003. But now I had the support of a Linda Lingle, our newly elected Republican governor. Lingle went to Capitol Hill to express support for the bill, and met separately with Attorney General Ashcroft and Interior secretary Gale Norton.

On February 25, a Tuesday, in room 485 of the Russell Senate Office Building, Lingle testified before the Senate Indian Affairs Committee, led by Ben Nighthorse Campbell. The committee had approved the measure last session, as had the House Resources Committee, so this was more a show of support than an effort to persuade members. She said recognition for Hawaiians was "a matter of simple justice."

Inouye, the ranking Democrat on the committee, also put in a word of support.

I said the bill would establish a political relationship between the United States and a Native Hawaiian government that would continue the process of reconciliation. I knew that several Republicans viewed the measure as benefitting a single ethnic group to the exclusion of others.

"This bill is not race-based," I insisted.

Ed Case, representing Hawai'i's Second District, called the legislation the most important to Hawai'i since statehood.

"The stakes are nothing more or less than the survival and prosperity not only of our indigenous Native Hawaiian people and culture, but of the very soul of Hawai'i as we know it and love it," he said.

Micah Kane, director of the state Department of Hawaiian

Home Lands, said the bill could eliminate legal uncertainties. In 2000, for instance, the U.S. Supreme Court had ruled that it was unconstitutional for the Office of Hawaiian Affairs to prevent non-Hawaiians from voting for the trustees.

"The risk of doing nothing puts us back in the courts," he said.

Several OHA trustees, including Chairwoman Haunani Apoliona, and leaders of the state Council of Hawaiian Homestead Associations and the Association of Hawaiian Civic Clubs, had come along on the trip.

Back home, some Hawaiians, notably Dr. Kekuni Blaisdell, my Kamehameha classmate, opposed the bill, saying that it would make Hawaiians subordinate to the federal government.

Over the next fourteen months, I picked up seven cosponsors—Inouye, Harry Reid, Ted Stevens and four other Republicans: Orrin Hatch of Utah, Gordon Smith of Oregon, Thomas Carper of Delaware and Campbell, the only other indigenous person in the Senate besides myself.

I was immensely honored, on August 29, to be subject of a Legacy Luncheon sponsored by the Council for Native Hawaiian Advancement. This was in concert with the council's second annual Native Hawaiian Conference. The council, organized in 2001, promotes the advancement of Hawaiians as a kind of a clearinghouse, or one-stop-shop, for information and outreach.

The luncheon program was a fourteen-page brochure with two flyleaf inserts. One of the inserts was a proclamation from Lingle that August 29 was "United States Senator Daniel Kahikina Akaka Day." I had never had my own day before. Most days, I can't find a spare minute. The brochure mentioned some of my legislation, including the Apology Resolution and the Hawaiian Home Lands Recovery Act, a 1995 measure that set up federal compensation for lands in Lualualei taken when Hawai'i was a territory. This had had wide ramifications elsewhere, including Alaska and American Samoa.

Throughout the program were testimonials as to my agreeable demeanor and sterling character. My high school classmate, Buzzy Agard, said, "At Kamehameha School for Boys, he was very well liked and popular. He had a pleasant personality and did well in everything." That serves as proof positive that memory fades with age. He was correct about one thing. Because our last names started with A, we always sat together at the front of the class. Oswald Stender, now an OHA trustee, said, "Senator Akaka is loved by all the people of Hawai'i and we honor him today as a true Hawaiian." Maybe Oz forgot the 85,000 votes for John Carroll—or the 23,000 blank votes—in my last election. Colleen Wong, acting chief executive officer of Kamehameha Schools, said, "Kamehameha Schools is honored and privileged to acknowledge Senator Daniel Akaka as a shining example of the 'good and industrious' man so envisioned by our princess," referring to Pauahi.

But one surprise brought a tear to my eye. It was the opening *oli* in Hawaiian by my son Kaniela. A digest:

> At the edge of night, as the sun approaches to pierce the darkness, a child emerges, born to Kahikina and Kahoa. He was given a name and was called Daniel Kahikina. The peaceful valley of Pauoa bore witness to his birth. A child raised with the unconditional love of his parents. The child grew into adulthood, was educated and nurtured in the love and faith of the ever-powerful God. He had become a person skilled in many tasks... He has accepted what life has placed before him and has been successful in his accomplishments. This is my song of praise for Daniel Kahikina Akaka. This is my song, my gift of love for my father.

I love my children so much.

My oldest, Millannie, went to Kamehameha Schools from kindergarten to twelfth grade. After graduation, she went to the University of Hawai'i at Mānoa. She then spent a career at Hawaiian Telephone Co., where she saw tremendous technological changes. When she retired she was handling all the new systems for the company. Her son, David Mattson, is a physician in Buffalo, New York, where he and his wife, Liz, started a nonprofit literacy program for children. Their initiative, which donates books to schools and arranges for authors to read to schoolchildren, has expanded to Hawai'i under the name Ohana100.

My eldest son, Danny Jr., Kaniela, is also a graduate of Kamehameha and UH Mānoa, where he got a degree in Hawaiian studies. He has always been passionate about Hawaiian culture. For Danny, music cannot be separated from life itself. During services at Kawaiaha'o, he took to heart his uncle Abe's frequent assertion, "We are all strings on God's 'ukulele." At age nine, he started playing my Martin guitar. He took lessons from Ellen Jane Hale, who taught him slack key. Two of his solo songs were included in a CD produced by the Lava Tracks recording studio. He also assiduously studies Hawaiian oli, chants. For years he has been director of cultural practices at the Mauna Lani Bay Resort, where his kuleana includes the famous Kalahuipua'a Fishponds. He has led thousands of tours for hotel visitors, sharing our culture with the wider world.

My next son, Gerard, graduated from UH and worked briefly for Aloha Airlines. When he was with Aloha Air, he played bass guitar at night for Al Harrington at his showroom in Waikīkī. Then he got a medical degree from UH. Then he decided he wanted to join the Air Force. I told him, "You should have joined the Air Force before you got your medical degree. They would have paid for your school!" So he served as a doctor in the Air Force and afterwards was selected as medical director of the Wai'anae Coast Comprehensive Health Center, the only medical facility serving Leeward O'ahu, mostly Hawaiian families. After a time, he moved on to become director of the Queen Emma Clinics at the Queen's Medical Center. In 2004, Queen's would name him outstanding physician of the year. Gerard believes strongly that compassion plays a big role in patient care. He maintains doctors should be "healers rather than technicians." Eventually, he would become a vice president of Queen's and set up clinics on the Neighbor Islands.

My son Alan went to Pauoa Elementary School and then in the seventh grade went to Kamehameha. Now, Danny, Gerard and Alan, when they were at Kamehameha, they would bring home their classmates and practice music. And so that became a regular thing at our house, usually on the weekends. One of the kids was Aaron Mahi, who went on to become director of the Royal Hawaiian Band. Another was Dennis Kamakahi, who became a celebrated slack key guitarist. Dennis spent the night at our place more than once. Another was Brian Hussey, who sang for Cyril Pahinui's Sandwich Isles Band. And we had Bruce Spencer, who went on to teach 'ukulele. Kalena Silva, another regular, got his doctorate and teaches Hawaiian at UH Hilo. Alan became a steel guitarist, and was at one time considered a top player in Hawai'i. Alan opened his own music school, Ke Kula Mele Hawai'i, on Auwaiku Street in Kailua, and teaches steel guitar, 'ukulele, bass guitar and has done a terrific job with his kids, all the way from elementary to seniors.

My last boy, Nick, is a decorated police officer. But his education took a different track. Millie felt, "Hey, so many of our kids went to Kamehameha!" She wanted Nick to go to another school, so she put him in Hanahau'oli on Nehoa Avenue in Makiki. For high school, he moved down the street to Roosevelt. Most recently, he joined the crime reduction unit in East Honolulu, where burglaries and car break-ins are a huge problem. I'm sure he'll retire as a police officer.

The Akaka 'ohana extends much farther, of course, to embrace staffers, former staffers and a legion of loyal campaign volunteers. ✤

CHAPTER

71

When it comes to environmental stewardship, the military has a mixed record.

At Mokapu Peninsula, the Marines have done a great job at preserving wetlands for native birds. Working with the Army Corps of Engineers, the base offers a variety of habitats for the birds to feed and breed. Mudflats, shallow ponds and vegetated shallows attract the black-necked stilt or *kukuluaeʻo*, the Hawaiian coot or *ʻalae kea*, the moorhen or *ʻalae ʻula*, Hawaiian duck or *koloa*, the red-footed booby or *ʻā* and the wedge-tailed shearwater, *ʻuaʻu kani*, all endangered. The base's Ulupaʻu Crater is one of only two main Hawaiian Island locations that have large red-footed booby colonies; the other is the Kīlauea Wildlife Refuge on Kauaʻi. First surveyed in 2002, the base includes the 517-acre Nuʻupia Ponds, eight interconnected ponds, marshes and scrubland. Each year since 1982, the 3rd Marines' Combat Assault Company, in advance of the stilts' breeding season, use their amphibious assault vehicles to break up the invasive pickle weed that covers the mudflats. The Marines call this exercise "mud ops." The base is home to about ten percent of the total Hawaiian stilt population. It also has an attractive beach, where occasionally a Hawaiian monk seal, green sea turtle or *honu*, or even a rare olive ridley turtle, takes up temporary residence. Kāneʻohe is also the only Marine base worldwide that has a coral reef.

Waikāne Valley on Oʻahu's windward side tells a different story. Between 1943 and 1953 the Army leased more than 2,000 acres in the Waiāhole and Waikāne Valleys for jungle training, live fire—artillery, mortars and small arms—and as a target for aerial bombing. In 1953, the Marines leased 1,061 acres for live-fire training. When the lease ended in 1976, a clearance effort removed 24,000 pounds of practice ordnance and fragments, and forty-two live rounds. The Marines came back in 1984 and removed 480 M28 anti-tank rockets from what has become known as the Waikane Valley Impact Area, 178 acres on the *makai* side of the parcel. For a while, the Marines considered using the area for blank-fire jungle warfare training. But they abandoned that idea in 2003 after concluding the area was simply too dangerous. For now, there is no solid plan for cleaning up Waikāne, although there has been plenty of discussion. At one point, the Corps of Engineers estimated it would take nearly $2 billion to clean up ordnance from 140 sites, including Waikāne in Hawai'i, American Samoa, the Northern Marianas, Guam and Palau. The target date to finish: 2134.

On July 22, 2003, the Army began what was to have been a "control burn" at its training area in Mākua Valley, on O'ahu's upper Wai'anae Coast. The idea was to clear 900 acres of vegetation so the Army could locate unexploded ordnance and clear pathways to Hawaiian cultural sites. Access to culture sites was a condition of an October 2001 settlement in a lawsuit by Mālama Mākua, a citizens advocacy group.

Unfortunately, the fire got out of control and burned 2,100 acres of brush, destroying seventy-one endangered plants. Fortunately, the cultural and archaeological sites in the valley remained largely untouched. But the fire nevertheless prompted calls for the Army to pull out of the valley completely. Frenchy DeSoto, a Mālama Mākua member and former trustee for the Office of Hawaiian Affairs, ranked among those opposed to more Army training. "It's virtually impossible at this point to trust the military," she said. "I say that with regret, but enough is enough."

The Mākua fire clearly was a mistake, which the Army admitted. But I felt the military was doing its level best to protect the lands under its jurisdiction and to make up for decisions made under duress in the distant past. Tom Brokaw wrote *The Greatest Generation* because heroes like Inouye and Robert Kuroda won World War II. But the leaders of my generation, after the war, also set off atomic bombs, with full mushroom clouds in the atmosphere, in the Nevada desert and at Bikini Atoll in the Marshall Islands. We scuttled chemical munitions at sea. Not much stewardship going on there. The end may justify the means, but the means can have other, unsuspected, dreadful consequences.

Institutional change takes time. Look at the civil rights movement: women in the voting booth, blacks in the front of the bus, gays in the military. If anyone had suggested in 2003 that gays and lesbians would someday marry, we would have laughed.

The environmental movement didn't really begin in earnest until the 1970s. The first Earth Day was April 22, 1970, inspired in part by the huge oil spill in the Santa Barbara Channel. Ultimately, the movement would embrace such diverse issues as nuclear testing in French Polynesia and oil drilling in the Arctic. When I was in the House, several members of the Protect Kahoʻolawe ʻOhana—Emmett Aluli and Walter Ritte among them—came to Washington to press their cause. They had no money, so the camped out on my living room floor. What a difference a decade makes. Or three.

In November 2003, on the grounds of ʻIolani Palace, the Navy officially turned over Kahoʻolawe to the state after a five-year, $460 million cleanup effort. The cleanup wasn't complete, mind you. And in fact the contractor, Parsons-UXB Joint Venture, would continue working on it until March 12, 2004. So far, ordnance had been removed from seventy percent of the surface (20,053 acres) and nine percent of the subsurface (2,600 acres) to a depth of four feet. The contractor also removed 4,500 tons of scrap metal—enough to build a small warship—and 12,700 tires. Some in the ʻohana weren't happy with these measures. After all, an executive order signed by President Eisenhower in 1953 guaranteed that the entire island would be returned in a condition safe for habitation. And a 1994 memorandum of understanding called for 100 percent surface clearance.

The Navy now was saying that was impossible. Some areas—steep ravines, gulches and gullies—were simply too dangerous for excavation work. But the bottom line was, time and money simply ran out. In a 1995 land use plan, the Kahoʻolawe Island Reserve Commission identified twenty-seven cultural centers and/or campsites that it intended to open to visitors. Seventeen of those had not been cleared of ordnance. Emmett, or Noa, as friends called him, took the long view. "Our major accomplishment has been serving as a model for the Native Hawaiian rights movement and a catalyst for grassroots activism and cultural resurgence," he said. "In a sense, the island is a beacon for the next generation."

※ ※ ※

I enjoyed my years in the House, but one thing I don't miss is running for reelection every two years. As usual, the 2004 election cycle had started early, with retired General Wesley Clark, an Arkansas native close to the Clintons, announcing his presidential candidacy in September 2003. He had had a distinguished Army career, serving as the commander of U.S. forces in Kosovo and as NATO commander. But the candidate with the most momentum early on was Howard Dean, former governor of Vermont. Also in the race were John Kerry, Senators John Edwards of North Carolina and Joe Lieberman of Connecticut, who had been Gore's running mate in 2000. Also, former senator Carol Moseley-Braun of Illinois, former House majority leader Dick Gephardt, Congressman Dennis Kucinich of Ohio and a couple of wild cards, the Reverend Al Sharpton and economist and "Star Wars" proponent Lyndon LaRouche. Senator Bob Gramm of Florida bowed out in October 2003 and endorsed Kerry.

Dean's star faded quickly as Kerry won the Iowa caucuses, with Edwards second. Dean ended up a distant third, with Gephardt behind him. I had known Gephardt and Kerry for a long time, particularly Dick, and had considerable confidence in their judgment. I thought either would make a fine president. I didn't know Dean or Edwards very well.

By early March, Kerry had clinched it. I thought he had a good chance with the revelations of torture at the Abu Ghraib prison camp in Iraq, run by the Army and the CIA. The pictures from the camp, first published by CBS in April, were simply horrific. But none of the scandal seemed to make it up the ladder to the commander in chief.

Working against Bush was the fact that, since he took office, 3 million Americans had lost their jobs. Much of the country was hurting economically. That's one of the reasons I cosponsored a bill to raise the minimum wage. The Fair Minimum Wage Act of 2003, introduced by Tom Daschle, would have increased it from $5.15 to $5.90 per hour and then to $6.65 a year later. By November, I expressed frustration on the floor of the Senate that the bill was going nowhere. I reminded my colleagues that the last hike in the minimum wage was in September 1997.

"The minimum wage would need to reach $8.38 an hour to equal the purchasing power of the statutory minimum wage in 1968," I argued. "A full-time worker paid the minimum wage earns about

$4,000 below the poverty line for a family of three. This is not right." But we wouldn't succeed in raising minimum pay until 2007, when it went up to $5.85, then to $6.55 the next year and $7.25 in 2009.

I also knew that in tough economic times, some people tended to fall back on their credit cards. This often proved disastrous.

One of my top issues as a senator was financial literacy—encouraging people, especially young people, to effectively manage their money and consumer credit. This campaign of mine began with the introduction of the Excellence in Economic Education Act of 2001. The Triple E Act was folded into the No Child Left Behind law, introduced in the House by John Boehner. The aim was to promote economic and financial literacy among students from kindergarten through twelfth grade by awarding a grant to a national nonprofit suited to that mission. The money in turn would be given to state and local agencies. The No Child measure was signed into law by Bush in January 2002. Unfortunately, it was severely underfunded from the outset.

In September 2003, I introduced an amendment to an appropriations bill to specifically provide funding for Triple E. Backing me up were Kennedy, Dodd, Sarbanes of Maryland, Debbie Stabenow of Michigan, Mark Pryor of Arkansas, John Corzine of New Jersey and one Republican, George Allen of Virginia. Ultimately, we were successful. Since 2004, the Triple E Act has funded a wide range of activities—teacher training, research and evaluation and school-based activities to underscore economic principles.

But I didn't want to limit financial literacy to K–12. In late October 2003, I introduced a bill to help college students. The College Literacy in Finance and Economics (College LIFE) Act evolved into a bipartisan compromise, the Financial Literacy in Higher Education Act, which had the support of Republican Mike Enzi of Wyoming. The bill proposed a pilot program for five higher education institutions to encourage students to take a personal finance course and participate in preventive annual credit counseling, working in conjunction with state or local public, private and nonprofit entities. But that measure never made it out of committee.

Keeping up my drumbeat, I introduced a resolution in March 2004 designating April as "Financial Literacy Month." That passed the Senate unanimously, but the House never took it up.

One of the mistakes that people make when they have credit

cards is to pay just the minimum every month. The interest will kill you. I wanted credit card statements to carry a clear warning about that. So on May 21, 2004, I introduced the Credit Card Minimum Payment Warning Act. This amended the Truth in Lending Act to require these words on every statement: "Minimum Payment Warning: Making only the minimum payment will increase the amount of interest that you pay and the time it will take to repay your outstanding balance." The statement also had to say how many years it would take to pay off the balance if only the minimum payment were made, and what the total cost would be. It also had to say what monthly payment would be necessary to drop the balance to zero within three years if no other charges were made. And finally it had to list a toll-free number for information about credit counseling and debt management services.

This bill had a long shelf life. I had to introduce it repeatedly before it gained any traction. On May 17, 2005, I made my case before the Committee on Banking, Housing and Urban Affairs. This was in Republican hands at the time, led by Richard Shelby of Alabama. I noted that credit card debt had risen from $54 billion in January 1980 to more than $800 billion in March.

"It is imperative that we make consumers more aware of the long-term effects of their financial decisions, particularly in managing credit cards at early ages, particularly since credit card companies have been successful with aggressive campaigns targeted at college students," I said.

Finally, in April 2009, the House passed the Credit Card Accountability, Responsibility and Disclosure Act, or Credit CARD Act. To me, accountability and responsibility are pretty much the same thing. But the sponsor, Carolyn Maloney of New York, apparently wanted to spell out CARD, with the first letter of the acronym standing for...card. The Senate, after adding my measure as an amendment, approved it 90–5. The House agreed to the new language and on May 22 it was signed into law by the new president, Barack Obama. In the consumer credit industry, the warning box on charge card statements is called the Akaka Box.

Of course, before the summer of 2004, few people had heard of Obama, a Hawai'i-born state senator in Illinois. That would change at the Democratic Convention. ❈

CHAPTER

72

In July, Inouye and I had great expectations for Senate Bill 344, the current incarnation of the Native Hawaiian Government Reorganization Act of 2004. After consulting with the Senate minority leader, Tom Daschle, and with the support of the Democratic Caucus, we tried to slip the Akaka Bill in as an amendment to another bill, Senate 2062, the Class Action Fairness Act, introduced by Republican Chuck Grassley of Iowa. We filed the amendment on July 7, and were on the Senate floor prepared to debate it when the majority leader, Bill Frist of Tennessee, used a procedural tactic called "filling the amendment tree" to block it. Essentially, he stacked amendments on the bill in a way that precluded other amendments, including ours. That closed off any possibility of passage this session, a very disappointing outcome.

On the second night of the Democratic National Convention, my close friend Dick Durbin of Illinois introduced Obama at the FleetCenter in Boston. Obama, wearing a dark suit, white shirt and light gray tie, stepped up to the lectern to wild applause and a sea of bouncing, blue and white Obama signs. In March, he had decisively won the Illinois primary for the U.S. Senate against a field of seven rivals. He now was clearly a young star in the party. Kerry, who had met Obama at a campaign stop in Chicago, had picked him to deliver the all-important keynote address at the convention.

"On behalf of the great state of Illinois, crossroads of a nation, land of Lincoln, let me express my deep gratitude for the privilege of addressing this convention," said the Punahou School graduate, now forty-two. "Tonight is a particular honor for me because, let's face it, my presence on this stage is pretty unlikely. My father was a foreign student, born and raised in a small village in Kenya. He grew up herding goats, went to school in a tin-roof shack."

After describing his own life as an example of American opportunity, he got around to values.

"Tonight, we gather to affirm the greatness of our nation not because of the height of our skyscrapers, or the power of our military, or the size of our economy; our pride is based on a very simple premise, summed up in a declaration made over 200 years ago: 'We hold these truths to be self-evident, that all men are created equal…'"

He was interrupted by cheering.

"'That they are endowed by their Creator with certain inalienable Rights, that among these are Life, Liberty and the pursuit of Happiness.' That is the true genius of America, a faith in simple dreams, an insistence on small miracles; that we can tuck in our children at night and know that they are fed and clothed and safe from harm; that we can say what we think, write what we think, without hearing a sudden knock on the door; that we can have an idea and start our own business without paying a bribe; that we can participate in the political process without fear of retribution; and that our votes will be counted—or at least, most of the time."

That dig at the chaos of the 2000 election in Florida brought a smattering of laughter.

"People don't expect government to solve all their problems," he said. "But they sense, deep in their bones, that with just a slight change in priorities, we can make sure that every child in America has a decent shot at life and that the doors of opportunity remain open to all. They know we can do better. And they want that choice.

In this election, we offer that choice. Our party has chosen a man to lead us who embodies the best this country has to offer. And that man is John Kerry."

As his speech proceeded, he couldn't utter two sentences without being interrupted by cheering.

"John Kerry believes in an America where all Americans can afford the same health coverage our politicians in Washington have for themselves."

Cheers.

"John Kerry believes in energy independence, so we aren't held hostage to the profits of oil companies or the sabotage of foreign oil fields."

More cheers.

"John Kerry believes in the constitutional freedoms that have made our country the envy of the world, and he will never sacrifice our basic liberties nor use faith as a wedge to divide us."

Cheers.

"And John Kerry believes that in a dangerous world, war must be an option sometimes, but it should never be the first option."

And it was on this theme that Obama received a standing ovation, a jab at Bush:

"When we send our young men and women into harm's way, we have a solemn obligation not to fudge the numbers or shade the truth about why they are going, to care for their families while they're gone, to tend to the soldiers upon their return and to never, ever go to war without enough troops to win the war, secure the peace and earn the respect of the world."

I hoped Ric Shinseki was listening to this.

Overall, it was an excellent address—only seventeen minutes long but just what the crowd needed—and many in the Hawai'i delegation agreed, including those committed to Ohio congressman Dennis Kucinich, who had come in second place in the Hawai'i caucuses. Abercrombie, who had known Obama's father at UH, was nearly bursting with pride and enthusiasm.

On August 18, Governor Lingle ordered the U.S. and state flags to fly at half-staff with news of the death of former U.S. senator Hiram Fong. He was ninety-seven. His son, Hiram Jr., a former city councilman and state lawmaker, said he died peacefully at home in 'Ālewa Heights. That made me happy, because I knew his final years had been difficult. For about two years, he had been undergoing dialysis for kidney failure. And he used a walker after slipping on the steps of his house and breaking some ribs in 2003. But his mind remained sharp to the end, his family said.

The elder statesman had had a remarkable career, serving in the territorial Legislature before becoming the first Asian American senator in history. He also led a rags-to-riches life in business. Hiram was a real institution, and an inspiration to public servants of any stripe.

I issued this statement:

"I am deeply saddened by the passing of Hiram Fong. My thoughts and prayers are with Ellyn and the Fong 'ohana.

"Senator Fong was a man of great integrity and a compassionate advocate for civil rights and workers' rights. In the United States Senate, he personified the spirit of bipartisan cooperation as he worked with Republican and Democratic colleagues and administrations to enact landmark civil rights legislation in the 1960s, reform U.S. immigration laws to end discrimination against Asian immigrants, improve job training programs for workers and fight for equal pay for women. A self-made man who worked his way through elementary school, McKinley High, the University of Hawai'i and Harvard Law School, he fought for the rights of workers to organize in the 1940s, and supported worker rights over three decades of public service.

"I always welcomed the opportunity to talk story with him after he retired from the Senate and appreciated his *mana'o*. I will remember his twinkling smile and gentle sense of humor. Many of my colleagues who served with Hiram Fong in the Senate speak to me about him with great fondness and admiration. The people of Hawai'i are truly fortunate that such a distinguished and upright gentleman dedicated much of his life to public service and represented our state so well in the U.S. Senate."

In July, I had had a freak accident on the golf course. While playing at a charity tournament in Northern Virginia, I was watching close by as my staffer John Tagawa addressed the ball. His swing went astray and chipped the ball at an odd angle. The ball flew directly into my left ankle. That hurt, I can tell you, but the bruise didn't look serious so I didn't have it checked. Eventually the bruise went away.

Back home in September, however, I mentioned it to my doctor during a regular visit. He took one look and alarm spread across his face.

"Senator, you need to get to the hospital right away," he said.

Apparently, I had developed an abscess of some sort. While the skin looked normal—at least to me—the underlying tissue was dead.

This required surgery, I was told. After the surgeon removed the decaying tissue, I needed a skin graft to cover the wound, so they took skin from my upper thigh.

As part of the healing process, I had to limit my movement. So my family set up a hospital bed in the living room, and there I spent what seemed like an eternity, a trying time for all of us. My daughter Millannie, son Gerard and the doctor looked in on me frequently and were very helpful because I couldn't do anything for myself except read. I will tell you, we don't appreciate what we have—like health or freedom of movement—until it is taken away.

Inouye was up for reelection in 2004, as were Abercrombie and Case, but the interesting race that fall was the one for mayor. Ten candidates took out papers in the nonpartisan contest. The best known were Fasi, Mufi Hannemann and Duke Bainum, a doctor and former city councilmember. In the primary on Saturday, September 18, Bainum won the most votes, just over 84,000, to Hannemann's 78,000. Fasi picked up just under 18,000. But since no one achieved a majority, Duke and Mufi had to face each other in a general election runoff. In the prosecutor's race, Peter Carlisle won election to a third term, beating former prosecutor Keith Kaneshiro.

Storm clouds built up over Oʻahu the night before Halloween. The trades had been weak of late thanks to a lingering low-pressure system. That allowed pillars of moisture to build up to altitudes conducive to lightning. After nightfall, the heavens broke, mostly over the southeastern Koʻolaus. At the height of the storm, 7 p.m., the gauge at Lyon Arboretum at the back of Mānoa Valley recorded more than five inches of rain per hour, a deluge that lasted two hours. Mānoa Stream simply couldn't handle that volume and overflowed its banks. The floodwaters picked up cars and swept them down Woodlawn Drive. The water flooded the basement of Hamilton Library at UH Mānoa to a depth of six feet, damaging valuable maps, books and documents. Students in a class in the basement had to smash a window to get out. In total, thirty-five buildings on campus were damaged. More than 190 houses and businesses were flooded, leaving inches of mud behind in the morning. So were Noelani Elementary School and Mid-Pacific Institute. The damage tally hit some $100 million from that one night of rain. Lingle, after surveying the destruction in the morning, promptly declared it a disaster.

Congress was in recess through the elections, so I was in Hawai'i to witness this catastrophe and its aftermath. Our home in the hills above Nu'uanu never was threatened, but I had tremendous concern for those in low-lying areas. It's a miracle no one was killed.

As a member of the Senate Committee on Government Operations, I was keenly interested in the response of FEMA, the Federal Emergency Management Agency, to this event. FEMA had been put under homeland security on March 1, 2003, and I wondered if the additional layer of bureaucracy would help or hinder its efforts. I wasn't encouraged that Bush failed to issue a federal disaster declaration for Honolulu until February 1, 2005—more than three months after the flooding. Only then did FEMA get involved, working with state civil defense.

On Election Day, November 2, Kerry handily won Hawai'i, 54–45 percent. He also won on the West Coast, in his native New England and the mid-Atlantic states, and the upper Midwest. But Bush beat him everywhere else, including New Mexico and Iowa, which Gore had taken in 2000. In the Senate, the casualties included Daschle, the minority leader, who lost to Republican challenger John Thune. In Illinois, Obama trounced Republican Alan Keyes. But the GOP had widened its lead to fifty-four seats.

In Hawai'i, Inouye picked up seventy-three percent of the vote against a little-known candidate. Abercrombie defeated former TV reporter Dalton Tanonaka and Case beat Republican Mike Gabbard. Again, the big upset came in the mayor's race, which Bainum had dominated in the primary. Mufi squeaked by him by a half-percent margin, or 1,345 votes out of nearly 300,000 cast. As happens too often, the blank votes outnumbered the winning spread: 5,664.

On the day after Christmas, a magnitude 9.1 quake off the west coast of Sumatra provided once again a potent reminder of the power of the sea. A massive tsunami hit coastlines all across the Indian Ocean, killing 230,000 people in one of the deadliest disasters on record. Humanitarian support poured in from around the world, including Hawai'i, no stranger to tsunamis. The frightening truth remained that a quake of that size was perfectly possible in the Pacific. ❖

CHAPTER

73

Wayne Hong joined the Hawai'i Army National Guard in the late 1960s, straight out of Kalani High School. While he was learning to shoot, salute and shine his shoes, his unit was called up, so suddenly he was regular Army. He had been hoping to become an MP, but with the Vietnam War in full fury, he found himself training as a medic at Fort Sam Houston in San Antonio.

"They just rushed us through medical training," he recalled. "From there a majority of us went to Vietnam."

He arrived in country in May 1969, just in time for Hamburger Hill. Ap Bia Mountain, or hill 937 to the Army, was a 3,000-foot edifice in a remote, lush valley near the border with Laos. The peak was heavily fortified but had otherwise little military value. Nevertheless, the U.S. generals ordered it taken by frontal assault. This took ten days and involved elements of the 101st Airborne Division and the 9th Marine Regiment, as well as South Vietnamese troops. The battle cost seventy-two American lives. Nearly 400 soldiers were wounded.

The injured were flown about thirty-five miles east to Phu Bai, a sprawling base near Hue and headquarters of the 101st Airborne and several Marine battalions. And that's where Hong waited, at the 85th Evac Hospital.

"I didn't have time to get any orientation or anything," Hong remembers. "We were just shoved right into the emergency room. To me, that was a big shock because I had never seen anything like that before. And the casualties came in for ten days straight. There was no stop, no stop for ten days... It was really a nightmare."

Previously, the only dead bodies he had seen were at funerals. Now he saw bodies every day.

"I'd put them in body bags and I never got used to it. They

always said, 'You get used to it.' But I never got used to it. I had a hard time up there. I really had a hard time."

One soldier's injuries struck him like a hammer blow.

"The first week I was there, there was one casualty that I'd never forget. His name was Anderson. He was nineteen or twenty and he was over six feet tall. Before he came to Vietnam, he got married and had a baby. I know that because I went through his belongings. He had both arms, both legs blown off and amputated. That really hit me. I was thinking, when he gets back home, I don't know how his wife—who must have been as young as he is—how she can live her life taking care of him the rest of his life?

"We gave out Purple Hearts there, and we had to read out this form from the president of the United States 'on behalf of a grateful nation.' And you try to read that to someone like that and it doesn't mean anything to them."

Hong was there for one tour, after which they shipped him out via Da Nang. He was in the first wave of a 25,000-troop withdrawal ordered by Nixon.

"When we got to Da Nang, there was an Army band there. There were generals and there were photographers. As we were walking up, the generals were shaking our hands and they were filming everything. I was toward the rear. When they stopped filming, the generals left, so I didn't get to shake anyone's hand. That was typical of Vietnam."

Stateside, things were worse. When the transport plane landed at McChord Air Force Base, Washington, the troops were met by protests.

"We got off the plane and were surrounded by demonstrators calling us murderers and widow-makers. We didn't know what was going on because we didn't know what was happening back in the United States. The first thought that came into my mind was, *What country am I in?* They started spitting at us, throwing things at us and we just couldn't understand it."

Back home in Honolulu, Hong joined his family's restaurant business. They owned House of Hong and Charley's Tavern. Wayne himself opened three fast food restaurants in Kāhala, Waikīkī and Kailua, and other businesses. But things never returned to normal. He was haunted by nightmares and flashbacks, startled by sudden sounds and had a hair-trigger temper.

He went to a series of psychiatrists and psychologists, but none knew how to help him. Wayne was a family friend—we had met at a party—but this was not the kind of thing that a veteran discussed with friends.

"Sometimes it feels very lonely because nobody understands how you feel," he admitted years later. "And if you try to explain it, they can't understand it."

I knew about post-traumatic stress disorder from my own wartime experience. As a lawmaker, one of my priorities was to make sure veterans got help for what we often call "the invisible wounds of war"—PTSD and chronic brain injuries. In the early 1990s, on a trip to Hilo, I learned that a large group of Vietnam veterans was living in the hills above town. They had built hooches, makeshift huts, some of them with thatched roofs, and would sometimes booby-trap them to keep intruders out. Some had gardens; others hunted, and they bartered for staples in Hilo. I strongly suspected that many if not all of them had PTSD, which was keeping them from properly reentering society.

But medical resources on the Big Island back then were few and far between. At my urging, the Veterans Medical Center in Honolulu set up a PTSD Residential Recovery Program in Hilo. This was initially a thirteen-week program at one of the hotels. It started accepting patients—all Vietnam vets—in 1993. One of them, unbeknownst to me, was Wayne, who had been referred by the VA. By that time, the program had been shortened to nine weeks.

He insisted it saved his life.

"I was there with eleven other Vietnam vets," he recalled. "Some of these guys, when they first got up there, they were really tough guys. That was all on the outside. When they left there, they left completely changed. After nine weeks they were a completely different person. One reason is because that place—we felt safe and we felt that we could talk to any of the other guys there, because they all understood.

"There are a lot of faults with the VA, but I appreciate what they did for me," he remarked. "Because if I hadn't gone there, I wouldn't be here today."

The Hilo program was the first in the country. Within a few years, they had them in nearly every major U.S. city.

In 2005, the VA decided to move the program to Honolulu. So the Hilo program closed in November and reopened in the spring of 2006 as a six-week program, still benefitting many, many veterans, and later active-duty troops as well, often with Persian Gulf experience. Initially, the graduation ceremonies were open to the public. More than once, I spoke at those ceremonies. When I couldn't make it, I sent Mike Kitagawa, my longtime Honolulu district manager, or another staff member.

Eventually, Wayne came to grips with his Vietnam War service.

"A Vietnam vet that was a good friend of mine, he asked me if I wanted to go back to Vietnam. Of course, I didn't. He went back and told me I should go back there."

In 2004, Wayne relented and returned with his friend for a visit. The country had changed profoundly. Now he could drive through areas outside Saigon that had been hostile. "Other than the PRRP program, that was probably one of the best things that ever happened to me," he said. On subsequent trips, he took other Vietnam veterans with him. All of the vets found the trips wonderfully cathartic.

"The first time I was there, I knew I wanted to do something. I didn't know what, but I looked around and I found this orphanage, and I started helping out at this orphanage. One day I was talking to one of the kids. This girl was about fifteen years old. I asked her, 'What are you going to do after high school?' And she said, 'I'd like to go to college, but the orphanage doesn't have the money to send us to college.' None of the students ever went to college. So I talked to one of the nuns and asked her, 'Can I sponsor her to go to college?' The nun said sure, so she went to college and graduated in to top ten in her class. Very smart girl.

"Then other kids started going and they started a fund there to raise money for the kids to go to college. Now there's a bunch of kids that go to college. After they get out, they start working and they give back some of the money to the fund." ❖

CHAPTER

74

Condoleezza Rice carried a powerful presence. She had *gravitas*, a popular phrase at the time. Tall, thin, energetic and articulate, she worked a reception room well. I had met her a few times, exchanging pleasantries. She offered her hand with a steady gaze. I believe she actually knew who I was.

That had not always been the case for the Hawai'i delegation.

Sparky, in 1981, attended a White House reception for Japanese prime minister Zenko Suzuki.

He ran into Alexander Haig, the new secretary of state.

Haig thought Sparky was part of Suzuki's entourage.

"Do you speak English?" Haig asked him.

"Yes, Mr. Secretary, I do," Matsunaga replied. "And I had the honor of voting for your confirmation the other day."

One of the first orders of business before the 109th Congress was the confirmation vote for Rice, whom Bush had appointed to succeed Colin Powell as secretary of state. In Bush's first term, Rice had served as national security adviser. I felt she had served poorly.

On January 26, 2005, I was one of thirteen senators, all Democrats, who voted against her confirmation. The others included Kennedy, Byrd, Boxer, Durbin, Jeffords, Levin and Kerry—a future secretary of state. Thirty-two Democrats voted for confirmation, including Inouye, Obama and Clinton—a future secretary of state.

I logged my reasons in the Congressional Record: "Today, I opposed the nomination of Dr. Condoleezza Rice to be the next secretary of state. While I believe that she has impressive credentials, we must not forget that as the national security adviser, she played a key role in analyzing the threat that Saddam Hussein posed to our security. Although I have strong support for our soldiers, sailors, airmen and marines who are deployed around the world in defense of the principles of democracy and our great nation, critical mistakes were made with dire consequences, which may have been avoided if Dr. Rice and the other members of the national security team worked more closely with the experts in the field.

"As secretary of state, one of the secretary's main responsibilities is to implement our diplomatic efforts, which include addressing regional and civil conflicts. I do not believe, given her past decisions and comments on the reasons to go to war in Iraq, that Dr. Rice will be able to represent the United States without a predetermined bias from the war."

I just hoped she could learn from her mistakes.

Lawmaking is a hit-and-miss business.

As Congress convened, I introduced a bill that would provide some badly needed help for veterans. This was the Fulfilling Our Duty to America's Veterans Act of 2005. First, it required more solid funding sources for Veterans Health Administration to ensure that all veterans have access to medical care. Second, it funded treatment for post-traumatic stress disorder for veterans of the Afghanistan and Iraq Wars and the war on terrorism. Third, it allowed pharmacies run by the Veterans Affairs Department to fill prescriptions written by civilian doctors. And it authorized the secretaries of the Army, Navy and Air Force to carry out epidemiological studies relating to any illnesses that developed as a result of military service. The classic example, of course, was Agent Orange. In Vietnam, the U.S. commanders didn't want the enemy to be able to hide in the jungle. So they sprayed a defoliant, or leaf-killing chemical, on the trees from aircraft. But Agent Orange proved to be toxic to humans as well as foliage. Decades later, many Vietnam veterans were coming down with cancer.

The bill attracted twenty-five cosponsors, including Inouye and Kennedy, but no Republicans. On January 24, it was referred to the Veterans' Affairs Committee, where I was now the ranking Democrat. The chairman was Larry Craig of Idaho, a staunch conservative. For his voting record, Craig consistently got high marks—say, ninety-six percent—from the American Conservative Union. He had served many years on the board of the National Rifle Association. In May 2003, he held up more than 200 officer promotions to try to pressure the Air Force, unsuccessfully, into basing C-130 Hercules cargo planes in his home state. He also supported the Federal Marriage Amendment, which barred the extension of rights to same-sex couples.

As a young congressman in 1982, Craig had been the subject of rumors that he had had inappropriate contact with male pages. He denied it, of course, issuing this statement: "Persons who are unmarried as I am, by choice or by circumstance, have always been the subject of innuendos, gossip and false accusations. I think this is despicable." In the late 1980s, he went after Congress's only openly gay member, Barney Frank of Massachusetts. He also sharply criticized Clinton over the Lewinsky scandal, calling him, among things, "a naughty boy." But there is a saying about people who live in glass houses. In June 2007, he was arrested for allegedly lewd conduct in the men's restroom of the Minneapolis-Saint Paul airport. In August of that year, he pleaded guilty to the lesser charge of disorderly conduct. When news of his arrest hit the Capitol Hill newspaper, *Roll Call*, Craig announced his intention to resign from the Senate. But he ended up finishing his term without running for reelection. That wasn't the end of it. The Federal Election Commission sued him for paying his lawyers with $242,535 from his campaign fund. He was ordered to pay it back.

So that was Larry Craig. Anyway, sadly, my bill never made it out of committee.

※ ※ ※

I also reintroduced the Native Hawaiian Reorganization Act, version 2005, and over the next six months drew nine cosponsors, including Inouye and five Republicans Ted Stevens and Lisa Murkowski of Alaska, Gordon Smith of Oregon, Norm Coleman of Minnesota and Lindsey Graham of South Carolina.

"As indigenous peoples, Native Hawaiians never relinquished their inherent rights to sovereignty," I said on the floor of the Senate. "We were a government that was overthrown. While the history of the Native Hawaiian government ended in 1893 with great emotion and despair, inspired by the dignity and grace of Queen Lili‘uokalani, Native Hawaiians have preserved their culture, tradition, subsistence rights, language and distinct communities. We have tried to hold on to our homeland."

The Akaka Bill, I held strongly, marked the next logical step after the Apology Resolution. The bill was referred to the Committee on Indian Affairs, now under the chairmanship of John McCain of Arizona, who held a hearing on it on March 1. Lingle joined me for the session.

"Danny, how are we going to do on this?" she asked.

"I don't know. McCain is on the fence."

But Lingle's presence lent credence to my insistence that the bill had bipartisan appeal.

Another piece of legislation I had high hopes for was the Tsunami Preparedness Act, introduced by Inouye. The bill called for improvements in tsunami detection and warning systems under the National Oceanic and Atmospheric Administration, and helping other nations to do the same. Seismic sea waves were a worry for Hawai'i, Alaska and the West Coast, part of the Pacific "Ring of Fire." So support from Patty Murray and Maria Cantwell of Washington, Gordon Smith and Ron Wyden of Oregon and Feinstein and Boxer from California came as no surprise. But Inouye and I were pleased to receive backing from many senators from states not at risk of tsunamis—including Montana, Minnesota and Nebraska.

"The world has learned valuable lessons in the past month about human suffering and loss, as well as generosity and good fortune in the face of impossible odds," I said in support of the measure. "We have also learned a great deal about the generation of tsunamis, the need to instrument the ocean and the need to assist in the development of a warning and civil defense system for vulnerable nations around the world."

The bill passed the Committee on Commerce, Science and Transportation, led by Stevens, then cleared the full Senate, with amendments, unanimously, on July 1. In the House, however, it ran into some snags. Ultimately, many of the provisions were folded into the Tsunami Warning and Education Act, introduced in April 2005 by Congressman Sherwood Boehlert, a Republican representing Syracuse,

New York. This passed the House and Senate in December 2006 and Bush signed it five days before Christmas.

Yet another successful measure was the Hawai'i Water Resources Act, which I introduced in February with Inouye as a cosponsor. This authorized a seawater desalinization plant in Kalaeloa on Oʻahu. This moved through Congress with relative speed and was signed by Bush in September 2005. On Oʻahu, the Board of Water Supply went ahead with site blessing and an environmental impact statement. But the board decided in 2006 that it had no immediate need for more fresh water and put the project on hold.

As I say, hit and miss.

On February 2, we held a hearing on the nomination of Michael Chertoff to be secretary of homeland security. Chertoff, a former federal prosecutor and judge, was Bush's second choice to succeed Tom Ridge. His initial pick, Bernard Kerik, a former New York City police commissioner and U.S. prefect for the Iraqi Coalition Provisional Authority, had to withdraw with the revelation that he had hired an undocumented immigrant as a nanny. Chertoff had a stellar record in the courtroom, but I had doubts that that would translate into running a multi-agency behemoth.

Just weeks earlier, in December, the department's inspector general had issued a report identifying a host of worrisome problems—some of which were to be expected when twenty-two entitles are combined under one umbrella.

Chertoff and I had met earlier in the week and I had raised the unique problems of Hawaiʻi. When disaster strikes, Hawaiʻi can't call on neighboring states for help. Our seven inhabited islands must be self-sufficient. Ridge had recognized that.

Running the hearing was Susan Collins of Maine.

"Senator Akaka," she said, signaling my turn to speak.

"Thank you, very much, Madam Chairman. Judge Chertoff, today the *Washington Post* reported on your role in the alleged retaliation against an employee of the Justice Department Professional Responsibility Advisory Office who disagreed with DOJ interrogation policies. As the author of legislation to strengthen protections for federal whistleblowers, this troubles me. My question to you is, will you pledge to protect whistleblowers and foster an open work environment that promotes the disclosure of government mismanagement and government illegality?"

"Senator, first, I had no part in any way, shape or form in any retaliation against this individual for any reason, let alone giving advice," he said. "I am pledged to support whistleblowers and to support candid assessments by employers when there are problems in the department. In fact I would like to hear about them first because, as I said previously, we all make mistakes and the only way we learn is if we get feedback and I would rather get the feedback to correct it than have people just simmer about it."

My next question had to do with protecting the nation's food supply.

"Since 2001," I said, "I have been urging the administration to develop a coordinated response to bioterrorism and agriculture security through legislation, which I reintroduced this session. Improving coordination among federal, state and local agencies is critical to the health and safety of Americans. What will you do to improve bioterrorism preparedness within the department and do you consider agricultural security to be a responsibility of DHS?"

"Senator, my understanding is that agricultural security is a joint responsibility of DHS and the Department of Agriculture as well as other agencies of the government. I believe, in fact, there is a sector council that deals with this in particular. The whole issue of nuclear, biological, chemical contamination and weapons is probably generally acknowledged as the most serious single threat that we face as a country. We have seen that when there have been contamination problems historically, in private industry, they can be deadly as well as disruptive on a wide scale. We have also seen though there are ways to respond to that in terms of confining the damage, being able to track the damage, building in protections within the system in terms of how we handle our food."

Another concern I had related to government snooping on its citizens.

"You have been characterized in the press as a defender of the use of data mining by the federal government," I said. "As you know, while data mining may identify terrorist threats and improve government efficiency, it may also collect personal data that could violate an individual's privacy rights. At my request, GAO reviewed the data mining activities of the federal government and confirmed the challenges data mining poses to the protection of privacy. If confirmed, how will you safeguard Americans' privacy rights while using data mining techniques to wage the war on terror? And how will you ensure the accuracy and quality of data mined from the private sector?"

"Senator, I think that is a very sensitive issue and needs a lot of thought and I look forward to talking to people in the department about the ways in which we can deal with that issue. Obviously, we are concerned about accuracy, we are concerned about not intruding unnecessarily into personal things. We are very concerned about when we do obtain data, even if it is publicly available data, that we not disseminate it widely or in a way that is inappropriate."

On February 7, the committee forwarded Chertoff's nomination, and the full Senate approved it a week later by a vote of 98–0, with only Max Baucus and Arlen Specter abstaining.

On July 25, I was delighted to watch on television the launch of the space shuttle *Discovery*, the first shuttle mission since the *Columbia* disaster in 2003. But apparently NASA hadn't worked out all the kinks. Launch video showed debris falling off the external fuel tank—the same problem that got the *Columbia* into trouble. At that point, the agency decided to postpone any future flights until they took a closer look at the hardware. We all breathed a sigh of relief when the crew landed safely August 9 at Edwards Air Force Base, California. Kennedy Space Center in Florida had been ruled out because of bad weather.

Tropical Depression 12 formed over the Bahamas on August 23. By the next day, it had strengthened into Tropical Storm Katrina. It reached hurricane strength, with winds of 74 mph, just before it reached Florida. Governor Jeb Bush declared a state of emergency as the storm bore down.

Landfall weakened Hurricane Katrina slightly, but it gained

more strength in the warm summer waters of the Gulf of Mexico. By August 27, it was a Category 3 storm, with winds of 111 mph. In only nine hours, it reached Category 5, with 157 mph winds. A true monster. But it wasn't finished growing. Eventually the wind speed would hit 175 mph. By contrast, Hawai'i's Hurricane Iniki in 1992 had maximum winds of 145 mph. On August 28, the National Hurricane Center issued a hurricane warning extending from Morgan City, Louisiana, to the Florida-Alabama border. New Orleans mayor Ray Nagin, perhaps a bit late, ordered the evacuation of the city's 1.3 million residents. There was serious concern that the city's system of levees would give way to the storm surge. Pandemonium broke out.

When Katrina hit Louisiana on August 29, its winds had dropped to 125 mph, still a strong Category 3. New Orleans was devastated, with whole sections of the city flooded. In the end, the damage extended from Texas to Alabama. More than 1,200 people died, and the damage tally eventually reached $108 billion.

While the Coast Guard had mounted a swift and efficient response, it became clear in the aftermath that the response from the Federal Emergency Management Agency, under Director Michael Brown, was woefully weak. Clear to everyone except Bush, who, when he toured the devastation, told him, "Brownie, you're doing a heck of a job." Brown would ultimately resign.

In a letter to Bush on September 8, I said, "Mr. President, my thoughts are with all of those from the Gulf Coast States affected by Hurricane Katrina as they mourn the loss of family and friends and neighbors. We wish them well. I know there are no words that can provide the needed comfort. I believe there must be an extensive examination of what went wrong with the government's response to this natural disaster.

"As hundreds of thousands of Americans look toward rebuilding their lives, our first priority must be to ensure that all possible federal resources are at their disposal. However, it is Congress's job to get to the bottom of what went wrong and to do whatever is necessary to ensure that it never happens again. I join those who say we must not engage in a blame game but, rather, we must come together to undertake responsible oversight.

"I say this from an interesting vantage point because throughout the debate over the creation of the Department of Homeland Security in 2002, I repeatedly expressed my strong concern that non-homeland security functions of the federal government would be diminished if included in the new department. I said that eliminating the Federal Emergency Management Agency's status as an independent agency to join this proposed department could seriously affect FEMA's traditional role of responding to natural disasters."

As with the Iraq War, I was once again very saddened to be right.

Unfortunately, Mother Nature wasn't done. On September 18, north of Hispaniola, Tropical Depression 18 became Tropical Storm Rita. ✤

CHAPTER

75

Millie and I lost a close friend and ally in early November with the death of Henry Giugni, Inouye's longtime chief of staff and later Senate sergeant at arms. A native of Pearl City and a former Honolulu police solo bike officer, he had been with Inouye since the days of the territorial Legislature. As sergeant at arms, he organized the inauguration of the first President Bush and escorted countless foreign leaders, including Margaret Thatcher, Nelson Mandela and Vaclav Havel, when they visited the Capitol. Referring to himself often as a "poor Hawaiian boy," he never graduated from college, but in 2003 the University of Hawai'i at Hilo awarded him a doctorate in humane letters for his long government service. From that point on, he jokingly insisted on being called "Dr. Giugni." Millie and I had chatted with him just a few weeks earlier. He died of congestive heart failure at Shady Grove Adventist Hospital in Rockville, Maryland, just outside Washington. He was eighty.

Inouye made the announcement in the Senate.

"His passing is a great loss for the people of Hawai'i, the United States and the Senate, an institution he loved dearly, and in which he served as its thirtieth sergeant at arms for four years, beginning on January 6, 1987. I had the privilege of knowing Henry for nearly fifty years, beginning in 1956 when he joined my reelection campaign to the Hawai'i Territorial House of Representatives. We quickly forged an unbreakable bond.

"With his tireless work, dedication and loyalty, he proved invaluable as the top aide on my staff when I served as a Hawai'i legislator, U.S. representative and U.S. senator. His keen political instincts also made him invaluable on campaigns."

I made a statement of my own.

"He was a well-recognized presence on the Hill, particularly in the Senate. After leaving the Hill, Henry joined one of the largest consulting firms in Washington where he was serving his clients effectively. I will remember Henry as one of the first friends who welcomed me and my family to Washington when I was elected to Congress nearly thirty years ago. His kindness continued over many years and we knew him to be a loving husband and father. Millie and I always appreciated his visits whether for business or a social call. We were extremely saddened to hear of his passing."

At his memorial service on November 15, Millie recalled having some spirited conversations with Henry.

"We were fighting partners," she said. "He had a big mouth, but his heart was big, too."

As 2005 closed, I remained deeply concerned about our intervention in Iraq. And I wasn't alone. In November, seventy-nine members of the Senate, including forty-one Republicans, voted for an amendment that said the year 2006 should see "significant transition to full Iraqi sovereignty," with Iraqi forces taking the lead for the security of a sovereign nation, and allowing the phased pullout of U.S. troops. But the means toward those ends remained unclear.

So on December 14, I joined Clinton and thirty-nine other senators in sending a letter to Bush, urging him to level with the American people about what loomed ahead in that tattered and ethnically divided nation. "We regret that the American people have still not been presented with a plan that identifies the remaining political, economic and military benchmarks that must be met in order to facilitate the phased redeployment of U.S. forces and a reasonable schedule to achieve them," we said.

Elections were on the near horizon for Iraq, and we emphasized the importance of women participating in a society where Islamic sharia often excludes them.

"Every day the women in Iraq are braving great odds to secure for themselves a political future that protects their rights and those of their daughters and granddaughters," the letter said. "Thousands of women have offered themselves as candidates in the upcoming elections, thousands more will come forward to monitor the polls. Women's groups and women from numerous political parties have joined together to advocate for strong protections for women's rights in the constitution, and that fight will continue until the language of that constitution is finalized next year. Women are already preparing to advocate for changes in social policy, greater transparency in government and laws to fight corruption.

"I hope that women will vote in large numbers in the December 15th elections, and that those who are elected will continue to push for strong protections for women in Iraq. Activists and leaders throughout the world know that their struggle will strengthen the cause of women everywhere."

Another worry was the role of security contractors in Iraq. An estimated 25,000 private guns-for-hire were working in the country, earning huge salaries—from $550 to $1,500 a day. One of the companies was Aegis Specialist Risk Management, which in 2005 was awarded a $1.3 billion Defense Department contract formally known as Reconstruction Security Support Services Iraq. In mid-December, the Pentagon launched an investigation into a video posted on a website affiliated with Aegis. The video is shot from the back window of a security detail vehicle. You can hear a machine gun being fired at cars to the rear. After a number of shots, the cars drift off the road, leaving one to assume the driver has been shot dead. During the entire video, the Elvis Presley song "Mystery Train" plays in the background.

"This behavior is offensive," I said on the Senate floor. "The actions of the individuals in the video put our troops at risk because such incendiary behavior only increases hatred towards Americans. Whether or not we agree with the troops' presence in Iraq, we all agree that the safety of our troops is paramount. Our troops in Iraq who wear uniforms are instant targets for retaliatory violence."

As the new year dawned, our country recoiled from the news of a preventable industrial disaster, the collapse of the Sago Coal Mine in West Virginia. An explosion and cave-in on January 2 trapped thirteen miners for two days; only one survived. In the ensuing weeks, we learned that the federal Mine Safety and Health Administration had cited the owners 208 times for safety violations. Ninety-six citations were considered "serious and substantial." I was flabbergasted that the agency had allowed the mine to continue operation, and could only conclude that the pro-business tack of the Bush administration had created the climate.

On January 23, the Arlen Specter's Senate Appropriations Subcommittee on Labor held a hearing on the accident. Among those testifying was David Dye, acting assistant secretary of labor for mine safety and health. He began with a conciliatory tone.

"It is with the heaviest of hearts that every MSHA employee grieves for the miners who died at the Sago mine and the loved ones who mourn their passing," he said. "MSHA's reason for being is to ensure that miners return home safe and healthy to loved ones at the end of their shifts. That is our mission and our focus, every day. That is our duty to America's miners and the reason we are conducting the investigation with the greatest care and diligence so we can uncover the full truth of why this tragedy happened and how we can better protect miners in the future."

He insisted the MSHA had stepped up enforcement in recent years, leading to a forty-two percent drop in fatalities in coal mines from the turn of the century to 2005.

"But that is cold comfort to the families of those who are killed, or to miners who suffer injuries," he admitted. "So we can never let up in improving mine safety, and we will not."

Specter noted that the 208 citations added up to only $27,000 in fines.

Byrd, who represented the state where the disaster happened, jumped in.

"Let me cut right to the chase," he said. "Is there too much opportunity here for cronyism? I wonder if the regulations are being enforced without fear of favor and the fines are being levied, are they heavy enough? They don't seem to be. Too often industry just seems to pay the fines and go right ahead and keep doing the wrongs. What do we have to do to fix that? It seems in part to have been the case here."

✳ ✳ ✳

In late January, I announced my opposition to Bush's latest Supreme Court pick, Samuel Alito. Bush's selections for the bench in general had caused Senate Democrats a lot of heartburn. The previous spring, outnumbered forty-five to fifty-five, we had held filibusters to prevent a vote on ten judicial nominees. That prompted majority leader Bill Frist to consider changing the Senate rules to ban filibusters. Outraged Democrats threatened a fight that could have hamstrung the Senate. The conflict ended when seven Democrats, including Inouye and Byrd, and seven moderate Republicans, collectively called the Gang of 14, reached a procedural compromise.

On July 19, 2005, Bush nominated John Roberts to the seat being vacated by Sandra Day O'Connor, who was retiring. I considered O'Connor a voice of moderation on the court, and she had provided the swing vote in a lot of 5–4 rulings. I wanted to see her succeeded by someone of similar stripe. Or at least someone less conservative than Roberts. But then, on September 3, chief justice William Rehnquist died. Bush immediately withdrew Roberts' nomination as associate justice and named him to replace Rehnquist.

The Senate Judiciary Committee, on September 22, approved Roberts' nomination 13–5, with Biden, Durbin, Feinstein, Kennedy and Schumer voting no. A week later the full Senate voted 78–22 to approve him. He got the support of every Republican and also Jim Sessions of Vermont, the Senate's only independent. The Democrats split, with the "no" votes coming from me, Inouye, Kennedy, Kerry, Feinstein, Boxer, Biden, Obama, Durbin, Clinton, Schumer, Reid and ten others.

An appellate judge, Alito was Bush's third pick to replace O'Connor, after White House counsel Harriet Miers dropped out amid bipartisan qualms. In the months since Alito's nomination, I had carefully considered his record and had followed his confirmation hearings closely. I concluded that his conservative views would lead the court in a direction hostile to privacy and civil rights.

"As a judge on the Third Circuit, he has repeatedly made it difficult for victims of discrimination to prevail or even receive a jury trial," I said in a statement. "I cherish our system of checks and balances in government, but Judge Alito's record shows that he would undermine Congress's authority to protect the public. On the Third Circuit, Judge Alito has ruled that Congress did not have the authority to pass the Family Medical Leave Act or to enact a federal ban on the possession or transfer of machine guns. In both cases, the Supreme Court disagreed with Judge Alito's conclusions and upheld these protections."

The Senate took up the Alito nomination in the last week of January, and approved him by a vote of 58–42, the narrowest margin since Clarence Thomas. Four Democrats voted yes, notably Byrd.

Jeffords and one Republican, Lincoln Chafee of Rhode Island, voted no, as did I, Inouye and thirty-eight other Democrats, including Kerry, who had tried but failed at a filibuster. ❖

CHAPTER

76

In January 2006, I got a call from Ed Case.

"Senator, this is an incredibly difficult call for me to make, as I have loved you and respected you all my life, but I think I need to put myself forward as a candidate."

We had heard rumors that he was going to run against me. Now here was confirmation.

I thanked him for letting me know. I told him I was certain we could keep the contest civil and that I looked forward to a spirited discussion of the issues.

"I do, too, Senator," he said.

He also called Inouye and Abercrombie, who told him they had to back me.

Inouye said in a statement: "I continue to give Senator Akaka my support. I hope Congressman Case will reconsider his decision to challenge Senator Akaka, and will instead seek reelection to the U.S. House of Representatives. Also, I have been advised that Senator Akaka has the full support of the leadership of the Democratic Senatorial Campaign Committee."

When contacted by reporters, my campaign chairman, Wayne Yamasaki, said, "We welcome challenges because challenges toughen the candidates."

"Gee, Wayne, I'm sorry you don't think I'm tough enough," I teased him privately later.

At an afternoon news conference with his wife, Audrey, on Thursday, January 19, Case said he felt the party needed a new generation of leadership. Inouye and I were both in our eighties, admittedly well past the typical retirement age but not so unusual in the Senate. Robert Byrd was eighty-eight; John Glenn had retired at eighty-seven; Strom Thurmond had served until age 100.

"I have the deepest aloha for Senator Akaka and truly honor his decades of selfless service," Case said. "But we all know that we are in a time of transition in our Hawai'i's representation in Congress and especially in the Senate. This transition requires that we phase in the next generation to provide continuity in that service."

So, for the first time in sixteen years, since Pat Saiki, I had a tough race ahead of me. It wasn't a sunny day.

※ ※ ※

Then the rains came. For six weeks, beginning in February, downpours drenched Hawai'i. Schools and roads closed.

In March, Mount Wai'ale'ale on Kaua'i—one of the wettest spots on Earth—set an all-time monthly record of 93.71 inches. During the midst of this, on March 14, the Kaloko Dam on Kaua'i breached its berm, sending 400 million gallons of water—in some spots twenty feet deep—down Waiakalua Stream. Seven people were swept to their death. It was the worst disaster on Kaua'i since Iniki.

Lingle asked the Legislature, then in session, for $14 million in emergency funds. Two days after the breach, I introduced the Dam Rehabilitation and Repair Act of 2006. It set up a grant program under FEMA to help states fix up deficient dams. Inouye and Jack Reed of Rhode Island signed on as cosponsors.

I made this statement in the Senate: "Mr. President, I rise today to express my sincere sympathy and deep concern for those affected by the collapse of the Kaloko Reservoir on the island of Kaua'i in Hawai'i. This tragic flooding has caused loss of life and substantial property damage. The people of Hawai'i have shown exceptional resolve in assisting their fellow citizens as emergency personnel and other volunteers have rushed to provide assistance to people in need."

The damage wasn't over. On March 31—the fortieth day of rain, biblical in its proportions—thunderstorms buffeted East O'ahu. In Kāhala, the storm drains on Hunakai Street couldn't handle the excess water, so it rushed down the emergency exits of the Kahala Mall theaters and through the rear, parking lot entrance. Soon moviegoers—watching glaciers melt in *Ice Age: The Meltdown*—found themselves calf-deep in water and fled. About ninety stores evacuated.

Finally, in early April, the skies cleared.

* * *

On April 14, *Time* magazine, with a national circulation of 4.1 million, ranked me among the five least-effective senators. Joining me on this list were Republicans Wayne Allard of Colorado, Jim Bunning of Kentucky and Conrad Burns of Montana and Democrat Mark Dayton of Minnesota.

"By all accounts, Daniel Akaka is an affectionate and earnest man," the magazine said. "Even a conservative fire-breather like Oklahoma's Jim Inhofe says his ultraliberal colleague 'is a lovable person, and most of us are not that lovable.' As a legislator, though, Akaka is living proof that experience does not necessarily yield expertise. After sixteen years on the job, the junior senator from Hawai'i is a master of the minor resolution and the bill that dies in committee... Akaka's seniority has placed him in positions of potential influence. At eighty-one he is the ranking Democrat on the Veterans' Affairs Committee and sits on four other committees that control such valuable political real estate as the armed services and homeland security as well as energy and natural resources. He did make a mark thirteen years ago by passing a resolution in which the U.S. apologized for invading Hawai'i in 1893. But he has struggled recently to get a bill approved that would provide increased autonomy to the islands." That last reference, apparently to the Akaka Bill, badly mischaracterized the measure.

And I felt that they had misread my style, which was not to go out and yell and argue with people but rather to talk to them personally, the Hawaiian way of working with people even when we disagree. With that approach, I made a lot of friends and built a lot of mutual respect. This was all done in the back rooms and the hallways, invisible to the public eye. Because I worked quietly, a journalist could look at me and say, "Hey, this guy doesn't do anything."

Of course, it should be noted that in 2000 Time Warner, the parent company of *Time* magazine, merged with AOL, becoming AOL-Time Warner. The executive chairman of the new company was the founder of America Online, Steve Case, Ed's cousin. Probably just a coincidence.

I did agree with some of their "best senator" selections, among them Kennedy, Durbin, Levin, Richard Lugar, McCain, Snowe and Specter.

Very shortly after Case's announcement, several Democrats expressed interest in running for his House seat. They included former lieutenant governor Mazie Hirono, state senator Colleen Hanabusa and state representative Brian Schatz, names that would remain familiar in the years ahead.

To help me prepare for the inevitable debate with Case, my legislative director, Melissa Hampe, a very bright young woman, put together a set of briefing papers. They set out precisely yet concisely my stance on key issues. Among them:

The Arctic National Wildlife Refuge. In March 2003, it had been widely misreported that Inouye and I had voted for a plan to drill for oil in this pristine Alaskan wilderness. The measure failed 52–48. To be clear, the portion of land set aside by Congress for oil exploration was outside the refuge. It is completely flat and barren of trees and covered with snow nine months of the year. Having said that, I felt it was important to balance environmental protection with our dangerous reliance on foreign oil.

Energy. As a member of the Energy and Natural Resources Committee, I had worked successfully toward advancing energy self-sufficiency in Hawai'i and the nation. This included promoting such renewable and alternate energy sources as wind, solar, wave, ocean thermal conversion, ethanol, photovoltaic and hydrogen. I had secured $36 million in funding for demonstration projects to convert sugarcane into ethanol. And I had secured $3 million for hydrogen energy research in fiscal year 2006. The beauty of hydrogen, the most abundant element in the universe, is that it makes up two of the three atoms that form water, readily available to an island state like ours.

Environment. I had consistently backed measures for clean air and water and against invasive species and ocean dumping. I had supported the creation of the Hawaiian Islands Humpback Whale Sanctuary and a marine sanctuary in the Northwestern Hawaiian Islands. My Hawai'i Tropical Forest Recovery Act had been signed into law in 1992. In more recent years, I had worked to expand or support Hawai'i Volcanoes National Park, the Pu'uhonua O Hōnaunau National Historic Refuge, the Kaloko-Honokōhau National Historic Park, the Ala Kahakai National Historic Trail and the Palmyra Island National Wildlife Refuge. Even before the Kyoto Protocol on global warming, I had supported carbon sequestration projects in forestry and credits for carbon dioxide reduction.

Consumer protection. I was proud of my efforts to promote financial literacy. These included the creation of the Financial Literacy and Education Commission to help more Americans make informed choices when it comes to credit cards, borrowing, saving and spending. I was also a leader in the national effort to ensure food safety. When mad cow disease, formally bovine spongiform encephalopathy, arrived in the United States in 2003, I introduced the Downed Animal Protection Act to make sure that the cattle most vulnerable to the disease—which could spread to humans—were euthanized humanely and kept out of the food supply.

Education. As a former teacher and principal, I was intimately aware of the challenges facing our teachers and schools. While asking them to maintain a high standard, we must also provide them with the tools and support to succeed in their mission. More importantly, for our schools to succeed, all of us, as a community, must be involved in some way. As Hillary Clinton famously noted, "It takes a village." Today's multicultural student bodies presented especially tough challenges. That's why I introduced the Teacher Acculturation Act of 2005, aimed to boost content knowledge and teaching methods among our primary and secondary school faculties. In 2005, I also introduced a bill to increase foreign language education. My bid to add $3 billion in funding to the No Child Left Behind Act failed in March by a slim 51–49 vote.

Health and social services. In a sense, we define who we are as a society and nation not by what we do for ourselves but what we do for others, especially those who cannot help themselves. Senior citizens and other beneficiaries, on limited and fixed incomes, depend on programs like Medicare and Medicaid for health care. I had worked hard to strengthen those programs and ensure access and affordability, including a comprehensive Medicare prescription drug benefit.

The Iraq War. The United States, I strongly held, needed a specific plan of action involving the Iraqi government that clarifies objectives and goals to secure peace and ensure democracy in Iraq. Since Bush had declared "mission accomplished" more than three years ago, more than 2,500 Americans had died, including more than 100 with Hawai'i connections. Before the war, Rumsfeld had estimated it would cost $60 billion. To date, the cost had hit $273 billion with no end in sight. Far from risking Iraq's collapse, setting a timetable for a phased withdrawal would signal America's clear intention to the Iraqi people and gives Americans a measure of certainty about ending a war that the majority of this nation no longer supports.

The Patriot Act. While we must be vigilant about terrorism, the effort must never come at the expense of the rights and privileges upon which this country was founded. History has shown us, over and over, that when those rights are dismissed for expediency, nothing good ever comes of it. Just look at the Japanese American internments during World War II. Or the McCarthy hearings to root out feared communists in America. I found quite chilling the sweeping new powers of the government to conduct domestic investigations and surveillance without constitutional checks and balances. I didn't think the Patriot Act, as employed by the Bush administration, strengthened the country. Rather, it weakened us by eroding the very freedoms that define us.

At the state Democratic Party Convention in May, Inouye repeated his full endorsement, mentioning my opposition to the Iraq War and push for Native Hawaiian recognition. He also raised the Jones Act, a 1920 law that protects the shipping industry from foreign competition. The Jones Act, which requires that cargo between U.S. ports move on U.S. ships, had emerged as a surprising policy difference between Case and me. He favored scrapping the law, arguing that it had created a monopoly favoring Matson Navigation Co. and Horizon Lines, the top cargo fleets in the market. "It's the concentration of power and the projection of power to reward your friends and punish your enemies simply to maintain the status quo," he said. He called the law "the modern-day incarnation" of the Big Five at its worst. "It's a monopoly over a key lifeline for Hawai'i." Inouye, Abercrombie and I favored the Jones Act as providing a reliable conduit for cargo between Hawai'i and the Mainland.

Meanwhile, my position on Iraq had hardened. I was now calling for a complete withdrawal of U.S. forces by July 2007. I felt like we needed to put pressure on the Iraqi government to take responsibility for its own security. British writer Cyril Parkinson famously observed, "Work expands so as to fill the time available for its completion." If we set no deadline, the Iraqis would take forever to get their act in order.

Case disagreed, urging more patience with the process.

Senate Bill 147, the Akaka Bill, which I had reintroduced in early 2005, approached a key hurdle on June 8, 2006. This was a vote in the Senate to invoke what is known as "cloture"—that is, closing debate, or a filibuster, on a bill and moving it forward for a make-or-break vote. Sixteen senators must sign a petition for cloture. We had that. Then the motion had to be approved by a sixty-vote majority. That was the rub.

I put in this last-minute appeal:

"Mr. President, I encourage my colleagues to vote with me to invoke cloture on the motion to proceed to S. 147, the Native Hawaiian Government Reorganization Act of 2005. I begin by expressing my deep appreciation to the cosponsors of this legislation and to the senators who spoke in support of bringing this bill forward for debate. I especially thank the senator from Illinois, Mr. Obama, and the ranking member of the Indian Affairs Committee, Senator Dorgan, for their support. I also thank the senators from Alaska who shared their experiences encountered thirty-five years ago when Alaska Natives sought to address similar issues when Congress enacted the Alaska Natives Claims Settlement Act. It is ironic that the same arguments used against that bill, which has been incredibly successful and has served to unite rather than divide the people of Alaska, are being used against our efforts today to bring parity in federal policies to Hawai'i's indigenous peoples."

The vote for me was a cliff-hanger. Years of hard work, of lobbying in the corridors, rode in the balance. The roll call began, as usual, in alphabetical order.

"Mr. Akaka."

"Aye."

"Mr. Alexander." This was Lamar Alexander of Tennessee, a Republican who had succeeded Fred Thompson, the *Law and Order* actor.

"Nay."

Two more Republicans followed, Allard of Colorado (see *Time*'s five worst senators, above) and George Allen of Virginia, son of the former head coach of the Los Angeles Rams. In 2000, Allen had beaten two-term incumbent Chuck Robb, LBJ's son-in-law. Both voted no.

"Mr. Baucus." This was the senator from Montana who had joined me on the trip to Cuba. I knew I could count on him.

"Aye."

"Mr. Bayh." Evan was the son of Senator Birch Bayh, a well-respected name in Indiana politics.

"Aye."

"Mr. Bennett." Bob Bennett of Utah was a staunch conservative, a card-carrying member of the National Rifle Association.

"Nay."

"Mr. Biden." Joe Biden was one of the Senate's most erudite members, a powerful voice on the Foreign Relations Committee. He commuted to Washington by train every day from Delaware.

"Aye."

"Mr. Bingaman." Democrat Jeff Bingaman of New Mexico was another brilliant senator, a graduate of Harvard and then Stanford Law School. With a steely jaw and steady gaze, he had a pleasant but no-nonsense demeanor worthy of a former attorney general and Army reservist.

"Aye."

"Mr. Bond." In the wake of Abu Ghraib, Kit Bond, a Missouri Republican, was one of only nine senators to oppose restrictions on CIA interrogation techniques. At one point, when asked if he thought waterboarding was torture, he said, "There are different ways of doing it. It's like swimming—freestyle, backstroke."

"Nay."

"Mrs. Boxer." A Brooklyn native and former stockbroker, Barbara Boxer got her start in California politics as an aide to my old friend Congressman John Burton. Like a lot of native New Yorkers—or maybe she picked this up from John—Barbara could be very direct. When she arrived in the Senate in 1993, women held seven out of 100 seats. The others were fellow Californian Dianne Feinstein, Nancy Kassebaum of Kansas, Barbara Mikulski of Maryland, Carol Moseley-Braun of Illinois, Patty Murray of Washington and Kay Bailey Hutchison of Texas. At Boxer's instigation, they all insisted on sharing space in the Senate gym. Well, of course we gave it to them. But, mind you, the Senate gym is much smaller than the one in the House. So, I didn't mind the women sharing the gym. But I kept my membership in the House gym, with a larger locker and twenty-five-meter heated pool, until I retired.

"Aye."

The next four Republicans voted no: Sam Brownback of Texas, Bunning of Kentucky and Burns of Montana. (See worst senators, above.) Also, Richard Burr of North Carolina.

"Mr. Byrd." I knew I could count on my fiddle-playing friend from West Virginia.

"Aye."

We picked up the next two votes, Democrats Maria Cantwell of Washington and Tom Carper of Delaware.

"Mr. Chafee." I had hopes for Lincoln, even though he was a Republican. He had sided with the minority on the 2002 Iraq War vote. In 2007, he would become a Democrat.

"Nay."

Republican Saxby Chambliss of Georgia also voted no.

"Mrs. Clinton." I had no doubt about Hillary, an old friend, close colleague and wife of my longtime golfing partner.

"Aye."

So there we were. Ten votes in favor, eleven against. Very close. I had hope.

In the end, all forty-four Democrats voted for Hawaiian recognition. And we brought aboard twelve Republicans, including Coleman of Minnesota, Specter of Pennsylvania, Stevens and Murkowski of Alaska, Kyl and McCain of Arizona, and Susan Collins and Olympia Snowe of Maine.

Four votes short of sixty. So the bill was dead.

"Today, across this nation, Native Hawaiians have been recognized as an indigenous people deserving of justice, equality and the recognition accorded to the other indigenous peoples of the United States," I said in a statement. "In the highest halls of our government, senators from all parts of our country and both sides of the aisle took up the cause to bring Native Hawaiians justice. For this, I am extremely grateful and extraordinarily proud.

"Sadly, the noble values of equality, fairness and strength in diversity, hallmarks of our state and our country, fell victim to politics, rhetoric and procedural maneuvering. The central issue of federal recognition for Hawai'i's indigenous people has yet to be given its fair examination.

"I am disappointed that we did not overcome the procedural obstacles to bring the bill to the floor, but I am heartened by the fact that fifty-six senators supported our efforts. I have always said that we had the votes to enact this bill on an up-or-down vote.

"I am extremely proud to have brought this issue to the forefront of the Senate and to have elevated the cause of the Native Hawaiians to a national level. We must continue to move forward for Native Hawaiians, the people of Hawai'i and everyone in this country who believe that ours is a nation which treats all of its people with an equitable hand." ❖

CHAPTER

77

A bit of encouraging news arrived in early July, when a poll commissioned by the *Advertiser* gave me a healthy lead over Case among likely Democratic voters, fifty-one to forty percent, with nine percent undecided. But the primary was still many weeks away. In the same poll, conducted by Ward Research, my job approval rating was sixty-four percent; Ed's also was high at sixty percent. I often wonder if he wishes he had stuck to the House.

On July 19, the Senate approved the Water Resources Development Act. It included provisions of the Dam Safety Act of 2006, which I introduced after the deadly Kaloko Reservoir breach in March.

"This tragic event serves as an important reminder of the responsibility held by the state and local governments and the leadership role of the federal government in supplementing state resources and developing national guidelines for dam safety," I said.

During the past two years, I had learned, there had been at least twenty-nine dam failures in the U.S. causing more than $200 million in property damage.

"This legislation will advance dam safety in the United States and prevent loss of life and property damage from dam failures at both the federal and state programmatic levels," I said. "Specifically, the reauthorization of the National Dam Safety Program Act will provide much-needed assistance to state dam safety programs that regulate ninety-five percent of the 80,000 dams in the U.S."

We had a crowded legislative calendar. The next day, Jim

Jeffords introduced the Global Warming Pollution Reduction Act of 2006 and I quickly signed on as a cosponsor, along with Bingaman, Boxer, Kennedy, Leahy, Lautenberg and Reed. The bill set the United States on a path to reducing emissions to 1990 levels by 2020 through a two percent annual reduction from 2010 through 2020, as well as achieving by 2050 emissions that are eighty percent below 1990 levels. I know 2050 seems like the distant future, but I recall my amazement at reaching the year 1984, the title of a futuristic novel by George Orwell, and 2001, another by Arthur C. Clarke.

Hawai'i has been at the forefront of global warming studies since 1958, when the first atmospheric carbon dioxide readings were taken at Mauna Loa Observatory. The site on Hawai'i's second tallest mountain makes sense because the air there is so pure, having been scrubbed by 2,500 miles of open ocean. It is also dry and too high to get any localized pollution or other particulates. Carbon dioxide concentrations fluctuate by season, but the first figures averaged about 315 parts per million. This figure has risen relentlessly over the decades in a line called the Keeling Curve, after Charles D. "Dave" Keeling, a researcher at the Scripps Institution of Oceanography, in La Jolla. By 2006, the concentration had grown to more than 380 ppm, an increase of twenty percent.

While there were some holdouts who believed climate change is a hoax, the international scientific community now concurred that human activities—burning fossil fuels, chopping down forests—were taking a potentially terrible toll. The U.S., the world's largest emitter of greenhouse gases, must be accountable as a leader, I felt, in reducing emissions.

What's more, Hawai'i is particularly susceptible to increases in sea level and ocean temperatures, to the detriment of public safety, economic development, cultural resources and our unique ecosystems and wildlife. Other coastal states clearly will face similar challenges—flooding of low-lying property, loss of coastal wetlands, beach erosion, saltwater contamination of the drinking water table and the undermining of near-shore roads and bridges. Climate models also forecast extreme weather. In the event of a disaster, remote and rural areas could be on their own for days.

"I am very concerned about the impact of fossil fuel emissions on the health of our planet and believe that we must actively seek solutions to curb the buildup of greenhouse gases," I said in a statement. "This bill sets energy efficiency targets to assist both the industry and energy consumers in meeting these standards. This legislation lays out ambitious goals to minimize U.S. emissions and assist in the stabilization of global atmospheric greenhouse gas concentrations."

In late July, I saluted—as would have Arthur C. Clarke—the successful landing of the space shuttle *Discovery*. NASA had finally fixed its hardware headaches, which had doomed the *Columbia* and threatened *Discovery* a year earlier. The shuttle soared skyward on Independence Day and spent thirteen days in orbit, delivering supplies and a European astronaut to the International Space Station. I was delighted the program was back on track. The renewed exploration, to me, meant that the astronauts lost in the *Columbia* and *Challenger* accidents, including Ellison, had not died in vain.

The growth of the air tourism industry in the last few decades had considerably interrupted the tranquility of Hawai'i's national parks. So, in early August, as the ranking member of the Subcommittee on National Parks, I introduced a measure to prohibit tour helicopter flights over Kalaupapa, Kaloko-Honokōhau, Pu'uhonua O Hōnaunau and Pu'ukoholā Heiau. I called this the Hawaiian Sacred Sites Noise Reduction Act of 2006. I felt strongly that prohibiting air tourism over these areas would allow residents and visitors the tranquility and peace necessary to enjoy these attractions.

Case and I appeared before a luncheon crowd of about 400 at a forum sponsored by the Hawai'i Publishers Association on August 8 at Dole Cannery Ballroom. It wasn't a debate. We each made statements in turn, followed by questions from the audience.

Ed revisited his transition pitch.

"We should start now to direct this transition to bring in the next U.S. senator while Senator Inouye can still serve, so that senator can build up ability, seniority and experience and relationships," he said.

I countered that seniors should not be dismissed as frail and disposable, of no use to society, seen only as a burden. Rather, they should be valued as *kupuna* with wisdom and long experience.

I was asked if I thought Case should have waited his turn.

"It's not just a matter of waiting your turn," I said. "It's a matter of gaining valuable experience and knowledge and insight."

Case pointed to the cloture vote as an example of my lack of clout.

"It was clearly a failure of effectiveness on the floor of the United States Senate," he said. "There have been no markers of national leadership in a thirty-year career. There has been a 'don't make waves' approach. That's not going to get our national problems solved. If we're just going to kind of go along to get along, we're never going to dig our way out of the problems that we face."

I argued that my style was collegial, not confrontational, and had worked to Hawai'i's advantage. On the Hawaiian recognition bill, I noted that the vote was close, that a few Republicans remained hostile and unaware of Hawaiian history. I wasn't giving up.

Case and I also voiced our differences over the Iraq War.

"To stay the course is no strategy at all," I insisted.

Case said, "To set a firm timetable unrelated to the conditions on the ground, I think, is a mistake. I think it is naïve and I think it is simplistic. You can't just set an arbitrary time frame and say, 'Everything is going to be OK.'"

We hugged at the end of the forum.

A national poll a few days later indicated the race had narrowed. A survey of 500 likely voters by Rasmussen Reports found me slightly ahead, 47–45, with eight percent undecided. The margin of error was 4.5 percentage points. The poll also found that the Iraq War and the economy were the most important issues for voters.

But the matchup results seemed to contradict another, locally run poll by the OmniTrack Group. That survey of 399 likely Democratic voters had me ahead 55–35, with ten percent undecided. The margin of error there was five percentage points.

I asked Wayne, my campaign manager, which one we should believe.

"We're not believing any polls," he said.

My campaign spokeswoman, Elisa Yadao, told the media, "We're going to continue to work hard every day. While we're grateful both of these polls showed us ahead, we're not taking anything for granted."

Later in the month, Ed and I agreed to a one-hour debate sponsored by AARP Hawaiʻi, to take place August 31 at PBS Hawaiʻi. The public would be invited to submit questions in writing. It would be moderated by Gerry Kato, a former *Advertiser* and broadcast reporter who was now chairman of the School of Communications at UH Mānoa. We would have five minutes for opening statements, two minutes to answer a question, one minute for a rebuttal and three minutes for closing remarks.

I looked over the briefing papers that Melissa had prepared, and before I knew it the date was upon us.

We tossed a coin to see who could choose to go first or second. I won, and I chose to go second, so my voice would be the last the voters heard.

After introductory remarks by Neil Hannahs, PBS Hawaiʻi chairman, and Barbara Kim Stanton, AARP Hawaiʻi executive director, we began under the studio lights.

"Gentlemen, good evening and welcome," said Kato, seated before us. "Senator Akaka has won the coin toss and has elected to go second. Congressman Case will now give his opening remarks."

Case leveled his gaze at the main camera.

"Senator Akaka, friends, good evening and aloha. In just twenty-three days, you will have a crucial choice. Who can represent you in our U.S. Senate, not just today but for the next generation. You must choose Dan Akaka or Ed Case, and it will be decided in the Democratic primary in which everyone can vote."

That was a clear appeal to independents and moderate Republicans. I think Ed knew he needed some crossover votes if he stood any chance.

"This is a crucial event so I asked for advice. I went to Mom and she said, 'Relax.' I went to our volunteers and they said, 'Smile.' I went to my wife, Audrey, and she said, 'Lighten up.' Well, I can take a hint. Lighten up. But that's hard to do when it's about our future. Because a U.S. senator should and must be a national leader, responsible for the well-being of all. A person who accepts the obligations of national leadership and is able to persevere through hard work and commitments to find workable solutions."

He argued for a balanced federal budget—"we've been running it into the ground, running up huge debts to countries like China"—and securing our homeland amid a dramatically changing landscape.

"Some threats are direct, like Iran, North Korea," he said. "Others are more difficult, like terrorism."

He called Iraq a "crucial, complex and tragic" engagement.

"Who doesn't mourn our losses? Who doesn't want to bring our troops home now? Who doesn't think we made a mistake? But a U.S. senator doesn't have the luxury of dwelling in the past or making decisions emotionally or based on what some want. Senator Akaka has misstated my views. I don't support a permanent occupation of Iraq, and I don't support an indefinite, status quo commitment. The question is not whether to disengage, but how and under what circumstances.

"The outcome in Iraq does matter, not just for Iraq but for the entire Middle East, and, yes, for our country. We and most Iraqis want a country that Iraqis can govern and secure. They are close to having a fighting chance of doing so, and we must get them there, and then disengage. We cannot simply pull out immediately, unilaterally, unconditionally, and on a firm timetable. That would guarantee chaos in Iraq and the entire region, and would come back to haunt us."

He went on to condemn gridlock politics in Washington and said I was part of the problem, not the solution.

"I've disagreed with our president in many areas from environment to energy, budgets, tax cuts and civil rights," he said. "But I refuse to live in Senator Akaka's party-first, party-always world. That's not going to get things done."

Kato said, "Senator Akaka, your opening remarks."

"Congressman Case, my fellow Americans, aloha," I said. "It is my pleasure to be here and to have this opportunity to speak to all of you today. What I like about appearing before an AARP audience is that my age is not necessarily a bone of contention. It's not something that is out of the ordinary or an excuse for not being able to participate in or contribute fully to society. Nor do I have to apologize for the more deliberate speed of my words, because it's not seen as a handicap, but rather a sign of thoughtfulness and care. Nor is the color of my hair a handicap."

By then it was fully gray, if not white.

"To the contrary. The fact that I have hair at all is a plus."

That drew a few chuckles.

I talked a little about my approach to the job, and Ed's frequent demand for more debates, which I knew he wanted because he felt he would come across more robustly.

"I'm a school teacher by profession, and communication has always been about listening and dialogue, and not about confrontation," I said. "I could not have been a very effective teacher if my primary method of communication was confrontational. Neither could I be an effective legislator today.

"The reason why I had been able to sponsor major legislation—and get people to support it, even people across the aisle—was that what takes place on the floor comes after the real work of deliberation, communication and compromise had occurred.

"That's why I believe the real strength of a legislator is in the ability to build relationships that matter. Showing respect to others. And even when their opinion may not be the same as his own, to work with and communicate with his peers. Many of my peers have spoken on my behalf, and I'm humbled and thank them for their support.

"This is not a boast," I went on. "This is about saying, 'This is my record,' and these are the people whom I work with, who will vouch for my effectiveness and my strength.

"But more than that, I would like to see this campaign move from discussing the need to talk about the issues to actually talking about the issues. And I, for one, don't need Congressman Case standing opposite me to talk about my record and my position on the issues. My opposition to the war in Iraq, my call for a timetable and a strategy for peace, my opposition to the Bush administration's dismissal of privacy and civil liberties. My opposition to tax cuts for the wealthy. And the need for a strong alternative voice in Washington to counter this administration's determination to undermine Social Security, Medicaid and Medicare benefits, and environmental protection laws, even while grandstanding on some of these issues."

Kato asked Case, "Given that the debate is sponsored by AARP, an organization of Americans fifty and older, I think it's appropriate to begin by asking about age. Do you feel age is an important criterion for judging effectiveness in the U.S. Senate?

"Not in and of itself," Case said. "This campaign and my candidacy have never been about age. They have always been about transition. It's a difficult issue for us to talk about in Hawai'i, but we do have two U.S. senators who are nearing the end of their careers. We want and need to provide that transition as we go forward. We want and need to bring in the next junior senator now, so that senator can build up seniority, experience, relationships, before the career of Senator Inouye ends."

I responded that longevity is an advantage in Congress.

"When I think of those who are up in age in the U.S. Senate, those men are considered to be the deans of the Senate. Other senators go to them for advice, and they are the ones that keep the Senate stable. Age makes a difference."

The rest of the debate touched on Bush's push to privatize Social Security; the high cost of health care; Medicare and Medicaid; the Akaka Bill, which we both supported; the Iraq War; military recruiting shortfalls; the Patriot Act; long-term care for the elderly and the shortage of nursing home beds; the Jones Act; Hawai'i's high inflation rate and gas prices; the Bush tax cuts; and prescription drug prices.

In his closing remarks, Case said, "Do you think our political culture is serving you well, or do you think it's broken? A culture that told me I should have asked permission before I decided to run... A culture of special interests too often making backroom deals and not looking out for Hawai'i's and our overall country's welfare, just their own. A culture that perceived any innovation, any advance, any progress and even any disagreement as a threat to their power. Senator Akaka is a product of that culture and is beholden to it."

I opted for a softer tone.

"In the U.S. Senate and in Hawai'i, you persuade by the wisdom of your words and not by the force of your voice. And in the end, it's your action that speaks louder than words. In Hawai'i, aloha means more than just a greeting. It dramatically affects your sensibilities and how you conduct your life. It defines how you treat others no matter how they treat you. In many ways, elections have always been about who we want to represent us. We need legislators who have character and believe in strong values, an integrity to support those values, no matter how unpopular, or how uphill the battle."

In the end, once again, we shook hands and hugged.

✳ ✳ ✳

Saturday, September 23, Election Day, dawned mostly cloudy but warm, with light northeast trades. I was up early, excited and optimistic, and after a modest breakfast Millie and I went down to vote at Central Middle School. We then waved some signs along Vineyard Boulevard.

As the polls closed, we joined about 200 supporters at the Dole Cannery Ballroom. They included Andy Winer, my campaign chairman, and George Yokoyama, my Hawai'i island mainstay, who had switched his allegiance from Case when the congressman challenged me.

"How are you, George?"

"Fine, my old friend," he said.

Before the first results, which typically include absentee and other mail-in ballots, I heard Case, on TV at his campaign headquarters on Cooke Street, call me "a good and decent and honorable man that I have loved and respected for thirty years." It was a noticeable change in tone from the debate, but a welcome one.

Cheers erupted in the room when the first printout showed me comfortably ahead. Case was doing well on O'ahu, leading 53,400 to 48,200, but I had large margins on the Neighbor Islands, especially Maui.

The crowd, waving tiny American flags, started chanting.

"Six more years! Six more years!"

With the second printout, which tallied 185,000 votes, I was leading by more than 15,000 statewide.

About ten minutes before midnight, Case admitted defeat.

"Realistically, there is no chance that this gap will narrow sufficiently for us to win, so now's the time for us to concede the race," he said. "I have to tell you that this loss is my responsibility. The decisions were mine to run and the responsibility and the result is mine. He won. I lost. That's democracy and we need to get on with it." ✤

CHAPTER

78

The island of Hawai'i encompasses the tallest mountain on the planet. Measured from the seafloor, Maunakea rises 33,000 feet, taller than Mount Everest at just over 29,000. The mass of the island actually depresses the seafloor. That generates stress—pent-up energy that must be released sooner or later. Usually, this is done in small ways, creaks and groans here and there.

On the morning of October 15, an otherwise quiet Sunday, a magnitude 6.7 earthquake rocked the island, followed by a second, magnitude 6.1 quake. The epicenter of the first was along the coast of South Kohala, about thirteen miles northwest of Kailua-Kona, while the second was centered just off Kawaihae Harbor. The shaking was felt as far away as O'ahu. Over the next four hours, twenty-eight aftershocks ranging in magnitude from 2.5 to 4.4 shook the Big Island and the seafloor to the northwest.

The north and west sides of the Big Island took the brunt of the blows, although East Maui also saw some serious damage. The south side of the Mauna Kea Beach Hotel collapsed and ultimately the hotel had to close for two years for repairs. Water pipes broke and flooded part of the Hapuna Beach Prince Hotel. The stone walls of Kalahikiola Congregational Church in Kohala collapsed, as did the iconic plantation smoke stack in Hāwī. Hulihe'e Palace in Kailua-Kona also suffered extensive damage.

Kawaihae Harbor, the hub of economic development and sustenance in South Kohala, would need to be rebuilt completely. Healthcare facilities also took a hit, including Kona Hospital, Honokaa Long Term Care Center, Hamakua Health Center and Kohala Hospital. A number of observatories on Maunakea, including the Keck I and II, suffered damage. The list of compromised structures went on. The final damage tally topped $200 million.

Power went out across the state, mostly on Oʻahu. Half of Hawaiian Electric Co.'s 290,000 customers remained without electricity some twelve hours after the quake.

Miraculously, there were no serious injuries.

The day after, Inouye and I toured the island by helicopter and on foot with the Hawaiʻi National Guard and state civil defense. We could not immediately know the extent of the damage, but it was obvious that federal assistance was needed. We saw cracked roads, fallen bridges and sunken terrain. One section of roadway near Hilo had just fallen away, leaving a gap like a first grader's missing tooth.

"This is bad, Danny," Inouye said.

"We're going to need help," I said.

Governor Lingle immediately declared a state of emergency, and I urged Bush by letter to do the same. He did so within days. But recovery would take years.

In Hawaiʻi, Election Day, November 7, produced few surprises. Lingle won, defeating her Democratic challenger, former state Senator Randy Iwase. Abercrombie beat a little known Republican opponent, 66–29. In the race to replace Case, Hirono, who had edged out Hanabusa in the primary by 844 votes, beat former sportscaster and state senator Bob Hogue. My leading Republican challenger had been Jerry Coffee, a retired Navy captain and a jet pilot and prisoner of war in Vietnam. But Coffee had a heart attack in the summer and dropped out. His name remained on the ballot in the primary, which he won with thirty-one percent of the vote. With Coffee out, the state Republican Executive Committee tapped longtime windward lawmaker Cynthia Thielen, seventy-three, to run against me in November. She attracted a respectable 126,000 votes, especially considering her late entry. On Maui, Charmaine Tavares, daughter of former mayor Hannibal Tavares, cruised past Alan Arakawa.

The welcome surprise came in the national elections. Largely due to disillusionment with Bush over the war and the weak response to Katrina and Rita, the Democrats won control of both the House and Senate. It was the first time we had both since 1994. Our advantage in the House now stood at 233 seats to 202, which led to the election of the first female Speaker of the House, Nancy Pelosi of California. In the Senate, the results remained unclear for a couple of days because of close races. Finally, in Virginia, Republican George Allen conceded to Jim Webb, former secretary of the Navy. And in Montana, Conrad Burns lost to Jon Tester, a farmer and former music teacher. That put us at a 49–49 tie, but two independents, Joe Lieberman and Bernie Sanders, pledged to caucus with the Democrats. So we had the power. Harry Reid of Nevada became majority leader. Byrd once again became Senate president pro tempore, replacing Ted Stevens. Mitch McConnell of Kentucky led the minority.

One piece of favorable fallout from the election, which Bush called "a thumpin'," was the resignation of Rumsfeld as defense chief. Rumsfeld had been increasingly under fire for the progress in Iraq—or lack thereof. Bush said he would name Robert Gates, former CIA director, to replace him.

On November 14, Reid announced the new committee assignments. I now had the chairmanship of the Committee on Veterans' Affairs, with jurisdiction over the $70.8 billion budget for veterans' benefits and services, including a $30 billion health-care budget. I was determined to work hard to help our next generation of veterans—returning from Iraq and Afghanistan—get the care and services they deserved. I also had seniority and therefore growing influence on my other committees: armed services, banking, energy and natural resources, homeland security and governmental affairs and indian affairs.

I was sad to learn of the passing, in late November, of one of my dearest friends, Masaru "Pundy" Yokouchi, at eighty-one. He had been involved in Governor Burns' campaigns on the Neighbor Islands in the 1960s. In 1966, Burns appointed him as founding chairman of the state Foundation on Culture and the Arts, where he served for twelve years. In 1994, he founded the Maui Arts and Cultural Center and also served as its chairman. This was a big loss for Hawai'i. Pundy made so many contributions in the areas of the arts, the economy and politics. He was a generous and humble man who was always looking out for others. Millie and I would miss him tremendously.

※ ※ ※

With Cheney and Pelosi seated above and behind him, Bush delivered his State of the Union address on January 23.

He noted a growing economy.

"We are now in the forty-first month of uninterrupted job growth—in a recovery that has created 7.2 million new jobs...so far. Unemployment is low, inflation is low and wages are rising. This economy is on the move—and our job is to keep it that way, not with more government but with more enterprise."

He called for a balanced budget without tax increases, a limit on earmarks in spending bills and better management of Medicare, Medicaid and Social Security. He proposed doubling the budget of the Border Patrol, and establishing a legal path for foreign workers to enter the country on a temporary basis.

"That will leave border agents free to chase down drug smugglers, and criminals, and terrorists. We will enforce our immigration laws at the worksite, and give employers the tools to verify the legal status of their workers—so there is no excuse left for violating the law. We need to uphold the great tradition of the melting pot that welcomes and assimilates new arrivals. And we need to resolve the status of the illegal immigrants who are already in our country—without animosity and without amnesty."

Nicely written.

He called for more diversified energy sources, including wind and solar, research into high-tech batteries and hybrid vehicles and the production of ethanol through agricultural waste. That drew applause.

"We made a lot of progress, thanks to good policies here in Washington and the strong response of the market. And now even more dramatic advances are within reach. Tonight, I ask Congress to join me in pursuing a great goal. Let us build on the work we've done and reduce gasoline usage in the United States by twenty percent in the next ten years."

More applause.

Eventually, he turned to terrorism and the Middle East.

"In Iraq, al-Qaeda and other Sunni extremists blew up one of the most sacred places in Shia Islam—the Golden Mosque of Samarra. This atrocity, directed at a Muslim house of prayer, was designed to provoke retaliation from Iraqi Shia—and it succeeded. Radical Shia elements, some of whom receive support from Iran, formed death squads. The result was a tragic escalation of sectarian rage and reprisal that continues to this day.

"This is not the fight we entered in Iraq, but it is the fight we are in. Every one of us wishes that this war was over and won. Yet it would not be like us to leave our promises unkept, our friends abandoned and our own security at risk. Ladies and gentlemen, on this day, at this hour, it is still within our power to shape the outcome of this battle. So let us find our resolve, and turn events toward victory. We are carrying out a new strategy in Iraq—a plan that demands more from Iraq's elected government, and gives our forces in Iraq the reinforcements they need to complete their mission. Our goal is a democratic Iraq that upholds the rule of law, respects the rights of its people, provides them security and is an ally in the war on terror.

"In order to make progress toward this goal, the Iraqi government must stop the sectarian violence in its capital. But the Iraqis are not yet ready to do this on their own. So we are deploying reinforcements of more than 20,000 additional soldiers and marines to Iraq."

I was vehemently against an increase in troop strength in Iraq. His plan called for a "surge" and additional funding without measurable goals and without an exit strategy to complete our mission. This is a war that we should never have gotten into and I opposed putting more American lives in jeopardy. Already, more than 3,000 Americans had died, including five just last month from Task Force Lightning, part of the 3rd Brigade at Schofield Barracks. We owed it to both our honored dead and wounded to ensure that their sacrifices were not in vain, that we stabilize the Iraqi government and that we withdraw our troops as soon as possible.

But I heartily supported Bush's proposals on alternate energy. And his call for a twenty percent reduction in fuel consumption was right out of the Democrats' playbook. If only it could happen.

The field of biotechnology holds such promise. I firmly believe that one day it will be possible to take a drop of blood or snip of skin and grow it into a kidney, heart, liver or pancreas, perhaps assembled by

3-D printer. The resulting organ will have the same DNA as the donor, rendering tissue rejection obsolete. This field today, still in its infancy, relies on stem cells—cells that have not yet committed themselves to a specific purpose. To support this important discipline, I cosponsored, along with forty other senators, a bill introduced by Harry Reid, the Stem Cell Research Enhancement Act of 2007. The measure required the secretary of health and human services to conduct and support research using embryonic stem cells—those from unborn babies. Now, we put tight restrictions on this. The stem cells could come only from embryos that had been donated by in vitro fertilization clinics because they were extra. Typically, a clinic will create several embryos in the lab, but once they implant one in a woman's womb, if the pregnancy takes, they don't need the others. Usually, they are destroyed, which is a tremendous waste. This bill would allow them to be used in research. The donors would have to agree and could receive no compensation or other inducements.

The bill had bipartisan support. The Republican cosponsors included Arlen Specter, Ted Stevens, Orrin Hatch, Gordon Smith, Olympia Snowe and Susan Collins, and we had the two independents, Lieberman and Sanders, on board as well.

On April 11, it passed the Senate by a vote of 63–34. The ayes included fifteen Republicans; only two Democrats, Bob Casey of Pennsylvania and Ben Nelson of Nebraska, voted no.

In the House, the measure went to the Rules Committee, then to the full House, which, on June 7, after some procedural wrangling, passed it 247–176.

On June 20, Bush vetoed it. In his accompanying message, he said he supported stem cell research, per se, but not studies that involved the destruction of embryos, which he apparently equated to abortion. Never mind that the embryos would be destroyed anyway.

"We cannot lose the opportunity to conduct research that would give hope to those suffering from terrible diseases and help move our nation beyond the controversies over embryo destruction," he said. "I invite policymakers and scientists to come together to solve medical problems without compromising either the high aims of science or the sanctity of human life."

We knew we didn't have the votes to override, so there the matter ended. ✣

CHAPTER

79

In communications technology, 2007 was an astonishing year, one that Thomas L. Friedman, writing in the *New York Times*, said left people feeling like they were "dancing in a hurricane." Apple released the iPhone, heralding an era in which nearly everyone would have the internet—and social media—at their fingertips. Twitter, launched the year before, gained crazy popularity in 2007. Facebook, which had been limited to the student crowd, now was open to anyone with email. Amazon introduced Kindle ebooks, and Google unveiled Android. And Intel moved beyond silicon in its quest for ever greater microchip memories.

All this would greatly alter the fabric of our society, and not all for the good. Many people ultimately would insulate themselves inside social media "echo chambers" where opinion held the same weight as truth, and a web of "false news" was permitted to thrive unchecked. It was almost enough to make you miss typewriters and the *Encyclopedia Britannica*.

In the Senate, once again, we tried to raise the minimum wage. Reid's bill, the Fair Minimum Wage Act of 2007, would raise it to $5.85 almost immediately and then to $6.55 a year later. I was among forty-three cosponsors—forty-two Democrats and Sanders. Even so, the measure was dead on arrival. Bad for business, the critics said.

We did manage to pass, 88–0, a resolution honoring former president Ford, who had died the day after Christmas. The resolution said Ford's "basic human decency, his integrity, and his ability to work cooperatively with leaders of all political parties and ideologies earned him the respect and admiration of Americans throughout the country."

The 2007 military spending bill already recommended that the Navy's next nuclear-powered aircraft carrier be named after Ford.

Soon after Ford's death, Bob Woodward of the *Washington Post* published an interview he had had with the former president in July 2004. Ford said he didn't want it in print until after his death. In the interview at his house in Beaver Creek, Colorado, Ford said he disagreed with the invasion of Iraq. He found fault not only with Bush but with Cheney, who had been Ford's chief of staff, and with Rumsfeld, who had been his chief of staff and defense secretary.

"I can understand the theory of wanting to free people," Ford told Woodward. "I just don't think we should go (hell bent for leather) around the globe freeing people unless it is directly related to our own national security."

I couldn't agree more. The nation could use more like Ford.

In the 110th Congress, I introduced or cosponsored several bill to help veterans. These included Jim Webb's Post-9/11 Veterans Educational Assistance Act, which expanded benefits under the G.I. Bill; Inouye's Filipino Veterans Equity Act, which would make Filipino veterans of World War II eligible for U.S. benefits; and an amendment, which I introduced on January 24, that would make Persian Gulf War veterans eligible for health care for five years after discharge rather than two. I also introduced the Disabled Veterans Insurance Act, which doubled the benefit, from $20,000 to $40,000, that veterans could get if they were totally disabled. But the only measure with traction was the Veterans' Compensation Cost-of-Living Adjustment Act, which increased the pay for veterans with service-connected disabilities or for their survivors. This bill cleared my Veterans' Affairs Committee on July 24, but was eventually folded in to a House bill introduced by freshman Democrat John Hall of New York. This passed the House, 418–0, with Abercrombie and Hirono voting aye, on March 21. The bill came over to the Senate Veterans' Affairs Committee and we moved it on October 18 to the full Senate, which approved it the same day. Bush signed it on November 5.

Hall, fifty-eight, was widely known in pop music circles. A guitarist and songwriter, he had worked with Janis Joplin, Seals and Crofts and Taj Mahal before starting his own band, Orleans, in 1972. Their hits included "Still the One," "Dance With Me" and "Love Takes Time." Later, in the 1980s, his John Hall Band didn't do as well. Along the way, he got involved in environmental activism in his home state of New York. He rejoined Orleans in 1985, working with his bandmates from time to time until 2006, when he won a seat in Congress from a traditionally Republican district outside Albany. In October 2004, Hall publicly complained that the Bush team had not asked for permission to use "Still the One" at campaign rallies. Bush dropped the tune. Four years later, McCain also adopted the song, and Hall had to repeat his objections.

I'm not one for pop music, but when it came to veterans' affairs, Hall and I sang in the same key.

On April 14, Hawai'i suffered a true loss with the death of legendary performer Don Ho, quite easily the most famous Hawaiian in the world. He was only seventy-six. Services for him three weeks later drew thousands of residents and tourists to Waikīkī. The private service, largely organized by Cha Thompson, was held on the beach at the Royal Hawaiian Hotel. Don had been an Air Force pilot in the 1950s, so he merited a military honor guard, a twenty-one-gun salute and a flyover by a Hawai'i Air National Guard F/A-18 Hornet fighter jet. The islands' entertainment community turned out to pay tribute, performing on two stages. By the end, I don't believe there was a dry eye in the audience.

The nation endured yet another paroxysm of violence on April 16, 2007, when a student at Virginia Tech, in Blacksburg, west of Roanoke, killed thirty-two people with Glock and Walther P-22 handguns. It was the deadliest shooting rampage in U.S. history. The gunman, Cho Seung-hui, twenty-three, a South Korean native majoring in English, opened fire at two locations on campus, first a dormitory, where he killed two people, then a classroom building where he went door to door. In between, he mailed a video to NBC News, which they got days later. Before he took his own life, Cho killed twenty-seven students, five faculty members and wounded another eighteen.

The news reached Washington very swiftly, and on Capitol Hill the sense of horror was universal and profound. Senator John Warner of Virginia sponsored a resolution offering our "heartfelt condolences to the victims and their families, and to students, faculty, administration and staff and their families who have been deeply affected by the tragic events that occurred today at Virginia Tech." The measure went on to express hope that the deaths would lead to a "shared commitment" to take steps to help communities prevent such tragedies from occurring in the future." It went on to recognize Virginia Tech as "an exemplary institution of teaching, learning and research." The resolution attracted ninety-nine cosponsors—that is, the entire Senate—and passed unanimously the same day.

A year later, Governor Tim Kaine announced that a large majority of the families of the slain and wounded had agreed to an $11 million settlement offering from the state. A judge approved the deal in June 2008 for families of twenty-four of those killed and the eighteen injured. But that wasn't the end of it. In 1990, Congress had passed the Clery Act, which required colleges to keep crime statistics and a public log of all crimes committed on campus. It also required campus officials to issue "timely warnings" when there is a threat to the safety of students or employees. In December 2010, the U.S. Department of Education released a report saying that Virginia Tech failed to warn students in a timely manner after the first two shootings at the dorm. And in March 2012 a jury agreed, awarding $4 million each to the families of two of the later victims. That sum later was cut to $100,000. The timely warning issue notwithstanding, this sad incident made me wish that more states had strict gun acquisition laws like Hawai'i's. In Hawai'i, if you have a history of mental illness, as did Cho, or a history of substance abuse, you can't get a permit to buy a firearm.

✻ ✻ ✻

I want to mention in passing the controversy over the admissions policy at my alma mater, Kamehameha Schools. In May 2007, the school paid a reported $7 million to settle a lawsuit by an anonymous student who contended that the Hawaiians-first policy violated his civil rights. The settlement ended a four-year attempt by the student, a non-Hawaiian known as John Doe, to matriculate to Kamehameha. The suit had similarities to *Rice v. Cayetano*, filed in 1996 by a Big Isle rancher, Harold "Freddy" Rice, against the state, claiming it was discriminatory to allow only Hawaiians to vote for the trustees of the Office of Hawaiian Affairs. In fact, attorney John Goemans at various junctures had represented both Rice and John Doe. That case went all the way to the Supreme Court, which in February 2000 ruled that the state could not restrict the voting to Hawaiians only.

U.S. district judge Alan Kay had dismissed the John Doe lawsuit in November 2003. He ruled that the policy helped address cultural and socio-economic disadvantages that Hawaiians have suffered since the overthrow of the monarchy. The plaintiffs appealed to the Ninth U.S. Circuit, and a three-judge panel overturned Kay's ruling, 2–1, in August 2005. That was an unpopular decision in Hawai'i, leading to protests and prayer vigils across the state.

I issued this statement: "I am proud to recognize my alma mater, Kamehameha Schools. In its halls and classrooms we learned to think critically and excel in all the ordinary disciplines that a school ought to provide. Our studies were also informed by the values of our ancestors and imbued with a sense of duty toward this land of ours and all of its people. Today's decision by the U.S. Court of Appeals for the Ninth Circuit fills me with a great sadness because there are those among us who will misinterpret the words of the court as a rejection of my alma mater, and the values it stands for."

As in *Rice v. Cayetano*, the court had remained silent on the political and legal relationship between Native Hawaiians and our federal government. The obvious answer was passage of my Native Hawaiian Government Reorganization Act, in 2005 known formally as Senate Bill 147.

But Kamehameha then appealed to the entire Ninth Circuit, and the full court in December 2006 overturned the three-judge panel's decision by an 8–7 vote. I responded: "Today's decision by the U.S. Court of Appeals for the Ninth Circuit sends a clear message reaffirming the values of Kamehameha Schools. While it was my alma mater's admission policy that was in question, there is no doubt that today's ruling recognizes the special circumstances of Native Hawaiians. As we progress into the 110th Congress, I remain committed to working with the Hawai'i congressional delegation to enact legislation that will formalize the existing legal and political relationship Native Hawaiians have with our federal government."

Eric Grant, an attorney for John Doe, then petitioned the U.S. Supreme Court to hear the case. But in May 2007, before the justices could decide whether they would hear the appeal, Kamehameha settled out of court.

"Obviously, a settlement is not exactly what either side wanted," Grant remarked at the time. "But it is something that both sides eventually came to terms on."

On the strength of the Ninth Circuit vote, Kamehameha was allowed to keep its preference for Hawaiians in admissions, which I felt was fair and just.

Of the news coming out of Iraq, some of the most disturbing was the gouging by contractors. Several private companies were making a mint out of the war. One of their key critics was Senator Byron Dorgan of North Dakota, who had my full support. To address that ongoing problem, the Senate Armed Services Committee held a hearing on April 19. When my turn came, I was recognized by the chairman, Carl Levin of Michigan.

"I continue to be very concerned about the contracting abuses and war profiteering in Iraq, and so, I thank you, Mr. Chairman, for calling this very important hearing today. No question, we feel that the resources in our country are not unlimited. And it is our duty to the taxpayers that our servicemen and women have all that they need, and to make sure that the tax dollars to be used for defense of our nation are not wasted. And that's where I am."

I put my question regarding the Iraq logistics contract, or LOGCAP, to Claude Bolton, assistant secretary of the Army for acquisition.

"Secretary, why is it that four years into the war in Iraq, we still haven't been able to provide adequate staffing to oversee this contract? Do you believe that the shortage of the contract oversight personnel is specific to this contract, or is it symptomatic of a broader shortage in the Department of Defense?"

"Senator Akaka, thank you very much for the question," Bolton said. "It's good seeing you again, sir. You know, I'll go back several years, when I was confirmed here, in front of Senator Levin and Senator Warner at the time. I made a statement during that particular confirmation hearing. I had a grave concern on the declining nature of the acquisition work force. I stated then, and it's come to pass, that within my tenure, a large number of professional acquisition types would retire. The demographics were against us, and they're still against us. What remains of my work force over the next three years, half of the civilian work force—that's roughly 45,000—are eligible to retire.

"Not a whole lot of folks are coming in behind them. The workload continues to increase. Rough numbers: When the Berlin Wall went down in 1989, the Army had about 140,000 people in this area. Today we have 45,000."

Pulling auditors out of the United States and sending them to Iraq is a limited option, he said, especially in "a very difficult environment, austere, hostile—without the infrastructure of having a computer system, a business system, a banking system... It's a hostile environment. Every person I send over there is a target, and unfortunately, I've had people hurt, and several killed."

I said, "But what are we doing to try to correct these problems? I'm saying this because this is my same concern with Katrina efforts. For twenty hearings, we discovered that many of the problems were because there were positions that were unfilled, and so they could not carry out what needed to be done. And if that's the case also here, then we need to make changes immediately to correct that."

Also appearing before the committee were Patrick Fitzgerald, auditor general for the Army, and Major General Jerome Johnson, commander of the U.S. Army Sustainment Command. I asked them why these problems were cropping up in Iraq and not in Afghanistan.

"The reason you hear more of that in Iraq than you do in Afghanistan is frankly the nature of the battlefield and the nature of the fight," said Johnson. "Iraq is an open country. It's a war that started off very much in maneuver warfare. And so, in many cases, the contracting kind of goes back to the de facto problem that we identified early on. A commander might say, 'Did I have objective A? It's in the western part of the country, and this brigade's heading there. I need food services, I need a base camp, I need laundry services, and I need food and fuel brought there as I execute the mission.'

"Well, in a maneuver operation, you may start out at objective A. You may get instructions in the middle of the process to move to objective B, C or D. And that happened in Iraq."

I guess I now knew the ABCs—and D—of maneuver operations, but still thought the system had failed. ✣

CHAPTER

80

On July 17–18, 2007, in a rare, all-night Senate session, we debated an amendment to the Defense Authorization Bill that would transition the mission in Iraq and bring U.S. troops home by April 30, 2008. Majority leader Harry Reid called the overnight session to highlight a GOP filibuster preventing the Senate from voting on the so-called Levin-Reed amendment, introduced by the armed services chairman Carl Levin and Senator Jack Reed of Rhode Island. I stood to speak at 12:45 a.m.

"Mr. President, I rise to express my deep concern about the administration's ongoing policy in Iraq. As a member of the Senate Armed Services Committee and chairman of the Subcommittee on Readiness, I have had the privilege to hear the testimony of our troop commanders, our soldiers and their families and now, more than ever, I insist we bring an end to this conflict. Already, too many lives have been lost, too many men and women have been wounded and permanently injured, and too many spouses, parents and children have suffered the pain of separation and, too often, permanent loss of a loved one. Yet, according to the new National Intelligence Estimate, al-Qaeda is growing stronger and we are no closer to achieving a sustainable security in Iraq. We must make it clear to the Iraqi political leaders: the future of Iraq is in their hands, and they must learn to reach the political compromises necessary for a functioning democracy.

"Once again, we are at a crossroads. We can either continue to pursue a policy that is no longer working or we can move forward and implement a strategy that will set us on a new course. The time is now to reevaluate the costs of this war. We must understand that the long-term responsibility for caring for those injured during their service—and for the families of those who died—is truly a cost of war. Over 3,600 members of the Armed Forces have given their lives in the service of this nation. Thousands more will come home with injuries, both physical and psychological, that will require treatment and rehabilitation, processes that can take many years. Invisible wounds that are difficult to detect—such as PTSD and mild to moderate traumatic brain injury—will affect a great many service members, making it difficult for them to adjust to civilian life, as they deal with long-lasting visions and experiences they encountered in combat. While we can help the brave troops by passing critical legislation that will provide much-needed counseling, these invisible wounds will take a long time to heal. Clearly, the total cost of the current conflicts includes both the loss of lives, and resources needed to help a new generation of young men and women combat veterans heal.

"The American people also believe that now is the time to begin the process of bringing our troops home. According to a recent poll, sixty-three percent of Americans believe that we should no longer continue in the present course of action set by the administration. They believe, as I believe, that the president's surge has not been a success."

In the end, the Republicans succeeded in blocking the vote. The bright young senator from Illinois, Barack Obama, issued this statement:

"It is a sad day for America when the United States Senate once again fails to vote to bring this war to a responsible end. The Levin-Reed amendment offers a responsible course to bring our troops out of Iraq, with a hard date to begin our drawdown and a hard date to complete it. I will continue to press my colleagues to turn the page on a war that should never have been fought. I will continue to insist that George Bush be denied the blank check he needs to continue this war. We also need to turn the page on a politics that puts divisive distractions ahead of the interests of the American people. It's time to leave behind the political posturing so that we can come together as Americans to end this war."

When Bush announced the "surge," he had set out eighteen benchmarks to measure its success. He said if the Iraqi government did not meet the benchmarks, it would lose the support of the American people. But the Iraqis were not meeting the benchmarks.

In early September, at a hearing of the Armed Services Committee, I had a chance to question Army General David Petraeus, the ground commander, and Ryan Crocker, U.S. ambassador to Baghdad, about why Iraq was not being held to greater responsibility.

"Why are we not holding the Iraqi government accountable for this?" I asked.

Crocker said, "These are, in many cases, very complex legislative initiatives that are difficult to do, particularly in conditions of significant violence. The reality has been that in many cases, it has been simply too hard to do as a straight-up national-level initiative."

Petraeus said the Iraqis have done better in meeting security-related benchmarks. But I told them I wasn't convinced that enough progress had been made to merit further sacrifices by our soldiers—or more spending.

"I remain committed to finding a new direction," I told them.

On September 15, a Saturday, the Capitol bore witness to a huge anti-war demonstration. Several thousand protesters marched from the White House to the Capitol, shouting slogans and carrying signs that called for an end to the war and the impeachment of Bush. The chief sponsors were Veterans for Peace and a group called the ANSWER Coalition, which stood for Act Now to Stop War & End Racism.

The Senate was in session, and many of us decided to lend support by greeting the demonstrators on the steps of the Capitol. These steps, largely ceremonial, led down to the West Front Lawn, with the Washington Monument in the distance. My staff recommended against this. For one thing, there was no railing. My press secretary, Jesse Broder Van Dyke, I think, was worried that I would slip and fall in front of the news cameras, a visual that would surely be broadcast around the world. But I had made up my mind.

I went up to Jesse, who was on the staff bench.

"All the senators are going out to this vigil," I said. "I'm going."

The senators all headed for one door, and the logistics were such that Jesse had to leave through another door and run around the building to meet me.

He did, and I grabbed his arm for support. We headed down the stairs toward the huge crowd, chanting and milling about, some arguing with pro-war activists. Blocking them from the Capitol steps were barricades and a phalanx of Capitol Police.

As we neared the bottom of the stairs, some protesters broke through the barricades and suddenly we were surrounded. Senator Barbara Boxer, who was right in front of us, turned and gave Jesse, who is quite tall, a silent plea for help. So Jesse got in front of us and acted as a wedge to get us out of the crush and up front where the cameras were waiting. It was quite a scene. The anti-war speakers included former presidential candidate Ralph Nader, former attorney general Ramsey Clark and activist Cindy Sheehan. A spokeswoman for the Capitol Police later said 189 protesters were arrested for crossing a police line.

Later in the month, on September 25, I opened a Veterans' Affairs Committee oversight hearing on Gulf War Illnesses research and treatment. The hearing was held at the request of fellow committee members Patty Murray of Washington and Bernie Sanders to focus on recent advances in research on Gulf War Illnesses. The witnesses included scientists and medical doctors. I laid out my concerns in my opening statement.

"As chairman, I must once again question whether DoD is protecting the health of troops, and whether they are adequately monitoring American service members' health before, during and after deployments," I said. "This is a legitimate focus for our committee; today's troops are tomorrow's veterans. As service members return from deployments abroad, many will separate from the military and become the newest generation of veterans. We need to ensure that VA has the capability to give these veterans the care they require. We have this recent study on brain damage, and evidence that suggests there may be an elevated rate of ALS (Lou Gehrig's disease) among Gulf War veterans. Further, the National Academy of Sciences has found that service in the Gulf places veterans at increased risk for anxiety disorders, depression and substance abuse problems. Unfortunately, as we have heard time and again, the reasons for these illnesses may never be known because important records were not kept or were lost. In addition, DoD did not track the location of individual troops, making it difficult to identify patterns among those who have fallen ill. In short, DoD was not prepared to monitor and protect the health of troops during the Gulf War."

An Army-funded study, published in January in the *American Journal of Psychiatry*, found that nearly twenty percent of combat veterans returning from Iraq suffered from post-traumatic stress disorder. One of them was Justin Bailey, a native of Las Vegas. Bailey had joined the Marines in 1998 at age seventeen. Even at that young age, he had a history of marijuana and alcohol abuse, and he and his family hoped that the corps would help straighten him out. By all accounts, he served honorably. But with the Iraq War looming his tour was extended and he was sent to Nasiriya, south of Baghdad. When he came home in April 2004, his parents sensed a difference. He never really detailed his experience, which is common for those with PTSD. It's also fairly common for PTSD sufferers have an increased risk of substance abuse.

"Mom, I shot women and children," his mother recalled him confessing. "I can't deal with this."

He had trouble keeping a job and couldn't pay his rent. He became addicted to prescription painkillers and street drugs. Finally, in November 2006, he checked himself in to the Los Angeles VA Medical Center. But he didn't get the help he needed. On January 26, he was found dead of an overdose in his room at the rehab center. He was one of five patients who died at that facility over a three-month period. Their deaths sparked outrage across the country and raised new questions about the ability of veterans' affairs facilities to deal with the warriors returning from Iraq. Already, Walter Reed Army Medical Center was under the gun for poor treatment and general squalor.

With Justin in mind, I introduced the Veterans' Mental Health and Other Care Improvements Act of 2008. The bill directed the secretary of Veterans Affairs to ensure the provision of the certain services and treatment to each veteran enrolled in the VA healthcare system. They included screening for substance use disorder in all settings, including primary care; short-term motivational counseling;

marital and family counseling; intensive outpatient or residential care; relapse prevention; ongoing aftercare and outpatient counseling; opiate substitution therapy; pharmacological treatments to reduce cravings for drugs and alcohol; detox; and coordination with groups providing peer-to-peer counseling. It also called for dedicated research and pilot programs for treatment, as well as help for family members of PTSD patients. And it increased from $130 million to $150 million the annual authorization of appropriations for VA service programs for homeless veterans.

I quickly attracted three cosponsors, Mikulski and Republicans Richard Burr of North Carolina and John Ensign of Nevada. ❖

CHAPTER

81

The Veterans Affairs Department was badly in need of an overhaul. Parts of it simply were broken. Despite my best legislative efforts, the department never had enough money or enough people in key positions. Active duty personnel leaving the service had a bumpy transition to the VA. Bush's second pick for the job of secretary, Jim Nicholson, a retired Army colonel, had resigned in October 2007. His deputy, Gordon Mansfield, was filling in.

After a couple of months, Bush nominated Dr. James Peake for the job. Peake, former Army surgeon general and a retired three-star general, had an excellent résumé and the backing of Inouye. He was a West Point graduate and Vietnam veteran. On December 5, I held a hearing on his nomination before the Veterans' Affairs Committee. I warned him that he faced a tremendous challenge.

"Heading VA is never easy," I said. "Indeed, it may be one of the most daunting tasks in or out of government. Doing so in a time of war is dramatically more difficult, and taking over, as you will—assuming your confirmation—when there is only a little more than a year left in the current administration, only compounds a demanding situation."

One area that needed immediate attention was the process by which an injured service member moves from DoD to VA, I said.

"A great deal of work had been done on that front, especially over this year, and much is being done now," I said. "I am hopeful that if you are confirmed, your long experience in the Army will enable you to continue to improve on those efforts. Returning service members, especially those who are seriously injured, must not be made to struggle as they work with both DoD and VA. We must strive for, and we must achieve, a truly seamless transition."

I also wanted to press him, as a longtime Army doctor, on the problems at Walter Reed Hospital, which I had toured on March 2 along with Levin, Mikulski, Lieberman and Reed. We found the accommodations appalling and the bureaucracy impenetrable.

As surgeon general, Peake had moved swiftly to address similar problems at Fort Stewart, Georgia, and Fort Knox, Tennessee: poor living conditions; an overwhelmed chain of command; poor case management; and difficulties with a complicated, out-of-date disability process.

"In connection with the initial problems of Fort Stewart, you immediately mobilized a team to respond to these concerns; mandated a case manager to stay with each soldier through the handoff to VA; and worked with the Army leadership to garner and reallocate resources to solve the problem. In your view, why did this fairly comprehensive action plan not translate then or later to Walter Reed?"

"You know, Senator, I asked myself what I could have done differently as part of that," he said. "I mean, when I saw that soldiers were living again in unsatisfactory conditions, that there was a sense of—or at least a perception of—a lack of caring of those who had transitioned to outpatient care, I was concerned as well. And when I look back at the Fort Stewart issues, our quick response did, in fact, do some of the things that would have helped if we had carried those forward with Walter Reed."

He noted that he had been retired for three years. "So I don't have direct knowledge of what was going on at Walter Reed—but I can tell you that when I was the surgeon general, we had not seen that large number of returning wounded from Iraq and Afghanistan at that point."

We were impressed with Peake and the committee approved him unanimously on December 13.

That same day, Kennedy and I introduced legislation to strengthen the employment and reemployment rights of returning servicemen and women. Recent hearings by the Veterans' Affairs Committee and Kennedy's Health Committee had shown that tens of thousands of returning troops had lost their jobs and benefits, and there was widespread dissatisfaction with the agencies that were supposed to help them.

"The administration's failure to help returning service members who have lost their jobs and benefits is a disgrace," Kennedy said in a statement to the media. "It is an insult to their courageous service to our country."

Our bill, the Kennedy-Akaka Uniformed Services Employment and Reemployment Rights Act, imposed deadlines on federal agencies to assist service members. It also codified the recommendations of the Government Accountability Office to increase efficiency at these agencies.

In early February, I introduced a new bill to keep veterans' compensation apace with inflation. It also expanded the benefits for families of veterans. I quickly picked up eleven cosponsors, including Obama and Bernie Sanders. Richard Burr of North Carolina, who had succeeded Edwards in the Senate, also was on board. So we passed this out of the Veterans' Affairs Committee in July and the full Senate approved it almost immediately. The House vote was 418–0, and Bush signed it September 24.

Several other of my pro-veterans measures fell by the wayside, but that's Congress. If I could not help veterans and their families in every way I could think of, it would not be for lack of trying.

In the spring of 2008, I became aware of a particularly disturbing trend: the high rate of suicides and suicide attempts among military personnel returning from the Middle East. In April, CBS News reported that the top mental health official at veterans affairs, Dr. Ira Katz, had withheld crucial information on the true suicide risk among veterans. Part of the disclosure came as evidence in a lawsuit that had gone to trial in San Francisco. An email from Katz to other VA officials began with "Shh!" and estimated 1,000 veterans a month attempt suicide while under department treatment. "Is this something we should (carefully) address ourselves in some sort of release before someone stumbles on it?" the email asks.

Patty Murray and I immediately called for Katz's resignation.

"Dr. Katz's irresponsible actions have been a disservice to our veterans, and it is time for him to go," said Murray. "The number one priority of the VA should be caring for our veterans, not covering up the truth."

I echoed her sentiments in a letter April 22 to Dr. Michael Kussman, VA undersecretary of health.

"Dr. Katz's personal conduct and professional judgment have been called into question by his response to the mental health needs of veterans, and in particular to veteran suicides," my letter said. "I believe veterans, and the Department of Veterans Affairs, would be best served by his immediate resignation. America's veterans deserve mental health care of the highest quality. Many veterans returning from combat have complex mental health needs, and VA must be fully able to meet those needs. VA cannot be complacent in its efforts to prevent veteran suicide. I look forward to working with you to provide veterans with the best services possible."

Murray, Tom Harkin of Iowa and Russ Feingold of Wisconsin promptly introduced legislation calling on the VA to track how many veterans commit suicide each year. Currently, VA facilities record the number of suicides and attempted suicides in VA facilities—but do not record how many veterans overall take their own lives. The new bill required the VA to report to Congress within 180 days the number of veterans who have died by suicide since January 1, 1997, and continue reports annually.

Harkin and CBS had numbers from the VA that showed that 790 veterans under VA care attempted suicide in 2007. That was a far cry from what Katz revealed in his email. In another email, to Kussman, Katz said that there are "about eighteen suicides per day among America's 25 million veterans." This was a figure that the VA had never made public.

On May 6, I met with the VA director, Dr. Peake, about ways to improve mental health care for veterans and the need for stronger outreach.

"Whether one person stays or goes, VA's entire mental health-care system needs to improve," I told him. "Without accurate information on veteran suicide, Congress cannot fulfill its oversight responsibilities."

I also thanked Peake for his decision to boost funding for the National Center for Post-Traumatic Stress Disorder. The National Center for PTSD consists of seven VA centers of excellence across the Mainland U.S. and Hawai'i, with a headquarters in White River Junction, Vermont. The center has taken on a larger mission in recent years, due in part to the ongoing wars and the increasing number of veterans suffering from PTSD.

In this climate, the bill I had introduced in the fall, the Veterans' Mental Health and Other Care Improvements Act of 2008, was making steady progress. I eventually attracted twelve cosponsors, including Hillary Clinton and Republicans Elizabeth Dole, Susan Collins and Ted Stevens. I passed it out of my Veterans' Affairs Committee in April 2008.

In testimony May 15 before the VA Committee, Peake said new studies had shown that male and female veterans were more likely than their nonveteran peers to commit suicide; male veterans commit suicide at a higher rate than female veterans, reflecting the general population as well; male veterans were more likely to commit suicide at a younger age than their general-population counterparts; and women veterans show a nearly twofold increase over the rate of suicide for women in the general population.

In a follow-up letter to Peake, I said, "We will not know the true cost of war until we know the true rate of suicides among veterans. Until the VA mental health-care system meets the needs of those who have served, we will continue to see the tragic consequence of veteran suicides."

The full Senate passed the bill unanimously in early June, and the House passed it by voice vote on September 24 after only forty minutes of debate. After a one-day conference, it went to the White House on September 30 and Bush signed it ten days later. ✤

CHAPTER

82

By the fall of 2007, the presidential campaign already had taken shape. Former senator John Edwards of North Carolina, Kerry's running mate in 2004, was the first to announce his candidacy, in late 2006. But early polling showed that my Senate colleagues Hillary Clinton and Barack Obama enjoyed the most popularity. Clinton announced on January 20, 2007; Obama on February 10. Few people gave Obama much of a chance in those early months because he had been in the Senate so short a time—just over two years. Before long, the Democrats had enough contenders to field a baseball team. They included Senators Joe Biden, Christopher Dodd and Evan Bayh, Congressman Kucinich of Ohio and Governor Bill Richardson of New Mexico. In the Clinton administration, Richardson had served as U.N. ambassador and secretary of energy. I knew him, of course, from his fourteen years in the House, where he was quite active in Indian affairs.

Most people thought the nomination was Clinton's to lose and, of course, she did. In the Iowa caucuses, she placed third, behind Obama and Edwards.

Obama's win felt big.

"They said this day would never come," he said in his victory speech, with reverberations back to the days of the Reverend Martin Luther King.

But Clinton bounced back and won the New Hampshire primary on January 8, outpacing Obama 39–37. Edwards came in a distant third and suspended his campaign on January 30, after losing his birth state, South Carolina. By the end of January, Biden, Dodd, Bayh, Richardson and Kucinich had all dropped out, leaving Clinton and Obama to slug it out.

❋ ❋ ❋

From his headquarters at Camp Smith, high above Pearl Harbor, Admiral John McCain Jr. faced a harsh choice as he assumed command of U.S. Pacific forces on July 4, 1968. His son, Lieutenant Commander John McCain III, had been shot down over North Vietnam the previous fall and was being held captive in Hanoi. Now the admiral's job included calling the shots in the Vietnam War. Neither officer was aware of the other's precise circumstances on that Independence Day in one of the century's most tumultuous political years.

Young McCain, badly injured and incommunicado at a prison camp, knew nothing of his father's promotion. Nor did he know the war had become contentious at home, leading in part to President Johnson's decision against a second full term.

He knew nothing of the assassinations of Martin Luther King or Robert Kennedy. There were no Voice of America broadcasts into the Hoa Lo ("Fiery Forge") Prison, which the inmates called the Hanoi Hilton, lodgings McCain shared with future senator Jeremiah Denton and Hawai'i Republicans Orson Swindle and Jerry Coffee.

If anything helped sustain McCain during this terrible time, it must have been thoughts of family. Both McCains had Navy blue in their blood.

The CINCPAC's father, Admiral John "Slew" McCain, was a legendary aircraft carrier strike force commander in the Pacific during World War II. His command of land-based aircraft around Vanuatu won mention in Michener's *Tales of the South Pacific*. Slew's otherwise stellar career went askew in December 1944, when, as commander of a task force of surface ships in the Philippine Sea, he proceeded into the face of an approaching cyclone, Typhoon Cobra. Three destroyers sank, and 800 lives and 146 aircraft were lost. Fires broke out aboard the carrier *Monterey* when its aircraft slid into each other during violent rolls and exploded. Among those fighting the flames was Lieutenant Gerald Ford, our future president. The storm was dramatized to great effect in Herman Wouk's 1951 novel, *The Caine Mutiny*, which won a Pulitzer Prize, and subsequent film starring Humphrey Bogart.

A Navy court of inquiry pinned the blame on McCain's boss, Admiral William "Bull" Halsey, commander of the 3rd Fleet, who was scolded but not fired. No commander, McCain included, takes such casualties lightly and he lost a great deal of weight under stress. He was among the brass who in 1945 witnessed the surrender of the Japanese aboard the battleship USS *Missouri*, today a floating museum at Pearl Harbor. Four days after the ceremony, McCain Sr. died in San Diego.

The senator's father, hard-drinking, cigar-chomping "Jack" McCain Jr., commanded the submarine *Gunnel* in the Pacific during World War II and went on to become the first son of a Navy four-star admiral to achieve that same rank. The Pacific Fleet destroyer USS *John McCain* is named for both admirals.

In his 1999 memoir, *Faith of My Fathers*, McCain recalls that a tradition of service weighed on him from an early age. His father, for instance, was an enthusiastic member of the Society of the Cincinnati, descendants of George Washington's officers.

"His evident pride in claiming such distinguished ancestry gave me the sense not only that I had a claim on my country's history, but that it would fall to me to represent the family when the history of my generation was recorded," he wrote.

As part of Navy life, McCain's parents moved from base to base every few years and landed at Pearl Harbor in the 1930s. "Every Saturday night," he wrote, "my father and mother, dressed in formal attire, attended a party at the Pearl Harbor Submarine Club, after spending their afternoon at the Royal Hawaiian Hotel's four o'clock tea dance."

There was never a doubt that he would attend Annapolis and, although admittedly a poor student, he graduated in 1958 and went on to become an aviator like his granddad. McCain was flying an A-4 Skyhawk off the carrier USS *Oriskany* on October 26, 1967, when a missile blew off his right wing. As he ejected, he broke his right knee, left arm and right arm in three places. Fractures notwithstanding, McCain was beaten and tortured for information, then inexplicably offered his freedom in 1968.

"Although I did not know it at the time, my father would shortly assume command of the war effort as commander in chief, Pacific," McCain wrote. "The Vietnamese intended to hail his arrival with a propaganda spectacle as they released his son in a gesture of 'goodwill.' I was to be enticed into accepting special treatment in the hope that it would shame the new enemy commander."

Even with the promise of medical care if he cooperated, McCain refused to go home ahead of those who had been in captivity longer. That was one of the codes.

And although he suspects he received less brutal beatings than some other POWs because of his father's position, McCain still endured atrocious treatment.

For years afterward, the sound of "jangling keys" at odd moments made him sit bolt upright at the feared approach of guards.

After McCain's release from the notorious Hanoi Hilton in March 1973, he talked to his father, then retired, about the war. The elder McCain insisted that it could have been won absent civilian interference.

"My father wasn't much of a believer in fighting wars by half measures," McCain recalled. "He regarded self-restraint as an admirable human quality, but when fighting wars he believed in taking all necessary measures to bring the conflict to a swift and successful conclusion. The Vietnam War was fought neither swiftly nor successfully, and I know this frustrated him greatly."

The elder McCain believed the United States had missed an opportunity to win the war in the aftermath of the Tet Offensive of 1968; and he chafed at the civilian reins that kept him from taking the fight into North Vietnam.

Finally, the Nixon administration relented.

"Late in the war, my father would give the order that sent B-52s to rain destruction upon the city where I was held prisoner," McCain wrote. "That was his duty, and he did not shrink from it."

The apple never falls far from the tree. Flash forward forty years and you had a senator named McCain strongly urging a surge. On that I couldn't agree. And he was consistently opposed to appropriations to keep the brown tree snake out of Hawai'i and such cultural programs as the *Hōkūle'a*, two efforts dear to my heart that he considered pork. However, I had profound respect for McCain for his devotion to duty under very difficult circumstances.

By the spring of 2008, McCain had pulled ahead of a large field of GOP presidential contenders, including former Massachusetts governor Mitt Romney, former Arkansas governor Mike Huckabee, former senator Fred Thompson of Tennessee, former New York mayor Rudy Giuliani and Congressman Ron Paul of Texas.

* * *

The second week of August, after Obama clinched the nomination but before the convention, he and his family came back to Hawai'i for a short vacation. Naturally, they were very well received. He jogged on the beach at Kailua, not far from his vacation rental, which was, of course, surrounded by Secret Service agents. He played golf with friends at Olomana. He, Michelle, daughters Malia and Sasha and sister Maya Soetoro-Ng brought a gift basket to Obama's grandmother, Madelyn Dunham. They snacked on shave ice at Island Snow in Kailua. They ate dinner at Alan Wong's Restaurant. The Obamas would repeat this pattern every Christmas during his eight-year presidency.

Even Governor Lingle, a Republican, had to acknowledge the fervor surrounding Obama's visit. But she made it clear her political support rested firmly with McCain. She said the excitement was "understandable," but added, "This is not *American Idol*. This is not voting for your favorite or your most popular. This is making an important decision on who should lead our nation."

On August 10, soon after he arrived in the isles, Obama came under criticism from Cokie Roberts of ABC-TV and National Public Radio. On ABC's *This Week*, a Sunday morning political talk show, Roberts said that Obama's vacation "has the look of him going off to some sort of foreign, exotic place." She repeated her complaint on NPR's *Morning Edition*, the next day, saying that Obama's presence in Hawai'i "makes him seem a little bit more exotic than perhaps he would want to come across as at this stage in the presidential campaign." The suggestion was that, with all the problems the nation was facing, it was inappropriate for Obama to go off to a tropical paradise that most Americans could not relate to.

I took exception to that characterization of Hawai'i, and said so.

"Saying our fiftieth state is somehow foreign does a great disservice to the hardworking, patriotic Americans who call Hawai'i home," I said in a statement. "For months people have been asking me, 'When is Senator Obama going to come home?' I'm so glad he found time to visit his sister and his grandmother, show his daughters more of his home state and relax a little."

I added, "Hawai'i is a great U.S. destination. Just ask the 5.5 million Americans who visited last year for business and pleasure."

* * *

On August 30, McCain made the surprise announcement that he had selected a relative unknown, Governor Sarah Palin of Alaska, as his running mate. Only two years earlier, Palin, forty-four, had been mayor of a small town.

"She's exactly what the country needs to help me fight the same old Washington politics of 'Me first and country second,'" McCain said at a rally in Dayton, Ohio. "She's got the grit, integrity, good sense and fierce devotion to the common good that is exactly what we need in Washington today."

By then, Obama had defeated Clinton for the nomination and tapped Biden as his running mate. So the stage was set for a historic presidential matchup. Either we would get our first black president or our first female vice president. ❖

CHAPTER

83

By 2008, the economy had already started to stagger. This had its roots in the subprime mortgage industry, but there was plenty of blame to go around. Investment banks like Goldman Sachs, Morgan Stanley, Merrill Lynch and Lehman Brothers began to rival federally insured commercial banks in their financial clout, but without the same level of regulation and scrutiny. Predatory lenders targeted people who really couldn't afford loans and didn't grasp the terms. The whole house of cards started to crumble when the inflated housing market collapsed in 2006, leaving securities backed by "bundled" subprime notes nearly worthless. Playing poker with investors' money might have worked out better. In December 2007, the Bush administration reached an agreement with the industry to freeze interest rates for certain subprime mortgages for five years to prevent more foreclosures. Still, a lot of hardworking Americans lost their savings—and their homes—in what became known as the Great Recession. When Lehman Brothers filed for bankruptcy on September 15, 2008, the hurricane flags went up. By then Congress was weighing a $700 billion bailout of the U.S. financial system. Some investment houses, the thinking went, were "too big to fail," a phrase that dated back to the S&L crisis. A rising tide lifts all ships, but the opposite is true. If some of these titans turned turtle, the economic ebb would be enormous.

The bottom line: Some people are focused exclusively on maximizing their wealth during their lifetime regardless of what it does to peace, stability, the environment, subcontractors or the taxpayers. And in fact, often they profit from instability. This makes me cherish all the more the Hawaiian principle of aloha.

Congressman Patrick Kennedy of Rhode Island introduced the bailout bill, the Emergency Economic Stabilization Act, in March 2007, with more than half the House, including Abercrombie and Hirono, as cosponsors. It passed the House a full year later, on March 5, 2008, by a vote of 268–148. Over the summer, it stalled in the Senate.

So great was the concern in America—and indeed the world—about the recession that the topic kicked off the first debate between Obama and McCain, even though the subject was supposed to be national security and foreign policy. This took place September 26 at the University of Mississippi, "Old Miss," in Oxford. The moderator was Jim Lehrer of PBS *NewsHour*.

"Let me begin with something General Eisenhower said in his 1952 presidential campaign," said Lehrer. "Quote, 'We must achieve both security and solvency. In fact, the foundation of military strength is economic strength,' end quote. With that in mind, the first lead question. Gentlemen, at this very moment tonight, where do you stand on the financial recovery plan?"

Obama went first.

"You know, we are at a defining moment in our history," he said. "Our nation is involved in two wars, and we are going through the worst financial crisis since the Great Depression. And although we've heard a lot about Wall Street, those of you on Main Street, I think, have been struggling for a while, and you recognize that this could have an impact on all sectors of the economy. And you're wondering, how's it going to affect me? How's it going to affect my job? How's it going to affect my house? How's it going to affect my retirement savings or my ability to send my children to college? So we have to move swiftly, and we have to move wisely."

He called the crisis "a final verdict on eight years of failed economic policies promoted by George Bush, supported by Senator McCain, a theory that basically says that we can shred regulations and consumer protections and give more and more to the most, and somehow prosperity will trickle down. It hasn't worked. And I think that the fundamentals of the economy have to be measured by whether or not the middle class is getting a fair shake."

Then McCain had his two minutes.

"We are seeing, for the first time in a long time, Republicans and Democrats together, sitting down, trying to work out a solution to this fiscal crisis that we're in," McCain said. "And have no doubt about the magnitude of this crisis. And we're not talking about failure of institutions on Wall Street. We're talking about failures on Main Street, and people who will lose their jobs, and their credits, and their homes, if we don't fix the greatest fiscal crisis, probably in—certainly in our time, and I've been around a little while."

* * *

On October 1, the Senate approved the bailout bill by a vote of 74–25 with amendments. Inouye and I voted yes, of course, as did thirty-seven other Democrats, thirty-four Republicans and Lieberman. Voting no were fifteen Republicans, nine Democrats and Bernie Sanders. Then it went back the House, where the bill with changes was approved again, 263–171, on October 3. Bush signed it the same day.

* * *

The economic crisis dominated the second debate on October 7, at Belmont University in Nashville, Tennessee, with NBC's Tom Brokaw moderating. But the third took a unique turn.

In the first two debates, three times each, McCain had blamed the financial crisis on "greed and excess" on Wall Street and Washington. In the third debate, on October 15, he mentioned greed only once, maybe because he had new fodder: Joe the Plumber.

Two days earlier, on Sunday, Obama made a campaign stop in rural Ohio. He was approached by a man in the crowd, Joe Wurzelbacher, who said he wanted to buy a small plumbing business. Obama had said he would raise taxes on people making $250,000 and up, and Wurzelbacher said the plumbing business would put him over the threshold.

"Your plan's going to tax me more," he said.

"It's not that I want to punish your success, I just want to make sure that everybody who is behind you, that they've got a chance at success, too," Obama told him. "My attitude is that if the economy's good for folks from the bottom up, it's going be good for everybody. If you've got a plumbing business, you're going to be better off if you've got a whole bunch of customers who can afford to hire you, and right now everybody's so pinched that business is bad for everybody, and I think when you spread the wealth around, it's good for everybody."

McCain and others leaped on that "spread the wealth" remark as showing that Obama was a socialist at heart.

The third debate, at Hofstra University in Hempstead, New York, was moderated by Bob Schieffer, chief Washington correspondent for CBS News and host of *Face the Nation*. After an initial question on the strength of their economic plans, the candidates were given five minutes to engage each other.

"All right," Schieffer said to McCain, "Would you like to ask him a question?"

"No," said McCain, "I would like to mention that a couple days ago Senator Obama was out in Ohio and he had an encounter with a guy who's a plumber, his name is Joe Wurzelbacher." He summarized the exchange and then looked directly at the camera.

"Joe, I want to tell you, I'll not only help you buy that business that you worked your whole life for and be able—and I'll keep your taxes low and I'll provide available and affordable health care for you and your employees. And I will not have—I will not stand for a tax increase on small business income."

Obama maintained that his plan would provide tax cuts to ninety-five percent of working Americans—three times the relief that McCain's plan called for. Then he mentioned Joe himself.

"Now, the conversation I had with Joe the Plumber, what I essentially said to him was, 'Five years ago, when you weren't in a position to buy your business, you needed a tax cut then.' And what I want to do is to make sure that the plumber, the nurse, the firefighter, the teacher, the young entrepreneur who doesn't yet have money, I want to give them a tax break now. And that requires us to make some important choices. The last point I'll make about small businesses. Not only do ninety-eight percent of small businesses make less than $250,000, but I also want to give them additional tax breaks, because they are the drivers of the economy. They produce the most jobs."

Altogether during the debate, Joe the Plumber's name came up twenty-six times, twenty-two times off the tongue of McCain. By comparison, Joe Biden, Obama's running mate, came up six times. It was extraordinary—and probably unprecedented—for a private citizen, unknown to the country just days earlier, to become an offstage character in a presidential drama, with the cast addressing him directly and by name. By the end of the campaign, Joe the Plumber had become a walking, unwitting symbol of our national dilemma.

* * *

Voters went to the polls on November 4. Turnout hit a record at 131 million nationally, compared to 122 million four years earlier. Obama beat McCain by about 9.5 million votes, 53–46. Obama also picked up states worth 365 electoral votes—ninety-five more than he needed. These included Florida, North Carolina, Virginia, Ohio, Colorado and Nevada, which Bush had taken in 2000 and 2004, and Iowa and New Mexico, which Bush had won over Kerry in 2004.

Riding Obama's coattails, down-ballot Democrats did well, picking up, at first blush, seven seats in the Senate. The race in Minnesota, where comedian Al Franken ran against Norm Coleman, was too close to call. The GOP incumbents who lost were Ted Stevens of Alaska, a longtime ally of Inouye's; Elizabeth Dole; John Sununu of New Hampshire; and Gordon Smith of Oregon. We also won open seats in Colorado, New Mexico and Virginia.

In the House, the Republicans ousted five incumbents, but lost twenty-six of their own. Basically, they reverted to where they were before the Gingrich Revolution of 1994.

In Hawaiʻi, Abercrombie and Hirono easily won reelection. And we had two new mayors: Billy Kenoi on the Big Island, and Bernard Carvalho, who beat former mayor JoAnn Yukimura on Kauaʻi. On Oʻahu, Hannemann beat city councilmember Ann Kobayashi.

But the real excitement of the night was Obama, our first Hawaiʻi-born president.

Almost everyone in Hawaiʻi, I suspect, watched his acceptance speech on TV. The rally at Grant Park in Chicago packed three punches of emotional power: the massive nighttime crowd, estimated at 240,000, the close-in videos of faces weeping with joy, and Obama's simple, well-considered, crafted words.

"Hello, Chicago," he said to roaring applause.

"If there is anyone out there who still doubts that America is a place where all things are possible, who still wonders if the dream of our founders is alive in our time, who still questions the power of our democracy, tonight is your answer," he said. "It's the answer told by lines that stretched around schools and churches in numbers this nation has never seen, by people who waited three hours and four hours, many for the first time in their lives, because they believed that this time must be different, that their voices could be that difference." ✤

CHAPTER

84

At the weekly Senate Prayer Breakfast, the speakers typically talk about a personal challenge, or something interesting about their family. We weren't allowed to share these discussions outside the breakfast venue. But I can offer an example of the type of thing we talked about. Over the years, we had a number of congressmen who had triplets: Dana Rohrabacker of California in April 2004, Vic Snyder of Arkansas in December 2008 and Pat Tiberi of Ohio in 2009. Snyder's wife, Betsy, an ordained Methodist minister, was diagnosed with congestive heart failure less than a week after she delivered the trio. "I was home for five days, and just feeling bad, and having trouble breathing," she told *The Hill*. She finally went back to the hospital, where she was diagnosed with cardiomyopathy. "I was in heart failure for five days before we even knew what it was... I was chosen to be a heart disease survivor, and that's something I live with every day." Her faith helped her overcome those daunting days.

In one of his last acts in office, Bush used his executive authority to designate the World War II Valor in the Pacific National Monument. At Pearl Harbor, that included the *Arizona*, *Utah* and *Oklahoma* memorials, bungalows on Ford Island and three mooring quays at Battleship Row. But it also included sites in Alaska and California, including the Tule Lake detention camp near the Oregon border. Inouye and I quickly praised this proclamation.

"We applaud the president for his decision to tie the history of World War II in the Pacific into a cohesive story through the national monument designation," we wrote on December 5. "It is crucial that future generations learn and remember the heroic actions of those who struggled on behalf of freedom and democracy. It is also necessary to tell the difficult stories, such as the internment of some 120,000 Japanese Americans, in order to learn from our nations' past mistakes. The president's declaration introduces a new way of thinking about national monuments as noncontiguous pieces of a larger narrative and we look forward to working with the Department of Interior on its implementation."

But Bush also made a less laudable move, issuing on November 26 an executive order revoking the collective bargaining rights of thousands of federal employees. Some of these employees had been represented by unions for decades, including those with the Bureau of Alcohol, Tobacco, Firearms and Explosives. But Bush cited national security concerns as justification for his action.

Kennedy, who had recovered from his earlier bout but was still battling cancer, joined me and three other senators—Lieberman, Leahy and Mikulski—in condemning the action.

"We reject the view that union membership undermines a worker's ability to effectively perform his or her job functions, particularly in regard to national security issues," we wrote. "Unionized employees serve with great distinction in a range of national and homeland security positions. Although federal law permits the president to exclude certain national security employees from collective bargaining when such rights are inconsistent with national security requirements, he should apply this exclusion narrowly and infrequently. This executive order fails that test."

From the president-elect, we got some great news on Sunday, December 7, the sixty-seventh anniversary of the Pearl Harbor attack. He named Shinseki to head VA.

"No one will ever doubt that this former Army chief of staff has the courage to stand up for our troops and our veterans," Obama said at a news conference in Chicago. "No one will ever question whether he will fight hard enough to make sure they have the support they need."

Obama, noting that Shinseki served two tours in Vietnam and lost part of his foot, said he "understands the changing needs of our troops and their families." And he predicted that he would be a veterans administration secretary "who finally modernizes our VA to meet the challenges of our time."

Later, on *Meet the Press*, Obama said Shinseki was "exactly the right person" for the job. The host, Tom Brokaw, said Shinseki lost his job as Army chief of staff because "he said that we would need more troops in Iraq than the secretary of defense, Don Rumsfeld, thought that we would need at that time."

"He was right," Obama said.

On December 9, I scheduled Ric's confirmation hearing before the Veterans' Affairs Committee for January 14.

"I am proud to support General Shinseki's nomination and I look forward to a long and productive relationship with him as secretary," I said in a statement.

The next day he stopped by my office. It was great to see my old friend again and I gave him my hearty congratulations. If confirmed, he would be the first Hawai'i-born person to lead a cabinet-level department.

I shared with him my goals for the VA: appropriate funding for the department as a cost of war; ensuring a seamless transition for troops from active duty to veteran status; restructuring VA for better delivery of services such as health care, benefits, education and housing; and increasing congressional oversight of VA programs and facilities. I also told him I want to see an increased emphasis on mental health care. VA needed more doctors trained to treat the invisible wounds such as post-traumatic stress. As a combat commander, he knew well what I was talking about.

As if to underscore how dysfunctional the department could be, I had recently been contacted by the widow of a veteran in Hawai'i. Under a 1996 law, when a veteran receiving benefits dies, the spouse is entitled to a payment for the month in which a veteran died. But her payment suddenly disappeared from her bank account, courtesy of the U.S. Treasury. Looking into this case, I found that the VA had failed to adjust its computer programs after the law went into effect. For almost twelve years, surviving spouses of veterans had been wrongfully denied benefits. When I told Peake about this problem, he vowed to fix it immediately.

In addition to Shinseki, Obama made some excellent cabinet picks, including Hillary Clinton as secretary of state. Robert Gates agreed to stay on at the Pentagon.

I knew Ken Salazar, Obama's nominee for secretary of the interior, from his years in the Senate, where he had replaced Ben Nighthorse Campbell of Colorado in 2005. Salazar and I differed on such issues as increasing fuel efficiency standards for cars and trucks. He also opposed an amendment to remove tax breaks for such major oil companies as ExxonMobil. He also voted to remove rules that limited offshore oil drilling along the environmentally sensitive Gulf Coast of Florida. But Obama's nominations for commerce and health and human services encountered the biggest resistance. For the latter, he first picked Tom Daschle, former Senate majority leader. But after it was revealed that he had picked up tidy sums from the health-care industry and lobbyists, Daschle withdrew. Obama then picked Kathleen Sebelius, the governor of Kansas, and she sailed through. For commerce, his first two nominations, Governor Bill Richardson of New Mexico and Senator Judd Gregg of New Hampshire, also were nonstarters. Obama then tapped former governor Gary Locke of Washington.

On January 14, the Veterans' Affairs Committee held a hearing on Shinseki's nomination. After my welcoming remarks, and those of Senator Burr, the committee's ranking Republican, Shinseki got two glowing introductions.

"Before we continue with opening statements of the committee, I would like to call on our two distinguished World War II veterans, my esteemed senior senator, Dan Inouye, and our former colleague, Senator Bob Dole, for their introduction of General Shinseki," I said. "I will leave it to the two of you to decide on the order of your introductions."

Inouye looked at Dole and said, "You are older."

That brought a laugh.

"Senator Dole?" I said.

Dole started off with a story.

"I am honored to be here, not only with you but with my former colleague, Senator Inouye," he said. "A little trivia. We were wounded a week apart, a mile apart or a hill apart in Italy near the close of the war.

We wound up in the same hospital, along with Colonel Hart, who the Hart Building is named after. So, here are three of us—we don't know whether it is politics or whatever—who found ourselves together in the U.S. Senate. They were both wonderful men; and the Hart Building is named after Phil Hart because he was the conscience of the Senate...

"Dan, as an aside, was the best bridge player at Percy Jones General Hospital. We had nothing else to do, so we stayed up all night, and I think he won the championship. I don't know how many entries there were, but he won the championship.

"I think one thing that ought to be noted here, we have General Shinseki succeeding General Peake and these guys have been longtime friends. It will be a seamless transition and they will be working together whenever they need each other. I don't know what General Peake has in mind, but I want to personally thank him for what he has done."

Inouye recalled that he and Oren Long, Hawai'i's first elected senator, had nominated Shinseki to West Point.

"Since that appointment and his acceptance, I have naturally followed his career," Inouye said. "In his initial tour of duty in Vietnam, he did well, but he suffered a grievous injury. Most Americans are not aware of this, but he has an amputated foot. Any other man would have justifiably resigned himself to civilian life and retired from the military. It would have been an honorable thing to do. However, General Shinseki pleaded to remain on active duty despite the hardship and physical pain. Well, this is just one measure of the man who appears before you today, an unflinching devotion to our country and to his duty."

He recalled Shinseki's estimate of the troop strength necessary to secure Iraq, an assessment immediately shot down by Rumsfeld.

"I think most of us expected the general to give the standard line that any administration would favor. But as we all know, he did not. He told the truth. It wasn't easy, and in so doing took a position contrary to his commander in chief. His honest assessment that more troops would be needed cost him his job, but it is the surest measure of his fitness to serve as a member of the cabinet. To speak the truth in the face of enormous pressure is not to take the easy way out. This is the kind of man I want to see as secretary of the Department of Veterans Affairs."

After the hearing, I also lent my support.

"General Shinseki is honest, distinguished and capable veteran who is well equipped to lead the Department of Veterans Affairs," I said in a statement. "He has a daunting task ahead of him, and I look forward to working with him and the incoming president to help veterans receive the care and services they have earned through their service. I urge my colleagues to support his confirmation as soon as he is formally nominated, so he can begin his work for America's veterans."

On January 20, Inauguration Day, the Senate confirmed Shinseki by voice vote.

In his address, Obama spelled out our troubles pretty well.

"That we are in the midst of crisis is now well understood," he said. "Our nation is at war, against a far-reaching network of violence and hatred. Our economy is badly weakened, a consequence of greed and irresponsibility on the part of some, but also our collective failure to make hard choices and prepare the nation for a new age. Homes have been lost; jobs shed; businesses shuttered. Our health care is too costly; our schools fail too many; and each day brings further evidence that the ways we use energy strengthen our adversaries and threaten our planet."

It was amazing to see a Hawai'i boy take the oath of office.

A couple of weeks later, in early February, Obama made another smart appointment at VA: Tammy Duckworth as assistant secretary. Tammy was born in Thailand to an American father, a Marine veteran, and a Thai woman, but the family moved to Honolulu when Tammy was sixteen. She graduated from McKinley High School in 1985 and then UH Mānoa. As a graduate student at George Washington University, she joined the ROTC program. She learned to fly UH-60 Black Hawk helicopters in the Army Reserve, and later transferred to the Illinois National Guard. She was working for Rotary International in Evanston and also on her doctorate in political science when she deployed to Iraq in 2004. On November 12, as a captain and copilot, her helicopter was hit by a rocket-propelled grenade and went down. She lost her right leg and her left leg below the knee, and her right arm was fractured in three places. She received her Purple Heart and a promotion to major while still recovering at Walter Reed.

In 2006, she ran for the congressional seat vacated by retiring Henry Hyde, but lost to Republican Pete Roskam. At that juncture, Governor Rod Blagojevich named her director of the Illinois Department of Veterans Affairs, a job in which she started programs to better address PTSD and traumatic brain injuries—two of my great concerns. So I saw this federal appointment as a fine choice. Tammy was a rising star and a source of inspiration for the latest generation of veterans. She easily won confirmation. ❖

CHAPTER

85

Manuel Braga was a staff sergeant with the Philippines Scouts, part of the U.S. Army, when World War II broke out in the Pacific. In fact, President Roosevelt had inducted all Philippines troops into the American forces on July 26, 1941, months before the Pearl Harbor attack. When the Japanese invaded on December 8, Braga and his fellow countrymen fought side by side with their U.S. brothers in arms, even after General MacArthur withdrew. Bataan fell, then Corregidor, but the troops fought on against a relentless and better-equipped enemy. Many were captured and sent to concentration camps, but many others fought on as guerrillas, surviving incredible hardships in the jungles and mountains and battling bugs, disease, snakes and starvation as well as the enemy. Braga was captured once and almost killed, but was rescued by his fellow Scouts.

Art Caleda was a guerrilla intelligence officer with the 11th Infantry Regiment, assigned in Northern Luzon. Like Braga, he also took his oath of allegiance under an American flag. He also survived the war with a shrapnel wound in his chin from a mission to rescue a downed American pilot.

In 1944, Congress passed the G.I. Bill, paving the way for Roosevelt to keep his promise to Filipinos of a just reward for their sacrifices. The measure entitled the Filipino soldiers, like all non-Americans who were serving in the U.S. Armed Forces, to full veterans' benefits, including naturalization as U.S. citizens. But two years later, Congress introduced a rider to the G.I. Bill, the Rescission Act of 1946, which unceremoniously took away from the Filipino veterans and members of the new Philippines Scouts, all benefits, rights and privileges under the G.I. Bill, declaring their wartime service as "not active service in the U.S. military." The Rescission Act specifically targeted Filipinos because all other aliens—Europeans and Asians from sixty-six nations—who served in the U.S. forces in the war were not affected.

Hawai'i's congressional delegation had long been active, passionately, in attempting to correct that injustice. It was a long struggle.

Among our early efforts was the Filipino Veterans Act of 1991, which Inouye introduced. I was his only cosponsor. The bill went nowhere. Inouye introduced the same bill in 1993 and 1995. By then we had three additional cosponsors: Boxer, Feinstein and Hollings. In 1997, the measure attracted fourteen cosponsors, including two Republicans, D'Amato and Gorton. In 1999, the Filipino Veterans' Benefits Improvements Act drew five cosponsors, including Boxer, Feinstein, Murray and Sarbanes. In 2001, that same bill got eleven cosponsors; in 2003, twenty-one. In 2005, Inouye changed the name to the Filipino Veterans Equity Act and Clinton and I were among the nine cosponsors. Two years later, fifteen senators signed on to cosponsor the Filipino Veterans Equity Act of 2007.

In April, on the fourth floor of the Russell Senate Office Building, I convened a hearing on the measure before the Veterans' Affairs Committee. Among the witnesses were Braga and Caleda, both in their eighties.

"Aloha," I said to open the hearing. "I am pleased to welcome all of the witnesses to this long-awaited hearing on the veteran status of Filipinos who fought alongside the United States military during World War II. I thank especially those of you who have traveled long distances to be with us here today. In the sixty-two years since the end of the Second World War, Filipino veterans have worked tirelessly to secure the veterans status they were promised when they agreed to fight under U.S. command in defense of their homeland and to protect U.S. interests in the region. Today, I am happy to say, many Filipino veterans enjoy eligibility to benefits and health-care services as U.S. veterans. However, as our distinguished witnesses here today will remind us, there is still work to be done in order to extend these eligibilities to all of those who served alongside the United States military during the World War II."

Braga, commander of the Filipino War Veterans of San Diego County, spoke with emotion.

"I plead with you on behalf of all my fellow Filipino WWII

veterans to enact this bill into law... All of us fought for America against a common enemy, and of all us should be entitled to the same benefits irrespective of our citizenship and/or place of residence. Most of us are now advanced in age, sick and frail and living in abject poverty, but we share one thing in common: We all willingly laid our lives on the line for this country in World War II."

But the measure never got a full vote in the Senate.

On May 7, 2007, I introduced the Senate Bill 1315, the Veterans' Benefits Enhancement Act, which contained a Filipino veterans equity measure. That provision faced considerable opposition from Republicans, notably Senator Richard Burr of North Carolina, who became the ranking member when Larry Craig was sidelined. In August, I passed the bill out of the Committee on Veterans' Affairs. But progress was slow. In April 2008, I picked up a single cosponsor, Ken Salazar of Colorado. But the Bush White House opposed the Filipino pension measure, which would give $300 a month to some 18,000 surviving members of the United States Armed Forces in the Far East and the Filipino Scouts.

Action came to a head in the third week of April. Burr tried to block the bill, but we brought it to the Senate floor with a 94–0 cloture vote on April 22. Not voting were Clinton, Obama, Mary Landrieu of Louisiana, and Republicans McCain, Domenici of New Mexico and David Vitter of Louisiana. The next day, Burr proposed an amendment to remove the pension provision. He and other Senate Republicans argued that the $166 million estimated cost would be better spent on U.S. troops returning from Iraq and Afghanistan. They argued out that the U.S. had invested heavily in the Philippines and that injured Filipino veterans got full benefits, including special burial rates and access to VA hospitals.

"I'm not sure anyone can say we didn't do our share," Burr said.

Burr also contended there had never been any U.S. promise to Filipino veterans.

"I can't find that promise," he said.

John Cornyn of Texas said, "The U.S. Treasury is not bottomless, and the funding that's being provided to create this new pension for these Filipino allies, which were, of course, fighting not only with us, but for themselves, for their freedom, for their country."

On April 24, Inouye and I rose to defend the bill.

"The junior senator from Hawai'i is recognized," said the acting Senate president pro tem, Sherrod Brown of Ohio.

"Mr. President, I see that my colleague is here, Senator Inouye of Hawai'i. Before I make my statement on S. 1315, I yield time to the senior senator from Hawai'i, Mr. Inouye."

"The senior senator from Hawai'i is recognized."

In the Philippines, Inouye said, "We had two tragic battles, Corregidor and Bataan. Before these battles were determined and ended, General MacArthur, the commander, was ordered to leave the Philippines, and he left with his staff and arrived in Australia. The Filipinos were left to do their part without proper armament, proper medicine and with inadequate food. But they fought."

He recalled the Bataan Death March, in which 75,000 American and Filipino prisoners of war were forced to march sixty-five miles without food or water. Only 54,000 survived. Of the 75,000, he said, 60,000 were Filipinos, many of them "bayoneted...slaughtered." That service alone merited the pension called for in the bill, he argued.

"Well, this veterans bill has a provision in it—a provision of honor—in which finally, after over sixty-five years, we will restore our honor and tell the Filipinos: It is late, but please forgive us."

Then it was my turn.

"As I have described in detail this week, further action on the bill has been blocked because of opposition from the other side of the aisle to certain benefits for Filipinos who fought under U.S. command during World War II," I said. "Mr. President, the people of the Philippines did not shy from the call to fight during World War II. They were true brothers in arms who fought valiantly under U.S. command in World War II. This bill, at long last, recognizes the valor of all Filipino veterans in sacrifice to this noble cause and loyalty to their American commanders."

Republican Ted Stevens of Alaska, who flew in the Army Air Corps in China-Burma-India during World War II, said the pension benefit for Filipino veterans of that conflict was long overdue.

"These people were the keys to the Pacific," he said. "Without them, we would have seen war for another few years. They gave us the time to survive."

He also called the measure "a matter of honor."

We shot Burr's amendment down by a vote of 56–41.

Later that day, we approved the bill by a vote of 96–1. The sole opponent was Vitter of Louisiana. Even Burr voted for it.

On September 22, 2008, after forty minutes of debate, the House approved the bill. But some eleventh-hour maneuvering in the House prevented it from getting it to Bush's desk before adjournment.

In late January 2009, Inouye and Congressman Dave Obey of Wisconsin introduced companion bills that would become known as the stimulus package. Formally the American Recovery and Reinvestment Act of 2009, this was intended to kick start the economy during the recession and keep jobs from vaporizing. Similar bills of the same name were introduced in the Senate by Harry Reid and Max Baucus, but all three were folded into Obey's bill. The measure ended up with more amendments than shells on a beach, but sped through Congress, where we all recognized the urgency of the matter. The House passed it on January 28 by a vote of 244–188, with Abercrombie and Hirono in the majority. The Senate received it the next day and proceeded with several days of amendment wrangling. Finally, on February 10, the Senate approved the bill, 61–37, with Inouye and I voting yes. The vote was almost precisely along party lines, with only two Republicans, Olympia Snowe and Arlen Specter, voting with the Democrats. No Democrats voted "nay."

Then it went back to the House. More wrangling and procedural votes. Then it came back to the Senate on February 13 and another vote, this time 60–38, with Republican Susan Collins of Maine joining the "ayes." But this time Kennedy, who was still battling brain cancer, did not make the vote. Obama signed it into law four days later in Denver, with Biden looking on.

This law, with a price tag of roughly $800 million, covered soup to nuts. Farms, rural development, defense, energy, water, small businesses, recovery programs after Hurricanes Katrina and Rita, information technology.

Under Title X, Military Construction and Veterans Affairs, was a section that seemed unrelated to the economy. This was Filipino Veterans Equity Compensation Fund. This authorized $198 million in payments to Filipino veterans who fought with U.S. forces during

World War II. U.S. citizens would get $15,000 and noncitizens $9,000 in a lump sum. It recognized such service as active U.S. military service. If they had died already—as many had—their surviving spouses got the money. So here was a measure of victory after many, many failed attempts. ✣

CHAPTER

86

The stimulus package also had money for the VA to help advance a number of projects that had been languishing for too long.

On February 12, I introduced a bill to further boost the VA health-care system, which had been chronically plagued by underfunding. This was folded into a bill in the House, introduced by Bob Filner of California. The Veterans Health Care Budget Reform and Transparency Act of 2009 was signed by Obama on October 22.

"With this legislation we're fundamentally reforming how we fund health care for our veterans," Obama said. "With advance appropriations, veterans' medical care will be funded a year in advance. For the VA, this means timely, sufficient and predictable funding from year to year. For VA hospitals and clinics, it means more time to budget, to recruit high-quality professionals, and to invest in new health-care equipment.

"And most of all, for our veterans it will mean better access to the doctors and nurses and the medical care that they need: specialized care for our wounded warriors with post-traumatic stress and traumatic brain injuries."

On March 7, 2009, NASA launched a seminal spacecraft, the Kepler Mission, designed to study a small, cross-shaped patch of sky near the right wing of Cygnus the Swan. In an orbit following the earth around the sun, the *Kepler* occupied an ideal perch to spot small variations in the brightness of stars with its ultrasensitive eyes. A slight dimming of a star indicated that a planet had passed in front of it, a so-called transit, mechanically much like a solar eclipse on Earth but on a vastly diminished scale. Modern telescopes have high-tech retinas that employ charge coupled devices, sensors that detect individual photons!

Over the next several years, *Kepler* would detect hundreds of extrasolar planets, or exoplanets, some of them around relatively nearby stars. The closest so far—although not a *Kepler* discovery—is Epsilon Eridani b, only 10.5 light-years away. But that planet is a Saturn-like gas giant—all atmosphere with no place to plant your feet. Amazingly, once these exoplanets are detected, astronomers using ground-based telescopes like the Keck Observatory on Maunakea are able to discern whether they are gas giants or rocky planets like Mercury, Venus, Earth and Mars. More intriguing still are those terrestrial exoplanets that are about the same size as Earth and have in an orbit in the Goldilocks Zone—neither too hot nor too cold—which makes the presence of liquid water a possibility.

Before year's end, astronomers would find the first exoplanet with a possible ocean, Gliese 1214 b, a so-called "Super Earth" because it is larger than Earth but smaller than a gas giant. Ultimately, astronomers would find that the closest star to our own, Promixa Centauri, only 4.3 light-years away, has a terrestrial planet, Proxima b, with a mass similar to Earth's. Its star, a red dwarf, is fainter than our own, but Proxima b is close in, so it occupies the habitable zone. Its tight orbit the day is only eleven hours long—which could mean that the radiation from the star is too intense for life as we know it. Eventually, I am confident, we are going to find Earth's twin. Andrew Howard, formerly at the University of Hawai'i Institute for Astronomy is a leader in this exciting field, which began in earnest with the launch of *Kepler*.

A less auspicious space development occurred on April 5, when North Korea tried to put a satellite into orbit. The launch failed, but North Korea under leader Kim Jong-il had shown great determination in improving not just its launch capabilities but in developing ICBMs and nuclear weapons. They conducted their second nuclear test on May 25. This won prompt condemnation by the United Nations Security Council, which is mostly bark and no bite. Unfortunately, Obama— adopting a policy of "strategic patience" toward the Pyongyang—would fare no better than Bush or Clinton in curbing this emerging threat.

※ ※ ※

Also in May 2009, for the sixth time, I introduced the Native Hawaiian Government Reorganization Act. Over the next year, I drew seven cosponsors: Inouye, Dodd, Durbin, Byron Dorgan of North Dakota, Roland Burris of Illinois and, from Alaska, Mark Begich and Lisa Murkowski, the only Republican. Dorgan was chairman of Indian affairs, so it had a shot there.

※ ※ ※

Ted Kennedy had been ailing for more than a year, since he suffered a seizure in May 2008. And his form of brain cancer, malignant glioma, ranked as one of the toughest to treat. Nevertheless, in August 2008, he wowed the crowd on the opening night of the Democratic National Convention in Denver. But during his treatments, he was absent from the Hill. In April 2009 he had stopped by the White House for a bill signing. I hadn't chatted with him in weeks.

On August 11, Ted's sister Eunice Shriver died on Cape Cod at age eighty-eight. Eunice was married to Sargent Shriver, the founding director of the Peace Corps and the creator of the Job Corps and Head Start programs. He was also McGovern's running mate in 1972 after Senator Tom Eagleton dropped out. Their five children included Maria Shriver, a respected journalist and First Lady of California. But Eunice had myriad accomplishments of her own. She founded what would become the Special Olympics. Reagan in 1984 had awarded her the Presidential Medal of Freedom, the nation's highest award for civilians, for her work for those with intellectual disabilities. Her funeral was held on August 14 at a Catholic church in Hyannis, Massachusetts. But Ted was too ill to go.

Then Ted himself died on August 25. He was seventy-seven.

Few people stayed in Washington for the month of August, a miserably muggy experience, so I was back home in Hawai'i when I got the news. In fact, as chairman of the Veterans' Affairs Committee, I had scheduled a series of field hearings in Hawai'i, including on the Neighbor Islands. We had the entire committee staff out there and some top VA officials. My press secretary, Jesse Broder Van Dyke, and I were sitting on an Island Air flight ready to go to either Moloka'i or Lāna'i when he got a call from my chief of staff, Joan Ohashi.

"Okay," she said, "they're doing the funeral Saturday in Boston."

To get there, we would have to catch a congressional delegation flight, called a "codel," in Washington at 5 a.m. Saturday. In order to make that flight, we would have to catch the red-eye to D.C. no later than Thursday. This was Wednesday. Then, after the funeral, we'd have to return to Washington and fly back to Honolulu on Sunday. And the Maui field hearing would have to be canceled. This was a painful decision for me.

"Tell her I'll think about it," I told Jesse.

I was silent during the entire flight, twenty-five minutes, staring at the seat in front of me.

When the plane touched down, I said to Jesse, "Call Joan and tell her I'm going."

I had to be there for Ted and his family.

Now, the rule for the codel flight was just members of Congress and their spouses, no aides. But Millie wasn't coming along, so she insisted Jesse accompany me. She called the Capitol logistics people personally.

"I'm not going to let Danny go there by himself," she said. "Jesse always travels with him."

"It's absolutely no staff," she was told.

"He can have my seat."

"It doesn't work that way."

"Okay, he's not going, then," she said and hung up.

A few hours later, we got an email.

"We'd be happy to accommodate Mr. Broder Van Dyke."

He was the only aide on the flight.

Under rainy skies, just outside Boston, the mourners gathered at Our Lady of Perpetual Help Basilica. This church had special significance. When Kennedy's daughter Kara had lung cancer, and was getting treated at nearby Brigham and Women's Hospital, he came here every day to pray. Sadly, Kara would die of a heart attack in 2011, possibly due to her cancer treatment. Fifty-eight senators, myself included, and twenty-one former senators had assembled at the JFK Library and arrived at the church around 10 a.m. That's when the music started—violins, a cello and clarinets. Then the vast Kennedy clan filed in. Then appeared President and Mrs. Obama, Vice President Biden and his wife Jill, President and Mrs. George W. Bush, President and Mrs. Clinton—the new secretary of state, and President and Mrs. Carter. This was a very gracious gesture by Carter, who had faced an internecine challenge from Kennedy in 1980. Then finally arrived Kennedy's widow, Vicki, and the immediate family. The archbishop of Boston, Sean O'Malley, was there, and a smattering of other clergy.

The procession began at 10:30 sharp with the hymn, "Holy God, We Praise Thy Name." The music was wonderful.

Obama delivered a fine eulogy.

"Mrs. Kennedy, Kara, Edward, Patrick, Curran, Caroline, members of the Kennedy family, distinguished guests and fellow citizens, today we say goodbye to the youngest child of Rose and Joseph Kennedy. The world will long remember their son Edward as the heir to a weighty legacy; a champion for those who had none; the soul of the Democratic Party; and the lion of the U.S. Senate—a man whose name graces nearly 1,000 laws, and who penned more than 300 himself."

He mentioned Kennedy's many travails—the death of siblings and nephews, surviving a plane crash, caring for two children with cancer—"a string of events that would have broken a lesser man."

As someone who had seen the tenor of the Senate change over the years, I found myself nodding at his next remarks.

"We can still hear his voice bellowing through the Senate chamber, face reddened, fist pounding the podium, a veritable force of nature, in support of health care or workers' rights or civil rights. And yet, while his causes became deeply personal, his disagreements never did. While he was seen by his fiercest critics as a partisan lightning rod, that is not the prism through which Ted Kennedy saw the world, nor was it the prism through which his colleagues saw him. He was a product of an age when the joy and nobility of politics prevented differences of party and philosophy from becoming barriers to cooperation and mutual respect—a time when adversaries still saw each other as patriots."

And he closed on this note: "Ted Kennedy has gone home now, guided by his faith and by the light of those he has loved and lost. At last he is with them once more, leaving those of us who grieve his passing with the memories he gave, the good he did, the dream he kept alive, and a single, enduring image—the image of a man on a boat;

white mane tousled; smiling broadly as he sails into the wind, ready for what storms may come, carrying on toward some new and wondrous place just beyond the horizon. May God bless Ted Kennedy, and may he rest in eternal peace."

After the Mass, an honor guard draped the casket with the American flag and covered it in plastic to protect it from the weather. Kennedy's body was flown to Andrews Air Force Base, just outside Washington, where a hearse took him for burial at Arlington National Cemetery. But on the way the motorcade stopped at the Senate chamber steps, where hundreds of staff members bade a final farewell.

Kennedy had served for nearly forty-seven years, the fourth longest of any senator, behind only Robert Byrd of West Virginia, Inouye and Strom Thurmond of South Carolina. The Senate wouldn't be the same without him. ❦

CHAPTER

87

At the end of September 2009, we lost one of our many stellar staffers. After working as a volunteer on my 2006 campaign, Tulsi Gabbard had joined our Washington office that November. My chief of staff, Joan Ohashi, had been impressed with Tulsi's energy and dedication as a volunteer, as well as her history as a legislator.

When she joined the Hawai'i Legislature in 2002, at age twenty-one, Tulsi became the youngest person ever elected to that body. Representing West Oʻahu, she did fine work on several committees: education, higher education, tourism and economic development.

She was also a member of the 29th Brigade Combat Team, part of the Hawai'i Army National Guard. In 2004, the brigade was due to deploy to Iraq. Tulsi was one of the few people not on the mandatory deployment roster. But she knew she could not sit back and watch nearly the entire Hawai'i Army Guard deploy without her. So she went to her commander.

"I'm going with you guys and volunteering to go," she told him.

"No," he said.

Tulsi is not one to take no for an answer. She persisted and finally her commanding officer relented. She halted her reelection campaign and resigned from the state House.

After six months of training on the Mainland, where she learned to enjoy crawling through mud and climbing over rock walls, she deployed on a twelve-month tour at Logistical Support Activity Anaconda, a large base near Balad, north of Baghdad, that came under regular fire. Tulsi served as a specialist in a field medical unit with the 29th Brigade Support Battalion. At the end of her tour, she received the Meritorious Service Medal.

The brigade returned to the United States between late

December 2005 and early January 2006. It was demobilized in March.

"A lot of my then former colleagues were saying, 'Great. You're back. You can run for your old seat, pick up life where you left off,'" she recalled years later. "For a lot of reasons I knew that that wasn't something I could do, and it wasn't something that I wanted to do primarily because already I wanted to find a way to take the experiences that I had had over those eighteen months both from the deployment itself, one of the lessons I learned from that whole experience working in that medical unit, seeing firsthand on a daily basis the incredibly high cost of war, the waste and abuse taking place by contractors."

She thought about working for the United Nations and the White House, but ultimately decided to volunteer for me in my tough race against Ed Case. She took a chance and sent an email through the campaign website. Luckily for me, it did not fall through the cracks.

As my Senate aide, Tulsi worked on energy independence, homeland security, the environment and veterans' issues. She lived nearby, so we would commute together into D.C., Jim Sakai driving, me in the front and Tulsi and Millie in the back. We would talk about everything from Wall Street to war to Wahine volleyball. Only one of those subjects was pleasant.

In 2007, she also graduated from the Accelerated Officer Candidate School at the Alabama Military Academy, and was commissioned as a second lieutenant. Her new Army Guard job was as a military police platoon leader with the Special Troops Battalion. In 2009, she deployed a second time to the Middle East, working on a variety of security missions and helping train the Kuwait National Guard. We were sad to see her go, but knew that she would continue her excellent work. And of course, she was by no means done with public service.

Two of my longtime staffers went on to accept appointments in the Obama administration.

Debra Wada, my legislative assistant in the 1990s, specialized in national defense, veterans' affairs, maritime issues, education, Social Security and welfare. She had a bachelor's degree in economics and political science from Drake University in Des Moines, Iowa, but also graduated from the Naval War College. When she left my staff in 1999, she worked as legislative liaison for the National Park Service, then on the staff of the House Armed Services Committee. Obama appointed her assistant secretary of the Army for manpower and reserve affairs.

Esther Kiaʻaina, who helped me on Hawaiian and Native American issues, graduated from Kamehameha Schools and earned a BA in political science and international relations from the University of Southern California. She got her law degree from George Washington University and a master's degree from the School of Advanced International Studies at Johns Hopkins University in Baltimore. When she left my staff, she worked as chief of staff for Congressman Bob Underwood of Guam (where Esther was born). She also worked for Ed Case, then as land asset manager for our alma mater, Kamehameha. Obama ultimately appointed her assistant secretary of the interior for insular affairs.

One of my longest-serving assistants was Pat Kim, later Pat Hill, a 1973 Kamehameha graduate. She started out as my scheduler in early 1979 but over the years her duties expanded to that of office manager and to executive assistant. She also handled a lot of personal things for me, but had been my appointments secretary since John Uchima brought her on board fresh out of the UH Mānoa with a degree in travel industry management. Having met Morrnah Simeona in 1982, Pat proved of particular help when I was trying to acquire the *Statue of Freedom* from the Smithsonian.

Pat moonlighted as a model. A graduate of the National Conservatory of Dramatic Arts in Washington, she was also an actor, with the stage name Leolani Hill, a singer and dancer and a member of the American Federation of Television and Radio Artists and the Screen Actors Guild.

On February 15, 1986, with *kumu* hula Kamaki Kanahele, she took part in a performance of traditional Hawaiian chants and dances at Carnegie Hall in New York City. About two months before the show, she was told by the house manager at Carnegie Hall, a Hilo boy named Kimo Gerald, that the 8:30 p.m. show was sold out, with 800 people still wanting tickets. The troupe asked if they could do a second show at midnight, and that also quickly sold out. In addition to Pat, who performed as Leolani Kim, the company included chanter Mahina Bailey, Karin Haleamau on slack key guitar, pianist and singer Jimmy Kaina, Clyde Sproat on slack key guitar and ʻukulele, and dancers Kaua Kahoʻonei, Lani Hidalgo, Makamae Erlich, Mohala Vadset, Pohailama Wong, Mark Tactay, Kalani Silva, Tracy Takaki and Ivan Hoʻopiʻi (twin brother of Ike Hoʻopiʻi, the Pentagon police officer).

Millie and I and the troupe made the trip up to New York in vans. It was cold but we were all very excited. As the narrator, I offered the welcoming remarks to the audience. Mahina and Pat performed four traditional chants, "No Luna O Ka Hale Kai," "Kona Kai ʻŌpua," "Pihanakalani" and "He Maʻi No ʻIolani." It was a wonderful experience for all of us.

In July 2011, Pat played Queen Liliʻuokalani in *Cry for the Gods: The Last Queen of Hawaiʻi*, at the Capital Fringe Festival, the equivalent of off-Broadway. The play had a five-night run at The Mountain theatre in the Mount Vernon Place United Methodist Church, on Massachusetts Avenue just north of the White House.

"Actress Leolani Hill is inspiring as the Queen Liliʻuokalani," wrote critic Laurel Elliott in DCTheatreScene.com. "Her portrayal of Hawaiʻi's last sovereign leader is a tribute to the woman who personified the strength and culture of a people struggling to hold on to their independence. Her nemesis is the arrogant J.L. Stevens, U.S. minister to Hawaiʻi. Actor Howard Wahlberg plays the arrogant politician hell-bent on ensuring the progression of the American way of life. What follows is an emotionally charged confrontation between the leaders of two radically opposed causes. *Cry for the Gods* accomplishes its mission to educate audiences about one of the most defining moments in the history of the Hawaiian Islands."

I went to the fourth performance, on a Saturday night. The dialog didn't actually happen in history, but I thought the play rang true. At the close, Pat sang a lovely "Aloha ʻOe," a song written by Liliʻuokalani. We gave her a standing ovation. So impressed was I with the performance that I had my staff arrange an encore in the U.S. Capitol auditorium. We invited the entire Congress and Capitol staff with the idea that many simply didn't know the history of the overthrow. Hundreds showed up that October, and, I think, came away with a better understanding of the travails of Hawaiians. Maybe, I thought, that would translate into more support for the Akaka Bill.

✳ ✳ ✳

I first met Jon Yoshimura in 1977, when I was a freshman in Congress and he was a freshman at Georgetown University. A Maui boy, Jon came by my office to drop off some Kitch'n Cook'd Maui potato chips, the kind in the bright red and yellow bag. He also stopped by the offices of Heftel, Matsunaga and Inouye, and chatted with Inouye. I wasn't in the office at the time, but was touched by the gift, a terrific addition to our Hawai'i-treats credenza.

So I decided to invite Jon and any other Georgetown students from Hawai'i over to the condo for dinner. He hadn't left any contact information, but the staff managed to track him down at his dorm, and I called what was apparently the one phone they had on the floor.

Some student picked up.

"Hello?"

"Hello, this is Congressman Dan Akaka. May I speak to Jon Yoshimura?"

"Just a second, sir."

I heard a knock on a door.

"Jon, your congressman is on the phone."

"What??"

Footsteps down the hall.

"Hello?"

"Jon, this is Dan Akaka."

"Hello, Congressman."

"Hey, thank you for stopping by my office. I'm sorry I wasn't there, but I'd like to invite you Hawai'i kids for dinner. Can you help me round them up?"

"Oh, yeah, sure."

"So how many do you have?"

"Well, maybe seven or eight."

"Oh, that's great. And if you have some friends you want to bring, please bring them."

So we set that up, and I sent over two cars to the campus, and had a great evening. I told them, "You know, I figure you kids have probably been here about a month, and you probably miss your rice."

They nodded eagerly.

As people familiar with the Mainland know, restaurants serve chili with cheese, not rice, and no one eats rice for breakfast. In Virginia, it's easier to get grits with eggs than rice.

So I made chicken hekka—skinless filet strips stir-fried with onions, carrots, mushrooms, shredded bamboo shoots and chopped watercress, and flavored with shoyu, sugar, ginger root and Japanese mirin.

Years later, when he worked for KHON Channel 2, first as a cameraman and then as a reporter, Jon thanked me for that dinner every time I saw him.

Uchima and I had a lot of Hawai'i people over for meals in those early House years. Sometimes I would cook, sometimes our guests would cook. Kaua'i mayor Eduardo Malapit, I remember, made a potent pot of pigs' feet. The pungent aroma got into the upholstery and lingered for days. Sometimes guests crashed on our couch or floor, including Walter Ritte, Emmett Aluli and George Helm of the Protect Kaho'olawe 'Ohana. Our office and home served kind of like the ninth and tenth Hawaiian Islands.

After a stretch with KHON, Jon went off to the UH Richardson School of Law.

As a Maui native, Jon was close to state representative Bob Nakasone, who represented Kahului, and had worked on Nakasone's unsuccessful 1982 campaign for mayor against Hannibal Tavares. In early 1994, as newly minted law school graduate, he was sitting in Nakasone's office when my chief of staff, Joan Ohashi, another Maui native, walked in.

"Hey, we are looking for a press secretary," she said. "You just graduated from law school and you've got a media background. Are you interested?"

"You know what?" Yoshimura said. "That sounds like a really great opportunity, but I'm going to run for office."

So Jon ended up on the Honolulu City Council in 1994. He served as chairman from 1999 to 2002, during which time he focused on renewing Waikīkī and ushered through the acclaimed Waikiki Beach Walk project. Jon was also the author of two city charter amendments approved by Honolulu voters in 2002, which created the Office of the City Auditor and set renewable five-year terms for the police chief. In his district, which included downtown and Papakōlea, he promoted community policing teams, worked on senior citizens issues and was active in the revitalization of Chinatown. Things were looking pretty good, notwithstanding a painful incident while playing softball in the Lawyers League: the ball hit him in the mouth and he lost an incisor. (His dentist simply put it back in, telling him, "This will either last a lifetime or it will last ten years.")

But in 1999 Jon learned an important lesson about drinking and driving. After an evening out, he hit a parked car and left the scene. But witnesses had seen him. He later publicly apologized and the Supreme Court suspended him from practice for six months for lying about the incident to the state Office of Disciplinary Counsel.

In 2002, Jon ran for the state Senate and won the Democratic primary, but lost in the general election to Gordon Trimble. He then spent a couple of years as an information specialist at the Honolulu Board of Water Supply.

In late December 2004, Jon and his wife, Yuki, newly married, were shopping for New Year's dishes at Marukai Market when they ran into Joan.

"Hey, you know," Joan said, "we're creating a position for a communications director. If you know anyone who might be interested, let me know."

"Hey, sure," Jon said.

Jon and Yuki went home, and he said to her, "Hey, I'm kind of interested in that job. Um, would you be willing to move to Washington, D.C.?"

Now, Yuki had only been living in Hawai'i about two years. Living in Hawai'i had been a lifelong goal for her.

"Okay, sure," she said.

So Jon called Joan.

"Hey, I'm kind of interested in that job."

"Oh, I don't think you'd want to move to D.C. at your age," she told him.

"No, I used to go to school there and sounds like a really interesting opportunity."

"Why don't you come in an interview with me and I'll let you know."

Joan worked out of our Hawai'i office in the federal building. Jon went down for the interview and two or three days later she called him back.

"You've got the job," she said.

Jon and Yuki moved to Washington in the early part of 2005.

He served ably for six years, working with my press secretary, Donalyn Dela Cruz, another former KHON reporter. Jon made it clear to Donalyn from the outset that he would not interfere with her press duties, that he was there to help if she needed it. They got along fine, as did Donalyn's successor, Jesse Broder Van Dyke.

Jon's responsibilities included a lot of work with constituents. In my office, the policy was that if we received a letter from a constituent, they would get a letter back. This was not just a toss-off effort; we always gave them a thoughtful response. We had a whole team of writers handling constituent correspondence and Jon proofread every letter, which only seldom required tweaking.

Moreover, I made it a point to greet every constituent who visited my office. My was feeling was, if they traveled 5,000 miles and took the time to stop by, I would meet them personally. Jon and often Millie, in her *mu'umu'u* and bare feet, greeted them initially, chatting them up, finding out where in the Islands they were from and offering homegrown refreshments. If I was busy he sometimes would let them visit the Senate cloak room, where they could see Hillary Clinton or John McCain or Fred Thompson coming and going. At some point, usually before 9 a.m., he would assemble them in my office and I would come in and he would introduce them all to me, having memorized everyone's name and home island. And we all would chat for fifteen or twenty minutes, sometimes longer. But I usually had to get to a committee hearing by 9:30 a.m. So if it looked like the time was getting away from us, Jon would pipe in:

"Senator, do you think we can take some pictures now?"

That was the cue.

"Sure," I'd say.

And Jon would take the pictures of us behind the desk in my ceremonial office.

Nine times out of ten, the visitors would then go on a tour of the Capitol. When they returned, their photos were ready, placed inside a nice card with the Senate seal and a preprinted note of thanks from me.

That was our system. ❖

CHAPTER

88

Walking back to my office one day, I saw Millie at the door, saying goodbye to a tall, good-looking man whom I didn't recognize. They seemed to be friendly.

"Who was that?" I asked her when we were alone in the office.

"One of my old boyfriends," she said.

"What does he do?"

"Oh, he's just a rubbish man."

For all I knew, this meant he was a high-ranking member of the United Public Workers, the union representing the trash pickup crews in Hawai'i.

"Well, he's quite handsome," I said.

"Yes," she quickly agreed.

"Why didn't you marry *him?*" I asked.

"Maybe I should have," she said.

I let that answer sit for a bit.

"Well, I guess if you had married him, you wouldn't be married to a senator," I said.

"If I had married him," she said, "he would be the senator and you would the rubbish man."

This was vintage Millie, part of our straight-faced humor in the bent of George Burns and Gracie Allen. Frank and Joyce Fasi had a similar repartee. I know because Millie and Joyce were good friends. Maybe the ability to tease one another is conducive to a lasting marriage. I don't know. On May 22, 2008, we celebrated our sixtieth anniversary.

❄ ❄ ❄

Vioxx.

The very word still gives me chills.

Manufactured by Merck & Co., Vioxx was an anti-inflammatory drug for people with osteoarthritis, a painful deterioration of the joints distinct from rheumatoid arthritis, an auto-immune disease in which the body's own defenses work against it. The Food and Drug Administration approved Vioxx in May 1999. But before long an epidemiologist with the agency, Dr. David Graham, began to notice a spike in heart attacks associated with the drug. He took his concerns to his superiors, but they essentially shut him down, a reflection of the then revolving door between the FDA brass and the drug companies.

The leadership even began a criminal investigation into leaks about safety concerns over another drug, Paxil, an anti-depressant for teenagers.

Graham finally took his concerns to Congress, testifying before the Senate Finance Committee on November 18, 2004, and offering a stunning revelation into the corrupt machinations of an agency whose primary mission was public safety. His research showed that the expensive painkiller had caused more than 88,000 heart attacks in the previous five years, about a third of them fatal. By then, Merck had already recalled the drug and eventually settled 27,000 lawsuits for nearly $5 billion.

"I would argue that the FDA, as currently configured, is incapable of protecting America against another Vioxx," he testified. "We are virtually defenseless."

Unfortunately, his words proved prophetic.

Dr. David Ross, another FDA scientist and safety officer, had serious concerns about a new drug being developed by a company called Sanofi-Aventis. The drug was Ketek, formal name telithromycin, an antibiotic designed to fight ear and respiratory tract infections by bacteria that were resistant to other medications.

During the first round of safety trials, the drug was shown to cause liver problems and blurred vision. A federal advisory committee then asked Sanofi-Aventis to conduct a study on likely patients. The study was junk science, even fraudulent. The company recruited more than 1,800 physicians and paid them $400 for every patient they gave the drug to, more than 24,000 in all. A routine inspection of the doctor who enrolled the most patients—more than 400—showed that he had fabricated his results. For that he went to federal prison for nearly six years. But despite that and other evidence of fraud—four in ten inspected sites were referred for criminal investigation, the FDA approved the five-month study, known as study 3014. When Ross and others raised more objections, they were threatened with termination by the FDA management, including then director Andrew von Eshenbach.

In April 2004, the FDA approved Ketek, and in 2005 it was prescribed more than 3 million times for sinusitis, bronchitis and pneumonia, grossing nearly $200 million for its manufacturer. The first case of fatal liver failure was reported in February 2005. Later that year, two more cases of acute liver failure occurred at the same medical center. Still, citing study 3014, the FDA insisted Ketek was safe.

That's when Ross and other whistleblowers went to Congress and the media.

But rather than conduct a global review of the drug's safety and efficacy—in many instances it worked no better than a sugar pill, the FDA ordered a useless warning label on the drug and continued its campaign to quiet its scientists.

On July 8, 2004, to ensure that federal workers do not face retaliation for "blowing the whistle" on mismanagement and bad practices, I introduced the Federal Employee Protection of Disclosure Act. My cosponsors included Republicans Susan Collins of Maine and Chuck Grassley, chairman of the Finance Committee, which would take Graham's testimony. Grassley and Carl Levin had sponsored the 1989 Whistleblower Protection Act. But that law had flaws. As a result of recent court decisions, legitimate whistleblowers had been denied adequate protection from retaliatory practices. I aimed to patch those pukas.

"As my colleagues know, the events of September 11, 2001, have brought renewed attention to the security lapses at our nation's airports, nuclear facilities, borders and law enforcement agencies," I said on the Senate floor. "However, in many cases, the current whistleblower system fails to protect those who would disclose information that could ensure the safety and welfare of the American people. As of May 2004, federal whistleblowers have prevailed on the merits of their

Queen Elizabeth II greets Dan and Millie before addressing
a joint session of Congress in 1991.

Top: Dan shares a toast with former Hawai'i governor John Burns and Abe Akaka. Above: Dan with Patsy Mink, who succeeded him in the U.S. House of Representatives.

Top: Texas congressman Henry Gonzalez looks on as Dan greets President George H.W. Bush. Above: In 1990, Dan and Senator Edward Kennedy visit a kindergarten class at The Early School at Church of the Crossroads in Honolulu.

Top: Vice President Al Gore (far left) and Hawai'i's congressional delegation (left to right: Daniel Inouye, Patsy Mink, Neil Abercrombie and Dan) look on as President Bill Clinton signs the Apology Resolution at the White House. Above (left to right): Honolulu mayor Frank Fasi, Dan, Hillary Clinton, Bill Clinton, Hawai'i governor John Waihee, Patsy and Neil greet the crowd on Waikīkī Beach in 1993. Opposite: Dan and Millannie with Bill and Hillary Clinton at a White House Christmas party.

Opposite top and above: Dan with President George W. Bush (holding the book *Hawaiʻi's Story by Hawaiʻi's Queen*) and President Barack Obama, the Hawaiʻi-born senator from Illinois, at an Akaka fundraiser in 2006. Opposite bottom: The Akaka family—(front, left to right) Millie, Dan and Millannie; (back, left to right) Dan Jr., Gerard, Nick and Alan—in August 2012.

Dan and Millie enjoy the cherry blossoms in Washington, DC.

claims before the federal circuit court of appeals only once since 1994. This record sends the wrong message. How can we expect civil servants to protect and defend the United States when we permit agencies to retaliate against them for doing their job?"

I knew the Justice Department had objected to previous legislation concerning this problem. But I felt that the department had an inherent conflict of interest. When a whistleblower sued their agency, it was the DOJ that defended the agency. But I had worked with my colleagues on the Governmental Affairs Committee to address some the concerns raised by DOJ. One of the most significant changes related to employees who find their security clearances stripped as a means of retaliation. Current law did not permit the whistleblower to have his or her case heard by an independent adjudicator when that type of retaliation happened.

On October 8, 2004, this bill passed out of the Senate Committee on Government Affairs, led by Collins, but never got a vote on the floor.

So I introduced it again on March 2, 2005, with a dozen bipartisan cosponsors. They included Grassley and Levin, Republicans Collins, George Voinovich of Ohio and Norm Coleman of Minnesota and seven other Democrats. Once again, on May 25, it cleared Collins' Committee on Homeland Security and Government Affairs, but then lost traction.

So I introduced it again on January 11, 2007, at the start of the 110th Congress. As cosponsors, I picked up Ted Kennedy and Barbara Mikulski of Maryland. It quickly drew support from the nation's largest union of federal employees, the National Treasury Employees Union, representing 150,000 workers in thirty agencies and departments. On November 16, it cleared the Homeland Security Committee, now in the hands of Joe Lieberman. Then, miracle of miracles, on December 17, the Senate passed it by voice vote. The House passed a similar bill, but we were unable to work out the differences before the 110th Congress adjourned.

In 2009, Mikulski's colleague Chris Van Hollen introduced the Whistleblower Protection Enhancement Act. On February 3, I launched a companion bill in the Senate. Joining the list of cosponsors were Democrats Jon Tester of Montana and Roland Burris of Illinois.

On June 11, I held a hearing on the bill before my Subcommittee on Oversight of Government Management, the Federal Workforce and the District of Columbia.

"The Whistleblower Protection Act (WPA) is an important cornerstone of our nation's good government laws," I said in my opening statement. "Federal employee whistleblowers play a crucial role in alerting Congress and the public to government wrongdoing and mismanagement, protecting our civil rights and civil liberties, helping to keep us safe and rooting out waste, fraud and abuse."

However, rulings by the U.S. circuit court and the Merit Systems Protection Board had created loopholes, I added.

"The law has become so weak that many employees, with good reason, fear they will not be protected from retaliation if the come forward to report wrongdoing," I said.

Testifying in favor were Angela Canterbury of Public Citizen, American University law professor Robert Vaughn, Danielle Brian of the Project on Government Oversight and Tom Devine of the Government Accountability Project. The latter organization had worked closely with Dr. Graham of the FDA.

However, Rajesh De, a deputy assistant attorney general, said that while the administration supported improvements to the law, it opposed offering jury trials for certain federal workers, particularly those with security clearances. And William Bransford, general counsel for the Senior Executive Association, argued that managers would be afraid to discipline "problem employees" if whistleblowers are allowed access to jury trials.

Lieberman guided it through the full committee in early December but it took more than a year to clear the Senate. In December 2010 we added some amendments, then sent the measure over to the House, still in the hands of lame-duck Democrats but not fully functional. Van Hollen plucked the bill from the grave, but we never managed to craft a coherent version acceptable to the administration.

If at first you don't succeed, the saying goes. On April 6, 2011, I introduced the Whistleblower Protection Enhancement Act of 2012. As cosponsors, I picked up Tom Harkin of Iowa, Mary Landrieu of Louisiana, Claire McCaskill of Missouri, Mark Begich of Alaska,

Ben Cardin of Maryland and Chris Coons of Delaware. This time, Lieberman took a year to pass it out of committee. But then it moved relatively rapidly, clearing the full Senate in May 2012. That vote won praise from the Union of Concerned Scientists, which mentioned Dr. Ross and Ketek and also environmentalist Jack Spadaro, who lost his job with the Mine Safety and Health Administration after he accused the agency of failing to fully investigate a toxic spill in Martin County, Kentucky, where more than 300 million gallons of coal waste burst through a containment facility and polluted nearby streams and rivers. In a 2011 survey by the union, 211 scientists at the FDA reported that they felt they could not discuss their work with the public or the media without fear of retaliation.

The House passed the measure on September 28, thanks to the hard work of Van Hollen, his Maryland colleague Elijah Cummings, and Republicans Darrell Issa of California and Todd Russell Platts of Pennsylvania. The House and Senate hammered out the differences over the next seven weeks. I was on hand in the Oval Office, of course, when Obama signed it on November 27, 2012. That marked one of the highlights of my legislative career.

The law clarified that any disclosure of gross waste or mismanagement, fraud, abuse or illegal activity was protected, but not legitimate disagreements over policy. It also suspended the role of the federal appellate court for two years. And it extended whistleblower protections to all employees of the Transportation Security Administration. The law also established an ombudsman to educate agency personnel about whistleblower rights.

"Federal employees who risk their careers to step forward and disclose waste, fraud and abuse save taxpayer money and make our government more efficient," I said in a statement. "They absolutely deserve our support and I am so proud that these new protections are now enacted into law." ❖

CHAPTER

89

There was nothing quite as big a treat as flying to and from Hawai'i on Air Force One with the Obamas, who rented a beach house in Kailua every Christmas from 2008 through 2016. I had known Obama from our Senate days, when we shared assignments on the Veterans' Affairs and the Homeland Security and Governmental Affairs Committees. Of course, in 2008, before his inauguration, he had no access to Air Force One. But after that he invited the congressional delegation to fly with him on every trip, and I took him up on it, I would say, three or four times, starting in 2009 and ending in 2012, my last full year in the Senate. On those trips, and on our occasional visits to the White House, I could see that he wanted to talk about Hawai'i news, but he refrained, sticking to official business.

That said, I did once hear him ask the Air Force One steward, "Do we have any li hing mui?"

So whenever I could—and especially when I was flying with him—I would bring along a box of papayas. But anything like that had to go through the White House gifts "system," and I wondered sometimes if he ever got his papayas.

One time, when we were coming home from D.C., I was surprised to see manapua as the main dish.

"Oh, wow," I said, attracting the attention of a colleague next to me at the table. "What's this?"

He looked at the menu.

"I've never seen that before."

Envisioning manapua from Chinatown, I wondered how many I would get.

When the plate came out, I saw that it held one giant manapua. It was hot and with all the char siu in there, I'm telling you, it was really good. But as a matter of etiquette—and practicality—we couldn't pick it up. We had to use a knife and fork. Obama tried to put local foods on the Air Force One menu whenever he could.

Obama called me "Senator" or often "Danny," but I always called him "Mr. President" as is customary, even though he is about the age of my youngest son, Nick. Millie and I could call Michelle Obama by her first name. And of course it was a delight to see their two girls, Malia and Sasha, grow from coltish kids to gracious young ladies.

One thing I never understood, though, is why the Obamas on their Hawai'i visits crossed the Ko'olau by motorcade instead of helicopter. Their Kailuana Place rental was only five minutes from Marine Corps Base Hawai'i, and it would seem an easy thing to fly between the Kāne'ohe air station and Joint Base Pearl Harbor-Hickam, where Air Force One landed. That would have avoided some of the freeway gridlock that sometimes happened when Obama and his entourage were on the move.

On December 11, 2009, Abercrombie announced he would be resigning from Congress to run full-time for governor. Neil had declared his candidacy in March, but initially said he would divide his time between Washington and Hawai'i. Waihee told me years later that he had softly cautioned Neil against giving up his seat, which he had held since 1991—almost as long as my time in the Senate. He was chairman of the Armed Forces Subcommittee on Air and Land Forces, and was a high-ranking member of the Natural Resources Committee, both areas of keen interest to Hawai'i.

"You know, Neil, you've gained quite of lot of seniority..." Waihee told him.

But Abercrombie was not to be dissuaded.

His decision to resign didn't sit well with Inouye, who remarked by email: "It leaves us a vote shy in the House at a time when major policy changes like health-care reform, a war spending measure, the Akaka Bill and others are shaping up for debate and passage."

Neil also caught some flak from his longtime political rival, Mayor Mufi Hannemann, who almost certainly would challenge him in the race.

"He is leaving the state in a lurch," Mufi told the newspapers. "He has become a very influential member of Congress. I think he put a lot of people in a difficult situation, including the city."

The likely Republican candidate for governor, Lieutenant Governor James "Duke" Aiona, fired a shot from a different angle, saying Abercrombie "has been a part of Washington politics for a very long time and has grown out of touch with our residents." He added that Neil "could use some time in Hawai'i to reacquaint himself with the issues facing our families and distance himself from his failed policies in Washington."

But Abercrombie ally John Radcliffe, a lobbyist and former union leader, defended the decision. "It will give him the opportunity to express some leadership close up," he said. "It will also give him the chance to be on the same ground as the mayor. It makes it a level playing field."

While Hannemann's campaign was still officially "exploratory," both he and Neil were busy raising money. Earlier in the month, Mufi had held a $1,000-a-plate fundraiser in Los Angeles.

Of course, Neil's decision to run for state office brought out a number of candidates interested in his U.S. House seat. They included Ed Case and state Senate president Colleen Hanabusa.

On January 7, 2010, I convened a hearing of the Veterans' Affairs Committee in Kahului, Maui. This was part of my long and continuing effort to make sure our veterans got the care and services they needed on the Neighbor Islands. I had had to cancel an earlier scheduled hearing because of the Kennedy funeral.

"Much has improved in recent years, for which I am grateful, but it is important for us to understand the present challenges," I said in an opening statement. "Both the clinic and vet center on Maui are tremendously busy, and must be available to those Maui veterans who rely on VA for their care, and to veterans living on Lāna'i and Moloka'i as well. I applaud the efforts of VA employees in Hawai'i—these men and women work hard to help the veterans who seek their assistance. There are many things that VA does well in Hawai'i. However, there is always room for improvement. Indeed, our unique geography, diversity and way of life require that VA develop a unique strategy to care for our island's veterans. Ensuring timely access to mental health services for veterans living on Maui has been a challenge due to reported shortages of VA and community health providers on the island. However, VA has established new mental health positions at the Maui Clinic and has expanded telehealth capabilities to other islands."

Telehealth was a relatively new term, similar to telemedicine, where doctors in remote areas could consult specialists—even have X-rays or CT scans read—in urban centers.

On January 26, on the eve of Obama's first State of the Union address (his speech to Congress the year before didn't qualify), I joined sixteen other senators in writing a letter urging him to place priority on clean energy and legislation to counter climate change. We really wanted him to see him improve on the dismal record of George W. Bush. The other senators included Barbara Boxer and Dianne Feinstein, Bernie Sanders and Patrick Leahy, Chris Dodd, Mary Landrieu, Ben Cardin of Maryland, and Kirsten Gillibrand of New York, who had succeeded Hillary Clinton, now secretary of state.

"Dear Mr. President," we wrote, "as you set your administration's priorities for the coming year, we urge you to place clean energy and climate legislation capable of creating new economic opportunities at the top of your list. Legislation that invests in clean energy and puts a meaningful limit on carbon pollution will be a major job creator. With unemployment still hovering around ten percent nationwide, our country desperately needs forward looking policies, such as clean energy and climate legislation, to reinvigorate our economy and achieve long term, sustained economic health.

"At this critical juncture in our nation's history, we face extraordinary economic, national security and environmental challenges. The solutions to these problems are intertwined with one another and begin with legislation that invests in clean energy technology and a new, twenty-first-century infrastructure. That investment will create good jobs, put us on a path toward energy independence and allow us to leave a healthy planet and economy to our children and grandchildren."

With Joe Biden and House Speaker Nancy Pelosi behind him, Obama delivered the address to a joint session of Congress the next day, January 27. We were gratified that he talked quite extensively about clean energy, especially regarding its role in job creation. He wanted to give tax rebates to people who make their homes more energy-efficient. And he wanted to encourage American innovation in the realm of clean energy. He called for more investment in advanced biofuels and clean coal technology. And he proposed an omnibus energy and climate bill to make green technologies profitable.

I issued this statement:

"I agree with President Obama that we must create private sector jobs through investments in small businesses, clean renewable energy and road and rail projects, because better jobs mean more security for working families. I share the president's commitment to reforming our health-care system and expanding access to quality health care. His proposed investments in education will lead to a more globally competitive workforce and greater economic prosperity.

"President Obama inherited many challenges, including two wars, threats of terrorism and an economic crisis. He has made tough decisions to set our country on the right track. Troops are coming home from Iraq, and our economy is beginning to recover. We have made progress but there is more to do. I look forward to working with him on it."

On February 1, 2010, much to my satisfaction, Obama signed the Veterans' Emergency Care Fairness Act. I had introduced this measure a year earlier with Roland Burris of Illinois as a cosponsor. Burris was an ally of Tammy Duckworth over at the VA. The measure allowed for a veteran to be reimbursed for the cost of emergency care at a non-VA facility. Previously, the VA could reimburse veterans or pay outside hospitals directly only if a veteran has no outside health insurance.

"For veterans with limited insurance, a trip to the emergency room should not result in financial ruin," I said in a statement the next day. "With this new law, VA will be positioned to help veterans who are enrolled in VA care whose insurance does not cover the full cost of emergency treatment."

The bill allowed for retroactive reimbursement, too. I had received correspondence from veterans who were unable to receive financial assistance under the old rules, and planned to share their information with Shinseki. The Congressional Budget Office estimated that this legislation will cover about 700 future claims per year and as many as 2,000 veterans retroactively.

In early February, we got word that longtime mayor Frank Fasi had died of natural causes at his home in Makiki. He was eighty-nine. Fasi served longer than any other mayor in history, but wanted very much to be governor as well. He ran five times—as a Democrat, as a Republican and at the helm of his self-styled Best Party, but never made the leap. Frank and I didn't agree on everything—the need for the H-3 freeway, for instance—but I always admired his tenacity and can-do attitude. After one of his many quixotic campaigns, reporters asked him what he would run for next.

"The pope is an elected office," Fasi quipped.

He would be missed. Millie's thoughts and mine went out to his widow, Joyce, and his eleven children.

By a vote of 245–164, the U.S. House on February 23 passed the Native Hawaiian Government Reorganization Act—the Akaka Bill. Abercrombie had introduced H.R. 2314 a year earlier with nine cosponsors, including Hirono, Madeleine Bordallo of Guam, Eni Faleomavaega of American Samoa, Gregorio Sablan of the Northern Marianas and Republicans Tom Cole of Oklahoma and Don Young of Alaska. Neil, who had resigned effective February 28, funneled it through the Natural Resources Committee and brought it to the House floor in his last week in Congress.

The vote was largely along party lines; four Democrats voted no and six Republicans voted yes. Partisanship notwithstanding, I considered this a huge milestone.

"We have a moral obligation, unfulfilled since the overthrow of Queen Liliʻuokalani, that we are closer to meeting today," I said. I expressed thanks to both Neil and Hirono for making it happen.

"Neil's unwavering support for federal recognition of Native Hawaiians over the past decade is greatly appreciated," I said. "I am optimistic about bringing the bill to the Senate floor this year."

The White House press secretary also remarked on the bill's passage.

"The president recognizes that Native Hawaiians are a vital part of our nation's cultural fabric, and they will continue to be so in the years to come."

Neil said, "We have a president who truly understands the importance and fundamental equity of Native Hawaiian self-determination, and today's vote demonstrates that Hawai'i has good friends in Congress. If we work together to push open the door to a future of respect and dignity for Native Hawaiians, we create a better future for all the people in Hawai'i."

The Hawai'i delegation had worked extensively with the U.S. Departments of Justice and the Interior on the language to make sure it passed constitutional muster. And we had had extensive consultations with Attorney General Mark Bennett and representatives of the Office of Hawaiian Affairs.

The trick now was getting it through the Senate.

Days later, on February 27, a massive magnitude 8.8 earthquake rocked south-central Chile, killing 550 people, causing widespread destruction and triggering a near-nationwide blackout. Here was yet another example of the powerful and unpredictable nature of the Pacific's volatile Ring of Fire. A tsunami swept over nearby coastal communities, causing extensive damage. The losses to the fishing fleet alone were estimated at $67 million. Tsunami warnings went out to fifty-three nations around the Pacific, but the United States suffered only minimal damage, in San Diego. In Hawai'i, tsunami waves arrived late that Saturday morning, but they were smaller than anticipated, in the one-to-three-foot range. They caused a surge in Hilo Bay and elsewhere around the state, but there were no reports of damage or injuries. Gerard Fryer, a geophysicist at the Pacific Tsunami Warning Center, remarked that Hawai'i had "dodged a bullet." What was a disaster for Chile was for Hawai'i an important reminder of the importance of being prepared. A little more than a year later, we would get another test of our nerves. ❊

CHAPTER

90

On April 20, 2010, another environmental disaster struck with the explosion and blowout at the Deepwater Horizon oil exploration rig in the Gulf of Mexico. This was even worse than the *Exxon Valdez* catastrophe. Eleven people were killed, and another 115 evacuated as the rig burned out of control. It sank two days later. Oil continued to gush from the uncapped well until July 15. Nearly five million barrels of crude spilled into the Gulf, fouling beaches from Texas to Florida and killing untold numbers of fish, marine mammals and seabirds. Here was another stunning example of lax federal regulation and safety shortcuts by corporate interests to maximize profits. The rig owner, Transocean Ltd., eventually agreed to pay $1.4 billion for violations of the Clean Water Act. British Petroleum would ultimately agree to pay nearly $19 billion in fines. And contractor Halliburton—of Iraq War and Dick Cheney fame—also was on the hook for more than $1 billion. Congressman Ed Markey of Massachusetts—later a senator—accused BP of lying in formal documents about the extent of the spill, a felony the company later admitted. In 2011, a White House commission blamed BP and its partners for a number of cost-cutting moves and safety lapses and predicted that similar incidents might occur absent improvements in federal policy and industry practices. Those of us watching this calamity play out at a distance could only shake our heads in dismay.

In May, Obama named Elena Kagan, U.S. solicitor general—the number three post in the Justice Department, to replace retiring justice John Paul Stevens on the Supreme Court. A Harvard educated

New Yorker, Kagan, fifty, had been a finalist for the high court a year earlier, when Obama named Sonia Sotomayor. I thought both were brilliant picks. If confirmed, Kagan would become only the fourth female justice in history.

Patrick Leahy, chairman of the Judiciary Committee, called her a "superb nominee" and predicted an easy confirmation. He was right. On August 5, the Senate voted 63–37 in favor, largely along party lines. Republicans Susan Collins and Olympia Snowe of Maine voted with the majority, as did Judd Gregg of New Hampshire and Richard Lugar of Indiana. One Democrat, Ben Nelson of Nebraska, voted no.

I put out this statement: "I was proud to support Elena Kagan's confirmation. She is highly qualified and exceptionally intelligent, and I know that she will do a tremendous job upholding our Constitution. Her confirmation is another example of the positive impact President Obama has already had on our country. When she is sworn in, there will be three sitting female justices on the court for the first time in history. The court is now closer to reflecting America."

Also in May, Obama signed another important piece of legislation that improved health care for veterans. I had introduced the Caregivers and Veterans Omnibus Health Services Act late in October with seven cosponsors, including Democrats Chris Dodd, Mark Begich of Alaska, Tim Johnson of South Dakota, Byron Dorgan of North Dakota and Jeanne Shaheen of New Hampshire, and Republicans Burr and Jim Inhofe of Oklahoma. The bill set up a system where family members in remote areas could care for wounded vets from Afghanistan and Iraq and get training and money for it.

In November, Republican Tom Coburn of Oklahoma introduced an amendment that would have paid for the program in part by diverting funds we send to the United Nations. We shot that down 66–32. On November 19, the bill passed 98–0 and went to the House. On April 21, after forty minutes of debate, the House passed the measure 419–0, with Hirono—our only member of the House with Abercrombie's resignation—voting "aye." A day later, the Senate agreed to a minor House amendment and the bill went to the president.

Later that month, I introduced another successful veterans'

measure, the Post-9/11 Veterans Educational Assistance Improvements Act of 2010. By year's end, the bill had attracted a whopping forty-nine cosponsors, so we had half the Senate on board. This provided a monthly stipend for veterans who were pursuing a college degree as a full-time student or at least more than half time. There was also help for active duty personnel trying to get an advanced education, either at a public or private college or foreign institution. I ushered the bill through the Veterans' Affairs Committee on October 26. The full Senate passed it by voice vote on December 13, and the House approved it three days later, 409–3. The lonely naysayers included Republican Don Young of Alaska. Obama signed in on January 4, 2011.

On June 28, the Senate lost an old and honored friend with the death of Robert Byrd of West Virginia. He was the longest serving senator and the then longest-serving member of Congress, having joined the House in 1953—fifty-seven years earlier. Byrd had replaced Ted Stevens as president pro tempore of the Senate in January 2007. But he had been in poor health since 2008 and died at a hospital in Fairfax, Virginia.

In many ways, Byrd epitomized the Senate and its tradition of polite, informed discourse.

"He was as much a part of the Senate as the marble busts that line its chamber and its corridors," Obama said. "His profound passion for that body and its role and responsibilities was as evident behind closed doors as it was in the stem-winders he peppered with history. He held the deepest respect of members of both parties, and he was generous with his time and advice, something I appreciated greatly as a young senator."

Secretary Clinton remarked, "It is almost impossible to imagine the United States Senate without Robert Byrd. He was not just its longest serving member, he was its heart and soul. From my first day in the Senate, I sought out his guidance, and he was always generous with his time and his wisdom."

When I joined the Senate twenty years earlier, to my great fortune, Byrd took me under his wing. He guided me through procedural rules and taught me how to preside over the floor. I still have the notes he gave me when I was a freshman senator. He was adamant that the presiding officer should always be respectful of the speakers, while maintaining strict adherence to the rules of the Senate. Byrd also was a spiritual man. He was a regular at the Senate Prayer Breakfast when he was well. His favorite hymn was "Old Rugged Cross" and I enjoyed singing it with him many times.

I made this statement on the Senate floor:

"Senator Byrd was the dean of the Senate, our foremost constitutional scholar. No one in the history of our country served longer in Congress. For more than a half century, Robert C. Byrd kept the Senate in line. He always kept a copy of the Constitution in his jacket pocket, close to his heart. He was meticulous, a master of the rules of this historic institution. Through hard work and dedication, Senator Byrd became an institution himself... We shared a love for music and the arts. His fiddle playing was legendary. He loved his family. He loved his children and grandchildren. He loved his dogs. Closest always was his wife, Erma, who was always by his side until her death in 2006. They spent many wonderful years together, and now they are together again. My thoughts and prayers are with the Byrd family. Senator Byrd, we love you and we miss you."

With Byrd's death, Inouye became Senate president pro tem, with full-on Secret Service protection.

This actually was the second death that month that hit close to home. About a week earlier, we lost former chief justice Bill Richardson, a dear friend. Millie and I were close to him and had the pleasure of spending a lot of time with him over the years. The "C.J.," as he was known, was a true Hawaiian, friendly, humble and down to earth, a pillar of the community. The year before, we had attended his ninetieth birthday fundraiser at the law school, named in his honor. He would be remembered for his many rulings that reflected Native Hawaiian culture and heritage. Perhaps his most famous decision preserved public access to the shoreline in Hawai'i: no beach could be considered private. He would be greatly missed.

* * *

Alaska, by virtue of a relatively small population, is one of a few states with only one U.S. House member. The others are Montana,

Wyoming, North and South Dakota, Vermont and Delaware. But Alaska has its own special brand of dynastic politics. Don Young, the former mayor of Fort Yukon—a tiny village above the Arctic Circle, had represented Alaska since March 1973. That's when he won a special election to fill the seat that belonged to first-term Democrat Nick Begich, who had disappeared (with Hale Boggs, see Chapter 19) in a plane crash just weeks before the November 1972 election. Begich, whose body never was found, still won the election—beating Young. But Young went on to show great staying power in the House, ultimately becoming the senior Republican and one of the longest-serving members.

In 1970, Begich had soundly beaten his Republican opponent, a banker named Frank Murkowski. Riding Reagan's coattails, Murkowski won election to the Senate in 1980 and served nearly four terms, rising to the chairmanship of the Energy and Natural Resources Committee. He tried but failed to allow oil drilling in the Arctic National Wildlife Refuge.

Murkowski ran for governor in 2002 and won, then resigned from the Senate and appointed his daughter Lisa, a member of the state House, to succeed him. This was widely criticized as blatant nepotism. But she went on to win a full term in 2004. Lisa is considerably more liberal than her father. She favored allowing gays to serve in the military and voted for same-sex marriage. This ultimately brought a challenge from the Tea Party, whose candidate, Joe Miller, beat Murkowski in the Republican primary in 2010. But Lisa launched a write-in campaign and, impressively, beat both Miller and the Democrat, Sitka mayor Scott , in the general.

When Frank Murkowski left the governor's office in December 2006, he was succeeded by Sarah Palin.

Alaska's other senator was Ted Stevens, first elected in 1968. During World War II, he flew cargo planes in the Asian theater, often without fighter escort, very dangerous duty. In December 1978, Stevens and his wife, Ann, were aboard a Learjet that crashed at Anchorage Airport. She and four others died. He survived, but later confided to friends that he had a premonition that he would die in a small plane crash.

With their seniority, Stevens and Young gave Alaska more clout in Congress than many bigger states enjoyed.

Stevens and Inouye were close friends and worked as allies on a lot of legislation benefitting Hawai'i. As majority whip, Stevens ran for the majority leader position when Howard Baker retired in 1984, but lost to Bob Dole. He ultimately became president pro tem, third in line to the presidency. Toward the end of his long and distinguished Senate career, Stevens ran into legal trouble. In 2008, when he was running for reelection, he got caught up in a federal corruption investigation and was found guilty shortly before the election. He narrowly lost to Mark Begich, son of Nick.

The conviction eventually was tossed out at the request of Attorney General Eric Holder, citing prosecutorial misconduct.

On August 9, 2010, Stevens and eight others were in a single-engine de Havilland Canada DHC-3 Otter, flying to a remote Alaskan fishing lodge. In rain and mist, the plane crashed in the southwestern Alaskan wilderness, not far from the Bering Sea, killing Stevens and four others. The survivors included former NASA administrator and Navy secretary Sean O'Keefe, who broke his neck but recovered.

Stevens was eighty-six.

"Irene and I are deeply saddened by the tragic death of our dear friend, and my brother, Ted Stevens," said Inouye. "His wife, Catherine, and his entire family are in our thoughts and prayers during this most difficult time. Our friendship was a very special one. When it came to policy, we disagreed more often than we agreed, but we were never disagreeable with one another. We were always positive and forthright. Senator Stevens and I worked together to ensure that the small noncontiguous states of Hawai'i and Alaska were not forgotten by the lower forty-eight and to ensure that the nation awoke to the importance of the Pacific for our economy and international relations.

"I will never forget him.

"Ted Stevens was an extraordinary American. He risked his life while serving in China with the Flying Tigers in World War II. He was a leader in the Senate, having served as chairman of the Defense Appropriations Subcommittee, chairman of the Commerce Committee, chairman of the Appropriations Committee and president pro tempore of the United States Senate.

"I have lost my brother."

In echoed Inouye's sentiments.

"Our country has lost a great American," I said. "Ted Stevens cared deeply for the people of Alaska and the United States. He dedicated his career to the security and well-being of the country. He brought strength and passion to the Senate for many decades. We worked together on issues facing our home states. He was a friend of Hawaiʻi and he understood the United States' responsibility to its indigenous peoples.

"He was a dear friend. We were ʻohana.

"Millie and I send out warm aloha and deepest condolences to Catherine and all of Ted's family."

In Hawaiʻi, two races dominated the political landscape in 2010.

On May 22, the state held a special election to fill the congressional seat left vacant by Abercrombie, that is to say, the remaining seven months of his term. This nonpartisan contest drew fourteen candidates, including Case, Hanabusa and Republican Charles Djou, who served on the Honolulu City Council and earlier in the state House. Case and Hanabusa effectively split the Democratic vote, handing Djou a victory with 39.4 percent. Hanabusa picked up thirty-one percent and Case just under twenty-eight percent.

At that point, Case graciously bowed out of the primary race, leaving Hanabusa facing only attorney Rafael Del Castillo, who had placed fourth in the special election.

The other interesting race was for governor, with historical rivals Abercrombie and Hannemann running in the Democratic primary, and Lieutenant Governor Duke Aiona facing token opposition from former state senator John Carroll on the GOP side.

Inouye was up for reelection but had no credible opponent.

On September 18, voters picked Hanabusa and Djou, who would face each other in November. Neil decisively defeated Mufi, 142,304 votes (fifty-nine percent) to 90,590 (thirty-eight percent), meaning he would face Aiona in November. In the lieutenant governor's race, state representative Brian Schatz, an Obama loyalist and former party chairman, dominated the Democrats, including respected fellow lawmakers Bobby Bunda, Norman Sakamoto, Gary Hooser and Lyla Berg. My former staffer Tulsi Gabbard, back from her second Mideast deployment with the Hawaiʻi Army National Guard, held off nine rivals to top the list of voter-getters in District VI of the Honolulu

City Council. The top two finishers would not face each other in the general election. On Maui, Mayor Charmaine Tavares, daughter of former mayor Hannibal Tavares, squeaked past Alan Arakawa, 7,313 votes to 7,041, a difference of 272, in a crowded field. The blank votes numbered 735.

※ ※ ※

In late September, the American Bar Association, representing 400,000 lawyers nationwide, took the extraordinary step of sending a letter to all 100 senators, urging them to support the Native Hawaiian Government Reorganization Act, the Akaka Bill. The letter said the organization "supports the right of Native Hawaiians to seek federal recognition of a native governing entity within the United States similar to that which American Indians and Alaska Natives possess under the U.S. Constitution. When the governing entity is formed, the letter continued, it would "serve, maintain and support their unique cultural and civic needs and advocate on their behalf at the federal and state levels." The association also affirmed the bill's constitutionality. "Our courts have upheld Congress's power to recognize indigenous nations," the letter said. "Native Hawaiians have the right to be recognized by Congress."

In July, Inouye and I had reached an agreement with Lingle to make four clarifying changes to the text of the bill, which then won her support.

On October 15 in Honolulu, I spoke to some 600 delegates of the ninth annual convention of the Council for Native Hawaiian Advancement.

"I know some people are concerned that we are running out of time to pass the bill in 2010," I said. "Let me set the record straight before all of you today. This bill is alive, and we have been working on it every day. I am optimistic that, with the strong support we have received, we will be able to schedule a vote and pass the bill this year, before Congress adjourns. I ask for your continued support and aloha as I return to Washington to continue to fight for our great state. *Imua!*"

The crowd gave me a standing ovation, and Robin Danner, president and CEO of the organization, tearfully thanked me for my efforts.

"Mahalo nui for all you do for us," she said. "We will never give up, Senator, and we are behind you."

In early December, Attorney General Holder and Secretary of the Interior Ken Salazar sent letters to Senate leaders Harry Reid and Mitch McConnell urging the Senate to pass the Native Hawaiian Government Reorganization Act and send it to Obama for his signature.

"Of the nation's three major indigenous groups, Native Hawaiians—unlike American Indians and Alaska Natives—are the only one that currently lacks a government-to-government relationship with the United States," the letter said. "The bill provides Native Hawaiians a means by which to exercise the inherent rights to local self-government, self-determination and economic self-sufficiency that other Native Americans enjoy."

Unfortunately, due to Republican intransigence, the bill did not get a Senate vote that year.

In the general election on November 2, Abercrombie beat Aiona, and Hanabusa defeated Djou. Schatz easily won election as lieutenant governor. Tulsi won her city council seat by more than 4,000 votes, 49.5 to thirty-five percent. The district covers downtown, Punchbowl, Pauoa Valley, Nu'uanu, 'Ālewa Heights, Papakōlea, Fort Shafter, Moanalua, Hālawa, Aiea, Kalihi Valley, and portions of Makiki, Liliha and Kalihi. So she was now my councilwoman. Lingle was out of office after eight years, but everyone expected her to mount a campaign for the Senate—that is, against me—in 2012. ✣

CHAPTER

91

Nationally, the midterm elections favored the Republicans, who picked up six seats in the Senate and sixty-three in the House. With the GOP in control of the House, 242–193, John Boehner of Ohio, who had been the minority leader, became Speaker, replacing Nancy Pelosi. Eric Cantor of Virginia became the House majority leader. We Democrats kept our majority in the Senate, barely—51–47, with two independents, Joe Lieberman and Bernie Sanders, caucusing with us. Harry Reid remained majority leader, with Dick Durbin as his whip. Mitch McConnell continued as minority leader, with Jon Kyl of Arizona as whip. Kyl was one of the major opponents of the Akaka Bill.

More and more, computers, smart phones, the internet and social media colored the fabric of our lives. No one remembers anyone's phone number anymore—perhaps not even our own—because it's stored in our Samsung, finger taps away. Few people use cameras these days; their phones take sharp, digital images, which then can be sent worldwide instantly. At the Pali Lookout or Makapuʻu, tourists used to be grateful when we offered to take their picture; that was before the selfie stick. The Kodak Hula Show, long a vibrant attraction at Kapiʻolani Park, vanished in 2002, a harbinger for color film itself. In the 1960s and 1970s, Rochester, New York, just south of Lake Ontario, was a vibrant city, headquarters of Eastman Kodak, Xerox Corp. and Gannett, the largest newspaper chain in the country. All those stars have faded.

For two decades, starting in 1971, Gannett owned the *Star-Bulletin*, the dominant daily in Honolulu. The afternoon paper had an advantage during the plantation era, when everyone went to work early and got off early. The paper was waiting for them when they got home. But in the 1980s the morning *Advertiser* overtook the *Bulletin* in circulation. In 1992, Gannett jumped ship, buying the *Advertiser* and selling the *Star-Bulletin* to Liberty Newspapers. Increasingly, it looked like the *Star-Bulletin* had been set out on a floe to die. In September 1999, when Liberty announced it was closing the paper, the community erupted in protest. Everyone understood the value of a two-newspaper town, with independent and competing voices. Such towns now were rare across America. Liberty backed down, and in 2001 sold the *Star-Bulletin* to a Canadian publisher, David Black, who also bought *MidWeek*. The daily flourished under Black Press, which in June 2010 bought the *Advertiser* and merged the two. So we lost our two-newspaper town. But at least we still had a newspaper, an industry struggling in the age of online information and advertising.

Twitter, once an engine of gossip or celebrity fanfare, had become a political tool. On December 14, 2010, McCain turned to Twitter to mock a $300,000 appropriation to the Polynesian Voyaging Society. He called it the number one worst pork barrel project in a $1.1 trillion federal spending measure. McCain and I agree on a lot of things, but this was not one of them. The voyaging society and its double-hulled canoe *Hōkūleʻa* were national treasures, linking ancient ways with a future that must embrace sustainability.

Inouye, through his press secretary, Peter Boylan, fired back a broadside.

"Rather than learn anything about the *Hōkūleʻa*, how the Pacific was populated by Polynesians sailing with nothing more than the stars, wind, sun, moon and currents as their guide, Senator McCain wants to vilify the Polynesian Voyaging Society as emblematic of wasteful government spending," he said.

Asked for a response, Nainoa Thompson, head of the society, said the senator should learn about voyaging firsthand.

"My comment to Senator McCain—just come sail," he said.

Personal computers and the internet have profoundly changed how we work. With that in mind, I introduced the Telework Enhancement Act of 2010. My cosponsors were Mary Landrieu and Republican George Voinovich of Ohio, a fellow member of the Federal Workforce Subcommittee, part of the Committee on Homeland Security and

Government Affairs. The bill was aimed at allowing more federal workers to "telecommute," that is, work on their computers at home. That would reduce roadway traffic and the need for office space. It would also allow the government to keep running during storms and other emergencies. Thousands of federal workers, for example, worked from home during the blizzard of February 5–6, when twenty inches of snow fell on Washington. Congressman John Sarbanes of Maryland—a state home to many federal workers—sponsored a companion bill in the House.

Lieberman ushered it through the Homeland Security Committee on May 3, 2010, and it cleared the Senate by voice vote later that month. Eventually, it was folded into Sarbanes' bill, which passed the House 290–131 on July 14. Hirono and Djou voted aye. Only one Democrat, David Wu of Oregon, voted no. In a bit of legislative ping-pong, the bill came back to the Senate, where it passed with an amendment, then went back to the House, which approved it 254–152 in November. Obama signed it December 9.

"This new law will reduce traffic and pollution by allowing more federal employees to stay off the road and complete their duties from home via telework," I said in a statement. "It will save the government money on office space and help recruit and retain top-notch employees that keep our country running strong. Senator Voinovich and I have worked together for years to give the federal government the tools it needs to keep functioning during emergencies, and to make it an employer of choice. We have one more accomplishment to add to our list."

On February 16, after having been nominated by Inouye and seconded by Republican John Barrasso of Wyoming, I took over as chairman of the Committee on Indian Affairs. Inouye expressed confidence that I would "focus on providing for indigenous people in rural communities all across America, and to help provide the same kind of recognition for Native Hawaiians already enjoyed by more than 500 indigenous groups." As part of the move, I gave up the chairmanship of veterans affairs, which was taken over by Patty Murray of Washington State. But I remained on that committee as a senior member.

I was looking forward to my new role. Native communities across the nation were facing unique challenges, including disparities in economic development, health care, public safety, education and energy development.

One of my first decisions was to bring aboard Loretta Tuell as committee staff director and chief counsel. Loretta had worked closely with me on a number of issues related to Indians, Alaska Natives and Native Hawaiians. She grew up on the Nez Perce reservation in northern Idaho, and graduated from Washington State and UCLA law school. She served as counsel to the committee when Inouye was chairman, and was a former partner at Anderson Tuell LLP, an American Indian-owned law firm in Washington, D.C. Loretta had practiced federal Indian law, represented American Indian tribal governments, and had experience in dealing with national legal and policy issues in Indian Country. She also had attended the Senior Executive Program at the John F. Kennedy School of Government at Harvard and served on the adjunct faculty at American University in Washington.

My new chairmanship was not the only change in the air. Back home over the holidays, I had come to the stark realization that my grandchildren were growing up without me. And without Millie. For some of the kids, I'm embarrassed to say, I couldn't recall their names! Largely for that reason—and partly due to my age—I decided that another six-year term simply was not in the cards. At the end of another term, in 2019, I would be ninety-four. This was a tough decision, because I felt I was poised to do some important work at the helm of Indian affairs. I also knew that in some quarters the move would be seen as politically charged, a way to let a younger candidate—maybe Hirono, Hanabusa or Case—take on Lingle. But that wasn't my motivation. I wasn't giving up. Just giving...in another direction.

I made the announcement well in advance, so that my staff would have plenty of time to seek other opportunities. The faces in the room were somber as I broke the news. Not every eye was dry, and I received more than a few hugs.

On Wednesday night, March 2, I made the formal announcement.

"After months of thinking about my political future, I am

announcing today that I have decided not to run for reelection in 2012," I said. "As many of you can imagine, it was a very difficult decision for me. However, I feel that the end of this Congress is the right time for me to step aside."

It was already clear that the next Congress would look much different than this one. I was the seventh senator so far to announce retirement. The others included three Democrats: Jim Webb of Virginia, Jeff Bingaman of New Mexico and Kent Conrad of North Dakota; Lieberman; and Republicans Kay Bailey Hutchison of Texas and Arizona's Kyl. I would miss our camaraderie.

Inouye released this statement: "I want to thank Senator Akaka for his service to Hawai'i and the nation. For nearly four decades, first in the House of Representatives and then in the Senate, Senator Akaka has fought hard for the people of Hawai'i. He is a tireless advocate for Hawai'i's residents and a true ambassador of aloha. He has been a willing and loyal partner and we have worked very well together over these many years. We have much more to do and I look forward to working with him over the next two years. Kaniela, thank you for your friendship and unwavering support. Irene and I wish you and Millie all the best in your future endeavors."

Despite the kind words from Inouye and others, I felt that my world had been upended. But sometimes events have a way of restoring your perspective. Days later, on March 11, a massive earthquake struck just off the coast of Tohoku, on the east side of Honshu, Japan. At magnitude 9.0, this was the most powerful quake ever to have hit that nation and the fourth largest quake anywhere at least since 1900. The devastation was vast and immediate, with the most famous and most alarming casualty being the Fukushima Daichi nuclear power plant. The quake hit at 2:45 p.m., Japan time, which was 12:45 a.m. in Washington, so we didn't see the astounding videos of the tsunami waves until the morning. In some spots, the walls of water washed six miles inland. It took years to tally the deaths, which the National Police Agency ultimately set at 18,000, with another 2,500 missing and presumed dead. That made it the deadliest tsunami since the magnitude 9.1 Sumatra earthquake and tsunami that caused nearly

230,000 deaths and $10 billion in damage in December 2004. More than 220,000 people were displaced.

Tsunami warnings went out all across the Pacific. In Hawai'i, where the first waves were expected to arrive just after 3 a.m., civil defense evacuated coastal inundation zones and the state opened a series of emergency shelters. The Pacific Tsunami Warning Center issued a warning for Hawai'i about 9:30 p.m. "Urgent action should be taken to protect lives and property," the center said. When the waves arrived—most in the two- to three-foot range, they battered boats in Ke'ehi Lagoon and washed one house into the middle of Kealakekua Bay. All you could see was the roof.

Now that's a world upended. ❖

CHAPTER

92

Jami Rozell, a Cherokee woman living in Tahlequah, Oklahoma, was brutally raped in 2003. At the local hospital, she underwent a sexual assault forensic examination. Photographs were taken of her injuries, and her clothes were confiscated as evidence. But because the culprit was a non-Indian, she could not take the case to tribal court. After five months, she went instead to the district attorney and testified at a preliminary hearing.

"It was the hardest thing I've ever done, get up there in front of my family with all these men I've grown up with all my life," she later told the *New York Times*.

But that's when she learned that her rape kit had been tossed out during a routine cleanup of the evidence room. That ended any chance of prosecution. The police later claimed they had permission to throw out the kit when the woman at first declined to press charges.

On October 9, 2003, in Shawnee, Oklahoma, another American Indian woman, forty-nine, accepted a ride home from two men she met at a bar. On the way home, they took her to a wooded area and raped and assaulted her. They then threw her off a highway bridge into a river. She testified at trial that she grabbed a log and floated down the river to shallow water, then hid until morning and sought help at a nearby house. But the jury was unable to reach a verdict against the primary defendant, Travis Foote, thirty-one. The reason: the woman had been drinking. After the judge declared a mistrial, one woman remarked: "She was just another drunk Indian."

The second trial in March 2005 resulted in a sixty-year sentence for Foote, who had previously raped at least four other women, and a ten-year sentence for the second defendant, Jeffrey Mellencamp.

In October 2005, an Alaska Native named Angelo Sugar went berserk in the village of Nunam Iqua, on the Yukon River near the Bering Sea. He beat his wife with a shotgun and hit a friend in the head with another firearm. He then barricaded himself in the house with four children. The remote village had no law enforcement presence. So the neighbors called the state troopers in the nearest town, Bethel, 150 miles away. The troopers had to charter a plane to get there, a process that took four hours. By the time they arrived, the man had abused a thirteen-year-old girl with other children watching. The next September, he was convicted and sentenced to eighteen years in prison.

These and other chilling incidents were chronicled in a scathing 2007 report by *Amnesty International*, "Maze of Injustice," that examined incidents in Oklahoma, Alaska and the Dakotas. Justice Department figures showed that more than one in three American Indian and Alaska Native women will be raped in their lifetime, almost double the national average of eighteen percent. In eighty-six percent of the cases, the report said, the perpetrators are non-Indian men. These sobering figures had been known for years, but jurisdictional disputes and other flaws in the law have kept the problem intractable.

When taking over the Indian Affairs Committee, I knew that I had only two years before I would retire, but as chairman I wanted to take every opportunity to advance the principles of self-determination and to strengthen the United States' trust responsibility to its first peoples. Just over 4 million American Indian and Alaska Native people make up 550 tribes scattered over reservations or other lands throughout the country—an incredibly complex and diverse system beset by many problems.

In 2009, Attorney General Holder had conducted a nationwide

"listening tour" involving tribal leaders. In part as a result of his recommendations, Congress in July 2010 passed the Tribal Law and Order Act, which increased the clout of tribal courts across the nation, allowing for jail sentences of three years, up from one. That was a major step toward improving justice in Indian Country. It was also aimed at increasing the accountability of federal prosecutors and improving training and coordination between law enforcement agencies, the judiciary and service providers. But that law alone was not enough to address the problem of abuse of native women.

So on July 14, 2011, I convened a hearing, "Native Women: Protecting, Shielding and Safeguarding our Sisters, Mothers and Daughters." Loretta, my staff director, helped me line up some excellent testimony. And the committee itself had senators with a keen interest in Indian issues. They included my vice chairman Barrasso of Wyoming, Inouye, McCain, Murkowski, Kent Conrad and John Hoeven of North Dakota, Tim Johnson of South Dakota, Maria Cantwell of Washington, Tom Udall of New Mexico and Al Franken of Minnesota.

In opening the hearing, I warned that the topics would be difficult but, unfortunately, affect native women every day in our country.

"For native peoples, women are sacred," I said. "They bring life and nurture us. They *mālama*, in Hawaiian, they care for our peoples, and we must mālama them.

"Many native peoples mark the important stages of a woman's life with ceremonies and community celebration. Yet, many of the native women find themselves in unbearable situations that threaten their security, stability and even their lives. Two in five native women will suffer domestic violence and one in three native women will be sexually assaulted in their lifetime. These statistics, these realities are unacceptable and we must act to change this."

Murkowski added that the problem was particularly acute in Alaska.

"I wish that I could tell you that we are making some progress, but I meet with far too many who tell me that there is still so much that is kept in the shadows, still so much that continues, and as it continues we know the destruction that it causes not only to the victim, but to the families, to those in the communities," she said. "Something that I never thought would be a situation in my state is that of a growing level of sex trafficking amongst our young native women. I am told that they are considered 'versatile' because they can be trafficked either as Asian or Hawaiian on the internet, and we have had some really frightening instances of young women coming into town, coming in from the villages, basically being picked up off the street and lost, gone forever into these sex trafficking rings, and the families never knowing where they are or if they will ever come back."

Our first witness, Tom Perrelli, associate attorney general, agreed that violence against native women had reached epidemic proportions.

"Not simply violence," he said. "We see in some communities murder rates of native women at ten times the national average. Tribal leaders, police officers, prosecutors tell us of an all-too familiar pattern of escalating violence that goes unaddressed, one beating after another, each one more severe than the last, ultimately leading to death or severe physical injury. Something must be done to end this cycle of violence. For a host of reasons, the current legal structure for prosecuting domestic violence in tribal communities is not well suited to combating this pattern of escalating violence. Federal resources are stretched thin and are often distant from where the violence occurs, and tribal governments, police, prosecutors and courts, which need to be an essential part of the solution, often lack authority to address many of the crimes."

He said there were three major legal gaps that Congress could address.

First, the patchwork of federal, state and tribal criminal jurisdiction in Indian Country had made it difficult for law enforcement and prosecutors to adequately address domestic violence—especially misdemeanor domestic violence, such as simple assaults and criminal violations of protection orders. New federal legislation could recognize certain tribes' power to exercise concurrent criminal jurisdiction over domestic violence cases, regardless of whether the defendant is Indian or non-Indian.

Second, at least one federal court had ruled that tribes lack civil jurisdiction to issue and enforce protection orders against non-Indians who reside on tribal lands. That ruling undermines the ability of tribal courts to protect victims. Accordingly, new federal legislation could confirm the intent of Congress in enacting the Violence Against Women Act of 2000 by clarifying that tribal courts have full civil jurisdiction to issue and enforce certain protection orders involving any persons, Indian or non-Indian.

Third, federal prosecutors lack the necessary tools to combat domestic violence in Indian Country. New federal legislation could provide a one-year offense for assaulting a person by striking, beating or wounding; a five-year offense for assaulting a spouse, intimate partner or dating partner, resulting in substantial bodily injury; and a ten-year offense for assaulting a spouse, intimate partner or dating partner by strangling, suffocating or attempting to strangle or suffocate.

Those were excellent suggestions.

Perhaps the most compelling testimony came from Sarah Deer, a member of the Muskogee Creek Nation and an assistant professor at the Mitchell College of Law in Saint Paul, Minnesota. Deer had devoted her career to ending violence against native women and had contributed extensively to the "Maze of Injustice" report. She had been working on a study, not yet published, with the Minnesota Indian Women's Sexual Assault Coalition on prostitution in Indian Country.

"Of the 105 women interviewed in the study, their ages ranged from eighteen to sixty, with an average of thirty-five," she said. "Two-thirds of the women had been used for sex by up to 300 men, with a third of the women reporting that they had been used for sex by between 400 and 1,000 men. The women also reported that seventy percent of the women that they knew in prostitution had been lured, tricked and trafficked into it, and ninety-five percent said they wanted to escape prostitution.

"As shocking as these statistics are, even more horrifying is that this information is but a glimpse into the unknown larger picture of which little research and data collection has been done, and we look forward to sharing the final report with the committee. In closing, I would like to impress upon you the importance of prioritizing native women's health and safety for the long term, and it will take many, many years, and perhaps even decades, to reverse the alarming trends that have only recently been documented, but have been ongoing for hundreds of years. We need to know that the federal government will stand with us for the foreseeable future, until such time that native women are restored to their traditional status of honor within tribal communities."

✷ ✷ ✷

On October 31, 2011, I introduced the Stand Against Violence and Empower Native Women Act, or SAVE Native Women Act for short. This amended the Omnibus Crime Control and Safe Streets Act of 1968 to include sex trafficking as a target of the federal grants to Indian tribal governments to combat violent crime against Indian women. The bill also amended the Violence Against Women Act of 2005 to increase federal cabinet-level consultations with Indian tribes to improve the safety of aboriginal women, including Alaska Natives and Native Hawaiians. I picked up fourteen cosponsors, including Inouye, Franken, Udall, Conrad, Murkowski and Begich of Alaska, Johnson of South Dakota, Harry Reid, Max Baucus and Bernie Sanders. In November, we held a hearing on the bill, with many of the same witnesses we had earlier. The bill itself went no farther than the Indian Affairs Committee, which passed it in December 2012—one of my last contributions in Congress. But the language became Title IX of the Violence Against Women Reauthorization Act. That was introduced by Pat Leahy of Vermont on January 22, 2013, and attracted sixty-one cosponsors. It cleared both chambers very briskly and Obama signed it on March 7. During the signing ceremony, he said, "Tribal governments have an inherent right to protect their people, and all women deserve to live free from fear. And that is what today is all about." ❖

CHAPTER

93

The space shuttle program, an institution for a generation, a source both of national pride and anguish, was winding down. On February 24, 2011, *Discovery* launched for the last time, carrying a module to the International Space Station and returning to Earth on March 9. Over its twenty-seven-year career, *Discovery* had spent a full year in orbit. On May 16, *Endeavour* made its swan song, landing June 1 after nineteen years in service. And on July 8, *Atlantis* took off for the final time, returning July 21 after thirty years of manned spaceflight. To me, it seemed like only yesterday that the shuttle program began, in 1981, with the launch of *Columbia*, back when Newt Gingrich and I were active with the House Space Caucus.

With our fleet retired, of course, we now had to rely largely on the Russians to resupply the space station. This was accomplished with the unmanned Progress M-series cargo ferry, which had been flying to the space station for more than ten years. On June 19, a Progress craft lifted off from Baikonur Cosmodrome in Kazakhstan via Soyuz rocket. Four days later, it successfully docked with the Zvezda service module on the space station, delivering 926 pounds of water, 110 pounds of oxygen, 2,800 pounds of food and equipment and 2,050 pounds of propellant. But things would not always go so smoothly. On August 24, another Progress vehicle launched for the station but less than six minutes into the flight, after the third stage ignited, the engine inexplicably shut down. The craft crashed in Siberia between Kazakhstan and Mongolia. Nothing irreplaceable was lost, only about three tons of food, fuel and supplies. The space station, with six aboard, had plenty of food, water and air—enough, at least, to last until March 2012, when a European cargo flight was due. Still, we had come to count on the Soyuz rockets for getting astronauts on and off the station. So this presented an unpleasant new wrinkle.

In the end, private industry came to the rescue. This was very rewarding for me as a longtime advocate of space commerce. This industry had expanded on several fronts since Reagan signed my Commercial Space Launch Act of 1984. GPS navigation had become an intricate part of our everyday lives, helping us drive to a certain street address or find the nearest notary. In 2001—a date that Arthur C. Clarke would have celebrated—Dennis Tito became the first space tourist, riding to the space station aboard a Soyuz. In June 2004, *SpaceShipOne*, developed by Scaled Composites, completed the first privately funded and operated manned spaceflight. After its launch from a mothership named *White Knight*, pilot Mike Melvill guided *SpaceShipOne* to an altitude of sixty-two miles before landing in Mojave, California. That and two later flights earned the team the $10 million Ansari X Prize for the first privately funded spaceflights. Based in Hawthorne, California, the Space Exploration Technologies Corp., or SpaceX for short, was founded in 2002 with the goal of cutting space transportation costs and getting humans to Mars. In 2008, SpaceX's Falcon 1 was the first private, liquid-fueled craft to reach orbit. The company's Dragon spacecraft in December 2010 became the first commercially built and operated craft to be recovered from orbit. In May 2012, a variant of the Dragon became the first commercial craft to dock with the space station, and the company began regular supply runs under contract with NASA in October 2012.

Happily, NASA kept active beyond Earth orbit as well. On March 18, 2011, the *Messenger* spacecraft became the first to orbit Mercury. On July 24, the *Dawn* spacecraft, launched in 2007, made a close approach to the asteroid Vesta, which it would orbit for fourteen months. Then it would take off for another asteroid, Ceres, ultimately becoming the first spacecraft to orbit two non-Earth bodies. On August 5, NASA launched the *Juno* probe to Jupiter, due to arrive in August 2016. That same day, NASA announced that its *Mars Reconnaissance Orbiter* had obtained images suggesting liquid water exists on Mars during the summer. The discovery of life on other planets—even microbial life—would be truly profound in terms of our thinking about our place in the universe. So great is our pace and breadth of exploration, it could easily happen for some of us alive today.

❋ ❋ ❋

In April 2011, in a sense, I came full circle with my visit to my old school, Kawananakoa Intermediate, to promote financial literacy. It felt great to be back in a classroom with youngsters.

"It all started here," I told the students in Jacob Johnson's math class, each wearing a black and red shirt with the school logo. "It was the beginning of my political career."

I told them about my acquaintanceship with Princess Kawānanakoa and how she had bought my May Day clothes.

I told them how my third grade teacher at Pauoa Elementary, Mrs. Dung, had told us to save our small change and how I had saved up for a yo-yo.

"It taught me how saving for things is important, and will be all your life," I said. "That carried me through life, and here I am in Congress."

I warned them about interest rates when you borrow money or use credit cards. I figured an iPod was a more meaningful example than a yo-yo for this generation. In 2011, the least expensive video-playing iPod touch was the 8 GB model with the new iOS 5 (iMessage, iCloud, Notifications and an improved Game Center). It retailed for $199. If you charged that at eighteen percent interest and paid only the $35 minimum per month, it would take six months to pay off and cost an additional $10.56. Imagine how much you'd pay if you bought a car that way! And people do. Every day.

If Congress had become financially literate years ago, I told the class, we would not have suffered the Great Recession of 2008.

In early May, we got the news that a team of Navy SEALs had killed Osama bin Laden, the mastermind of the 9/11 attack. On May 2, I issued this response: "Osama bin Laden, who orchestrated the worst attack on U.S. soil since Pearl Harbor, is dead. As a senior member of the Senate Armed Services and Homeland Security Committees who has closely examined the terrorist threat in the decade since 9/11, I commend the tenacity of the intelligence and military personnel that led to this victory. I applaud President Obama for his unwavering commitment to bring bin Laden to justice. I am pleased to see the nation unite around this significant milestone. However, we must not lose sight of the many national security challenges that still confront us. Our dedicated service members remain on the front lines in Afghanistan, and al-Qaeda continues operations across the globe. We must remain vigilant and determined in our efforts to protect the American people."

This was followed shortly by the news that the architect of the 1998 bombings of our embassies in Kenya and Tanzania, Fazul Abdullah Mohammed, died in a shootout at a roadway checkpoint in Somalia. Sometimes the wheels of justice turn slowly. Don't get me wrong: I oppose capital punishment. I would rather have had these men captured and convicted. But having them dead was better than having them loose.

The wars in Afghanistan and Iraq dragged on, of course, longer than anyone expected, but at least Iraq was winding down. By summer we had a new defense secretary to manage these conflicts. Leon Panetta, former CIA director, White House chief of staff and my 1977 U.S. House classmate, succeeded Robert Gates in July. The Senate had confirmed him 100–0. To replace him at CIA, Obama had named General David Petraeus, former commander of U.S. forces in Afghanistan. Obama was expected shortly to announce a draw down in Afghanistan, but the country remained dangerous. On August 6, the Taliban shot down a NATO helicopter in Wardak Province, killing thirty-eight troops, including twenty members of SEAL Team 6, which had carried out the bin Laden operation. This was the deadliest day for American forces since the war began in 2001.

On March 20, 2011, for the last time, I again introduced the Native Hawaiian Reorganization Act. My cosponsors were Inouye, and Murkowski and Begich of Alaska. On April 7, the Indian Affairs Committee approved it, which won immediate acclaim from many quarters.

"I fully support the Native Hawaiian Government Reorganization Act, and would like to laud the leadership and efforts of Chairman Akaka, who remains committed to seeing this historic piece of legislation through to passage," Inouye said. "This measure begins a process of establishing a government to government relationship between the U.S. and the native people of Hawaiʻi. We have held public hearings, made revisions and debated this issue for more than a decade. There is strong support for this bill—from the White House, Washington Place, native country and from the people of Hawaiʻi. I urge my colleagues in the Senate to bring this bill to the floor and vote in favor of it. Federal recognition for the Native Hawaiian people is long overdue."

Also issuing statements of support were Abercrombie; Collette Machado, chairwoman of the Office of Hawaiian Affairs; and Alapaki Nahale-a, director of the Hawaiʻi Department of Hawaiian Home Lands; Jefferson Keel, president of the National Congress of American Indians; Julie Kitka, president of the Alaska Federation of Natives; and Tex Hall, chairman of the Mandan, Hidatsa and Arikara Tribe.

Nahale-a said, "With the Native Hawaiian Government Reorganization Act of 2011 heading to the full United States Senate for consideration, Native Hawaiians should feel heartened that self-determination is on the horizon. The Hawaiian Homes Commission continues to support Senator Akaka's efforts and we congratulate and extend a heartfelt mahalo to him for his tenacity in seeking passage of this important measure for the Hawaiian people."

But the bill then entered a long legislative limbo. In the Senate, under the rules, any member can put a "hold" on a bill. With a hold in place, I needed sixty votes—not just a majority—to move it to the floor. And I could never get the sixty. If I had gotten it to the floor, I could have passed it. And the opponents of the bill knew that. So they held it, several of them in turn. I made it my mission to find out who had the hold on the bill and go talk. I felt that if they really understood Hawaiian history, they would agree to passage. But the Republican floor leaders would never tell me who had placed the hold. Often, by the time I finally found out who it was, that senator had passed it on to someone else, like a schoolyard game of keep away. That way, they could avoid having a discussion on the merits. So then I had to go look for the next person. And as soon as I found out who it was they would switch again. This went on for more than a year. With another four Republicans on my side, I could have brought the bill to the floor and passed it. But four would prove to be an elusive number.

A second bill, Senate 676, which I introduced in May, addressed an unfortunate 2009 high court ruling involving the Narragansett Tribe, based in Rhode Island. After a long battle, the Narragansett won federal recognition in 1983. In 1991, they bought thirty-one acres for housing for elderly tribe members, then asked the federal Bureau of Indian Affairs to take over that land in trust. The bureau agreed, under the terms of the 1934 Indian Reorganization Act. In response, Rhode Island governor Donald Carcieri sued the Interior Department, naming Secretary Ken Salazar as defendant. The U.S. district court, then a three-judge appellate panel, and then the full First Circuit Court of Appeals all ruled in favor of the tribe and the bureau. But then the Supreme Court, in a decision crafted by Clarence Thomas, voted 6–3 to overturn the lower court decisions, in 1991.

My measure meant to remedy that.

"This bill," I said, "will allow tribes to meet the economic and basic needs of their members for housing, elder centers, schools and tribal businesses. S. 676 ensures that all tribes are treated equally and have the same abilities to function as governments and meet the needs of their people. I want to be clear that this legislation does not grant any new authorities to the secretary. It merely reaffirms the intent of the Indian Reorganization Act as it has been carried out for the past seventy-five years."

Again, Inouye and Salazar weighed in favorably, but I will quote Larry Echo Hawk, assistant secretary of the Interior for Indian Affairs. "I am pleased with the Senate Indian Affairs Committee's fair and just decision to fix this crucial act so that American Indian and Alaska Natives can advance economic development through the restoration of their homelands. This issue has been an ongoing challenge and brought into question our authority to take land into trust as part of the Department of the Interior's trust responsibilities."

Unfortunately, the Carcieri remedy, as this bill became known, never gained any traction.

I had better luck with two other pieces of legislation, both important in their way. On July 18, I introduced a bill that fine-tuned the court system in the District of Columbia. For one, it authorized the top judge to delay court deadlines in the event of emergencies like the blizzard of 2010. Although I had no cosponsors, this met with no opposition and Obama signed it into law on December 28, 2012. At the same session, Obama signed a measure that clarified some of the provisions of the Hatch Act, the law that prohibits federal employees from participating in most political activity.

❋ ❋ ❋

On a bright and balmy Tuesday in August, the first signs of distress came from the animals at the Smithsonian National Zoological Park off Connecticut Avenue. In the Ape House, the primates abruptly left their afternoon meal and climbed to the top of their treelike jungle gym. The lemurs shrieked. The flamingos grouped tightly together. The duck-like hooded mergansers all took to the water. They all felt it coming.

At 1:51 p.m. on August 23, a section of the Virginia Piedmont groaned under low-level but relentless tectonic stress. The resulting magnitude 5.8 quake—modest by Pacific Basin standards—shook the eastern third of the United States, rattling people from Florida to Canada. The epicenter was between Richmond and Charlottesville, about eighty miles southwest of Washington and not far from Spotsylvania, an 1864 battleground. The Virginia Seismic Zone, as it's known, has its origins in the process that formed the Appalachians eons ago, and is extremely inactive, as is the entire East Coast, which hadn't felt a jolt like this since 1944.

Millie and I were in Hawai'i for the August recess, but it was all over the news.

I called the office to make sure everyone was all right. No answer. The Capitol and offices had been evacuated, as had the White House, Pentagon, the Justice Department and other federal buildings.

I finally reached Jon Yoshimura, who told me everyone was fine, if unnerved. The staff initially feared the shaking was from a bomb, but he said it was soon obvious that it was not. The tremors lasted less than a minute, but still longer than you would feel from an explosion. The staff filed out to Upper Senate Park, the staging area for our emergency drills, which we conducted every month or two. The park is across Constitution Avenue from the Capitol and just west of the Russell Senate Office Building, so it was a short walk. After thirty or forty-five minutes, the Capitol Police told everyone that it was going to be a long time before they got back in to the offices. The integrity of the structures had to be assessed. So my staff went home. Jon took a couple of coworkers with him because he lived nearby, at 5th and Massachusetts. They had beers and pupus and from the balcony watched the evening commute turn into gridlock due to the many dead traffic lights. The largest aftershock weighed in at 4.5.

The quake cracked the top of the Washington Monument, which was closed until May 2014 for $15 million in repairs. Pieces of masonry fell off the National Cathedral. In all, the damage along the Eastern Seaboard topped $200 million. Incredibly, no one was seriously hurt.

When my staff returned to the office the next day, every picture hung crooked. ❊

CHAPTER

94

Back home, tremors of a different sort shook the political landscape in large part due to my decision to retire. On August 24, Hanabusa announced that she would not be running for the Senate but instead would run for reelection to her First District House seat. I think there was some legitimate concern that, should she give up the seat, it might fall back into the hands of Republican Charles Djou.

"The challenges that confront our nation are many," began her official statement on the matter, "and the risks to Hawai'i are great. At this moment, stability in Hawai'i's congressional representation is critical. I believe that a change in both Hawai'i seats in the U.S. House of Representatives, along with a seat in the U.S. Senate, could seriously undermine our efforts to preserve such cherished programs as the East-West Center and continue vital funding for the military in Hawai'i, while threatening other federal support that has helped keep our economy moving in these difficult times. I hope that my continued service in Congress will support that stability, and that the relationships I have developed will assist our state and our residents."

Ed Case had expressed interest in my Senate seat, of course, but most people gave the inside track to Hirono, who had the support of the Democratic Party establishment. A Lingle-Hirono matchup would echo the governor's race in 2002, which Lingle had won comfortably, 51.6–47. But that was back when a Republican occupied the Oval Office. Now it was a Democrat—born in Hawai'i—who had long coattails.

Then there was the race to fill Hirono's Second District House seat. That had attracted two of my former aides, Tulsi Gabbard and Esther Kia'aina, and former mayor Mufi Hannemann, who had the most experience and name recognition.

On the national level, the field as usual formed early. Gingrich these days had his eyes not on the skies but the White House. Also in the running on the GOP side were former Massachusetts governor Mitt Romney, former Minnesota governor Tim Pawlenty, Minnesota congresswomen Michelle Bachman, former Pennsylvania governor Rick Santorum, former Texas congressman Ron Paul and Texas governor Rick Perry. Pawlenty dropped out in August 2011—more than a year before the election—after the first straw poll, which Bachman won. As summer turned into fall, it became clear that Romney was the likely nominee. But elements of the GOP found him too liberal, so a number of anti-Romney candidates emerged, including Sarah Palin, New Jersey governor Chris Christie and businessman and reality TV star Donald Trump.

On the Democratic side, Obama and Biden had a clean shot, no competition.

※ ※ ※

A number of events that fall stand out.

On September 11, we marked the tenth anniversary of the terrorist attacks. My thoughts were with Pentagon police officer Ike Hoʻopiʻi when I said, "We honor the countless acts of heroism that day—the selflessness and courage of the first responders who ran into burning buildings and through unstable passageways, throughout the day and night, to save lives. The 9/11 heroes who simply did what needed to be done. Some risked their lives to help coworkers to safety. Others rescued complete strangers. If there is a positive to be taken out of this tragedy, it is the spirit of unity and brotherhood seen in our nation's response to the attacks. Responders from every state, including Hawaiʻi, came together to aid their fellow Americans at their time of need. It was that same spirit we demonstrated nearly seventy years ago on December 7, 1941, and the same our forefathers used to found this country over two centuries ago.

"Our country is a different place than it was ten years ago. It is a place more mindful of the threats around us, but it is a safer place because Americans have been willing to work together. As we mark this solemn anniversary, let us remember what makes this country great, that when we are united there is no challenge we can't conquer, and no problem we can't solve. May God bless America."

Later that month, Obama repealed the "Don't Ask, Don't Tell" policy, allowing gays to serve openly in the military. I applauded that landmark decision.

"Today is a historic day for our military and for our nation," I said. "The 'Don't Ask, Don't Tell' policy, which prevented brave members of our armed services from openly expressing their true identity, is finished. Never again will sexual orientation prevent service in our military. The well-being of our troops is incredibly important to me and I was pleased to see the results of a Pentagon study last year showing that a majority of our troops are prepared to serve with openly gay members. This repeal is a major step toward ensuring equal rights for all Americans. Our nation and our military will be stronger because of it."

On October 31, the United Nations proclaimed, the world population had officially reached 7 billion. That's a scary Halloween. It had taken only twelve years to rise from 6 billion. This took me back to my days with the House Select Committee on Population. Back then we were worried about 5 billion. How much more can planet Earth take? I guess our future generations will find out.

On December 15, the United States formally declared an end to the Iraq War, with the last of our troops withdrawn. This was in accordance with an agreement that Bush had signed with the Iraqis in 2008. Actual combat operations—Operation Iraqi Freedom—had ended in August 2010, but about 50,000 troops remained in country as part of a transitional force under Operation New Dawn. Now New Dawn was done. But we left behind a heavily fortified embassy in Baghdad with about 17,000 personnel, consulates in three other cities and more than 4,000 defense contractors. Within a few short years, a new menace, the Islamic State, would emerge, requiring the United States once again to intervene. But for now the news was good.

"I am so pleased our combat troops will be home from Iraq in time for the holidays," I said on December 15. "Our service members and military leaders worked diligently for years to help the Iraqi government take responsibility for its own security, and it is now up to Iraqi people to succeed as an independent nation. I offer my warmest aloha and mahalo to all of those who served and their families for their commitment and sacrifice. Now that the war is over we must continue to honor our sacred obligation to our veterans and their families and ensure they receive the care and benefits they earned, need and deserve. Our nation will never forget those who made the ultimate sacrifice in service to their country."

In another seismic shift, we got word in late December of the death of longtime Korean dictator Kim Jong-il. He was about sixty-nine, his precise age not certain. Initial reports said he died of a heart attack on a train outside Pyongyang. At least the "outside Pyongyang" part proved true. A South Korean newspaper, *Chosun Ilbo*, later reported that he died during a "fit of rage" over construction problems at a hydroelectric dam in a province along the Chinese border. The project was viewed as bedrock to North Korea's economic future, and Kim was by all accounts incensed at the serial snafus.

State media announced that Kim's younger son, Kim Jong-un, then thought to be about twenty-eight, would succeed him. Nobody knew much about the young Kim, except that he had gone to school for a time in Switzerland and liked American movies and basketball. What this foretold about the North's nuclear and missile programs was anyone's guess. North Korea had already conducted two underground tests, in 2006 and 2009. More would come.

For me, it was like the Japanese soldiers in caves who refused to surrender on Saipan and other islands after the war. They didn't know the war was over. We couldn't communicate with them. We couldn't assess their firepower. Our choices were: attack, or, assuming they had rations, wait. Obama and Secretary Clinton chose to wait with the North Koreans. But the policy of "Strategic Patience" didn't seem to be working. It would soon become our most intractable problem, with tremendous stakes.

On a lighter note, I want to thank *Star-Advertiser* columnist Dave Shapiro for his year-end "Flashback" column. Dave observed that Inouye and I had celebrated our eighty-seventh birthdays during the same week in September. "The candles on the cake set off fire alarms in the U.S. Capitol that hadn't sounded since the War of 1812," he said. Millie and I got a very warm chuckle out of that. I look forward to telling Shapiro about my efforts, with Dolley Madison, to save Washington's portrait from the advancing Redcoats.

✳ ✳ ✳

In his third State of the Union address on January 24, Obama set the tone for the final year of his first term. This year's speech was special to me. It was my last as a member of Congress. Over my thirty-six-year career, I had attended speeches from six different presidents. With Vice President Joe Biden and House Speaker John Boehner seated behind him, the president spoke with his typical eloquence and energy.

"Mr. Speaker, Mr. Vice President, members of Congress, distinguished guests and fellow Americans: Last month, I went to Andrews Air Force Base and welcomed home some of our last troops to serve in Iraq. Together, we offered a final, proud salute to the colors under which more than a million of our fellow citizens fought—and several thousand gave their lives. We gather tonight knowing that this generation of heroes has made the United States safer and more respected around the world."

That drew applause.

"For the first time in nine years, there are no Americans fighting in Iraq."

More applause.

"For the first time in two decades, Osama bin Laden is not a threat to this country. Most of al-Qaeda's top lieutenants have been defeated. The Taliban's momentum has been broken, and some troops in Afghanistan have begun to come home. These achievements are a testament to the courage, selflessness and teamwork of America's armed forces. At a time when too many of our institutions have let us down, they exceed all expectations."

In a wide-ranging speech, Obama went on to talk about the economy, taxes, manufacturing and keeping the American dream alive—the fundamental principle that hard work brings rewards in terms of raising a family, owning a home, sending your kids to college and affording retirement. He supported extended tax breaks to help small businesses, grants to medicinal and technological research projects and tapping America's natural gas reserves—enough to last America 100 years.

He ended with a tribute to the American flag.

"Each time I look at that flag, I'm reminded that our destiny is stitched together like those fifty stars and those thirteen stripes," he said. "No one built this country on their own. This nation is great because we built it together. This nation is great because we worked as a team. This nation is great because we get each other's backs. And if we hold fast to that truth, in this moment of trial, there is no challenge too great; no mission too hard."

I quickly added my endorsement of those sentiments.

"I am proud of the way our *keiki o ka ʻāina* president, Barack Obama, is making progress towards rebuilding the slowed economy he inherited and putting Americans back to work, although there is still much more to do. I agree with the president that we must defend the American dream by increasing fairness in the tax system and giving all Americans a chance to succeed... Some students spend years paying off loans, while millionaires and large corporations with tax shelters use loopholes to lower their tax rates. That's not right, and we must fix it."

I also backed Obama's call to make us a leader in clean, renewable energy; technology that reduces our need for imported oil, puts less pollution in the air we breathe and creates American jobs that cannot be outsourced. And I fervently agreed with the president's call for Congress to work together and find common ground. This had been one of the most partisan, dysfunctional Congresses of my career, but I remained hopeful that we could work together for the good of our country.

The presidential campaign, meanwhile, was in full swing. In the Iowa caucuses in early January, Santorum eked out a thin victory over Romney—by thirty-four votes. At that point, Bachman dropped out. Romney had won the New Hampshire primary on January 10, with Ron Paul second. In late January, Gingrich took South Carolina decisively, and Perry withdrew. Fairly quickly, the race boiled down to Romney, Santorum and Gingrich. On Super Tuesday, March 6, Romney won six states, Santorum three and Gingrich only his home state of Georgia. But Santorum dropped out on April 10, at which point Newt declared himself "the last conservative standing." But there was no catching Romney. Newt dropped out May 2.

On May 8, the Senate got a shock when six-term Senator Richard Lugar lost the Republican primary in Indiana to a little-known

Tea Party member, Richard Mourdock, 61–39. It was clear that the Senate next year would have quite a number of new faces.

Meanwhile, more and more states were legalizing gay marriage, although the nation remained sharply divided on the issue. In February, Washington State had joined the pack, becoming the seventh so far. On March 1, Maryland became the eighth. On May 8, however, North Carolina by voter referendum amended the state constitution to ban same-sex marriage. A day later, Obama became the first president to announce his support for gay marriage. In an interview on ABC-TV, he said, "I've just concluded that for me personally it is important for me to go ahead and affirm that I think same-sex couples should be able to get married." He admitted that his views on the issue had "evolved." That put him at odds with Romney. "My view is that marriage itself is a relationship between a man and a woman," he said at a campaign stop in Oklahoma. "That's my own preference, and I know other people have differing views. This is a very tender and sensitive topic." A Gallup Poll released May 8 showed the nation almost evenly split, with fifty percent of Americans in favor of legalizing same-sex unions and forty-eight percent opposed.

This rift had played out in Hawai'i, where in May 1993 the state supreme court ruled that the state could not ban gay marriages absent a "compelling reason." The Legislature responded by codifying such a ban. In 1997, Hawai'i became the first state to offer domestic partnership benefits to same-sex couples. Then, a year later, voters approved a constitutional ban on gay marriages. But by 2012 you could sort of see the tide turning, in Hawai'i and elsewhere. On January 1, 2012, Hawai'i began accepting civil unions and by year's end more than 140 such unions, all or nearly all of them same-sex, had been granted. Hawai'i eventually became the fifteenth state to legalize same-sex marriage, in November 2013.

For myself, I had voted against the Defense of Marriage Act in 1996 and had supported efforts to repeal it. I was an original cosponsor of Dianne Feinstein's Respect for Marriage Act of 2011, and was a strong supporter of the repeal of "Don't Ask, Don't Tell."

With Obama's announcement on ABC, I issued this statement:

"I strongly agree with the president that all Americans deserve the equal opportunity to have their loving committed partnerships legally recognized as marriage, with the same rights and responsibilities. I am proud of President Obama for taking this courageous stand, and I know his upbringing in diverse Hawai'i helped to shape his understanding that everyone should be treated with equality.

"No religious institution should ever be forced to conduct a ceremony that is against their beliefs, but as a legal matter all Americans deserve the same rights. As someone who has been happily married for sixty-four years, I believe every American who loves another person should have the same right to form the bond of marriage and commit to living a life together, for better or for worse." ✤

CHAPTER

95

On June 26, we got the sad news that my former chief of staff, Jimmy Sakai, had died at age eighty-four at home in Wahiawa. Our thoughts went out to his wife, Florence, and daughters Colleen and Cheryl.

And on August 25, we lost a true American hero with the passing of Neil Armstrong, the first man on the moon, in Cincinnati, Ohio, from complications from heart bypass surgery. He was eighty-two. On September 13, Armstrong was remembered at a ceremony at the Washington National Cathedral—still damaged from the quake. The cathedral has one of my favorite stained glass windows, the Space Window, which contains a small moon rock that Armstrong and his fellow crewmen donated in 1974. I was unable to make it to the service, but two dozen members of Congress attended. Armstrong's cremated remains were scattered the next day in the Atlantic from the deck of the cruiser USS *Philippine Sea*.

In Hawai'i, the fall election matchups had been set since the primary on August 11. Lingle easily defeated former state senator John Carroll in the race for U.S. Senate. And Hirono held off Case, 57–40, on the Democratic side. In the race for the First District House seat, Djou won the Republican primary and would face Democrat Hanabusa in the general. But the big surprise of the night was Tulsi Gabbard's huge upset over former mayor Mufi Hannemann in a six-way race for the Second House District seat. She won by a whopping fifty-four percent to Mufi's thirty-four percent. Esther Kia'aina came in third at 5.7 percent. Since Tulsi's Republican opponent, Kawika Crowley, was a freelance handyman who lived in his van, her general election prospects looked excellent. The other interesting development was in the Honolulu mayor's race, essentially a three-way contest pitting incumbent Peter Carlisle against former acting mayor Kirk Caldwell. Running as an anti-rail transit candidate was former governor Ben Cayetano, who got the most votes of the three. But because he received less than a majority, he would face the number two vote-getter, Caldwell, in a runoff in the general.

On September 11—my eighty-eighth birthday—our mission in Benghazi, Libya, came under attack by rocket and mortar fire, and Ambassador Christopher Stevens and three other Americans were killed. The initial thinking was that this was the work of a mob angry about a U.S. video that made fun of Islam and the prophet Mohammed. But it turned out to be another instance of 9/11 terrorism. This prompted several inquiries by the State Department and Congress.

On September 19, on the third floor of the Dirksen Building, Joe Lieberman convened a hearing of the Homeland Security and Government Affairs Committee. The topic: homeland threats and agency responses. Joining us on the panel were Tom Carper of Delaware, Susan Collins of Maine and Jerry Moran of Kansas. We each had our say.

"I join all Americans in mourning the loss of the four brave and dedicated American public servants who died as a result of the senseless attacks in Libya last week," I said. "I honor them and the thousands of civilian federal employees overseas, as well as members of the military, who risk their lives every day in service to this country.

"I am troubled by the recent violence that has targeted U.S. facilities across the Muslim world. These incidents raise concerns about the protection of Americans working abroad, including questions about U.S. efforts to secure our 270 posts around the world. I applaud President Obama's action sending marines to secure diplomatic posts in Libya and Yemen, and I recognize the important work the State Department's Diplomatic Security Bureau is doing to protect American posts overseas."

Kevin Perkins, associate deputy director of the FBI, delivered a sobering assessment from FBI director Robert Mueller.

"We face a fluid, dynamic and complex terrorist threat," the assessment said. "We have seen an increase in the sources of terrorism, a wider array of terrorism targets, a greater cooperation among terrorist groups and an evolution in terrorist tactics and communications methodology. In the past decade, al-Qaeda has become decentralized, but the group remains committed to high-profile attacks against the West. Records seized from Osama bin Laden's compound more than one year ago confirm al-Qaeda's intent. The May 2012 conviction of an al-Qaeda operative who plotted to conduct coordinated suicide bombings in the New York City subway system emphasizes the reality of the threat."

Increasingly, he said, the threat has been coming not from organizations but unaffiliated fanatics.

"These individuals have no typical profile; their experiences and motives are often distinct. But they are increasingly savvy and willing to act alone, which makes them difficult to find and to stop. For example, in February 2012, the FBI arrested Amine El Khalifi, a twenty-nine-year-old Moroccan immigrant, for allegedly attempting to detonate a bomb in a suicide attack on the U.S. Capitol. According to court documents, Khalifi believed he was conducting the terrorist attack on behalf of al-Qaeda, although he was not directly affiliated with any group."

Another example, he said, was Rezwan Ferdaus, a twenty-six-year-old U.S. citizen and graduate student in Boston. During the fall of 2011, Ferdaus planned to use drones to attack the Capitol and other locations in Washington. Although he espoused loyalty to bin Laden, Ferdaus was not affiliated with any group. He had become radicalized on his own, influenced by websites advocating militant fundamentalism.

In short, homegrown terrorism was not going to go away anytime soon, and would require not just the best efforts of the FBI but vigilance by local law enforcement officers, thousands of whom had received federal training on recognizing risks. Overseas, the picture proved equally murky. I don't believe we ever got a satisfactory answer on why we were caught flat-footed at Benghazi. And the issue would dog Hillary Clinton, our secretary of state, well into the next election cycle.

※ ※ ※

On October 5, in Honolulu, I delivered my final speech as a senator to the annual Native Hawaiian Convention at the Hawai'i Convention Center. I had made remarks at every convention since its inception in 2001.

"When it was written, the broad terms 'Indian' and 'tribe' were used in the Constitution to mean indigenous peoples, with their diversity of unique cultures, languages and traditions. Each with their own ways of governing themselves. The consistent use of these terms, Indian and tribe, results in the federal government treating all federally recognized native peoples equally, with the same tools to address the unique needs and priorities in their own communities.

"It is long past time for the Native Hawaiian people to have the same rights, the same privileges, and the same opportunities as every other federally recognized native people." The painstakingly revised Akaka Bill was one avenue, I said. But there was another.

"I was proud to be the first person to sign up for the Kana'iolowalu registry—the new roll of Native Hawaiian voters. If you haven't already, I urge you to do the same, to participate in this incredible process to reorganize our Native Hawaiian government. I'm told there is a booth here where you can sign up, or you can visit their website. I truly believe that as the indigenous people of Hawai'i, our ability to chart our own course and define our own future will never be secure until we have parity with all other native peoples."

I recalled the words of our beloved Queen Lili'uokalani, a woman of great character. She said, "You must remember never to cease to act because you fear you may fail." Those words had guided my conduct over the years.

"Serving as your senator has been my greatest privilege, honor and duty. I am thankful to all the people of Hawai'i for putting their trust in me. This voyage we are on together, advancing the cause of our people, is far from over. Like those who set the course before you: Grab your paddle and *hoe a mau*. There may be rough seas along the way, but I am confident that you possess the ability to successfully navigate our people into the future." ❖

CHAPTER

96

It was with immense pride but also humility that I accepted, on October 18, the Denali Award from the Alaska Federation of Natives. This is the federation's top honor for non-Alaska Natives who have contributed to the growth and development of the community's culture, economy and health. I was the first person from outside Alaska to receive it. This was at a luncheon at the Downtown Marriott Hotel in Anchorage. The other honoree was Kevin Washburn, a member of the Chickasaw Nation of Oklahoma and assistant secretary of the interior, overseeing the Bureau of Indian Affairs. It was good to see my old friend again under such pleasant circumstances.

Later, I had a chance to express my appreciation at the federation's annual meeting at the Dena'ina Convention Center.

"Alaska and Hawai'i have a long, successful relationship working together, both in the halls of Congress—and home in our communities," I said. "I am proud of all that we have accomplished together."

In Hawai'i, one example was the building of the *Hawai'iloa* double-hulled canoe. For the hulls, we used 400-year old Sitka spruce logs donated from Alaska Natives from the southeast and the Sealaska Corporation. But the special relationship between Alaska and Hawai'i goes back much farther. It was not impossible—in fact, in some circles it is considered likely—that ancient Hawaiians visited Alaska and the Pacific Northwest. Some of the indirect evidence comes from names. One chief of the Tyoneks on the Moquawkie Reservation was Albert S. Kaloa. On the Kobuk River, the Alaskans have a village named Kiana. And one river in the Arctic National Wildlife Refuge, flowing into the Arctic Ocean, is called the Hulahula. Becky Cann, a molecular geneticist at the University of Hawai'i, has found DNA links between Polynesians and the Nuu-chah-nulth Tribe on Vancouver Island and elsewhere in the Americas. Native Hawaiian and Alaska Native leaders, young and old, were engaging in cultural exchanges and building new relationships for the future.

"Throughout my career, the Hawai'i and Alaska congressional delegations have worked across party lines, in support of each other, to advance issues important to each of our noncontiguous states. Especially for our native peoples. Over the thirty-six years I have served in Congress, I have collaborated with my good friends Congressman Don Young, Senators Ted Stevens and Frank Murkowski, and now Senators Lisa Murkowski and Mark Begich. We come together to pass bills and sustain programs critical to both of our unique states."

Stevens and Inouye, in particular, had been effective allies.

"Lisa Murkowski is a powerful voice on the Indian Affairs Committee," I said. "Whether she is speaking in support of reforms in native education, addressing health and social issues that contribute to the tragic rate of youth suicides in native communities or highlighting the critical role of subsistence in your daily lives, Lisa's work on behalf of native peoples is well respected in the Senate." Murkowski was also a strong supporter of my provisions to protect native women from rape and abuse—now part of the Senate's bill to reauthorize the Violence Against Women Act.

"I have seen many changes across the country, and I have been amazed at the resiliency of native peoples, our cultures and our languages," I said. "Since I was a boy, the United States has grown and evolved. I have witnessed profound change in the status and treatment of all indigenous peoples. Gone are the days when our languages were banned, when our cultures and traditions were deemed unimportant, or worse, considered liabilities.

"We have proven time and time again that our native cultures and traditions hold incredible wisdom about how best to live in harmony and build a sustainable future. Throughout my life, and my career in public service, I have worked to bring the Hawaiian culture and the aloha spirit, love and respect, with me at all times. I have sought to remain focused on what is pono, what is right and proper. I set my goals around what can be achieved in the spirit of *lōkahi*, unity, to *holo i mua*, move forward.

"In these changing times, it is critical that all Native Americans—American Indians, Alaska Natives and Native Hawaiians—continue to stand together, and move forward together, to advance native sovereignty and self-determination in the United States. There is strength in that solidarity."

At my insistence, in fact, the Senate Indian Affairs Committee in 2011 and 2012 had worked tirelessly to advance tribal priorities and improve programs and services for American Indians, Native Hawaiians and Alaska Natives. We held a total of forty-four hearings, including thirty-six oversight hearings and eight legislative hearings on eighteen bills for numerous tribes. We also reported out twenty-six bills to the Senate, and five became law. The committee staff also would hold seventeen roundtables and listening sessions to hear directly from tribal leaders and other stakeholders. I firmly believed that meaningful, direct consultation with tribes was necessary if the committee were to be effective, and I fervently hoped that would continue after my departure.

As cooperative as the Alaska delegation was on indigenous peoples issues, there comes a time when politics inevitably takes priority. Congressman Don Young, a Republican, had backed Hirono against Case in the primary. That prompted Hirono to produce a ninety-second ad, "Opposites Attract," that played up their bipartisan cooperation. Young told Hawai'i voters that if they were "looking for a United States senator who doesn't just talk about bipartisanship but actually knows how to work with both Republicans and Democrats to get things done, Mazie Hirono will be that senator."

Lingle fired back quickly. Her campaign manager, retired major general Bob Lee, former state adjutant general, released a statement belittling the veteran congressman.

"It should be troubling to the people of Hawai'i that Mazie Hirono's first attempt to convey any example of bipartisanship is a video advertisement with one of the House of Representatives' most controversial members, who even Mazie's fellow Democrats have criticized on a range of ethics and spending issues. This is not the leadership Hawai'i needs."

But after the primary, on October 15, Young jumped ship, endorsing Lingle. At this point, the Lingle campaign conveniently forgot its earlier swipe at Young's ethics and spending.

* * *

Don invoked the ubiquitous federal budget brinksmanship.

"Bipartisanship leadership is what is lacking in the U.S. Senate and is what has brought our country to the edge of a fiscal cliff," he declared. "Now more than ever Hawai'i needs a real bipartisan leader to provide common sense governance to Washington, D.C." And that leader, he said, was Lingle.

He also blasted Democrats for blocking oil exploration in the Arctic National Wildlife Refuge. "As the only noncontiguous states in the union, Alaska and Hawai'i are connected through a unique set of issues facing each state," he wrote. "Energy is on the minds of both Alaskans and Hawaiians. Harry Reid and his cohorts continue to stand in the way of responsible development of Alaska's resources."

But Lingle discovered she had more Alaska resources than Young. In mid-October, Murkowski personally went to Hawai'i to campaign for her. Lisa also played the bipartisan card an interview with the *Star-Advertiser* at Lingle's campaign headquarters on Dillingham Boulevard.

"I think it's critical for good governance," she said. "Last I checked, the Republicans didn't have the monopoly on good ideas. Nor did the Democrats. Legislating, by its very definition, requires coming to agreement, forming a consensus amongst disparate interests and groups and approaches and philosophies. I think part of what you're seeing with the gridlock in Washington, D.C., right now is you have folks lining up on either side of the political spectrum and saying, 'It's my way or the highway.' And so, as a consequence, we don't get anything done."

In response, the Hirono campaign dug up the Alaska senator's earlier criticism of Sarah Palin, whom Lingle had nominated for vice president at the GOP convention in 2008.

Murkowski on Palin: "I just do not think that she has those leadership qualities, that intellectual curiosity that allows for building good and great policies. I don't think that she enjoyed governing."

Lingle on Palin: "Sarah is a person with proven leadership skills and strong moral character."

So now, Betsy Lin, Hirono's campaign manager, whipped out a statement.

"While Palin's own U.S. senator has questioned Palin's qualifications, Lingle told the world that she believed Palin was, in fact, qualified to be a heartbeat away from the presidency," she said. "History, as well as Murkowski, tells us that Lingle's assessment was flat out wrong."

These were classic political ripostes. And enough to make me glad I was out of politics!

But Election Day itself, November 6, felt a bit bittersweet. This was the first election I had spent on the sidelines since 1972—forty years earlier. So much water under the bridge: Vietnam, the Watergate scandal, Nixon waving goodbye, the Iran hostages, Reagan and Iran-Contra, "Star Wars," the shuttle program, the Savings and Loan crisis, the end of the Cold War, China on the rise, the decline of sugar and pineapple, the blight of foreign and domestic terrorism, wars in Afghanistan and Iraq, the communications revolution, the subprime mortgage morass and the Great Recession.

Locally and nationally, the election pretty much matched expectations. In Hawai'i, Obama crushed Romney, 70–28. In the Senate race for my old seat, Hirono soundly defeated Lingle, 62–37, sending the former governor into political exile, although she surfaced some time later as an adviser in the Illinois statehouse. In the First District House race, Hanabusa beat Djou by ten points, 54–44. In the Second District, Tulsi won with seventy-seven percent of the vote. In the Honolulu mayor's race—after Cayetano was smeared by pro-rail interests—Caldwell won 51–45. And in the Big Island mayor's race, Billy Kenoi narrowly edged out Harry Kim, 31,806 to 30,368 votes, a difference of 1,438 votes. That razor-thin margin was topped by the blank votes, 1,619, which happens all too often in Hawai'i, where turnout traditionally is abysmal.

In the Senate, the Democrats gained two seats for a total of fifty-three. With two independents—Bernie Sanders and Angus King of Maine—caucusing with the Democrats, the battle lines were drawn at 55–45. In the House, the Democrats gained eight seats, but the Republicans still had control at 234–201. So Tulsi and Colleen would find themselves in the minority, a spot I knew well. ✤

CHAPTER

97

With Millie and the staff watching from the office on closed-circuit TV, I rose in the Senate chamber on December 12, a Wednesday, to bid aloha to my colleagues. As I looked around, I saw so many familiar faces—Mikulski, Durbin, Reid, Leahy—but also sadly marked faces absent: Kennedy, Wellstone, Byrd. Inouye also was not there, as he had been admitted for evaluation to Walter Reed Army Medical Center two days earlier. As Senate president pro tempore, he had named Senator Kirsten Gillibrand of New York as acting president pro tem.

"Before I begin," I said, "I would like to take a moment to wish my good friend, my colleague of thirty-six years, my brother, Dan Inouye, Hawaiʻi's senior senator, a speedy recovery and return to the Senate."

Recalling how I had been helped immeasurably by the G.I. Bill, I put in a pitch for continued support for veterans.

"When I was blessed with the opportunity to lead the Senate Committee on Veterans' Affairs, I dedicated myself to helping our service members and veterans and their families, and worked with my colleagues to expand VA services and pass a new twenty-first-century G.I. bill. So I want to take this moment to urge all of my colleagues and all of the incoming senators and representatives to do everything they can for our veterans and their families because we ask them to sacrifice so much for us. They put their lives on the line while their wives and husbands watch over their families. Caring for them is one of our most sacred obligations as a nation."

I also called for recognition and support for the civilian federal workforce.

"Not everyone on the frontlines making our nation stronger wears a uniform," I said. "In many critical fields the federal government struggles to compete with the private sector to recruit and retain the skilled people our nation needs: experts in cybersecurity and intelligence analysis, doctors and nurses to care for our wounded warriors and accountants to protect taxpayers during billion-dollar defense acquisitions. These are just a few examples. After I leave the Senate, it is my hope other members will continue to focus on making the federal government an employer of choice. We need the best and brightest working for our nation."

And finally I urged parity for indigenous peoples.

"The United States is a great country," I said. "One of the things that makes us so great is that though we have made mistakes, we change, we correct them, we right past wrongs. It is our responsibility as a nation to do right by America's native people, those who exercised sovereignty on lands that later became part of the United States. While we can never change the past, we have the power to change the future.

"Throughout my career I have worked to ensure that my colleagues understand the federal relationship with native peoples and its origins in the Constitution. The U.S. policy of supporting self-determination and self-governance for indigenous peoples leads to native self-sufficiency, resulting in our continued ability to be productive and to contribute to the well-being of our families, our communities and our great nation. That is why I worked to secure parity in federal policy for my people—the Native Hawaiians. The United States has recognized hundreds of Alaskan Native and American Indian communities. It is long past time for the Native Hawaiian people to have the same rights, same privileges and same opportunities as every other federally recognized native people."

I thanked my current and former staff members—too many to name. I thanked the Office of the Architect of the Capitol, the sergeant at arms and also Senate chaplain Barry Black, who had provided me so much guidance and strength. He had done more to bring the two rancorous sides of the chamber together and find common ground than just about anyone. And I thanked my prayer breakfast colleagues.

Finally, Millie.

"There is no one I owe more to than my lovely wife of sixty-five years, Millie. She is literally there for me whenever I need her. Nearly every day that I have served in the Senate for the past twenty-two years, Millie has come to the office with me. She helps me greet constituents, she makes me lunch, she keeps me focused and she makes sure I know what is happening back home. She means the world to me. Every honor I have received belongs to her and to my family, my children, my grandchildren and great-grandchildren. This speech is their farewell speech, too.

"So mahalo, Millie and my 'ohana, my family. In life there are seasons. While leaving Congress is bittersweet, I am looking forward to spending more time with our five children and getting to know our fifteen great-grandchildren, and—can you believe this?—we are expecting our sixteenth great-grandchild next year, and I will be home to see it."

I said I hoped I had succeeded in bringing a bit of the aloha spirit to the Capitol.

"As I come to the end of twenty-two years in this chamber, and a total of thirty-six years serving in Congress, I offer my profound gratitude and humble thanks to the people of Hawai'i for giving me the opportunity to serve them for so many years. It truly was an experience of a lifetime. All I ever wanted was to be able to help people, and you gave me that opportunity. So mahalo nui loa. Thank you very much. In Hawai'i, when we part, we don't say goodbye. Instead, we say, 'A hui hou,' which means 'until we meet again.' Although I am retiring, I see this as the start of a new chapter, a new season. And I am blessed to have made friendships and partnerships that will last forever. God bless Hawai'i, and God bless the United States of America with the spirit of aloha. A hui hou. Madam President, I yield the floor."

Five days later, I was on a call with my chief of staff, Joan Ohashi, and during our conversation she received an email from Jesse Broder Van Dyke informing her that Senator Inouye had passed away. This was a tremendous shock, because we had no idea that his condition had deteriorated so badly. He had had good color and seemed in fine spirits.

We later learned that he died of respiratory complications just past 5 p.m. at Walter Reed, where he had been hospitalized since December 6 after a fainting spell in his office. His staff said his wife, Irene, and his son, Ken, were by his side. His staff said his last word was "aloha." He was eighty-eight. It's no exaggeration that Inouye was a towering figure, not just in Hawai'i politics, but nationally. From the Watergate Committee to the Iran-Contra hearings, to our wars of intervention, to our budget battles, he had a powerful voice, an influential role, in every major issue before the nation.

Senator Patrick Leahy of Vermont, a good man, would succeed Inouye as Senate president pro tempore, third in line to the presidency.

※ ※ ※

Of course, the condolences came from every quarter.

Obama said, "Tonight, our country has lost a true American hero with the passing of Senator Daniel Inouye. The second longest serving senator in the history of the chamber, Danny represented the people of Hawai'i in Congress from the moment they joined the union. In Washington, he worked to strengthen our military, forge bipartisan consensus and hold those of us in government accountable to the people we were elected to serve. But it was his incredible bravery during World War II—including one heroic effort that cost him his arm but earned him the Medal of Honor—that made Danny not just a colleague and a mentor, but someone revered by all of us lucky enough to know him. Our thoughts and prayers are with the Inouye family."

Biden said, "Everyone in the Senate not only admired Danny Inouye, but they trusted him. We all knew he would do the moral thing regardless of the consequences—whether it was passing judgment on a president during Watergate or on another president in the Iran-Contra hearings. And Danny always remembered where he came from—and how hard his family had to struggle. From having to fight for the right to fight for his country in the all-Japanese-American 442nd, to his keynote speech at the Democratic National Convention in 1968, he always spoke of the country's struggles with racism and bias, and his call for a 'new era in politics.' And to his dying day, he fought for a new era of politics where all men and woman are treated with equality."

I remarked: "It is very difficult for me to bid aloha to my good friend, colleague and brother, Dan Inouye. Senator Inouye was a true patriot and American hero... His legacy is not only the loving family he leaves behind; it can be seen in every mile of every road in Hawai'i, in every nature preserve, in every facility that makes Hawai'i a safer place. He leaves behind him a list of accomplishments unlikely to ever be paralleled... Every child born in Hawai'i will learn of Dan Inouye, a man who changed our islands forever."

The next day, December 18, I introduced Senate Resolution 624, which drew ninety-eight cosponsors—that is, everyone. We expressed our "profound sorrow and deep regret" at Inouye's death and ordered that a copy of the resolution be delivered to his family.

On December 20, a chilly, overcast Thursday, Inouye's flag-draped mahogany casket went on display in the U.S. Capitol Rotunda, where colleagues and aides lined up to say goodbye.

"Senator Daniel Inouye was a noble soul—one of the finest men I've ever met," said Harry Reid, the majority leader, in opening remarks at the memorial service. "It is with a heavy heart that we bid aloha." My good friend Barry Black, the Senate chaplain, praised Inouye for the "laudable footprint he left in the sands of time."

After the service, under the watchful eye of four Capitol Police guards, members of the public filed by all day to pay their respects.

On Friday, Inouye's funeral was held at the National Cathedral, after which his body was flown back to Honolulu for burial at the National Memorial Cemetery of the Pacific, Punchbowl. I attended every event.

In a letter delivered at the state capitol the day he died, Inouye had asked Abercrombie, as his "last wish," to name Hanabusa to the seat. Under the rules, the Democratic Party's State Central Committee had until December 28 to forward three names for the governor's consideration. From early on, Schatz, the lieutenant governor, made it clear he wanted to be among those three. The committee heard pitches from fourteen interested parties, including Case and my former aides Tulsi Gabbard and Esther Kia'aina, now deputy director at the state Department of Land and Natural Resources. On Wednesday, the day after Christmas, the panel picked Colleen, Brian and Esther.

With a fiscal crisis looming, Reid had called Abercrombie to urge him to name a successor as soon as possible. Abercrombie immediately tapped Schatz. At a news conference with Abercrombie at the Capitol, Schatz said, "I'm humbled and honored by this opportunity and obligation to serve the people of Hawai'i and the people of America. No one can fill Senator Daniel K. Inouye's shoes, but together—all of us—we can try to walk in his footsteps."

Obama was in Hawai'i for his Christmas getaway, but made it known he was flying back to Washington Wednesday night to deal with the "fiscal cliff." He invited Schatz to fly back with him. Schatz later said he slept most of the way, but did chat briefly with the commander in chief.

As president of the Senate, Biden administered the oath to Schatz in the chamber the next day. I was on hand, of course, having flown back on my own earlier Wednesday. As we walked up to the well, following Harry Reid, the majority leader, Brian took my right hand to keep me steady. That kind gesture as much as anything captured the generational shift underway in our delegation. With my official retirement on January 3, 2013, Brian would become, at forty, Hawai'i's senior U.S. senator.

Several Democrats and a few Republicans looked on as Biden greeted us, shaking my hand. I took his hand in both of mine. It was always great to see Joe.

He then had Brian raise his right hand.

"Do you solemnly swear to support and defend the Constitution of the United States against all enemies, foreign and domestic?" Biden asked. "That you bear true faith and allegiance to the same, that you take this obligation freely, without any mental reservation or purpose of evasion, and that you will well and faithfully discharge the duties of the office upon which you are about to enter, so help you God?"

"I do," said Schatz.

"Congratulations, Senator," said Biden.

"Thank you."

"Welcome."

Generous applause erupted around the chamber.

Brian and I then shook hands and shared a one-arm embrace.

Then I stood for a brief floor speech.

"Mr. President, I rise today to welcome Hawai'i's new United States senator, Brian Schatz. Brian is a leader, for Hawai'i's present and for our future. And I welcome him with much aloha *pumehana*, which is with warm love. I also welcome and congratulate Senator Schatz's wife, Linda, the children, Tyler and Mia, and his brother, and Senator Schatz's proud parents, Dr. Irwin and Mrs. Barbara Schatz."

I didn't know Irv Schatz well, but knew he was one of the founders, with Kekuni Blaisdell, of the UH medical school.

"Senator Schatz arrived in Washington during a sad time as we continue to mourn the loss of our champion, Senator Dan Inouye," I said. "Dan Inouye will always be a legend in Hawai'i. He will never be replaced. At Dan Inouye's memorial service in Honolulu this past weekend, I was reminded of how many people he touched in Hawai'i and across the country. We must honor his legacy by working together for the people of Hawai'i.

"I thank Brian for volunteering for this incredible responsibility. He only learned of his appointment yesterday and did not have any time to spare so he hopped on Air Force One and flew straight to Washington to be sworn in here today. We need him here now because we are facing a major challenge, one that regrettably has been created by Congress and in our inability to thus far compromise. The looming spending cuts and tax increases known as the fiscal cliff must be fixed within the next five days.

"Mahalo—thank you—Brian, for accepting this challenge. I'm here to help you in any way I can. While there are other talented leaders in Hawai'i who stepped forward and who would also have been excellent appointees, I know that my colleagues will join me in supporting Senator Brian Schatz for the good of Hawai'i."

I talked briefly about his legislative and community service, then brought it to a close.

"I say to my friend, the new junior senator from Hawai'i, never forget that you are here with this solemn responsibility to do everything you can to represent the people of Hawai'i, to make sure that their needs are addressed in every policy discussion, to speak up and seek justice for those who cannot help themselves. God bless you, Senator Schatz. God bless Hawai'i. God bless the United States of America. Aloha."

I started to take my leave, but our Democratic leader rose.

"Mr. President," Reid said to Biden.

"The senator from Nevada."

"Mr. President, before my friend from Hawai'i leaves the floor..."

He paused, as if caught up with emotion.

"We have all come and given speeches—a lot of us, at least—about Senator Akaka, but we have not had a lot of people on the floor when we have done that. The presentation just now is typical for Dan Akaka: never a word about himself, always about somebody else. If the new senator has Senator Akaka's qualities—the kindest, gentlest person I have ever served in this body with—it is something for which he should strive. The shoes he has to fill, we all know—Akaka and Inouye—are significant to fill, but he can do that.

"For you, Senator Akaka—with these people on the floor—we are going to miss you so much. You are a wonderful human being and have been a great senator."

And with those kind words in my ears, my congressional career came to a close. ❖

Epilogue

The Light after Twilight

On a beautiful sun-splashed day above Laupāhoehoe, on the slopes of Maunakea, a group of young conservationists and I took spades in hand to plant 'ōhi'a saplings in the rich, dark soil. This was in October 2014 in the fenced-in Kupua'e 'Ōhi'a Common Garden, part of the Kahikina Learning Center. The center, which bore my middle name, was established by the U.S. Forest Service and is supported by the Akaka Foundation for Tropical Forests. Joining us were two members of the Forest Service: Christian Giardina, a research ecologist, and Melissa Dean, a biological sciences technician. Also on hand were two Akaka Foundation board members: my good friends Bob Masuda, the foundation president, and Paul Nakayama, a retired nuclear engineer and director of the Hawai'i Preparatory Academy. But the real thrill for me was to see the young people getting sweaty with this vital work: James Akau, Kainana Francisco, Makalani Pina, Riley DeMattos and Aleysia-Rae Kaha. These were members of the Ulu Lehulehu initiative, established by my foundation in 2012 and aimed at protecting and restoring 'ōhi'a trees statewide through replanting programs that enlist students in high school and college. 'Ōhi'a, of course, is a pillar of the Hawaiian culture and a keystone species that makes up more than eighty percent of Hawai'i's native forests. Yet it is threatened with extinction because of invasive species, unwise land-use practices and introduced plant diseases, notably a new scourge called rapid 'ōhi'a death.

After the planting work, we held hands and enjoyed the cool mountain breeze. We offered our mana'o, or our breath and life force, in the form of an oli, in gratitude to the forest elements that keep our island communities healthy. It was a reminder that we are all connected through the heat between our palms, and in the firm stance that keeps us rooted in the place we call home.

I ola ʻoe, i ola makou nei!
My life is dependent on yours,
and your life is dependent on mine!

My interest in tropical forests dates back decades, but I guess the pivotal year was 1992 with the passage of the Tropical Forest Recovery Act, which I introduced in May of that year with Inouye as a cosponsor. Signed by the first President Bush, this measure established the Hawaiʻi Experimental Tropical Forest on the Big Island, and directed the secretary of agriculture to promote the protection of habitat for native plants and animals, develop biological controls for invasive species, establish a baseline by which to measure long-term changes, and detect and assess stress factors such as insects, disease and pollution. This task, under the Forest Service, fell to the Pacific Southwest Research Station, part of the Institute of Pacific Islands Forestry.

To build on that, we established the Akaka Foundation, which supports efforts to protect and restore native forests, including reducing or eliminating threats to Hawaiʻi's unique species, so important to our culture. The initial geographic focus was the Laupāhoehoe and 39,000-acre Puʻu Waʻawaʻa units of the Hawaiʻi Experimental Tropical Forest. We pulled together a terrific group of people. Chief among them is Robert Masuda, whom the young folks call Uncle Bob, a longtime YMCA executive who also served as director of the city Department of Parks and Recreation and first deputy director of the state Department of Land and Natural Resources. Our vice presidents are my son Kaniela, director of cultural affairs at the Mauna Lani Bay Resort, and Michael Chun, former president of Kamehameha Schools. I won't go through the whole list, but the board also includes Giardina, my son Gerard, former Office of Hawaiian Affairs trustee Oz Stender, current OHA trustee Bob Lindsey and several stellar scientists.

Tropical forestry is but one of the causes I have taken up since retirement. As throughout my career, I remain devoted to promoting health and education among Hawaiians.

Studies by the Centers for Disease Control and Prevention and other organizations have shown unequivocally that Hawaiians and other Pacific Islanders have higher rates of certain ailments than Asians or Caucasians. More than fifteen percent, for instance, have diabetes—compared to 8.7 percent nationally. Since most cases are adult-onset type 2 diabetes, they are almost entirely preventable through proper diet and exercise. Of course, diabetes carries an increased risk of kidney disease, as does high blood pressure or hypertension. That's part of the reason I became active with the National Kidney Foundation of Hawai'i. Nationally, a whopping thirty percent of the Medicare budget is spent on kidney-related diseases. But in Hawai'i, the prevalence of the disease is about thirty percent worse than on the Mainland. Here we have more than 168,000 people with chronic kidney disease and another 100,000 at risk. Of some 450 people on the organ donor waiting list, more than ninety percent are waiting for kidney transplants. Sadly, most will die before they get one. Hawaiians and other Pacific Islanders, Asians, especially Filipinos and Japanese, and those over sixty regardless of ethnicity have up to four times the risk of having kidney disease. As Western diets and lifestyles become more common, the Chinese and Korean populations are expected to become more susceptible as well.

The problem is particularly acute in fast-growing West O'ahu, where more than 40,000 residents suffer from this ailment. So, on July 29, 1916, the Kidney Foundation broke ground on a new $12-million kidney resource center in Kapolei. The 20,000-square-foot center is aimed at increasing the foundation's ability to offer help individuals and families better manage kidney disease. As part of the new facility, the Senator Daniel K. Akaka Community Center will provide a spot where local organizations can hold their own meetings. Its mission includes the promotion of healthy lifestyles and better education about kidney disease. "The idea behind the new facility will not be just offices or a headquarters, but to have an impact on peoples' lives," says Glen Hayashida, foundation president and CEO. "In the early days the most we could do was raise awareness; now what we really want to do is change their lives."

The center will include a fitness area and a teaching kitchen emphasizing healthy meals.

The opening target date is January 2018.

At the University of Hawai'i, meanwhile, some of my closest supporters in 2014 helped establish the Senator Daniel K. Akaka

Regents Scholarship Endowment. The cochairs of the endowment committee were Walter Dods, Bert Kobayashi, Lawrence Okinaga and my longtime chief of staff, Joan Ohashi. The overall scholarship program, established by the Board of Regents in 1986, was created to help Hawai'i's most promising students pursue their higher education ambitions right here at home. The Akaka endowment further supports those promising students. In announcing the endowment, Okinaga, a partner in the Carlsmith Ball law firm, said, "We aspire to increase the number of future Hawai'i leaders like Senator Akaka, by expanding these prestigious scholarship opportunities. The scholarship honors the senator's passionate commitment to growing Native Hawaiian and Hawai'i's scholars and leaders. Throughout his career from public school teacher and administrator to public office, Senator Akaka was intent on finding solutions and strengthening the futures of America's native peoples through vehicles including education, access to opportunity and financial literacy." Donations to the endowment included $300,000 from OHA and $250,000 from Kamehameha Schools. Along with individuals and pledges the initial total topped $1,142,000.

Along the way, I picked up a few prizes of my own. Soon after my retirement, I was awarded the first-ever Aloha Order of Merit from the Legislature and Governor Abercrombie. The award, established by the Legislature in 1993, recognizes individuals who have "distinguished themselves nationally or internationally and who contributed to the attainment of statehood or have provided extraordinary service to, devoted themselves to the betterment of, or brought honor to the state." Flanked by Abercrombie and Lieutenant Governor Shan Tsutsui, I accepted this honor in the state House chambers on January 14, 2013.

"To me, the aloha spirit exemplifies what makes Hawai'i so special, so unique in this country," I said to those assembled. The ceremony included an oli and *pule* by my son Kaniela, who flew over from Hawai'i island. "Anyone who was born in Hawai'i or lives in Hawai'i captures that spirit, but we've got to share it."

I was also honored, a year later, to accept the Ellison S. Onizuka Memorial Award from the National Education Association. This award goes to someone whose activities in Asian and Pacific Island affairs "significantly impact education and the achievement of equal opportunity for Asians and Pacific Islanders." The citation mentioned my role in establishing Pohakea Elementary School, my support for the Ke Kula

Kaiapuni O Anuenue Hawaiian language immersion program, and my sponsorship of the 1988 Native Hawaiian Education Act, which, the association said, "creates innovative education programs to enhance the education of Native Hawaiians." Previous winners included Haunani Apoliona.

I also was proud to have my name associated with a recognition program established by state senator Brickwood Galuteria in collaboration with singer Marlene Sai. They wanted to spotlight those in the community who champion our kupuna and provide them with the knowledge and support to age with purpose and dignity. So in 2015 they set up what has become known as the Kūpuna Power initiative and each year they recognize someone in the community with the Daniel Kahikina Akaka Award for Outstanding Senior Service. This typically take a place in early April at the state capitol and includes a high school color guard and entertainment by the likes of Marlene, Danny Kaleikini and, while he was still alive, Jimmy Borges. Jimmy passed away in May 2016. I present this award myself. The early recipients included state senator Suzanne Chun Oakland; Alan Kumalae, an RSVP volunteer; Jerry Rauckhorst, president and CEO of Catholic Charities of Hawai'i; Jimmy Lee of Senior Medicare Patrol Hawai'i; entertainer and community leader Carole Kai and AARP Hawai'i.

While my Native Hawaiian Government Reorganization Act never cleared the Senate, a separate process arose that could achieve the same goals. In July 2011, Governor Neil Abercrombie signed Act 195, creating the Native Hawaiian Roll Commission. Led by former governor Waihee, the commission includes Naalehu Anthony, a member of the Polynesian Voyaging Society and an award-winning documentary producer; Robin Danner, founding president of the Council for Native Hawaiian Advancement; Mahealani Perez-Wendt, former executive director of the Native Hawaiian Legal Corporation; and Lei Kohoi, also a lawyer. On July 2012 at Washington Place, the commission kicked off Kana'iolowalu, its campaign to create a registry of eligible Native Hawaiian voters. I wasn't at the ceremony, but was among the first to sign up online. Over the next year or so, nearly 123,000 Hawaiians joined the registry.

The registrants in turn elected delegates to a constitutional convention, or Naʻi Aupuni Aha, held in February 2016 at the Royal Hawaiian Golf Course in Maunawili. After thoughtful debate, the delegates voted 88–30 to adopt a governing document. The proposed constitution allows room for recognition by the U.S. government while holding out for the possibility of independence. That would extend to Hawaiians recognition enjoyed by many American Indian tribes for decades. Among Native Hawaiians, support for this process is by no means universal. Many object to being equated to a "tribe" rather than a sovereign nation. Of course, Hawaiians have lived under six different forms of government. First there were the *aliʻi*, the chiefs. Then the islands were unified under Kamehameha I. In the late 1800s, we had a brief, provisional government under American businessmen. Then we were annexed as a U.S. territory. During World War II, civilian leadership gave way to martial law. Then came statehood. Whatever comes next—and there are a rainbow of possibilities—our indigenous people, for the first time, will have a say in forging.

Waihee was leading the drive to raise funds to spread the word on the constitution, register new voters and stage a ratification vote. For its part, the U.S. Interior Department has published a regulation allowing a Native Hawaiian nation to apply for formal recognition by the United States. The move in the waning days of the Obama administration offered a path to the nation-within-a-nation status that had been blocked by Senate Republicans for years.

In February 2015, on Presidents Day, my daughter, Millannie, and I stopped by the Maple Garden restaurant in McCully for a meeting of the Akaka ʻohana. This is a group of my former campaign volunteers and other political supporters and former staff members. Some, like Gladys Karr, were all of the above. This group, founded by my longtime campaign office manager, Liz Rathburn, had been meeting for lunch on every federal holiday for twenty-five years. Many had been with me since the beginning. These were the people who mailed out the brochures and Christmas cards and answered the phones.

"We kept this group together and we enjoyed it," organizer Faith Kaneshiro explained to one newcomer. "It started off small. At first it was to help Uncle Danny. We became a social thing. We welcome everyone."

I made the rounds, greeting as many of the ninety-plus attendees as I could.

"Good to see you, good to see you," I said. And it was very good to see them all.

Here was Haunani Apoliona, an OHA trustee and mainstay, with Jerry Santos of the musical group Olomana. Here was former (and future) congresswoman Colleen Hanabusa. Here was Ken Inouye, son of Senator Dan. I shook hands with council chairman Ernie Martin and Councilmember Joey Manahan. I had a chance to say a few words to Kekoa Kaluhiwa, one of my former aides in Washington and now up for the number two position at the Department of Land and Natural Resources under our new governor, David Ige.

"I just came to say I love you," he said, kissing me on the cheek.

"Aw, you're in a good spot," I said.

"Still need to be confirmed by the Senate," he said.

He would be.

At a back table sat retired Brigadier General Irwin Cockett, former commander of the Hawai'i Army National Guard. Cockett was on hand to pay tribute to a fellow soldier of the Korean War, Herbert Pililaau, who won the Medal of Honor for his actions at Heartbreak Ridge in September 1951. For the tribute, Faith had invited Pililaau's family members: Agnes Pililaau, Yolanda Kala and Lani Sullivan.

"We do mahalo things," Faith explained.

That was the abiding spirit of this group.

A different kind of Akaka 'ohana assembled later that week at my alma mater. That was when our family donated the papers of my brother Abe to Kamehameha Schools. These included his spiritual writings, but Abe also composed music, wrote prayers and plays and penned an epic Hawaiian creation chant that was recorded in part by Aaron Mahi, conductor of the Royal Hawaiian Band from 1981 to 2005. When the Reverend Abraham Akaka Ministries Foundation was launched in the mid-1980s, it had four stated purposes—"bringing hope and help to those in need," uplifting the lives of Native Hawaiians, supporting the church and promoting world peace. When Abe died in 1997, the foundation members added a fifth purpose: preserving his archival spiritual works, which now had been accomplished.

Toward the end of the ceremony at the school's chapel, we sang one of Abe's compositions, "Mahalo Nui," which begins:

> *Mahalo nui for your sweet laughter*
> *Mahalo nui for thoughts sincere*
> *May blessings smile and God be with you*
> *Until we come to laugh again.*

At the close, the entire family—more than 100 of us—posed for a huge group photo. It was so great to be with the extended family. And I was delighted that I now could recognize my grandchildren! And know them by name.

On October 12, 2015, in a ceremony at Punchbowl, I was delighted to take part in Tulsi Gabbard's promotion to major in the Hawai'i Army National Guard. Brass from all four branches attended, with the Army Guard represented by Major General Gary Hara, assigned to Camp Smith, and Brigadier General Keith Tamashiro. After the usual opening pomp and ceremony, Tulsi's mom, Carol, pinned the new bronze oak leaf on Tulsi's black beret. Her dad, Hawai'i senator Mike Gabbard, pinned the leaf on one shoulder, and her husband, Abraham Williams, did the other.

I led her in the oath of office:

"I, Tulsi Gabbard, having been appointed an officer in the Army of the United States, as indicated above in the grade of major, do solemnly swear that I will support and defend the Constitution of the United States against all enemies, foreign and domestic, that I will bear true faith and allegiance to the same; that I take this obligation freely, without any mental reservations or purpose of evasion; and that I will well and faithfully discharge the duties of the office upon which I am about to enter; So help me God."

Then she took the podium.

"Standing here today," she said, "amongst veterans at the Punchbowl National Cemetery, I'm again reminded of what aloha truly means. Ultimately, aloha means respect, love and caring. Some people think love and caring means weakness, but I assure you that the exact opposite is true. The truth is, nothing is as strong as love. It was their love for liberty and freedom that gave our country's founders the courage and strength to fight for independence. It is that love for country that motivates our men and women in uniform to be ready and willing to put their lives on the line for the freedom and liberty that is the foundation upon which America stands. Punchbowl Cemetery is sacred. It exudes the aloha of those who have given their lives for America. I am humbled, honored and inspired to be here with them—and with all of you."

It was from Henk Rogers, millionaire owner of the wildly popular Tetris video game and founder of the Blue Planet Foundation, that I first learned of the International Union for Conservation of Nature. Henk had graciously invited Millie and me to his house near the Puʻu Waʻawaʻa Forest Reserve, a beautiful location on the Big Island. Also on hand was Mark McGuffie, executive director of the Hawaiʻi Island Economic Development Board and another strong environmental advocate. Created in 1948 and based in Geneva, the IUCN has become one of the world's largest and most diverse environmental networks, with 1,300 member organizations, both governmental and nongovernmental. With access to 16,000 experts on science and the environment, the IUCN, by its own admission, is the "global authority" on the status of the natural world and steps required to protect it. The organization holds a meeting every four years called the World Conservation Congress. In 2012, at Jeju Island, South Korea, the group published a list of the world's 100 most threatened species, including *Hibiscadelphus woodii*, a small tree found only in Kalalau Valley on Kauaʻi. Yet I was astounded to discover that never once had the meeting been held on U.S. soil. Over the next couple of years, Henk and I, along with Tim Johns, former state land board chairman and head of the Bishop Museum, explored the possibility of inviting the group to hold its meeting in Honolulu. We secured the support of the governor and the mayor. And I got some much-needed impetus from Secretary of State John Kerry, whom I knew well from our Senate years.

In 2014, we put together a National Host Committee to support Hawai'i's commitment to host the 2016 Congress. I served as one of two honorary cochairman, along with Thomas Lovejoy, a professor of environmental science and policy at George Mason University in Virginia. The fourteen-member committee included Johns as chairman and, as vice chairman, Chipper Wichman, president and CEO of the National Tropical Botanical Garden on Kaua'i. Honolulu finally made the list of finalists. Our competition included Rio de Janeiro and Istanbul, Turkey and five other major cities. Finally, in May 2014, the much-anticipated announcement came from the IUCN: Honolulu had won. The meeting, which carried the theme "Planet at the Crossroads," ran from September 1–10, 2016, and was the best-attended ever, with 10,000 participants, and by all accounts the most successful.

After careful deliberation, the conferees adopted what became known as the Hawai'i Commitments. This was an action plan addressing such issues as sustaining world food supplies, maintaining the health of the oceans, fighting the trafficking of wildlife, getting help from the private sector and building resilience to climate change. Incredibly, some people—some powerful people—still write off global warming as a hoax. Tell that to the low-lying islands in the Pacific and Indian Oceans that are underwater at high tide or during a storm surge. The Hawai'i Commitments underscored nature-based solutions to climate change. That includes the restoration of forests and peatlands. The document also emphasized the role of indigenous peoples—including women—in implementing the Paris Agreement. "Nature-based solutions have been shown—in many different settings, in both developed and developing countries to mitigate greenhouse gas emissions, help communities adapt to climate change impacts, reduce the risk of natural disasters and support sustainable livelihoods," the conferees concluded.

Imagine if every person on the planet planted one tree. Seven billion trees would remove a lot of carbon from the atmosphere. Now imagine if they planted one tree per year.

As night falls over upper Hāmākua, the stars stand out in wondrous display. In cities, due to light pollution, we cannot see the brilliant sheen of the Milky Way Galaxy, our home. But here, we realize that this band of light, on every cloudless night, informed our culture for thousands of years. I find it astounding that most of what we view as stars—pinpoints of light—are actually galaxies, a collection of billions of stars like our own Milky Way. Our ancestors identified Hōkūpaʻa, the North Star, a steadfast guidepost. They learned that Hōkūleʻa, Arcturus, reaches its zenith over Hawaiʻi, a beacon for countless Polynesian migrations. We identified Hikianalia, or Spica, in the constellation Virgo, a sister star to Hōkūleʻa, also helpful when plying the vast Pacific seas. What the Greeks called the Pleiades and the Japanese Subaru, we call *makaliʻi*, "little eyes," as if the heavens are looking back at us. Perhaps they are. The canoe *Makaliʻi* embarked on its maiden voyage in 1995 to Raiatea and Nuku Hiwa. In the Hawaiian renaissance, we named our canoes after stars for good reason. Stars form the underpinning of our culture.

On the slopes of Maunakea, it is easy to see why some people consider the mountain sacred. It carries tremendous *mana*. But like opinions on Hawaiian self-governance, that view is not universal. Is the entire island, down to the seafloor, sacred? Or is it the part of the mountain above sea level? Or is it just the top of the mountain? And if so, sacred to whom?

The opponents of the proposed Thirty Meter Telescope have mustered a number of arguments against it. But there is no question that the telescope would generate huge educational opportunities—and jobs—for the Hawaiian community. I feel certain that in the decades ahead—perhaps soon—astronomers using space-based observatories, in concert with telescopes like the Keck on Maunakea, will find evidence of life on planets orbiting nearby stars. That will be a truly monumental discovery. This quest by astronomers conforms with, rather than undercuts, our traditions. The search for other habitable planets shares much in common with the Polynesians' canoe-borne exploration for habitable islands. In hula, the ancient, *kahiko*, and modern, *ʻauana*, not only coexist but complement one another. The old need not be the enemy of the new. Let's allow Maunakea, rightfully, to become a bridge between our past, as Hawaiians, and our future.

Students of stars are who we are. ✤

APPENDIX A

Major legislation sponsored by Senator Dan Akaka

H.R. 4416 (96th): A bill to clarify that the SS United States may operate in the domestic and/or foreign commerce of the United States and between foreign ports.
Introduced: June 11, 1979
Referred to Committee: June 11, 1979

H.R. 6374 (96th): A bill to authorize the President of the United States to present on behalf of the Congress a specially struck gold medal to Ambassador Kenneth Taylor.
Introduced: January 30, 1980
Enacted—Signed by the President: March 6, 1980

H.R. 3942 (98th): Commercial Space Launch Act
Introduced: September 21, 1983
Enacted—Signed by the President: October 30, 1984

H.J.Res. 17 (99th): A joint resolution to consent to an amendment enacted by the legislature of the State of Hawaii to the Hawaiian Homes Commission Act, 1920.
Introduced: January 3, 1985
Enacted—Signed by the President: October 27, 1986

H.R. 4614 (99th): A bill to amend an Act to add certain lands on the Island of Hawaii to Hawaii Volcanoes National Park, and for other purposes.
Introduced: April 17, 1986
Referred to Committee: April 17, 1986

H.R. 4480 (100th): A bill to change the name of the Pacific Tropical Botanical Garden, a federally chartered organization, to the National Tropical Botanical Garden, and for other purposes.
Introduced: April 28, 1988
Enacted—Signed by the President: October 28, 1988

S. 3032 (101st): A bill to designate the planned Department of Veterans Affairs Medical Center in Honolulu, Hawaii, as the "Spark M. Matsunaga Department of Veterans Affairs Medical Center".
Introduced: September 12, 1990
Enacted—Signed by the President: October 31, 1990

APPENDIX A   605

S.J.Res. 198 (102nd): A joint resolution to recognize contributions Federal civilian employees provided during the attack on Pearl Harbor and during World War II.
Introduced: September 18, 1991
Enacted—Signed by the President: December 11, 1991

S. 2679 (102nd): Hawaii Tropical Forest Recovery Act
Introduced: May 7, 1992
Enacted—Signed by the President: October 29, 1992

S.J.Res. 19 (103rd): A joint resolution to acknowledge the 100th anniversary of the January 17, 1893 overthrow of the Kingdom of Hawaii, and to offer an apology to Native Hawaiians on behalf of the United States for the overthrow of the Kingdom of Hawaii.
Introduced: January 21, 1993
Enacted—Signed by the President: November 23, 1993

S. 1194 (104th): Marine Mineral Resources Research Act of 1996
Introduced: August 11, 1995
Enacted—Signed by the President: October 19, 1996

S.J.Res. 10 (105th): A joint resolution to consent to certain amendments enacted by the Legislature of the state of Hawaii to the Hawaiian Homes Commission Act, 1920.
Introduced: January 22, 1997
Referred to Committee: January 22, 1997

S. 714 (105th): Veterans' Benefits Act of 1997
Introduced: May 7, 1997
Enacted—Signed by the President: November 21, 1997

S. 2129 (105th): Hawaii Volcanoes National Park Adjustment Act of 1998
Introduced: June 2, 1998
Enacted—Signed by the President: November 12, 1998

S. 700 (106th): Ala Kahakai National Historic Trail Act
Introduced: March 24, 1999
Enacted—Signed by the President: November 13, 2000

S. 938 (106th): Hawaii Volcanoes National Park Adjustment Act of 2000
Introduced: May 3, 1999
Enacted—Signed by the President: November 13, 2000

S. 1334 (106th): Organ Donor Leave Act
Introduced: July 1, 1999
Ordered Reported by Committee: August 3, 1999

S. 1694 (106th): Hawaii Water Resources Reclamation Act of 2000
Introduced: October 6, 1999
Enacted—Signed by the President: December 23, 2000

S. 2722 (106th): A bill to authorize the award of the Medal of Honor to Ed W. Freeman, James K. Okubo, and Andrew J. Smith.
Introduced: June 13, 2000
Enacted—Signed by the President: June 20, 2000

S. 1822 (107th): A bill to amend title 5, United States Code, to allow certain catchup contributions to the Thrift Savings Plan to be made by participants age 50 or over.
Introduced: December 13, 2001
Ordered Reported by Committee: March 21, 2002

S. 254 (108th): Kaloko-Honokohau National Historical Park Addition Act of 2003
Introduced: January 30, 2003
Enacted—Signed by the President: December 2, 2003

S. 678 (108th): Postmasters Equity Act of 2003
Introduced: March 20, 2003
Enacted—Signed by the President: September 30, 2003

S. 1145 (108th): A bill to designate the facility of the United States Postal Service located at 120 Baldwin Avenue in Paia, Maui, Hawaii, as the "Patsy Takemoto Mink Post Office Building".
Introduced: May 23, 2003
Ordered Reported by Committee: June 17, 2003

S. 264 (109th): Hawaii Water Resources Act of 2005
Introduced: February 2, 2005
Enacted—Signed by the President: September 21, 2005

S. 2089 (109th): A bill to designate the facility of the United States Postal Service located at 1271 North King Street in Honolulu, Oahu, Hawaii, as the "Hiram L. Fong Post Office Building".
Introduced: December 13, 2005
Enacted—Signed by the President: March 20, 2006

S. 423 (110th): Veterans' Compensation Cost-of-Living Adjustment Act of 2007
Introduced: January 29, 2007
Ordered Reported by Committee: June 27, 2007
Enacted via H.R. 1284 (110th): Veterans' Compensation Cost-of-Living Adjustment Act of 2007
Enacted via S. 2617 (110th): Veterans' Compensation Cost-of-Living Adjustment Act of 2008

APPENDIX A 607

S. 550 (110th): A bill to preserve existing judgeships on the Superior Court of the District of Columbia.
Introduced: February 12, 2007
Enacted—Signed by the President: April 18, 2008

S. 2162 (110th): Veterans' Mental Health and Other Care Improvements Act of 2008
Introduced: October 15, 2007
Enacted—Signed by the President: October 10, 2008

S. 2617 (110th): Veterans' Compensation Cost-of-Living Adjustment Act of 2008
Introduced: February 8, 2008
Enacted—Signed by the President: September 24, 2008

S. 3023 (110th): Veterans' Benefits Improvement Act of 2008
Introduced: May 15, 2008
Enacted—Signed by the President: October 10, 2008

S. 252 (111th): Veterans Health Care Authorization Act of 2009
Introduced: January 15, 2009
Ordered Reported by Committee (Enacted Via Other Measures): May 21, 2009
Enacted via S. 1963 (111th): Caregivers and Veterans Omnibus Health Services Act of 2010

S. 404 (111th): Veterans' Emergency Care Fairness Act of 2009
Introduced: February 10, 2009
Enacted—Signed by the President: February 1, 2010.

S. 407 (111th): Veterans' Compensation Cost-of-Living Adjustment Act of 2009
Introduced: February 10, 2009
Enacted—Signed by the President: June 30, 2009

S. 574 (111th): Plain Writing Act of 2009
Introduced: March 11, 2009
Ordered Reported by Committee (Enacted Via Other Measures): April 1, 2009
Enacted via H.R. 946 (111th): Plain Writing Act of 2010

S. 707 (111th): Telework Enhancement Act of 2010
Introduced: March 25, 2009
Passed Senate (Enacted Via Other Measures): May 24, 2010
Enacted via H.R. 1722 (111th): Telework Enhancement Act of 2010

S. 801 (111th): Caregiver and Veterans Health Services Act of 2009
Introduced: April 2, 2009
Ordered Reported by Committee (Enacted Via Other Measures): May 21, 2009
Enacted via S. 1963 (111th): Caregivers and Veterans Omnibus Health Services Act of 2010

Enacted via S. 509 (111th): A bill to authorize a major medical facility project at the Department of Veterans Affairs Medical Center, Walla Walla, Washington, and for other purposes.

S. 1310 (111th): A bill to authorize major medical facility projects for the Department of Veterans Affairs for fiscal year 2010, and for other purposes.
Introduced: June 19, 2009
Referred to Committee: June 19, 2009
Enacted via S. 1717 (111th): A bill to authorize major medical facility leases for the Department of Veterans Affairs for fiscal year 2010, and for other purposes.
Enacted via S. 509 (111th): A bill to authorize a major medical facility project at the Department of Veterans Affairs Medical Center, Walla Walla, Washington, and for other purposes.

S. 1717 (111th): A bill to authorize major medical facility leases for the Department of Veterans Affairs for fiscal year 2010, and for other purposes.
Introduced: September 25, 2009
Enacted—Signed by the President: October 26, 2009

S. 1963 (111th): Caregivers and Veterans Omnibus Health Services Act of 2010
Introduced: October 28, 2009
Enacted—Signed by the President: May 5, 2010

S. 3107 (111th): Veterans' Compensation Cost-of-Living Adjustment Act of 2010
Introduced: March 11, 2010
Ordered Reported by Committee: August 5, 2010
Enacted via H.R. 4667 (111th): Veterans' Compensation Cost-of-Living Adjustment Act of 2010

S. 3447 (111th): Post-9/11 Veterans Educational Assistance Improvements Act of 2010
Introduced: May 27, 2010
Enacted—Signed by the President: January 4, 2011

S. 743 (112th): Whistleblower Protection Enhancement Act of 2012
Introduced: April 6, 2011
Enacted—Signed by the President: November 27, 2012

S. 1379 (112th): D.C. Courts and Public Defender Service Act of 2011
Sponsor: Sen. Daniel Akaka [D-HI, 1990–2012]
Introduced: July 18, 2011
Enacted—Signed by the President: December 28, 2012

S. 2170 (112th): Hatch Act Modernization Act of 2012
Introduced: March 7, 2012
Enacted—Signed by the President: December 28, 2012

Appendix B

Senate floor tributes to Senator Dan Akaka
December 2012

Senator Harry Reid, Nevada

Mr. President, I want to spend a little time today talking about the junior senator from Hawai'i, Daniel Akaka, as he retires from a life dedicated to his community and this country.

Senator Akaka's service to this nation began during wartime, when he was a teenager. He graduated from high school and the war was ongoing. Of course, people were watching Hawai'i very closely because they had such a huge Asian population—a huge Japanese American population. So it was watched very closely, and for reasons that weren't valid, but that is what we did then. Dan Akaka spent two years as a civilian worker with the U.S. Army Corps of Engineers and two years on active duty in the U.S. Army. His duties with the Army, as I recall, having talked to Dan Akaka, were to protect the water in Honolulu.

After the war, Dan attended the University of Hawai'i, using the original G.I. Bill. Years later, he would receive his master's degree from the University of Hawai'i as well as his bachelor's degree. Senator Akaka believes he would never have become a U.S. senator if not for the G.I. benefits he received through his service in the military. That is why, as a member and past chairman of the Veterans' Affairs Committee, he has worked to make important improvements to the twenty-first-century G.I. Bill.

Today's G.I. Bill is modeled after the work done by Jim Webb, after the educational opportunity program that Dan took advantage of when he was a young boy. Senator Akaka was chairman of the Veterans' Affairs Committee from 2007 to 2010, as thousands and thousands of Iraq and Afghanistan veterans were coming home from combat. As Democrats collectively worked to bring our troops home from Iraq, Dan Akaka labored with the Veterans Administration to meet the needs and challenges of a new generation of veterans. The twenty-first-century G.I. Bill ensures those veterans get the educational opportunities they deserve.

Dan so valued his own education that he went on to serve his community as a teacher after he graduated from college. He became a principal, worked for the Department of Health, Education, and Welfare, and the Hawai'i Office of Economic Opportunity. He served fourteen years in the House of Representatives before he was appointed to the Senate in 1990. He won election to the Senate later that year.

As chairman of the Indian Affairs Committee, Dan has been a strong voice and tireless advocate for Native Americans. He has taught us all about history—the history of Hawai'i and its native communities, as well as the issues facing indigenous Hawaiians today. Senator Akaka is a descendant of Native Hawaiians. He is seventy-five percent Hawaiian and he has Hawaiians on both sides of his family. He is very proud of his heritage. Dan was the first Native Hawaiian in the Senate.

He is also a deeply religious man who comes from a strong faith tradition. His devout mother taught her children a custom of charity. His mother was really a soft touch. If anyone came by with a sad story, she would invite them in. Sometimes her hospitality only allowed her—because she had nothing else—to give them something to drink. His family was very poor when he was young. But Dan was able to work through this. Even if his mother had spent the grocery money for the month, strangers were always welcome at her table.

A friend of Dan's brother came to Hawai'i from Chicago for a very brief period of time, and his mother took him in. He never left. He basically was raised in the Akaka home. Anthony became such a part of that family that, before he died, he wanted to make sure he was buried in Hawai'i. He wanted to be buried with Dan's siblings and family in Hawai'i. And he was.

Senator Akaka served as choir director of the Hawai'i Christian Mother Church, where his brother was minister for some seventeen years. Senator Akaka is still a member of that church. He is blessed with a wonderful family as well as a rewarding career. He and his wife, Millie, have five children, fifteen grandchildren and fourteen great-grandchildren.

Senator Akaka has served his constituents well and with distinction. He has served not only his constituents and the state of Hawai'i but our country with distinction. He has enjoyed a long and productive career and his presence in the Senate will be missed.

I offer congratulations to Senator Akaka on his dedicated military and public service and wish him and Millie happiness in their retirement.

Senator Dick Durbin, Illinois

Mr. President, I add my comments in chorus to what the majority leader said about Senator Dan Akaka of Hawai'i. I came to know him—and I have spoken about this on the floor—and Millie who are the perfect Senate family. They have devoted a major part of their lives to serving Hawai'i and serving in the national interest. The legacy Senator Akaka leaves behind is substantial when it comes to legislation, particularly in helping veterans and agricultural issues. But, more important, what Dan Akaka leaves behind is the feeling of kinship and camaraderie that he has with so many members of the Senate. He is a stalwart at the Senate Prayer Breakfast, leading the singing every Wednesday morning, and it is heartfelt and very genuine.

As Senator Reid mentioned earlier, his family background of Hawai'i—which he shared with us one afternoon at a lunch—is a tradition of giving and hospitality, which we find built in to Danny Akaka. We are going to miss him.

Senator Dan Inouye, Hawai'i

Mr. President, today I would like to honor the legacy and service of my colleague and dear friend, Senator Daniel K. Akaka. My brother, Senator Daniel Akaka, has been my friend and partner in Washington for thirty-six years. During that time, he has fought hard for Native Hawaiians, veterans and the needs of Hawai'i.

I am sad at the thought of the Senate without him and I am sorry I am unable to join him on the floor today.

Dan Akaka is the spirit of aloha.

I have always relied on his even keel and hard work to help me represent the people of Hawai'i. I have never, ever heard him utter a harsh word or do anything to harm another person. There are few words to describe a kind man of his stature, but I assure you, Hawai'i and this nation are better because of his work.

On behalf of the people of Hawai'i, thank you, Danny.

There will never be another like you.

Senator Kent Conrad, North Dakota

Mr. President, I rise today to pay tribute and recognize the accomplishments of a colleague and dear friend who will be retiring from the U.S. Senate at the end of the term. Senator Akaka has represented the state of Hawaiʻi with distinction for thirty-six years. He has been a firm advocate for his constituents, especially for Native Hawaiians. I have had the honor and privilege to work alongside Senator Akaka on the Indian Affairs Committee. During this time and throughout his tenure as chairman, I have witnessed his commitment to improving the overall well-being of Native Hawaiians as well as all indigenous people. He has been a tireless advocate for their rights, and, with his leadership and bipartisan dedication, he has brought many issues they confront to the forefront. For more than a decade, Senator Akaka has championed the Native Hawaiian Government Reorganization Act, which establishes a process for Native Hawaiians to gain federal recognition. He has also been the driving force in advancing the Native Hawaiian language movement. His dedication and leadership has ensured survival of the language.

As part of the Greatest Generation and a veteran, Senator Akaka also used his time as chairman of the Committee on Veterans' Affairs to champion laws to improve health care and benefits for countless veterans, service members and their families.

Known for breaking down barriers and building relationships, Senator Akaka has served the people of Hawaiʻi with integrity and humility. He is a true statesman, gentleman and patriot, and our country is better for his service. He leaves a distinguished legacy and will be greatly missed by us all. I thank Senator Akaka for his friendship and service to our nation, and I wish him and his wife, Millie, all the best for the future.

Senator Barbara Mikulski, Maryland

Madam President, I rise to comment about some wonderful men in the Senate who are retiring on both sides of the aisle. Earlier today I spoke about my deep affection and sorry-to-see-go friends Olympia Snowe and Kay Bailey Hutchison, but I want to rise as the dean of the women in the Senate to say some very special words about very special men on both sides of the aisle. Because when I came to the Senate, it was only Nancy Kassebaum and me, and yet we worked on so many issues together. There are really wonderful men here who supported me, supported our issues, but really stood up for those states and their communities.

I want to say goodbye, aloha, to my very good friend Danny Akaka, a wonderful man with whom I have served in both the House and the Senate. He has been a real advocate not only for the people of Hawai'i but, wow, I salute the way he stood up for the federal workforce, the civil servants who do such a great job and the outstanding job he has done on the veterans' committee.

Lives are better off, particularly for our veterans. I want to say a wonderful goodbye and give a hug to him because he demonstrates that you do not have to be loud to be powerful...

I wanted to be sure that the day would not end without me acknowledging these wonderful people who have given a big part of their lives to making this country a better place. I want to, in the most heartfelt way—I am so sorry we did not have a bipartisan dinner or party to be able to express this. I would have liked to have been in the same room, breaking bread with them, in order to be able to tell them how much we appreciate them, across party lines, across those lines that ordinarily divide us. They came from different parts of the country, they arrived in the Senate with different objectives, they will leave under different circumstances. I want to again let them know that each and every one of them had a positive impact on me and I think a wonderful impact on the future of this country. So I wish them well. God bless and Godspeed.

Senator Tom Harkin, Illinois

Mr. President, we are bidding farewell to one of our most respected and beloved members, Senator Daniel Akaka of Hawai'i or, as we all know him, "Danny." With his retirement, our friend is bringing to a close a remarkable and distinguished career in public service spanning nearly seven decades. Having witnessed, as a seventeen-year-old boy, the Japanese attack on Pearl Harbor, he took a civilian job with the Army Corps of Engineers before joining the U.S. Army in 1945. We honor him, along with his senior colleague from Hawai'i, Senator

Inouye, and Senator Lautenberg, as the only veterans of World War II still serving in the Senate.

Not surprisingly, Senator Akaka has been a leader on veterans issues. He served as chairman of the Committee on Veterans' Affairs in the 110th and 111th Congresses, and he remained active on that committee despite relinquishing his chairmanship in the current Congress in order to chair the Committee on Indian Affairs.

We will not soon forget Senator Akaka's retort when another senator was holding up a package of veterans benefits, demanding that the costs of the veterans benefits be offset.

Senator Akaka calmly, very deliberately argued that the costs did not need to be offset, stating, "The price has already been paid, many times over, by the service of the brave men and women who wore our nation's uniform." Needless to say, Senator Akaka carried the day.

Senator Akaka has played a leading role in demanding improvements in the handling of post-traumatic stress disorder and traumatic brain injuries sustained by service men and women. In 2009, he joined with Senator Inouye in securing compensation for Filipino veterans of World War II who fought for the United States.

Senator Akaka is the only ethnic Native Hawaiian to serve in this body. Throughout his congressional career, including fourteen years in the House and twenty-two years in the Senate, he has been a determined and impassioned advocate for the people of his state of Hawai'i. He has fought for legislation that would grant federal recognition to ethnic Native Hawaiians, the same recognition we have granted to American Indians and Native Alaskans.

In 1993, President Clinton signed a resolution sponsored by Senator Akaka officially apologizing on behalf of the U.S. government for overthrowing Hawai'i's last monarch a century earlier.

In so many ways, Senator Akaka represents the Senate at its very best—the Senate the way it used to be in less partisan times. He works tirelessly behind the scenes, and he shuns the media limelight. He prides himself on reaching across the aisle and forging honorable compromises. He is the ultimate gentleman, and his word is his bond. Across these many years Danny Akaka has been a wonderful friend and colleague. Of course, that friendship will continue, and I will miss him in the Senate.

I join with the entire Senate family in wishing Danny and Millie all the best in the years ahead.

Senator Carl Levin, Michigan

Mr. President, for the last twenty-two years, Daniel Akaka has represented the people of Hawai'i in this body. They have been the better for his service, and I have greatly appreciated the wisdom, humility, and passion with which he has served here.

One issue on which we have been able to work closely as fellow members of the Homeland Security and Governmental Affairs Committee is oversight of the federal workforce, a key issue for his state and for taxpayers everywhere.

Senator Akaka's passion for federal workforce issues comes from his passion for public service and for effective government. Just in this Congress, I was an original cosponsor of his federal Whistleblower Protection Act to strengthen the law protecting federal employees who bring to light fraud, waste and abuse in federal programs. That Akaka Bill is expected to be signed into law before the end of the year. Also this Congress, I was proud to cosponsor his Hatch Act Modernization Act to allow hardworking employees of state and local governments, who are covered by the Hatch Act, to serve as elected officials in their communities.

In addition to his focus on federal workforce issues, Senator Akaka has long been a valued member of the Armed Services Committee. We have worked together on legislation to reform Defense Department business and financial management systems; strengthen oversight and accountability of wartime contracting; and strengthen the Defense Department's management of the substantial funds it spends to acquire property and services.

In 2002 Senator Akaka joined with Senator Inhofe to form the Senate Army Caucus, and through this bipartisan group they have focused welcome attention on the programs and needs of our army. Senator Akaka, himself an army veteran, has been an important source of insight into the challenges facing our soldiers and their families.

Of course, as the former chairman of the Veterans' Affairs Committee, Senator Akaka has long demonstrated an intense dedication to those who have helped defend our nation. His steadfast advocacy for veterans' health programs, education benefits and other important programs has made a significant and lasting impact on the lives of veterans and their families.

When people describe Daniel Akaka, one of the first words used to describe him is "humble." He is indeed that. He has been a dedicated and principled servant of the people of Hawai'i and our nation, an unfailing ally of our veterans and their families, and a valued colleague and friend. I will miss him, and I will always remember how he taught us that gentleness and effectiveness are not mutually exclusive characteristics.

Danny, as I have come to know him, has been one of the strongest and most loyal parts of our Senate Prayer Breakfast. That regular gathering that many of us attend gives us an opportunity to come together to share our faith and discuss the difference it has made in our daily lives.

No one has played a more important role in those weekly meetings than Danny. His faith has brought him through some very difficult situations in his life and it has also helped him to pursue policies and programs that have made a difference in more lives than we will ever know.

When Danny was in the House he was the song leader. His understanding of the importance of music helped him to better express his faith. He led our singing of the hymns by providing us with the history of each song as he explained the meaning of the words that were used to bring its message to life. His faith also showed itself with his work on a sailing ship that helped to bring missionaries around the Pacific to share their faith with those who might otherwise have never heard such stories.

Danny is a veteran of World War II. His experience during the war gave him an understanding of the sacrifices our veterans made during their service and the importance of ensuring that we as a nation take good care of them and address their medical needs. That is why one of Danny's great accomplishments here in the Senate has been his efforts on behalf of his fellow veterans. Whenever an important bill was taken up and passed, Danny immediately got to work, trying to determine the impact each bill would have on our veterans and how any negative impacts could be addressed and reversed. Just as we owe our veterans a great debt of gratitude for their service, veterans everywhere have a special place in their hearts for everything Danny has done over the years to protect and preserve the benefits they have earned with their service.

In addition to his great faith and his concern for our nation's veterans, Danny also brought to the Senate his love of Hawai'i and its great culture and history. It was a gift he shared with us over the years that increased our awareness of Hawai'i's past and the great traditions of his home state.

Through the years Danny has made a reputation for himself here in the Senate as a careful, thoughtful legislator who works quietly but effectively. The good work he has done on a number of issues has had an impact that will continue to be felt for many years to come.

Thank you, Danny, for your service both here in the Senate and in our armed forces. You can be very proud of all you have achieved. You have represented your state very well. Thank you most of all for your friendship and for sharing your faith and the impact it has had on your life. You will be missed and not just by those of us in the Senate who have enjoyed having a chance to come to know you. You have been a great friend to our nation's veterans, too, and they will always remember your commitment to them.

Senator Jack Reed, Rhode Island

Madam President, at this time, I wish to take a few minutes to salute my colleagues who are retiring at the end of this year with the conclusion of the 112th Congress: Daniel Akaka of Hawai'i, Jeff Bingaman of New Mexico, Scott Brown of Massachusetts, Kent Conrad of North Dakota, Jim DeMint of South Carolina, Kay Bailey Hutchison of Texas, Herb Kohl of Wisconsin, Jon Kyl of Arizona, Joseph Lieberman of Connecticut, Richard Lugar of Indiana, Ben Nelson of Nebraska, Olympia Snowe of Maine and Jim Webb of Virginia. They have all worked ceaselessly to give their constituents the best representation and give the country the benefit of their views, their wisdom and their experience. They are men and women who are committed to the nation, and they have every day in different ways contributed to this Senate and to our great country.

I wish to thank them personally for their service, and, in so many cases, their personal kindness to me; for listening to my points and for, together, hopefully, serving this Senate and this nation in a more positive and progressive way.

In particular, let me say a few words about some of the members with whom I have had the privilege to work more closely.

Senator Daniel Akaka, like his colleague, the late and revered Senator Daniel Inouye, proudly served our nation during World War II. I am stepping into the huge shoes of Danny Akaka as the cochair of the Army Caucus. From one soldier to another, I salute him.

He has also been an extraordinarily forceful advocate not just for active duty personnel but for veterans and, of course, for the men and women of his beloved Hawaiʻi...

I could go on with all of my colleagues, just thanking them for their friendship, for their camaraderie and for their commitment to the nation and the Senate. As they depart, they have left an extraordinary legacy. Now it is our responsibility to carry on in so many different ways, and I hope we measure up to what they have done. If we do, then we can go forward confidently.

With that, I yield the floor.

Senator Susan Collins, Maine

Mr. President, in his farewell message to the people of Hawaiʻi, Senator Daniel Akaka wrote that his dream was always to work in a job in which he could help people. In his thirty-six years in Congress—fourteen in the House of Representatives and twenty-two here in the Senate—Danny Akaka has done that job exceedingly well.

He has done it with statesmanship and perseverance. As just one example, just a few weeks ago, President Obama signed into law landmark legislation to better protect federal employees who come forward to disclose government waste, fraud, abuse and other wrongdoing. The Akaka-Collins Whistleblower Protection Enhancement Act would not have passed without Danny's determination to help both our dedicated federal workers and the citizens they serve.

Serving with Danny on the Homeland Security and Governmental Affairs Committee, I appreciate the priority he always placed on making the federal government more efficient and transparent, and on advancing policies to attract, recruit and retain the skilled workforce needed to meet today's challenges. From safeguarding our nation against terrorist attacks to supporting the first responders in our communities, Danny has been a great ally and a true leader.

It also has been an honor to work with Danny on the Armed Services Committee. As a World War II veteran, he brought to the committee a deep and personal understanding of the sacrifices made by our men and women in uniform, and by their families. He is a champion of efforts to ensure that our active National Guard and reserve personnel have the equipment and training to remain the best fighting force in the world, and he is dedicated to providing our veterans with the services they earned and deserve.

Danny Akaka has been described as the "Aloha Senator." To most of us, that multipurpose word can mean anything from "hello" to "goodbye." To the Hawaiian people, it is a word of deep spirituality and profound meaning. The late Reverend Abraham Akaka, Danny's oldest brother and one of Hawai'i's most beloved clergymen, defined the "aloha spirit" this way: "God first, others second, yourself last." As a patriot and statesman, Senator Daniel Akaka embodies that spirit through his desire to promote the true good of others and to help people. Aloha pumehana, Senator Akaka, farewell with my deepest regards and affection. Thank you for your friendship and for your service to our country.

Senator Lisa Murkowski, Alaska

Mr. President, I was watching my friend and colleague Senator Akaka as he was delivering his comments earlier about Senator Inouye and the legislation that both he and our dear friend and former colleague have worked so hard on over the years, and I wanted to come to the floor this evening and tell my friend that I am deeply appreciative of the words he has delivered as the chairman of the Senate Committee on Indian Affairs. I would certainly hope the Senate would respect the thinking the senator has outlined as it relates to the Native Hawaiian Government Reorganization Act...

Senator Inouye and Senator Akaka have worked valiantly to create programs for Native Hawaiians that parallel those available to American Indians and Alaska Natives, but this is not enough. Justice demands that the native people of Hawai'i earn the federal recognition that is rightfully theirs...

We began our morning paying tribute to our friend and former colleague Senator Inouye. As we think about Hawai'i and its peoples, and as we remember the contributions of Senator Inouye, and as we recognize Senator Akaka as he departs from this body after years of honorable service, I would hope that within this body we would not forget the efforts they have worked on so valiantly.

I will commit to my friend, Senator Akaka, that the cause the senator has taken up, that he has worked on so hard with Senator Inouye, will not die until justice for the native people of Hawai'i is achieved. I thank the senator for his leadership.

Mr. President, I was going to yield the floor, but I would like to take a moment to provide my remarks regarding Senator Akaka and his contribution here, if I may.

(Written remarks)

Mr. President, I rise to speak on behalf of my friend, my colleague, Senator Daniel Akaka, who is set to retire after twenty-two years of dedicated service in the Senate. He has been a personal friend to me, he has been a personal friend to my family and to my parents. He and his wife, Millie, a wonderful, beautiful woman, have been leaders on behalf of the people of Hawai'i and have long been friends and partners to the people of Alaska.

Senator Akaka has served our nation and the great state of Hawai'i honorably for nearly seventy years. That is an incredible contribution. His service began in 1943, immediately following his graduation from the Kamehameha School for Boys in Honolulu. The Japanese attack on Pearl Harbor had taken place a year earlier, only five miles from his dormitory steps. In the hours immediately following that attack, Senator Akaka, who was a seventeen-year-old ROTC cadet, helped his classmates search for paratroopers in the fields above his school grounds. Like so many others of his generation, Senator Akaka answered the call of duty, joined the U.S. Army, first with the Corps of Engineers as a mechanic and a welder and later as a noncommissioned officer.

In 1952, Senator Akaka used the G.I. Bill to earn his degree in education from the University of Hawai'i and began his lifelong dedication to our nation's students, first as a teacher, then as a principal at a high school in Honolulu, and later with the Department of Health, Education and Welfare.

Senator Akaka was first elected to the U.S. House of Representatives in 1976 and then went on to win six more elections. It was clearly evident the people of Hawai'i within that Second Congressional District valued his passion and his dedication for the office. In 1990, after the death of Senator Spark Matsunaga, Senator Akaka was appointed and then subsequently elected to the seat in the Senate that he has held for twenty-two years now.

Senator Akaka's fortitude and his determination have not waned in these seventy years. As the first Native Hawaiian ever to serve in the Senate, and the only indigenous person currently serving in the Senate, he is a proven champion for American Indians, Alaska Natives and Native Hawaiians. It was just in October of this year that Senator Akaka came to Alaska and was honored by the Alaska Federation of Natives with the Denali Award. This award is presented to an individual who is not an Alaska Native for their contributions to the growth and development of the Alaska Native community's culture, economy and health. Senator Akaka has done that repeatedly over the years. The efforts he has worked on, whether it was bigger initiatives or whether to ensure the people in King Cove had access to an airport so their lives weren't threatened in a medical emergency and they could get out, Senator Akaka has stepped up to ensure the people of Alaska are cared for.

It has truly been a pleasure to work with Senator Akaka over these past ten years on the Senate Indian Affairs Committee. The chairmanship he has administered has been admired and appreciated by all of us who are on that committee.

Senator Akaka's leadership, wisdom and grasp of issues has helped us work together toward many visions and goals that we shared. The SAVE Native Women Act—a bill to help protect native women and children across our 565 federally recognized tribes—was largely incorporated into the Senate version of the 2012 Violence Against Women Act. We need to make sure that legislation passes. Again, as we think about the statistics that so many of our native peoples face, we need to make certain we are making appropriate gains and strides to help address them, and Chairman Akaka has worked with us on that. We fought to ensure the preservation of native languages not only in our communities but within our classrooms.

As I mentioned, I have long supported the concept that Senator Inouye and Senator Akaka have championed with regard to federal recognition of Native Hawaiians.

Senator Akaka is also special to two other constituencies—our federal employees and our veterans. He is one of this body's leading experts on some of the more arcane laws that apply to federal civil service. Alaska's federal employees clearly appreciate his leadership on the Non-Foreign AREA Act, which made them eligible for locality pay that counts toward retirement. This is an issue in my state that took some time to negotiate and to move through, but the federal employees in Alaska—as they are seeing the benefits of that locality pay—owe thanks and gratitude to the work of Senator Akaka. And he knows well the laws that govern the U.S. Postal Service probably as well as anyone in this body.

During Senator Akaka's tenure as chairman of the Senate Veterans' Affairs Committee, this body has made great progress in ensuring that the VA had a budget commensurate with its needs. His contributions to ensuring that post-9/11 veterans had access to critically needed health and education resources will endure.

As neighbors in the Pacific, Alaska and Hawai'i have always shared a very special bond, not only because of our geography and our time differences. Every time I endure a twelve-hour flight across the country to go home—and home is four time zones away—I am reminded that it takes Senator Akaka a couple hours more and one time zone more to get home. It is not only our geography that binds us; we have many other similarities: our indigenous peoples, the relative youth of our states, our unique landscapes and for years our delegations have worked together across the aisle for the good of our people.

Senator Akaka's bipartisan approach, his willingness to work toward success, will be missed by me and so many of our colleagues. Of course, I don't think Senator Akaka would call it bipartisanship. He would call it aloha. We work in the aloha spirit.

With that, I wish to tell my friend and my colleague, mahalo. From the bottom of my heart, mahalo. I am going to miss you, Senator Akaka. I am going to miss your wife, Millie, and your entire extended family. As you return home to your beloved Hawai'i, know that you have left an impression on so many.

With that, Mr. Chairman, I yield the floor.

Senator Ben Cardin, Maryland

I have been privileged to work with Senator Akaka on efforts to protect the federal workforce. Federal employees have no greater champion than Senator Akaka, who has chaired the Homeland Security and Governmental Affairs Subcommittee on Oversight of Government

Management. Senator Akaka is committed to making the federal government an employer of choice capable of attracting and retaining the best and the brightest. In 2009 he introduced the Telework Enhancement Act, which became law in 2010 and expands telework opportunities at executive agencies. Senator Akaka has also fought to create a culture of transparency and fairness in the federal government, authoring the Whistleblower Protection Enhancement Act, which I was proud to cosponsor. President Obama signed that bill into law last month. Senator Akaka has been a civil rights champion, partnering with Senators Lieberman, Collins, me and others to support domestic partner benefits.

I also appreciate Senator Akaka's determined advocacy for financial literacy and consumer protections. His Credit Card Minimum Payment Warning Act was included in the 2009 Credit CARD Act. Now, thanks to Senator Akaka, credit card bills must include a disclosure box to show consumers how long it will take to repay their entire balance if they only make minimum monthly payments. The so-called "Akaka Box" also lets consumers know how much it will cost to pay off their outstanding balance within thirty-six months, which is a typical length of a debt management plan. Senator Akaka was also an author of portions of the Dodd-Frank Act addressing financial literacy (establishing the Office of Financial Education within the Consumer Financial Protection Bureau) and investor protections.

Throughout Senator Akaka's long and distinguished career in Congress, he has also been an ardent environmentalist. As a former chairman of the Subcommittee on National Parks, legislation he authored has created, expanded or otherwise improved each of Hawai'i's national parks. His Hawai'i Tropical Forest Recovery Act established the Hawai'i Experimental Tropical Forest in order to promote the recovery of tropical forests in Hawai'i and undertake needed research to better protect tropical forests around the world.

A hallmark of Senator Akaka, like Senator Inouye, is his soft-spoken and courteous manner. The senators from Hawai'i have always treated the rest of us with respect and graciousness. They have reached across the aisle to foster bipartisan cooperation. They have exhibited a rare and calming serenity when partisan tempers have boiled over. I will miss the warm and gentle and friendly personalities of Senators Akaka and Inouye, their wise counsel, and their service here in the U.S. Senate on behalf of Hawaiians and all Americans. ✤

INDEX

A

Abercrombie, Neil 176, 178, 185, 222, 225, 231, 244–246, 275, 281, 283, 288–289, 291, 294, 296, 298, 300, 302, 304, 307, 310, 312, 315, 337, 339, 362, 380, 413, 415, 416, 437, 442, 456, 462, 486, 490, 502, 524, 533–534, 537–538, 540, 545, 547, 564, 589–590, 596, 597
Adams, Brock 265
Aea, Richard 40, 54
Affleck, Ben 133
Afghanistan war 19, 162, 336, 366–367, 372–373, 395, 423, 457, 467, 476, 500, 540, 563, 572, 584
Agard, Louis "Buzzy" 40, 176, 401
Agbayani, Amy 236–237
Agsalud, Joshua 79
Aiona, James "Duke" 534, 545, 547
Akaka, Abraham 6, 16, 25, 30, 36–37, 49, 59–60, 62, 69, 71, 78, 82, 116–117, 222, 249, 254–256, 322–324, 390–391, 403, 522, 599–600
Akaka, Alan Limaikaika 58, 67, 82, 101, 403–404, 526–527
Akaka, Annie Kaleiānuenue (née Kāhoa) 16, 23, 25–26, 54, 402
Akaka, Daniel Kahikina Jr. 55, 67, 72, 82, 101, 402, 403, 526–527, 594, 596
Akaka, Fenner Marie 62, 249, 323
Akaka, Gerard Kāpena 58, 67, 82, 101, 403, 415, 526–527, 594
Akaka, Godfrey 116–117
Akaka, Jeff 323
Akaka, Joe 30, 116–117, 322, 324
Akaka, John 30, 322
Akaka, Kahikina 16, 23, 25–26, 30, 32, 113, 117, 323, 402
Akaka, Mary Louise (née Jeffrey) 116–117, 323
Akaka, Mary Mildred "Millie" (née Chong) 8, 18, 20–21, 44, 48, 54–55, 58, 72, 79, 80, 99, 101, 116–117, 123, 128, 135, 163, 165, 186–187, 211, 214, 222, 250–251, 254–255, 258, 260, 280, 288, 322–323, 327, 329, 353, 380, 386, 404, 431–432, 454, 457, 507, 511, 513, 517–518, 521, 526–528, 533, 537, 542, 545, 551–552, 566, 571, 585–587, 601
Akaka, Mikey 386
Akaka, Nicholas Kalāohikina 64, 67, 82, 101, 404, 526–527, 533
Akaka, Phoebe 30
Akaka, Pualani 113, 116–117, 323
Akaka, Pulu 323
Akaka, Sally 323
Akaka, Sandy 323
Akaka, Simeon 323
Akaka, Violet 116–117
Akana, Annie (née Akaka) 27, 30, 322, 324
Akana, Bernard 202
Akana, Francis 322
Akana, Harriet "Wunnie" Lau 54
Akau, James 593
Albert, Carl 84, 102–104
Albright, Madeleine 319, 332
Alexander, Lamar 345, 443
Ali, Muhammad 313
Alito, Samuel 435–436
Allard, Wayne 439, 443
Allen, George 409, 443, 457
Allen, Gracie 518
Aluli, Emmet "Noa" 93, 235, 407, 515
Aluli, Kimo 93
al-Zawahiri, Ayman 336–337
Amaral, Annelle 316
Amemiya, Ron 95
Amiyoka, Shiro 95
Amougezar, Jamshid 125
Anderson, D.G. "Andy" 81, 153, 168, 175–176, 182, 382
Anderson, Eileen 18, 140, 168, 180
Anthony, Naalehu 597
Aoyagi, Mary Beth 215
Apana, James "Kimo" 337
Apoliona, Haunani 401, 597, 599
Arakawa, Alan 337, 456, 546
Arakawa, David 315
Arashiro, Steve 228
Archer, Bill 312
Aristide, Jean-Bertrand 298–299
Ariyoshi, George 56, 74–86, 94, 96–98, 100, 129, 140, 153, 175–176, 180, 183–185, 254–255, 292, 325, 325–326, 388
Ariyoshi, Jean 84, 254–255
Armey, Dick 341
Armstrong, Neil 576
Arnold, Henry "Hap" 121, 315
Ashcroft, John 354, 400

Index

Ashley, Tom 107
Asimov, Isaac 146
Askew, Reuben 167
Aspin, Les 177
Atwater, Lee 199
Awana, Henry 40

B

Babbitt, Bruce 195
Bachman, Michelle 569, 573
Bailey, Justin 473
Bailey, Mahina 513
Bainum, Duke 415, 416
Baker, Howard 90, 142, 544
Baltazar, Gabe 288
Barnhart, Ray 181
Barrasso, John 550, 556
Barr, Bob 309
Bates, Jim 208
Baucus, Max 332, 354, 356, 357, 428, 443, 502, 559
Bayh, Birch 443
Bayh, Evan 338, 443, 480
Bazargan, Mehdi 133
Beamer, Billie 231, 243
Beamer, Kapono 91
Beamer, Keola 91
Beamer, Nona 321
Beaumont, Robert 91
Begich, Mark 506, 530, 540, 544, 559, 563, 581
Begich, Nick 104, 543–544
Benham, Roy 321
Bennett, Bob 443
Bennett, Charles 177
Bennett, Mark 538
Benny, Jack 61
Bent, Dan 281
Bentsen, Lloyd 202, 274, 275
Bergland, Bob 129
Berg, Lyla 545
Bermudez, Leilani 62
Bertie, George Allen Jr. 267
Bessette-Kennedy, Carolyn 344
Bessette, Lauren 344
Bevill, Tom 148
Biden, Joe 195, 199, 216, 220, 265, 294, 435, 444, 480, 485, 489, 502, 508, 535, 569, 572, 588, 590, 592

Bingaman, Jeff 22, 338, 444, 447, 552
Bingham, Hiram III 14
Bingham, Hiram Jr. 14
bin Laden, Osama 336–337, 366–367, 562–563, 572, 578
Bishop, Bernice Pauahi (princess) 31–32, 59, 321, 402
Bitterman, Mary 196, 201, 202, 204
Black, Barry 586, 589
Black, David 549
Black Eagle (smuggler) 36–37
Black, William 206
Blagojevich, Rod 497
Blair, Russell 196
Blair, Tony 399
Blaisdell, Neal 59
Blaisdell, Richard Kekuni 38–40, 401, 591
Blitzer, Wolf 345
Bode, Carl 40
Boehlert, Sherwood 425
Boehner, John 378, 409, 548, 572
Bogart, Humphrey 481
Boggs, Hale 104, 543
Boland, Ed 178
Bolling, Dick 102, 104–107
Bolton, Claude 466–467
Bond, Kit 444
Bonk, Keiko 361
Bordallo, Madeleine 537
Boren, David 265
Borges, Jimmy 85, 597
Borlaug, Norman 122
Bornhorst, Marilyn 181, 202
Borreca, Richard 80
Borthwick, William 224
Boschwitz, Rudy 221, 380
Bowles, Erskine 296–297
Boxer, Barbara 22, 310, 358, 422, 425, 435, 444, 447, 472, 499, 535
Boylan, Peter 549
Brademas, John 108
Bradley, Bill 265, 345
Brady, James 143
Braga, Manuel 498–500
Brandt, Gladys 321

Bransford, William 530
Breaux, John 359
Bremer, Paul 399
Brennan, William 265
Breyer, Stephen 362
Brian, Danielle 530
Bright, Teresa 288
Broder, David 106
Broder Van Dyke, Jesse 471–472, 506–507, 517, 587
Brokaw, Tom 11, 373, 406, 488, 493
Bronster, Margery 322
Brooks, Jack 105, 294, 301
Brown, Boyce 180
Brown, George 156, 208
Brown, Hank 282
Brown, Jerry 70, 264, 273–274
Brown, Kenny 239
Brown, Michael 429
Brown, Pat 70
Brown, Ron 217, 302
Brown, Sherrod 501
Brownback, Sam 377, 444
Bryan, Richard 311
Brzezinski, Zbigniew "Zbig" 133–136
Buchanan, Pat 263, 345–346
Buchli, James 168
Bunda, Bobby 545
Bunning, Jim 439, 444
Burdick, Quentin 168–169, 265
Burke, Yvonne 106
Burmeister, E.R. 38
Burns, Anne "Flo" 30
Burns, Bea 84, 86
Burns, Conrad 283, 439, 444, 457
Burns, George 518
Burns, Jim 84
Burns, John A. "Jack" 30, 40, 56, 58–59, 71–79, 81–82, 84–86, 97–98, 102, 325, 457, 522
Burris, Roland 506, 529, 536
Burr, Richard 444, 474, 477, 494, 500–502, 540
Burton, John 103, 130, 145, 156
Burton, Michele 103

Burton, Phil 103–108, 130, 142, 144–145, 160–161, 444
Burton, Sala 161–162
Bush, Barbara 232, 266
Bush, George H.W. 19, 139, 362, 431, 523, 594
Bush, George W. 19–21, 195, 197, 199, 201–202, 204–205, 208, 214, 216–219, 221–223, 226–227, 230, 233, 233–239, 242–246, 263–264, 266–267, 275–280, 298, 305, 308, 314, 345–346, 354, 361–364, 372–373, 375, 379, 381, 383, 394–399, 408–409, 413, 416, 422, 426, 429, 432, 434–435, 441–442, 452–453, 456–460, 462–463, 470–471, 475, 477, 479, 486–488, 490–492, 500, 502, 505, 508, 526–527, 535, 570
Bush, Jeb 428
Bush, Laura 508
Buyers, J.W.A. "Doc" 318
Byers, Terri 215
Byrd, Erma 542
Byrd, Robert C. 19, 22, 142, 186, 214, 220, 271, 311, 375, 383, 422, 434–437, 444, 457, 509, 541–542, 542, 585

C

Caldwell, Kirk 577, 584
Caleda, Art 498–499
Campbell, Ben Nighthorse 361, 400–401, 494
Campbell, Kim 288
Campbell, William 40
Cann, Becky 580
Canterbury, Angela 530
Cantor, Eric 548
Cantwell, Maria 362, 425, 444, 556
Carcieri, Donald 565
Cardin, Ben 531, 535
Cardus, Paul 215

Carlisle, Peter 315, 415, 577
Carnahan, Jean 21, 362, 381
Carnahan, Mel 21, 362, 381
Carpenter, Dante 202
Carper, Thomas 401, 444, 577
Carroll, John 346, 361, 402, 545, 576
Carter, Eleanor Rosalynn 135, 508
Carter, Herbert 307
Carter, James Earl III "Chip" 135
Carter, Jimmy 93, 106–107, 109, 111, 122–123, 127–128, 130, 134–141, 145, 161, 167, 176, 180, 220, 274, 298–299, 345, 378, 387, 508
Carvalho, Bernard 490
Carver, George Washington 161
Case, Audrey 450
Case, Ed 382, 400, 415, 416, 437–440, 442, 446, 448–454, 456, 511, 512, 534, 545, 551, 568, 576, 582, 589
Case, Steve 360, 439
Casey, Bob 460
Casey, William 188
Castro, Fidel 354–356, 357
Cayetano, Ben 79, 176, 210–211, 222, 231, 292, 296, 300, 302, 307, 315–317, 322, 325, 337, 379, 577, 584
Cedras, Raoul 298–299
Chafee, John 340, 342
Chafee, Lincoln 22, 217, 283, 311, 436, 445
Chamanan, Kriangsak 125
Chambliss, Saxby 382, 445
Chapman, Mark David 144
Cheney, Dick 226, 235, 245, 266–267, 361–362, 381, 395, 458, 462, 539
Cheney, Lynne 266
Chertoff, Michael 426–428
Ching, Donald 74
Chisolm, Shirley 106, 144, 156
Cho, Seung-hui 463–464

Christie, Chris 569
Christopher, Warren 316
Chun, Dave 374
Chun, Michael 594
Churchill, Winston 12
Ciampi, Carlo 288
Clarke, Arthur C. 447, 448, 561
Clark, Ramsey 472
Clark, Wesley 408
Cleghorn, Archibald 54
Cleland, Max 382
Clift, Montgomery 44
Clinton, Bill 10, 19, 21, 109, 263, 273–274, 277–280, 282–283, 285–286, 288–296, 298, 302–304, 305–308, 310–312, 314, 316–317, 319–320, 327, 329–334, 336–339, 342, 346–347, 349–352, 359, 362–363, 363, 366–367, 381, 397, 422, 424, 432, 435, 480, 485, 499–500, 505, 508, 524–525
Clinton, Chelsea 289, 292, 332
Clinton, George 274
Clinton, Hillary 289–292, 327, 329–330, 332–333, 338–339, 362, 441, 445, 479–480, 494, 508, 517, 524–525, 535, 541, 571, 578
Cobb, Steve 176
Coburn, Tom 540
Cochran, Thad 283
Cockett, Irwin 599
Coelho, Tony 177
Coffee, Jerry 277, 456, 481
Cohen, William 217, 293, 311, 319, 350
Coleman, Norm 380–381, 424, 445, 490, 529
Coleman, William 180
Cole, Tom 372, 537
Collins, Susan 340, 426, 445, 460, 479, 502, 520, 529, 540, 577, 618, 623
Como, Perry 166
Conlon, Richard 160
Conrad, Kent 22, 552, 556, 559

INDEX 627

Conte, Silvio 109
Cook, James 169
Coons, Chris 531
Coppola, Francis Ford 90
Cormack, Maribelle 51
Cornyn, John 500
Corzine, John 22, 409
Couch, John 224
Courtney, Reneisha 240
Crabbe, William 40
Craig, Larry 320, 423–424, 500
Cramer, Ken 148
Cranston, Alan 167, 206, 228, 265
Cranston, Bryan 133
Craven, John 94, 100, 286, 296
Crocker, Ryan 471
Crockett, George 163
Cronin, Dave 199
Crosby, Bing 62
Crosby, Gary 62
Crossley, Randy 77
Crowder, Richard 219
Crowley, Kawika 576
Crozier, Michael 204, 225, 231
Cummings, Elijah 531
Cunningham, Helen 57

D

Daley, William 332
D'Amato, Alphonse 311, 320, 338, 499
Danforth, John 217, 282
Daniels, Joseph 40
Dannemeyer, William 282
Danner, Pat 310
Danner, Robin 546, 597
Darden, George "Buddy" 162
Darvill, Jack 195
Daschle, Tom 272, 320, 341, 346, 362, 373–376, 408, 411, 416, 494
Davila, Rudolph 352–353
Davis, Charles K.L. 62–63
Davis, Jefferson 270
Day, Doris 62
Dayton, Mark 22, 439
De, Rajesh 530
Dean, Howard 408

Dean, Melissa 593
DeConcini, Dennis 206, 265, 301
Deer, Sarah 558
Defense of Marriage Act 309–311, 574–575
De Guair, John 40
Dela Cruz, Donalyn 517
de la Garza, Kika 123
Del Castillo, Rafael 545
Deloso, Alfred 316
DeMattos, Riley 593
DeMocker, Wendy 219
Denny, Martin 63
Denton, Jeremiah 276–277, 283, 481
DeSoto, Frenchy 235, 406
Devine, Tom 530
Dicke, Robert 393
Diehl, Leo 105
Dingell, John 332
Dixon, Alan 265
Dixon, Don 206
Djou, Charles 545, 547, 550, 568, 576, 584
Dodd, Christopher 216, 274–275, 409, 480, 506, 535, 540
Dods, Walter 596
Doi, Nelson 56, 77–78, 80–83, 100, 388
Doi, Paul 80
Dole, Bob 157, 195, 224, 227, 243, 283, 301, 314, 494, 544
Dole, Elizabeth "Liddy" 157, 181, 243, 314, 345–346, 479, 490
Dole, Sanford B. 54
Domenici, Pete 217, 283, 500
Donlin, Von Hulu 44
Doo, Arthur 40
Doo, Leigh-Wai 181, 201
Doolittle, Jimmy 42
Dorgan, Byron 443, 466, 506, 540
Dougherty, Ralph McClearn 267
Douglas, Robert 40
Doyle, Mike 341
Dubs, Adolph 123
Duckworth, Tammy 496–497, 536

Dukakis, Michael 195, 199, 201–202, 274
Duke, David 263
Dung, Mrs. (third-grade teacher) 28–29, 562
Dunham, Madelyn 484
Dunn, Anita 219
Durbin, Dick 22, 215, 411, 422, 435, 439, 506, 548, 585
Durenberger, Dave 217, 275
Dwyer, Bernard 266
Dye, David 434
Dylan, Bob 381

E

Eagleton, Tom 506
Earhart, Amelia 34–35
Echo Hawk, Larry 565
Eckhardt, Bob 105
education issues 409, 441, 541
See also Native Hawaiian affairs: education
Edwards, John 338, 408, 477, 480
Edwards, Webley 91
Ehrlich, Paul 122
Eisenhower, Dwight D. 59, 223, 236, 265, 327, 407, 487
Elizabeth II (queen) 258–260, 521
El Khalifi, Amine 578
Elliott, Laurel 513
Emerson, Ralph Waldo 260
energy issues 140, 208, 216, 221, 263, 275, 286, 440. *See also* environmental issues: alternative/clean energy
Ensign, John 474
environmental issues
  alternative/clean energy 221, 243, 447–448, 535–536, 573
  chemical weapons disposal 237–238
  climate change 208, 221, 239, 359, 447–448, 535–536, 601–602
  environmental protection 247–248, 263, 293–294,

358–359.
  See also H-3 freeway
  Tropical Forest Recovery
    Act 275–276, 440,
    594
  marine sanctuaries 230, 440
  National Parks and wildlife
    refuges 286–287, 293,
    336, 342, 405, 440
  ordnance removal
    405–406.
    See also Kahoʻolawe
  pollution 128, 189–190,
    358–359
  environmental disasters
    203–204, 539
  sustainability 286, 549
  aquaculture development
    127–128, 286, 302, 312
  water resources 160, 342,
    426, 446
Enzi, Mike 409
Ertel, Allen 105
Ervin, Sam 90
Exon, Jim 265, 311, 315

F

Faleomavaega, Eni 537
Fallon, William 365
Fargo, Tom 365
Fasi, Frank 18, 76, 80–81,
  83, 96, 100, 140–141, 153,
  168, 180, 180–182, 202,
  204, 237, 239, 243, 289,
  296, 300, 302, 315, 337,
  361, 415, 518, 524, 537
Fasi, Joyce 243, 518, 537
Fawcett, Welcome 181
Fazio, Vic 208
Feingold, Russ 22, 310, 383,
  478
Feinstein, Dianne 293, 310,
  358, 425, 435, 444, 499,
  535, 574
Ferdaus, Rezwan 578
Ferraro, Geraldine 142, 144,
  167
Filner, Bob 504
Finney, Ben 91
Fitzgerald, Patrick 467
Flippo, Ronnie 156
Flores, Carlene 216

Foley, Tom 106, 110, 130,
  142, 186, 206, 215, 258,
  271, 301, 364
Follett, Ken 276
Fong, Ellyn 414
Fong, Hiram Jr. 413
Fong, Hiram Sr. 84, 93–94,
  135, 218, 232, 237, 378,
  413–414
Foote, Travis 554
Forbes, Steve 345–346
Ford, Gerald 90, 93, 106,
  141, 188, 195, 362,
  461–462, 481
Ford, Wendell 311
Foreman, Michele 375
Fort, Cornelia 121
Francisco, Kainana 593
Francis, Russ 361, 362
Frank, Barney 310, 424
Frankel, Chuck 175
Franken, Al 490, 556, 559
Franklin, Benjamin 333–334
Fraser, Malcolm 134
Free, James 123
Friedman, Thomas L. 461
Frist, Bill 399, 411, 435
Fritts, Amelia 128
Fryer, Gerard 538
Fujimoto, Amy 215
Fukunaga, Carol 233

G

Gabbard, Carol 600
Gabbard, Mike 416, 600
Gabbard, Tulsi 510–511,
  545–546, 547, 568, 576,
  584, 589, 600
Gagarin, Yuri 65
Galdeira, Pae 111
Galuteria, Brickwood 597
Gates, Robert 457, 494, 563
Gayler, Noel 84
Gearan, Mark 332
George, Mary 227, 237
Gephardt, Dick 109, 122,
  142, 177, 195, 206, 315,
  341, 379, 408
Gerald, Kimo 512
Gerardo, Sonny 154
Geren, Pete 310
Gevirtz, Don 328

Gevirtz, Marilyn 328
Giardina, Christian 593–594
Gillibrand, Kirsten 535, 585
Gill, Tom 74, 76–78, 80–81,
  83, 96
Giltner, John 118
Gingrich, Newt 146–148,
  156–159, 274, 302, 309,
  338, 341, 490, 560, 569,
  573
Ginsburg, Ruth Bader 362
Giugni, Henry 431–432
Giuliani, Rudy 483
Glenn, John 66, 167, 206,
  293, 338, 437
Glickman, Dan 109, 220,
  332
Godfrey, Arthur 69
Goemans, John 313, 465
Goldschmidt, Neil 180
Gomard, Robert 40
Gomez, Edward Jr. 267
Gonzalez, Henry 523
Gorbachev, Mikhail 197
Gore, Albert III 264
Gore, Al Jr. 8–10, 109,
  129, 156, 195, 199, 209,
  216, 220, 264, 274, 283,
  327–330, 331, 338–339,
  345–346, 361–362, 363,
  381, 408, 416, 524
Gore, Tipper 327–328, 330,
  338
Gorton, Slade 282–283,
  340, 499
Graham, Billy 328, 330
Graham, Bob 22
Graham, David 519–520,
  530
Graham, Lindsey 424
Graham, Phil 174
Gramm, Bob 408
Granger, Raymond Edward
  267
Grant, Eric 466
Grassley, Chuck 411,
  520–521
Graulty, Rey 316
Gray, Kenneth 199–200
Greenspan, Alan 305
Green, Steve 110
Greer, Gerald 79, 96
Gregg, Judd 494, 540

Grisham, Wayne 148, 156, 158
Guarini, Frank 163
Guerrero, Joe 61
Gulf War 226, 230, 245–246, 472–473

H

H-3 freeway 80–81, 179–185, 325–326
Hagel, Chuck 315
Haig, Alexander 195, 422
Hajiro, Barney 352
Haleamau, Karin 513
Hale, Ellen Jane 403
Hall, Jack 103
Hall, John 462–463
Hall, Katie 162
Hall, Tex 564
Halsey, William "Bull" 481
Halvorson, Richard 210
Hamilton, Lee 332
Hampe, Melissa 440, 450
Hanabusa, Colleen 440, 456, 534, 545, 547, 551, 568, 576, 584, 589, 599
Hand, Learned 200
Hanks, Tom 106
Hannahs, Neil 450
Hannemann, Mufi 176, 204, 222, 225, 231, 361, 415, 416, 490, 533–534, 545, 568, 576
Haʻo (chiefess) 25
Hara, Gary 600
Harkin, Tom 209, 260, 263, 273, 275, 381, 478, 530
Harrington, Al 403
Harris, Blase 176
Harris, Eric 343
Harris, Jeremy 204, 302, 307, 315, 361
Harris, Katherine 362
Hart, Gary 167, 195
Hart, Philip 495
Haselbush, Paul 369
Hasemoto, Mikio 352
Hastert, Dennis 341, 382, 395
Hastings, Alcee 310
Hata, Frank 79
Hatch, Orrin 275, 345, 401, 460

Hatfield, Mark 216–217, 220, 283, 311
Havel, Vaclav 431
Hawaiian renaissance 91–92
Hawaiʻi statehood 59–60
Hayashida, Glenn 595
Hayashi, Joe 352
Hayashi, Shizuya 352
Hayes, Bully 52
Hayes, James 310
Hays, Wayne 103
Heen, Walter 321
Heflin, Howell 315, 358
Heftel, Cecil "Cec" 94, 100, 109, 111, 129–130, 144–146, 156, 167, 173–177, 180, 386, 514
Height, Dorothy 328
Heine, Leinaʻala Kalama 82
Heinlein, Robert 146
Heinz, John 217
Helbig, Otto 57
Helm, George 93, 110–112, 515
Helm, Mae 111
Helms, Jesse 144, 161, 314, 354
Hemmings, Fred 227, 231, 237, 296, 300
Hemmings, Suzy 243
Henry, Geoffrey 238–239
Heu, Herbert 40
Hicks, David 350
Hidalgo, Lani 513
Higashi, Roland 99
Hill, Anita 264
Hill, Pat "Leolani" (née Kim) 215, 374, 512–513
Hills, Carla 204
Hinckley, John 143–144
Hirata, Teichiro "Tim" 95, 98
Hirohito, Emperor 134
Hirono, Mazie 296, 300, 302, 382, 440, 456, 462, 486, 490, 502, 537, 540, 550, 551, 568, 576, 582–584
Hirten, John 183
Ho, Don 31, 82, 86, 463
Hoeven, John 556
Hogue, Bob 456
Ho, Hannah 31
Holbrook, Hal 276

Holder, Eric 544, 547, 555
Holiday, Billie 85
Hollings, Ernest F. "Fritz" 167, 174, 320, 358, 383, 499
Holmes, Tommy 91
Holschuh, Fred 361
Holt, Milton 316
Hongo, Andrew 329
Hongo, Gae 328–329
Hongo, Randy 328–329
Hong, Wayne 418–421
Hoʻopiʻi, Bess 367
Hoʻopiʻi, Emily 367
Hoʻopiʻi, Gigi 367
Hoʻopiʻi, Isaac "Ike" 367–369, 513, 569
Hoʻopiʻi, Ivan 367, 513
Hoʻopiʻi, Jeff 367
Hooser, Gary 545
Hoover, Herbert 21, 45, 141
Hopkins, Charles 111
Horio, Don 73
Hormel, James 310, 380
Horton, Willie 199
Houston, Sam 130
Howard, Andrew 505
Howard, James 189
Howard, Rita 307
Hoyer, Steny 156, 200, 215
Hoyt, Diana 146–147, 149, 156, 158–159
Hua, Guofeng 134
Huang, Qin Shi (emperor) 332
Hubbard, Carroll 161
Huckabee, Mike 483
Hudson, Rock 62
Humphrey, Hubert 70, 274
Hurricane Iniki 277, 289, 297, 429
Hurricane Iwa 153–155
Hussein, Saddam 19, 226, 228, 230, 246, 395–396, 398, 422
Hussey, Brian 403
Hustace, Maria 175–176, 195, 201, 202, 225, 295, 300
Hutchinson, Frank 225
Hutchinson, Tim 315
Hutchison, Kay Bailey 444, 552
Hyde, Henry 339, 497

I

Ige, David 599
Ige, Marshall 316
Ikeda, Donna 316
Inhofe, Jim 439, 540
Inouye, Daniel 9, 22, 56, 66, 77, 90, 111, 129–131, 142–143, 167, 174, 180, 180–181, 185, 188–192, 199, 209, 211, 214–217, 220–223, 227, 230, 235, 237, 245–248, 260, 264, 266, 274, 276, 281–283, 285, 288, 291, 298, 304, 307, 310–312, 314, 320, 336–338, 341–342, 350–353, 358, 360, 365, 368, 374–375, 379, 383, 386, 397, 400–401, 406, 411, 415–416, 422–426, 431, 435–438, 440, 442, 449, 453, 456, 462, 475, 488, 490–491, 494–495, 499–502, 506, 509, 514, 524, 533, 542–546, 549–552, 556, 559, 563–564, 565, 571, 581, 585, 587, 587–592, 594, 599
Inouye, Irene 544, 552, 587
Inouye, Ken 587, 599
internment camps 40–41, 209, 346, 349, 352, 491–492
Iran-Contra scandal 186–188
Iraq War 18–22, 380, 395–399, 423, 432–433, 441–442, 449, 451–453, 457, 458–459, 466–474, 563, 570–571
Irons, Andy 377
Isa, Mary 79, 84
Isaak, Charlie 128
Ishimoto, Art 154
Issa, Darrell 531
Ito, Masashi 15
Ivins, Bruce 374
Iwase, Randy 182, 456
Izutsu, Satoru 57, 118

J

Jackson, Jesse 167, 195, 381
Jacobs, John 105
Jeffords, James "Jim" 22, 129–130, 217, 265, 293, 311–312, 320, 340, 375, 383, 422, 436, 446–447
Jervis, Gerard 321
Jiang, Zemin 331, 333
John Paul II (pope) 163–165
Johns, Tim 601–602
Johnson, Andrew 339
Johnson, Jacob 562
Johnson, J. Bennett 280
Johnson, Jerome 467
Johnson, Larry 317
Johnson, Lyndon B. 58, 65, 68–70, 269, 274, 301, 443, 481
Johnson, Tim 315, 320, 540, 556, 559
Jones, James 44
Jones, Jim 130–131
Jones, John Paul 76
Jones, Walter 203
Jossem, Jared 295

K

Ka'ahumanu, Queen 25
Kaanoi, Martial 111
Kaapana, Ledward 91
Kaapana, Nedward 91
Kagan, Elena 539–540
Kaha, Aleysia-Rae 593
Kahale, Edward 54
Kahanamoku, Duke "Paoa" 28, 69, 277
Kahanu, David 182
Kahanu, Henry 40, 237
Kaho'olawe 92–93, 110–112, 223–224, 230, 235–236, 239, 407, 515
Kaho'onei, Kaua 513
Kai, Carole 597
Kaina, Jimmy 513
Kaina, William 322
Kaine, Tim 464
Ka'iulani, Princess (née Cleghorn, Victoria) 54–55
Kaiwa, Bill 82
Kala, Yolanda 599
Kalākaua, David 54
Kalaniana'ole, Jonah Kūhiō 31, 100
Kaleikini, Danny 82, 266, 296, 300, 597
Kaloa, Albert S. 580
Kaluhiwa, Kekoa 599
Kamakahi, Dennis 403
Kamakawiwo'ole, Israel 288
Kamāmalu, Victoria 59
Kamehameha III 92, 329
Kamehameha the Great 73, 322, 342, 598
Kanahele, Kamaki 512
Kane, Herb Kawainui 91
Kane, Micah 400
Kaneshiro, Faith 598–599
Kaneshiro, Keith 240, 415
Kantor, Mickey 316
Kapi'olani, Queen 31
Karr, Gladys 215, 598
Kasich, John 345
Kassebaum, Nancy 232, 275, 283, 312, 444
Kato, Gerry 450–452
Katz, Ira 477–478
Katz, Mitchell 316
Katz, Suzanne 316
Kauhane, Francis 110–111
Kauinui, Kelli 215
Kauka, Donald 40
Kawānanakoa, Abigail Kapi'olani 31, 562
Kawānanakoa, Abigail Kekaulike 31
Kawānanakoa, David 30
Kawasaki, Duke 78
Kay, Alan 465
Kealoha, Thomas 40
Keating, Charles 206
Keel, Jefferson 564
Keeling, Charles D. "Dave" 447
Keir, Gerry 78
Kekumano, Charles 84, 86, 321
Kelly, Robert J. 292
Kemp, Jack 156, 195, 228, 314
Kennedy, Anthony 362
Kennedy, Caroline 508
Kennedy, Curran 508

Kennedy, Edward Jr. 508
Kennedy, Edward Moore "Ted" Sr. 20, 22, 137–138, 141, 215–217, 220, 234, 240–244, 265, 275, 301, 310–312, 344, 380, 383, 409, 422–423, 428, 435, 439, 447, 476–477, 492, 502, 506–509, 523, 529, 534, 585
Kennedy, Jackie 269
Kennedy, John F. Jr. 344
Kennedy, John F. Sr. 20, 64–65, 104, 158, 242, 264, 274, 344
Kennedy, Joseph 508
Kennedy, Kara 507–508
Kennedy, Patrick 486, 508
Kennedy, Robert Francis 20, 70, 344, 481
Kennedy, Rory 344
Kennedy, Rose 508
Kennedy, Vicki 508
Kenoi, Billy 490, 584
Kent, Mrs. (chaperone) 62
Keppeler, Doris 32
Keppeler, Herbert 32
Kerik, Bernard 426
Kerr, Deborah 44
Kerrey, Bob 263, 273, 294, 310, 350–351
Kerry, John 216, 265, 310, 358, 408, 411–413, 416, 422, 435, 436, 480, 490, 601
Ketchum, Creston 53
Keyes, Alan 416
Khomeini, Mustapha 125
Khomeini, Ruhollah 125, 132–133
Kiaʻaina, Esther 247, 304, 512, 568, 576, 589
Kim, Donna Mercado 182
Kim, Harry 361–362, 584
Kim, Jong-il 505, 571
Kim, Jong-un 571
Kim, Leolani. *See* Hill, Pat "Leolani" (née Kim)
Kim, Pat. *See* Hill, Pat "Leolani" (née Kim)
Kimura, Shunichi 72, 78
King, Angus 584
King, Charles E. 62

King, Jean 153
King, Martin Luther Jr. 70, 161, 167, 480–481
King, Sam 74, 77, 179–180, 321
Kitagawa, Mike 421
Kitamura, Michael 216
Kitka, Julie 564
Kiyosaki, Ralph 68, 74, 95
Kleber, Herbert 207
Klebold, Dylan 343
Kobashigawa, Yeiki 352
Kobayashi, Ann 490
Kobayashi, Bert 317, 596
Kobayashi, Les 79
Kobayashi, Paul 79
Koga, George "Scotty" 57, 118
Kohl, Helmut 288
Kohoi, Lei 597
Koki, Stan 296
Konetzni, Al 364
Kong, Lily 99
Koresh, David 284–285
Koyonagi, Karen 110
Kresnak, Bill 211
Kucinich, Dennis 408, 413, 480
Kumalae, Alan 597
Kuna, Steve 139
Kunimura, Tony 154, 202
Kuroda, Joe 64, 95, 97–100, 353
Kuroda, Robert 348–349, 352–353, 406
Kusaka, Maryanne 337
Kussman, Michael 478
Kusumoto, Kristy 215
Kuwata, Kam 228, 234
Kyl, Jon 301, 445, 548, 552

L

Lake, Tony 319
Lancaster, Burt 44
Landrieu, Mary 359, 500, 530, 535, 549
Langley, Nancy 215
Lansing, Clarabelle 198
Lapic, Tom 380
LaRouche, Lyndon 408
Larson, Charles 266–267, 289, 292

Larson, Sally 266
Lautenberg, Frank 265, 447
Leahy, Patrick 22, 374–375, 447, 492, 535, 540, 559, 585, 588
Lee, B. Glen 295
Lee, Bob 582
Lee, Jimmy 597
Lee, Kui 86
Lehman, Bill 184–185
Lehman, John 150
Lehrer, Jim 487
Lemke, Herman 80–82
Lennon, John 144
Leolani Kim. *See* Hill, Pat "Leolani" (née Kim)
Leong, Glenn 215
Lesher, Richard 224
Levin, Carl 22, 383, 397, 422, 439, 466, 469–470, 476, 520–521
Lewin, Jack 296
Lewinsky, Monica 339
Lewis, Jerry 200
Lewis, Price 14, 16, 49–51, 53
Li, Peng 280, 331
Li, Victor 239
Lieberman, Joe 221, 311, 361, 408, 457, 460, 476, 488, 492, 529–531, 548, 550, 552, 577
Likelike, Miriam 54
Liliʻuokalani, Queen (née Kamakaʻeha, Lydia) 54, 59, 62, 281, 424, 513, 537, 579
Lin, Betsy 583–584
Lincoln, Abraham 377
Lind, Ian 93
Lindbergh, Charles 47
Lindsey, Bob 594
Lindsey, Lokelani 321
Lingle, Linda 244, 287, 337, 382, 400, 401, 413, 416, 425, 438, 456, 484, 546, 547, 551, 568, 576, 582–584
Linish, Al 15
Linish, Joe 15, 17
Liu, Mike 225, 227, 231, 237, 316
Lloyd, Alan 65

Lloyd, Jim 101
Locke, Gary 315, 494
Long, Oren 495
Lorber, John 307
Lott, Trent 312, 341, 344, 362, 375, 381
Lovejoy, Thomas 602
Lowry, Mike 159
Ludloff, Keanahou 40
Ludlum, Robert 104
Lugar, Richard 439, 540, 573
Lujan, Manuel 159
Lyman, Richard 205

M

MacArthur, Douglas 42, 498, 501
MacDonald, Albert 40
Machado, Collette 564
Machtley, Ronald 294
Mack, Connie 282–283, 328, 330
Mack, Michael 330
Mack, Priscilla 328
Macke, Richard 307
Madison, Dolley 571
Mahi, Aaron 403, 599
Mahikoa, Ainsley 39–40
Major, John 288
Malapit, Eduardo 515
Mallan, Lloyd 202
Maloney, Carolyn 410
Manahan, Joey 599
Mandela, Nelson 431
Mansfield, Gordon 475
Mao, Zedong 134
Marcos, Ferdinand 124
Markey, Ed 332, 539
Markusun, Marcia 380
Marshall, Thurgood 264, 358
Martin, Ernie 599
Masuda, Robert 593–594
Mathis, Dawson 107
Matsunaga, Helene 210
Matsunaga, Matt 222, 225, 231
Matsunaga, Spark 20, 56, 77, 94, 100, 111, 129, 167, 174, 180–181, 190, 195, 201, 202, 204, 209–211, 214–215, 220–222, 247–248, 286, 378–379, 379, 386, 422, 514
Mattingly, Ken 168–169
Mattson, Alika 386
Mattson, Anthony 386
Mattson, David 402
Mattson, Elizabeth 402
Mattson, Millannie Kahōkūaonani (née Akaka) 54, 58–59, 67, 101, 113, 116–117, 250, 386, 402, 415, 524–527, 598
Mattson, Renard 386
Mau (Hawaiian Electric welder) 33–34, 43
Maugham, Somerset 48
Mavroules, Nicholas 177
McAdams, Scott 543
McAuliffe, Christa 171
McCain, John III 206, 276, 319, 345–346, 359, 425, 439, 445, 463, 481–484, 485, 487, 487–490, 500, 517, 549, 556
McCain, John "Jack" Jr. 481–483
McCain, John "Slew" 481–483
McCarthy, Eugene 69–70, 264
McCarthy, Joseph 442
McCarthy, Robert 316
McCaskill, Claire 530
McClaran, Peter 215
McCloskey, Pete 93, 122, 130, 144
McClung, David 76, 80–81, 83
McConnell, Mitch 457, 547, 548
McCormack, John 309
McDermott, Bob 382
McDonald, Kathy 162
McDonald, Larry 161–162
McEvoy, Mary 380
McFall, John 102, 104–107
McFarlane, Robert "Bud" 188
McGarey, Patrick 171, 215
McGovern, George 70, 167, 506
McGuffie, Mark 601
McKay, Gardner 53
McKenzie, Tara 313
McLaughlin, Will 380
McVeigh, Timothy 306
Meese, Ed 188
Mellencamp, Jeffrey 555
Melvill, Mike 561
Menor, Ron 204, 225, 231
Metzenbaum, Howard 216, 275, 301
Michener, James 53, 152, 481
Midler, Bette 360
Miers, Harriet 435
Miho, Kats 135
Mikulski, Barbara 8, 22, 216, 232, 265, 275, 444, 474, 476, 492, 529, 585
Mikva, Abner 106
Miles, Ellen 93
Miller, Amoi 96
Miller, Joe 543
Miller, Loren 14–15, 17, 119
Minagawa, Bunzo 15
Mineta, Norman 107, 134, 142, 145, 148, 156, 346, 379
Mink, John 18, 94, 100, 175, 181, 182, 204, 225, 228, 231, 232, 233, 237, 244, 246, 275, 281, 283, 288, 289, 291, 294, 298, 300, 302, 304, 310, 312, 316, 337, 339, 361, 362, 366, 378, 379, 380, 381, 382, 522, 524, 606
Mink, Patsy 18, 94, 100, 175, 181–182, 204, 225, 228, 231, 231–233, 237, 244, 246, 275, 281, 283, 288–289, 291, 294, 298, 300, 302, 304, 310, 312, 316, 337, 339, 361–362, 366, 378, 378–382, 522, 524
Mitchell, George 214, 301
Mitchell, Kimo 112
Mitterand, Francois 288
Miyazawa, Kiichi 288
Mizuguchi, Norman 222, 225, 231
Mizuguchi, Takeshi 365
Mohammed, Fazul Abdullah 563

INDEX   633

Mondale, Walter 139, 141, 167, 274, 380–381, 392
Montgomery, Sonny 200, 310
Moran, Jerry 577
Morgado, Arnold 182, 315
Mori, Yoshiro 364
Morita, Ed 79
Morrison, Theodore 40
Morrow, Tom 316
Morse, Stephen 93
Moseley-Braun, Carol 310, 408, 444
Moses, Mark 316
Mossman, Bina 62
Moto, Kaoru 352
Mourdock, Richard 574
Moynihan, Daniel Patrick 310, 358
Mueller, Robert 577–578
Muller, Lionel 40
Muncy, James 146–147, 156, 158
Muranaga, Kiyoshi 352
Murata, Susumu 46
Murkowski, Frank 283, 312, 336, 342, 358, 383, 543, 581
Murkowski, Lisa 424, 445, 506, 543, 556–557, 559, 563, 581, 583–584
Murphy, Jack 156
Murray, Patty 22, 425, 444, 472, 477–478, 499, 550
Muskie, Edmund 134–136, 188

N

Nader, Ralph 362, 472
Nagin, Ray 429
Nahale-a, Alapaki 564
Nakae, Masato 352
Nakamine, Shinyei 352
Nakamura, William 352
Nakasone, Bob 515
Nakayama, Paul 593
narcotics trade 122–126, 163–165, 206–207, 331
Narvaes, Tony 182
Native Hawaiian affairs
  Akaka Bill (federal recognition) 360–361, 400–401, 411, 424–425, 442–445, 506, 537–538, 546–547, 563–565, 586, 597
  Apology Resolution 282–283
  education 131, 190–191, 596–597
  Hawaiian Home Lands Recovery Act 401
  health care 192, 594–595
  Office of Hawaiian Affairs 139, 401
  Rice v. Cayetano 464–466
  sovereignty 313, 598
  voter registry 579, 597–598
Neary, Blossom 62
Nelson, Ben 460, 540
Nelson, Myrtle 102
Nichols, Terry 306
Nicholson, Jim 475
Nishimoto, Joe 352
Nixon, Richard 70, 80, 90, 93, 167, 419, 483, 584
Noonan, Fred 34–35
North, Oliver 188, 301
Norton, Gale 400
Norvo, Red "Mr. Swing" 62
Nunn, Sam 283, 285, 299, 311

O

Oakland, Suzanne Chun 316, 597
Oba, Sakae 15
Obama, Barack 41, 292, 354, 410, 411–413, 416, 422, 435, 443, 470, 477, 480, 484, 485, 487–490, 492–494, 496, 500, 502, 504, 505, 508–509, 512, 527, 532–533, 535–536, 539–541, 545, 547, 550, 559, 562, 563, 565, 569–575, 577, 584, 588, 590, 598
Obama, Malia 484, 533
Obama, Michelle 484, 508, 533
Obama, Sasha 484, 533
Obey, Dave 502
O'Brien, Jack 40
O'Connor, Dennis 227, 234, 288
O'Connor, Sandra Day 362, 435
Ogawa, Bob 110, 216, 304
Ogawa, Sharon 304
Ogawa, Shigeo 79
Ohashi, Jimmy 118
Ohashi, Joan 215, 506–507, 510, 515–516, 587, 596
Ohashi, Rose 79, 216
Ohata, Allan 352
Ohira, Masayoshi 134
Okata, Russell 79
O'Keefe, Sean 544
Okinaga, Lawrence 596
Okubo, James 352
Okutsu, Yukio 352
O'Leary, Hazel 316
Olson (Hawaiian Electric superintendent) 34, 43–44
O'Malley, Sean 508
O'Neill, Tip 101–106, 108–109, 122, 130, 142–143, 159–160, 162, 177, 186, 390–391
Onizuka, Clyde 171
Onizuka, Darien 171
Onizuka, Ellison 168–172, 448
Onizuka, Janelle 171
Onizuka, Lorna 171–172
Onizuka, Masamitsu 170
Onizuka, Mitsue 170–171
Ono, Champ 79
Ono, Frank 352
Ontai, Calvin 40
Orwell, George 166, 447
Osaki, Masao 79
Oshiro, Bob 76, 97
Ossipoff, Vladimir 55
Otani, Kazuo 352
Owens, Major 379

P

Pace, Peter 399
Packwood, Bob 217, 265
Pahinui, Cyril 404
Pahinui, Gabby 91
Pahlavi, Reza 125

Palin, Sarah 485, 543, 569, 583–584
Palmer, Arnold 269
Panetta, Leon 109, 145, 563
Parker, Mike 310
Park, Tong-sun 102
Parkinson, Cyril 442
Paul, Ron 483, 569, 573
Paulsen, Pat 263
Pavao, Dennis 91
Pawlenty, Tim 569
Payton, Gary 168
Peake, James 475–476, 478–479, 494–495
Pell, Claiborne 221, 310
Pelosi, Nancy 457, 458, 535, 548
Penzias, Arno 393
Perez-Wendt, Mahealani 597
Perkins, Kevin 577
Perot, Ross 276–277, 279, 314
Perrelli, Tom 557
Perry, Rick 569, 573
Perry, William 298, 316
Peters, Henry 204, 224, 321
Petraeus, David 471, 563
Philip, Prince 258
Piailug, Mau 92
Pico, Tom 316
Pililaau, Agnes 599
Pililaau, Herbert 599
Pina, Makalani 593
Platts, Todd Russell 531
Poepoe, Andy 225, 237
Poindexter, John 188
Poindexter, Joseph 39
Powell, Colin 22, 230, 245, 266, 267, 285, 299, 364, 396, 399, 422
Prejean, Gail 93
Presley, Elvis 277, 433
Pressler, Larry 283, 315
Proxmire, William 138
Pryor, David 311, 315
Pryor, Mark 409
Pyle, Ernie 171

Q

Quayle, Dan 109, 131, 202, 258, 345–346

Quinn, Bill 94, 224, 382

R

Radcliffe, John 534
Rahall, Nick 310
Rahman, Ziaur 134
Railsback, Tom 123
Rains, Claude 383
Randall, Tony 62–63
Randolph, Jennings 220
Rangel, Charlie 110, 123–124, 130, 142–144, 163
Rathburn, Liz 598
Rauckhorst, Jerry 597
Ray, Elizabeth 103
Rayburn, Sam 102, 309
Reagan, Nancy 300–301
Reagan, Ronald 41, 122, 133, 139, 141–143, 147–149, 150–151, 157–158, 162–163, 167–168, 173–174, 177–178, 185, 186–192, 195, 197–198, 205, 217, 220, 271, 288, 300–301, 314, 362, 378, 389, 506, 543, 561, 584
Recca, Joe 61–62
Reed, Jack 22, 438, 447, 469–470, 476
Reed, Rick 196
Rehnquist, William 339, 362, 435
Reid, Harry 341, 401, 435, 457, 460, 461, 469, 502, 547, 548, 559, 583, 585, 589–590, 592
Reyes, Art 346
Rice, Condoleezza 399, 422–423
Rice, Harold "Freddy" 465
Richardson, William S. 84, 224, 480, 494, 542
Richter, Scott 215
Rickover, Hyman 150, 155
Ridge, Tom 373, 383, 426
Riegle, Donald 206
Riley, Ken 271
Ritte, Loretta 111
Ritte, Walter 93, 110–111, 236, 407, 515

Robb, Chuck 301, 310, 443
Roberts, Cokie 484
Roberts, John 435
Robertson, Pat 195
Roberts, Pat 354, 357
Robinson, Kaloa 215
Rockefeller, Jay 293, 319, 332
Rockefeller, Laurance 72
Rockefeller, Nelson 93
Rodine, Sharon 232–233
Rodino, Peter 106, 123, 144
Rodrigues, Gary 229
Rogers, Harold 163
Rogers, Henk 601
Rogers, Will 187
Rohrabacker, Dana 491
Romney, Mitt 301, 483, 569, 573–574, 584
Roosevelt, Franklin 45, 141, 351, 498
Rose, Charlie (Hawai'i Island) 99
Rose, Charlie (N. Carolina) 107
Rosenthal, Ben 132
Roskam, Pete 497
Ross, David 519–520, 531
Ross, Donald 267
Rostenkowski, Dan 104–108, 142, 301
Roth, Randy 321
Rowland, John 199
Rowland, Richard 295
Rozell, Jami 554
Rubin, Robert 305, 332
Rudman, Warren 174
Rukavina, Martin 380
Rumsfeld, Donald 195, 364, 398–399, 441, 457, 462, 493, 495
Russo, Marty 177
Rutherford, Skip 292
Ryan, Leo 130–131

S

Sabey, John 40, 225
Sablan, Gregorio 537
Sadat, Anwar 390–391
Sagan, Carl 147
Sagum, Juliette 216
Sai, Marlene 597

Saiki, Pat (née Fukuda) 153, 176, 190, 191, 192, 195–196, 201, 202, 203, 210, 214, 218–228, 229, 230, 232–237, 239, 243–244, 296, 300, 302, 438
Sakai, Cheryl 576
Sakai, Colleen 576
Sakai, Dale 215
Sakai, Edward 64
Sakai, Florence 576
Sakai, Jim 18, 141, 215, 511, 576
Sakamoto, Norman 316, 545
Sakata, Norman 171–172
Sakato, George 352–353
Salameh, Mohammed 284
Salazar, Ken 494, 500, 547, 565
Sanders, Bernie 306, 457, 460, 461, 472, 477, 488, 535, 548, 559, 584
Santorum, Rick 569, 573
Santos, Jerry 91, 599
Sarbanes, John 550
Sarbanes, Paul 22, 383, 409, 499, 550
Sasser, Jim 283, 301
Sawyer, Harold 163
Sawyer, Richard 110–111
Sawyer, Zenadia 111
Scalia, Antonin 362
Schatz, Barbara 591
Schatz, Brian 440, 545, 547, 589, 590–592
Schatz, Irwin 591
Schatz, Linda Kwok 591
Schatz, Mia 591
Schatz, Tyler 591
Scheuer, Jim 122, 131–132, 144, 156
Schieffer, Bob 489
Schoolland, Ken 176, 195, 227
Schornstheimer, Robert 198
Schroeder, Pat 188
Schulz, George 188
Schumer, Chuck 338, 358, 435
Schwarzkopf, Norman 245, 267

Scott, Bobby 328
Scowcroft, Brent 188
Seacrest, Patrick 363
Sebelius, Kathleen 494
Senate Committee on Indian Affairs 550–551, 555–559, 563–565, 581–582
Sessions, Jeff 315
Sessions, Jim 435
Shaheen, Jeanne 540
Shakespeare, William 11
Shalala, Donna 350
Shapiro, Dave 571
Sharp, Phil 275
Sharpton, Al 408
Sheardown, John 133
Sheehan, Cindy 472
Shelby, Richard 283, 340, 410
Shelton, Carolyn 328
Shelton, Hugh 327–328
Sherman, Eddie 62
Shida, Jeanne 79
Shigeta, Jimmy 57
Shimabukuro, George 57
Shinseki, Eric "Ric" 351, 397–399, 413, 492, 492–496, 537
Shinseki, Lori 351
Shore, Dinah 60–63, 253
Short, Walter 39
Shriver, Eunice 506
Shriver, Loren 168, 171
Shriver, Maria 506
Shriver, Sargent 506
Silva, Kalani 513
Silva, Kalena 404
Simeona, Morrnah Nalamaku 269–272, 512
Simonds, John 175
Simon, Paul 216, 282, 310, 338
Simpson, Alan 311
Simpson, Carole 277–278
Sinatra, Frank 44
Sinclair, Wayne 368
Sisk, Bernie 106
Skeen, Joe 148, 156
Skelton, Ike 310
Slack, John M. 142
Slom, Sam 316
Smith, Bob 275, 345–346

Smith, D. Gordon "Don" 138, 141
Smith, Gordon H. 401, 424–425, 460, 490
Smith, Neal 184
Smyser, Bud 175
Snider, Paul 225
Snowe, Olympia 301, 311, 340, 439, 445, 460, 502, 540
Snyder, Betsy 491
Snyder, Vic 491
Sobin, Judy 233
Soetoro-Ng, Maya 484
Soon, Cheryl 182
Sotomayor, Sonia 540
Souki, Joe 72
Souter, David 264–265, 362
space technology 146–149, 151–152, 156–159, 166, 168–172, 384–386, 428, 448, 504–505, 560–561
Hawai'i-based telescopes 455, 505, 603
Spadaro, Jack 531
Specter, Arlen 217, 283, 311, 320, 340, 428, 434, 439, 445, 460, 502
Spencer, Bruce 404
Sproat, Clyde 513
Sproat, Manny 52
Stabenow, Debbie 22, 409
Stafford, Robert 180–182, 185
Stanley, Anne 228
Stanton, Barbara Kim 450
Stark, Pete 123
Starr, Kenneth 338–339
Stassen, Harold 167, 263
Stender, Oswald 205, 224, 321, 402, 594
Stenholm, Charlie 310
Stevens, Ann 543
Stevens, Catherine 544–545
Stevens, Christopher 577
Stevens, Edna 64
Stevens, J.L. 513
Stevens, John Paul 362, 539
Stevens, Ted 142, 217, 283, 340, 358, 382, 401, 424–425, 445, 457, 460, 479, 490, 501, 541, 543–545, 581

Stockdale, James Bond 276
Stockman, David 122
Stokes, Louis 163
Stone, Scott 78
Sugar, Angelo 555
Sullivan, Lani 599
Sumimoto, Arlene 96
Summers, Larry 305–306
Sutton, Richard "Ike" 225, 296
Suzuki, Zenko 422
Swindle, Orson 277, 285, 295–296, 300, 302, 315, 481
Symms, Steve 161

T

Tactay, Mark 513
Tagami, John 215
Tagawa, John 414
Taira, Norman 128
Takabuki, Matsuo 224
Takahashi, Pearl 216
Takaki, Tracy 513
Takayama, Gregg 215
Talent, Jim 381
Tamashiro, Keith 600
Tanaka, Michael 128
Tanga, Ellen 64
Tanonaka, Dalton 416
Tanouye, Ted 352
Tavares, Charmaine 456, 546
Tavares, Hannibal 235, 287, 456, 515, 546
Taylor, Betty Loo 85
Taylor, Gene 310
Taylor, Kenneth 133
Taylor, Mack 40
Taylor, Patrick 113, 116–117
Taylor, Susan (née Akaka) 30, 116–117, 322
Teague, Olin 122
Tenet, George 367, 396
Tester, Jonathan "Jon" 457, 529
Thach, Nguyen Co 132
Thatcher, Margaret 431
Thielen, Cynthia 181, 456
Thomas, Clarence 264–265, 358, 362, 436, 565
Thompson, Cha 463

Thompson, Fred 301, 340, 443, 483, 517
Thompson, Myron S. "Pinky" 73, 91, 191, 224
Thompson, Nainoa 91, 549
Thompson, Tommy 381
Thornburgh, Dick 206
Thune, John 416
Thurmond, Strom 349, 358, 437, 509
Tiberi, Pat 491
Tinsulanonda, Prem 134
Tito, Dennis 393, 561
Togo, Ellen 58
Togo, Hiroshi 58
Togo, May 58
Tokioka, Darci 215
Tokita, Turk 79
Tompkins, Mimi 198
Tong, Nick 135
Tower, John 188
Trask, David 79
Trible, Paul 146–147, 158
Trimble, Gordon 516
Truman, Harry 45–46, 96, 383
Trump, Donald 569
Tsongas, Paul 263, 273–274
Tsuji, Clift 80
Tsutsui, Shan 596
Tuell, Loretta 551, 556
Twain, Mark 47
Twigg-Smith, Thurston 224

U

Uchima, John 79, 95–96, 101–102, 128, 141, 186, 512, 515
Udall, Mo 156–157
Udall, Tom 556, 559
Underwood, Bob 512
Ushijima, John 84

V

Vadset, Mohala 513
Van Hollen, Chris 529–531
Vaughan, Palani 288
Vaughn, Robert 530
Ventura, Jesse 381
veterans affairs 192, 320, 348–353, 420–421, 423–424, 457, 462, 472–479, 492–504, 534–535, 536–537, 540–541, 585
Villalba, Karla 93
Vitter, David 500, 502
Voinovich, George 529, 549–550
Volkmer, Harold 310
von Eshenbach, Andrew 520

W

Wada, Debra 215, 511
Waddle, Scott 363–365
Wahlberg, Howard 513
Wai, Francis 352
Waihee, John 6, 20, 79, 153, 171, 175–176, 204, 210–211, 222–223, 228, 231, 235, 241, 244, 281, 286, 288–289, 291–292, 296, 302, 316–317, 325, 378, 524, 533, 597, 598
Waihee, Lynne 302
Wakatsuki, James 84
Wang, Dan 331
Ward, Gene 337
Warner, John 283, 340, 464, 467
Warner, Leonard 40
Warrington, Charles 110–111
Washburn, Kevin 580
Washington, Booker T. 161
Washington, George 21–22, 274, 482
Webb, Jim 457, 462, 552
Wei, Jingsheng 331
Weinberger, Caspar 188
Wellstone, David 380–381
Wellstone, Mark 380–381
Wellstone, Paul 22, 275, 320, 380–381, 585
Wellstone, Sheila 380
West, Togo 350
Whistleblower Protection Act 520–523
White, George M. 270–271
Whitten, Jamie 142, 183–185
Wichman, Chipper 602
Wilcox, Leslie 223

Wilder, Douglas 263, 273
Williams, Abraham 600
Williams, Benjamin 40
Wilson, Charlie 106–107, 142, 158
Wilson, Eleanor 51, 53
Wilson, Robert 393
Winer, Andy 454
Wirth, Tim 106, 142, 147–148, 221
Wolff, Lester 123
Wolfowitz, Paul 398
Won, Abraham 40
Wong, Colleen 402
Wong, Dickie 321
Wong, Llewellyn 40
Wong, Pohailama 513
Woo, Doug 81
Woods, Bill 296
Woodward, Bob 462
Wouk, Herman 481
Wright, E. Alvey 180, 325
Wright, Jim 103–108, 131, 142, 186, 193, 197, 200–201, 206
Wu, David 550
Wurzelbacher, Joe "Joe the Plumber" 488–489
Wyden, Ron 22, 310, 425

Y

Yadao, Elisa 57, 450
Yadao, Eppy 57, 118
Yamada, Rose 79
Yamamoto, Cora 215
Yamasaki, Audrey 437
Yamasaki, Wayne 181, 437, 449
Yanagihara, Ted 57, 118
Yasin, Abdul Rahman 284
Yellen, Janet 332
Yeltsin, Boris 260
Yeutter, Clayton 220
Yokoi, Shoichi 15
Yokouchi, Masaru "Pundy" 457
Yokoyama, George 72, 79–80, 96–100, 454
Yokoyama, Mieko 96
Yokoyama, Paul 96
Yoshimura, Jon 514–517, 566–567
Yoshimura, Yuki 516–517
Young, Don 104, 537, 541, 543, 581–583
Young, Frank 194
Young, Jackie 296
Young, Zillah 61–62
Yukimura, JoAnn 202, 490

Z

Zimmerman, Bob 225
Zinni, Anthony 366

Daniel K. Akaka served in the United States Congress for thirty-six years—in the House of Representatives from 1976 to 1990 and in the Senate from 1990 until his retirement in 2013. Born in Honolulu in 1924, he attended the Kamehameha Schools and served with the U.S. Army Corps of Engineers during World War II, before earning his bachelor's and master's degrees in education at the University of Hawai'i at Mānoa. He was a high school teacher and principal and later held several positions in state government, including that of chief program planner for the state Department of Education and director of the Hawai'i Office of Economic Opportunity. He resides in Honolulu with his wife, Millie. Dan and Millie Akaka have five children—Millannie, Dan Jr., Gerard, Nick and Alan.

Jim Borg first saw Hawai'i from the decks of the SS *Lurline* in 1961 as his family was moving to Japan. After studying at the University of Hawai'i at Mānoa in 1974–75, he earned a journalism degree at Northwestern University and worked in Chicago, Georgia and Rochester, New York, before returning to the Islands as a reporter for the *Honolulu Advertiser* in 1979. At the *Advertiser*, Jim covered science and the military and won a yearlong science journalism fellowship at MIT in 1986–87, taking classes at MIT and Harvard. In 1990, he won the top prize in U.S. science reporting—the Westinghouse Award from the American Association for the Advancement of Science—for a series on tsunamis. A year later he won a second fellowship, from the Alicia Patterson Foundation in Washington, D.C., to write about chemical weapons. Jim has also taught news writing and magazine writing at UH Mānoa and was editor of *Hawaii* magazine for three years. He joined the *Honolulu Star-Bulletin* full-time in 2001, working as a copy editor, then as a reporter and currently as assistant city editor of the *Honolulu Star-Advertiser*.